★ ★
= MAJOR =
PHILIP M. ULMER

A Hero of the American Revolution

PATRICIA M. HUBERT

FOREWORD BY ARTHUR COHN

Charleston London

THE
History

Published by The History Press
Charleston, SC 29403
www.historypress.net

Cover: General Arnold's fleet coming ashore at Ferris Bay on Lake Champlain, October 13, 1776. *Courtesy of Ernest Haas, Lake Champlain Maritime Museum, Vergennes, Vermont.*

First published 2014

Manufactured in the United States

ISBN 978.1.62619.514.1

Library of Congress CIP data applied for.

Notice: The information in this book is true and complete to the best of our knowledge. It is offered without guarantee on the part of the author or The History Press. The author and The History Press disclaim all liability in connection with the use of this book.

Contents

CONTENTS

CONTENTS

CONTENTS

Contents

Foreword

Born in December 1751 and passing in 1816 at age sixty-five, Philip Ulmer was of the generation of citizens whose lives encompassed the formative events that gave rise to the United States of America. This study of Ulmer's life provides a new window into the transformation of a sparsely settled frontier colony into what became the states of Maine and Massachusetts. A review of Ulmer's life also provides insights into the birth of a new nation resting on concepts of liberty, commerce and freedom. Patricia Hubert's research has resulted in a narrative filled with dramatic accounts of events in Ulmer's lifetime and his efforts and sacrifice to bring about that new nation. He was, from the beginning, a Patriot and active militia member. When the War for Independence began in April 1775 with the shot heard around the world, Philip Ulmer quickly marched to Boston, and until the end of the war, he devoted himself to supporting the American effort.

My personal and professional interest in Philip Ulmer is focused on his role as captain of one of Benedict Arnold's gunboats on Lake Champlain in 1776. When exactly Philip Ulmer's relationship with Arnold began is not known for certain. His younger brother George served under Arnold in May 1775 when Fort Ticonderoga was seized, and Arnold directed the capture of the only large ships operating on the strategic lake. In this early action of the war, Arnold demonstrated all the skill, courage and contentiousness that were to mark his career. Just a few weeks later Arnold was back at Boston lobbying General Washington to let him lead an army through the wilderness of Maine and Canada for a surprise attack on the British stronghold at Quebec City. As a shipwright before the war, Philip Ulmer had helped build the schooner *Broad Bay* that transported Arnold's ill-fated invasion force from Massachusetts to its embarkation point on the Kennebec River. For the remainder of the fall, Ulmer was assigned to use his maritime skills to convert merchant vessels into some of the nation's first naval ships. As the ring of rebels around Boston strengthened, the soldiers awaited news about the fate of their bold invasion of Canada.

When news from the north finally arrived, it was all bad. The combined armies of General Richard Montgomery and Colonel Arnold had attacked Quebec City during a New Year's Eve snowstorm with disastrous results: Montgomery was dead, Arnold was wounded and hundreds were made prisoner. Philip Ulmer was among the first troops Washington sent north to support what was left of the Northern Army in Quebec. Arriving at Montreal in April, just about the time the recovering Benedict Arnold arrived from Quebec City to take charge, Ulmer was attached to Arnold's command. Recognizing Philip Ulmer's strong maritime experience, Arnold assigned the twenty-four-year-old the command of the captured British eight-gun sloop *Isabella*. In this capacity, Ulmer actively participated in the final weeks of the failing Canadian invasion.

When a British relief convoy arrived at Quebec City in early May, the rout of the American army began. Confusion, sickness and setbacks didn't allow the Americans to catch their breaths until they reached the forts of Crown Point and Ticonderoga on Lake Champlain. Forced to hastily invent a strategy to contain the British and Hessian forces from invading the colonies via the strategic Lake Champlain corridor, a decision was made to also fortify the mount across the lake to the east of Fort Ticonderoga. The point of this defensive spear would be American control of the lake. In addition to the vessels captured from the British in 1775, the Americans began building new warships at Skenesboro (today Whitehall, New York) at the southern end of Lake Champlain to ensure that the British force amassing at the northern end of the lake could not pass south. In this effort, Benedict Arnold would have one of his finest hours, with Philip Ulmer as one of his captains.

Arnold was first assigned to superintend the construction of the new gunboats and row galleys at the Skenesboro shipyard and then assigned to become commodore of the American fleet. Arnold was constantly in need of experienced shipwrights, sailors and mariners, and by the end of July, as the first four gunboats were launched and fitted out, Arnold assigned Philip Ulmer to take command of the gunboat christened *Spitfire*. This is confirmed in an order signed by "Philip Ulmer Capt" to Ezekiel Farrow, appointing him mate of the gundelo *Spitfire* "by virtue of the Authority vested in me…by the Command of the Honorable Brigadier General Arnold…in the fleet in the Service of the United States of America."

Just ten weeks later, on October 11, 1776, *Spitfire*—along with the rest of the "wretched, motley crew," as Arnold had described them—fought the British navy with determination and "Spirited Conduct" at the Battle of Valcour Island. As darkness brought the intensive five-and-a-half-hour contest to an end, Arnold assessed his casualties and the strength of the enemy and put forward a bold plan for a daring nighttime escape. Ordering his thirteen surviving vessels to wrap their oars with rags to muffle their clatter and to hang a single, shrouded light in the stern, as darkness fell the battle-weary men were ordered to weigh anchor and slip past the British ships deployed in a blockade. Remarkably, with night to shield them, Arnold, Ulmer and the surviving sailors and marines succeeded in rowing undetected past the British line and south toward the safety of Crown Point.

We know from Arnold's October 15 letter to General Philip Schuyler that during this desperate escape two gunboats had to be abandoned in the vicinity of Schuyler's Island. One of these gunboats was the *Jersey*, which was found abandoned and awash the next day by the British and taken by them into their service. We also now know that the second gunboat was Captain Philip Ulmer's *Spitfire* and that it did sink as intended and came to rest upright on the deep, dark lake bottom. The gunboats' crews were taken aboard other vessels as the desperate race to escape the pursuing British warships continued into October 13. It was then that the far less damaged British fleet caught the fleeing Americans and a second battle, dubbed in modern times the battle of Split Rock Mountain, took place. For more than two hours Arnold and his rearmost five warships fought the British while running for their lives until it was clear that the action could not be sustained. Arnold then ordered the four remaining gunboats to accompany his row galley *Congress* into a small bay on the eastern shore. Here, with their flags still flying, Arnold ordered his ships blown up, and their surviving crews marched with him overland to safety. Among the survivors was Captain Philip Ulmer.

Philip Ulmer had been made an ensign by a commission signed by John Hancock, had been promoted to lieutenant by George Washington, had been assigned as a sloop and gunboat captain by Benedict Arnold and had served as a translator with General Lafayette and General De Kalb. After Valcour Island, Ulmer served at the Battle of Saratoga and wintered with the army at Valley Forge before returning home to Maine, where his service continued until the war's end. Active in community civic and commercial affairs, Ulmer was called to serve again during the War of 1812. During this latter service, Ulmer was wounded leading an assault against a strong British position. Philip Ulmer died shortly after the end of the War of 1812, some years before Maine achieved the statehood for which he had worked so hard. Today, the impact and legacy of his contributions to his state and country can still be felt and are chronicled in Patricia Hubert's new biography.

There is another, tangible legacy connected to Philip Ulmer and his life and contribution to the formation of our nation. It is the gunboat *Spitfire*, intact, upright and archaeologically untouched since it sank in the early morning hours of October 12, 1776. Historians who studied the Battle of Valcour Island had long believed that perhaps one vessel, usually referred to as the "missing gunboat," was unaccounted for and might still remain beneath the waters of Lake Champlain. Over several decades, a number of institutions launched efforts to search for the missing gunboat. In June 1997, the Lake Champlain Maritime Museum's sonar survey team found an intriguing target on the deep lake bottom. The museum was in the second year of an ambitious ten-year "Whole Lake Survey" to locate and document all the lake's shipwrecks, initiated in response to an infestation by zebra mussels. And so it was that the "missing gunboat" was found, and after almost two years of intensive research, this gunboat was conclusively identified as Captain Philip Ulmer's *Spitfire*. Patricia Hubert invested an additional five and a half years of research, documenting and writing to compile Ulmer's story.

I have often preached that finding shipwrecks is easy but managing these complex and irreplaceable cultural resources is hard. *Spitfire* has been recognized as the most significant underwater cultural resource in Lake Champlain and is listed on the National Register of Historic Places, but its future is by no means secure. It is my sincere hope that the publication of this new biography of Captain Philip Ulmer will encourage and promote discussion about how best to preserve the *Spitfire* to inform and inspire future generations.

Art Cohn
Senior Scientist, Lake Champlain Maritime Museum
February 24, 2014

Preface

A small boat left Snug Harbor Marina, located on the western shore of Lake Champlain, several miles south of Plattsburg, New York. Our guides were Eric Pabst and his son. It was a harbor workboat not built for sightseeing but comfortable enough for the four of us. We crossed the open water of the small channel and passed over the site where the Battle of Valcour Island had taken place on October 11, 1776. This first major naval battle of the new republic was between a small American naval fleet commanded by General Benedict Arnold and the powerful British Royal Navy fleet commanded by Sir Guy Carleton, the governor general of British forces in North America. The intense three-day battle on Lake Champlain began at Valcour Island on the western shore of the lake, and it ended two days later on the eastern shore. While four vessels escaped, the remaining remnants of General Arnold's naval fleet were scuttled at Ferris' Bay (present-day Arnold's Bay in Panton, Vermont). The boats were abandoned and left in billowing flames with their colors still flying. The American survivors of the lake battle made their way to safety following a narrow bridle path through the dense woodlands that led southward along the lake toward Fort Ticonderoga while being pursued by hostile Mohawk Indians and fired upon by the warships of the powerful British fleet.

Our guides related the dramatic stories of the battles that took place on Lake Champlain during the American Revolution and the War of 1812, the second British invasion of the United States of America. My husband and I were intrigued to learn more about Lake Champlain and specifically about the Battle of Valcour Island since my husband is the direct descendant of John Thacher, who had participated in the battle as captain of the galley *Washington*. We learned that the gunboat *Philadelphia* had been salvaged from the underwater battlefield at Valcour Island and was placed permanently on display at the Smithsonian in Washington, D.C., as part of the National Museum of American History. Lake Champlain Maritime Museum at Basin Harbor in Vergennes, Vermont, has constructed an exact replica of the *Philadelphia* by hand, and it is presently used as a floating classroom for public education and historical enrichment programs every summer. We completed our boat tour of Valcour Island and decided that we needed to visit the Lake Champlain Maritime Museum to learn more about the Valcour Island maritime battlefield and the museum's marine archaeological research and preservation efforts.

We were very pleasantly surprised by the rewarding experience that we had at Lake Champlain Maritime Museum. After enjoying the beautifully displayed and informative exhibits, we saw the inspirational video *Key to Liberty* about the Battle of Valcour Island on October 11–13, 1776, as told by Revolutionary War veterans. Another video showed the discovery of the gunboat *Spitfire* at the bottom of Lake Champlain. The *Spitfire* had been in the Battle of Valcour Island and was scuttled by a Captain Ulmer, on General Arnold's orders, due to extensive damage by the British guns on the first day of battle. Lake Champlain Maritime Museum's 1997 discovery of the last vessel that belonged to America's first naval fleet, lost in action shortly after the Declaration of Independence was proclaimed by the Continental Congress on July 4, 1776, sent shockwaves through the quiet lake community and great excitement through the U.S. Navy Department. The use of a side-scanning sonar device, similar to the device that was utilized in the discovery and exploration of the *Titanic*, made the discovery of the *Spitfire* possible. The cold lake water and the gunboat's location in the deep lake had kept the gunboat in excellent condition, with only the top five or six feet of the mast having been snapped off. Some of the armaments and equipment remained in place since it sank on October 12, 1776. Since the discovery, Lake Champlain Maritime Museum has worked closely with the U.S. Navy to preserve the integrity of the site and protect the location of the gunboat. Efforts to document, preserve and protect the integrity of the underwater battlefield at Valcour Island have also been ongoing. The importance of the preservation of the gunboat *Spitfire* and the historical significance of the discovery cannot be overstated, especially when considered in the context

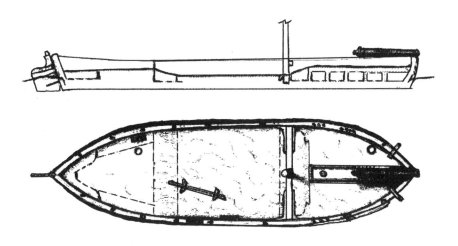

Drawing of the gunboat *Spitfire* at the bottom of Lake Champlain. *Courtesy of the Lake Champlain Maritime Museum.*

of understanding American naval history and archaeological practices since the early years of the American Revolution.

After speaking with several of the staff members at the Lake Champlain Maritime Museum who were preparing artifacts for display, I asked more questions about the discovery of the gunboat *Spitfire*. The primary challenge was to try to discover who Captain Ulmer of the *Spitfire* was. What role did he play in the naval fleet on Lake Champlain and in the battle at Valcour Island? Where did this military officer come from, and how did he become involved in the American Revolution? What kind of a person was the captain, and what was his story? All that was known at the time of my visit to the maritime museum in the summer of 2007 was simply that Ulmer was the captain of the gunboat *Spitfire*. Research was needed to discover more about the man. No one knew Captain Ulmer's first name; his regiment; the state in which he lived; his involvement in the Revolutionary War; or his life and military experience during the war. I contacted the director of the Lake Champlain Maritime Museum, Art Cohn, who referred me to the lead researcher, Peter Barranco, who was starting to search for information about the captain of the gunboat. Since the last name "Ulmer" is a familiar last name on my father's side of the family, I became curious to learn more about Captain Ulmer and if he might be related to me. I volunteered to assist with any research that might be helpful to the museum. Could one of my family's ancestors possibly have been involved in the Battle of Valcour Island in 1776 with my husband's family ancestor, Captain John Thacher? What was discovered about the *Spitfire* captain became a personal quest, and the book that resulted from the research became a labor of love and discovery.

Like the layers of an onion, as one layer was pulled away, another layer was discovered. The story of Philip Ulmer's life has been uncovered layer upon layer from the military rank of a common enlisted foot soldier to the officer's rank of major, through his personal performance, sacrifice and dedication to duty. The political and international events that happened on the world stage around the time of the American Revolution also had an impact on the American colonies on the national and state levels. The events that occurred on the state level in colonial Massachusetts also had an impact on the local level in the eastern frontier District of Maine, and then on a personal and human level. The story of Philip Ulmer and the life and times in which he lived has been unveiled layer by layer against the backdrop of colonial Massachusetts and national events—politically, militarily and economically. The character and personality of Philip, as a man, has been gradually revealed. The material reflects Philip Ulmer's personal contributions and challenges against the backdrop of his local community and county involvement in the eastern frontier of Massachusetts, as well as his involvement in the Massachusetts colony and in national and international events. Major Ulmer's personal courage, leadership, dedication to duty and public service and his perseverance in the face of fear, threats of violence, conflicts with enemies locally and regionally, the danger of death and the devastation of war was humbling and inspirational.

Philip Martin Ulmer grew up during the turbulent times of the French and Indian War, the Revolutionary War, the quasi-war with France and England and the War of 1812. Philip was directly or indirectly involved in conflicts and wars with England and/or France all of his life. The value and importance of freedom, liberty, justice, independence and sovereignty from oppression and foreign domination was impressed upon his life by his German-immigrant family from his birth in 1751 until his death in 1816. The values and principles upon which the United States of America was originally founded became an integral part of his life and belief system. Having experienced the lessons of slavery in his family's ancestry in Europe, the values of freedom and liberty were ingrained in his life from an early age. He was willing to fight for freedom and to give his life and fortune to preserve the democratic ideals of the new American republic for his posterity. This was Major Philip Ulmer's legacy and one that every American patriot since the founding of the United States can readily understand and support. He stands as an example of the quintessential American military serviceman, businessman and public servant of his time.

The bravery and determination of our early American patriots in resisting oppressive foreign domination and uniting as a nation under the common cause of freedom, justice and liberty—in spite of numerous cultural, religious, political and diverse racial issues—is a most valuable lesson for American citizens, immigrants and foreign countries to learn. By preserving the memories and honoring the servicemen and servicewomen of the past and present, we encourage the next generation of American citizens to also become honorable, courageous and brave in the defense of the American homeland and our American way of life. The underwater battlefield on Lake Champlain deserves to have a proper memorial recognizing the valor and personal sacrifices of the American soldiers and seamen who fought and died during the first official naval battle of the American Revolution. The site of the battlefield and the gunboat *Spitfire* deserve to be preserved for future generations of Americans as other sites and historical artifacts and relics have been throughout our American history. The gunboat, which is standing upright on the lake bottom with its cannon and munitions still in place, is the last of the Revolutionary War naval fleet to be discovered and probably the oldest intact naval war vessel to be discovered in modern times in America.

Acknowledgements

M any individuals have helped over the years since the initial research began for the manuscript of Philip Ulmer's life and the times in which he lived. Some individuals offered help by extending advice and encouragement, while others shared information, and still others helped by reading parts of the manuscript and commenting. I have come to appreciate the extraordinary generosity of the people on whom the historical researcher depends. I have learned through my experience that one of the joys of writing about American history is that many doors are opened to the serious inquirer. Nothing was known about Captain Ulmer, not even his first name, his company, his regiment or his state prior to my research. It has been a great challenge to discover who he was, where he came from and how he got involved in the Revolutionary War. Who was Captain Ulmer as a person, and what was his story? Although there may be unintentional faults or oversights made within the book, I have tried to be faithful and true to the historical facts and events (as they are presently known) that happened during Philip Ulmer's life and the turbulent times in which he lived.

I must gratefully mention a few individuals who gave their support and encouragement during the challenging years of research, documentation and writing of Major Philip Ulmer's biography. My husband, Richard Hubert, was a most valuable and constant assistant in the writing of this book by offering his suggestions, encouragement and his assistance in editing, formatting and proofing the finished manuscript. He is a direct a descendant of Captain John Thacher, captain of the galley *Washington*, who fought beside Captain Philip Ulmer in the Battle of Valcour Island on Lake Champlain in October 1776. Sincere appreciation and gratitude is given to my friend Judy Craven for her willingness to read and edit the book manuscript in its initial written form. My appreciation is also extended to Robert Manness, John Treleaven and Herman and Rhonda Davenport for their support and suggestions during the writing of the book manuscript. I would also like to acknowledge the encouragement of my children, Christopher Hubert and Carolyn (Hubert) Murray, as well as my grandchildren, Kyle, Julia and Ryan Murray, who are descendants of the original Ulmer family from Ulm and Enzberg, Germany. They are related to Major Philip M. Ulmer through his grandfather, Johannes Jakob Ulmer, an original founder of the Broad Bay settlement in Waldoboro, Maine. The town of Ulm was named for the early von Ulm family, descendants of the Baron von Ulm.

Art Cohn, past director of the Lake Champlain Maritime Museum (LCMM), receives my thanks for the opportunity to work with his research team and for giving me suggestions and technical directions in writing the manuscript. He is presently heading up the *Spitfire* Project Management Plan for the preservation of the gunboat *Spitfire* and other historical artifacts for the LCMM. Erick Tichonuk and Adam Kane, co-directors of the LCMM, gave their encouragement and provided information that helped with the documentation of the research material. Erick Tichonuk, the present director, has been a source of support in the final stages of the book preparation.

Peter Barranco is gratefully acknowledged as the lead researcher on the *Spitfire* project in its initial form until his eyes failed him. I felt strongly about continuing the research work, and I committed myself to carrying on the work that he initiated with the discovery of the gunboat *Spitfire*. Peter was helpful with the early research information on Captain Philip Ulmer's name and military service with the captured British armed transport vessel *Isabella* during the Canadian Expedition in 1776 on the St. Lawrence River and with Philip Ulmer's later involvement with the gunboat *Spitfire*, which was involved in the three-day battle on Lake Champlain in October 1776.

Artist and devoted volunteer Ernest Haas has donated years of his time and talent to the enrichment of the education programs that are given during the year at the LCMM. His impressive artwork depicting the discovery of the gunboat *Spitfire* at the bottom of Lake Champlain and his other artist renderings of the Battle of Valcour Island add interest and value to the excellent work that goes on at the LCMM. Thanks and gratitude is given to Eloise Biel, director of collections and exhibits, who helped provide the images and advice for the final image preparation of this book.

The dedicated team of people involved in the Lake Champlain Underwater Historic Preservation efforts must be mentioned with great appreciation for their efforts in bringing maritime history alive for present and future generations of Americans to enjoy. The divers and recovery crew of the Nautical Archaeological Program have spent many years searching for sunken ships and unexpectedly discovered the gunboat *Spitfire*, the last of Commodore and General Benedict Arnold's American naval fleet, which was scuttled and sank to the bottom of Lake Champlain on October 12, 1776, near Schuyler Island.

My thanks are given to Darren Brown of the Beverly Historical Museum, who provided early research materials in documenting the Ulmer family in Salem and Marblehead, Massachusetts, and to the Peabody-Essex Museum staff for providing further documentation on the Ulmer lineage in the Salem area. Gratitude is given to Cynthia Alcorn, librarian for the Grand Lodge of Masons in Massachusetts, who provided valuable information on Philip Ulmer and his brother, George, and their involvement as Grand Representatives from the Grand Lodge of Massachusetts to the District in Maine. She provided information on Philip Ulmer's early association as a Charter Member of the Hancock Lodge, No. 4 at Castine, Maine, where he served as Grand Treasurer pro tem at the constitution of the Masonic lodge in 1794. Thanks are also given to Emily Schroeder of the Maine State Historical Library, who provided resource information and copies of Philip Ulmer's masonic record in frontier Maine as a Charter Member of the Amity Lodge No. 6 in Camden, Maine, at its constitution in 1801. The original date of Philip Ulmer's initiation into the Masonic Fraternity of Free and Accepted Masons and his elevation to the sublime degree of Master Mason has yet to be discovered, but it was likely in a military traveling lodge with other officers during the Revolutionary War. Many valuable documents and historical records have been destroyed over the generations by fires, water damage and deterioration from neglect or discarded because of disinterest and the need for more space.

Historian James Nelson, education associate at the Maine Maritime Museum in Bath, Maine, provided support and encouragement during my early research on Philip Ulmer's involvement during the siege of Boston and the Battle of Valcour Island on Lake Champlain in October

1776. I give my thanks to him for reviewing the manuscript, giving permission to use some of his maps and for lending his encouragement for having the manuscript published.

My sincere gratitude is given to writer and historian Carol Fisher of Camden, Maine, who was a knowledgeable resource and provided support and information during my research in the towns of Waldoboro and Lincolnville, Maine. Carol Fisher's cousin Rilla Whiteneck of Concord, New Hampshire, amiably researched archive documents on Philip Ulmer's involvement in the Massachusetts state militia and provided valuable information about Philip's movements and the involvement of his detached militia company in frontier Maine during the Revolutionary War from April 1778 until the end of the conflict.

I am indebted to Connie Parker, past director of the Lincolnville Schoolhouse and Historical Museum, who provided valuable support, encouragement and information about Philip and George Ulmer's lives at Ducktrap Harbor and cove in Lincolnville, Maine. She graciously researched and discovered the long-hidden burial site of Major Philip M. Ulmer and his wife, Christiana, beside the shores of the Penobscot Bay at the small private cemetery at Osgood Point on Ducktrap Harbor-cove. Thanks are given to Christopher Osgood for permission to visit Major Ulmer's gravesite at the Ulmer and Wade Cemetery. Connie Parker and Diane O'Brien are gratefully acknowledged for their support and documentation that was valuable in the accurate understanding of Philip Ulmer's life and contributions as a public servant to the town of Lincolnville and his service to the county and local communities as a congressman in the House of Representatives in the Massachusetts Provincial Congress located in Boston.

I extend my appreciation to Larry Koolkin, assistant to Art Cohn on Special Projects, for his willingness to encourage and shepherd Major Philip Ulmer's manuscript thorough some uncertain times to its final publication.

Without the contributions of dedicated writers, historians and caring individuals, little information and historical documentation would be available for future researchers and writers. It is from the study of our cultural and historical roots from past generations that our present-day society can learn valuable lessons about successful endeavors. Learning the lessons of American history empowers and enables present-day and future generations to build a more secure and productive future for all of its citizens.

Timeline

1743	Ulmer family comes to America from Germany
December 25, 1751	Philip Ulmer born at Broad Bay settlement
1754–63	French and Indian War
1755	Philip and his family move to Marblehead/Salem
April 19, 1775	Lexington and Concord, Massachusetts, attacked by the British raiders
April 1775	Philip Ulmer enlists as sergeant with Colonel Gardner/Bond's regiment
April 1775	Siege of Boston begins with a "Call to Arms"
May 1775	Capture of Fort Ticonderoga by Benedict Arnold and Ethan Allen
June 17, 1775	American Revolution begins with the Battle of Bunker Hill
July 3, 1775	General George Washington takes command of army at Cambridge

September 11, 1775	Expedition to Canada under command of Colonel Arnold
March 1776	Philip Ulmer sent with first relief troops to Canada
March 5, 1776	Siege of Boston ends with Continental occupation of Dorchester Heights; British evacuation of Boston on March 17
April 1776	Philip Ulmer enlists as ensign with the Massachusetts Twenty-fifth Regiment in Canada
April 1776	General Arnold assigns Philip Ulmer as captain of the ship *Isabella*
June 1776	American army retreats from Canada to Fort Ticonderoga, New York
Summer 1776	American navy fleet built at Skenesboro, (Whitehall) New York
July 28, 1776	Declaration of Independence read at Fort Ticonderoga
August–October 1776	Arnold's American naval fleet defends Lake Champlain
October 11–13, 1776	Battle of Valcour Island, defeat of the American naval fleet
November 1776	Sullivan and Gates's troops ordered to join Washington's army in Pennsylvania
December 25, 1776	Delaware crossing and the Continental Army attack on Trenton, New Jersey
January 1, 1777	Philip Ulmer advanced in rank to lieutenant
January 2, 1777	Battle at Assunpink Creek, the second battle at Trenton

January 3, 1777	Battle of Princeton
January–May 1777	Washington's Continental Army in winter quarters at Morristown, New Jersey
April 26, 1777	British General Tryon's raid on American supply depot at Danbury, Connecticut
May 1777	Lieutenant Philip Ulmer, Colonel Vose's regiment, assigned New York Highlands
August 1777	Colonel Vose's regiment with Lieutenant Philip Ulmer sent to Stillwater to defend Saratoga, New York
September 19, 1777	First Battle at Saratoga, Lieutenant Ulmer with General Glover's regiment
October 7, 1777	Second Battle at Saratoga; surrender of British General Burgoyne's army on October 17
October 1777	Lieutenant Ulmer chosen as translator and escort for German POWs to Boston
December 1777	Lieutenant Ulmer returns to General Washington's troops at Valley Forge
January 1778	Lieutenant Philip Ulmer seeks to resign from the Continental Army
February 1778	General Washington grants resignation six weeks later
February 1778	Lieutenant Ulmer remains on Valley Forge muster rolls, given special assignment
February 1778	Lieutenant Philip Ulmer, translator for General DeKalb with General Lafayette's troops
February 6, 1778	Franco-American Alliance signed between king of France and Congress

March 1778	Lieutenant Ulmer remains with DeKalb in General Lafayette's Canadian Expedition
April 1778	Lieutenant Ulmer returns to Valley Forge with American forces under Lafayette
April 1778	Lieutenant Ulmer returns to Waldoboro, Maine, in the Eastern Department
April 1778	Philip Ulmer enlists as captain with General McCobb's state militia
April 1778	Captain Philip Ulmer given detached company to build seacoast defenses
June 28, 1778	Battle of Monmouth, New Jersey
July 1778	Focus of war shifts to the Southern Theater
July 24–August 12, 1779	Penobscot Bay Expedition, Captain Ulmer with McCobb's Regiment
July 28, 1779	Captain Philip Ulmer, Continental Marines, attack cliffs at Dyce's Head
Summer 1779	Philip Ulmer shot by a British soldier, never fully recovers
August 12, 1779	American fleet destroyed along the shores of the Penobscot River
October 19, 1781	Battle of Yorktown, General Cornwallis's British army surrenders
September 3, 1783	Treaty of Paris signed
January 14, 1784	U.S. Congress ratifies the Treaty of Paris; approves the articles of peace on January 15

April 1784	British troops leave Fort George in frontier Maine
1784	The Ulmer brothers build new sawmill and dam at Ducktrap Harbor
1784	Generals Knox, Lafayette and Lincoln and Colonel Jackson visit Ulmer brothers
1785	Ulmer brothers build business complex along the Ducktrap River
1786–1806	Henry Knox becomes a business patron of the Ulmer brothers
September 1787	George Washington presides over the Constitutional Convention
1788	Ulmer brothers purchase the Ducktrap watershed from General Knox
1789–97	George Washington elected to serve as the first U.S. president
1796	Ulmer brothers build new houses for their families
1797, 1800	Several valuable Ulmer shipments captured by French privateers
1798	Henry Knox forecloses on the Ulmer brothers' mortgages
1801	Ulmer shipbuilding, shipping, loan and credit records burned in a house fire
June 23, 1802	Lincolnville incorporated as a town
1802–16	Philip enters a career of public service in town government

1804	Philip dissolves business partnership with his brother
1806	Philip serves as Massachusetts legislator in Boston; taken to jail for nonpayment of taxes and debts
1806	General Henry Knox dies under suspicious circumstances
1809	Philip recalled to active duty as a sailing master in the U.S. Navy
1811	Philip elected to the House of Representatives in Massachusetts Congress
1812–15	Philip serves as Lincolnville town selectman during the War of 1812
1814	Philip appointed as deputy customs official by the State of Massachusetts
1814	Philip Ulmer involved in actively defending Lincolnville from British invasion
December 24, 1814	Treaty of Ghent signed ending the War of 1812
1815–16	Philip continues to serve in Lincolnville town government
October 3, 1816	Philip Ulmer dies and is buried at "the Point" on Ducktrap cove
March 15, 1820	Congress grants statehood to Maine as the twenty-third state

Overview of Philip Ulmer's
Military Life

These are the times that try men's souls.
The summer soldier and the sunshine Patriot will
In this crisis shrink from the service of his country;
But he that stands it NOW deserves the love and thanks of man and woman.
—The American Crisis *by Thomas Paine, December 1776*

Philip Martin Ulmer's military experiences, like those of many other American Patriots of his time, shadows the story of America's struggle for freedom, liberty, independence and the opportunity to pursue one's own destiny in the sparsely settled colonies in North America. After the French and Indian War ended with the Treaty of Paris in 1763, England's King George III and the British Parliament were determined to continue their exploitation and imperial colonization in Canada and in the Province of Maine, as well as in the Great Lakes region and in the Northwest Territories. The British government employed great military and naval efforts to forcefully crush the rebelling colonists of New England who opposed England's repressive taxation without representation. The British government, in order to rebuild its own failing economy and to finance the wars in which England had been engaged for many years around the world, decided to exploit the American colonists and America's natural resources for its own economic and military gains. The British government's foreign policy and imperialistic mindset came into direct conflict with the American colonists' desire for independence and to seek their own destiny and God-given rights to freedom, liberty and opportunity in America's frontier colonies.

The Ulmer family, like many first- and second-generation immigrant Americans, sought to escape the feudalistic society in Europe and to seek a new life in America, where life, religious freedom, liberty and the pursuit of happiness and prosperity were respected and encouraged. The original Ulmer (von Ulm) family of Germany had suffered the loss of many family members from devastating illnesses and plagues that swept through Europe. The Ulmer family, like many immigrant pioneer settlers, had a deep abiding faith in divine Providence. They believed in the values of hard work, sacrifice, perseverance and constancy to the principles of freedom, liberty and mutual respect for their fellow man. Like other immigrants from European countries, the Ulmer family sought freedom from powerful kings, oppressive rulers and brutal dictators, as well as an opportunity to escape from starvation and disease that was rampant in Europe at the time. In America, freedom from Europe's harsh feudal system of servitude, exploitation of the population and slavery was made possible. New immigrants had the opportunity to own land, worship as they pleased, develop their own livelihood and build family prosperity for future generations. The original Ulmer family, immigrants from the vicinity of Ulm in the district of Baden-Württemberg, Germany, rose in social standing and leadership in the new frontier settlement of Broad Bay (later called Waldoborough) in the District of Maine in the eastern frontier of Massachusetts. The Ulmer family's financial success was made possible through their hard work, education, ingenuity, business enterprise, financial investments and land speculation. The Ulmer family managed to become one of the wealthiest families in the Broad Bay settlement and the Penobscot Bay region.

Philip Martin Ulmer was an unknown American Patriot who served as a Massachusetts state militia foot soldier, rose to the rank of a lieutenant Continental Line officer and later became a state militia major during the Revolutionary War. He came from humble beginnings in the coastal frontier settlement of Broad Bay (hereafter Waldoboro) in the Province of Maine. After the Revolutionary War, he moved to the small, sparsely developed pioneer settlement of Ducktrap, where he and his younger brother, George Ulmer, struggled to establish a lumbering and shipbuilding business. Through hard work and perseverance, Philip and George became successful lumbering and shipping agents and wealthy business entrepreneurs in Ducktrap (renamed Lincolnville in 1802) in the eastern frontier of Massachusetts in the district of Maine Province. After many successful years in the shipbuilding and merchant trading businesses, the Ulmer brothers suffered a reversal of fortune from marauding enemy privateers in the West Indies. To survive the devastating financial business losses, both Philip and George Ulmer became involved in local and state politics. George Ulmer became a senator in the Massachusetts General Court, where he served a number of terms, and afterward made an unsuccessful political bid for the governorship of Massachusetts. Philip served as a justice of the peace and town leader in various governing roles for many years. He was elected by his district as a congressman to the Massachusetts House of Representatives prior to the War of 1812. After leaving the Massachusetts Congress when his term was completed, Philip Ulmer continued to act as a public official for the town of Lincolnville during the War of 1812. He also served as a town selectman, veteran militia leader and military strategist in his community during this period. He was appointed and served as a U.S. customs official in the Penobscot Bay region of frontier Maine from 1814 until the end of the war. He became involved in a potentially explosive incident with the captured British supercargo vessel *Mary* in November 1814 that almost caused the burning of several seaport towns along the Penobscot Bay.

Philip Ulmer's story as a Revolutionary War soldier began quite unexpectedly on April 19, 1775, when a British raiding party was sent from the British-controlled city of Boston, Massachusetts, to attack and destroy the arms and munitions that were being stored by farmers and merchants at Lexington and Concord. Paul Revere and several other Patriots, which included William Dawes and Samuel Prescott, rode through the Massachusetts countryside to alert the local towns and villages that a British raiding party of seven hundred men, led by Lieutenant Colonel Francis Smith, was coming to destroy the military arms and supply depot at Lexington and Concord. The local militiamen met the advancing British raiding party, led by Major John Pitcairn, and engaged them in a skirmish. The American militia and local minutemen were successful in forcing the British raiders to retreat back into the city of Boston. There were losses on both sides. This incident was credited as the beginning of the American Revolution with "the shot heard around the world." The Salem and Marblehead communities were greatly alarmed since they had also been storing arms and military supplies in a depot on the outskirts of Salem Village. On April 23, 1775, the Massachusetts Provincial Congress gave instructions to General Artemas Ward, who was in command of the militia forces outside of Boston, to issue a general "call to arms" to the American colonies for an army of thirty thousand militiamen to be formed to repel the British forces that were intent on securing Boston and setting up a British military stronghold there.[1]

Among other measures, the Massachusetts Provincial Congress strengthened its defensive position with wavering and indifferent towns by setting up a Central Committee of Correspondence and Safety in each county to coordinate the actions of smaller town committees and prod them into conformity and action. In 1760, Wiscasset (the Abenaki Indian name for the village town) was incorporated as Pownalborough and named for colonial governor Thomas Pownal (also appears as Pownall). In the District of Maine, Pownalborough (hereafter Pownalboro) was the seat of operations for the Central Committee of Safety in the Lincoln County vicinity of frontier Maine Province. The militia leadership was made up of Samuel McCobb, Joseph Waldo, Timothy Langdon, Dummer Sewall and James Howard.[2] It was this central committee that asserted pressure upon the frontier settlement at Broad Bay to declare itself either in support of the British Crown or in support of the rebelling New England colonies. Pownalboro was located several miles to the west of Broad Bay, and it was renamed Wiscasset in 1802. The local Massachusetts state militiamen from the frontier District of Maine responded the next day by sending a company of sixty fully equipped militia soldiers to Cambridge, which was the central army headquarters for the American resistance outside of Boston. In a few days, the first company of Massachusetts state soldiers was followed by other militiamen and volunteers from the Province of Maine. Militia troops gathered for service in seacoast towns from Kittery (in York County) to the eastern frontier settlement of Machias (in Lincoln County) on the Penobscot Bay.

Philip Ulmer and his younger brother, George, usually wintered in the Salem/Marblehead vicinity with their Ulmer relatives. On April 19, 1775, a British raiding party was sent from Boston to arrest Samuel Adams and John Hancock, who were considered Revolutionary leaders. General Artemas Ward, following the orders of the Massachusetts Provincial Congress, issued a universal call to arms. Philip Ulmer, being a trained twenty-three-year-old militia sergeant from Waldoboro at the time of the raid on Lexington, marched with his fellow Massachusetts militiamen from Salem to Cambridge in April 1775. He was assigned to Colonel Thomas Gardner's regiment with other Massachusetts soldiers who had responded to the call to arms. Philip Ulmer enlisted as an infantry sergeant for one year in Colonel Gardner's Fifteenth Regiment, and he served with his militia company at Prospect Hill[3] under the command of General Israel Putnam at Cambridge, the American military headquarters. (Salem and Waldoboro were both credited with his enlistment.) Captain Abraham Hunt, in whose company Philip Ulmer served during the siege of Boston, was adjutant for Colonel Gardner's regiment.

While fishing in the harbor off Marblehead in early May, Philip Ulmer's younger brother, George, was captured by British impressment troops on the warship *Lively*. After a dangerous and daring escape, he made his way to the American lines and enlisted as a private in Colonel Paterson's regiment. (Salem was credited with his enlistment.) On May 2, Captain Benedict Arnold received a colonel's commission from the Massachusetts Provincial Congress and was given orders to raise a body of men, not to exceed four hundred, for the purpose of capturing Fort Ticonderoga and Crown Point in northern New York on Lake Champlain.[4] Arnold and a small number of junior officers helped recruit men for the mission in Massachusetts. Ethan Allen and his Green Mountain militiamen, along with Arnold's small detachment of soldiers, successfully captured Fort Ticonderoga with little resistance. In the days that followed, the Green Mountain Boys slowly drifted back across the lake and returned to their farms. Arnold's recruits started to arrive, and his situation began to improve when his friend Eleaser Oswald arrived with a small schooner named the *Katherine*, which had belonged to the wealthy Loyalist Philip Skene and named for his wife. The schooner had been captured at its berth by Ethan Allen's men, who did not know how to sail the ship and turned it over to Oswald and Arnold's recruits. The *Katherine* was renamed the *Liberty* and was quickly converted to an armed ship by piercing the ship's sides with four carriage guns and mounting eight swivel guns on the side rails. The guns had been some of those captured at Fort Ticonderoga and Crown Point. Private George Ulmer apparently volunteered to be a new recruit on this mission to northern New York.[5] George remained with General Schuyler's and General Montgomery's regiments in the New York Department and did not return to Boston with Colonel Arnold. He was not involved in the Battle of Bunker Hill. (Private George Ulmer would later participate with General Montgomery's forces in the Canadian Expedition in the fall of 1775, the American attack upon Fort St. John and the capture of Montreal.[6] It is unlikely that he participated with General Montgomery's and General Arnold's forces in the attack upon Quebec City on December 31, 1775, since his enlistment had terminated and many of the Massachusetts soldiers left Montgomery's and Arnold's army troops in Canada and had returned home by that time.)

Colonel Thomas Gardner's Fifteenth Regiment and Colonel John Paterson's (also written Patterson) Twelfth Regiment served as the rear guard for General William Heath's regiment on June 17, 1775, and these regiments were involved in the heat of the battle at Bunker Hill.[7] Sergeant Philip Ulmer became actively involved in the heavy fighting in the afternoon during the final action with Colonel Gardner's and Colonel Paterson's regiments. These regiments were a part of the fierce battle at Bunker Hill with General Ward's and Colonel John Nixon's regiments. Colonel Nixon's regiment included Captain Samuel McCobb's company, with whom Philip Ulmer had served at Waldoboro prior to the British raid on Lexington and Concord. Samuel McCobb's company was from the frontier district of Cumberland and Lincoln Counties where the original Ulmer family lived. The combined troops of General Ward's and Colonel Gerrish's regiments with Major Henry Jackson's company (also part of Colonel Gardner's regiment) covered the American retreat.[8] The American militia forces under the command of General Putnam withdrew from Bunker Hill to the high ground at Prospect Hill, where the American forces regrouped.[9] Colonel Gardner was mortally injured during the fierce battle at Bunker Hill and was taken to the home of his sister, Elizabeth, the wife of Thomas Sparhawk, where he languished for two weeks.[10] A defensive fortress was rapidly erected upon the top of the prominence at Prospect Hill overlooking Charlestown and the city of Boston. The fortress was described as the strongest work in the besieging line and withstood nine months of British bombardment from June 17, 1775, to March 17, 1776.[11] Sergeant Philip Ulmer was involved in the fighting with Colonel Gardner's, Colonel Paterson's and Colonel Nixon's regiments. Some of his fellow Waldoboro militiamen were Isaiah Cole, Conrad Heyer and John Stahl, who also gave continuous military service during the siege of Boston.[12] (The bloody battle actually took place on and around Breed's Hill but was incorrectly called Bunker Hill.)

Sergeant Philip Ulmer was present with Colonels Paterson, Nixon and Gardner's regiments at the Prospect Hill encampment when General George Washington arrived at the American militia army headquarters at Cambridge, Massachusetts, on Sunday, July 2, 1775.[13] The soldiers who had been digging ditches, reinforcing the siege lines and burying their dead from the recent battle at Breed's Hill and Bunker Hill were assembled for General Washington and his staff officers to review. General Washington, fully dressed in his military uniform, was an impressive sight riding on his white horse, which had a leopard-skin blanket and a fine leather saddle on its back. The soldiers, dressed in their dirty work clothes, stood silently at attention as the new commander in chief rode past them in review. Because of the weather conditions, the soldiers were soon dismissed and returned to their assigned tasks. The newly arrived general and his staff retired to the military headquarters at Cambridge to unpack and settle into their lodgings after their long overland journey from Philadelphia.

On July 3, 1775, General Washington assumed command of the American militia army, renaming it the Continental Army. General Washington and the commanding officers of the militia army troops made a formal review of the siege troops that were present outside of Boston. It was the same day that Colonel Thomas Gardner finally died from the musket ball injuries that he received during the bloody battle at Bunker Hill. General Washington's General Orders, issued on July 4, 1775, read in part, "Colonel Gardner is to be buried tomorrow, at 3 o'clock, P.M., with the military honours due to so brave and gallant on officer, who fought, bled, and died in the cause of his country and mankind. His own regiment, except the company at Malden, to attend on this mournful occasion. The place of the companies, in the lines on Prospect Hill, to be supplied by Colonel Gardner's regiment, till the funeral is over."[14]

On July 5, General Washington spoke at the burial of Colonel Thomas Gardner. General Washington praised Colonel Gardner's bravery, valor and his sacrifice to the American cause and to mankind. The review of the militia troops was a sad and solemn occasion. Colonel William Bond, who had been a lieutenant colonel in Colonel Gardner's Fifteenth Massachusetts Regiment, was soon assigned to command Gardner's regiment (renamed Colonel Bond's regiment) in which Philip Ulmer served at Prospect Hill. Major Jackson, who served in Colonel Gardner's regiment, was moved up in rank to second-in-command. On July 18, 1775, a flag was presented to General Putnam and his brave soldiers at Prospect Hill bearing the motto of Massachusetts, "An Appeal to Heaven," and the motto of Connecticut, "Qui Transtulit Sustinet" (He Who Transplanted Still Sustains).[15] In November 1775, the Continental Army was reorganized by General Washington, and Colonel Bond's regiment was designated as the Twenty-fifth Continental Massachusetts Line.

Sergeant Philip Ulmer's first involvement with the Canadian Expedition may have been in helping to provide ship transportation for Colonel Arnold's Canadian expeditionary forces in the fall of 1775. The *Broad Bay* schooner was a cargo and transport vessel that Philip Ulmer helped to build with his uncles in the Ulmer shipyard at Broad Bay Cove in 1770, prior to the Revolutionary War.[16] This schooner became the flagship for Colonel Arnold's flotilla that sailed up the Kennebec River to Fort Western[17] on the first leg of Arnold's expedition into Canada in September 1775. It is quite likely that Sergeant Philip Ulmer, who knew the transport vessel well, was among the volunteer soldiers involved in the expedition and was on board the schooner at this time. The transport vessel *Broad Bay* served as a water base for Arnold's troops, and it brought the soldiers who were too sick to continue on the expedition with Colonel Arnold back to Newburyport for care at the army hospital.[18] The *Broad Bay*, which was anchored in the river near the primitive outpost of Fort Western, was to serve as the support vessel and evacuation base for Colonel Arnold's expeditionary forces. It continued to serve as a water base for operations and to transport supplies and correspondence for a number of weeks before returning to port and resuming further orders.[19] Operating on Washington's orders, the military seamen (called marines since they fought on land and sea) who transported Colonel Arnold's detached volunteer brigade to Fort Western would deliver the heavy munitions, supplies and military goods to Canada for General Montgomery's and Colonel Arnold's American forces once they arrived in Canada.[20] Upon their return from this assignment, the soldiers were to be assigned the task of converting merchant vessels into armed warships for service in Washington's Continental Navy at Beverly and Plymouth.[21] Colonel John Glover's merchant schooner *Hannah* was the first of the converted naval transports to become outfitted as an armed fighting vessel at Beverly, Massachusetts, for service in General Washington's "secret" Continental naval fleet. The Continental Congress had given General Washington broad powers to appoint ships' captains and to direct their orders, but developing armed vessels to defend the seacoast was to be kept secret.

Another possibility is that Philip Ulmer was among the German American soldiers (which included his cousin, George Ulmer Jr., the son of his uncle John) that served with Captain Samuel McCobb's detached company of volunteers from the Kennebec and Lincoln County area that participated in the Canadian Expedition.[22] Captain McCobb's company of volunteers from Cumberland and Lincoln Counties in frontier Maine was one of the New England companies in the brigade of Lieutenant Colonel Enos that made up the rear of Colonel Arnold's Canadian Expedition in 1775. Colonel Farnsworth, who likely came from the Waldoboro community, served with Colonel Arnold on the Canadian Expedition as quartermaster. His assignment was to collect and forward provisions and supplies for the soldiers to use on their trek through the wilderness of Maine Province to Quebec, Canada. His assignment was also to provide for the needs of any returning sick soldiers from the expedition and to take them to Newburyport, where they would be transported by land to the nearest army hospital. Another duty of Colonel Farnsworth was to forward Colonel Arnold's reports and messages to General Washington and the outside world.[23] Other Farnsworth men belonged to the local militia company that was commanded by Captain Samuel Gregg and composed of young soldier recruits from the Waldoboro and St. George (appeared as St. Georges in the old spelling) settlements in Lincoln County. Some of the young Farnsworth soldiers included fifer James Farnsworth and Private William Farnsworth Jr.[24] Documents indicate that militia soldiers from this same company served at Camp Prospect Hill during the siege of Boston during the winter of 1775–76 with Sergeant Philip Ulmer.

Sergeant Philip Ulmer could have participated in Colonel Roger Enos's division with Captain McCobb's volunteer company with other detached volunteer soldiers and marines he knew from frontier Maine. Sergeant Ulmer could have remained with the schooner *Broad Bay*, which completed its supply and transport mission as General Washington had instructed. The schooner returned to its home port, and the crewmen returned to their previous assignments. The soldier volunteers who participated in the fall invasion of Canada with Colonel Arnold's brigade suffered terribly on their trek through the Maine wilderness in 1775. About half of the militia volunteers who started on the Canadian Expedition eventually died of starvation, illness, exposure to the harsh environmental conditions and accidents. After a council of war with Colonel Christopher Greene at the Dead River encampment in the wilderness frontier of Maine, Colonel Enos decided to abandon the expedition and left for home, leaving Colonel Arnold's Canadian Expedition on the night of October 25. He took with him his three companies and their commanders, Captain Thomas Williams (from Colonel John Paterson's regiment), Captain Samuel McCobb and Captain Scott (of Connecticut) with several other officers—about 150 men—plus another 150 invalids and weak stragglers (including forty-eight sick men from Greene's division), totaling about half of Arnold's expeditionary forces.[25] The boat repair crew commanded by Reuben Colburn also turned back with Colonel Enos's division. By October 30, after five days of traveling, the first of the returning soldiers reached the first Kennebec River settlements below the Norridgewock Falls. They enjoyed warm, dry living conditions and the best meal that they had had in a long time. Those soldiers with McCobb's company who had relatives in the frontier vicinity and access to boat transportation were able to return to Cambridge in a timely manner. The other companies had to march for about two weeks before completing their return to the army headquarters at Cambridge. They all arrived back from the Canadian Expedition by November 23. Upon their return to Cambridge, the division of soldiers was disbanded and returned to their former regiments. In any case, Sergeant Philip Ulmer was present at Prospect Hill with his regular company with Captain Fuller by mid-November 1775.

Although the circumstantial evidence is strong, it cannot be absolutely confirmed that German family names from Waldoboro and Lincoln County appeared on the list of militiamen who were killed or taken prisoner during General Montgomery's and Colonel Arnold's attack on Quebec City on December 31, 1775.[26] This is because General Washington ordered that the names of the militia volunteers involved in the "secret" Canadian Expedition be removed from the duty rolls at Cambridge prior to the invasion of Canada in September 1775. The Revolutionary War service records stated that "Waldoborough soldiery [was] a tangled nightmare"[27] since the enlistment of the militia soldiers was for such short durations. Overall, the records showed that soldiers from Waldoboro served honorably and far above average.[28]

Colonel Bond's regiment (formerly Colonel Gardner's regiment) was renamed the Twenty-fifth Massachusetts Continental Regiment in November 1775, and several companies were detached from the regiment to serve on special assignment at Plymouth to convert merchant ships to armed war vessels. As part of this regiment, Sergeant Philip Ulmer became involved in the conversion of merchant sloops and schooners into armed fighting vessels for General George Washington's Continental naval fleet at Plymouth.[29] Dr. John Manvide, who was a French volunteer surgeon at Philip Ulmer's encampment at Prospect Hill, wrote in his journal, "On the 8 November we left Prospect Hill at 4 o'clock in the afternoon with 80 men, arms and baggage to go to Plymouth, where the Brig [Washington] was."[30]

Sergeant Philip Ulmer was involved with Captain Fuller's detached company in the conversion and outfitting of the two galleys *Spitfire* and *Washington*, which were sanctioned by the General Assembly of Rhode Island in late 1775.[31] Philip Ulmer probably served with the seamen and other soldiers in Captain Fuller's detached company from Prospect Hill on one of the converted armed Continental naval vessels at Plymouth. The General Assembly of Rhode Island, which had ordered the conversion of the merchant vessels, was able to put the two armed vessels into service in January 1776 with John Grimes as commodore. They sailed in the defense of American shipping in Narragansett Bay, acted as troop and supply transports and assisted landing parties engaged in seeking forage and provisions.[32] These two vessels were engaged in confrontations with British ships-of-war along the New England seacoast and captured British prize transports with supplies headed for the British-held stronghold in Boston. (Philip Ulmer's early associations with the refitted and armed galley *Spitfire*, on which he likely served briefly with Captain Fuller's company, might also explain why, a year later, he named the armed naval gunboat on which he served as captain on Lake Champlain in the fall of 1776 the odd name of *Spitfire*. The galley *Spitfire* had probably been the first armed warship that he had been associated with as part of Washington's Continental Navy, and the odd name had a special meaning to Philip.)

Colonel Bond's regiment stayed in winter quarters at Prospect Hill during the siege of Boston in 1775–76. On January 1, 1776, General Washington ordered that the flag of the United Colonies, bearing thirteen stripes and the crosses of Saint George and Saint Andrew, be raised at Prospect Hill in defiance of the British forces in Boston.[33] Sergeant Philip Ulmer was personally identified in a letter written by his cousin, Philip Reiser of Waldoboro, who served as a soldier at Prospect Hill with Philip during the winter encampment in late February 1776. After the battle at Dorchester Heights, Sergeant Philip Ulmer was among the first detached relief forces that were sent by General Washington to Quebec and Montreal, Canada, following the defeat of General Montgomery's and Colonel Arnold's American expeditionary forces at the city of Quebec on December 31, 1775.[34] Colonel Benedict Arnold was advanced in rank and commissioned as a general by the Continental Congress following his heroic leadership in the wilderness trek through Maine and the unsuccessful attack on Quebec City. Philip Ulmer had enlisted as a sergeant in the Massachusetts state militia for one year at the beginning of the siege of Boston in 1775, and he received a congressional commission as an ensign on April 20, 1776.[35] The commission was signed by John Hancock, president of the Continental Congress.[36] Ensign Philip Ulmer reenlisted in Colonel Bond's detached Twenty-fifth Continental Regiment, and he served with General Arnold's detached brigade in April 1776 in Canada. General Arnold appointed Ensign Philip Ulmer as captain of the captured British sloop *Isabella* on the St. Lawrence River.[37] Ensign Philip Ulmer's assignment as captain of the *Isabella* was to guard the captured fortress at Montreal, to observe and report movements of the British forces and to transport the American troops and supplies wherever they were needed. In late April 1776, Captain Philip Ulmer helped to transport General Arnold's troops on the armed sloop *Isabella* from Quebec to Montreal, where Arnold took command of the fort. Captain Philip Ulmer operated under the command and direction of General Arnold at Montreal. Captain Ulmer became involved with the protection of the fort at Montreal and the naval transport and defense of General Arnold's troops in their maneuvers in the vicinity of the American strongholds at Sorel and Montreal on the St. Lawrence River.

An outpost called "The Cedars" was built by Colonel Bedel's troops at the rapids to the west of Montreal at the junction of the Ottawa and St. Lawrence Rivers. It was a strategic landing point that controlled the navigation on the St. Lawrence River in both directions. Colonel Bedel's soldiers were captured by the British troops commanded by Captain George Forster and their Mohawk Indian allies. The Indian allies were led by Chief Brant, the principal war chief of the Confederacy of the Six Nations. Colonel Paterson, who was at Montreal, sent Major Henry Sherburne with a detached company of 140 men from his regiment toward The Cedars in an attempt to rescue Colonel Bedel's troops, but they were captured too. Captain Joseph Vose's journal, written in 1776, stated that he and his company of soldiers who were part of Colonel Paterson's regiment were stationed at the fort at Montreal in early May. Captain Vose wrote that troops led by General Arnold attempted a daring rescue mission in May 1776 to free Colonel Timothy Bedel and Lieutenant Isaac Butterfield's troops that had been surrendered at The Cedars. Captain Philip Ulmer was involved with the transport of General Arnold's forces in their attempt to rescue the American soldiers who had been captured. The Indian chief wanted some of the soldiers for slaves, and other Indians wanted to torture and kill some of the American captives. The captured American troops were eventually released after a tense confrontation and negotiations between General Arnold and Captain Forster. They were transported back to Montreal aboard the armed sloop, where their rescue was celebrated.

General John Thomas, who had only been in command of the American forces in Canada since the first of May, contracted smallpox. He suffered a miserable death a month later, like so many other soldiers during the American Revolution. He was buried near the fort at Chambly along the Richelieu River in Canada. General John Sullivan, who had been the commanding officer at Winter Hill during the siege of Boston, received orders from the Continental Congress to lead the American army's retreat from Canada in June 1776, after the death of General John Thomas on June 2. Philip Ulmer continued to be an active participant with General Arnold's detached brigade (part of Colonel Bond's Twenty-fifth Continental Regiment) during the retreat from Canada and during the summer of 1776. Ensign Philip Ulmer served with Brigadier General Arnold's Continental naval fleet being assembled at Fort Ticonderoga and Skenesborough (hereafter Skenesboro) at present-day Whitehall, New York. General Arnold appointed Philip Ulmer as the captain of one of the armed gunboats (referred to as gondolas or gundelos) to defend against the British and Hessian invasion forces advancing southward on Lake Champlain from Canada.[38] The rest of Colonel Bond's regiment was kept busy at Fort Ticonderoga with various construction projects to fortify the fort and the local hills in the immediate vicinity. Colonels Bond, Paterson and Greaton and General Poor's regiments were encamped at Rattlesnake Hill across the river from Fort Ticonderoga. They were involved in the building and preparation of the barracks, storage sheds and the army hospital. The hospital was quickly being filled with sick and diseased smallpox victims. The American troops constructed a floating bridge to connect Rattlesnake Hill to Fort Ticonderoga, and they built a log-boom that had been strung across the river to protect the fort from an incursion by the British forces from the north.

On July 28, 1776, after divine worship on Sunday, Colonel St. Clair read the Declaration of Independence to the assembled troops.[39] At the end of the reading, Colonel St. Clair said, "God save the free independent States of America!"[40] The army troops expressed their joy with three cheers. Rattlesnake Hill was renamed Mount Independence in celebration of the joyous occasion. Philip Ulmer became an active participant with General Benedict Arnold's detached American fleet in the first naval engagement against the Royal British Navy and Hessian forces on Lake Champlain in October 1776.[41] Captain Ulmer, who was in command of the gunboat *Spitfire*, appeared in a communication from General Arnold to General Horatio Gates written on August 31, 1776. The letter reported that "Captain Ulmer weathered a violent storm though exposed to the rake of Cumberland Bay, fifty miles long. The hard gale made an amazing sea."[42] In all of General Arnold's and General Gates' military communications and in references by soldiers who served with him at the time, Philip Ulmer was referred to as Captain Ulmer of the gunboat *Spitfire*.[43] Ezekiel Farrow of Windham, Massachusetts (and later Bristol, Maine), was taken out of Colonel Bond's regiment at Fort Independence and was appointed as a lieutenant by Brigadier General Arnold to serve with "Captain Ulmer." Lieutenant Ezekiel Farrow served as a first mate on Captain Philip Ulmer's gunboat *Spitfire*.[44]

On the first day of battle against the British and Hessian naval fleet at Valcour Island, the naval gunboat *Spitfire* received intensive gunfire for many hours, and by the end of the day, the gundelo began taking on water. Under cover of darkness and fog, the badly damaged American naval flotilla made a daring escape from the British fleet, which had anchored near the island for the night and expected to completely destroy the little American fleet the next morning. The British fleet commander, General Sir Guy Carleton, was irate the next day when he discovered that the American fleet had disappeared during the night. The British scouts and armed reconnaissance vessels searched almost the whole day before finally discovering the hidden American fleet, which had taken refuge behind Schuyler Island to make repairs. By the end of the second day, the *Spitfire* was determined to be too severely damaged to be repaired, and General Arnold directed Captain Philip Ulmer and his crew to sink the vessel in deeper water near Schuyler Island. The gunboat *New Jersey* was beyond repair and was ordered to be scuttled as well. The *New Jersey* was scuttled near the island in more shallow water than the *Spitfire*. (The *New Jersey* was later salvaged, repaired and used by the British navy as a transport vessel on the lake.) The crewmen of the *New Jersey* were taken on board Captain John Thacher's row galley *Washington*. The crewmen from the sloop *Lee*, which had been run aground in an inlet and made unserviceable, were also taken aboard the galley *Washington*. General Arnold took Captain Philip Ulmer, his crewmen and the swivel guns, cannon and munitions from the *Spitfire* on board his flagship *Congress*.[45]*

On the final day of battle, the *Congress* was engaged in a heated running gun battle for about two and a half hours against the British Royal Navy and Hessian forces. Brigadier General Arnold was kept busy aiming all of the cannons due to the inexperience of the surviving crewmen who were left to man the guns.[46] The little rebel fleet was ordered by General Arnold to beach their boats in the bay on the eastern side of Lake Champlain and to destroy them by setting them on fire so that the British could not use the vessels later on the lake. Captain Philip Ulmer and the crewmen of the galley *Congress*, along with the crews of the remaining four gunboats, beached their

---

* *Author's comment*: Many soldiers who served on the flagship *Congress* were part of Colonel Vose's troops with whom Philip Ulmer served in the war. Philip Ulmer may have become the acting captain of the galley *Congress* since the experienced naval officers on board, except for General Arnold, had been wounded, severely injured or killed in battle by the third day.[47] Although direct evidence is inconclusive, circumstantial evidence indicates that Captain Philip Ulmer, an experienced mariner who served under Arnold's command as the captain of the captured British vessel *Isabella* in the spring of 1776 in Canada, became the acting captain of the galley *Congress* since there was no one else who was as experienced or capable of sailing the badly damaged vessel.

battered vessels in Ferris Bay (known later as Arnold Bay). General Arnold and his few remaining officers set the boats on fire with their colors still flying.[48] Sergeant Cushing, one of the marines with Captain Philip Ulmer's crew, assembled his men at the top of the high sand embankment at Ferris Bay. The marines covered General Arnold's and the officers' efforts to set the battered vessels on fire just as the British warships came into cannon range.[49] The exhausted, battle-weary soldiers gathered up their supplies and their injured crewmen, and they started southward through the thick woodlands, following a narrow bridle path toward Crown Point with the frightened lake settlers guiding the way.

Following the disastrous defeat of Benedict Arnold's naval fleet on October 13, 1776, Philip Ulmer was among the American survivors who made their way southward toward Crown Point, about ten miles away. They hoped to find safety and assistance from the American troops who had been stationed at Crown Point. At Chimney Point, located at the southern end of Lake Champlain, the lake settlers and surviving crewmen climbed into the small boats and raft that were normally used to ferry people across the river tributary to the western side of the lake and the fort at Crown Point. The remains of General Arnold's naval vessels that had not been involved or destroyed during the three-day battle on the lake were resting at anchor when the weary survivors arrived. Finding only Lieutenant Colonel Thomas Hartley's Sixth Pennsylvania Regiment entrenched in the old fortification and barracks at Crown Point, it was decided that there was insufficient food and medical supplies to handle the injured soldiers and marines. With the powerful British flotilla descending upon Crown Point from the north, Colonel Thomas Hartley and General Arnold decided that the British and Hessian forces were too heavily armed for an adequate defense at Crown Point. The Sixth Pennsylvania Regiment was directed to assist the surviving men from General Arnold's naval fleet and the fleeing lake residents and make a retreat back to the safety of Fort Ticonderoga by boat and by foot another fifteen miles to the south. The fort at Crown Point was quickly abandoned and left in flames. Upon their arrival at Fort Ticonderoga, the men of Arnold's fleet and the soldiers of Colonel Hartley's Sixth Pennsylvania Regiment were assigned to the outpost and barracks at Fort Independence.

Several days after their narrow escape from death at the hands of the British and Hessian forces and their Indian allies, Philip Ulmer and other survivors of the battle at Valcour Island were among the combined American forces who participated in a great show of military strength at Fort

Ticonderoga and at Fort Independence.[50] The impressive American display of military soldiers and cannons caused General Carleton and his British advisors to decide to return to Canada, where the British forces spent the winter of 1776–77 in Montreal and Quebec City. During the winter months in Canada, the British prepared another invasion plan to divide the colonies for the summer campaign of 1777. The American invasion campaign was to be led by General John Burgoyne.

Without the heroic delaying tactics of the little American naval fleet on Lake Champlain, the combined forces of the British Royal Army and Navy, the German Hessians and their Indian allies would have been able to push southward to Albany, New York, and unite with the British forces from New York City who had planned to push northward up the Hudson River to Albany. The New England colonies would have been divided from the colonies to the south, and the American Revolution against Great Britain's power and control of the colonies would have ended. General Arnold's little naval fleet on Lake Champlain was destroyed; however, it provided a year of precious time that the colonies needed to unite in a common goal. The crucial period of one year that was provided by the brave men who stopped the first British invasion on Lake Champlain during the summer of 1776 enabled the Continental Congress and General George Washington to rally public support for independence and freedom from Great Britain. They were able to inspire public opinion and alter Loyalist public opinion toward American sovereignty from Great Britain. It gave Washington time to enlist soldiers in the American cause and to supply and arm the American troops for the Continental Army. The American troops were given time to prepare, to rally and organize, to confront and defeat the powerful British Royal Army and Hessian forces at Saratoga in October 1777.

Remnants of Colonel Bond's Twenty-fifth Continental Regiment were split up, combined and reorganized at Fort Ticonderoga in November 1776. With the death of Colonel Bond, remnants of the detached troops with Philip Ulmer were combined with the Fifteenth Continental Regiment commanded by Colonel John Paterson and with Colonel Joseph Vose's newly formed regiment. Other soldiers from Bond's Twenty-fifth Regiment remained with Bond's second-in-command, Lieutenant Colonel Ichabod Alden, until the next month, when Alden's company was redistributed and combined with other New England companies. The regiments of Colonels Paterson and Vose often operated together, and often apart, but they were later combined to become the First Massachusetts Regiment.[51]

In late November 1776, General Washington ordered the American forces who had recently arrived at Fort Ticonderoga to march southward through western New Jersey and join with the main Continental Army at the winter encampments along the Delaware River in Pennsylvania.[52] These combined regiments of Colonel Paterson and Colonel Vose marched from Fort Ticonderoga with General Sullivan and joined General Washington's Continental Army at their encampment in Pennsylvania prior to the Delaware River crossing on Christmas night. Colonel Ichabod Alden's regiment, which contained remnants of the Twenty-fifth Regiment and other companies that had injured and sick soldiers, marched directly to Morristown, New Jersey, to prepare the area as a winter encampment for General Washington's Continental Army. The remnants of the regiment remained in service until January 1, 1777, when it was reorganized as the Third Massachusetts Regiment of the Continental Line, and it later became part of Glover's brigade at Saratoga. The reorganized regiments of Colonels Paterson and Vose actively participated in the attack on Trenton and Princeton in General Arthur St. Clair's brigade.[53] Philip Ulmer participated in conflicts and skirmishes in New Jersey and Pennsylvania that included the Battles of Trenton, Assunpink Creek and Princeton.[54] With his bilingual abilities in communications, translating and speaking fluent German and English, Philip Ulmer became a valuable asset to his regiment and commanding officers, facilitating communication with captured Hessian soldiers and assisting with instructions, directions and the interrogation of the prisoners.

Because of his long military service, his valuable assistance with detached reconnaissance troops and his German American linguistic skills with the captured Hessian troops, Philip Ulmer was advanced in rank to lieutenant by General Washington on January 1, 1777, following his participation in the battle at Trenton. These skills were valuable assets at the Battles of Assunpink Creek and Princeton. Lieutenant Philip Ulmer served with Captain Abraham Hunt's company in both Colonel Vose's and Colonel Paterson's combined regiments during this time.[55] Lieutenant Philip Ulmer and his combined regiments wintered with General Washington's Continental Army troops in Morristown, New Jersey, during the winter of 1776–77.[56] It is probable that Lieutenant Philip Ulmer became a Freemason in the traveling Masonic military lodge during this time while in winter quarters with General Washington's troops. There were ten working lodges operating in the Continental Army during the American Revolution. One of these lodges was called the "Movable Lodge" and met during the time of the siege of Boston. Another traveling lodge, called the "American Union Lodge," was often led by General Paterson, who frequently served as the Master of the traveling lodge.[*]

General Washington often served as Worshipful Master of the traveling Masonic military lodge. Washington supervised and oversaw the initiation ceremony for new candidates, as well as the Masonic rituals and the Masonic degrees taken by his chosen officers who were the rank of lieutenant and above. They promised their loyalty until death and were then included as lodge brothers in his trusted military family.[57] According to General Lafayette, "Washington never willingly gave independent command to officers who were not Freemasons. Nearly all members of this official family, as well as most officers who shared his inmost confidence, were his brethren of the mystic tie."[58] Lieutenant Philip Ulmer received independent duties and assignments from this time forward in Paterson's and Vose's regiments and in other detached operations.

While on furlough in early 1777, Lieutenant Philip Ulmer was involved in the recruitment of new soldiers in the Lincoln County vicinity for the Continental Army. Colonel Vose, who was on furlough at the same time, sought new recruits in various towns and villages south of Boston. Colonel Vose received word by messenger that the main army depot in Danbury, Connecticut, had been burned by a British raiding party led by British General William Tryon. Colonel Vose's regiment was ordered to the Highlands Department near Peekskill and Newburgh, New York, on the Hudson River to defend against further incursions by British forces encamped in the vicinity of Pound Ridge and New Castle villages in White Plains. Colonel Vose notified Lieutenant Philip Ulmer of the reassignment. Lieutenant Ulmer and his new recruits from the frontier district in Maine responded to the orders and hastily proceeded to the lower Hudson River Valley area, where they were reunited with the rest of Colonel Vose's troops under the command of General Israel Putnam. In mid-June 1777, Colonel Vose's regiment was assigned to McDougall's brigade for a short time before being reassigned to the Second Connecticut Brigade stationed in the Highlands Department located in the vicinity of New Castle and Peekskill, New York.[59] Further British raids were expected in the summer campaign from the British stronghold in the New York City vicinity. The British planned to capture the fort and main resistance headquarters at Peekskill on

---

[*] *Author's comment*: The American Union Lodge exists to this day under the Grand Lodge of Ohio as American Union Lodge No. 1.

the Hudson River. In July 1777, prior to the battles at Saratoga, the First Massachusetts Regiment was reassigned to the Second Massachusetts Brigade under General John Glover in the Northern Department.[60] Part of Colonel Vose's regiment, which had remained with Washington's main Continental Army, was sent to the Northern Department on July 24, 1777. General Burgoyne's British and allied forces advanced southward from Canada in their summer invasion campaign via the Lake Champlain and Hudson River Valley waterways. General Burgoyne's goal was to divide the New England colonies from the southern colonies and bring the American rebellion to an end.

Lieutenant Philip Ulmer served with Colonel Vose's regiment in General Glover's brigade at Saratoga, New York, in the late summer and fall of 1777.[61] Lieutenant Ulmer participated with Colonel Vose's detached reconnaissance company and fought with Colonel Paterson's and Colonel Vose's regiments wherever his detached soldiers were needed in battle. The heroic actions of the American troops at Saratoga led to the surrender of General Burgoyne's British and Hessian army forces.[62] Lieutenant Philip Ulmer's translation and communication skills served as a valuable resource during the surrender ceremony at Saratoga between the German and American officers. He was able to translate and interpret information to the Hessian officers and captured German prisoners and give instructions and directions to them. General Glover's regiment was assigned the honor of accompanying the captured British and Hessian army to Boston to be held as prisoners of war. Lieutenant Philip Ulmer was among the escorts from General Glover's troops. After the defeat of the British forces at Saratoga, the American troops were ordered to reinforce General Washington's Continental Army, which had taken a stand outside Philadelphia, Pennsylvania, having lost the city to General Howe's British forces.

During the winter of 1777–78, Lieutenant Philip Ulmer served in Colonel Vose's regiment with General Glover's brigade at Valley Forge, Pennsylvania, as part of General Washington's main Continental Army troops in winter quarters.[63] Lieutenant Ulmer served with General Lafayette's Canadian invasion campaign in early 1778. He was probably involved as an intelligence officer and German American translator as part of General DeKalb's division.[64] General DeKalb, second-in-command to General Lafayette, spoke only German and a little French. Lieutenant Philip Ulmer's bilingual abilities would once again have made him valuable as a translator for General DeKalb and a liaison and interpreter with the American army forces participating in the Canadian Expedition of 1778.

The second Canadian invasion was ordered by General Horatio Gates, the newly appointed president of the Board of War. The Board of War was a newly created committee of the Continental Congress to oversee the American Continental Army's administration. Lieutenant Philip Ulmer's proven leadership abilities early in the American Revolution, his facility as a fluent translator and interpreter in German and English and his reconnaissance and fighting experience would certainly have made him a valuable asset for General Lafayette and General DeKalb to utilize during the early organization and operation of the Canadian campaign.

American troops led by Generals Lafayette and DeKalb began their Canadian campaign from Valley Forge and proceeded to Albany, New York, during the winter of 1778. During this critical time of preparation and decision-making, Generals Lafayette and DeKalb made a personal connection with Lieutenant Philip Ulmer. After an investigation by Lafayette's reconnaissance officers and advice from the American generals in the Northern Department, the Canadian Expedition of 1778 was aborted by the Continental Congress due to the lack of proper preparation, insufficient troops and inadequate supplies and hard currency. The soldiers returned to Valley Forge, and Lieutenant Ulmer was released from further military duty. Lieutenant Ulmer likely suggested that his brother might help as a German-English-speaking replacement and translator for General DeKalb or General von Steuben, who was training the American soldiers in military skills and maneuvers at Valley Forge. General DeKalb and General von Steuben spoke primarily German and no English. They would need to have a versatile interpreter and translator to help with directions and instructions for the American troops. Before leaving Valley Forge, Philip likely helped to facilitate his brother's advancement to sergeant and his new assignment with General DeKalb, who was second-in-command to General Lafayette's division.

Upon Lieutenant Philip Ulmer's return home from Valley Forge in early April 1778, he enlisted in the Massachusetts state militia in Lincoln County, and he was advanced in rank to captain in General McCobb's regiment. His assignment was to lead a detachment of soldiers (many from Waldoboro) and construct defensive fortifications and barracks in vulnerable shoreline locations from Falmouth[65] to the outposts of Belfast and Machias in frontier Maine. The objective was to defend against British raiding parties and attacks from British warships. The British warships regularly patrolled along the frontier coastline, firing upon the coastal outposts and settlement communities at will. British raiding parties sporadically attacked the towns and villages, plundering and pillaging the local citizens and kidnapping prominent citizens for ransom. Captain Philip Ulmer and his detachment of militiamen were involved in the building of the militia headquarters at Fort Pine Hill (near present-day Rockland) and defensive fortifications at Cambden (the old colonial spelling, hereafter Camden). He supervised the mounting of the eighteen-pounder cannon on a fortified ridge located near the fort at the entrance of the Penobscot Bay. The large cannon was capable of causing the British warships to be wary of coming too close to the militia headquarters and nearby village.

During the Penobscot Expedition in the summer of 1779, Philip Ulmer held the rank of militia captain in Colonel McCobb's regiment. Captain Ulmer led a company of volunteer militia soldiers with a detachment of Penobscot Indians and U.S. Continental Marines in climbing the steep cliffs at Dyce's Head on the Bagaduce Peninsula while under heavy gunfire from the British snipers above them.[66] He received a serious wound in his thigh from grapeshot during the siege outside the British-held Fort George.[67] Captain Philip Ulmer refused to leave the field of battle and continued to lead his men in the attack on the British fortification at Bagaduce.[68] While leading his company of militiamen with a company of U.S. Marines in a siege at Fort George, Captain Ulmer distinguished himself with valor while under continuous and heavy gunfire in spite of his serious leg injury.[69] Captain Philip Ulmer was the only American officer who was able to keep his regiment together after the disastrous defeat of Commander Saltonstall's American naval fleet and the frenzied retreat up the Penobscot River in the fall of 1779.[70] (Bagaduce, interchangeably called Maja-bagaduce, is located on the Bagaduce Peninsula at present-day Castine.)

Captain Philip Ulmer, while in great pain from his leg injury, was able to rally his company of troops. He attached their militia flag to the end of a long stick for the soldiers to follow. Using the stick to help him walk, he bravely led the soldiers along an Indian path through the dense woodlands toward Fort Pine Hill.[71] He not only led his own militia company back to the safety of Fort Pine Hill (which he had been actively constructing and arming prior to the Penobscot Expedition) but other disoriented soldiers and U.S. Marines who were unfamiliar with the Maine wilderness and saw his flag and followed it. Captain Philip Ulmer saved the lives of several soldiers during the bloody days of the siege at Fort George, during the chaotic retreat up the Penobscot River and during their escape through the dense forest to Fort Pine Hill. Among those soldiers whom Philip Ulmer brought to safety were his commanding officers—General Peleg Wadsworth, General

Solomon Lovell and Adjutant Jeremiah Hill—who were unfamiliar with the Maine wilderness and the Penobscot region. Philip Ulmer directed the Penobscot Indians who operated with his company to take General Lovell to the safety of their Indian village above Treats Falls (at present-day Bangor). In order to protect General Lovell from being captured by the enemy, the Penobscot Indians were directed to take him to their Indian village at Old Town, where they safely kept him for about five weeks. When the danger of enemy capture and retribution had subsided, a small party of Indians would return him safely to Boston.

As a result of his heroic service and leadership during the Penobscot Expedition, Captain Philip Ulmer was advanced in rank to major by General Peleg Wadsworth.[72] He was given the command of his own detached company of selected soldiers from York, Cumberland and Lincoln Counties. Their assignment was to build defensive fortifications, earthworks and barracks in important locations for the "Defense of the Eastern Frontier." Major Philip Ulmer operated under the command and direction of General Peleg Wadsworth.[73] Major Philip Ulmer served in many capacities, and he was involved in numerous encounters against British raiding parties from the British strongholds at Castine and Halifax, Nova Scotia. He continued to fight against British incursions in frontier Maine while stationed at Fort Pine Hill and at other seacoast locations where reconnaissance and special defensive fortification operations were needed until the end of the American Revolution.[74]

The American Revolution ended in 1783. However, the conflict in frontier Maine did not end until April 1784, when the British troops finally left the fort at Castine and returned to the British stronghold at Halifax. Major Philip Ulmer returned to his home and devoted his time and energy to his community at Waldoboro. The townspeople of Waldoboro elected him as a town selectman for their community in 1783–84. In 1784, Philip and his brother, George Ulmer, purchased a land claim from an illiterate squatter named James Getchell at Ducktrap watershed and cove, about twenty miles from their hometown of Waldoboro. The Ulmer brothers proceeded to establish a milldam on the Ducktrap stream, and they began to develop the Ducktrap watershed into a viable business complex. Philip and George moved to the small settlement of Ducktrap after the Revolutionary War to pursue their business opportunities. Their families remained in Waldoboro until the Ducktrap settlement was more habitable.

In 1784, the Ulmer brothers received some very interesting visitors who sought them out at Waldoboro and Ducktrap. General Henry Knox and several other veteran officers escorted General Lafayette on a brief tour of New England and the coastline of Maine. It was Lafayette's first visit to the Province of Maine. Henry Knox wanted to show the vast opportunities for business investment and land speculation in the eastern frontier of Massachusetts. Knox wanted to show off the enterprising developments that were taking place at Ducktrap cove with the Ulmer brothers. Lafayette had already made a personal connection with the Ulmer brothers during the Revolutionary War, and he wanted to make a brief visit to Waldoboro to meet with Philip Ulmer (who was a major by this time) and George Ulmer (who was a militia captain by this time) to thank them for their personal service to him and to General DeKalb (now deceased) during the war. Philip, George and their cousin George Ulmer Jr. had served honorably as soldiers in Colonel Vose's First Massachusetts Regiment that became a part of General Lafayette's brigade. George Ulmer and his cousin had enlisted in the army for three years in early 1777 and had participated in the battles at Germantown, Brandywine and Monmouth in New Jersey with General DeKalb's division under General Lafayette's command. The First Massachusetts Regiment in which they served was also involved with the unsuccessful American attempt to recapture the British-held seaport of Newport, Rhode Island, in August 1778. Lieutenant Philip Ulmer had returned to Waldoboro from Valley Forge in early April 1778, prior to those battles. George and George Jr. returned home in early 1780 having completed their enlistment service. General DeKalb was killed at Camden, South Carolina, on August 19, 1780. The news of his death was met with great sadness at Waldoboro by Philip and George Ulmer and their cousin George Ulmer Jr. in the fall of 1784.

General Knox had another motive in mind when he escorted General Lafayette on a tour of the Maine frontier. He wanted to show Lafayette some of his vast Waldo Patent acreage in frontier Maine, as well as the Ducktrap watershed and harbor-cove where the enterprising Ulmer brothers were busy developing a lumbering and sawmill business, a shipyard and a commercial trading and shipping complex. Lafayette was impressed by the beauty of Maine's wilderness coastline with its various natural resources and its potential for investment and business development. After the Revolutionary War, Henry Knox frequently sought to entice wealthy Europeans, land speculators and venture capitalists to invest in his vast property holdings in frontier Maine. Wealthy investors in America, Great Britain and Europe speculated on potential land development and business growth on the world market. The Ulmer brothers and their business expansions at Ducktrap

Harbor showed great potential for savvy investors with venture capital. They received political and business patronage from Henry Knox, with whom they had served during the American Revolution.

Once the Ulmer business complex at Ducktrap was successfully underway, Philip focused his energies on developing the small settlement into a town. He served as a leader and town official of the Ducktrap community, a similar leadership role that he had held as a town selectman in Waldoboro prior to his move to Ducktrap. Philip, his brother, George, and a friend, Abner Milliken, were given the task of writing to the Massachusetts Congress in Boston for permission to organize the Ducktrap and New Canaan plantations into a town. They framed a code of bylaws for the governing powers and incorporation of their settlement into a town. Permission was granted by the Massachusetts General Court, and the town of Lincolnville came into being in October 1802. Philip Ulmer's concerns for the well-being and the protection of the seaport towns and communities remained constant throughout his adult life. As a first-generation German American, Philip Ulmer was a religious and principled person whose grandfather had greatly influenced him in his youth as a town official and spiritual leader for twenty years. Like his grandfather, Philip devoted his adult life to his family and to the welfare of his community. He was willing to fight to retain the principles of freedom, liberty and independence. He represented the best qualities and values of a first-generation American citizen. Having learned from his youth about human bondage that occurred to one of his ancestors and the evilness of slavery and persecution, he respected all ethnic and cultural backgrounds. This was demonstrated throughout his life.

Philip Ulmer was elected by the townspeople of Lincolnville and the surrounding communities to serve as their congressional representative to the Commonwealth of Massachusetts in Boston on the Democratic-Republican platform in 1807.[75] Congressman Philip Ulmer served for several years in the House of Representatives; however, early records of the town are sketchy about the amount of terms. The political responsibilities of the Congressional Legislature in Boston kept Philip Ulmer away from his large young family and from his wife, Christiana, in Lincolnville. The obligations and responsibilities of Philip's public service in the House of Representatives proved to be a hardship for him. He decided that the political life in Boston was expensive, contentious and difficult to sustain. The British presence at Castine kept the local community in fear and anxiety from the unexpected British raiding parties and kidnappings for ransom. Philip chose to return to Lincolnville and devote his energies to the concerns and protection of

Lincolnville, the local communities and his family. He continued to represent and support the interests and the well-being of Lincolnville's townspeople and county communities with his written legal communications to the Massachusetts General Court.

Philip Ulmer was called back into military service as a sailing master with the U.S. Continental Navy in January 1809 to enforce the unpopular embargo orders of President Jefferson.[76] However, Major Philip Ulmer had his sailing warrant revoked several months after it was issued. This was due to Philip's moral and ethical beliefs concerning the president's Embargo Acts that forced the closure of the seaports in America and stifled trade and navigation. The trading policies of the administration threatened the survival of his family and local community in frontier Maine, which depended upon commercial trading, fishing, transportation and navigation for their livelihood and existence. The Embargo Acts of President Jefferson obstructed the economy of the nation and had devastating effects on merchants and trading vessels in coastal towns and communities throughout the United States. Smuggling became necessary for many areas in order for the inhabitants to survive. Controlling the smuggling activities in New England became an unsuccessful and losing effort. It was later discovered that William King (who later became the first governor of the state of Maine in 1820 and the first Grand Master of the Grand Lodge of Masons in Maine) was heavily involved in the illegal smuggling trade along with other prominent merchants, statesmen and congressmen.[77] Illegal trading was the only way to maintain their wealth and position and support the fragile state and federal economy. The Embargo Act of 1809 was repealed in the final days of Jefferson's administration, but it came too late to salvage Philip Ulmer's career as a sailing master. Unable to perform in a more active role in the state militia, Philip was subsequently assigned as a U.S. deputy customs inspector stationed at Lincolnville and Camden for captured British prize shipping vessels.[78] He remained in this position until the end of the conflict with Great Britain in December 1814 with the signing of the Treaty of Ghent.

America struggled to recover from the debts and expenses of the long and drawn-out Revolutionary War. Since the 1790s, there were hundreds of American sailors and seamen from the District of Maine who were captured by the British warships or enemy privateers and forced to serve on enemy vessels to fight against their own countrymen. Those who refused to serve the British demands were killed and thrown over the side of the vessel. Other men were abducted from their homes and used for political leverage, for bargaining purposes in ransom demands and for other prisoner exchanges. Fear and distrust of the British, as well as a multitude of other political and economic issues, had festered for many years after the Revolutionary War. The continuing rivalry between England and France in Europe and in the West Indies gave rise to an undeclared quasi-war over the exploitation of America's land and natural resources. They vied for their own economic gains with America's international trading and treaty agreements in Europe, the West Indies and other countries in the world. America's Declaration of Neutrality in the 1790s and early 1800s was basically ignored by both European countries and their allies, resulting with all parties pointing fingers at each other over treaty violations and threatening to declare war. America tried to avoid involvement in the political manipulations of conflicting foreign policies in European countries and their efforts to disrupt and collapse one another's economies. Both England and France tried to draw America into the European conflict on their own sides. President George Washington didn't want to be caught up in the conflict between these two countries and their struggle for power and dominance in the world.

The American economy was based on its fishing, lumbering and food-producing industries, as well as its national and international interests in the merchant trading businesses and its sale of western land to frontier settlers and investment speculators. The practice of impressments of American citizens into the service of foreign and enemy powers continued to increase and eventually led to the start of the War of 1812. European countries had not yet recognized America's fierce desire for sovereignty as a free and independent country and its claim to neutrality on land and sea. Both France and England thought that the American experiment as a republic composed of many free and independent states would eventually collapse. The rulers, dictators and ruling authorities of the powerful European countries wanted to make a claim on the lands and resources in America when the struggling new nation finally failed. Both France and England worked quietly behind the scenes to manipulate and undermine trading in the world and speed up the collapse of the American economy. If the American economy faltered and failed, the country would be plunged into anarchy and chaos, making it more certain for the stronger European countries to take over the United States and divide the various states and waterways among them.

Although war was declared between England and the United States on June 18, 1812, the conflict was mostly limited to skirmishes along the northern border of New England and the disputed borders in the Great Lakes region. The mission of the British invasion in the Passamaquoddy and Penobscot

Bay region in the summer and fall of 1814 was to reestablish British title to the border region and to control the frontier District of Maine, restoring it to British hands. The British claimed territory in the eastern frontier of Massachusetts from the mouth of the Penobscot River to the St. Croix River in New Brunswick, Canada. The Ducktrap watershed at Lincolnville, where the Ulmer families lived, was included in the British plan. This frontier region had been renamed "New Ireland" by the British authorities with Castine serving as the port of entry. Claiming title to New Ireland from the New England colonies had been a goal of the British government and settlers of Nova Scotia ("New Scotland") prior to the American Revolution.[79]

Major Philip Ulmer became involved as an officer with the veteran militia company of retired Revolutionary War soldiers in the Penobscot region of Camden, Lincolnville, Northport and Belfast. He served periodically as a veteran militia leader and U.S. Volunteer of detached units at several locations in the local Penobscot Bay area when he was needed.[80] The local militia company served under the command of Brigadier General John Blake in the Penobscot region near Bangor, Maine. Major Jacob Ulmer, eldest son of Major Philip Ulmer, was assigned the command of Fort Sullivan at Eastport in the fall of 1812. Reports at Eastport indicate that Major Philip Ulmer actually held the command at this time.[81] In any case, the militia troops were relieved from duty within the year by George Ulmer, then holding the rank of colonel commandant. Colonel George Ulmer, Philip's brother, retained command of the fort at Eastport until late summer of 1813. As a result of a heated confrontation between George and his officers and soldiers during a Fourth of July celebration, he was relieved of his military command, placed under house arrest and held for military trial for misconduct. Philip Ulmer assumed the responsibilities of protecting and defending the town of Lincolnville as well as the protection of his own family, his brother's family and the families of his two sons, Major Jacob Ulmer and Lieutenant Charles Ulmer, who were actively involved with the militia troops fighting the British invasion forces. The weight of family responsibilities, the needs of the town governments to protect its citizens and the defensive regional stresses rested heavily upon Philip Ulmer's shoulders as he bravely struggled with his leadership responsibilities as Lincolnville's wartime selectman during the War of 1812.

In July 1814, Sir John Sherbrooke, lieutenant governor of Nova Scotia, had overall command of an invasion force of eight British warships and ten transport vessels with 3,500 British regular military troops from Halifax.

The powerful British forces invaded frontier Maine District and attacked Fort Sullivan at Eastport and Fort Madison at Castine, located at the mouth of the Penobscot Bay. Sir Sherbrooke sent an expeditionary force of three warships and one transport carrying 500 veteran soldiers under the command of British captain Robert Barrie in the battleship HMS *Dragon* to Hampden and Bangor. The towns were quickly captured in spite of the efforts of General Blake's militia forces, who tried to stop the British troops unsuccessfully. In spite of pleas for mercy from many of the townspeople, Captain Barrie reportedly declared, "I have none for you. My business is to sink, burn, and destroy. Your town is taken by storm, and by the rules of war we ought to lay your village in ashes and put its inhabitants to the sword. But I will spare your lives, though I mean to burn your houses."[82]

Captain Barrie was prevented from totally destroying the towns of Hampden and Bangor by the timely intervention of Sir Sherbrooke. The alarm spread quickly throughout the Penobscot Bay region, and militiamen and volunteers hurried to assemble to defend the coastal towns and river communities from the invasion of British forces. The British raiding expedition was part of a larger British plan to invade America and reclaim American territory and the colonies for Great Britain.

During July of 1814, the British naval and marine invasion forces from Halifax captured the town of Eastport and forced the surrender of Fort Sullivan. The American militia troops from Eastport made a hasty retreat through the woods toward Machias, which was easily captured by the British invasion fleet in their heavily armed warships. General Blake's militia soldiers continued to be pursued by the British troops from one seacoast village to another. A British detachment of enemy troops sailed up the Penobscot River and attacked the shipyards at Hampden and Bangor, where Major Philip Ulmer's son Charles was stationed with state militia troops repairing and constructing armed vessels to fight against the British. General Blake's militia soldiers fought the heavily armed British detachment as long as they could, but they were soon forced into a fighting retreat through the woods toward Belfast. The shipyards and the towns of Hampden and Bangor were set on fire by the British raiding detachment. The British fleet in the Penobscot Bay sailed on to Belfast, which was quickly overrun and captured. The American troops retreated southwestward toward Lincolnville and Camden, where they planned to make a defensive stand against the British forces. Major Philip Ulmer, who had served as the town leader, veteran military volunteer and wartime selectman of Lincolnville since the spring of 1812, was involved in overseeing the evacuation of the non-essential townspeople to a safer location inland. He hastily prepared the veteran militiamen and volunteers of the town for the British invasion forces that were descending upon them.

The Massachusetts General Court and the federal government were unable to defend the Penobscot region of frontier Maine since there was little or no money in either treasury to do so. The inhabitants of frontier Maine were left on their own to provide for their own defense against enemy raiding parties and invading British forces. Philip Ulmer had anticipated future conflicts with the British forces at Halifax. His primary focus since his return from Valley Forge in 1778 had been on the defense of coastal towns and villages in the frontier region of Maine and the well-being of the local inhabitants in his hometown. Prior to the War of 1812, Philip Ulmer and several militia veterans (which included his brother, George) petitioned the Massachusetts government for permission to salvage cannons and other military armaments from the wreckage of the American fleet at Cape Jellison (and several other sites known to him) that had been destroyed in the American retreat up the Penobscot River in 1779.[83] Permission for the salvage operation was granted by the Massachusetts General Court. Many of the cannons, howitzers and mortars were repaired, and the heavy equipment was distributed throughout the different communities to protect the towns and villages from further British raiding parties. Several years after the Massachusetts General Court granted Philip Ulmer's petition for salvage rights, Philip's foresight and planning came into play in the defense of the Lincolnville and Camden village communities.

The salvaged, refurbished and repaired cannons and other military equipment and munitions had been distributed along the main road from Belfast/Northport, where the first barricades and a battery had been set up, and southward along the Penobscot Bay shoreline to Lincolnville's hills at Ducktrap Harbor-cove and the Lincolnville beach. Philip Ulmer, as the leader of the town of Lincolnville and as an experienced defensive officer in the local veteran militia, had directed that the repaired cannons and heavy field pieces should be placed in strategic locations along the Lincolnville shoreline and the surrounding hills overlooking the important harbor-coves and beach areas. The interspersed barricades and small batteries then continued southward along the shoreline to the Camden hills and Camden harbor area on the Penobscot Bay. To make the British believe that Lincolnville and Camden were more heavily armed than they actually were, logs were cut to resemble cannons and mortars and mounted on wooden pilings or stacked rocks and placed with the real pieces. From a distance the logs resembled heavy guns and appeared formidable to the British reconnaissance scouts. This strategic ploy had worked previously against the invading British and Hessian forces during the American Revolution, and Major Philip Ulmer hoped that the same deceptive technique would work again against the British forces from Halifax that were sweeping through the Penobscot Bay region upon their poorly defended town.

There was a narrow fourteen-mile water passage between the island of Long Island (hereafter referred to by its present-day name of Islesboro) and the western shore of the Penobscot Bay at Lincolnville, which was just three miles away. A battery of heavy military equipment was placed on the island of Islesboro to cover the narrow water passageway between the island and the mainland at Lincolnville harbor and beach. Once the British fleet entered the narrow passageway between Lincolnville and Islesboro, the enemy fleet would be unable to maneuver effectively and would be caught in the crossfire from the shoreline batteries at Lincolnville and the island battery at Islesboro. The British fleet would be sitting ducks caught in the narrow waterway and would be unable to maneuver their warships or put up an effective defense. The trap for the enemy fleet was set, and the defensive militia troops and townspeople waited for the trap to be sprung.

After attacking Belfast and leaving the town in flames, the British admiral had sent out reconnaissance troops to determine the next objective in the plan to subdue the Penobscot Bay region. The British scouts discovered the clever plot that had been set by Major Philip Ulmer and his militia veterans and volunteers at Lincolnville to trap the unsuspecting British fleet in the narrow water passage between Islesboro and the Lincolnville mainland in a well-armed crossfire attack. The British admiral changed his plans and decided to proceed to Castine on the eastern side of Islesboro, which was not well defended. The British forces attacked and quickly captured the poorly defended American-held fort. After leaving a battalion of British soldiers on Castine to secure the captured Penobscot area, the British fleet sailed on to Fort Pine Hill near Clam Cove (present-day Rockport) and unleashed a heavy barrage of cannon fire and mortars. The British fleet successfully destroyed the fort, which had served as the American militia headquarters in the Penobscot Bay region, leaving behind the flaming wreckage. The massive British invasion in 1814 continued to sweep southward along the eastern coast of the United States as well as from Canada using the Great Lakes and major river waterways into the heart of America. After many conflicts and battles and much destruction, peace was finally achieved with the American success at the Battle of New

Orleans by General Andrew Jackson's troops and the signing of the Treaty of Ghent on December 24, 1814.

Sir John Sherbrooke, who had declared New Ireland as a province of the British in North America, did not enforce the Treaty of Ghent, which had been signed in 1814. Sir Sherbrooke did not order the British forces to abandon the fort and barracks at Castine until late April 1815. The Penobscot Bay region of frontier Maine was the very last area that the British forces vacated after the signing of the peace treaty. Peace finally began to return to the Penobscot Bay region, and commercial trading and fishing quickly returned to the Maine frontier. Benedict Arnold returned to North America from England, and he set up a trading and mercantile business in the New Brunswick (Canada) area. Benedict Arnold was banned from returning to the United States because of his treachery during the Revolutionary War, but Arnold's trading company and sailing vessels conducted business in the Passamaquoddy Bay area, in Quebec and Montreal and in the West Indies. Commerce was soon renewed with the British merchants at Halifax and New Brunswick, Canada. Smuggling and covert trading of goods was conducted between the towns of Eastport and Lubec (Maine) at the entrance of the Passamaquoddy Bay with questionable parties who lived and conducted business in the New Brunswick area. Some of the covert activities in the Passamaquoddy and Penobscot Bay areas may have included dealings with Benedict Arnold's trading and mercantile company in New Brunswick. The dispute over the border territory between Canada and the United States, specifically in frontier Maine, continued for many decades after the signing of the Treaty of Ghent. The final boundary between the Maine Province and the Province of Canada would remain in open dispute until 1842, when the Webster-Ashburton Treaty finally resolved the contentious issue of the northern border of the United States.

Philip Ulmer and his brother, George, supported the efforts of politicians and town leaders in frontier Massachusetts to gain statehood and become self-reliant. Some of these early discussions about statehood had taken place at Philip's house or at other homes within the town when Philip served the town as moderator. The first calls to make Maine a state appeared in a Portland newspaper, *The Eastern Herald*, on April 9, 1792. Philip Ulmer did not live long enough to see his efforts toward statehood granted to frontier Maine. Long governed by the General Court of Massachusetts Bay, the Province of Maine finally became the twenty-third state in the Union as part of the Missouri Compromise in 1820. William King became Maine's first governor.

Major Philip Ulmer, who had been permanently injured in the Revolutionary War during the Penobscot Bay Expedition of 1779, received a government pension as an invalid from the United States Congress in 1815 for his military service. His government pension was again granted by Congress in February 1816.[84] Philip continued to serve the town of Lincolnville during his elder years until days before his death.[85] According to his wife, Philip suffered complications and varying degrees of pain during his adult life, but especially in the final months before his death. He died on October 3, 1816, and was buried with military and Masonic honors in the small private Ulmer Cemetery at "The Point" at Ducktrap Harbor-cove overlooking the Penobscot Bay in Lincolnville, Maine.[86] Several other war veterans who had served with Major Philip Ulmer during America's early struggle for freedom and independence are buried near him.

Chapter 1

The Ulmer Family
Comes to America

The [ship of pioneers] *contained a cross-section of values that would become quintessential America: the insistence on following the heart rather than the law* [of rulers]; *the inability to tolerate injustice; the audacity to demand authority over authorities; the courage to pursue a better life no matter how much worse it might be; the wisdom of working together as a society for mutual benefit and personal profit. They believed in the power of the congregation. They would do their own thinking and make their own decisions. They would pray their own prayers. They would dig in their heels. The strong would bury the weak, perhaps suffer a moment of doubt, then remember the mercy of their God, and then get back to work.*[87]

ANCESTRAL BACKGROUND OF THE ULMER FAMILY

The name "Ulmer" has been traced back through many generations to the "von Ulm" family, an ancient, knighted and noble family who formerly came from the area of Bavaria and settled in the medieval duchy that became Swabia, Germany. Swabia was located in the strategic position between the upper reaches of two of Europe's most important rivers, the Danube and the Rhine. Baden-Württemberg is located in the historic region known as Swabia situated on the borders of Switzerland and Austria. The original ancestor was Gottfried von Ulm, who lived at the beginning of the Crusades and died in AD 1127. He served King Henry IV in the late eleventh century in his efforts to remain as king of Germany. Gottfried von Ulm supported King Henry IV in his conflict with the Pope in Rome. Through leadership and bravery, Gottfried von Ulm's military and diplomatic actions eventually led to King Henry IV being crowned as the Holy Roman Emperor. Because of his bravery and military service to Henry IV, Gottfried von Ulm was knighted and rewarded with a castle from the king, and he received the title of "Baron" or "Duke" von Ulm with a coat of arms. The coat of arms was displayed as a black field with a yellow lion rampant with claws and tongue painted red, the standard of the Elector Palatinate.[88] The family motto on the coat of arms was *Inter fortissimos*, which translated means "Among the Bravest."[89] Baron (or Duke) von Ulm and his wife, Kunnigunde von Salm, settled in Swabia, a part of Bavaria that was located between Switzerland and Alsace (now part of France). This area consisted of the duchy of Baden-Württemberg, Germany, part of the Holy Roman Empire. They had four surviving sons: Kuno, Albert, Gottfried and Conrad. The three elder sons unfortunately lost their lives in the Holy Lands during the Crusades. The youngest son, Conrad, remained at home with his parents and was not involved with the Crusades. Conrad became overseer in the employ of German emperor Barbarossa, who was also known as King Friedrick (Frederick) I. The descendants of Conrad von Ulm were large in number during the reign of German King Louis IV, the Duke of upper Bavaria and the Count Palatine of the Rhine until 1329.

By the eighteenth century, the von Ulm family coat of arms evolved to reflect a chevron on the center of the shield, and it had three eagles that were displayed above and below the chevron, indicating the male descendants of the von Ulm family. The chevron indicated the region of Baden-Württemberg, Germany, where the family once flourished. The symbol of the eagle came from the reign of King Friedrick I Barbarossa in 1155, and it became a symbol of the Holy Roman Empire in its one-headed image. In medieval heraldry, eagles were said to indicate that the armiger (person bearing the arms) was courageous, a man of action and demonstrated sound judgment. The motto under the shield was *Aquila Non Captat Muscas*,[90] translated to "The Eagle Catches Not Flies," meaning that the wise and courageous leader doesn't worry about insignificant things.[91]

In the year 1348, the majority of the von Ulm family members who had settled in the vicinity of present-day Ulm died from the plague in Europe called the Black Death. Only Reginald von Ulm survived the devastating effects of the plague. Grateful for having survived the plague, he made a religious pilgrimage to Jerusalem, where he was seized by Turks along

Drawing of the Ulmer family crest. Artist unknown.

the road and sold into captivity in Egypt. After fifteen years in captivity, he was at last freed by Venetian merchants, and he returned to his home in Germany. By this time, the ancestral von Ulm castle had deteriorated and was in great disrepair. He met and married Johanna Felandt, and they settled in Donanworth, a part of Swabia, Germany. They had two sons, Waldemar and Friedrick (Frederick) Ulmer, who survived to adulthood. From these two sons, the von Ulm family divided into two branches.[92] The elder son, Waldemar, retained the noble title as "Sir" von Ulm, and his many descendants remained in the area and flourished. The vicinity where the von Ulm family settled and flourished became known as the village or town of Ulm. The von Ulm castle, located on a high hill overlooking the town of Ulm, was eventually repaired and stayed in the family for many generations. The younger son, Friedrick von Ulm, did not retain the title and moved away from the developing town of Ulm to the village of Altheim, about seven miles to the southwest. His family was simply called "Ulmer."[93] Subsequent generations of descendants from Friedrick (Frederick) von Ulm and from Waldemar von Ulm who remained near the developing city of Ulm within the region of Baden-Württemberg were simply known as "Ulmer" from the vicinity of Ulm.[94] (Example: Johann Ulmer was literally John from Ulm.)

During this period of time, Europe was suffering from the effects of the "Little Ice Age" that caused extremely cold weather that killed off vegetation and crops and resulted in great famines. The resulting deaths of massive numbers of people and animals caused the spread of disease and pestilence, and this resulted in the deaths of millions more people. Wars and conflicts resulted because of scarcity of crops, provisions and supplies throughout Europe. The Ulmer families suffered from the extreme conditions in Europe as well, and family relatives moved to other areas in Germany that might provide food and better living conditions. The great-grandfather of Philip Martin Ulmer was Georg Ulmer. He was born about 1661 in Altenstadt, Germany, a village to the north of Frankfurt about two hundred miles from the town of Ulm. Eventually, Georg Ulmer returned to Altheim near the city of Ulm, where other von Ulm (Ulmer) relatives lived.

In August 1684, Georg Ulmer married Barbara Hornung in Altheim. She was born in February 1663 to Hans and Margareta Finck Hornung. Johannes Jakob (Jacob) Ulmer (the grandfather of Philip Martin Ulmer) was born on October 5, 1688, to Georg and Barbara (Hornung) Ulmer in Altheim, located about seven miles southwest of the city of Ulm. He grew up in an educated family and served as a drummer in the citizen-militia army in the service of King Frederick William I. Georg Ulmer (great-grandfather of Philip Martin Ulmer) died on March 16, 1706, in Altheim, Germany.[95] Johannes Jakob Ulmer was married on March 8, 1710, to Anna Catharina Kopp, the daughter of Hans Jakob Kopp, who was a schoolmaster and baker of Enzberg, a village near Stuttgart, Germany, about fifty miles from Ulm. They had four children, two of whom died before reaching adulthood. Anna Kopp died on February 28, 1722, at age forty-two while "extremely pregnant" and was buried in Enzberg. Johannes Jakob Ulmer (now a widower) married on September 8, 1722, to Anna Margareta Weeber in Enzberg Parish, Germany.[96] They had eight children, many of whom died in infancy or before they reached adulthood. Johannes Jakob Ulmer was first listed as a schoolmaster in 1733, and he served as a spiritual leader in the town, following the teachings of Martin Luther, who initiated the Protestant Reformation movement in Europe. Johannes Ulmer was well respected in the town and became a leader of the community in which he lived in Germany.[97]

IMMIGRATION OF THE ULMER FAMILY TO AMERICA

The earliest known ancestor of Philip Martin Ulmer in America was his grandfather Johannes Jakob Ulmer, who originally brought the Ulmer family to America in 1742 from a small town near Ulm in Württemberg, Germany.[98] Colonel Samuel Waldo, a Boston merchant, was a land agent for the Massachusetts Bay-Plymouth Company, and he was seeking inhabitants to settle and develop a community on a land grant located in the eastern frontier of Massachusetts in the wilderness Province of Maine. Samuel Waldo had petition ads circulated in the 1740s in Germany, Switzerland and Holland for plentiful land available in America located in his Waldo Patent (land grant) in the Province of Maine, where the settlement of Broad Bay was being developed. In the spring of 1742, Captain James Abercrombie took German and Swiss passengers on board the sailing vessel *Lydia* at Württemberg, Germany, bound for Samuel Waldo's new Broad Bay frontier settlement in the Province of Maine, part of the Massachusetts-Bay Colony's northern frontier.[99] Johannes Jakob Ulmer and others in the German community responded to the Waldo circulars promising abundant land, housing, provisions and support from Samuel Waldo and the investors of the Massachusetts Bay-Plymouth Company. The circular advertisements promised the frontier settlers opportunity and prosperity in the new Broad Bay settlement.

Johannes and Anna Ulmer boarded the sailing ship *Lydia* in Württemberg with their family. Having lost his first wife and unborn child and a number of other children to disease and starvation in Germany, Johannes Jakob Ulmer (hereafter referred to as Captain John Ulmer or John Ulmer Sr.) decided to move to America and start a new life with his surviving three children and his second wife.[100] The three surviving Ulmer children— Sedonia, Johann Jakob and Johannes Ulmer Jr.—were all born in Enzberg, Germany, prior to the Ulmer family's voyage to America. Anna and John

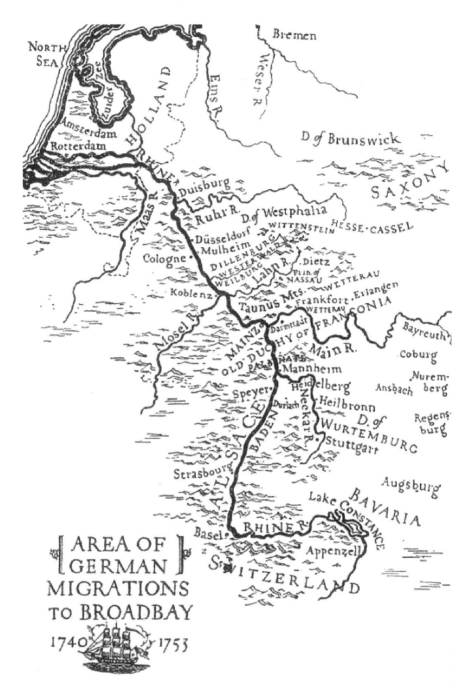

Map of the German migration region from Germany to America. Artist unknown; In the public domain.

Ulmer Sr. would eventually have children of their own who were born at the Broad Bay settlement.[101] Johann Jakob Ulmer (referred to hereafter as Jacob) was sixteen years old, Sedonia Elizabeth was nineteen years old and Johannes Ulmer Jr. (referred to hereafter as John Ulmer Jr.) was six years old. Sedonia married Georg Werner (old German spelling) about 1752 or 1753 at the Broad Bay settlement.[102] (Werner also appears in the military records as Varner.) Jacob Ulmer would become the father of Philip Martin Ulmer and George Ulmer who fought in the American Revolution and the War of 1812. Hans Martin Ulmer, who was the eldest son of John Ulmer Sr. by his first marriage, would not immigrate to the Broad Bay settlement with other members of the Ulmer family until 1753.

The *Lydia* first sailed from Württemberg in April 1742, but the ship and the passengers were delayed at Cologne and Rotterdam, Holland, where the ship stayed for four months while more immigrants eventually joined the voyage to America.[103] The ship eventually sailed from Rotterdam on August 18, 1742, for the long voyage across the Atlantic Ocean to Salem, Massachusetts. First landfall was on September 24, 1742, at Marblehead, a part of Salem at the time.[104] The passengers stayed for several days at Salem while a "state reception," given by the wealthy merchants and Massachusetts land agents, was held for the newly arrived German, Swiss and Dutch settlers.[105] Massachusetts governor William Shirley, some of his staff members and Colonel Samuel Waldo (who later became a general) attended the reception. A number of honorable Massachusetts state legislators and members of the General Court of Massachusetts were also in attendance.[106] The new settlers were wined and dined, and their depositions were recorded concerning their treatment and future plans. Their depositions were used at a later time for recruitment of more settlers back in Europe.

THE BROAD BAY SETTLEMENT

By the beginning of October, the German, Dutch and Swiss immigrants were moved from Marblehead to the sparsely prepared wilderness settlement along the Medomak River in the Massachusetts frontier Province of Maine. The promises of land, food, supplies, housing and a viable livelihood in the Waldo circulars and in the Massachusetts Bay Settlement Company ads proved to be dismally inaccurate. The hastily constructed settlement at Broad Bay lacked food and proper shelter for the settlers to survive the extremely harsh winter conditions at the end of the Little Ice Age in North America. Many people who remained at the Broad Bay settlement during the winter of 1742–43 died of starvation or illness or were frozen to death.[107] It was a miserable and devastating year for the new German, Swiss and Dutch settlers at the Broad Bay frontier settlement. An appeal for support was made to the parent company in Boston to comply with the conditions that had been promised by the promoter, Samuel Waldo, who was associated with the Lincolnshire Settlement Company and the Massachusetts Bay-Plymouth Company. The Lincolnshire Company also established a Scots-Irish community along the St. George River across from the settlement of Broad Bay (Waldoboro).[108]

John Ulmer Sr. and his family, seeing the primitive conditions at the new Broad Bay settlement, moved back to Salem/Marblehead with other families who had young children. They needed to find work, food and sufficient living conditions for their young families for the winter. John Ulmer Sr. worked for about a year blowing glass for windows and making glass items for a Salem merchant while his son, Jacob, worked as a sailor and fisherman with mariners from Marblehead. Anna Ulmer, John Ulmer Sr.'s wife, and six-year-old John Ulmer Jr. became quickly involved in the colonial lifestyle of the Salem and Marblehead communities. When the living conditions in the Broad Bay settlement improved the following year, the Ulmer family returned to the Broad Bay settlement, where John Ulmer Sr. and his older son, Jacob, built a log cabin on the plot of land granted to the Ulmer family by Colonel Samuel Waldo and the Massachusetts Bay Company. John Ulmer Sr. was assigned lot No. 4; his younger son, John Ulmer Jr., was assigned lot No. 5; and his older son, Jacob Ulmer, was assigned lot No. 15.[109]

In late 1743, John Ulmer Sr. and his family moved back to the Broad Bay settlement. John Ulmer Sr. and Jacob began to help develop the Broad Bay settlement and the expanding new settlement on the eastern side of the river named St. George (also written as St. George's). John Sr. and Jacob helped to design and construct dams on the local streams for the development of various kinds of mills. They constructed a shipyard at Broad Bay Cove like those they had seen in the busy and prosperous communities at Salem and Marblehead. As early leaders in the Broad Bay village, John Sr. and Jacob helped to develop the settlement into a trading community, and they helped to develop a commercial shipbuilding business center for Colonel Samuel Waldo and the Massachusetts Bay Company.[110]

As forest land was cleared to enlarge the frontier settlement, logs were cut to build a fort and stockade. Additional log houses were built for the new frontier settlers, and more land was cleared for crops and for animals to graze. Fishing boats were built to provide food and a livelihood for the community as well as for transportation. Timber was harvested, and firewood, wooden boards and other wood products were sold to the seaport communities in the Boston and Salem areas and towns to the south. The Indians, who did not believe that land could be owned or settled permanently, realized the threat that the frontier settlements posed to their livelihood and way of life. The danger of Indian attacks became a great concern to the settlers. The settlers were attacked while attending to their crops, hunting for game or while collecting firewood for cooking and warmth. Some young women and children disappeared while outside the settlement stockade, never to be seen again. The Indians would attack without warning and slip back into the forest, unseen. Because of the constant threat of Indian raids, a militia guard was needed for protection for the settlement. Colonel Samuel Waldo appointed John Ulmer Sr., an experienced former Prussian soldier, to serve as captain and the commander of the Broad Bay Guard.[111] Captain John Ulmer Sr. organized the militia and trained the men of the settlement in the methods and techniques of German warfare and defense that he had learned as a citizen-soldier in Germany. He and other settlers who were former German soldiers held regular training sessions and organized drills for the inexperienced men and boys of the community. They learned discipline, cooperation, self-reliance and self-defense tactics. Captain John Ulmer Sr. trained the Broad Bay Guards to maneuver and function as a unit, and he conducted competitions of skill and accuracy among the militiamen and boys of the settlement.

John Ulmer Sr. became an important leader in the Broad Bay community. Having been a schoolmaster in Germany before immigrating to America, he taught the Ulmer children and other young children of the community how to read, write and do simple arithmetic problems.[112] Penmanship was very important to Captain John Ulmer Sr., and he made certain that the children he taught wrote legibly. Being educated and able to communicate well was extremely important to Captain John Ulmer Sr., and he insisted that his grandsons were properly educated and prepared to be responsible and productive individuals. John Ulmer Sr. brought with him letters of commendation from his town's minister in Germany, his town's mayor, the district judge and the state procurator, John William Fischer of Enzberg, in the duchy of Württemberg, Germany.[113] Samuel Waldo, who represented the Massachusetts Bay Company, appointed Captain John Ulmer Sr. as the primary village official and also the spiritual leader of the German-speaking Lutheran Brethren in Broad Bay.[114] He was called "Brother" Ulmer by the church congregation who followed the teachings of Martin Luther. "Brother" or "Elder" Ulmer administered to the moral and spiritual needs of the settlement for about twenty years. He delivered sermons regularly at the homes of friends and neighbors until a proper church could be built. Jacob Ulmer faithfully assisted his father in his duties as spiritual leader and village official in the Broad Bay community.

John Ulmer Sr. had learned about the merchant business during his first year in America while living and working in Marblehead and Salem. He learned English while in Salem so that he could communicate and conduct business in the Massachusetts colony. He had made valuable business contacts in those busy commercial trading towns along the Massachusetts seacoast. As the leader of the Broad Bay settlement, he made business contacts in Boston with wealthy merchant investors, land speculators and venture capitalists with the Massachusetts Bay-Plymouth Company. During his first year in America, sixteen-year-old Jacob Ulmer (who would later become Philip Ulmer's father) learned fishing and sailing techniques at Marblehead, and he learned about shipbuilding and navigation techniques on coastal merchant trading ships while living and working in the Salem, Massachusetts area.

WAR BETWEEN ENGLAND AND FRANCE SPREADS TO THE PROVINCE OF MAINE

In March 1744, France declared war on Great Britain (called the War of Austrian Succession, 1740–48, in Europe), but the conflict spread across the Atlantic and affected France's claims in Canada and in North America (called King George's War in North America). The trade routes between the developing Canadian cities of Quebec City and Montreal and the American colonies were affected greatly by the war between these great rivals. The mouth of the St. Lawrence River near Nova Scotia opened up the center of the North American continent to trade and colonization and became a contentious issue between France and England for domination. The Grand Banks near Newfoundland held the world's greatest fish hatcheries and provided abundant supplies of fish for the New England colonies and for Europe.

With the outbreak of war in Europe, the governor of Massachusetts, Sir William Shirley, issued a call to arms and made Sir William Pepperell the commander of American colonial forces in New England. The governor ordered an expedition of colonial troops to attack the French citadel of Louisbourg, which was built upon a point of land on Cape Breton Island that protected the mouth of the St. Lawrence River in Canada. New England furnished the soldiers (mostly fishermen and farmers), while Pennsylvania sent some provisions and New York sent a small amount of artillery. Many of the families from the Broad Bay settlement were moved to the safety of the fort at Pemaquid, while others went with the soldiers as camp followers. Captain John Ulmer Sr., his son, Jacob, and the militiamen of the Broad Bay Guards (sometimes referred to as the Broad Bay Rangers) participated in the early battles against the French King Louis XV's land claims in Canada, the Province of Maine and other territories in America. General Sir William Pepperell led one army division, and newly appointed Brigadier General Samuel Waldo led another army division to Cape Breton Island. The small American fleet, composed of over one hundred vessels of various types that were transporting the army troops, was joined by four British warships from the West Indies commanded by Commodore Warren. General Waldo and Captain John Ulmer Sr., who led the Second Massachusetts Regiment from Broad Bay and St. George, proceeded to the French fortress on Nova Scotia, where they conducted a siege at Fort Louisbourg from 1744 (some sources say 1745) to 1748.[115]

On May 1, 1745, the assorted sailing vessels of the American fleet came to the high stone walls of the Louisbourg fortress, and a landing was made. It was reported that "the men flew to shore like eagles to their quarry."[116] It was recorded that on the night of May 2, 1745, Captain John Ulmer Sr. led the Broad Bay militiamen, including his teenage son Jacob, in a successful attack on the arsenal northeast of the harbor at Louisbourg and captured great stores of military and naval supplies.[117] Captain John Ulmer Sr. led the Second Massachusetts Regiment courageously in battle and earned the respect of General Samuel Waldo. After the war, the troops returned to their Broad Bay settlement, which had been destroyed by Indian raids. They buried the dead and started to rebuild their lives and community. Those settlers who had been left behind in the settlement had either moved away, been killed, taken refuge at Fort William Henry at Pemaquid (present-day Bristol, Maine) or been taken as prisoners—never to be seen again. When hostilities between Britain and France erupted during the French and Indian War, the fortress at Louisbourg was taken again after a seven-week siege in 1758. John Sr. and Jacob were involved in this second successful siege at Louisbourg with the Second Massachusetts Regiment.[118]

Upon their return to Broad Bay, Captain John Ulmer Sr., Jacob and several other men from the settlement represented the villages of Broad Bay and St. George in an Indian peace ceremony with the delegations from the Sagamores and all the eastern Indian tribes except the Mickmacs and those of the St. Francois. Dummer's Treaty, as it was called, was ratified and executed under seal and witnessed by thirty-two persons. The treaty agreed upon stated: "…the English were to inhabit as far as the salt-water flowed, and the Indians to have the rest."[119] Presents were distributed, belts of wampum were delivered and an ox was given for a feast of celebration. The wampum exchanged by the representatives from the Kennebec and Penobscot Indian tribes conferred authority and a duty to be truthful and was considered a pledge of honor that sealed the words and promises given during the ceremony with the settlement representatives.[120] After the French and Indian War, the friendship bonds between the Native Americans in the Penobscot and Passamaquoddy tribes and the frontier settlers of the growing Broad Bay and St. George communities would last for many generations. To the Native Americans, wampum belts were considered to be of great value when shared between people and cemented a bond between them. Over time, the value of the Indian wampum shell-beads took on a different value—a trading value of coinage. The purple beads were valued as gold, the white beads were the equivalent of silver and the black beads were the copper equivalents of English coinage.[121] Trading in beads became a means to purchase or barter for wanted goods. For those in frontier Maine who had been bound by their pledge of honor and trust, their family and tribal friendships remained for many generations.

FRIENDSHIPS FORGED WITH
CAPTAIN JOHN ULMER SR.'S FAMILY

The friendships forged between the local Penobscot Indians (part of the Abenaki Nation) and Captain John Ulmer Sr.'s family members would be extended to the future generations with his grandsons, Philip and George Ulmer. The Algonquin-speaking Wabanaki people (Confederacy), which included the local Penobscot, Abenaki and Passamaquoddy Indians, were active participants on the side of the colonists in frontier Massachusetts during the American Revolution, or they remained neutral.[122] Having been exposed during his formative years as a child, as a teenager and as a young man through his extended families in Salem, Marblehead and Waldoboro, Philip Ulmer understood and spoke several languages. Philip Ulmer had been exposed to transatlantic commerce and merchant business trading practices in Europe, the West Indies and in cities along the eastern seacoast of America through his prosperous family members in Salem, Marblehead and Waldoboro. He was fluent in English and German,[123] and he was somewhat familiar with Dutch and Swiss from his family's connections in the local community. Philip was exposed to the local Indian dialects through his grandfather's and father's involvement with the local Indian tribes and with the Dummer's Treaty following the French and Indian War. Local Penobscot Indians maintained their loyalty to the American settlers in the communities of the frontier Maine district. They shared their hunting techniques while continuing to respect their ancestral traditions and hunting grounds.

It is important to note that the strong personal relationship that developed between Brigadier General Samuel Waldo, Captain John Ulmer Sr. and his son, Jacob Ulmer, seemed to have remained through several generations. Jacob Ulmer became friends with Samuel Waldo Jr., and John Ulmer Sr.'s grandchildren, Philip and George Ulmer, became childhood friends of Lucy Flucker, granddaughter of General Waldo. Lucy Flucker later became the wife of General Henry Knox, who served as artillery commander for Washington's Continental Army during the Revolutionary War. Philip Ulmer, who was advanced in rank to first lieutenant on January 1, 1777, after his participation in the Battle of Trenton, got to know General Knox well during the American army's military campaigns in New York, New Jersey and Pennsylvania. Family intermarriage, community and business connections, military comradeship, Masonic affiliations and personal friendships were important in the life of Philip Ulmer during the Revolutionary War and in his business connections and political career as a public servant after the war.

It is also important to note that there were Native Americans from the Penobscot Indian tribe in frontier Maine district who were involved in General Montgomery's and Colonel Benedict Arnold's 1775 expedition to Canada as couriers and guides.[124] The Native Americans were involved with the Delaware River crossing in late December 1775, and they were involved in the battle at Saratoga and at Valley Forge with Washington's Continental

Army forces.[125] The Penobscot Indians were actively involved with Captain Philip Ulmer's company during the Penobscot Bay Expedition in 1779 when Captain Philip Ulmer's militia company climbed the cliffs at Dyce's Head. They supported and assisted the American forces during their disastrous retreat up the Penobscot River.[126] General Lovell was protected and given assistance after the American retreat by the Penobscot Indians at their village at Old Town (near Bangor, Maine) until it was safe for him to return to Boston many weeks later. After the Revolutionary War, the Penobscot Indians became workers at Philip Ulmer's shipyard, and they were paid a salary equal to that of the other men of the Penobscot community who worked in the Ulmer brothers' shipping and trading businesses at Ducktrap Harbor and cove (now Lincolnville, Maine).[127]

BROAD BAY DEVELOPS
INTO A PRODUCTIVE SEAPORT VILLAGE

As the settlement at Broad Bay became more organized and productive, trade developed on a regular basis with the markets in Boston, Salem and other seacoast towns. Business in the Broad Bay community was carried on by smaller sailing vessels called coasters. Frequent trade brought people from the larger towns and villages in the Massachusetts Bay to Broad Bay, St. George and other developing settlements in frontier Maine. Many Massachusetts merchants, tradesmen and sea captains began to realize the potential of the region and the possibilities for development, land speculation and business investments. Once the Indian problem was settled after the French and Indian War, there was a large migration of Englishmen and Puritans from Salem, Boston and other towns in the Massachusetts Bay area to Broad Bay, St. George and other frontier settlements.[128] There were a number of reasons for this migration to the Province of Maine and to the settlements at Broad Bay and St. George. One reason was the availability for venture investment capitalists to develop various commercial businesses and trading opportunities with the abundance of raw timber and mineral resources readily available in the frontier region. Another reason for the increased migration was the result of officers and soldiers who had repeatedly appealed to the Massachusetts General Court for payment for their military services or given bounty land warrants (land grants) in the unoccupied areas of Massachusetts state land in frontier Maine Province. A considerable number of people became established in this way or received state government land in lieu of payment for military services given during the French and Indian War (the Seven Years' War).

Still another reason why there was a large migration of settlers to the district of Maine after the war was that land was abundantly available and considered better than the soil in Massachusetts. Land was much cheaper than in the more developed towns of Boston and Salem, and new settlers could acquire more land and natural resources than they could in other parts of Massachusetts. Wealthy merchants and land speculators expected to reap large profits from the sale of land in the frontier regions of Maine Province when the state land was surveyed and sold to new settlers and investors. Business and financial opportunities for the venture capitalist would reap great rewards for a wise investor and developer. The Broad Bay and St. George communities were made up largely of people who wanted to sell their property in the Boston area, purchase a farm in Maine and have a considerable amount of money left over to live comfortably. These were well-to-do, hardworking and highly capable people who recognized a good opportunity and were willing to take a risk and reap great rewards and profits.[129] Through foresight and enterprise, these early entrepreneurs became the wealthiest families at the Broad Bay and St. George villages in the early days.

Growing Up in America

Jacob Ulmer, upon his return from the siege of Louisbourg, married Christiana Rügner (also written as Riegner) in 1748 at the Broad Bay settlement.[130] Christiana (also appears as Christine or Christina) was born at Klingenberg in Swabia, Germany, where her father had been the mayor of the city. She was a petite woman who wore her light-colored hair up on her head in a Swabian braid. She came to America aboard the ship *Lydia* with her family in 1742, and the family settled in Broad Bay with other emigrants from Germany.[131] Christiana Rügner's father, Johann Rügner, was a veteran German soldier with experience during the Louisbourg Expedition and during the French and Indian War with Captain John Ulmer Sr.[132] Jacob and Christiana Ulmer had two children who lived to become adults. Philip Martin Ulmer was born on December 25, 1751, and his brother, George Ulmer, was born on February 25, 1755 (some records say 1756), in their log house at the Broad Bay settlement.[133] The family spoke primarily German with other German pioneers at the settlement.[134] They learned to speak English in order to interact and transact business and commerce in Salem and Boston. They needed to communicate with other English-speaking people in the colonial seaport communities throughout the Massachusetts Bay Colony and other coastal towns to the south.

A severe earthquake occurred in November 1755 that affected the seacoast of America from Nova Scotia to the Chesapeake Bay.[135] Great fear was generated by the earthquake in the Broad Bay settlement, which caused Jacob and Christiana Ulmer to pack up their small family and move back to the Salem and Marblehead area permanently.[136] Jacob's younger brother, John Ulmer Jr., also moved to Marblehead at the same time, and he lived with Jacob's family for several years.[137] Hans Martin Ulmer, the son of Captain John Ulmer Sr. by his first marriage, sailed to America from Enzberg, Germany, on the vessel *Elizabeth*. Hans arrived with his wife, Maria Barbara (Steinmetz) Ulmer, and their four children in the Broad Bay settlement on October 9, 1753, eleven years after his father and second wife and his Ulmer stepbrothers and stepsisters.[138] Hans (also written as Johann or John) Martin Ulmer and his family remained in the Broad Bay community for several years. They moved to Marblehead with other Ulmer family members at the time of the great earthquake. Hans Martin Ulmer was Jacob Ulmer's half brother from Germany and Philip Martin Ulmer's uncle. Hans and his family became active participants in the Salem community. Philip and George Ulmer grew up being very close to their uncles and their extended families in Waldoboro, Salem and Marblehead.

Once the Ulmer family moved, young Philip Ulmer (who was not yet four years old) learned to speak English in the Salem and Marblehead communities, and he spoke German with his relatives and friends in Broad Bay. George Ulmer, who was an infant at the time his family moved to Salem, grew up speaking English and German fluently. Since they were young, languages came easily to the Ulmer brothers. Being fluent in both German and English would become important for Philip and George Ulmer in later years while serving with the American military forces during the Revolutionary War. Since Massachusetts was a multicultural and an abolitionist colony, the young Ulmer children learned to pray, play, sail and fish with children of diverse cultural and ethnic backgrounds. Interaction between white children and black children was readily acceptable, and they never had any qualms about sailing or fighting alongside African sailors or militia soldiers. In Broad Bay (later renamed Waldoboro), the young Ulmer boys learned to play, fish, hunt, navigate and communicate with local Indian children from the migrating Abenaki tribal families.

John Ulmer Jr., who lived with Jacob Ulmer's family, became a Marblehead mariner and learned about the shipping and trading business as well as shipbuilding and construction. Since most men were involved in the fishing industry in Marblehead, the Ulmer men were probably also involved in fishing as well. After several years, John Ulmer Jr. married his Broad Bay childhood girlfriend, Mary Catherine (also written as Katherine) Remilly, on July 27, 1759, in Marblehead, Massachusetts.[139] She was the daughter of Captain Matthias Remilly, an officer in the Dutch Rangers militia in the St. George and Broad Bay settlements.[140] She was born on board the ship *Lydia* during the Atlantic crossing in 1742 when the family immigrated to America.[141] Her family name was originally Römele in the ship's early listings at Broad Bay but was anglicanized to Remilly (also appears as Remiley, Remilee and Remely).[142]

Jacob Ulmer became involved with sailing on merchant trading and cargo vessels, while his younger brother, John Ulmer Jr., became involved with shipbuilding and the cod-fishing business. The family likely became familiar acquaintances with John Glover, Samuel Tucker and other merchants of Marblehead and Salem. Several cousins who relocated with Hans Martin Ulmer, with Jacob Ulmer's young family and with John Ulmer Jr. married into wealthy and successful seaport families such as the Beckett and Orne (sometimes appears as H'orne or even Horne) families in Salem and Marblehead.[143] These families were shipyard owners and coastal and international merchant traders who owned numerous commercial ships and businesses in the Salem and Marblehead communities. These marriages opened up opportunities for Jacob Ulmer and John Jr. in the merchant trading, commercial fishing and shipbuilding communities. These opportunities were later extended to Jacob Ulmer's sons, Philip and George, as well as to other Ulmer family relatives who moved to the area.

Hans Ulmer, Jacob Ulmer and John Ulmer Jr. lived and worked in the Salem/Marblehead/Beverly area. Beverly was the shipbuilding center of the area, Salem was the merchant and commercial shipping center and Marblehead was the commercial fishing center of the communities. The Ulmer brothers maintained connections with their father, John Ulmer Sr., in Broad Bay, where his shipbuilding, commercial trading, shipping business and venture investment opportunities remained. In 1760, Jacob Ulmer sold his Broad Bay lot (No. 15) below the Medomak Falls, and he never returned to the Broad Bay settlement to live.[144] By 1760, John Ulmer

Sr. had constructed the largest private residence at Broad Bay near the shore.[145] The large house later became an inn called The Ulmer located at Ulmer Point near the Broad Bay village.[146] Young Philip Ulmer would often spend many weeks at a time in the Broad Bay community with his many cousins as he grew up, learning the shipbuilding trade at the shipyards and helping his grandfather in the merchant trading and shipping business. When he returned to Marblehead, Philip enjoyed going fishing or sailing with his father and his uncle John Jr. He sometimes helped at the main wharf in Salem when the merchant ships arrived and the cargo was unloaded. Young Philip and John Jr. occasionally sailed with Jacob Ulmer on business voyages to transport cargo and deliver goods between the Salem and Boston markets and coastal towns and cities along the eastern seacoast of New England. Philip's father, Jacob, would sometimes sail to the West Indies on trading or commercial business voyages with goods that were needed in the islands. He would return in the sailing schooner laden with spices, fruit and exotic goods from ports in the islands of the West Indies or from other places in Europe and around the world. It was an exciting and enriching life for the young Ulmer boys beyond their own small community. Philip and George grew up knowing, appreciating and working with people of all races and ethnic backgrounds.

In 1761, Jacob Ulmer, who was thirty-five years old, went on a merchant voyage from Salem to the West Indies and unexpectedly disappeared.[147] He was presumed dead when his sailing ship was lost at sea somewhere near the Bahamas. Jacob Ulmer's two young boys, Philip and George, were just nine and a half and five years old, respectively. Their mother, Christiana (also appears Christine or Christina), was devastated by the loss of her husband. The following year, Philip and George's mother remarried, but sadly she lost her new husband in less than sixteen months of the marriage.[148] She married again in Salem to a merchant seaman whose name was probably John Ropes. The facts of her life after this time are unclear, but she apparently remained in the Salem vicinity. Their grandfather Captain John Ulmer Sr. took responsibility for his two young grandsons and took them to Broad Bay, where their grandmother, cousins, several aunts and uncles and extended family members lived. Philip and George Ulmer would visit the Marblehead/ Salem area to see their Ulmer relatives whenever their grandfather sailed to Salem to conduct business in the vicinity. As young boys, Philip and George watched the militia drills and exercises at Broad Bay and at the Salem green while staying with their relatives at those locations. The lessons and skills that the boys learned in their formative years in Waldoboro and in the

Marblehead/Salem/Beverly vicinity would become important parts in their future choices and success as adults.

Philip, who was several years older than George, spent much of his time learning sailing techniques, shipbuilding and the merchant business trade.[149] He was a hardworking and responsible person; he had good organizational skills and business instincts; and he was an intelligent person with a quiet confidence that inspired trust and confidence from others. He was probably lean, strongly built and short in stature, about five-foot-five or five-foot-six, which was slightly below the average size for men at the time. He would probably have had slightly wavy, sandy-colored hair; blue eyes; and fair skin. He had a broad nasal bridge and a rather prominent nose. Philip was a quiet, serious person who, through unfortunate circumstances, had been required to grow up quickly and assume responsibility at a very young age. He was a serious student and a logical and creative thinker. He excelled in mathematics, and he had good administrative skills.

George was taller than his older brother at about six feet tall. He had broad, muscular shoulders and a prominent nose, another family characteristic. He probably had sandy-colored hair, blue eyes and fair skin like his older brother. These traits were inherited genetically through the Ulmer family, if one can judge from inherited traits of future successors. George was spirited and determined and sometimes got himself into trouble as a youth. On several occasions during George Ulmer's lifetime, his anger got the better of him. These heated confrontations sometimes resulted in fighting and his being reprimanded or even jailed in order to cool down the situation. He had a quick, confrontational and sometimes volatile temper that led to some tense personal encounters. George's temper led to verbal altercations, threats of bodily injury for questioning his views and his authority and on several occasions led to threats of a duel to assuage his self-esteem. His experience in the military service during the war taught him many valuable lessons. He learned by observing wealthy merchants and military leaders and how they conducted business and developed political relationships. He quickly learned the value of political contacts and the power that wealth could bring in providing personal opportunities, public respect, prosperity and authority. George was an outgoing person who developed political charm and oratory savvy. He could be quite diplomatic by ingratiating himself to powerful men, and he was a self-promoter when the circumstances called for it. George styled and conducted himself with a military air that later carried over into his elderly years.[150]

Philip and George Ulmer learned to have self-confidence and to seize opportunities when they presented themselves. The boys were bright and intelligent people, and they learned quickly. The Ulmer brothers learned valuable character traits from their grandfather such as their loyalty and devotion to duty, as well as a deep religious faith. They learned perseverance and determination to weather the risks and challenges placed before them in life.[151] Philip and George Ulmer learned early from their grandfather to become independent-minded and to develop a good work ethic; however, they also became reliant on each other. The young brothers, like other young families from Broad Bay, generally spent the cold winters in the Salem area, where their mother, Christiana, and extended Ulmer relatives lived. The French and Indian War had little effect on Philip and George Ulmer as young boys since this time was spent in the Salem/Marblehead vicinity with their family, friends and relatives.

Philip and George's grandfather John Ulmer Sr. was an innholder at Broad Bay (like a bed-and-breakfast inn today) in November 1762.[152] It was considered the largest house in the Broad Bay settlement. This large house, called The Ulm or sometimes The Ulmer, became a popular place for gatherings and lodging in the community. While visiting Marblehead sometime after September 27, 1763, John Ulmer Sr. died unexpectedly, leaving his two little grandsons, ages eleven and seven and a half, to be raised by relatives.[153] With the death of Philip and George's grandfather, Hans Martin Ulmer (the half brother of Jacob Ulmer and John Ulmer Jr.) inherited the Ulmer family holdings at Broad Bay as the eldest Ulmer son. He returned to Broad Bay to settle his father's business accounts and see to the needs of the relatives living there. Unfortunately, Hans Ulmer's life also ended early, several years after his father, John Ulmer Sr. By the time Philip was about twelve years old, the young Ulmer brothers had lost their father, their grandfather and their uncle Hans Ulmer, who had assumed the role as the head of the Ulmer family clan. Their mother struggled with her own emotional losses as a widow with two young boys in the Salem vicinity. She needed to find a new husband and to build a new life in the community. Philip and George had a very deep bond with each other and with their uncle John Jr., who had lived in their home as a teenager. He had helped Philip's mother raise the young boys after the death of their father, Jacob. The Ulmer brothers were devoted to each other all of their lives.

Philip and George's uncle John Ulmer Jr., who lived in Marblehead with his own young family at the time, was a twenty-seven-year-old mariner and fisherman. He took responsibility as the principal guardian for the two young boys, and he served as their male parent mentor and guardian. The young brothers lived with John Ulmer Jr. and their aunt Mary Catherine, where they appeared with their uncle's family in the activities of the town.[154] (Note: Historians have often confused Philip and George Ulmer's uncle, [Johannes] John Ulmer Jr., as the *father* of the brothers, but this is incorrect. Uncle John Ulmer Jr. was ten years younger than his older brother, [Johann] Jacob Ulmer, who was the *actual* father of Philip and George Ulmer. John [Johannes] Ulmer Jr. was only fifteen years old when Philip Ulmer was born in December 1751 and couldn't possibly have been Philip's father.) With the death of Hans Martin Ulmer, who was the eldest son of Philip's grandfather, the Ulmer holdings in Broad Bay were passed by inheritance to John Ulmer Jr., the surviving male member of Captain John Ulmer Sr.'s family at the Broad Bay settlement. It was decided that John Ulmer Jr., his wife, Mary Catherine, their young children and their nephews, Philip and George, would move back to Broad Bay and assume the management of the Ulmer family businesses at Broad Bay Cove and at Ulmer Point where other Ulmer family members lived.

The most important legacies that John (Johannes Jakob) Ulmer Sr. gave to the Ulmer family members were a firm religious faith and belief in freedom, liberty, justice, equality, hard work and enterprise. There was no evidence of illiteracy in the Ulmer family. Philip and George's uncle John Ulmer Jr. briefly assumed his father's responsibilities as a spiritual leader in the Broad Bay community, where he served as a lay pastor for several years, and he schooled the children in the local community. Like his father, John Ulmer Jr. emphasized the importance of education, industry and commerce in the villages of Broad Bay and St. George.

SHIPBUILDING

After the death of John Ulmer Sr. and Hans Martin Ulmer sometime after 1763, Philip and George's uncle John Ulmer Jr. assumed guardianship of the two boys. He moved the young Ulmer family back to Broad Bay to pursue the shipbuilding and the commercial trading business at the Broad Bay Cove shipyards that the Ulmer family had established there. As the last surviving son of his father, John Ulmer Jr. was able to carry on his father's business enterprises in lumbering, shipbuilding, cargo shipping, merchant trading and real estate development.[155] Lumbering and shipbuilding were the fastest-growing industries in New England following the French and Indian War due to the abundance of forests, wood supplies and natural resources in the eastern frontier of Massachusetts. The merchants and businessmen sought to purchase sailing ships as fast as the shipyards could produce them. Wood products were greatly needed in the larger towns such as Boston, New York City and Philadelphia, and these products were desired in the West Indies and in Europe as well. The District of Maine in the eastern frontier of Massachusetts had abundant forest timber for ships and other needed goods and natural products. Maine had an abundance of tall "King Pine" trees needed for the main masts of the sailing vessels. The lime, granite and marble quarries in frontier Maine were among the best to be found anywhere in North America. Shipping was the major form of transportation since roads and bridges were mostly nonexistent. It provided a primary means for earning a profitable income through trading, navigation and commerce. There were secure, regular and free-flowing commercial business dealings among Boston, Salem, Broad Bay (Waldoboro) and Newburyport during this time. Broad Bay became incorporated in 1773, and the name was changed to Waldoborough (hereafter Waldoboro) in honor of General Samuel Waldo, the founder of the settlement. Waldoboro became a busy shipbuilding and commercial seaport community. The Ulmer shipyard in Waldoboro built coastal ships (called coasters) that carried supplies, lumber products and cargo to seaport towns and cities along the eastern coast of North America from Nova Scotia to the West Indies. There were also seagoing vessels that made transatlantic trips to countries in Europe, the Mediterranean and other foreign ports.

The Ulmer family knew other shipbuilders, ship owners and businessmen in seaport towns and villages all along the eastern seacoast of New England and the Penobscot Bay region, as well as some merchants in the southern states and the West Indies. The merchant traders, ship owners and shipyard owners knew one another either through their business dealings or by reputation. The trading merchants, ship owners and shipyard owners depended on one another as a support network to maintain their business livelihoods as well as their leadership and social status in their local communities and counties. While maintaining his shipbuilding, cargo transport and land investment businesses, John Ulmer Jr. became more and more involved with investments and land speculation. He purchased property from people unable to pay their taxes or took promissory notes or collateral from people who needed money for the support of their families.

He sold acquired land at a sizable profit. He co-owned several gristmills, sawmills and other business enterprises in Waldoboro and the surrounding inland areas, which added to his wealth.[156] By 1794, John Ulmer Jr. was a wealthy man through investments in merchant vessels and cargo transports. Through land speculation and acquisition, he held many valuable pieces of property in the Waldoboro vicinity, the backcountry inland areas and land as far eastward as the Penobscot Bay. He sold his business investments and land holdings in the Waldoboro around 1796, and he moved his large family from Waldoboro to the Thomaston vicinity (in present-day Rockland), where they settled near Clam Cove at the entrance to the Penobscot Bay. The family descendants of Philip's uncle John Jr. built a very profitable shipbuilding, shipping and lime-burning business complex.[157]*

In 1771, John Ulmer Jr. and his nephew Philip (almost twenty years old) built the *Yankee Hero* at the Broad Bay Cove shipyard. It was a 150-ton merchant schooner built for the Tracy brothers, ship owners and trading merchants from Newburyport, Massachusetts.[158] Philip Ulmer and Nathaniel Tracy were the same age and became friends over the years through their families' business contacts. He also developed a friendship with the other Tracy brothers: John, Patrick and James. James Tracy later became the captain of the *Yankee Hero*. In 1775, Nathaniel Tracy was appointed by General Washington to provide the necessary transports for Colonel Arnold's expeditionary forces on their "secret mission" to Canada.[159] Nathaniel Tracy's prior relationship

---

* *Author's comment*: Uncle John Ulmer Jr. had two sons who have often been confused with their cousins over the years. One of Uncle John Jr.'s sons was also named Philip, and he was born in the fall of 1775. He later became a militia major with the cavalry during the War of 1812. He is often mistaken for his cousin Major Philip Martin Ulmer of Lincolnville. Another son of their uncle John Jr. was also named George Ulmer. Uncle John Jr.'s son George was born two years after Philip Ulmer's brother George. In the Massachusetts military records, this younger cousin was referred to as George Ulmer *Jr.* to distinguish between the two cousins. It has been a daunting task to try to sort out, and keep separate, the individual Ulmer cousins and Ulmer relatives who carried the same first and last names but were born on different dates and years. Of course, Philip's uncle John Ulmer Jr. was named for his grandfather. Uncle John Jr. had a son also named John, which has only added to the confusion of separating and distinguishing between the various Ulmer family members who carried the same first and last names. The Ulmer cousins were frequently referred to by their middle names, which were different.

with Philip Ulmer, a family friend and knowledgeable shipbuilder, would serve him well in locating and obtaining sufficient vessels for this service for General Washington. John Jr. and Philip, along with other relatives and friends in the community, were responsible for the construction of the *Broad Bay* schooner at Broad Bay Cove prior to the Revolution.[160] This schooner would serve in an important way in transporting American troops on a special secret expedition to Canada in 1775.

Between the years 1765 and 1775, the migration of Massachusetts Bay Puritans from the Boston and Salem areas had an important influential effect on the culture of the German/Swiss/Dutch settlements of St. George (near present-day Thomaston) and Broad Bay (present-day Waldoboro).[161] The two different cultures and patterns of life had influenced and changed each other through interaction and intermarriage over the years. The Puritan influence became the more dominant culture of New England, and over time, the Puritan culture gradually transformed the old European feudal practices and viewpoints of Broad Bay, St. George and other early frontier settlements into more democratic communities that were English in thought, organization and action. The settlers in the new communities in the District of Maine were strong in their evangelistic views and had definite divisions between right and wrong and good and evil, which imparted rigorous moral disciplines to their everyday lives.[162]

Many people in frontier Maine's seaport communities were more open and worldly in their viewpoints since their livelihoods depended on trading of commercial goods and services, transportation of cargo and people by sailing vessels and the interaction with people in other colonial seaports and in countries around the world. Many early settlers in New England still had friends, family and relatives in England, Germany and other European countries with whom they still communicated and sometimes visited by sailing vessel. This was certainly true with the Ulmer family of Broad Bay since other Ulmer family members from Germany also immigrated to the Broad Bay settlement in later voyages to join those relatives who were already settled there. Other Ulmer relatives also moved to Salem at this time and did not return to the Broad Bay settlement to live. These Ulmer relatives remained in the Marblehead, Salem and Beverly communities permanently. Following the French and Indian War, inhabitants of Broad Bay and other frontier settlement communities moved to warmer and less dangerous places. Several Ulmer relatives and a number of other Broad Bay German Lutherans moved to the outskirts of Philadelphia, Pennsylvania (Germantown); other frontier settlers moved to New Bern, North Carolina (the capital and principal trading seaport at the time); and later Broad Bay settlers moved to the Charleston, South Carolina vicinity, where they established new settlement communities. Some Ulmer relatives and inhabitants of Broad Bay, with their spiritual leader, Pastor Cilley, moved to the Carolinas and started new settlements on rich, fertile lands and started commercial trading businesses.[163] The German and Swiss settlers felt their religious and cultural beliefs and customs could be preserved in new settlements in the sparsely settled southern colonies.

Chapter 2

The Revolution Begins

If force is to be used at length, it must be a considerable one, and foreign troops must be hired, for to begin with small numbers will encourage resistance, and not terrify; and will in the end cost more blood and treasure.[164]
—*General Thomas Gage*

THE PRE-REVOLUTIONARY BRITISH RAIDS

In order to pay for the various wars that England had conducted against France and other European countries in different parts of the world, the British government determined that the American colonies would be a good source of tax revenue and industrial and commercial wealth for their own economy. The British government, wealthy merchants and venture capitalists in England decided to exploit the colonists and the natural resources in America for their own financial gain. By early 1770, the relationship between the American colonies and Great Britain became increasingly strained due to the many restrictive acts and resolutions that the British Parliament imposed upon the American colonies in the form of more taxes and decrees. Royal Governor Thomas Hutchinson was a strong supporter of the British king and Parliament and imposed restrictive British acts and decrees upon the Bostonians in Massachusetts. On February 22, 1770, a petty British customs official in Boston, while being harassed by a small group of young people over newly imposed taxes, turned and fired his weapon into the small crowd. A little eleven-year-old German boy who had thrown a snowball was unexpectedly fired upon and shot dead in the snowy street by the customs official. This young German boy, whose last name was Seider (Seiders), came from the Broad Bay settlement in the frontier district of Maine. He became the first martyr of the American Revolution.[165] He had been the friend of Philip Ulmer's brother, George, and the boys had known each other in the Broad Bay community. The needless killing of the young boy inflamed the emotions of the Massachusetts community, especially those living in the settlement of Broad Bay. The Seiders' son was given an impressive funeral in Broad Bay and was hailed as a "Martyr to the cause of liberty."[166] The British twist on the young Seider boy's death was that "it was [due] to the lawlessness of the mob and the recklessness of the agitators."[167] The following month, the Boston Massacre took place near the statehouse in Boston and resulted in a great emotional outpouring of indignation.

THE BOSTON TEA PARTY

Friends! Brethren! Countrymen!—That worst of plagues, the detested tea, shipped for this port by the East India Company is now arrived in this harbor— the Hour of Destruction or Manly Opposition to the Machinations of Tyranny stares you in the Face.[168]
—Dr. Joseph Warren

The American resentment toward British armed occupation troops in the New England colonies continued to simmer and erupt in escalating events that became increasingly violent. In Massachusetts, other confrontations followed as the American colonies chafed under the succession of new taxes and restrictions imposed on them by King George III and Parliament on the opposite side of the Atlantic Ocean, more than three thousand miles away. The colonists in the Massachusetts colony rebelled against the new duties and taxes that had been placed upon tea and other imports. They would not allow the tea to be brought ashore. The owner of the ship *Dartmouth* offered to send the ship out to sea until the conflict could be resolved, but the royal governor, Thomas Hutchinson, would not allow it and refused to give the ship clearance to sail back to England without paying any import duties. In December 1773, Royal Governor Thomas Hutchinson gave orders to the harbor officials in Boston that no ships were to sail out of the harbor until the tea taxes and import duties had been paid. The city of Boston was tense as officials frantically tried to negotiate a resolution for the tea dispute. In December, Samuel Adams told a large gathering of Bostonians that Governor Hutchinson had repeated his demands upon the seaport. The result was the Boston Tea Party, in which colonial activists who called themselves the "Sons of Liberty" disguised themselves as Mohawk Indians. They boarded the cargo ship *Dartmouth*, where they seized the tea, owned by the East India Company, and carried the boxes of tea to the rails of the ship, where they dumped the 342 containers into the Boston Harbor. This was a great financial loss to the company and a great embarrassment to the British government. In March 1774, an angry British Parliament imposed a series of Coercive Acts (called Intolerable Acts by the colonists) in response to the rebellion in Boston. The Boston Port Act was issued against the Bostonians that effectively shut down all commercial shipping in Boston Harbor until the Massachusetts citizens paid the duty taxes owed on the tea dumped into the harbor and reimbursement to the East India Company for the financial loss of the tea. Bostonians called for a boycott of British imports in response to the Boston Port Act.

In May 1774, General Thomas Gage, commander of all British forces in the colonies, arrived in Boston, replacing Royal Governor Thomas Hutchinson and putting Massachusetts under military rule. In mid-April 1775, Thomas Gage, now the British governor of Massachusetts, was secretly ordered by the British Ministry to enforce the Coercive Acts and suppress open rebellion in the colony by all necessary force. On April 19, 1775, British governor Thomas Gage, who represented the British government in Boston, sent raiding parties to attack Lexington and Concord and confiscate military arms and supplies that were being accumulated and stored for defensive purposes by the townspeople. The British soldiers returned to the relative safety of Boston having lost some of their soldiers. Thomas Gage was concerned about the city's vulnerable position, lying as it did in the shadows of surrounding hills. The wisdom of securing those heights was considered but not acted upon. This would prove to be a big mistake.

Word of hostile confrontations and bloody encounters in Massachusetts was received with astonishment in England. Edmund Burke, one of America's most ardent supporters in Parliament, expressed a minority view when he urged the withdrawal of British soldiers from Boston. His plea made little headway with Prime Minister Lord Frederick North, who dispatched additional soldiers to the rebellious New England colony.

Lord North hoped that a more aggressive British response to the unrest in Massachusetts would result from new military leadership. The War Ministry sent three generals—William Howe, Henry Clinton and John Burgoyne—to subdue the rebellion. Lord Effingham addressed the British Parliament in a daring speech supporting the American colonies' grievances against Great Britain's oppressive taxation, and he voiced recognition of America's desire for independence from England's rule. He expressed a warning to the British government that if England's policy of exploitation of the colonies continued and their grievances went unchanged, America would have no choice but to declare war against the mother country. He offered his resignation from the British army, saying that he would not fight against his fellow Englishmen in America, but the resignation was refused. The Ministry of War decided that the American colonies must be controlled and opposition to British rule had to be crushed. The colonies served England's economic interests as a source of revenue, as a source of exploitation of America's natural resources, as a source of land speculation and personal and business investment opportunities. The American colonies were too valuable to lose.

For more than a year, the people of Massachusetts, and especially the Marblehead mariners, had taken every opportunity to make life as difficult as possible for the British troops and Admiral Samuel Graves, who commanded the North American station of the Royal Navy at Boston. On May 13, 1774, the HMS *Lively* arrived in Boston Harbor as part of the British Royal Navy fleet that blockaded the port to enforce the Boston Port Act, a punishment of that city for the Boston Tea Party in December 1773. The warship brought with it General Sir William Howe (who would replace General Thomas Gage in October 1775), Major General John Burgoyne and Major General Henry Clinton. The royal governor declared that all trade and shipping "is henceforth transferred to Salem and Marblehead."[169] General Gage's flagship HMS *Lively* joined the other British warships blockading the New England coast and anchored off Marblehead and Salem Harbor.[170] Its commander, Lieutenant William Lechmere, had orders to "harass and impress at will, all sailors of Salem and Marblehead."[171] These "press warrants" were issued by Vice Admiral Graves, commander of the British Royal Navy forces in America. "Press gangs" were sent out periodically to capture Marblehead fishermen and seamen in order to force the young men into British naval service. Other seaport communities were also visited by these press gangs; however, Marblehead seems to have been targeted most frequently. Philip and George regularly spent the winters in the Salem and Marblehead communities with relatives and extended family members since they were children. Their widowed mother remarried but was widowed again soon thereafter. She married a third time and remained in the Salem area.[172] Philip and George were aware of the restrictions and deprivations experienced by these local towns and the dangers of possible kidnappings. Philip and George Ulmer, who often went fishing together or went sailing to other nearby seaports on business, had to be cautious not to become captives of these marauding British press gangs or by British warships and raiding parties. As it would happen, George Ulmer became a victim of such an encounter while living with his Ulmer relatives in Marblehead and Salem at this time.

Powder Alarm: British Raid on Salem

The town officials and militia leaders in Salem had constructed a fort, called Fort Lee, where the militia troops could conduct their military training. Military equipment and munitions were stockpiled and stored at the fort in case arms were needed for defensive purposes to defend their town and their economic commercial interests from British raiding parties. Philip and George were probably present when a British raiding party marched on Fort Lee, which was located in the countryside outside the town of Salem. The British learned from an informer about Fort Lee at North Field (present-day Danvers), where military arms and munitions were being stockpiled and heavy artillery equipment was being stored. A regiment of British soldiers under the command of Colonel Alexander Leslie was ordered to capture the eight cannons, arms and powder supplies stored on Salem's fort at North Field. About 250 British troops disembarked at Holman's Cove in Marblehead in the afternoon of February 26, 1775, and marched to the river dividing Marblehead from the town of Salem. An alarm was spread throughout the seaport community that the British were coming to attack the fort and confiscate the military equipment. Captain John Felt of the Salem militia and a large crowd of townspeople confronted Colonel Leslie and the British raiding troops at North Bridge.[173] Colonel Leslie demanded that the drawbridge over the river connecting the two towns be lowered. British soldiers could not cross over the river because two Salem men had sunk the two barges nearby, preventing their passage.

Colonel Leslie threatened to have his British raiding party fire upon the gathered Salem and Marblehead townspeople. When several British soldiers poked their bayonets at two defiant men, they bared their chests in the frigid cold air and dared the British soldiers to proceed. One of the men received a superficial wound, drawing the first blood of the American Revolution. The tense situation remained for much of the afternoon until the British colonel received word that thousands of American militiamen were on the way to lend support to Salem. Colonel Leslie negotiated a face-saving agreement with the townspeople that if they would permit some of the British troops to cross over the drawbridge and to advance about 165 yards into the outskirts of Salem, then the British troops would turn around and proceed back to their ships at Holman's Cove. The face-saving agreement was made, and the British soldiers returned to their boats amid constant catcalls and insults.[174] The British returned to Marblehead, led by their fifers playing "The World's Turned Upside Down." In retaliation for this British incident, Captain Samuel Trevett led a successful nighttime raid on the HMS *Lively* and removed a large quantity of weaponry and powder, all of which went to outfit the Marblehead Militia Regiment.[175]

LEXINGTON AND CONCORD

The clash of arms at Lexington, Awoke the martial fires, That slumbered in the sturdy hearts, Of our New England sires…To arms! To arms! Avenge the lives of our brothers who have fallen at Lexington!…They felt the justice of their cause; And when the tempest broke, Though tyrants made the wrongful laws, God made their hearts of oak. No weight of years their feet could stay, Nor tender age restrain, When foreign musketry blazed forth, O'er Concord's hallowed plain…[176]

With the Boston Port Act in effect, Philip Ulmer and his brother, George, likely had remained in the Salem and Marblehead vicinity with relatives at this time. Philip Ulmer responded to the call to arms for state militiamen and volunteers issued by the Massachusetts Committee of Safety following the British raid at Lexington and Concord on April 19, 1775, with other state militiamen from the local area. Philip Ulmer probably enlisted in the Massachusetts state militia from the Salem area. Philip had previously been in the local Massachusetts militia in frontier Maine district, called the Broad Bay Guards, under the command of Matthias Römele (Remilly), who was commissioned as captain of the local militia, and with Martin Reiser as militia lieutenant.[177] Since Philip was already a militia soldier with the rank of sergeant in the Broad Bay Guards, Waldoboro was credited with his enlistment in the government records. George Ulmer would later enlist for military service; however, Salem received credit for his recruitment as a new militia soldier with the rank of private since he had not served in the state militia before. Soldiers in the Massachusetts state militia usually enlisted for service up to one year. Sergeant Philip Ulmer was assigned with David Fuller to Captain Phineas Cooke's company, a part of Colonel Gardner's Fifteenth Regiment at Prospect Hill in 1775. Meanwhile, back in the frontier district of Maine, a company of state militiamen from the York and Cumberland County areas responded the next day and sent sixty fully equipped soldiers to Cambridge. They were followed a few days later by other militiamen from the frontier region of Maine. Lieutenant Colonel Samuel McCobb led a volunteer company of militiamen from frontier Maine district to Cambridge in the third week of April 1775, and they became part of Colonels Read and Nixon's regiments at Winter Hill. The militia soldiers and volunteers from the frontier District of Maine were distributed among the regiments at Prospect Hill and Winter Hill to furnish support and troop strength, wherever needed, in order to conduct the siege upon British-held Boston.

News of the April 1775 conflict at Lexington and Concord reached Machias, located in frontier Maine on the Penobscot Bay, just as the settlers were anxiously expecting supplies from Boston. When the cargo transports *Polly* and *Unity* arrived carrying the long-needed supplies, they were accompanied by the armed British schooner *Margaretta*, under the command of Lieutenant Moore. The job of the armed escort vessel was to see that in exchange for supplies, lumber was brought back to Boston to build barracks for British troops. The British commander demanded that all Machias settlers were to sign a petition promising to protect British property at all times in exchange for the right to buy supplies. Since many settlers were opposed to aiding the British war effort, the residents were angered by this demand. A group of men from the seaport village decided to strip the two British sloops of the supplies and to also capture Captain Ichabod Jones, Lieutenant Moore and his officers following the Sunday church service. The British officers and crew avoided capture and fled on the *Margaretta*. The village settlers lined the shore demanding that the British "surrender to America!" The British commander replied, "Fire and be damned!" Forty men, armed with swords, axes, guns and pitchforks, headed by Jeremiah O'Brien, went aboard the sloop *Unity* while twenty men under the direction of Benjamin Foster boarded a small schooner, and they pursued the *Margaretta*. During the chase, the attacking sailors put up planks and other material to defend against the *Margaretta*'s cannons. On June 12, 1775, near Round Island in the Machias Bay, the rebel Patriots crashed into the *Margaretta* and engaged in hand-to-hand combat. The British crew lost the one-hour battle, and their captain was mortally wounded. The rebel Patriots claimed "four double fortified three pounders and fourteen swivels" and other smaller military guns. This encounter is considered the first sea engagement and the start of the merchant marines' role during the American Revolution.[178] Following this incident, Jeremiah O'Brien, as captain of the Machias privateer *Liberty*, captured two armed British schooners and delivered the prisoners to General George Washington at the military headquarters at Cambridge, Massachusetts. On the recommendation of General Washington, the Massachusetts governing body appointed Captain O'Brien to command his two prize British schooners.

BRITISH IMPRESSMENTS

Vice Admiral Samuel Graves of the British Royal Navy was particularly angry with the people of Marblehead and Salem for their defiance of British rule. In the early spring of 1775, Admiral Graves had ordered wax candles from a shop in Marblehead, and the town fathers had confiscated them and refused to let the Admiral have them. In retaliation, Admiral Graves sent Lieutenant Lechmere, aboard the HMS *Lively*, out on an assignment to capture two fishermen just outside the harbor and impress them into the British service as seamen. On one such occasion in early May 1775, two teenaged fishermen who were fishing just outside the entrance to the harbor at Marblehead were confronted and captured by the British warship HMS *Lively*. The two young fishermen were unaware that Admiral Graves of the British Royal Navy had issued an order to the British fleet that any fishermen found fishing off the New England coastline were to be captured and brought to Boston, where the young men would be pressed into the British service as seamen to fight against their own countrymen. The young teenagers were standing helplessly on the deck of the HMS *Lively* being addressed by the ship's captain, Lieutenant William Lechmere, about either choosing to die or serve as seamen aboard a British warship.

Without warning, some one hundred Marblehead fishermen in ten whaleboats came out of the harbor and approached the British vessel and demanded to have the two boys released. Lechmere ordered his marines at the warship's gunwales to aim at the approaching fishing boats. The Marblehead fishermen aimed their guns at Lieutenant Lechmere and his British sailors. There was a tense standoff as the British and the Marblehead mariners faced one another, prepared to fire. Suddenly, one of the teenagers made a dash for the side of the ship and leaped overboard. The Marblehead fishermen cheered for him. Lieutenant Lechmere fired his pistol at the boy as he tried to swim away from the British ship, but the pistol misfired. The men in one of the fishing boats hauled the teenager into their boat and quickly started rowing him back into the harbor. The other teenager also tried to escape by jumping overboard, but he was wrestled to the deck, put into chains and dragged down below decks. It was a standoff. Both sides slowly retreated, each getting only half of what they wanted. The frightened teenager was brought back to the docks amid cheers of the gathered crowd. He was hoisted onto the shoulders of the fishermen and carried back to his house.[179] This event made a great emotional impact upon George Ulmer, Philip's younger brother, who was believed to be involved in this incident. Vice Admiral Graves was furious when he heard about the Marblehead fishermen in the rowboats who had dared to challenge the commander of one of His Majesty's flagships. He warned the Marblehead town fathers that he would retaliate with harsh measures. A few town fathers with Tory leanings decided it might be wise to send a letter of apology to the vice admiral and agreed "to pay all costs for damages, and promised in the future there never shall be any cause of complaint."[180] The town fathers gave Admiral Samuel Graves his candles, which ended the episode.

George Ulmer was one of those taken in another encounter by the British press gangs and forced to board the HMS *Lively* that patrolled the Massachusetts northeastern coastal areas in 1775. According to historical accounts and a newspaper report: "George Ulmer who in his twentieth year had been captured on a fishing trip by the frigate, *Lively*. The vessel and crew were taken to Boston, where Ulmer made his escape into the town and over the Charles River to the American lines at the imminent hazard of his life. There he enlisted in the American Army and served through the remainder of the campaign."[181]

After this encounter with the press gangs from the HMS *Lively*, George Ulmer enlisted for three years to serve with the First Essex Company from Salem and was sworn into service by Joseph Sprague, the first military officer of the town of Salem in the spring of 1775.[182] George Ulmer's residence was given as Salem at this time. He was assigned to Captain Abraham Hunt's company at Prospect Hill, in Colonel John Paterson's regiment. Sergeant Philip Ulmer and Private George Ulmer's two companies and regiments were stationed together near Camp Prospect Hill. George Ulmer's first assignment in military service was apparently with a detachment of four hundred volunteers under the command of Captain Benedict Arnold, whose objective was to capture the forts at Ticonderoga and Crown Point in northern New York colony.[183] These volunteers in the detached corps would remain in the Northern Department under the command of General Schuyler until ordered on the Canadian Expedition under the command of General Montgomery in the fall of 1775.

James Easton was an influential Connecticut militia colonel and a friend of Herman Allen of Salisbury, Connecticut, the younger brother of Ethan Allen. Colonel Easton and militia captain Edward Mott of Connecticut, with approximately seventy recruited volunteers (which included the Pittsfield, Massachusetts activist lawyer John Brown), met and joined forces with Ethan Allen and his 175 militiamen in the town of Bennington, located in the center of the New Hampshire Grants. (The New Hampshire Grants later became the state of Vermont.) Bennington was the headquarters of Ethan Allen's militiamen, who were called the "Green Mountain Boys." They had devised a plan to attack and capture the poorly defended British-held fort at Ticonderoga. Captain Benedict Arnold had been commissioned as a colonel by the Provincial Army of Observance on May 2, 1775, and he also had a plan for an attack on Fort Ticonderoga that had been endorsed by the Massachusetts Committee of Safety. Colonel Arnold's volunteers for the expedition were recruited at the military headquarters in Cambridge, Massachusetts, and apparently included George Ulmer. The detached troops met and joined forces with the two militia detachments from Connecticut and the New Hampshire Grant at the settlement of Shoreham (in present-day Vermont) across from Fort Ticonderoga on May 9, 1775. In the early morning hours of May 10, the American troops led by Captain Benedict Arnold and Ethan Allen entered the poorly guarded and sleeping fort, taking about forty-eight British soldiers and two officers captive without firing a shot. George Ulmer, who was a private at this time, stayed with the troops occupying Fort Ticonderoga, while Colonel Arnold and some of the other Massachusetts officers arranged for a number of field pieces to be transported back to Boston to help with the siege.[184] Colonel Arnold continued his expedition up Lake Champlain with his volunteers on the schooner *Liberty*, and they were able to capture a large sloop that was anchored at Fort St. John (also referred to as St. Jean or St. Johns). They managed to get away with the prize sloop, *George* (renamed *Enterprise*), before the British troops fired upon them. They sailed the vessel to Crown Point, where it was then anchored. (The unlaunched vessel at Fort St. John, the *Royal Savage*, would later be captured by General Montgomery's American troops in the fall of 1775 and, following the American retreat from Canada, would become involved in the Battle of Valcour Island in the fall of 1776.) Many of these volunteer troops from Massachusetts remained at Fort Ticonderoga under the command of General Philip Schuyler, and they later served with General Montgomery during the Canadian campaign in the fall of 1775.[185]

In the early weeks of June 1775, Philip Ulmer was with Colonel Thomas Gardner's Fifteenth Massachusetts Provincial Regiment. He served as a militia sergeant at Camp Prospect Hill near the Provincial Army headquarters at Cambridge under the command of Generals Israel Putnam and Nathaniel Greene.[186] The volunteers and state militiamen in Colonel Gardner's regiment would later be incorporated with Lieutenant Colonel Bond's infantry troops following the death of Colonel Gardner on July 3, 1775. General Washington promoted William Bond to colonel in July 1775 and assigned him as regiment commander of Colonel Gardner's soldiers. Colonel Bond's regiment was assigned to General Greene's brigade on July 22, 1775, an element of General Washington's Continental Army. They operated with General Charles Lee's division. Colonel Bond's regiment was later designated as the Twenty-fifth Continental Regiment by General Washington in early 1776.

THE REVOLUTION BEGINS

Lord George Germain, the secretary of state of the American colonies and minister of trade to King George III, received support from many Royal Army officers and leaders in the British Parliament to pursue a policy of deliberate violence and extreme fear to break America's independent spirit and bring about submission to the power and control of Great Britain. Several British officers applied this brutal strategy in 1775 at the start of the American Revolution and continued throughout the war. Admiral Graves ordered the town of Falmouth to be burned in retribution for the support that the townspeople had given to the Sons of Liberty and the incident in Boston with the Boston Tea Party. General John Burgoyne deliberately ordered the town of Charlestown, Massachusetts, burned during the British attack on Bunker Hill to eliminate the American defenses in the town. While some British generals took a hard line against the rebellion, others took a softer approach, with varying results. General William Howe and his brother, Admiral Richard Howe, rejected the systematic destruction of civilian life and property, which they considered unlawful and inhumane.[187] General Washington, like the Howe brothers, believed that there were rules of civility and decent behavior, even in war, and he strove to live by those basic principles of civility.

The Provincial Congress of Massachusetts Bay issued a call to arms for militiamen from the various colonies to come to the defense of the colony following the British raid on Lexington and Concord on April 19, 1775. The call stated:

> *...that the result of the action of the council of war on this resolution of the Committee of Safety was* [General] *Ward's order to fortify Bunker Hill—and the resolution and order have been variously interpreted: as a step of almost blind recklessness, a desperate hazard, occasioned by the urgent necessity to do something to check the British plans to raise the siege; as a move to offset the British intention to take Dorchester Neck; as an act of defiance calculated to bring on a general engagement; as the first step in the contemplated expulsion of the English from Boston.*[188]

One day after the British raid at Lexington and Concord, a company of sixty men fully equipped with arms, ammunition and food marched from the Province of Maine to Cambridge, Massachusetts. The first company was followed by other militiamen from the Maine province. These companies formed up with other militiamen at Cambridge and were present at the Battle of Bunker Hill.[189] During the siege of Boston, practically every able-bodied man in frontier Maine was present. An old letter found in the Massachusetts Archives stated that during the siege of Boston, an urgent call for additional volunteers was made to the inhabitants of Maine Province. The Committee of Safety from the state militia command in frontier Maine sent the reply: "Every man who can leave home is gone or is going to Cambridge. They must draw upon this part of the province for women instead of men, and for knives and forks instead of arms."[190] These New England militia soldiers, who made up approximately two-thirds of General Washington's Continental regiments, served willingly in the years 1775 to 1777.[191] These militiamen, some of whom were first-generation immigrants like Philip and George Ulmer of Waldoboro, were raised with a unique idea of liberty as independence and freedom as a right of belonging to a community. These rights of liberty and freedom entailed a sense of mutual obligation to protect these basic principles. They dearly loved their new country of America, and they were willing to risk their lives and fortunes to defend it from foreign domination and oppressive exploitation. Other colonial settlers wanted to retain their rights as Englishmen and not become a separate and independent country. The conflict caused great divisions among the American population.

In the early months of the siege of Boston, General Artemas Ward served as commander of the Massachusetts, Connecticut, Rhode Island and New Hampshire regiments as commander in chief of the New England colonies' militia forces. The militia army headquarters was located at Cambridge at this time. On June 14, 1775, the Second Continental Congress created the Continental Army and advanced Colonel George Washington to the rank of major general. Congress appointed four other major generals: Artemas Ward, who was leading the militia forces besieging Boston; Israel Putnam, an older veteran soldier with experience in the French and Indian War; Philip Schuyler, a wealthy and influential man from New York who had vast landholdings in the Albany area; and Charles Lee, a British officer who had recently retired from the British army and had settled in America to seek his fortune. The next day, the Continental Congress unanimously named George Washington as commander in chief of the Continental Army forces, and General Ward was named second-in-command at Boston. Congress also appointed nine men as brigadier generals, including Horatio Gates, another former British officer who had retired to America looking for fame and fortune. (It is interesting to note that British officers Charles Lee, Horatio Gates and Thomas Gage, who commanded the advanced unit in the unsuccessful Braddock campaign, had all served with young George Washington during the French and Indian War in their efforts to capture the French Fort Duquesne, which is located in present-day Pittsburgh, Pennsylvania.)[192] General Washington had requested that the Congress appoint Horatio Gates to serve as his adjutant general, which was the top staff position in the new Continental Army. George Washington convinced two young politicians from Pennsylvania to serve on his staff. Joseph Reed was persuaded to serve as General Washington's military secretary, and Thomas Mifflin was to be Washington's aide-de-camp.[193] General Artemas Ward was not a healthy person at this time, so General Charles Lee, General Washington's rival, effectively became second-in-command of the Continental Army.[194] Washington referred to him as "the first officer in military knowledge and experience we have in the whole army…but he is rather fickle and violent [and] I fear in his temper."[195] Charles Lee was passionate about the principles of the American cause, but he did not respect the leaders of the Revolution.

On June 20, the assembled delegates of the Second Continental Congress gave the new commander of the Continental Army his orders: "You are to repair with all expedition to the Colony of Massachusetts Bay, and take charge of the army of the United Colonies."[196] Several days later, amid great fanfare with flags flying, bands playing and people cheering, General Washington left Philadelphia with Lee, Schuyler, Gates, Reed and Mifflin for New York City. General Washington proceeded on to the military headquarters at Cambridge to assume his command of the American troops outside of Boston. General Schuyler left the military party at New York City and proceeded to Albany, where he was to assemble the Northern Department of the Continental Army in the Northern Theater. He was also charged by Continental Congress with the responsibility of organizing an expedition into Canada to liberate the settlers in Montreal and Quebec City from British control and to encourage the Canadians to become part of the United Colonies as the fourteenth colony. Of the six men who left Philadelphia in June with General Washington, only General Schuyler would remain Washington's friend and supporter.[197] Unlike the other men who had been appointed to serve with Washington, Schuyler would not become one of the deceptive adversaries and detractors who would attempt to remove General Washington from his leadership role in the Continental Army. Most of these same men who served on General Washington's staff would also become bitter foes of both George Washington and Benedict Arnold. Philip Ulmer would eventually come into contact with, and serve under, many of these same men during his time of military service in the Continental Army.

The first battle in which Sergeant Philip Ulmer participated was the Battle of Bunker Hill with Colonel Gardner's regiment that was under the supreme command of General Artemas Ward at Cambridge.[198] In June 1775, the records of the First Massachusetts Provincial Congress listed Thomas Gardner as a colonel who commanded a regiment with two field pieces and who had answered the Lexington Alarm on April 19, 1775.[199] Colonel Gardner's regiment at this time was designated the Fifteenth Massachusetts Regiment. General Ward ordered Colonel Gardner's regiment to Lechmere Point (East Cambridge) to guard the road to Cambridge. Colonel Paterson's regiment was located at Fort Three at the base of Prospect Hill near Union Square. General Heath's regiment

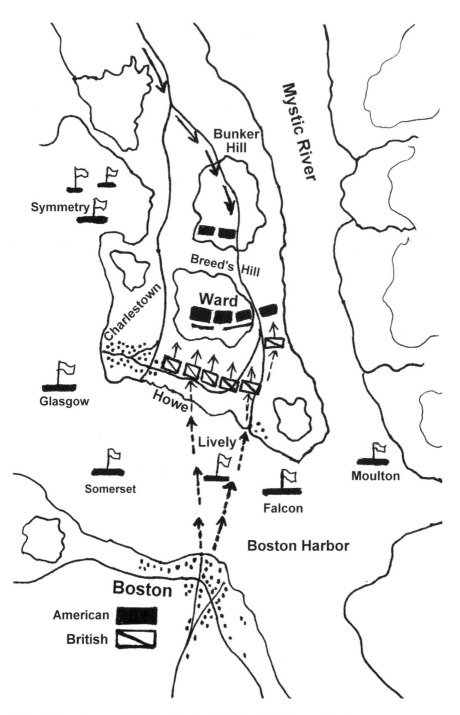

Map of the actions at the Battle of Bunker Hill (Breed's Hill) near Charlestown, Massachusetts, on June 17, 1775. *Courtesy of the author.*

was stationed at Fort Two near the Putnam defenses. Colonel Edmund Phinney's regiment from Cumberland County (Maine) was at Fort Two on Dana Hill, and Colonel James Scammon's regiment from York County (Maine) was at the Riverside works called Fort One. The regiments of Colonels Prescott, Glover, Frye and Bridge were assigned to Cambridge, with Woodbridge's regiment located at the Charlestown Road west of Prospect Hill and Sargent's regiment at Inman's Farm. Leaving a small company of soldiers to guard the road to Cambridge, Colonel Gardner realized that the major part of the engagement had started on Breed's Hill, and he advanced his regiment toward Bunker Hill, where he was met by General Israel Putnam's Third Connecticut Regiment troops.

General Israel Putnam, who served as a brigadier general of the Connecticut militia forces, ordered part of Colonel Gardner's regiment to assist in fortifying Bunker Hill while another company was sent to reinforce the troops at the rail fence. Another part of Colonel Gardner's regiment served with Colonel John Paterson's regiment as rear guard for Colonel Heath's brigade. They were all a part of Israel Putnam's division at this time. The larger part of Colonel Gardner's regiment advanced to the redoubt on Breed's Hill just as the third attack was launched by the British forces. As the regiment moved forward toward the redoubt, a musket ball struck Colonel Gardner, and another hit General Joseph Warren, mortally wounding him.[200] During the heat of the battle at Bunker Hill, Phineas Cooke of Hingham, Massachusetts (Philip Ulmer's company captain at the time), sustained a wound from which he would never fully recover.[201] Phineas Cooke was carried from the field of battle and was replaced by Captain Fuller, who continued to lead the militia company. Colonel Gardner, the regiment commander, was severely wounded and was carried off the field of battle by several of his soldiers. After lingering for almost two weeks, Colonel Gardner finally died on July 3, 1775, leaving Philip Ulmer's regiment without a regiment commander.[202]

In a letter to Lord Stanley (Burgoyne's nephew) in June 1775, Major General John Burgoyne wrote of his observations of the Battle of Bunker Hill from his safe location at Copp's Hill across the Charles River in Boston:

> *The action of the 17th establishes the ascendancy of the King's troops though opposed by more than treble numbers. It comprised, though in a small compass, almost every branch of military duty and curiosity. Troops landed in the face of the enemy; a fine disposition; a march sustained by a powerful cannonade from moving field artillery, fixed batteries, floating batteries, and*

The Death of General Warren at the Battle of Bunker Hill, 17 June 1775. By artist John Trumbull. *Courtesy of the Library of Congress.*

broadsides of ships at anchor, all operating separately and well disposed; a deployment from the march to form for the attack of the entrenchments and redoubt; a vigorous defense; a storm with bayonets; a large and fine town set on fire by shells. Whole streets of houses, ships upon the stocks, a number of churches, all sending up volumes of smoke and flame, or falling together in ruin, were capital objects. A prospect of the neighbouring hills, the steeples of Boston, and the masts of such ships as were unemployed in the harbour, all crowded with spectators, friends, and foes, alike in anxious suspense, made a background to the piece. It was great, it was high spirited, and while the animated impression remains, let us quit it.

General Washington arrived at Watertown, the seat of the Massachusetts Provincial Congress, on Sunday, July 2, 1775, with the men he had chosen to serve on his military staff. General Washington, wearing his blue and buff uniform of the Virginia militia, took command of the New England militia troops at the Continental Army headquarters at nearby Cambridge on July 3. He was met with reserved celebration from the troops.[203] It was uncertain as to how the New England militia forces would receive the southern officers and designated officials who had been appointed to take command of the Continental Army. There were black freemen and soldiers among the troops from Marblehead and Salem, which caused unrest and negative comments among the southern officers and troops. The Continental Congress wanted an army that was drawn from all the colonies. Congress expected that this would unite all the thirteen colonies in the common American cause. It was hoped that Canada (namely the inhabited areas of Montreal and Quebec City) would become the fourteenth colony and unite with the lower thirteen colonies in the effort to expel the British forces from North America. The Continental Congress had not actually voted to go to war but had established the army for the protection of American freedoms and the redress of their grievances, not for a permanent separation from the mother country, England.[204]

Sergeant Philip Ulmer served among the military regiments who were drawn up and standing at attention with their muskets on their shoulders for General Washington's review at Prospect Hill. There was no real parade of troops or assembly of the army to greet the new commander in chief. It was expected that the British would launch an attack at any time, and the militiamen and volunteers could not leave their positions for a parade ceremony. General Washington approached the camps at Prospect Hill riding his white horse and accompanied by General Ward, the commander

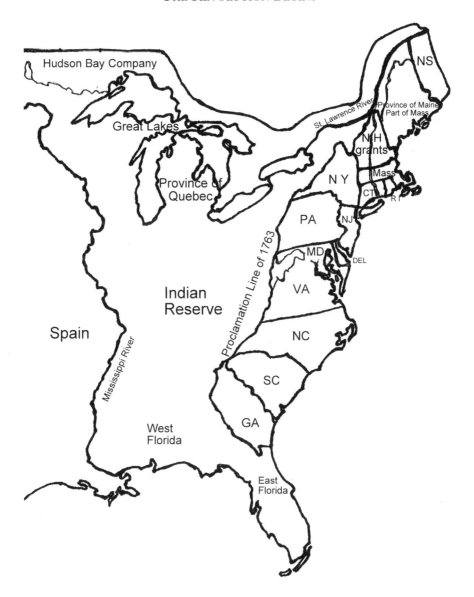

Land claims in America in 1776. *Courtesy of the author.*

of the militia forces. He rode slowly down the line of men and noted their lack of uniforms and that the clothes they did have were sweaty, ragged and dirty from the near-constant work of improving the defensive lines. The American troops were called out in such haste that the militiamen, boys and black men in the ranks had few tools, supplies, clothing or arms. It was a subdued time for the colonial troops. The American militia soldiers were burying the last of the fallen officers from the Battle of Bunker Hill: Dr. Joseph Warren and Colonel Thomas Gardner, the commander of Philip Ulmer's regiment. General Washington assumed the role of commander in chief of the American army. The men who composed the militia troops were mostly untrained and poorly equipped militia regiments whose local towns had provided for their own militia soldiers' needs as best as they could, with varying degrees of effectiveness.

William Bond had held the rank of lieutenant colonel, and he was second-in-command to Colonel Gardner in early July 1775.[205] Following the death of Gardner, Bond was promoted to colonel and took over the command of Colonel Gardner's regiment. Abraham Hunt, who had served as adjutant in 1775 in Colonel Gardner's regiment, was advanced in rank and leadership along with Major Henry Jackson and Captain Fuller, all officers with whom Sergeant Philip Ulmer served during the siege of Boston and later during the Revolutionary War.[206] General Washington assigned Brigadier General Nathanael Greene as the commander in chief of the regiments stationed at Prospect Hill.[207] Colonel Bond's regiment became part of Brigadier General Nathanael Greene's Sixth Brigade, in Major General Charles Lee's Second Division, on the left wing of General George Washington's Continental Army during the siege of Boston.[208] Colonel Bond's regiment served on picket duty at Prospect Hill overlooking the burned-out remains of the small town of Charlestown. They guarded against an enemy attack from the Mystic River, where the British ships were anchored. They also served as guards for the British prisoners taken during the fighting and held at Camp Cambridge near General Washington's military headquarters.[209]

Prior to 1775, Washington had never commanded anything larger than a regiment during the French and Indian War. Even more important, although the colonial militias had trained using European manuals, George Washington had not personally faced the European style of in-line warfare in which soldiers closed ranks and maneuvered in unison in open country. All of George Washington's experience in warfare had involved fighting in the backwoods of the American frontier, where soldiers or Indians hid behind trees, rock walls and convenient structures. These were the types of irregular combat and mobile tactics that were necessary to counter the European style of warfare. Washington was battle-tested in this type of conflict during the French and Indian War, but it had nothing to do with the sort of fighting that he faced as commander in chief of the Continental Army. Besides the sheer size of his command, Washington had battle issues that he had never dealt with before. He had no experience in the use of field artillery, siege warfare or with the excessive use of entrenchments and fortifications. There was no way for General Washington to predict if the British might choose to attack the American lines head-on with artillery and hand-to-hand warfare or that the siege at Boston might become a stalemate with no resolution for the land troops.

For the first time in his career, these new elements had to be considered in his strategic thinking. With his new command, Washington encountered another factor that was unfamiliar to him—the sea. Every major port city in colonial America was directly associated with the sea and was dependent on navigation and commerce. The British enjoyed a naval superiority that was unequaled anywhere in the world. Washington realized that his position around Boston was vulnerable to the British Royal Navy forces. Their complete command of the water would enable the British to attack any point along the American coastline, from Georgia to the Canadian border. As they moved from one theater to another during the conflict, the reinforcement troops and supply lines for the Continental Army would be in jeopardy. As General Washington looked out over the expanse of land from Camp Cambridge, located on the hilltop overlooking Boston and Boston Harbor, he realized that he was looking at the sea in a very different way. The great expanse of ocean in which the British fleet lay safely anchored was the open back door into Boston. His siege of Boston was only half a siege with no chance of becoming something more as long as the British controlled the sea lanes. Washington's appreciation of the naval side of the equation became more evident as his General Orders began to change.

General Washington learned quickly that he had to be innovative and somewhat unorthodox in his plans and decisions as to how he and his advisors chose to conduct the conflict with England. As tensions began to mount through 1775, the British and American supply lines needed to be addressed since this would be a war for necessary army materials and troop supplies. Although the American forces could contain British supplies and movement on land during the siege of Boston, goods and supplies were delivered by sea on a regular basis since the British held sea superiority with their armed ships-of-war. General Washington realized that the real war in New England was not a fight for land but for matériel, and it would be fought at sea.[210] The battles would be fought along the American seacoast, on the rivers and on the lakes in upstate New York, as well as on the St. Lawrence River in Canada. Colonel John Glover, whose Marblehead militia troops were at Cambridge, suggested the conversion of his merchant vessel

Hannah into an armed warship to counter the British warships patrolling off the New England coastline. Strategic plans for a naval defense of the New England colonies began to be formulated and take shape among the staff officers in the inner circle of General Washington's strategic command center at Cambridge. A return was made on July 17, 1775, of the number and name of men in the late Colonel Gardner's regiment who were "expert in managing whale boats in the following companies."[211]

Colonel John Glover was directed by General Washington to convert his seventy-eight-ton merchant schooner *Hannah* into an armed vessel to be leased to the Continental Army in the naval service for American defense against the hostile British Royal Navy fleet. Washington agreed to the lease of Glover's schooner for "one Dollar per Ton per Month."[212] The colonel selected a crew of forty-three, mostly men from Marblehead, who were to receive army pay and would split amongst themselves one-third of whatever cargo they captured except "military and naval stores…which with vessels and apparel are reserved for publick service."[213] General Washington issued a commission to Nicholson Broughton of Marblehead and ordered him to take Colonel Glover's schooner *Hannah* to sea "to cruise against the enemy and to seize such Vessels as may be found on the High seas or elsewhere, bound inward and outward to or from Boston in the Service of the [British] ministerial Army, and to take and seize all such vessels, laden with soldiers, arms, ammunition, or provisions…which you shall have good reason to suspect are in such service."[214]

Through the summer of 1775, the blockade around the city of Boston was so tight that no supplies or provisions could reach Boston from the surrounding countryside. Most of the British stores had to be sailed into Boston from Halifax, Nova Scotia. The British supply line stretched along the coastline of frontier Maine. The seaport communities that were harassed by British raiding parties from Halifax took action against the British supply ships, which led to the fitting-out of small dories and fishing boats into armed privateering vessels. Many of these small vessels were manned and commanded by men from the coastal towns of frontier Massachusetts. The harassment and capture of supply transports became a thorn in the side of the commanding British general in Boston, General William Howe. The British ordnance brig *Nancy* became one of the richest prize captures for Washington's "secret" naval fleet. The brig *Nancy* contained two thousand rifles and bayonets, eight thousand fuses, thirty-one tons of bullets, several hundred barrels of powder and military tools of every description. This captured British prize was recognized by General Washington as "an instance of divine Providence"[215] because these ordnance stores were used by Washington's forces to support the siege of Boston. The captured British ordnance supplies were used in the spring of 1776 to force the British troops out of Boston. (These ordnance supplies were later taken to Canada with the American relief troops to resupply and equip General Arnold's brigade and other troops who were besieging Quebec City in early 1776.)

General Washington had not notified Congress previously that he had given Colonel John Glover the orders to start converting merchant vessels into armed vessels at the shipyard at Beverly, Massachusetts.[216] When Congress finally came around to the understanding that something had to be done about the threat of the British armed fleet and its devastating effect on the colonial commerce, navigation and economy, they were surprised to discover that General Washington had already gone ahead with his plans for a "secret navy," and the ship conversions were already underway. General Washington felt that "without a constant naval superiority upon these coasts, the struggle will be over."[217] Congress gave its support for this new phase of naval defense on October 13, 1775. The Continental Congress resolved that "each colony, at their own expense, make such provision by armed vessels or otherwise…for the protection of their own harbours and navigation of their own coasts, against all unlawful invasions, attacks, and deprivations, from cutters and ships of war."[218]

Chapter 3

Expedition to Canada

GENERAL WASHINGTON'S PLANS FOR AN EXPEDITION TO CANADA

The design of this Express is to communicate to you a plan for an Expedition,
which has engrossed my Thoughts for several Days. It is to penetrate into Canada
by way of Kennebeck River, and so to Quebec…He [General Carleton] *must*
either break up [abandon Montreal] *or follow this party to Quebec, by which*
he will leave you a free passage or suffer that important Place [Quebec] *to fall*
into our Hands….Not a Moment's Time is to be lost in the Preparation for this
Enterprise, if the advices from you favor it.[219]
—*General Washington*

In August 1775, plans were being made by General Washington to aid and assist General Schuyler in the orders issued from the Continental Congress in July 1775 to invade Canada.[220] One of the objectives of the expedition into Canada was to attempt to bring the people of the Canadian territory into union with the American colonies and to be the fourteenth colony in the United States of America.[221] General Washington's scheme was to give assistance to General Schuyler, but he contemplated a diversionary move—a strike against the British in Canada through the Province of Maine. By diverting some of the British troops away from General Schuyler's thrust at

Montreal, the British forces would be divided as some of the troops would be needed to defend Quebec City, the capital. The occupation of Quebec City would give the Americans additional leverage in their anticipated negotiations with the British government to bring a quick end to fighting.

In a letter to General Schuyler on August 20, 1775, General Washington outlined his idea to assist in his assignment from the Continental Congress to invade Canada and remove the growing British threat in Montreal and Quebec. Washington's letter included his belief that a second assault on Canada in support of General Schuyler's American army troops would force General Sir Guy Carleton and his British Royal Army forces from Montreal to defend Quebec City. General Schuyler responded to Washington's letter, writing, "I thank your Excellency for the honour you have done me in communicating me your plan for an expedition into Canada. Your Excellency will easily conceive that I felt happy to learn your intensions, and only wished that the thought had struck you sooner."[222]

In late August, General Philip Schuyler, commanding officer in the Northern Department, led the American troops from Fort Ticonderoga on an expedition against the British forces in Canada. General Richard Montgomery took over General Schuyler's role of leading the American army forces in the fall invasion because of Schuyler's health issues. Philip's younger brother, Private George Ulmer, was among the New England troops who marched on the Canadian expedition to capture the British forts at St. John and at Chambly (also appeared as Chamblee) in Canada.[223] These volunteer troops had been part of Colonel Benedict Arnold's troops who had captured Fort Ticonderoga in May 1775 with Ethan Allen and his Green Mountain militiamen. The fort at Chambly was captured by Major John Brown's American troops and James Livingston's three hundred Canadian troops in October. The military supplies taken at Fort Chambly facilitated the successful siege on Fort St. John by General Montgomery's troops. The siege on Fort St. John took fifty-five days and was finally accomplished by Montgomery's American forces on November 2, with approximately seven hundred British soldiers taken prisoner. Led by General Montgomery, the American forces proceeded twelve miles northwest to Montreal and captured the fortress on November 11, 1775.

While these actions were taking place in the Northern Theater, by September 5, 1775, General Washington had chosen Captain Benedict Arnold to conduct and coordinate the expedition into Canada with General Schuyler's forces as a second front. Arnold was advanced in rank to colonel, which was the appropriate designation for his mission. He actively recruited volunteers for his "secret" mission to lead an expedition to capture the cities of Quebec and Montreal in Canada. Upon General Washington's orders, "Three days after the call for volunteers went out, the names of those accompanying Arnold were removed from the duty rolls, and told to report to Cambridge no later than Saturday morning, September 9."[224]

The Arnold expedition was referred to in the General Orders of the day for September 8, 1775. The General Orders read: "The Detachment going under Command of Col. Arnold to be forthwith taken off the Roll of duty, and to march this evening to Cambridge Common: …Such Officers & men are taken from Genl Green's brigade, for the above detachment, are to attend Muster of their respective regiments tomorrow morning at seven O'clock, upon Prospect hill, when the Muster is finished, they are forthwith to rejoin the Detachment at Cambridge." [225]

At Cambridge, Colonel Arnold selected his officers first, and he chose men who had distinguished themselves in the recently fought battle at Bunker Hill. A number of these veteran officers were chosen to participate and lead companies on the "secret" expedition to Canada. Samuel McCobb and Henry Dearborn, who had led soldiers from frontier Maine during the battle at Bunker Hill, were among the officers chosen. These men were known to Sergeant Philip Ulmer, who served with these same officers in the York, Cumberland and Lincoln County state militia companies in frontier Maine prior to and during the Revolution until the secession of the war.

The following is a list of officers on the Arnold expedition as they appeared in Captain Henry Dearborn's Journal:[226]

Officers of the First Battalion: Lieutenant Colonel Christopher Greene (cousin of General Nathaniel Greene, on General Washington's staff), Major Timothy Biggelloe (also spelled Bigelow), Captain Samuel Ward, Captain Simeon Thayre (also spelled Thayer), Captain John Topham, Captain Samuel McCobb, Captain Jonas Hubbard.

Officers of the Second Battalion: Lieutenant Colonel Roger Enos, Major Return J. Meigs, Captain Thomas Williams, Captain Henry Dearborn, Captain Scott, Captain Oliver Hanchett, Captain William Goodrich.

Hundreds of soldiers participating in the siege of Boston, including many in Colonel Bond's regiment, were chosen and became part of Colonel Arnold's brigade. A large portion of the chosen soldiers for the expedition were from the Kennebec area in frontier Maine. A report had been made to

General Washington on July 17, 1775, listing the names of men in the late Colonel Gardner's regiment who were proficient in handling whale boats and would be included as soldiers assigned to Colonel Arnold's brigade on the expedition to Canada to capture Quebec and Montreal.[227] Many of these young soldiers from frontier Maine were recruits whom Sergeant Philip Ulmer knew from the Kennebec area near Falmouth and from other local coastal communities in Cumberland and Lincoln Counties prior to the outbreak of the war. They were knowledgeable about the sea and about survival in the Maine wilderness.

PHILIP ULMER'S EARLY INVOLVEMENT IN THE REVOLUTIONARY WAR

In such a Cause every Post is honourable in which a Man can serve his Country.
—General George Washington[228]

Philip Ulmer was in a unique position to aid General Washington in acquiring vessels needed as transports for Colonel Arnold's volunteer brigade on the Canadian Expedition and still actively participate in the Canadian campaign himself. General Washington chose Nathaniel Tracy, a wealthy merchant in Newburyport, Massachusetts, to be contracted to supply the vessels on the initial start of Colonel Arnold's "secret" expedition to Canada. Philip and his uncles had built vessels at the Broad Bay Cove shipyard for a number of ship owners in Massachusetts and for Nathaniel Tracy's family of Newburyport (located about thirty-four miles from Washington's headquarters at Cambridge) prior to the start of the Revolution.[229] Sergeant Philip Ulmer knew Colonel John Glover and many of the mariners and militiamen from his younger years, when he lived in Salem and Marblehead with his father and mother, Jacob and Christiana Ulmer, and with his uncles, John Ulmer Jr. and Hans Martin Ulmer. They had been involved with the shipping and fishing trades and had also been involved with the militias at Marblehead and Salem in defense of the local Massachusetts towns and coastal villages.

Prior to the Revolutionary War, Philip Ulmer had been trained in the Prussian style of combat with the militiamen in the Broad Bay (Ranger) Guards under the command of his German (Prussian) relatives, Captain

Matthias Remilly and Lieutenant Martin Reiser, veterans of the French and Indian War.[230] Over the years, Philip had witnessed the military training of citizen-soldiers under his grandfather's direction (Captain John Ulmer Sr.) at the Broad Bay settlement. He had observed the training of the Salem/Marblehead militiamen when he lived in the area as a youth. Philip Ulmer would have been able to use his shipbuilding, his sailing and navigation knowledge, his merchant trading experience and his family contacts[231] to coordinate many of the needs for transport vessels and supplies for Arnold's brigade by assisting Colonel Glover to move Washington's plans forward for an armed naval fleet. Prior to the Revolution, Philip Ulmer had developed a friendship with Nathaniel Tracy and the Tracy brothers, John, Patrick and James (who became captain of the *Yankee Hero* built at the Ulmer shipyard in Broad Bay for the wealthy Newburyport family).[232] Philip's connections to other shipyard owners and merchant traders through his family's connections at Marblehead, Salem, Beverly, Newburyport and Waldoboro would have been useful to launch General Washington's plans for the fall Canadian campaign as well.[233] Militia major Reuben Colburn owned a sawmill and shipyard on the Kennebec River and was certainly known to the Ulmer family at Waldoboro through their service with the local militia and as shipbuilders and business associates in frontier Maine.

A letter dated September 7, 1775, and sent to Nathaniel Tracy by Joseph Reed, Washington's military secretary from his headquarters at Cambridge, alerted him that "seven small ships had already been located at several coastal towns near Newburyport fitted out for another Purpose, but will answer the Present equally well…It will be a saving in Time & Expence [*sic*] to make use of these, You will therefore be pleased in your Transaction of this Matter to consider these seven Vessells as Part of the Transports, & only extend your Care to the Remainder."[234]

Within a short time, sufficient vessels were acquired and taken to Newburyport in readiness for Colonel Arnold's Canadian Expedition. A number of the transport vessels included on the expedition were those which Philip Ulmer, his relatives and villagers had built at the shipyards at Broad Bay Cove. Seven sloops and schooners were involved in the transporting of the expeditionary troops up the Kennebec River to Fort Western, which protected the northernmost navigation on the river. Colonel Arnold did not accompany his volunteer brigade on the march from General Washington's headquarters in Cambridge to Newburyport but assigned the command of the route to Lieutenant Colonel Christopher Greene and Lieutenant Colonel Roger Enos.[235] By Saturday, September 16, Colonel Arnold's entire corps of riflemen and two army divisions headed by Enos and Greene (cousin of General Nathanael Greene, General Washington's closest friend and staff aide who came from Rhode Island) had arrived in Newburyport after their march from Cambridge. Colonel Arnold, accompanied by his volunteer aide, Eleazer Oswald, proceeded to the seaport of Salem, where he made personal purchases of provisions that he would use on the Canadian Expedition. While he was at Salem, he received 270 blankets for his troops from the Committee of Safety.[236] Having completed his shopping and received the needed supplies, Arnold hired a small rented coach to take them to Newburyport, where they joined the troops. Colonel Arnold, Eleazer Oswald and several of Arnold's senior officers were guests at the mansion of Nathaniel Tracy, located a short distance from the waterfront at Newburyport. Some officers were housed across the street from the Tracy mansion in the large home of Tristram Dalton, a patriotic and wealthy member of the thriving Newburyport business community.[237] Other officers were lodged at the Wolfe Tavern owned by William Davenport. Eleazer Oswald, who later became the printer and publisher of the *Independent Gazetteer*, was likely the first imbedded news reporter and publisher who wrote about his wartime experiences with General Washington's Continental Army during the American Revolution.

On Sunday, September 17, 1775, Colonel Arnold's corps of detached troops paraded in an open field early in the morning. Several diarists recorded the parade event, which was assembled in full martial array and was a stirring sight for the pro-rebellion citizens of Newburyport. Ebenezer Wild, who later appeared in Colonel Vose's regiment with officer Philip Ulmer, recorded in his journal, "This day [September] 17th had a general review, and our men appeared very well and in good spirits, and made a grand appearance…"[238] The American troops liked flags and standards with patriotic and martial images with slogans that expressed their sentiments. There were red flags with the word "LIBERTY" written across in bold letters and white flags with the outline of a pine tree above the words "An Appeal to Heaven."[239] Music was played during the parade. Colonel Arnold's fifers and drummers were likely grouped together during the muster at Newburyport for the best effect. The musicians had a practical role of relaying commands to the troops through specific fife tunes and drumroll calls.

Following the Sunday morning muster in the field, Colonel Arnold's corps of soldiers proceeded to the First Presbyterian Church to attend a special service as patriotic townspeople lined the way. According to several journals, many soldiers marched to the church with the expedition's colors flying and drums beating. The men formed two ceremonial lines inside the church and presented arms. As drums rolled, Chaplain Spring walked solemnly between the lines of soldiers to the pulpit. The arms were on display in the aisles, and the chaplain gave an impromptu patriotic sermon. Following the service, the church sexton led Chaplain Spring, Colonel Arnold and his senior officers down a flight of stairs to the crypt below the sanctuary, where the remains of the English evangelist George Whitefield (also written Whitfield) lay entombed. The sexton removed the lid from Reverend George Whitefield's coffin, and Colonel Arnold and his officers gazed upon the remains of the great cleric. Although his body was decayed, some of his clothing remained intact. The sexton solemnly reached inside the coffin and removed the clerical collar and wristbands from the corpse. He cut them into little pieces with a pair of scissors and gave a piece of the precious relic to each officer to take with them to Quebec. As the coffin closed, they prayed for the success of their Canadian Expedition.[240]

Colonel Benedict Arnold and his brigade of detached volunteer soldiers from General Greene's Division at Prospect Hill proceeded to the wharves, where Nathaniel Tracy had the eleven fishing boats, small transports and merchant vessels provisioned and waiting. Arnold's brigade of soldiers boarded their transport vessels at Newburyport on the first leg of their wilderness journey up the Kennebec River to Fort Western in the wilderness of frontier Maine.[241] Colonel Arnold's flagship on the Canadian Expedition was a schooner built at the Ulmers' Broad Bay Cove shipyards named the *Broad Bay*.[242] Other vessels that served as transports on the Canadian Expedition with the *Broad Bay* were the *Swallow*, *Betsy*, *Houghton*, *Eagle*, *Conway*, *Abigail* and others from Waldoboro, Beverly (the shipbuilding section of Salem) and Newburyport shipyards.[243] The *Broad Bay* sailed from Newburyport with Colonel Arnold, his chosen officers and his "gentleman volunteers," including Aaron Burr. They were followed by the rest of the small flotilla of eleven sloops and schooners carrying about 1,150 chosen militia volunteers who were woodsmen and experienced in handling canoes and whale boats. Although General Washington had already given Benedict Arnold informal orders, on September 14, 1775, he sent Benedict Arnold, now commissioned a colonel in the detached militia army, official notice that he was to lead his detachment from Washington's Continental Army through the Maine wilderness to invade Quebec, Canada. It read, "You are intrusted [sic] with a command of the utmost consequence to the interest and liberties of America."[244]

By September 19, all the transport ships were safely out to sea except for the schooner *Swallow*, which had run aground on a sandbar in the entrance to the harbor. The expedition lost valuable time as the soldiers aboard the *Swallow* were transferred to other ships.[245] The sailing crew remained aboard, and Arnold instructed them to proceed to the Kennebec River with their cargo as soon as possible. Being unarmed and unable to defend itself, if Arnold's little flotilla was discovered and attacked by British warships, the entire expedition would be a failure before it had scarcely begun.

Arnold's transport vessels sailed northward toward Penobscot Bay and then proceeded up the Kennebec River to Ruben Colburn's sawmill and shipyard at Gardiner, Maine, where the two hundred bateaux and twenty additional cargo boats for Arnold's expedition had been hurriedly constructed of green wood. Ruben Colburn was a businessman who was known to the Ulmer family, and he served as a militia officer in the Lincoln County area, which included Waldoboro and communities on the western side of the Penobscot Bay. Colonel Wheaton and Lieutenant Colonel Farnsworth were top commanders in this unit. Additional Kennebec militia troops (from Lincoln County) led by Captain Samuel McCobb[246] were taken aboard the topsail schooner *Broad Bay* along the way up the Kennebec River toward Fort Western, where the march to Quebec was to begin. Sergeant Philip Ulmer probably sailed aboard the schooner *Broad Bay*, the ship that he had helped to build at Broad Bay Cove prior to the war. He was likely among the volunteer soldiers in Captain McCobb's company from the Lincoln County area (which included men from Waldoboro and St. George) who were part of the First Battalion, commanded by Colonel Christopher Greene.

General Washington and Colonel Arnold had selected Fort Western (located near present-day Augusta) as the starting point for the Canadian Expedition. This was the farthest point upstream that a merchant transport could safely travel on the Kennebec River, about forty-five miles from the sea.[247] Fort Western was situated on a strategic rocky bluff overlooking the Kennebec River channel, which was especially low in the fall. Several of the transports grounded, and this problem caused a delay of several days. Dr. Isaac Senter, who was the surgeon on the expedition, estimated the cargo that Arnold had accumulated for the troops to be a total of one hundred tons when the supplies and cargo were finally offloaded at Fort Western. There was no time to set up advance supply bases. Speed was essential. All of the expedition's troops, food, equipment and additional supplies had to be moved with the men through the Maine wilderness at the same time.[248] The artillery and heavy equipment would be delivered to Canada by sailing transport as General Washington had ordered. The route seemed straightforward, according to the map that Colonel Arnold had been given by General Washington. (British captain John Montresor was the British chief army engineer in North America who had mapped the wilderness route through Maine during the French and Indian War.) It was believed by the advocates of the Canadian Expedition that a lightly equipped, fast-moving army, without artillery and heavy equipment to haul with them, could cover the distance from Fort Western to Point Levy (a small settlement and ferry port that was located across the St. Lawrence River from Quebec City) in twenty days.[249]

Several Penobscot Indians had appeared earlier in Cambridge to express their concerns and grievances about the tensions that were escalating along the frontier border in Maine with the British at Nova Scotia. Penobscot chief Orono Williamson, Poveris, Joseph Pease and one other tribal leader needed assurance from the Massachusetts Provincial Congress that the American government would continue to meet their needs so their tribes would be able to remain neutral in the conflict against Great Britain. Captain John Lane led the small company, and Lieutenant Andrew Gilman served as their interpreter at Cambridge. They received strong words and assurances by General Washington and by a letter from the Provincial Congress that stated: "…our Liberty and your Liberty are the same, we are brothers and what is for our good is for your good."[250] Support for General Washington and the Provincial Congress was given, and a pledge of Indian support was given.

Colonel Arnold's troops were joined by a number of Penobscot Indians on the Canadian Expedition. The Indians were identified as Chief Orono Williamson, Poveris, Joseph Pease, Soncier, Eneas, Sewanockett, Metagone and Sebatis (Sabattis), who was the brother of the Abenaki English-speaking Indian leader from northern Maine's Norridgewock tribe named Natanis (Nattanis), and other Indian braves.[251] (Some of these same Indians would later serve with Captain Philip Ulmer's company during the Penobscot Expedition in 1779.) In order to receive assistance and friendship from the Abenaki Indians on the expedition, Colonel Arnold met with the Indian leaders and spoke of the conflict that had broken out between Great Britain and the American colonies. After the speech was delivered with much pomp and circumstance by one of the chiefs (probably Chief Orono), he was surrounded by his followers, and Arnold returned the following diplomatic, simple and candidly truthful reply:

Friends and Brethren: I feel myself very happy in meeting with so many of my brethren from the different quarters of the great country, and more so as I find we meet as friends, and that we are equally concerned in this expedition. Brethren, we are the children of those people who have now taken up the hatchet against us. More than one hundred years ago we were all as one family. We then differed in our religion and came over to this country by consent of the King. Our fathers bought lands of the savages and have become a great people,—even as the stars in the sky. We have planted the ground and by our labor grown rich. Now a King and his wicked great men want to take our lands and money without our consent. This we think unjust and all our great men from the River St. Lawrence to the Mississippi, met together at Philadelphia, where they all talked together, and sent a prayer to the King, that they would be brothers and fight for him, but would not give up their lands and money. The King would not hear our prayer, but sent a great army to Boston, and endeavored to set our brethren against us in Canada. The King's army at Boston came out into the fields and houses, and killed a great many women and children, while they were peaceably at work. The Bostonians sent to their brethren in the country, and they came in unto their relief, and in six days raised an army of fifty thousand men and drove the King's troops on board their ships, and killed and wounded fifteen hundred of their men. Since that they durst not come out of Boston. Now we hear that the French and Indians in Canada have sent to us, that the King's troops oppress them and make them pay a great price for their rum, etc., and press them to take up arms against the Bostonians, their brethren, who have done them no hurt. By the desire of the French and Indians, our brethren, we have come to their assistance with an intent to drive out the King's soldiers; when drove off we will return to our own country, and leave this to the peaceable enjoyment of its proper inhabitants. Now if the Indians our brethren, will join us, we will be very much obliged to them, and will give them one Portuguese per month, two dollars bounty, and find them their provisions, and their liberty to choose their own officers.

Colonel Arnold's speech to the Indian chiefs and scouts had the desired effect, and about forty of the Indians took their canoes and joined the troops moving on the river. The Indians were quick to find a name for Colonel Arnold, and they called him the "Dark Eagle" (perhaps by the cast of his features and his keen and penetrating eyes). Chief Natanis, at the first interview, had, according to Indian tradition, addressed him in this way: "The Dark Eagle comes to claim the wilderness. The wilderness will yield to the Dark Eagle, but the Rock will defy him. The Dark Eagle will soar aloft to the sun. Nations will behold him and sound his praises. Yet when he soars highest, his fall is most certain. When his wings brush the sky, then the arrow will pierce his heart. Mark my words and go in peace, my friend."[252] With friendship secured, the expedition continued toward its goal northward through the wilderness of Maine Province toward the Canadian border and the settlement of Point Levi across the St. Lawrence River from Quebec City.

Colonel Arnold moved ahead with his plans and assigned the leadership of the four divisions in his brigade. The first division was led by Captain Daniel Morgan and consisted of several musket companies. The second division was led by Lieutenant Colonel Greene. The third division was led by Major Return Meigs's company and commanders that included Henry Dearborn, who kept an important journal of the expedition, and Samuel Ward Jr., whose father was a former governor of Rhode Island. The fourth division was led by Lieutenant Colonel Roger Enos and included three musket companies and Captain Reuben Colburn's company of twenty boat repairmen.[253] Colonel Arnold and his gentleman volunteer, Eleazer Oswald, were transported in a large canoe manned by Penobscot Indians (part of the Abenaki Confederation) from frontier Province of Maine.

Colonel Arnold needed mobility to quickly move between the advancing divisions who had been allowed by Arnold to spread out and advance at their own pace. Arnold kept the Indians near him to use as guides and couriers and for special assignments. The Indian couriers—Soncier, Eneas, Sebatis, Metagone and Sewanockett—maintained communications between the four divisions.[254] Once the troops entered Canadian territory, the divisions faced a greater possibility of being attacked. Arnold had designated the rendezvous point for the expedition as Lake Magentic, the large body of water that lay just over the border in Canada. On September 25, 1775, Colonel Arnold wrote to General Washington from Fort Western: "I design Chaudiere Pond [Lake Magentic] as a general Rendevouze, and from thence to march in a Body."[255]

On September 28, Colonel Arnold ordered Lieutenant Colonel Roger Enos "to send along any men still left behind (at Gardiner's Town) with the last of the bateaux and supplies…and to send the sick back to Newburyport aboard the schooner, *Broad Bay*."[256] The *Broad Bay* vessel was involved in transporting Colonel Arnold's troops and supplies and returning the sick men to Newburyport, where they would receive medical care at the army's

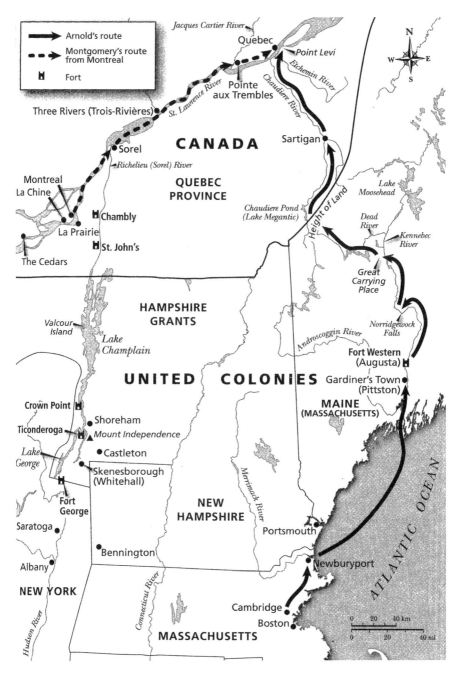

Map of the American assault on Quebec City, Canada, during the fall campaign of 1775.
Courtesy of James Nelson; Maine Maritime Museum, Bath, Maine.

hospital. The *Broad Bay*, a coastal trading transport, remained the expedition's water base while the other transports were dismissed.[257] The story of the role of the schooner *Broad Bay* is briefly told in Colonel Arnold's express from Fort Western to Nathaniel Tracy of Newburyport on September 28, 1775, which stated: "To Capt. Clarkson I am under many obligations for his activity, vigilance and care of the whole fleet, both in our passage, and since our arrival here…he has really merited much."[258] The schooner remained at Fort Western for a period of time and then proceeded with the rest of its assigned transport duties as indicated in Colonel Arnold's orders to Colonel Enos on September 29, 1775, from Fort Western, which read: "You will bring up the rear and order all stragglers, except those sick, which you will send on board the Broad bay—Capt. Clarkson."[259]

General Washington had given orders to Colonel Arnold prior to leaving on the expedition that

> *the expedition's prodigious supply of food, ammunition, tents, tools, medical supplies, and personal baggage would be transported to Quebec by boat, while the troops would use the Indian paths and frontier traces that paralleled the route's waterways…The seamen who had assisted in taking the expeditionary corps and those who had completed their mission of delivering supplies to Quebec…should be put to work converting other vessels into the armed privateering service of the military fleet upon their return…*[260]

This order from General Washington would have included Sergeant Philip Ulmer, who probably sailed aboard the schooner *Broad Bay*. Having completed their assignment to deliver the expedition's military supplies, food and dry goods to Canada, Sergeant Philip Ulmer and the other detached volunteers would have returned to their regiments to continue the siege on Boston. Philip would have rejoined Colonel Bond's regiment, where he served in Captain Fuller's company at Prospect Hill.*

---

* *Author's comment*: Information about the destination of the shipment for Arnold's detached forces is vague on this issue since the secrecy of the mission to Canada was of the utmost importance. Some historians think that Washington's supply shipment for Arnold's expeditionary forces was sent to American supporters at the outpost at Point Levi on the southern shore of the St. Lawrence River across from Quebec City. This was unlikely since Arnold did not have field pieces or the necessary military supplies when they later arrived at the village settlement. The military supplies, food and dry goods sent by General Washington for the

American expeditionary forces in the early fall of 1775 were most likely shipped on Arnold's cargo sailing ship, *Polly*, to Arnold's American business friend and pro-rebel supporter in Quebec City, John Mercier. The cargo ship was known to have made a delivery of molasses and rum in Quebec City about that time. The plan was that John Mercier and his companions would open the gates at Quebec City for Arnold's troops when they made their attack on the city. The city would be seized and held by Arnold's American troops until General Schuyler's army was able to seize the British forts at St. John (St. Jean) and Montreal and could rendezvous with Arnold's army at Quebec City. Colonel Arnold's and John Mercier's plan was disclosed by a British spy and double agent, John Hall, who was embedded with Colonel Arnold's troops. John Mercier was seized and placed under arrest as a rebel supporter and spy by the acting commander of Quebec, British lieutenant governor Hector Cramahé, on October 28, 1775.[261] Arnold and the Connecticut, New Hampshire and Massachusetts soldiers who had completed the trek through the wilderness of Maine lay siege to Quebec City unsuccessfully. Since John Mercier's help was no longer available due to his capture, Arnold's troops soon had to abandon their encampment outside the city gates. They made their way to Pointe-aux-Trembles to await General Montgomery's forces and military supplies.

Another possible scenario was that military supplies for Arnold's Canadian Expedition had been shipped to the village outpost at Sorel, where American troops with Colonel James Easton and Major John Brown received them. More troops eventually joined Montgomery and Arnold in Canada. There were about 160 Massachusetts troops under the command of Major John Brown camped at Sorel on the St. Lawrence River. Some of the soldiers were the same Massachusetts troops raised and commanded by Arnold early in the war to defend the Lake Champlain region in May 1775.[262] These troops had bypassed Fort St. John and taken control of the outposts at Chambly and Sorel during the siege of Fort St. John with General Montgomery's forces. Colonel Easton and Major Brown's troops, who were under the command of Generals Schuyler and Montgomery, had set up a blockade on the St. Lawrence River with a floating gun battery to block the channel and capture enemy vessels. Major Brown's blockade managed to capture Governor General Guy Carleton's heavily loaded British flotilla that was attempting to escape from Montreal in mid-November 1775, just days before General Montgomery and his American forces triumphantly entered the city on November 13. Under cover of darkness, General Carleton, who was in disguise, and Captain Bouchat of the armed sloop *Isabella*, with several attending crewmen, made their escape over the side of Carleton's flagship *Gaspee* into a small workboat. Staying close to shore, they made their way down the St. Lawrence River to the British brig *Fell*, which was anchored for the night downstream. They boarded the brig and successfully made

Colonel Arnold's trek through the wilderness of Maine was much more difficult than anyone had imagined and lasted longer than the anticipated twenty days. On October 25, 1775, Lieutenant Colonel Enos and his three company commanders—Captain Thomas Williams, Captain Samuel McCobb and Captain Scott—during a council meeting with Colonel Christopher Greene and his company commanders, voted not to continue on the mission with Colonel Arnold's expedition to Quebec. They felt it was a doomed mission. Colonel Enos and his three companies of 150 soldier volunteers, plus 150 sick and feeble men and 48 sick men from Colonel Greene's division, abandoned the expedition at the Dead River, turned back to Fort Western and then proceeded to the Kennebec seaport settlement. If Sergeant Philip Ulmer had been among the volunteers chosen for the Canadian Expedition, he would likely have been with Captain McCobb's company of militiamen from Lincoln County in frontier Maine with Colonel Enos's division. The boat repair crew commanded by Reuben Colburn of Kennebec also turned back with Colonel Enos's division and helped transport the men back to Fort Western in three bateaux. When they finally found their way back to Fort Western, the schooner *Broad Bay*, having completed its mission, was gone, along with the other fishing boats and coastal vessels that had transported the expedition from Newburyport to Fort Western weeks before. The returning officers and soldiers made their way downstream to Colburn's shipyard in the Kennebec settlement. The invalids and most feeble soldiers were ferried in the three returning bateaux to the nearest settlement. These sick and feeble soldiers went to the hospital at Newburyport, where their needs could be addressed. The returning soldiers in Captain Colonel Enos's division returned to Newburyport, where they continued their march back to Cambridge, arriving on November 23, 1775.[263] The General Orders for the army for November 25, 1775, from General Washington included the following: "The

---

their escape to Quebec City. Ironically, after Arnold and his troops arrived at the village of Pointe-aux-Trembles and had set up camp, they observed the British brig *Fell* on the St. Lawrence River sailing downstream in the opposite direction.[264] Unknown to Arnold and his troops, Governor General Guy Carleton was on board and sailing to Quebec City, having abandoned Montreal to General Montgomery's advancing American invasion forces. If Arnold's troops had seized the British brig and captured Governor Carleton in November 1775, the course of history in North America would have been changed.

Commissioned, Non Commission'd Officers & Soldiers, lately arrived in Camp from Kenebeck river, are to join their respective Corps."[265] The returning companies on the expedition were disbanded, and the men returned to their prior regiments.

If Sergeant Ulmer returned to Cambridge with Captain McCobb's company from Colonel Enos's division, he would have rejoined Colonel Bond's regiment with Captain Fuller's company in the construction and refitting of merchant ships and transports into armed warships and privateering vessels for Washington's naval fleet at Plymouth.[266] Colonels Benjamin Lincoln and John Thomas, who became generals during the Revolution, both came from Plymouth County. During the time when Sergeant Philip Ulmer was stationed with his company near Plymouth, he became familiar with these officers and their troops, who were also engaged in refitting and arming vessels at Plymouth for privateering activities against the British supply ships. Philip's uncle John Ulmer and his wife, (Mary) Catherine, who were living in the vicinity of the military encampment at Pembroke, Massachusetts (near Plymouth), during this period, delivered their ninth child, whom they named Philip Ulmer after his cousin, Sergeant Philip Martin Ulmer. (These two individuals were often confused in later historical records since both of them became majors in the state militia in Camden Township in Lincoln County [Maine], shared the same first and last name and were closely related. Only the middle name was different.) During the siege of Boston, detached companies of soldiers were deployed on particular assignments, but the main part of Colonel Bond's regiment remained encamped with Washington's army near Cambridge and Prospect Hill during the winter of 1775–76.[267]

By mid-December 1775 and the early part of 1776, the Massachusetts Provincial Congress had again authorized the raising of militia regiments in all counties of the seacoast communities. They were to be sent to the military headquarters in Cambridge. A fourth militia regiment was raised with men from Waldoboro, Falmouth, Machias and other Kennebec settlements from the frontier Province of Maine.[268] Many of the troops from Waldoboro and the Kennebec area included friends and cousins of Philip and George Ulmer. There are few records of these men before 1777. This is because the Continental Congress ordered that the names of soldiers who had served under Colonel Arnold's command prior to his defection be removed from the military records to protect them from any association that would connect them with Benedict Arnold.[269] What is known of Philip Ulmer was that he served in the Continental Army and Massachusetts state militia throughout the Revolutionary War (1775–83).[270] The federal government's archives do not have Philip Ulmer's military service recorded until January 1, 1777.

After the return of Colonel Enos's division from Arnold's expedition, General Washington quickly moved to have Enos court-martialed since his commission as an officer expired at the end of 1775. Washington ordered a Court of Inquiry to investigate the circumstances of the defection. The court met on November 29 with Major General Charles Lee as the president, completing its inquiry investigation in just one day. A court-martial was held a few days later with thirteen officers appointed to try Colonel Enos on charges of abandoning the expedition without permission from Colonel Arnold. The court-martial board heard testimony from Colonel Enos and his officers (including Captain McCobb), who found themselves in the same position as their commander. Without testimony from some of the men whom Enos abandoned at the Dead River, the court had insufficient evidence to convict Enos and his officers, and the court acquitted them of wrongdoing. General Sullivan expressed his opinion that the colonel was justified in returning with his troops because he had sent forward so many provisions to support the other divisions. General Washington mentioned Enos's court-martial verdict in a letter written to Colonel Arnold on December 5, 1775. General Washington wrote, "You could not be more Surprised than I was, at Enos return with the Division under his Command. I immediately put him under Arrest & had him tried for Qui [quitting] the Detachmt [sic] without your Orders—He is acquitted on the Scor [score] of provisions [having no food to continue into Canada]."[271]

Washington understood that Enos's defection reduced the chances of Colonel Arnold's success in the Canadian Expedition. Writing to General Schuyler on November 30, he wrote that the impact of Enos's action had severely jeopardized the success of the mission in Canada. He wrote, "Colonel Enos who had Command of Arnold's Rear Division is returned with the greater part of his Men, which must weaken him so much as to render him incapable of making a successful attack on Quebec without the assistance from General Montgomery."[272]

Upon hearing of Arnold's successful arrival opposite Quebec City, General Washington, whose commendation was always a badge of honor and whose experience as a frontiersman and as a soldier did not underestimate Arnold's achievement, wrote to General Schuyler: "The merit of this gentleman is certainly great, and I heartily wish that fortune may distinguish him as one of her favorites. I am convinced that he will do everything that his prudence and valor shall suggest to add to the success of our arms, and for reducing Quebec to our possession."[273] To Arnold himself, General Washington wrote: "It is not in the power of any man to command success, but you have done more—you have deserved it."[274] Colonel Arnold's trek through the harsh wilderness of Maine to the outskirts of Quebec City with his troops was heralded in newspaper articles as humanly remarkable and heroic. Samuel Adams, who served in the Massachusetts Provincial Congress during this time, referred to Colonel Arnold as "America's Hannibal" in a letter dated December 5, 1775, and compared the wilderness trek through Maine to "Hannibal's crossing over the Alps."[275]

THE SIEGE OF BOSTON CONTINUES

As the siege of Boston continued, the British authorities became more frustrated and brutal in their dealings with the New England seaport communities that were defying the imposed British taxes, harassing the tax officials and showing demonstrations of sympathy for the defiant American activists in Boston. On October 13, 1775, George Washington wrote to his brother, John: "I have fitted out several privateers, with soldiers, who have been bred to the sea, and have no doubt of making captures of several British transports, some of which have already fallen into our hands, laden with provisions…"[276] This was a reference to the privateering activities in frontier Massachusetts, which were starting to become effective against the supply lines of the occupying British forces in Boston. Vice Admiral Graves decided to terrify and punish some of the Massachusetts seaport towns by using superior British power and might to crush the rebel resistance and force the settlers into submission. The entire month of September had been used by carpenters, under orders from Admiral Graves, to convert and prepare the British army transport sloops HMS *Symmetry* and HMS *Spitfire* into ships-of-war. They were to be fitted out to receive mortars and howitzers for naval bombardment. Preparations were slowed by Admiral Grave's insistence that the ordnance ships would be loaded under cover of darkness to preserve the secrecy of the mission.[277] Four British warships—the *Canceaux*, with Captain

Henry Mowat aboard; the *Halifax*; the *Spitfire*; and the *Symmetry*—were ordered by Vice Admiral Graves to "destroy all shipping in the harbors of Marblehead, Salem, Newburyport, Gloucester, Portsmouth, and all ports in Maine, and make a most vigorous effort to burn the Towns. First burn Gloucester…"[278] On October 6, 1775, Admiral Graves's orders read: "burn destroy and lay waste the said Town together with all Vessells and Craft in the Harbour."[279]

This impressive fleet of British warships arrived at Gloucester Harbor just as the *Hannah* and its new crew were sailing out of the harbor, having completed the conversion of Colonel John Glover's schooner to an armed vessel in the shipyard at Beverly, Massachusetts. The British warships, under the command of Commander Mowat, did not engage the armed *Hannah* but sailed on to Falmouth (present-day Portland, Maine), a neighboring town of Waldoboro where Philip Ulmer's family lived. On October 18, Commander Mowat ordered that the four British warships should open fire upon the unarmed town and burn it to the ground with red-hot cannonballs. Captain Mowat told the townspeople before he started firing: "You are guilty of the most unpardonable Rebelion [*sic*] and [he was there] to execute a just punishment"[280] for the town's rebellion. Eyewitness Daniel Tucker, a Falmouth resident, reported: "Mowat hoisted a red flag and fired the first gun."[281] Reverend Jacob Bailey wrote: "The flag was hoisted to the top of the mast, and the cannon began to roar with an incessant and tremendous fury."[282] Another eyewitness reported: "The firing began from all the vessels with all possible briskness, discharging on all parts of the town…a horrible shower of balls from 3 to 9 pounds weight, bombs, carcasses, live shells, grapeshot, and musketballs [*sic*]…The firing lasted, with little cessation, until six o'clock."[283]

According to the master's log of the *Canceaux*: "… at 10 the fire broke out with great violens [*sic*] in houses of the Somost [southernmost]…at Noon the fire begun to be general both in the town and vessels but being calm the fire did Not Sprede [*sic*] as wished for…"[284] The barrage of cannons and mortars continued through the afternoon. Mowat decided it was "…absolutely necessary for some men to land, in order to set fire to the vessels, wharfs, storehouses, as well as many parts of town that escaped the shells and carcasses."[285] With the sun close to setting, "…the body of the town was in one flame."[286] After nearly nine hours of constant gunfire from the four warships, Captain Mowat's ammunition was almost expended. The *Spitfire* was "much scattered" from the constant concussion of the guns.[287] The converted transport vessel was not designed to take heavy pounding. Falmouth had received the devastating treatment that Admiral Graves had hoped to inflict upon the unarmed townspeople. Nearly every structure that faced the water was left as a smoldering ruin. There had been thirteen ships in the harbor at the time of the British attack upon Falmouth. Two vessels were captured, and the rest were sunk, some with valuable cargoes aboard. Many people of Falmouth were looking at a long, hard winter ahead with no home, no resources and no town. Americans were outraged and shocked by the extreme force and brutality that was inflicted by British men who had been looked upon until recently as countrymen.

In Falmouth's neighboring settlements, the thunderous, incessant percussion of the broadside cannons from the four British warships sent great alarm and fear through the seaport communities. The militia soldiers from nearby Waldoboro, which included Philip and George Ulmer's uncles, cousins and neighbors, became involved in the defense and rescue of the many frightened Falmouth townspeople after the town was set on fire.[288] The people in nearby Waldoboro would have heard the thundering roar of the cannons and would have seen the smoke from the British attack billowing into the sky. They would have seen the British warships finally departing and sailing out to sea having completed their devastating mission. From the waterfront, the alarmed state militiamen and settlers continued to shoot at the departing British warships, with no effect. General George Washington stated that the attack upon Falmouth was "an outrage, exceeding in barbarity and cruelty every hostile act among nations."[289] The attack on Falmouth stimulated the Continental Congress to take action. The incident was mentioned on November 25, when the Continental Congress passed legislation to advance its plans to establish a Continental Navy to protect American citizens from British attacks and deprivations. The legislation, passed in response to the unprovoked British attack upon Falmouth, was described by John Adams as "the true origin of the American Navy."[290] The Continental Congress authorized the commissioning of two naval ships-of-war for the protection and defense of the United Colonies of North America on October 30, 1775.[291]

Reaction to the Burning of Falmouth

*The British navy attacked Falmouth with every Circumstance of Cruelty
and Barbarity, which Revenge and Malice could suggest. We expect every
Moment to hear other Places have been attempted and have been better
prepared for their Reception.*[292]
—*General George Washington to General Philip Schuyler*

Americans were shocked and outraged with the news of the British naval
attack upon the defenseless village citizens and the burning of Falmouth.
Rather than bringing the radical elements of the American colonies into
submission, the unprovoked attack fed the fires of revolution that were
sweeping across colonial America in 1775. Events such as this one inspired
Thomas Paine to write his pamphlets, *Common Sense* and *American Crisis*.
These pamphlets stirred the hearts and minds of the colonists as well as
those in Europe who also read the pamphlets. The pamphlets focused on
the true cause for which people would be willing to struggle and sometimes
die: preserving their freedom, liberty and sovereignty as a nation.

A month after Falmouth was burned and left in ashes, the editor of the
New England Chronicle boldly declared: "The Savage and brutal Barbarity
of our enemies…is a full demonstration that there is not the least
remains of virtue, wisdom, or humanity in the British court…Therefore
we expect soon to break off all kinds of connections with Britain, and
to form into a Grand Republic of the American Colonies."[293] Coastal
port communities and towns that could be accessed from the sea began
frantically to construct defenses against British raiding parties and
attacks by enemy warships and armed vessels. This was true for coastal
towns such as Waldoboro, St. George and other communities in the
northeastern frontier of Maine District.

One of the delegates for Rhode Island presented before the Continental
Congress a part of the instructions given to them by the House of Magistrates
on August 26, 1775, which read:

*Whereas, notwithstanding the humble and dutiful Petition of the last
Congress to the King and otherwise, and pacifick [sic] measures taken for
obtaining a happy reconciliation between Great Britain and the Colonies,
the Ministry, lost to every sentiment of justice, liberty, and humanity,
continue to send troops and ships of war into America which destroy our*

trade, plunder and burn our towns and murder the good people of these Colonies: Resolved, That this Colony most ardently…requires us to obey that great and fundamental law of nature, self-preservation, until peace shall be restored upon constitutional principles…this Assembly is persuaded that building and equipping an American fleet, as soon as possible, would greatly and essentially conduce to the preservation at lives, liberty, and property of these Colonies, and therefore instruct their Delegates to use their whole influence at the ensuing Congress for building, at the Continental expense, a fleet of sufficient force for the protection of these Colonies…and they are also instructed to use all their influence for carrying on the war in the most vigorous manner, until peace, liberty, and safety, are restored and secured to these colonies, upon an equitable and permanent basis.[294]

The destruction of Falmouth did not seem to cause much interest or excitement in England, and reports of the incident were dismissed as "rebel propaganda." Secretary of state for the North American colonies, Lord George Germain, received a report with the simple facts surrounding the burning of Falmouth from General Howe, and he was apparently satisfied with the explanation.

The French foreign secretary of state, Charles Gravier, the Comte de Vergennes, closely watched the events unfolding in America and realized the British blunder for what it was: "I can hardly believe this absurd as well as barbaric procedure on the part of an enlightened and civilized nation…more especially as the perpetrators of this terrible crime allegedly declared that the order had been given to burn all maritime towns from Boston to Halifax."[295]

General Washington felt anxiety and the need for armed vessels to be put to sea as soon as possible against the British supply and transport ships arriving regularly at Boston. Washington wrote a series of pleas to John Hancock, president of the Senate: "Should not a Court be established by Authority of Congress, to take Cognizance of the Prizes made by Continental Vessels?[296]…I should be very glad if Congress would, without delay, appoint some mode by which an examination into the captures made by our armed vessels may be had as we are rather groping in the dark till this happens."[297] Glover had trouble finding enough carpenters to build and refit merchant vessels to carry cannons for Washington's naval fleet. As anxiety mounted, delays caused frustration at the headquarters in Cambridge. Joseph Reed, Washington's secretary aide, wrote: "We are very anxious to hear of the armed Vessels being ready for Sea. Every Day, nay every Hour is precious. It is now fourteen days since they [Glover's four refitted schooners] were set on Foot, Sure they cannot be much longer in preparation."[298]

By the end of October 1775, the British command was growing more irritated and frustrated by the increasing attacks and successes made upon the British shipping and supplies by the American privateers and seamen operating along the coast of frontier Massachusetts. The converted American merchant warships and transports had captured the British naval supply ships *Nancy, Dolphin, Industry* and *Prince George* containing valuable cargos. The privateering ship *Yankee Hero* was captured with its commander, Captain James Tracy (Philip Ulmer's friend), and 170 crewmen by the frigate HMS *Lively*.[299] This was the same British warship that had captured Sergeant Philip Ulmer's brother, George, several months before in an attempt to impress him into the British naval service as a seaman. General Thomas Gage, like General Washington, had come to understand that the real struggle between the British Royal Army and the American Continental Army was a war for matériel and supplies.

In November 1775, Colonel Bond's regiment was designated the Twenty-fifth Massachusetts Regiment and consisted of men from Captain Phineas Cooke's company and Captain Fuller's company within Colonel Bond's regiment. Captain Cooke's company had been involved at the Lexington Alarm, and he suffered an injury at the Battle of Bunker Hill from which he never fully recovered, causing his early death. Captain Fuller took over the leadership of the companies in which Sergeant Philip Ulmer served in Colonel Bond's regiment.[300] This company became involved in defensive activities for Washington's secret navy against the British supply and troop transports and the British warships.[301] Captain Fuller's company was sent to Plymouth in the fall of 1775 to outfit sailing vessels with arms to defend against the British forces. They were involved in the building and arming of the two American warships that Rhode Island sent to sea in January 1776. The encampment was located near Pembroke, between Plymouth/Duxbury Harbor and Scituate, Massachusetts.

In the fall of 1775, the General Assembly of Rhode Island ordered the reconstruction of two galleys into warships, the *Washington* and *Spitfire*.[302] Captain Fuller's company became involved in the building and outfitting of General Washington's Continental Navy vessels.[303] The refitting and ship conversions were done primarily at Beverly and Plymouth,

Massachusetts. Sergeant Philip Ulmer had knowledge and experience in shipbuilding and sailing most of his life prior to the war. He served in a leadership position with the young sailors and soldiers in Captain Fuller's company. Captain Fuller's company was sent from Prospect Hill to Plymouth in November 1775 to convert and refit two galleys at the shipyards there. Philip Ulmer became involved in refitting and converting the *Washington* and *Spitfire* vessels at Plymouth with his company. Philip Ulmer and other young and experienced sailors and fishing mariners in Captain Fuller's company, many men from the coastal towns of Broad Bay and St. George in frontier Maine, also became privateers aboard the armed naval vessels.[304]*

Dr. John Manvide was a French volunteer surgeon at Philip Ulmer's encampment with Captain Fuller's company at Prospect Hill. Manvide and other volunteers sailed with Captain Martindale aboard the *Washington*, where he wrote in his journal, "On the 8 November we left Prospect Hill at 4 o'clock in the afternoon with 80 men, arms and baggage to go to Plymouth, where the Brig [*Washington*] was."[305]

The soldiers from Captain Fuller's company at Prospect Hill arrived at Plymouth three days later[306] and discovered that the *Washington* (formerly named the *Endeavour* and was supposed to be renamed the *Eagle*)[307] and the *Spitfire* were still in the process of being refitted and far from ready to go to sea. Bad weather had caused delays for many days, and Plymouth carpenters, artificers and riggers refused to work on Sundays, like those at the shipyards in Beverly. There were long delays in receiving needed supplies. Toward the end of November, the guns, water and provisions were at last being assembled and stowed in the refitted schooner warships. The *Harrison* (formerly the schooner *Triton*)[308] had already set sail, and the soldiers and seamen left behind were impatient to get to sea and encounter British prize transports and supply vessels. The British occupation of Boston had served to the economic advantage of Providence, Rhode Island, which became New England's main entry point for European goods imported by way of the West Indies. European commodities, mercantile and domestic goods and foodstuffs from other colonies, as well as arms from the West

---

* *Author's comment*: This would likely explain why Philip Ulmer, who later served as captain of the gundelo *Spitfire* in the fall of 1776 on Lake Champlain, chose to name his gunboat the same odd name *Spitfire*. The vessel was probably the first armed naval vessel that Philip worked on and sailed on with other men from Captain Fuller's company.

Indies that included cannons, gunpowder and other military supplies (mostly from France) for the American military depot (armory) in Springfield, Massachusetts, mainly came through Rhode Island.[309] The British invasion of Newport, Rhode Island, in December 1777 sealed off Narragansett Bay and abruptly severed Providence, Rhode Island's route to the Atlantic Ocean and its access to markets in the southern colonies, in Europe and in the West Indies. Ships carrying military supplies and arms for the American army forces had to deliver their goods to Portsmouth, New Hampshire, for the northern troops.

In the meantime, back in Canada, Colonel Arnold and his small army of American volunteers had managed to make their way through the wilderness of Maine Province by way of the Kennebec and Chaudière Rivers to Point Levi, a settlement across from Quebec City on the southern shore of the St. Lawrence River. In a letter dated November 8, 1775, Colonel Arnold described his volunteer army's terrible trek to Canada: "I cannot give you particular detail, but can only say we have hauled our batteaux over falls, up rapid streams, over carrying places; and marched through morasses, thick woods, and over mountains, about 320 miles [actually 270 miles]—many of which we had to pass several times to bring our baggage."[310]

Arnold described to General Montgomery in the same letter that Colonel Enos returned to Cambridge from the Dead River, "contrary to my expectation, he having orders to send back only the sick, and those that could not be furnished with provisions…" Arnold further wrote that his letter to General Schuyler on October 13 had fallen into the hands of the enemy and his movements and mission had been betrayed. He stated that all the canoes around Point Levi (Pointe de Lévy) had been destroyed, and there were two small, armed vessels "lying before Quebec, and a large ship or two lately arrived from Boston." In closing, Arnold told Montgomery, "I propose crossing the St. Lawrence as soon as possible…otherwise shall endeavor to join your army at Montreal."[311] Although Arnold and his six hundred volunteers attempted a siege upon Quebec in mid-November 1775, Arnold's letters demanding the surrender of the city were rejected by Lieutenant Governor Hector Cramahé, who was in command of the city while Governor General Carleton was at Montreal.

Many of the American soldiers whose enlistments had expired in mid-December began to leave the army and return to their hometowns. Some soldiers were given strong inducements to stay until April, when more reinforcements were expected. Private George Ulmer was among General Montgomery's troops who captured the forts at St. John (St.

Jean) and Montreal. He was among those soldiers whose enlistment would expire by the end of the month.[312] He and other soldiers whose enlistments were completed returned to their homes for the winter. On December 31, 1775, before more soldiers' enlistments expired and the army lost more strength, the combined forces of General Montgomery and Colonel Arnold made an unsuccessful assault upon the British-held city of Quebec in the middle of a heavy snowstorm. Though the attack was made courageously by the American forces, it failed. General Montgomery and several officers were killed at point-blank range by grapeshot from an unexpected location, and Colonel Arnold received a severe leg wound. With the death of General Montgomery and several of his key officers, the American troops were confused and blinded by the snowstorm and were forced to retreat. Arnold and Montgomery's successor, General David Wooster, regrouped Montgomery's scattered troops, and they retreated to a safer location away from the city. Hundreds of New England soldiers were killed or taken as prisoners by General Carleton's British soldiers. Many of these men came from the Kennebec area in frontier Maine district. The enlisted soldiers were put into the dungeons below the fortress at Quebec City, while the officers were separated and put into the convent under heavy guard.

General Wooster and his troops returned to the safety of Montreal, where they remained until early April 1776 recuperating from the unsuccessful attempt to capture Quebec City. The American siege outside Quebec City continued during the winter months under the command of Colonel Arnold, who was still recovering from his injuries at the American hospital under the care of Dr. Isaac Senter. It was a brutal and snowy winter for Arnold's soldiers outside the city of Quebec on the Plain of Abraham. The American troops had to deal with great suffering from the extreme cold, various kinds of illness including smallpox and pneumonia, starvation and with few supplies. The Congress provided little or no aid or support for the troops in Canada on the expedition. Arnold's agent in the city of Quebec, who was positioned to give aid to Arnold's troops when they arrived, was arrested by the British authorities prior to their arrival, and the American supplies were confiscated. It was a desperate situation for Arnold's troops. In early April, American reinforcements began to trickle into Arnold's encampment outside of Quebec City. As the month of April proceeded, American troop strength increased enough to support another attack upon Quebec City. The second attempt to capture Quebec City had to be made by the middle of April before enlistments again ran out and Arnold's volunteer army would disperse and return home. British reinforcements were expected to arrive in early May when the ice melted and passage could be made on the St. Lawrence River.

Back in Rhode Island, the General Assembly of Rhode Island in January 1776 appointed John Grimes as commodore of the two armed warships that were placed into service in Narragansett Bay. They were the *Washington* (carrying ten carriage guns), with Captain Martindale in command, and the *Spitfire*, commanded by Esek Hopkins.[313] It was Commodore Esek Hopkins, commander in chief of the Continental Navy, who issued instructions for the U.S. Continental Navy vessels to fly the U.S. Navy Jack, which consisted of thirteen horizontal alternating red and white stripes (representing the thirteen colonies) with a rattlesnake superimposed upon it. The motto "Don't Tread on Me" was printed below, symbolizing resistance to British repression of colonial America. They patrolled in defense of American shipping, acted as military transports and assisted landing parties seeking forage and supplies. Soon thereafter, these two armed vessels recaptured the brig *Georgia Packet* and the sloop *Speedwell*, which the British warship HMS *Scarborough* had captured previously. They brought the two vessels into the Narragansett Bay, braving the fire of *Scarborough*'s guns as they took the prizes from under its stern.[314*]

Sergeant Philip Ulmer was probably involved with Captain Fuller's company from Prospect Hill on special assignment in defense of American shipping and in the building and conversion of transports into armed vessels.[315] In mid-December, more young recruits from Waldoboro enlisted in Captain Fuller's company with Sergeant Philip Ulmer, and they served aboard a privateering vessel sailing against the British.[316] Sergeant Philip Ulmer remained with Captain Fuller's detached company

---

* *Author's comment*: In July 1776, the row galleys *Washington* and *Spitfire* were ordered to New York City to help protect the Hudson River. The armed vessels cooperated with a small flotilla created by General Washington to defend and transport the troops on the river. On the afternoon of August 3, 1776, the *Spitfire* joined *Washington* and *Lady Washington* in a daring attack upon the British warships *Phoenix* and *Rose* in the New York City area, during which time the little flotilla engaged the warships for over two hours. The two galleys returned to Providence, Rhode Island, at the end of August. The *Spitfire* continued to be engaged in the defense of Narragansett Bay and was sent to New London, Connecticut, in early October 1776 to strengthen the naval defenses there. Little is known about the vessel until the summer of 1778, when the *Spitfire* galley was destroyed by the enemy in a conflict on the Hudson River.[317]

with Colonel Bond's regiment in winter quarters during the siege of Boston in 1775–76. Colonel Bond's regiment protected the fortress on Prospect Hill, and they were also involved in the defense of the Winter Hill redoubt. Philip Ulmer's cousin Philip Razor (also appears as Reiser) identifies Sergeant Philip Ulmer as being assigned to Colonel Bond's Twenty-fifth Continental Regiment at Prospect Hill in a letter to his family in Waldoboro (Broad Bay) on February 28, 1776.[318] Philip Razor's letter to his father, Major Razor in Waldoboro, gives some insight into army life around Boston in February 1776.

Camp Prospect Hill. February 28, 1776

Honoured father and mother. I take this opportunity to write to inform you that I am now in Good health hoping these few lines may find you the Same. I hope you will not think hard of my not writing to you before for I have been with Lieutenant Smith to take care of him for he has been almost at Deaths Door but he is now well and I have been sick but am now hearty and like the Army Very well and like my officers well, all that I dislike is that everything is exceedingly Dear and cloathes [sic] in a particular manner. I expect to Go to battle every minute and if my life is Spared me I hope to be with you to pay you A visit next Spring with Sergt. [sic] Ulmer. Give my love to my Brothers all Enquiring friends. I should be glad if you would write to me every opportunity and if you send letters you must Direct them to Prospect Hill in Col. Bond's Regiment and in Capt. Fuller's Company which is the Company I Belong to. Sergt. Ulmer Remembers his love to you all and all his Uncles and aunts family. No more at present. But I remain Your Dutiful Son,

—*Philip Razor*
—*Address: Mr Martin Razor in Waldoborough,*
—*By favour of Mr. Acorn.*[319]*

---

* *Author's comment*: Young Philip Razor (Reiser) died of illness or infection sometime later in 1776.[320] He lost his life while serving with Colonel Bond's Twenty-fifth Massachusetts Regiment, possibly at Fort Ticonderoga in the fall of 1776.

DORCHESTER HEIGHTS

British general William Howe had long been aware of the importance of the Dorchester Heights, which, along with the heights of Charlestown, had commanding views of Boston and its outer harbor. The British planned to seize both of these heights, beginning with those in Dorchester, which had a better view of the harbor than the Charlestown hills. It was the leaking of this plan that precipitated events leading to the Battle of Bunker Hill (which was actually fought on Breed's Hill).[321]

The idea of bringing the cannons from Ticonderoga to provide heavy guns for the siege at Boston was raised by Colonel Henry Knox soon after George Washington took command of the army in July 1775. The original idea of using the cannons from Fort Ticonderoga as artillery pieces for the use of the Continental Army had first been raised by Benedict Arnold, who had been dispatched in May 1775 to secure the fort and outposts on Lake Champlain, which he accomplished in partnership with Ethan Allen and his Green Mountain Boys. Colonel Knox had eventually been given the assignment by General Washington of transporting heavy military weapons from Fort Ticonderoga to Cambridge, Massachusetts, in November 1775. Over the course of three winter months, the detached company of American troops with Colonel Knox moved sixty tons of cannons and other military armaments by using boats and rafts and by horse and ox-drawn sledges.[322] (The sledges were basically wagons that had their wheels removed and fitted with flattened wooden boards or staves that were curved on the front.) The impressive feat took heavy manpower along poor-quality roads, across two semi-frozen rivers (only losing one or two cannons, which broke through the ice into the Hudson River) and through the forests and swamps of the lightly inhabited Berkshire Mountains to the army headquarters at Cambridge, Massachusetts.

Sergeant Philip Ulmer, his friends and cousins from Waldoboro and other soldiers stationed at Prospect Hill were tense with anticipation that a confrontation with the British enemy would occur at any time.[323] By the end of January 1776, Colonel Henry Knox and his troops had arrived with the cannons from Ticonderoga. They had also brought additional supplies of powder and artillery shells.[324] General Washington decided the time was right to act. Washington, seeking to end the siege, formulated a plan to draw at least some of the British out of Boston, at which point he would launch an invasion of the city across the Charles River. Heavy field pieces were distributed to several locations overlooking Boston and the harbor. Hushed whispers and rumors swept through the encampments that military action against the enemy would occur very soon.

Unknown to the British generals in Boston, artillery batteries and impressive fortifications on wheels were being constructed by the soldiers out of the sight of the British forces at Dorchester Heights. This was being carried out under the direction of the American chief army engineer of the Massachusetts forces, Colonel Richard Gridley. Hay bales were placed between the path taken by the troops and the harbor in order to muffle the sounds of the covert activities. Logs were painted to look like cannons to make it appear that the American defenses were stronger than they really were. Throughout the night, these troops and relief soldiers labored at building earthworks and hauling cannons to the location overlooking Boston and the harbor. General Washington was present to provide moral support and encouragement, reminding them that March 5 was the sixth anniversary of the Boston Massacre.[325]

General Washington first placed some of the heavy cannon from Ticonderoga at Lechmere's Point (Colonel Bond's location near Prospect Hill where Philip Ulmer served as sergeant), at Cobble Hill near Cambridge and on Lamb's Dam in Roxbury.[326] As a diversion against the planned move on the Dorchester Heights, General Washington ordered these batteries to open fire on the town on the night of March 2, which the British returned, without significant casualties on either side. These cannonades were repeated on the night of March 3 while preparations for the taking of the heights continued. Sergeant Philip Ulmer, his cousin Philip Razor and the other soldiers in Captain Fuller's company were involved in the cannonades and diversionary tactics at this time. On the night of March 4, 1776, the batteries opened fire again, but this time the fire was accompanied by action.[327] Under cover of darkness, General George Washington ordered General John Thomas's division to position dozens of cannon on top of Dorchester Heights. The code word that night was "Boston," and the reply was "Saint Patrick" in honor of the many Irish involved in the assignment.

By four o'clock in the morning, the soldiers had constructed fortifications that were sufficient protection against small arms and grapeshot. Work continued on the positions, with troops cutting down trees and constructing abatis to impede any British assault on the works. The outside of the works also included rock-filled barrels that, while appearing to be a part of the defensive structure, could be rolled down the hill at attacking troops. Washington anticipated that General Howe and his troops would either flee or try to take the hill, an action that would have been reminiscent of the Battle of Bunker Hill, which was a disaster for the British.[328] If Howe decided to launch an attack on the heights, Washington planned to launch an attack against the city from Cambridge. The sudden appearance of the formidable structure and strategically placed cannons upon the heights overlooking Boston and the harbor caused alarm to the British leadership. A Salem ship's captain who had been previously taken prisoner by the British escaped during the confusion and reported to General Washington that "Bombardment and Cannonade caused a good deal of Surprize [*sic*] and alarm in Town [Boston], as many of the Soldiery said they never heard or thought we [the Americans] had Mortars or Shells."[329] On March, 5, 1776, General Howe wrote that "The rebels have done more in one night than my whole army would have done in a month."[330]

On March 9, the cannons continued to roar during the evening and night as mortar rained upon Boston from the Dorchester lines and lines on Boston Neck, as well as the American batteries at Roxbury, Cobble Hill and Lechmere's Point. Unknown to the British forces, some of the figures and cannons that were seen through the British spyglasses from their boats were stuffed scarecrow figures and logs mounted on rocks behind the breastworks to resemble cannons. The appearance gave the impression to the British generals inside Boston that the American troop strength was more forceful than it actually was. General Howe sent an express message to General Washington that if the British were permitted to leave Boston unmolested, they would not burn the city to ashes. An agreement was reached. The British Royal Army, Royal Navy and Loyalists were directed to leave Boston. They set sail on March 17, 1776, for Halifax, Nova Scotia, where the British had their naval shipyard and formidable military fortress. Brigadier General Heath wrote in his journal: "The position of General Howe had become untenable. On the 17th of March, in the morning, the British evacuated Boston. The American troops moved rapidly into the city by foot or in boats. On the Americans entering the town, the inhabitants discovered joy inexpressible."[331] The siege of Boston came to a close. General Washington became concerned that the British forces were going to seize New York City in a spring offensive. Washington prepared to move his main army forces from Boston to western Connecticut and White Plains in Westchester in an attempt to secure the Long Island Sound, New York City and the harbor areas and the mouth of the Hudson River.

PHILIP ULMER BECOMES INVOLVED IN THE CANADIAN CAMPAIGN, 1776

In the waning days of 1775, General Montgomery made a special appeal to the soldiers whose enlistments were up at the end of December to continue to fight until April 15, and then they could return in time for spring planting. These troops had been involved in the unsuccessful campaign to capture Quebec City. This agreement had saved the winter army, but it would later cause General John Thomas great difficulty just as the spring campaign season was about to begin. Many soldiers whose enlistments had terminated in mid-December or on the first of January 1776 left the conflict and headed for home. This left the American troops in Canada at a great disadvantage without enough soldiers to engage the British forces effectively.[332] Colonel Arnold and General Montgomery were in the difficult position of having to rush the attack on Quebec before they were fully prepared. This resulted in a terrible defeat in which General Montgomery was killed, Colonel Arnold was wounded, many brave young soldiers died and hundreds of American soldiers were captured and held in the fort prison, under miserable winter conditions, in Quebec. Many of the captured soldiers were from the Kennebec vicinity of frontier Maine and were part of Colonel Arnold's Kennebec corps. Their story of captivity at the citadel in Quebec in the winter of 1776 and their nearly successful escape from British imprisonment is one of intrigue, ingenuity and, sadly, betrayal by a British spy from within their ranks. The traitor, John Hall, had been with Arnold's Canadian Expedition through the wilderness of Maine in the fall of 1775 and the attack on Quebec City on December 31, 1775. He alerted the British prison guards just hours before the clever American escape plan was to go into effect in the early morning hours of April 1, 1776. It was later discovered that Dr. Benjamin Church Jr., who had served in the Massachusetts Provincial Congress and other sensitive leadership positions and was a trusted friend of General Washington, turned out to be a British spy. He was an informer for General Gage in Boston prior to the British raid on Lexington and Concord. He continued to inform General Gage during the siege of Boston and notified him about the plans for an American expedition to invade Canada and capture Quebec and Montreal. The information about the American invasion plans was sent to General Carleton in Quebec so that the British army would be prepared to disrupt and confront the advancing American expedition and defeat them.

During the Canadian campaign and the siege of Quebec City, many of Colonel Arnold's Kennebec militiamen and General Montgomery's New York soldiers and volunteers had been either captured, had been sidelined with injuries and illness, had frozen to death or had been killed by the British in the attack on Quebec City on December 31, 1775. The American troops were severely depleted due to many reasons. Some reasons for the loss of troop strength were due to sicknesses from a smallpox epidemic within the army ranks, dysentery, pneumonia, malnutrition and infections from frostbite. Deaths occurred daily from starvation and from exposure to the extreme Canadian cold caused by the lack of necessary winter supplies, clothing, food and shelter. Companies of soldiers left the army because their enlistments had ended after a few days, weeks or months. Many men simply deserted from the army and returned to their homes for the winter. Recruiting, reenlistments and keeping good soldiers and qualified officers were continuous problems for General Washington as the commander in chief of the Continental Army. Finding qualified or experienced seamen for the armed naval vessels was also a challenge for his seagoing naval forces. How to finance the American Revolution, to pay the soldiers and officers for their military service and to provide necessary arms and military supplies were continuous problems for the Continental Congress, which relied on the colonial states to provide tax revenue and troop support. Reinforcements were desperately needed to replenish Colonel Arnold's troops in Canada. British governor Carleton had strongly encouraged desertions within the American lines, and he sent agents to promote defections. Printed material was circulated offering food, warm clothing, comfortable quarters and other generous inducements. Governor Carleton's work was made easier prior to the signing of the Declaration of Independence on July 4, 1776, because many of the American soldiers still considered themselves loyal Englishmen who hoped to eventually resume their allegiance to the mother country. Deserters were a valuable source of manpower and information, and they tended to be welcomed by both sides during the Revolution.[333]

Inside Quebec City, British general Sir Guy Carleton aggressively tried to recruit captured American prisoners to increase the size of his own garrison. Colonel MacLean of the Royal Highland Emigrants focused his recruiting efforts on his English- and Irish-born prisoners. Governor Carleton and Colonel MacLean threatened to ship the men back to England in chains to be tried and hanged as traitors.[334] Eventually, the bribes and threats worked, and seventy-eight men from the Arnold expedition joined the Highland Emigrants. After taking an oath of allegiance to serve the king, they were given uniforms and weapons, and they were absorbed into the regiment.[335] The captured Kennebec corps of officers should not have worried that so many of their captured soldiers had switched sides because those who had joined the British forces soon ran for freedom at the first opportunity.

Following the request from General Gates in the Northern Department for more American troops, the Continental Congress issued orders to General Washington that relief troops should be sent to Canada. The detached relief troops marched from Cambridge to Montreal to replenish Arnold's and Montgomery's volunteer expeditionary forces that had been depleted when enlistments had terminated at the end of December 1775. Having participated at Dorchester Heights in early March 1776 outside Boston, Sergeant Philip Ulmer was among the first American relief troops who arrived from Montreal.[336] Sergeant Philip Ulmer marched and snowshoed over icy and snowy terrain with the first American relief companies from Cambridge.[337] The detached American relief troops in early March 1776 likely used the same military route taken by General Montgomery's troops in the Canadian Expedition to capture Fort St. John on the northern end of Lake Champlain and to capture the fortress at Montreal in the fall.[338] The American relief regiments used the natural waterway of the Hudson River and probably proceeded to the town of Albany. At Albany, General Philip Schuyler and his military forces were prepared to receive the relief troops with supplies to be transported to the American troops in Canada.

By the time Sergeant Philip Ulmer and the first detached relief troops arrived at Albany, the military munitions and supplies, provisions and other dry goods for the American forces in Canada were already assembled by General Schuyler and his command. The supply train was ready to move northward with seventy-six ox-drawn sleds over the snow and frozen northern water route.[339] These first relief troops from Cambridge continued northward to the fort and outpost at Lake George. From the northern end of Lake George, the troops progressed along a primitive roadway through several miles of frozen woodlands and along the La Chute River, which separated Lake George from Lake Champlain. Once at Fort Ticonderoga, the troops progressed to Crown Point on Lake Champlain, where they continued their trek northward over the ice and snow through the Lake Champlain Valley. Transportation was made easier when the rivers and lakes were frozen and supplies could be transported by ox-drawn sleds.

These first American relief troops navigated over the ice of Lake Champlain to the captured British fort of St. John. The fort had been captured several months earlier and was held by some of General

Montgomery's American invasion troops. The detached relief forces continued overland along the rugged La Prairie route to the docks on the St. Lawrence River across from Montreal. The American troops were able to cross the frozen St. Lawrence River and arrived at the fort in Montreal, where General Montgomery's American invasion forces held the captured city. General David Wooster of Connecticut was in command of Montreal at this time while General Arnold was with the siege forces outside of Quebec City. The remnants of Montgomery's troops, who had retreated in the confusion of the attack on Quebec City in late December 1775, were among the American troops at Montreal. These relief troops, including Philip Ulmer, began to arrive at the fortress at Montreal in April before the ice thawed in early May. The food, clothing and medical and military supplies were received with great joy by the American troops stationed in Montreal: "…fresh American troops were trickling in, and that they were being prepared for action in an April offensive upon Quebec. General David Wooster joined Arnold at Quebec with relief troops from Montreal in early April 1776. Arnold's army grew to 2,500 men."[340] Colonel Arnold was promoted by the Continental Congress to brigadier general in January 1776, and he commanded the American troops laying siege outside the gates of Quebec City.[341] Quebec City was buried under four or five feet of snow by late March/early April 1776. The American relief troops proceeded from Montreal down the frozen St. Lawrence River shoreline to General Arnold's camp located on the Plains of Abraham outside Quebec City, supplementing Arnold's depleted American troops who continued to lay siege outside Quebec City on the Plains of Abraham.[342] A spring offensive in April 1776 was planned against General Carleton's British troops in Quebec City before the British reinforcements from England could arrive when the St. Lawrence River thawed in early May. With the arrival of American reinforcements, General Arnold instructed his troops to construct a battery of four guns on Point Levi and another battery of eight guns, one howitzer and two mortars on the Plains of Abraham. Colonel Haskell, in his correspondence, further related: "A hot firing began this morning in the city (Quebec) upon our men at Point Levi." Arnold wrote that he "hoped the batteries would have the desired effect and cause Carleton to surrender the city, but if they failed, they had ladders and other items to help them storm the walls of the city."[343]

General Arnold had prepared a fire ship—his own schooner *Peggy* that had been stranded in the harbor outside Quebec City prior to the outbreak of war. His cargo vessel had recently delivered a shipment of dry goods and rum from the West Indies.* Arnold planned to send the fire ship, packed with explosives, against the small British fleet anchored at the wharves of the lower village below the cliffs outside Quebec City. The increased rebel activity and the cannon fire from the newly arrived American batteries could be heard inside Quebec City, and it brought hope to the American prisoners being held inside the fortress that they would soon be liberated. Hoping to lure General Arnold into attacking, General Sir Guy Carleton (the royal governor of the Province of Quebec and commander of British forces in Canada) staged a false prison break inside the walls of Quebec with shouting and gunfire. General Arnold's battery at Point Levi opened fire upon Quebec City in response to the alarm. General Arnold's startled horse reared up on his hindquarters and fell upon the general in the confusion. General Arnold's leg that had sidelined him in the army field hospital since the attack on Quebec City at the beginning of the year was re-injured. General Wooster took over command of the American forces again with Arnold unable to lead his men due to his disabling leg injury. General Arnold requested that General Wooster make him commander of the fortress at Montreal, where he would at least be able to be useful. The request was readily granted by General Wooster.[344] On April 12, 1776, General Arnold rode away from the encampment outside Quebec City, taking with him some of the sick and injured soldiers, as well as other soldiers who were needed to move and care for them. Colonel Arnold took over the command of Montreal and immediately started to reorganize his troops. He made arrangements to tighten the defenses around the fortress and to use the captured armed British vessels that were taken in the fall to defend Montreal and other outposts on the river against further British attack. [345]

Philip Ulmer, whose one-year enlistment had expired in April, reenlisted with the Twenty-fifth Massachusetts Regiment in General Arnold's detached brigade in mid-April 1776. Sergeant Philip Ulmer was advanced in rank and commissioned as an ensign.[346] He received his commission on April 20, 1776, by an act of the Continental Congress, and the document was signed by President John Hancock.[347] Philip Ulmer was appointed by General Arnold as captain of the captured British warship of eight guns, the *Isabella*, in April 1776 for the defense of Montreal and for the transport and support of the American troops.[348] His assignment was to defend the fortress at

---

* *Author's comment*: This might have been the same sailing vessel that was meant for Arnold's agent inside the city and carried disguised supplies for Arnold's troops when they arrived at Quebec City in late 1775.

Montreal, the outposts at Pointe-aux-Trembles, the American battery and outpost at Sorel and the outpost at Trois-Rivieres (hereafter Three Rivers) from the British forces. He was to provide transportation for the American troops, their provisions and their munitions on the St. Lawrence River between Montreal and Quebec City. The captured British sloop *Isabella*, whose British captain had been Captain Bouchat (Bouchet, Bouchette)[349] and the aide-de-camp to General Sir Guy Carleton, was the first vessel that Philip Ulmer officially commanded as captain for the American army troops.

Heavy snow and ice had often stopped the soldiers and supplies from moving through the Champlain Valley from Fort Ticonderoga to Canada for the American troops. Although weather conditions had changed, with milder weather toward the end of April, melting snow and the lack of thick ice became a hazardous problem for the American supply lines and for new troop reinforcements making their way northward. Colonel John Haskell reported in his communications: "By then the ice was too thin. Some horses and one man have already been drowned on Lake George and Lake Champlain. They would have to wait for the ice to break up enough to allow bateaux to cross the lakes before men and supplies could be moved north again."[350]

THE AMERICAN RETREAT FROM CANADA IN 1776

The Continental Congress, after numerous requests from General Arnold, sent a committee of three congressional commissioners in the spring of 1776 to assess the American troop strength, the supply line difficulties and the monetary issues and concerns that caused great hardship for the American forces in Canada. The congressional delegation consisted of Benjamin Franklin, Samuel Chase and Charles Carroll. Father John Carroll (a Catholic priest and cousin of Charles Carroll) had also become part of the delegation in hopes of having a positive effect upon the large Catholic population within Quebec City and surrounding settlements. The delegation sailed up the Hudson River and arrived in Albany on April 7, 1776, where they stayed for two days as guests of General Philip Schuyler. General John Thomas, who was en route to Canada to assume the command of the American forces in Quebec, and the congressional delegation proceeded northward to Saratoga, where General Schuyler and his family had a country residence. On April 11, Generals Thomas and Schuyler set off for the fort at Lake George, followed five days later by the three commissioners. General Thomas was eager to assume his command of the American forces in Canada from General Wooster at Quebec City. General Schuyler was prepared to send military stores and supplies with the next American relief troops, which were in transit up the Hudson River on sloops. More relief troops were soon expected to arrive in Albany with General Thompson.

General Thomas arrived at Montreal at the end of April 1776 to assume his command in Canada. He pushed on to the besieged city of Quebec, arriving at the American encampment on the Plains of Abraham on May 1, 1776.[351] Ensign Philip Ulmer, now the captain of the armed transport vessel *Isabella*, would have known General John Thomas from his activities at Plymouth in late 1775 in refitting (and probably sailing on) armed vessels for Washington's naval fleet in operations along the New England seacoast. He had certainly known General Thomas during the siege of Boston and the altercation at Dorchester Heights that resulted in the British forces evacuating the city on March 17, 1776. He probably knew General Thomas and his family prior to the war since General Thomas had relatives who lived at Waldoboro in Philip Ulmer's hometown.

What General Thomas discovered on May 1 when he arrived at the army headquarters outside Quebec City was considered a disaster. The American forces numbered fewer than one thousand, and over three hundred of the soldiers were overdue for discharge from their enlistment (the agreement that the soldiers had made with General Montgomery before the attack on Quebec). Smallpox was raging through the encampment, and few soldiers were fit for duty. General Thomas immediately sent the sick soldiers (mostly afflicted with smallpox) to Three Rivers for hospital care at the American military post. He began to organize the remainder of the American troops for a withdrawal to the American military post at Sorel, which was manned by Major John Brown and the remnants of Colonel Arnold's former Connecticut regiment.[352] Philip Ulmer was probably involved with transporting the troops to these locations since he had been placed in a position of defending Montreal and the outposts along the St. Lawrence River with his armed transport.

After the British forces evacuated the city of Boston on March 17, 1776, the Continental Congress, at the request of General Horatio Gates in the Northern Department at Albany, ordered that General Washington send four American relief regiments to reinforce the American army forces in Canada. These relief troops were sent in late March 1776 following the evacuation of the British troops and Loyalists. They were led by Colonels William Bond,

John Paterson and John Greaton, along with the New Hampshire regiment led by General Enoch Poor. These four relief regiments were under the command of Brigadier General William Thompson. They were sent along with six more regiments under Major General Sullivan to further reinforce Brigadier General John Thomas's new command in Canada. Fearing that the British command had plans to capture Long Island and New York City, General Washington ordered the four relief regiments bound for Canada to divert to the White Plains and Westchester County vicinity to support the Continental forces that were trying to repulse the British forces from Long Island Sound and New York City at the mouth of the Hudson River. George Ulmer, who had enlisted in the army for three years, appeared with Paterson's regiment at White Plains, New York,[353] prior to the regiment's orders to go to Canada with the relief forces. After a short time, these four regiments were released from Washington's diversion orders at White Plains and ordered to proceed on their original assignment to Canada as relief forces for the Canadian Expedition.

The situation in Canada changed dramatically on the evening of May 5, when rumbling sounds were heard in Quebec City from downriver. The sounds grew louder during the night and were identified as cannon fire. The St. Lawrence River was beginning to thaw, and the British warships were forcing their way through the ice. The following morning, the Royal Navy frigate *Isis*, commanded by Captain Douglas, approached the besieged city of Quebec. The Royal frigate was followed soon afterward by several other British ships with reinforcements of supplies, British army troops and Hessian mercenary soldiers. The siege of Quebec was lifted with the arrival of the new British relief forces. The American Continental soldiers retreated rapidly toward the fort at Montreal, leaving behind tons of valuable equipment and hundreds of sick soldiers who were too weak to travel. American forces had lost the race to capture Quebec City, the last stronghold of the British forces in Canada.

While all of these incidents were happening, the three congressional commissioners (Benjamin Franklin, Charles Carroll and Samuel Chase) had arrived at the La Prairie wharf the first week of May. Philip Ulmer, captain of the *Isabella*, had been directed by General Arnold to give a welcoming salute to the three congressional commissioners, and the salute would also signal their arrival to General Arnold and his welcoming delegation. The guns of the *Isabella* roared out a welcome, announcing the arrival of the delegation. Since Captain Ulmer's responsibilities were to transport troops and defend Montreal from the British ships, he was probably involved in helping to transport the three commissioners and Father Carroll across the St. Lawrence River to Montreal, where the congressional delegation was met by General Arnold and the welcoming officials at the dock. The delegation was ceremoniously escorted into the fortress on Mount Royal. The cannons inside the fortress responded and fired off a salute to the three congressional commissioners as a welcome.[354] General Arnold and his officers paraded the commissioners to their headquarters while the guns continued to roar out a salute.[355] In the fall of 1775, Generals Montgomery and Arnold had sent letters and pleas to the Continental Congress for diplomats to come to Canada and to assess the situation and negotiate a solution to the British-American conflict. The congressional delegation had finally arrived. After assessing the situation, the three commissioners decided that the American situation in Canada was tenuous at best and determined that a retreat was the proper solution. The commissioners recognized that without a war chest, they could do little to affect the action. The three congressional commissioners determined that the American presence in Canada was no longer viable. The Continental Congress was unable to provide sufficient funds, supplies or men necessary to support the American military troops in Canada. It determined that a report had to be made in person to inform the delegates in Congress about the desperate shortages and conditions that constrained every effort of the American troops in Canada.[356]

The American relief troops, which included the regiments of Colonel Bond, Colonel Paterson, Colonel Greaton and the New Hampshire regiment with General Poor, had arrived in Canada by mid-May. These relief troops from Cambridge had been delayed at the fort on Lake George because of thin ice and thawing conditions.[357] These relief troops had to wait for the icy lake to adequately thaw enough before they could safely proceed in bateaux through the cold water and ice chunks to the landing at the northern end of the lake. Supplies for the American forces in Canada had to be transported over dreadful and slippery roads by wagons and oxcarts from the landing at the north end of Lake George to Fort Ticonderoga. At this point, the relief troops again reloaded the bateaux and small boats with supplies, soldiers and equipment, and they proceeded northward down Lake Champlain to Fort St. John. The bateaux were again unloaded, and the supplies and provisions were carried around the rapids of the Richelieu River to the outpost at Chambly. They proceeded northward with all of their baggage and supplies to the outpost at Sorel on the St. Lawrence River.

The American relief troops with General Thompson eventually arrived in time to assist in the evacuation of the American forces in their retreat from Canada in June 1776.[358]

In order to protect the American forces in the Northern Theater and to prevent the British forces from proceeding south along the Richelieu River to Fort St. John on Lake Champlain, General Thomas had determined that a great iron chain should be placed across the river at Chambly. Large chains strung across navigable rivers were not a new idea, but one that was very effective. American ironworkers made portions of the chain, and the sections of large chain were shipped to Canada in mid-May 1776.[359] Because of the American retreat from Canada, the large chain was never installed. The chain sections were evacuated from Canada, and the chain was later assembled at Fort Montgomery on the Hudson River near the American military headquarters at West Point in the upper Highlands Department under the command of General Heath. On July 21, Robert Yates, chairman of the committee of New York State for the defense of the Hudson River, wrote about the chain to Major General Gates, who commanded the American field army at Fort Ticonderoga. On July 25, Major General Schuyler, commander of the Northern Theater of operations, forwarded a request to General Gates that "if the chain can be spared, I wish you would send it without delay, under the care of a careful officer to attend to it, to Poughkeepsie."[360] The large chain was sent to Poughkeepsie, New York, in late July 1776. In order to support the massive chain, 150 logs were sawed and attached to it. This chain would become an important deterrent to British armed vessels on the Hudson River, and it was instrumental in keeping British forces from capturing West Point and Albany, New York, during the American Revolution.

Although General Thomas had been a doctor from Plymouth County, Massachusetts, and was familiar with the smallpox disease and skilled in its treatment, he never had been inoculated against the disease.[361] This was most unfortunate since it cost him his life within the first five weeks of his arrival and shortly after assuming the command of the American forces in Canada. On June 2, 1776, while awaiting army reinforcements at the fort at Chambly, General Thomas died of smallpox, which had left him totally blind for several days before his death.[362] General Thompson assumed command of the American forces in Canada after the death of General Thomas. General Thompson was later replaced by General Sullivan when Thompson, his senior officers and two hundred soldiers were captured by the enemy along with most of the ships used for an expedition at Three

Rivers (Trois-Rivières) near Quebec City on June 8, 1776. The arrival of British reinforcements and large amounts of supplies at Quebec City brought about the retreat of American troops at Sorel who were under the command of General Sullivan. General Thompson's American forces were defeated at Three Rivers. This major defeat, along with the American defeat at The Cedars by British general Forster's troops and their Mohawk Indian allies, dramatically hastened the end of the American presence in Province of Quebec and the retreat of the American forces from Canada.

General Sullivan became the commander of the American forces in Canada following the capture of General Thompson and his soldiers by the enemy at Three Rivers. General Sullivan received orders to withdraw the remnants of the battered American army from Canada and to retreat to the safety of Fort Ticonderoga, where he was directed to establish new defensive positions. It was learned that General Guy Carleton intended to push his British and Hessian forces southward, deep into the New York colony, using vessels suited for fighting on Lake Champlain that had been prefabricated in Great Britain and shipped in pieces to Quebec.[363] The ten prefabricated gunboats were to be transported by boat to a location near the Richelieu River, and then the parts were to be conveyed through the woods by wagons around the waterfalls to Fort St. John on Lake Champlain. Carpenters and artificers would assemble the gunboats and build new warships at the shipyard at St. John. Experienced sailors, trained artillerymen and veteran British soldiers were sent as reinforcements to arm, prepare and man the warships on the lake.

The retreating American regiments that were transported by bateaux and by captured British transport vessels from Three Rivers reached the fort at Sorel by June 14.[364] A British fleet of approximately thirty-six sailing ships appeared near the American fort at Sorel. General Arnold had written a letter to General Sullivan that the troops must be evacuated from Sorel and moved south along the Richelieu River to Chambly. He suggested that the troops withdraw to Fort St. John, where boats had been secured for such a retreat. The American forces could make their evacuation to the safety of Crown Point and Fort Ticonderoga. General Arnold wrote that he would hold Montreal until the troops could be brought out, and then he would withdraw to the fort at St. John as well.[365] General Sullivan, Arthur St. Clair and other officers called a council of war, and all who were present agreed that Sorel should be abandoned. However, the American troops had to continue to move quickly since the British fleet with their Royal Army and Hessian forces were in close pursuit. The American troops at Sorel broke camp and made their way up the Richelieu River just hours ahead of the British grenadiers and light infantry troops. In his haste during the American retreat, General Sullivan failed to send word to Arnold in Montreal about what was happening and what had been decided in the council of war at Sorel. On June 15, General Arnold, unaware that Sorel had been abandoned, sent his aide, James Wilkinson, with an express message to General Sullivan. While crossing the St. Lawrence River, Major Wilkinson and his small company of men ran right into an advanced guard of the British soldiers who were moving toward Montreal.[366] Before they were discovered, Wilkinson and his men leaped over a fence and scrambled quickly toward the woods. They made their way back to their boat, and by late afternoon, they were back in Montreal, where they warned General Arnold of the danger of advancing British infantry troops.

Philip Ulmer remained with General Arnold's brigade and helped to transport American troops and supplies aboard the *Isabella* and continued to guard Montreal from the advancing British and Hessian troops. General Arnold directed that his entire garrison of soldiers at Montreal should be taken across the St. Lawrence River to the dock at La Prairie. Through the dark and rainy evening, the soldiers were evacuated by the transport vessels from the wharves at Montreal and Longueuil across the river to the La Prairie dock. Even as the last of the American troops were leaving Montreal on June 15, the British transports made their way up the St. Lawrence River toward Montreal.[367] By the time General Arnold, Wilkinson, the rear guard soldiers and sailing crew reached the dock at La Prairie across the river from the fortress, word was received that the British had retaken Montreal. The *Isabella* had been used for the purpose of protecting Montreal and for transporting, evacuating and protecting the troops at Longueuil, La Prairie, Sorel and Montreal. The *Isabella* was abandoned and rendered inoperable (probably burned or scuttled near the wharf). In a letter sent by General Guy Carleton to Lord George Germain at the War Ministry in England concerning the American retreat, he wrote, "Had not the wind failed, this column might have arrived at Longueuil the same night and about the same time with Mr. Arnold and the remainder of the Rebels."[368]

It took most of the night to acquire the thirty carts that were needed to transport the baggage, the supplies, the sick and the injured to the fort at St. John.[369] The American relief troops who had arrived recently in Canada (which included the rest of Philip and George Ulmer's troops with Colonels Bond and Paterson's regiments) became involved in the retreat to Fort St. John and then further southward to Crown Point and

Fort Ticonderoga. On June 18, 1776, the last of the American troops hastily destroyed whatever could be useful to the British troops who were in close pursuit of the retreating American soldiers. General Arnold and Captain Wilkinson rode their horses back up the pathway to check on the advancing British soldiers at Fort St. John. Upon their return, the saddles were removed from Arnold's and Wilkinson's horses, and the horses were shot.[370] Ensign Philip Ulmer may have been with the small detachment of anxious crewmen who waited for Colonel Arnold and his aide to board the bateau that was waiting at the wharf to make their escape from the approaching enemy troops.[371] Colonel Arnold, accompanied by Captain Wilkinson, boarded the last bateau, and the crewmen pushed away from the shore just as a rifle shot was heard ahead of the advancing British troops.[372] When the British regiment arrived at Fort St. John, they could see the last of the Americans' bateaux pushing away from the shore, leaving behind the burning remnants of the British fort. In anger, the British pursuers fired their muskets at the escaping rebel bateau with Arnold on board. The garrison buildings, store houses and boats under construction were still in flames.[373] Benedict Arnold was reported to have been the last American to leave Canada.[374] The British troops under the command of General Burgoyne took possession of Fort St. John on June 18 and began rebuilding the barracks and docks. They salvaged what they could use and prepared for the next phase of the fall campaign on Lake Champlain.

By June 18, the American troops withdrew to Isle aux Noix, where they waited for further orders from General Schuyler, the Continental Congress and General Washington (located near New York City). The sick and injured soldiers were taken to Crown Point, where Colonel John Trumbull, deputy adjutant general, was serving as commanding officer at the time. The invalid soldiers were sent down the river tributary by boat to the army hospital at Fort Ticonderoga for care. General Arnold finally caught up to his commanding officer, General John Sullivan, who was very anxious and stressed over the defeat of the American troops by the British forces led by General Burgoyne. He had no plans for recovery, and he was uncertain of his next orders for the American troops. General Sullivan sent General Arnold and his aide, James Wilkinson, to confer with General Schuyler about further orders for the retreating troops. On June 24, not finding General Schuyler at Fort Ticonderoga, General Arnold, Captain Wilkinson and his small detachment of soldiers continued toward Albany. They arrived at the home of General Schuyler, where they were welcomed to spend the night. The next morning, they proceeded to the headquarters of the Northern Department at Albany.[375]

General Schuyler and General Arnold conferred upon the precarious situation of the American troops. Couriers were sent with letters to update General Washington and to direct General Sullivan to withdraw his battered army to the safety of Crown Point and Fort Ticonderoga. A recovery plan was decided upon to establish a new defensive position at Fort Ticonderoga with the retreating American troops from Canada and with reinforcements from the New England colonies. They recognized the immediate need for naval superiority on Lake Champlain if the British and Hessian invasion forces were to be stopped and held at Ticonderoga. The American counter-strategy was to make a decisive stand to prevent the New England colonies from being divided from the southern colonies through the Lake Champlain and Hudson River Valleys. The American army needed time to prepare for the anticipated conflict against the superior British forces that were bearing down upon them from Canada. By using a delaying strategy, the British forces might be held back long enough for General Washington's Continental Army to grow stronger, to become better armed and to be trained in proper military procedures. By using a prolonged delaying tactic, the British supply lines and reinforcements could be stretched thin, the enemy's morale and war finances would be affected and the efficiency of the invading enemy army would become greatly weakened.

John Hancock informed General Washington on June 18 that after the unfortunate death of General Thomas, Congress had appointed Major General Horatio Gates to the command of American forces in the Northern Theater. General Washington ordered General Horatio Gates "to the important command of the troops of the United Colonies in Canada."[376] Unfortunately for General Gates, by the time he arrived in Albany to assume his command, there were no more military operations in Canada. General Gates was under the impression that he had command of all the troops in the army of the Northern Department, regardless of wherever they were. General Schuyler disagreed with General Gates's assumption. General Schuyler wrote in protest to General Washington, stating, "If Congress intended that General Gates should command the Northern Army, wherever it may be, as he assures me they did, it ought to have been signified to me…"[377] General Schuyler would not serve under General Gates, whose commission was more recent than his. Congress attempted to settle the conflict between the two generals by informing General Gates that the intention was "to give him the command of the Troops whilst in Canada, [but had not intended to] vest him with superior command to General Schuyler whilst the Troops should be on this side [of] Canada."[378] John Hancock further admonished that both of the generals were expected to carry on operations in harmony. The generals came to an agreement, of sorts, to maintain the balance of power earlier established between General Schuyler and the commander at Fort Ticonderoga, who was now General Horatio Gates.

When General Sullivan learned about General Gates's appointment upon his return from Canada with the American troops, he was displeased. Although General Horatio Gates had more military experience, General Sullivan was the more senior officer in rank and commission. He felt that Congress' decision implied that "he was not equal to the trust they [Congress] were pleased to repose in me."[379] General Sullivan felt that if Congress put a junior officer ahead of his senior position, then he was compelled by honor to resign from his post, which he did. Animosity over seniority and authority between the generals began to fester and become contentious. The animosity between the generals never fully ended, but remained beneath the surface, only to resurface later at an inopportune time. The lower-ranking officers who served closely with the disgruntled generals and senior officers could not help but be affected by their discontent and rancor. Throughout the Revolutionary War, a number of leaders and officers (like Washington, Schuyler and Arnold, until his defection, as well as Hancock and Franklin) rendered extraordinary service to the American cause of independence. Their valor gave some of them the image of greatness and even made some leaders seem larger than life. The war also brought forward other officers and leaders (like Gates, Wilkinson and the Lee brothers) who were small-minded, ambitious and unable to see beyond their own personal pettiness and opportunism to the greater good for the American people and the new nation as a whole. Jealousy, innuendos, lies, plots, intrigue and vitriol crept into the military command structure and into the halls of the Continental Congress. The Conway plot to replace General Washington with Gates as commander in chief of the Continental Army is one example. Blind ambition and desire for power threatened to undermine the very success of the Revolution and the American cause. Ambitious European nobles and foreign military officers (like the Marquis de Lafayette, Baron DeKalb, Baron von Steuben, Horatio Gates, a retired British soldier living in America and others) were made generals by the Continental Congress and given leadership roles in the American army above experienced American officers. General Washington, his devoted inner core of officers and dedicated delegates in the Continental Congress tried to keep harmony within the army and cooperation within the Congress.

General Schuyler tried to maintain control over the growing animosity between Gates and himself. He directed General Gates to concentrate his efforts on the defenses of the Lake Champlain area while he (Schuyler) retained authority over the overall direction of the entire Northern Theater. General Gates felt that the operations on Lake Champlain were two distinct operations.[380] General Gates decided to focus his attention on preparing the land defenses and strengthening his ground troops, where he felt most competent. He decided to appoint General Arnold to deal directly with the naval affairs, in which Arnold was more competent. General Arnold, who had years of nautical experience and was battle-tested in the Northern Theater already, was appointed as commodore of American Naval Forces on Lake Champlain. In late July 1776, General Gates reported to General Washington and to John Hancock, the president of the Continental Congress, that "Arnold has most nobly undertaken to command our fleet upon the lake [Lake Champlain]. With infinite satisfaction, I have committed the whole of that department to his care, convinced he will thereby add to that brilliant reputation he has so deservedly acquired."[381]

By July 2, the Northern division of the American army from the Canadian retreat had arrived back at Crown Point, and by July 11, the remaining troops had arrived at Fort Ticonderoga. General Schuyler's efforts to construct an American naval fleet for the defense of Lake Champlain were fully underway at Skenesboro.[382] There was a desperate attempt to build vessels capable of offering resistance to the British ships. A number of British prefabricated and traditionally constructed vessels were in the process of being assembled at Fort St. John at the northern end of Lake Champlain. Commodore Arnold arrived at Skenesboro on July 23 and was pleased to find the construction of the little flotilla of gunboats and conversion of several captured British vessels to warships was going well. Trouble again erupted in the American command when Commodore Jacobus Wynkoop claimed command of the region and refused to take orders from General Benedict Arnold. When harmony and cooperation were needed the most, animosity between the two ranking officers caused many problems for the command structure at a critical time. The problem was eventually resolved when Jacobus Wynkoop was removed from his command in mid-August 1776.

The American forces in the Northern Department strove to quickly put together a naval fleet before the British army forces could complete the construction of their naval fleet at Fort St. John. The British forces were equally involved in building a commanding naval fleet to secure their control and authority of Lake Champlain before the American fleet could be built.

British warships were assembled on the St. Lawrence River and hauled overland to be reassembled on Lake Champlain. Prefabricated sections of sailing vessels sent from England were also hauled overland through the woods on crude pathways to be reassembled at Fort St. John. A wilderness arms race had begun, and the impending collision course between the two opposing military forces was soon to be determined. In the shipbuilding race, there was never any doubt that the British forces would produce a vastly superior fleet. But the fact that the American troops were building vessels to defend Lake Champlain, however inferior, made the British general Sir Guy Carleton pause and delay the invasion plans into the heartland of the New York colony in the early fall of 1776.

Perhaps the most important result of the Canadian campaign in 1775–76, and Colonel Arnold's expedition in general, was that it validated General Washington's efforts to build a naval fleet to defend the American coastline, to cut off enemy reinforcements and supply lines and to organize a professional army with long-term professional soldiers that the Continental Congress was reluctant to provide and unable to adequately support. More than any other event, the death of General Montgomery shocked the congressional delegates into understanding the shortcomings of their ideological and impractical policy of a citizen army composed of enlistees for one year. John Hancock, who served as president of the Continental Congress at Philadelphia, wrote a letter to General Washington on the subject on September 24, 1776. John Hancock wrote, "The untimely Death of General Montgomery alone, independent of other Arguments, is a striking Proof of the Danger and Impropriety of sending Troops into the Field, under any Restriction as to the Time of their Service."[383]

The congressional delegates in Philadelphia had not properly supported the expedition in Canada in a timely way, although they had sanctioned it. The delegates argued over unification with Great Britain or independence from England. Congress was generally uncertain about the direction it should pursue in the United Colonies' foreign affairs with Great Britain. The American forces who participated in the Canadian Expedition lacked sufficient troop strength, sufficient military arms and supplies, necessary field support and money to carry out the mission in Canada. These were all responsibilities of the Continental Congress. The failure of General Montgomery and Colonel Arnold's hasty attack on Quebec City was primarily due to a hurried decision regarding the large numbers of soldiers who would soon return to their homes having completed their enlistments on December 31, 1775. The harsh weather conditions (a blinding windblown snowstorm) during which the assault on Quebec City occurred caused confusion and uncertainty among the American troops, who were unprepared for the weather conditions. This resulted in bewilderment among the soldiers and a disorganized, hasty retreat by Montgomery's troops outside the gates of Quebec City following the deaths of General Montgomery and a number of his officers. Hundreds of Kennebec soldiers from the frontier district of Maine and the other volunteers who served with General Montgomery and Arnold's invading troops were quickly surrounded by enemy troops. Resisters were killed, and others were taken captive by the British soldiers outside the gates of the city. They were taken into Quebec City, and the officers were separated from the militia soldiers, who were then held in the fortress dungeon. Their disposition was determined at a later time.

Except for the American success at Dorchester Heights in early March 1776, which forced the British forces to evacuate their stronghold at Boston, the year of 1776 can best be characterized as a series of many defeats and retreats for General Washington's army forces. Washington's troops were defeated and retreated from enemy engagements at Long Island, White Plains (in Westchester County), at New York City and through New Jersey to the western shore of the Delaware River in Pennsylvania. The value of a naval fleet was beginning to be recognized by the war critics and the public, although how to pay for a colonial navy was still uncertain. By the end of 1776, the Continental Congress began recruiting men who agreed to serve for three years or for the duration of the war. This policy was instrumental in the creation of trained, experienced soldiers who served in regiments of "Continentals" and made up the central core of the American army for the remainder of the Revolutionary War. Although the Canadian campaign failed to achieve its mission, it proved to be a training ground for American combat officers who later successfully led the American army in a series of victories that eventually brought about the end of the war with Great Britain.

Chapter 4

Defense of Lake Champlain

THE DECLARATION OF INDEPENDENCE IS READ TO THE AMERICAN TROOPS AT FORT TICONDEROGA

Preamble of the Declaration of Independence
July 4, 1776

We the People of the United States, in Order to form a more perfect Union, establish Justice, insure domestic Tranquility, provide for the common defence, promote the general Welfare, and secure the Blessings of Liberty to ourselves and our Posterity, do ordain and establish this Constitution for the United States of America.

The Declaration of Independence was printed on Thursday, July 4, 1776, by local Philadelphia printer John Dunlap. Congress ordered that copies be sent "to the several Assemblies, Conventions, and Committees or Councils of Safety, and to the several Commanding officers of the Continental Troops, that it be proclaimed in each of the United States, and at the head of the Army."[384]

Articles appeared in the *Pennsylvania Evening Post* on July 15, 1776. On July 28, 1776, immediately after worship services, Colonel Arthur St. Clair had the honor of reading the Declaration of Independence before the assembled troops at Fort Ticonderoga. After the reading, Colonel St. Clair said, "God save the free [and] independent States of America!"[385] The army troops expressed their great happiness with three cheers and shouts of joy. Ensign Philip Ulmer was among the young officers and soldiers who rejoiced at the exciting news. Newspaper articles appeared with Colonel St. Clair's public reading of the document to the army troops at Fort Ticonderoga on July 28. The *Boston Gazette* printed an extract from a letter on August 29, 1776, that reported:

> *We hear from Ticonderoga that on the 28th of July. Immediately after divine worship, the Declaration of Independence was read by Colonel St. Clair, and having said "God save the free independent States of America!" the army manifested their joy with 3 cheers. It was remarkably pleasing to see the spirits of soldiers so raised after the calamities, the language of every man's countenance was,… "Now we are a People! We have a name among the states of this World." A salute of 13 guns was fired and the neighboring eminence was christened Mount Independence.[386]*

The *New York Journal* ran articles about readings of the Declaration of Independence on August 15, 1776; the *New York Packet* on August 15, 1776; and the *New York Gazette and Weekly Mercury* on August 19, 1776. The United Colonies were set upon a new course toward sovereignty and independence from Great Britain and as a new nation.

The Lake Champlain Valley and the Hudson River Valley had for many centuries been used by the Indians and traders as the highway for commerce, transportation and fur trading in North America. It had also been used for generations as an invasion route between Canada and the American colonies. General Washington's countering strategy in 1776 was simple but bold in its mission. It was determined that Fort Ticonderoga must be held at any cost to prevent the colonies from being divided in half by enemy invasion forces from Canada. If the British and Hessian forces captured Fort Ticonderoga, they would be able to advance southward and capture the American headquarters of the Northern Command at Albany. From Albany, the invasion forces could easily sweep down the Hudson River Valley to New York City, which was held by the British Royal Army under General William Howe's command. The rebellion against Great Britain's exploitation and repressive hold on the American colonies could be quashed by dividing and conquering the weakened and mostly defenseless colonies.

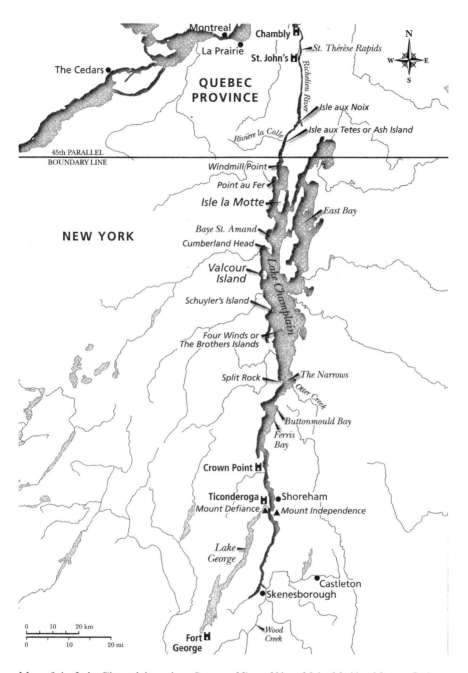

Map of the Lake Champlain region. *Courtesy of James Nelson; Maine Maritime Museum, Bath, Maine.*

General Schuyler and the commanding officers at Fort Ticonderoga understood that when the clash between General Carleton's larger, well-supplied, regular army forces actually happened against the remnants of the poorly supplied and depleted American troops, there was little doubt in anyone's mind as to the outcome. It was urgent that an American fleet should be built to take the offensive and prevent the enemy forces from reaching the southern end of Lake Champlain, or at least delay the British and Hessian troops until the American army had sufficient defensive strength to withstand an assault. It was decided that General Carleton's advancing forces had to be confronted "at sea" on Lake Champlain. Naval superiority on the lake would be crucial in determining the future success or failure of the American Revolution. It was decided that delaying the enemy fleet until the onset of winter might be just as effective as defeating it outright. Everyone recognized that this mission to delay the enemy was a suicide mission. Those who served in the daring mission would have contributed more courage and patriotism to the American cause of freedom and liberty than could ever be expressed in words of gratitude.

During the summer of 1776, the American troops and volunteers were continuously kept busy with numerous projects to fortify Fort Ticonderoga and to build a naval fleet for the defense of the Lake Champlain Valley. On July 30, 1776, the returning American troops with Generals Arnold and Sullivan from the Canadian Expedition were assigned to four brigades. The first brigade was composed of soldiers from Greaton's, Bond's, Burrell's and Porter's regiments. The second brigade was made up of soldiers from Stark's, Wind's, Maxwell's and Poor's regiments. The third brigade was composed of soldiers from Reed's, Paterson's, Wynkoop's and Bedel's regiments. The fourth brigade was composed of soldiers from St. Clair's, De Haas's, Wayne's and Irvine's regiments. They joined other troops that had participated in the siege of Boston the year before.[387] Supplies were distributed from the commissary officer to those men who were fit for duty and needed shoes, shirts and moccasins.

The American fleet was built at Skenesboro by carpenters and shipbuilders from many states, especially from Connecticut, Massachusetts and Pennsylvania. The vessels were made of "green" wood—newly cut timber that had not had time to "cure." The boats were turned out as quickly as possible. Once completed, the vessels were taken to Fort Ticonderoga, where they were fitted with equipment for sailing and armed with cannons, swivel guns and given military munitions for active service. The military engineer, Colonel Jeduthan Baldwin, acquainted the commanding officers of each brigade with the work that was expected to be done by that brigade.

TABLE 1

CONTINENTAL ARMED VESSELS ON LAKE CHAMPLAIN (as of August 5, 1776)

Vessel	Captain	Guns	Swivels	Men	Status
Schooner *Royal Savage*	Hawley	12 4-lbs	10	50	Sailed
Sloop *Enterprise*	Smith	12 4-lbs	10	50	Sailed
Schooner *Revenge*	Seaman	4 4-lbs 2 2-lbs	10	35	Sailed
Schooner *Liberty*	Primmer	2 4-lbs 6 2-lbs	8	35	Sailed
Gondola *New Haven*	Mansfield	1 12-lbs 2 9-lbs	8	45	Sailed
Gondola *Providence*	Simonds	3 9-lbs	8	45	Sailed
Gondola *Boston*	Sumner	1 12-lbs 2 9-lbs	8	45	Sailed
Gondola *Spitfire*	Ulmer	3 9-lbs	8	45	Almost rigged
Spanish-built row-Galley not rigged					
Total		**52**	**70**	**350**	

Source: Peter Force, *American Archives,* Series V, Vol. 1, (Washington, D.C.; 1837–1853.) page 797. See: Correspondence, Proceedings, &c., August 6, 1776

Philip Ulmer's brother, George, was among the soldiers with Colonel Paterson's regiment who were involved in construction of buildings at Fort Independence. The barracks and parade ground at Fort Ticonderoga were finished in early September 1776. The breastworks, which included entrenchments, redoubts and other fortifications, were still under construction in November. In accordance with a resolution of the Continental Congress, a general hospital, troop barracks and storage structures were erected on Rattlesnake Hill (also called East Point at the time). The fortified outpost on Rattlesnake Hill was renamed Mount Independence following the reading of the Declaration of Independence by

Colonel St. Clair, the commandant of Fort Ticonderoga.[388] General Gates assigned Dr. Stephen McCrea to serve as the first surgeon of the fleet.[389] The mountain just southwest of Ticonderoga, called Sugar Loaf Hill, was renamed Mount Defiance. Fort Ticonderoga was a strong, star-shaped fort that was erected and surrounded by pickets. In the center of the fort was a square of barracks. Roads and bridges were made under the direction of Lieutenant Colonel John Barrett of the Cumberland County militia from frontier Massachusetts (Maine).[390] On August 9, 1776, Arthur St. Clair was elected as a brigadier general by the Continental Congress, and by the order of Congress, General St. Clair left the Northern Department in November to join General Washington's Continental Army, which was in a retreat southward through New Jersey.[391]

THE FIRST NAVAL BATTLE FOLLOWING THE DECLARATION OF INDEPENDENCE

Upon your arrival at Crown-Point you will proceed with the Fleet of the United States under your Command, down Lake Champlain…It is a defensive War we are carrying on; therefore, no wanton risqué [sic], or unnecessary Display of Power of the Fleet, is at any Time, to influence your conduct…You are to act with such cool determined Valour, as will give them Reason to repent their Temerity.
—Major General Gates's letter to General Arnold
August 7, 1776[392]

Ensign Philip Ulmer, part of Arnold's brigade, was actively involved in the support of Commodore Arnold's naval fleet at Ticonderoga and in training exercises at Crown Point with the little flotilla. The American fleet consisted of three galleys (the *Trumbull*, the *Washington* and the flagship *Congress*, which Arnold had chosen to command prior to the battle), two schooners (the *Revenge* and the *Royal Savage*, which was captured earlier at St. John), two sloops (the *Enterprise* and the *Lee*, which was actually believed to be a cutter) and eight gunboats that were armed gondolas (the *Spitfire*, the *Philadelphia*, the *Providence*, the *Boston*, the *Connecticut*, the *New York*, the *New Jersey* and the *New Haven*). Commodore Arnold, who was familiar with Philip Ulmer's sailing and leadership abilities on the St. Lawrence River in Canada, assigned command of one of the gunboats

The *Spitfire* manifest of Captain Phillip Ulmer, 1776. *National Archives and Records Administration, Washington, D.C.*

to Ulmer, who became the captain of the gondola.[393] Once assigned to command the vessel, Philip Ulmer was thereafter referred to as "Captain" regardless of his official rank. The captain and crew of the vessels were given the choice of naming their own gunboat. They often chose the name of the town or colonial state from which they came. The only oddly named gunboat was the *Spitfire*, which was probably named for the first armed vessel on which Philip Ulmer served and worked. Each gunboat carried three carriage guns and eight swivels and was manned by a crew of forty-five men. They were mostly soldiers from the Northern Army who were drafted to serve as crewmen for the vessels and had little or no experience aboard sailing vessels.[394] Because the proper size cannon was unavailable when it was needed, the *Spitfire* was cut down on the starboard side to accommodate a smaller six-pounder cannon instead of the nine-pounder that it was designed to have.[395*]

---

* *Author's comment*: Philip's brother, George Ulmer, who was with Paterson's regiment, might have served either as a volunteer on the crew of the *Spitfire* or he might have remained at Fort Ticonderoga with his regiment fitting out the sailing vessels. A good guess might be that he served as a volunteer crewman with his older brother aboard the gunboat *Spitfire*, but this scenario is unproven, and his participation might never accurately be known.

On August 24, the American fleet, under command of Commodore General Benedict Arnold, raised their anchors and set sail on a light southerly wind to run down Lake Champlain. By the beginning of September, the American army forces at Fort Ticonderoga and Crown Point were impressed with the rapid assembly of their little naval fleet. The progress in construction of the British naval vessels went more slowly because the materials from England had to be hauled by carts from the St. Lawrence River through the woods and around the Richelieu falls to the docks at Fort St. John for assembly. General Philip Schuyler wrote to John Hancock, president of the Continental Congress, that "We are however so much a Head of the Enemy in our Naval Force, that I do not comprehend they will be able to equal our strength this Campaign…"[396] Others in the Northern Theater agreed with this assessment, including General Horatio Gates and Colonel Anthony Wayne, who had been in Canada as part of General Thomas's brigade. No one in the Northern Command seemed to have any idea how powerful the British and Hessian forces actually were, but that lack of intelligence was soon to change.

Captain Philip Ulmer was engaged in the "sailing-trials" (practice in maneuvering the gondolas and firing the guns) and in reconnaissance duty on Lake Champlain to assess and report the position of the British troops and the building progress of the British fleet at Fort St. John. Learning to work together and how to handle and maneuver the sailing vessels was important for the success of the fleet's mission on Lake Champlain. Changing weather conditions often caused sudden storms and violent squalls on the large lake, and it was important for the inexperienced crewmen to know how to handle their boat under varying weather conditions. At the end of August, there was a violent storm on the lake that swept in from the northeast and threatened the safety of Arnold's fleet. Realizing that the vessels could not weather the storm on the western shore, Arnold sent the order to be ready to sail for the shelter of Button Mould Bay on the eastern shore. The wind picked up suddenly with great force. Arnold fired a gun as the signal to get underway. The schooners and clumsy gondolas weighed anchor and set their sails. General Arnold reported that "the hard gale made an amazeing [sic] Sea."[397] All the vessels except the *Spitfire*, which was closest to the western shore on reconnaissance duty, were able to make their way to open water. The *Spitfire* was driven closer to the rocks on the western shore by the mounting waves and violent gusting winds. The *Spitfire* was left behind to its fate by the desperate naval fleet. General Arnold, the officers and the crewmen held little hope that the *Spitfire* would survive the intense storm.

With the *Enterprise* in the lead, Arnold's naval fleet sailed south on the stiff and blustery northeastern gale past Split Rock and through The Narrows in the attempt to reach the shelter of Button Mould Bay. The straining canvas sails on the *Connecticut*'s rigging proved to be too much, and halfway to the bay, its mast broke with a loud crack and collapsed, covering the bow under torn cordage and canvas sail. The dismasted gondola was taken under tow by the *Revenge*. The *Enterprise* went aground and was stranded in the muddy shallows as it was trying to make its turn into the bay. The *Enterprise* became a marker for the other vessels, which sailed around it and came to anchor in the sheltered bay. Before dusk, the crewmen of the *Enterprise* were able to get the vessel free from the shallows, and they managed to bring the *Enterprise* to anchor with the rest of the fleet at Button Mould Bay. All through the next day, the fleet was kept at anchor by the intense northerly gale winds and driving rain. The crewmen on the gondolas remained huddled beneath their canvas awnings. They found little shelter or protection from the gusting gale winds and blowing rain. Word in some way reached Arnold's anchored flotilla that the *Spitfire* had filled with water and was lost.[398]

General Arnold wrote in a letter to General Gates from Button Mould Bay on August 31, 1776, that, to everyone's amazement, Captain Ulmer of the *Spitfire* had somehow weathered the heavy wind and torrential rainstorm the night before on Lake Champlain. Captain Philip Ulmer surprised everyone in Arnold's fleet when his gunboat and crewmen managed to join the rest of the fleet at Button Mould Bay. Everyone had been certain that the *Spitfire* had been dashed against the rocks and had sunk on the western shore of the lake in the horrific storm. Skillful handling and leadership by Captain Philip Ulmer had made it possible for the gunboat and crewmen to survive. Arnold reported in his letter to Gates that "Captain Ulmer of the *Spitfire* having rode out the Storm, tho [*sic*] exposed to the rake of Cumberland Bay…Fifty miles long, [and] to survive the fifty mile rake of the wind and rain storm on Lake Champlain having lost only their small work boat."[399] Captain Philip Ulmer earned the respect and confidence of General Arnold, the other naval officers and the fleet crewmen. Even after the storm had passed, the fleet stayed at anchor for two more days as the wind continued to blow from the northeast. General Arnold invited all the captains and lieutenants ashore for a social gathering. The officers competed in target practice and developed close comradeships. The officers enjoyed a feast of roast pig, cider, punch and wine, most likely provided by the Ferris family who lived nearby and whom Arnold had known and visited with prior to the war. The officers toasted the Continental Congress and General Arnold. They named the nearby point of land Arnold's Point. The diversion ashore provided a boost in morale and helped develop a spirit of friendship among the fleet's officers. The violent storm on Lake Champlain occurred on August 24, 1776, and was just days before Colonel William Bond, the commander of Philip Ulmer's Twenty-fifth Continental Regiment, died of illness at Mount Independence.[400]

The same storm that almost sank General Arnold's fleet on Lake Champlain had also affected Washington's army troops near Long Island, New York. The storm had prevented the British naval warships in New York Harbor from sailing into the East River and cutting off Washington's troops that were retreating from Brooklyn. During the stormy night, General Washington's army troops were able to retreat across the East River to Manhattan with the help of Colonel John Glover's regiment from Marblehead, Massachusetts. Glover's regiment of skilled mariners was able to save Washington's army from capture and complete destruction. The escape of the American troops was made possible by the same terrible storm that ironically had battered General Arnold's fleet on Lake Champlain.[401] General Arnold's naval fleet knew nothing about the storm event that had also impacted General Washington's army near New York City, to the south.

General Arnold called a strategy meeting with the boat captains in early September to develop information about the British forces on the lake and the vessels being constructed at the British-held fort of St. John. With a fresh breeze, the fleet sailed down the lake on September 3, and the naval vessels came to Cumberland Head in the early afternoon.[402] Several picket gunboats that were sent in advance of the fleet discovered a scouting party of twenty enemy soldiers, and they fired upon them with swivel guns. When riflemen were sent ashore to search for the enemy scouts, they discovered nothing. This was the first indication that enemy forces were in the woods. They soon discovered that the northern end of the lake was swarming with British soldiers, Loyalist Canadians and hostile Indians who were allied with the British forces.

Captain Philip Ulmer had instructed his crew on the *Spitfire* to fashion fascines (bundles of branches tied together) and lash them onto the sides of their gondola in order to protect the men from being fired upon by small arms and from being boarded by the enemy. The crewmen from other vessels also used fascines and small trees as camouflage and lashed them to their gondolas as well. The gunboats could hide from the enemy along the shoreline or near an island and blend in with the wilderness flora. The fascines would give protective coverage to the body of the gunboat and would protect the crewmen from enemy gunfire and Indian arrows while they were working on the deck of the boat.[403] (As a young boy in Waldoboro, Philip had learned many techniques of camouflage for hunting and defensive protection from the local Abenaki Indians. Philip Ulmer had also learned many other valuable survival lessons as a young man from his grandfather John Ulmer Sr. and other relatives who had established a binding peace with the local Indians since the French and Indian War.)[404] General Arnold, observing this method of defensive protection, ordered that other vessels of the flotilla also gather fascines and do the same thing to protect and camouflage their boats as well.[405] On September 5 and 6, the crews of the gondolas went ashore to gather fascines. Arnold ordered that "They were to be fixed on the Bows and Sides of the Gondolas to prevent the Enemies boarding and to keep off small shot."[406] Arnold's little flotilla would be able to camouflage itself and blend in with the wilderness environment and become virtually invisible to the passing enemy bateaux, canoes and British warships.

COMMODORE ARNOLD'S FLEET PREPARES FOR A CONFRONTATION ON LAKE CHAMPLAIN

In Philadelphia on September 9, 1776, the Continental Congress resolved that "[whenever] the words 'United Colonies' have been used, the stile [sic] be altered for the future, to the 'United States.'"[407]

On September 24, Arnold's little naval fleet moved to the protected channel of Valcour Island from their prior location at Isle la Motte to make a stand against the British invasion forces. General Arnold explained in a message to General Gates that "…if the Americans succeeded in their attack, the British could not escape, and if the Americans were bested, their retreat would be 'open and Free.'"[408] The next day, Arnold invited his captains and lieutenants to share dinner and a social gathering with him on Valcour Island. This would enable the officers to bond with one another and develop comradeship and mutual support, as they had done at Button Mould Bay several weeks before. Captain Philip Ulmer and his first mate, Ezekiel Farrow, would have been among the officers at Valcour Island who shared dinner with General Arnold and the other commanders, captains and lieutenants. The officers competed in target practice and again enjoyed roast pig, wine, punch and cider.[409] Lieutenant Bayze Wells of Farmington, Connecticut, recorded in his journal that "the gathering on Champlain's [island] shore was a moft Genteel feaft [feast] and provided a great boost to the esprit de corps for the fleet's officers."[410]

General Arnold had appealed numerous times to General Schuyler and General Gates for greatly needed supplies, for gunpowder and other munitions for the men who were serving with him in his little naval flotilla on Lake Champlain. Arnold complained to General Gates that he needed more qualified and experienced seamen to serve with his fleet. Arnold wrote: "We have but very indifferent men, in general…a great part of those who shipped for Seamen know very little of the matter."[411] Many of Arnold's men began to fall ill from disease and exposure, and he had to send twenty-three men back to Ticonderoga. He pleaded for more men with real sailing experience to be sent immediately to serve with his naval fleet at Valcour Island in preparation for the expected encounter with the British naval forces massing at Fort St. John. A violent and bloody battle was expected to occur at any time. In a plaintive letter sent to General Gates from Valcour Island on October 1, 1776, General Arnold wrote:

Dear General: Last night the Trumbull *arrived here, and Captain Warner delivered me your letter of the 26th ultimo. I was rejoiced to hear she brought a reinforcement of seamen. I expected at least one hundred but was much surprised when Captain Warner informed he had not save his own ship's company. I hope to be excused (after the requisitions so often made) if with five hundred men, half naked, I should not be able to beat the enemy with seven thousand men, well clothed, and a naval force, of the best accounts, near equal to ours. The* Trumbull *is a considerable addition to our fleet, but not half finished or rigged; her cannon are much too small. I wrote in July for cordage sufficient for eight galleys; I then supposed that number would be built. I am surprised at their strange economy or infatuation below* [referring to Congress's lack of money, supplies, seamen and support of the basic needs of the naval troops]. *Saving and negligence, I am afraid, will ruin us at last…*

Enclosed is a list of sundry articles which I have sent Lieutenant Calderwood to bring down, if to be had. Great part of my seamen and marines are almost naked. The weather has been very severe for some time. I don't expect to be able to keep my station above a fortnight longer. We have continual gales of wind, and the duty very severe. I ordered the Captain of the Liberty *to stay no longer than to overhaul his vessel, which might be done in forty-eight hours. I beg you will be kind enough to order him back immediately. If he brings materials his vessel may be done here in a day.* [The *Liberty* did not return to the flotilla with provisions or supplies and was not present at the Battle of Valcour Island.]

This minute Sergeant Stiles is returned from a scout to the Isle-aux-Noix, where he was sent this day week. Enclosed is his examination, by which it appears the enemy are exerting every nerve to augment their navy, doubtless with a design to cross the Lake [Champlain] *this fall or be an over-match for us next spring...*

I am, dear General, your affectionate and obedient humble servant,
To Hon. Major-General Gates From: B. Arnold[412]

The members of Congress continued to argue and posture for political advantage among themselves in spite of repeated requests for support with enlistments, additional carpenters and artificers, as well as other needed material supplies (such as rope, sails, oakum, warm clothing and many other items needed for Arnold's men) and military munitions (cannons, howitzers, arms, gunpowder) for the military generals and troops fighting the war on the ground. The Congress did not respond in a timely way to the needs of the generals, fighting soldiers and volunteers on the front line of conflict. Political posturing and maneuvering among the military officers lobbying for support from congressional members weakened and undermined the military structure. Generals, officers and delegates who were dedicated to the American cause were undermined by jealous and disgruntled underlings seeking power and privileges for themselves. The country had not yet come together in the common cause that was based upon merit, hard work, freedom, liberty and the opportunity to seek one's own destiny in America.

Following the American retreat led by General John Sullivan in June 1776, the British governor in Canada, General Sir Guy Carleton, was determined to pursue the American troops southward from Canada using the water highways through the Lake Champlain and Hudson River Valleys. The strategy was to crush the American rebellion in a fall invasion campaign. The goal of the British fleet was to destroy the little American fleet on Lake Champlain; capture the American-held forts at Crown Point, Ticonderoga, Mount Independence and Mount Defiance; and drive a military wedge down through the heartland of the New York colony from the Canadian border to the Atlantic Ocean. At Fort St. John, the British troops had assembled the largest naval fleet to sail on Lake Champlain. The British Royal Navy consisted of approximately thirty major vessels with about seven hundred experienced seamen. Several days behind this naval force was the combined forces of the British Royal Army and Hessian soldiers with their artillerists and their Indian allies. This was an invading British allied army of approximately seven thousand troops in about four hundred bateaux.[413]

The Battle at Valcour Island

The escape was done with such secrecy that we went through them undiscovered.
—*General Waterbury's report to the president of the Continental Congress, 1776*[414]

The *Royal Savage* had served as General Arnold's flagship for the American fleet up to this time. However, Arnold decided with the impending conflict that the better vessel for him would be the galley *Congress*, although his papers and personal effects remained on the *Royal Savage*. A council of war was called for the night of October 10. General Arnold (commander of the American naval fleet), General David Waterbury (second-in-command) and Colonel Edward Wigglesworth (third-in-command) did not agree upon a strategy for engaging the British naval fleet when the weather and conditions on the lake improved. General Arnold listened to the arguments of Waterbury and Wigglesworth to fight the British forces on the open lake rather than remaining at Valcour Island, where they would be trapped between the island and the New York mainland. The boats could not escape northward around the island due to rocky shoals, hidden underwater boulders and shallow water. Waterbury and Wigglesworth felt that their little fleet of fifteen vessels would be trapped in the narrow channel with no escape. Arnold considered their concerns and made the decision that the American fleet would remain at Valcour Island and engage the British from that location. The strategy was to force the British vessels to fight them in the narrow channel using only a few boats at a time since the channel was difficult for large warships to maneuver. The full fighting force of the little American fleet could be levied upon a couple British warships at a time.[415] General Arnold instructed the captains and first mates to use the lines of their crossed anchors to swing and maneuver their boats to fire the cannons with more accuracy or to deliver a more effective broadside attack. He instructed the officers to make themselves prominent to their men and encouraged them to fight vigorously during the battle.

General Waterbury went aboard Arnold's galley *Congress* early the next morning and called a hasty council of war. He entreated General Arnold that the American fleet ought to immediately set sail and fight the British in the main lake on their retreat to Crown Point. General Arnold was determined to fight within the narrow channel at Valcour Island. He ordered the battle lines to be tightened and told his commanders and captains to prepare for battle. The wind was brisk, and the inclement weather had improved on the lake. The trees were bright with their vibrant autumn colors with hues of red, yellow and orange. The Battle of Valcour Island began on the morning of October 11, 1776, when the alarm-guns were fired by the American scouting boats, which alerted Arnold that the enemy's fleet was approaching off Cumberland Head. The British fleet sailed south with the *Inflexible*, fitted with eighteen guns, followed by two schooners—the *Maria*, with fourteen guns, and the *Carleton*, with twelve guns. They also had the *Thunderer*, which was a huge radeau bristling with heavy weapons; the *Loyal Convert* (also called the *Royal Convert*), which was a large armed gondola; and approximately twenty gunboats and two dozen longboats.[416]

The British Royal Navy sailed in formation past Valcour Island for about two miles. General Arnold ordered that the three galleys—*Washington*, *Trumbull* and *Congress*—as well as the schooner *Royal Savage* be moved out into the open lake. Dr. Robert Knox, the British fleet surgeon aboard the schooner *Carleton*, looked back and saw the Americans' *Royal Savage*.[417] The four American vessels confronted the British fleet by firing upon them. The British had been challenged to a fight! The British warships had to come about, tack and sail into the heavy wind coming from the north. The four American vessels raced back into the protection of the bay, using their sweeps to maneuver, and resumed their defensive positions in the battle line. Arnold barked orders through his speaking horn to the other boat captains, who tensely waited in their defensive line to fire their bow cannons. The schooner *Royal Savage*, like the British warships, was struggling to tack and get to windward, but it ran aground off the southern end of the island while maneuvering to come about.[418] Floundering, the schooner was heavily fired upon at close range by the well-trained British and Hessian artillerymen in gunboats.

The British Royal fleet pressed hard into the heavy north wind and with difficulty drew close to Valcour Island. The hidden American flotilla was discovered arrayed for battle in a crescent formation in the narrow channel behind Valcour Island and the New York mainland on the western side of the lake. General Sir Guy Carleton gave an order to form in battle lines across the southern end of the bay while under the full fire of the American fleet. British lieutenant James Hadden wrote of this battle in his journal:

> *An order was given by the Commanding Officer for the Boats to form across the Bay: this was soon effected tho' under the Enemies whole fire and unsupported, all the King's Vessels having dropped too far to Leeward. This unequal combat was maintained for two Hours without any aid, when the Carleton Schooner of 14 Guns 6Prs got into the Bay and immediately received the Enemies whole fire which was continued without intermission for about an hour, when the Boats of the Fleet expended their Ammunition when they were withdrawn, having sunk one of the Enemies Gondolas, and considerably damaged others...the Boats having received a small supply of Ammunition were unaccountably order's to Anchor under cover of a small Island without the open of the Bay.*[419]

The schooner *Carleton*[420] and the armed British gundelos were forced to engage the American flotilla in the shallow bay. The larger warships could not enter the narrow channel, as General Arnold had foreseen. Except for the *Carleton*, which had sweeps as well as sails, none of the larger British warships with their numerous heavy guns managed to engage in the fighting until late in the day. The constricted and unfamiliar maneuvering space, the hidden rocks and shoals and the heavy gusting wind limited the ability of the British warships to hurl shells a long distance. In time, the billowing smoke of battle made it difficult to distinguish where the opposing boats were maneuvering. The British gunners didn't want to fire upon their own gundelos and crewmen. The point-blank barrage continued until the British gunboats had exhausted their grapeshot, and at that point, the gunboats backed away for several hundred yards and switched to firing solid shot.

With the *Royal Savage* inoperable, Captain David Hawley and many of the crewmen jumped overboard and waded ashore onto Valcour Island.[421] The Mohawk Indians and British soldiers who were ashore on both Valcour Island and on the western shore of the lake kept up a constant firing on the American fleet, but with little damage.[422] The British gunboats turned their fire on the escaping patriot crewmen from the stranded schooner and unwittingly made themselves a target. British lieutenant James Hadden wrote in his journal: "The firing at one object drew us into a cluster and four of the Enemy's Vessels getting under way to support the Royal Savage fired upon the boats with success."[423] Some of the American crewmen from

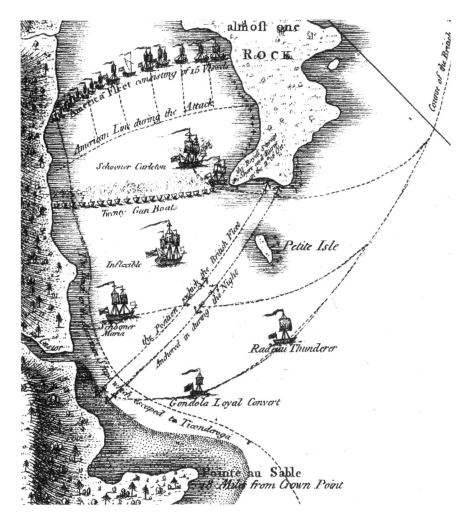

Array of the American and British fleets at Valcour Island on Lake Champlain, October 11, 1776. By artist William Faden. *Courtesy of the Boston Public Library.*

the *Royal Savage* took refuge in a small, cave-like structure among the rocks at the waterline on the southern end of the island. The men in the cave and those hidden in the thick woods above fired upon a large British gondola that had been sent by Sir Guy Carleton to retrieve important papers from the grounded American schooner that had served as General Arnold's flagship prior to the battle. The *Royal Savage* contained General Arnold's important personal papers, military maps, documents and communications, as well as his personal belongings.

The remaining crewmen on the *Royal Savage* and those in nearby gondolas kept up sporadic firing on the *Loyal Convert* as it stubbornly tried to reach the grounded schooner. Those still aboard the schooner quickly fled to the island and continued to shoot down at the approaching vessel from the thick woods above the rock cave. The British boarding party led by Lieutenant Edward Longcroft was determined to take back the *Royal Savage*, which had been previously captured by the American troops. The British sailors grabbed the rammers and sponges abandoned by the Americans, and they turned the *Royal Savage*'s six- and four-pounder broadside guns on the American fleet. Half the men in the British boarding party had been killed by American gunfire. Lieutenant Longcroft and his soldiers abandoned the *Royal Savage*, and they rowed back to the safety of the British lines through a storm of gunfire.[424] Two detachments of Mohawk Indians and one hundred Canadian soldiers under the command of Captain Christopher Carleton (nephew of General Guy Carleton) and Colonel Simon Fraser went ashore on Valcour Island and the western shoreline of New York, respectively, and kept up a constant crossfire upon Arnold's flotilla.[425] The Indians who landed in canoes on Valcour Island proceeded through the woods in an attempt to kill the crewmen of the *Royal Savage*. Guns from American boats near the island and those of the *Congress* sporadically sprayed the woods with gunfire to keep the Indians at bay and to provide cover for the stranded Americans.

During the battle, Captain Philip Ulmer stood out prominently at the stern of the *Spitfire* like the other captains in the little flotilla. Captain Ulmer actively participated throughout the heat of the conflict, giving orders to his crew and encouraging his inexperienced crew to continue to fight vigorously. The thick gunsmoke and loud firing of the swivel guns and cannons were deafening. Captain Ulmer directed the first mate, Ezekiel Farrow, to pull on the anchor ropes with him to swing the gunboat from side to side, enabling the crew to aim and fire the bow and side cannons more effectively. The swivel guns were also made more effective against the smaller British boats that came close within range. Musket fire from the British soldiers and arrows shot by their Indian allies on the New York mainland and on Valcour Island caused additional danger to the crewmen of the small American fleet.[426] The fascines along the bow and sides of the boats gave the men some needed protection from enemy boarding parties, musket fire and Indian arrows. Black smoke from the swivel guns and musket fire burned their eyes and blackened their faces as the men shot at the British gundelos and longboats that came into range of their guns. The clouds of smoke from the cannon fire made it difficult to breathe. Flying grapeshot, bar shot and cannon balls splashed all around the trapped vessels, sometimes sending sprays of cold water onto the men. Captain Philip Ulmer's gunboat *Spitfire*, located near the middle of the crescent formation, received a heavy amount of cannon fire and grapeshot, and the vessel slowly began to take on water. Fear and anxiety mixed with a rush of adrenaline kept the men fighting vigorously against the overwhelming odds and the vigorous gunfire from the British naval vessels. Several beleaguered men rowed in small workboats through the gunfire, collecting the wounded and bringing them to the sloop *Enterprise*, which served as the hospital ship. The journal of Jahiel Stewart, who was aboard the sloop during the battle, recorded that "They brought the wounded abord of us and the Doctors Cut off great many legs and arms and I See Seven men threw overboard that died with their wounds."[427]

The hours passed in thunderous exchanges, and both sides dealt out and absorbed heavy punishment. The very hot engagement continued most of the day until about sunset.[428] Human casualties were severe on both sides. As the fighting tapered off, the heavily damaged gunboat *Philadelphia* filled with water and was sinking. Captain Benjamin Rue and the surviving crew were taken aboard the *Washington* galley, which was heavily damaged, "hulled a Number of Times, her Main Mast Shot thro [through]…both Vessels [*Congress* and *Washington*] are very leaky & want repairing."[429] Several of the American gunboats were barely afloat, and every vessel had sustained damage. General Arnold's fleet had lost the schooner *Royal Savage*, which had run aground at the onset of the engagement, and one gundelo, the *Philadelphia*. The gundelo *New York* had been swept time and again by enemy fire until all the officers were killed except for Captain John Reed. When one of the gunners touched his slow match to the touchhole on the cannon, the barrel exploded, sending shards of thick, hot metal through the closely packed gunboat, injuring and killing many of the crew.

Arnold's flagship *Congress*, which was at the center of the battle line, had been hulled by iron cannonballs nearly twenty times, with seven of those hits at or below the water line.[430] Round shot had gouged two sections from the mainmast and damaged the main yard. Most of the ammunition had been expended on all the vessels, and many experienced gunners and seamen were wounded or dead. The British fleet lost one gunboat and the schooner *Carleton*, which was almost destroyed. Captain Georg Pausch, a German professional artilleryman who was involved in the battle at Valcour Island, wrote in his journal: "The cannon of the Rebels were well served, for as I saw afterwards, our ships were pretty well mended and patched up with boards and stoppers."[431] The bloody engagement had ended in a draw. The

177

British and Hessian forces would be ready the next day for another fight, but the American forces would not.

At dusk, after many hours of heated fighting, Captain Thomas Pringle, commander of the warship *Maria*, made the signal for a recall and ordered the British fleet to form a semicircle to the south of the channel at Valcour Island and the New York mainland.[432] General Carleton ordered the *Royal Savage* to be burned. The Indians on Valcour Island carried out the order and set fire to the stranded schooner.[433] The British vessels withdrew about six hundred or seven hundred yards away and anchored out of range from the rebel fire, but they continued their longer-range cannon firing until darkness started to descend over the lake. Gradually, the *Royal Savage*'s crewmen on Valcour Island, who had fought off the Indians' attacks until darkness, were removed by several small boats and were taken aboard the galley *Washington* and several nearby boats. The injured were taken to the *Enterprise*, the hospital sloop, where Dr. Steven McCrea was kept busy attending to the wounded and dying.

The crackling flames from the *Royal Savage* towered high into the air, sending glowing sparks in all directions. Before long, there were loud explosions from the barrels of gunpowder as the intense fire reached the magazine, which dramatically blew up, carrying away the upper part of the schooner in a massive fireball. The fire continued to burn all night and kept the attention of the British soldiers and the Indians who were still on the island and on the western shore. The exhausted British and Hessian troops who had been engaged in deadly combat most of the day were finally able to rest and sleep in preparation for the anticipated defeat of the American fleet the next day. The British and German forces were so confident of the American flotilla's capture and defeat that scarcely any watchmen were posted during the night.[434] Only the hammering of the repair crew could be heard as they struggled to repair the most severely damaged parts of the vessels in preparation for the battle that was to come when the fog lifted from the lake the next morning.

A council of war was called by Colonel Arnold aboard the *Congress* to determine the status of each ship's damage, injuries and deaths. The munitions and gunpowder situation aboard each vessel was of great concern since two-thirds of their supply of gunpowder had been exhausted during the battle on the first day. There were some reports that indicated that Captain Philip Ulmer received an injury to his leg from flying shrapnel through the side of his wooden gunboat during the intense battle on the first day. It was reported in the journal of one of the officers on the galley that:

"Little Ulmer of the *Spitfire* wore a bandage on his thigh."[435] Captain Ulmer reported that a number of the crewmen on his gunboat were injured, several men had been lost and his ammunition was very low. It was determined by General Arnold, General Waterbury and Colonel Wigglesworth that every vessel's ammunition was nearly three-quarters spent. It was thought that the best decision was to return to the safety of Crown Point.[436] Arnold and his ship captains discussed their situation and developed a strategy for an escape during the cover of darkness. They would make their daring escape between the western mainland on the New York side of Lake Champlain while the British fleet rested at anchor just to the south of Valcour Island. The northerly wind was dying, and that would make it more difficult for the little fleet to go north. It would require the vessels to use their sweeps alone with no sail to assist them. In the darkness, it would be difficult to "feel their way" around the northern end of the island and avoid the submerged boulders, rocks and the shallow shoals. It was decided that the *Trumbull* would lead the way southward along the shoreline and the battered little fleet would proceed past (some reports say *through*) the British fleet. Colonel Wigglesworth wrote: "It being calm, we row'd out clear of the Enemy without being discovered."[437]

The schooner *Royal Savage* was still burning as the battered American fleet got underway. The night was moonless and very dark with thick fog setting over the lake. The burning schooner impaired the night vision of the few British and Hessian guards. The exhausted British and Hessian sailors and artillerymen slept in their quarters, ready to resume the fight if an alarm was given. British captain Pringle had poorly positioned his vessels outside the bay, which enabled the American fleet to slip past the anchored British vessels. Through the night, the constant thundering roar of the British ships' cannons—fired from several hundred yards out of range of the American fleet's guns in Valcour Bay—worked to the advantage of the escaping American vessels.

At approximately eight o'clock in the evening, the orders from General Arnold were given to the captains of the flotilla to prepare to proceed with the daring escape plan. With muffled oars and a shielded lantern light held in the stern of the vessels, the damaged American fleet weighed anchor and quietly made their escape undetected. The *Trumbull*, with Wigglesworth on board, ran out the muffled sweeps and led the way past the British fleet. One by one, the rest of the American fleet followed in a ragged line. The night was cold and moonless as Arnold's men wordlessly manned the long canvas-wrapped sweeps and worked their way through the water, which was strewn with wreckage and dead bodies from the day's battle. The *Trumbull* was followed by the *Enterprise*, which managed to go aground. The sloop was quickly freed, and it got under way again. The *Lee* and the remaining gunboats followed the ragged procession along the western shore. The badly damaged galley *Washington*, commanded by Captain John Thacher, who had been badly injured when the ship's main mast collapsed, with General Waterbury on board, followed the gunboats. The *Congress*, commanded by Captain James Arnold, with General Benedict Arnold on board, was at the rear of the little flotilla. The hungry and exhausted men, who had been locked in deadly combat during the day, rowed and sailed their vessels into the brisk and gusting southerly wind. They were only able to proceed about nine to ten miles up the lake as far as Schuyler Island. The little flotilla anchored and stayed hidden on the mainland side of Schuyler Island to make repairs on their badly damaged vessels. Their camouflaged boats helped them to blend into the woodland environment. Bayze Wells, on board the gunboat *Providence*, wrote of the battle in his journal: "the Enemy Came hard againft [*sic*] us So that we ware Oblig'd to Leve [*sic*] three Gondolas and make the beft [*sic*] of our way with boats…[and they] made thare Efcape [*sic*] this Day by Rowing all night."[438] In a letter to John Hancock, the president of the Continental Congress, General Waterbury wrote of the escape, "It was done with such secrecy that we went through them undiscovered."[439]

After the heavy fog finally lifted in the later part of the morning on the second day, General Guy Carleton, aboard the *Maria*, was in a rage when he discovered that the entire American fleet had escaped. Frustrated and angry, a pursuit was begun in great haste by General Carleton in his flagship, *Maria*. However, Carleton neglected to issue orders to the land forces, and he had to break off his pursuit after sailing several miles and returned to Valcour Island to give the rest of the British forces their orders.[440] The British scouting boats were sent out to pursue the escaping Americans up Lake Champlain, but they had difficulty finding any signs of Arnold's little fleet. The camouflaged American vessels had disappeared. The damaged British naval vessels remained anchored near Valcour Island to make repairs until evening, when the scouting boats returned and reported that the rebel fleet had been sighted. British lieutenant James Hadden wrote of the daring escape by General Arnold's fleet: "This retreat did great honour to Gen'l Arnold who acted as Admiral of the Rebel Fleet."[441]

On the second day, General Arnold's battered fleet tried to put as much distance as possible between themselves and the Indian scouts and British fleet. The objective was to make their way to Crown Point, where the fleet could be resupplied with ammunition, provisions and reinforcements and make another stand. Unfortunately for the galley *Washington*, the sails that had the bolt ropes shot through on the first day of battle could no longer handle the pressure of the wind and gave out entirely. The galley was heavily damaged, taking on water and was in danger of sinking. A message was sent to Arnold about their condition. General Arnold's reply was to sail (as best they could) and row to Schuyler Island, where repairs could be made. The *Trumbull*, which had led the way through the British fleet during the night, passed Schuyler Island and continued south for another six miles, coming to anchor at Ligonier Point. At Ligonier Point, Colonel Wigglesworth decided to wait for the fleet, stop the leaks and sew up the main sail, which had been shot and split in half.[442] The rest of Arnold's little fleet came to anchor at Schuyler Island with the vessels able to sail arriving first. Arnold's fleet remained hidden at Schuyler Island, plugging and repairing leaks on the boats and sewing up the sails of the *Washington* galley. In the meantime, General Arnold wrote a message to General Gates informing him about the action at Valcour Island against the British fleet and about the heavy damage that the American fleet received. The message further stated his intent to proceed to Crown Point as quickly as possible. He requested that ammunition be sent to the fort and a dozen well-manned bateaux be dispatched immediately to help tow the fleet toward Crown Point in case the southerly wind persisted.[443]

On October 12, Benedict Arnold reported in his letter to General Gates from Schuyler Island that "The captain thought it prudent to run her [the *Royal Savage*] on the point of Valcour, where all the men were saved. They boarded her, and night set fire to her. Most of the fleet is underway to Leeward and beating up. As soon as our leaks are stopp'd the whole fleet will make the utmost dispatch to Crown Point, where I beg you will send ammunition & further orders for us. On the whole, I think we have had a fortunate escape."[444] Bayze Wells of Farmington, Connecticut, wrote in his journal that "With boats at Sun Set they [the British] Blow'd up our Schooner and Set her on fire and Seaft [ceased] firing and Retreated."[445] General Arnold wrote to General Schuyler on October 12 that he was happy to be alive: "On the whole, I think we have had a very fortunate escape and have great reason to return our humble and heady thanks to Almighty God for preserving and delivering so many of us from our more than savage enemies."[446]

It was determined at Schuyler Island (about ten miles to the south of Valcour Island on the western side of the lake) that the *Spitfire* was too badly damaged at the waterline to be repaired, and it was rapidly taking on more water. The equipment, swivels and smaller cannon were removed, and Arnold directed that the *Spitfire* should be taken into deeper water and scuttled. Another vessel, the *New Jersey*, was abandoned in shallow water.[447] The crewmen from the *New Jersey* were taken aboard the galley *Washington* with those of the *Philadelphia*.[448] The crewmen from the *Spitfire* were taken on board the *Congress*, Colonel Arnold's row galley and flagship. The crew of the sloop *Lee* abandoned the vessel on the western shoreline.[449] (The *Lee* and the *New Jersey* were recovered by the British and later used for service on the lake.) General Arnold's exhausted men had not slept or eaten for more than thirty hours. They had fought desperately and valiantly for six hours without intermission on the first day of battle. They had spent the entire night of October 11 sailing and rowing against a brisk southern wind to escape from the British fleet and their allies. Arnold did not want to remain any longer than necessary at Schuyler Island.

The weather on October 12 was blustery and cold with a rain/sleet mixture. The windswept lake had choppy waves with white caps and turbulent currents. The men of Arnold's fleet were wet, cold, hungry and exhausted from lack of sleep after their long day and night ordeal of trying to stay alive and escape from the enemy. The sailing vessels *Revenge* and *Enterprise*, whose men had not done as much rowing as those in the gunboats (gondolas), would have been the first of the American vessels to get underway again. They caught up to the *Trumbull*, still at anchor at Ligonier Point, around sunset. The galley *Congress* was underway around two o'clock in the afternoon, but the galley *Washington* was unable to get underway until sunset. The *Washington* had received such severe damage during the first day of battle that it continued to slowly wallow through the lake water in an effort to catch up with the rest of the fleet. The gunboats, which were lightly made from green timber, were slowly coming apart. They had to be mostly rowed into the brisk southerly wind through the night (their second night at the sweeps) in order to catch up with the rest of the fleet that was headed for Split Rock to regroup.

Around midnight, the gunboat *Boston* caught up with and passed the galley *Trumbull*, still at anchor and making repairs. An hour later, the gunboat *Providence* caught up with the galley at Ligonier Point, and Captain Isaiah Simonds informed Colonel Wigglesworth that "…the Enemy had pursued us & had taken 1 gondola, Capt. Grimes [of the *New Jersey*]."[450] * The galley

---

* *Author's comment*: This report was inaccurate, since the *New Jersey*, which had been rapidly taking on water, was abandoned by its American crewmen at Schuyler Island and was not recovered by the British for another day.

Trumbull finally got underway about one thirty in the morning and headed toward Split Rock. The brisk wind from the south increased in intensity causing a heavy chop on the lake, making it very difficult for Arnold's little fleet to sail and row into the heavy wind. The little fleet slowly made their way into the persistent headwinds toward the safety of Crown Point. The same southerly wind conditions that were hampering Arnold's fleet in their flight toward Crown Point were also frustrating the British pursuit. Finally, the violence of the wind and the swells of water forced the British fleet to come to anchor. The American fleet was in view, but the weather conditions made it unsafe to continue the pursuit.

During the night, the wind decreased and enabled Arnold's desperate little fleet to make some progress. About an hour after sunrise, the British fleet was sighted moving quickly up the lake. The shift in the wind from the north enabled the British fleet to set sail and make rapid headway down the lake in their pursuit of Arnold's battered fleet. All through the morning hours of October 13, the persistent little American fleet continued to struggle southward toward Split Rock. General Arnold's galley *Congress* caught up with the *Enterprise*, whose crew had all manned the oars with three men to each oar. General Arnold ordered the sloop to proceed with haste and to try to reach the safety of Crown Point with the sick and injured.[451] The *Congress* managed to proceed to about twenty-eight miles north of Crown Point, and the *Trumbull* was ahead of them. Colonel Wigglesworth reported that "In the morning on Sunday, the 13th, the Hospital Sloop & Revenge were ahead & the two galleys in the rear & the rest of the gondolas rowing up the Shore & the Enemy's fleet in chase of us, the wind dying away."[452] Arnold sent a small boat to the *Trumbull* and ordered Wigglesworth to wait for the rest of the fleet so that the galley's guns could give protection and support to the gunboats. The galley *Washington* had spent the entire night rowing and sailing up the lake, and it was still taking on more water. At sunrise, the *Washington* had made little progress, and it was two miles astern of the galley *Congress*. The rest of the fleet were scattered over a distance of seven miles as the desperate little fleet struggled to reach the safety of Crown Point.[453]

On October 13, just twelve miles to the north, the British fleet was experiencing a favorable northern breeze that was driving them rapidly toward the retreating American fleet. The galley *Washington*, which was listing badly to the side and rapidly taking on water, observed the British warships bearing down on them. General Waterbury dispatched a boat to General Arnold to ask permission to send the *Washington*'s wounded men up to Fort Ticonderoga by boat and then run the galley ashore and blow it up.[454] General Arnold sent back word that Waterbury should not destroy his ship, but they should to try to sail to Split Rock as soon as possible and the fleet would make a stand against the British forces there. Unfortunately for the *Washington*, the northerly winds soon brought the British fleet within range of the badly damaged American galley. The British schooners and the *Inflexible* were too fast for the *Washington*. The water-logged galley was about five miles south of Split Rock before the enemy overtook the *Washington* and began firing into it. General Waterbury could not fight back because he had brought the vessel too close to the eastern shore of the lake and could not maneuver.

Three British vessels surrounded the galley *Washington*, and after a short encounter with broadsides, General Waterbury had to "strike their colors," and he surrendered the galley to the British warships *Maria*, *Carleton* and *Inflexible* that surrounded the vessel. The *Washington* was badly damaged, with its first lieutenant dead and Captain John Thacher and the sailing master severely wounded.[455] The *Washington* had taken such a beating that the damaged sides of the galley would not sustain the recoil of the cannons. General Waterbury reported that the *Washington* galley was "so torn to pieces that it was almost impossible to keep her above the water; my sails was [*sic*] so shot that carrying sail split them from foot to head."[456] General Arnold would later report to General Schuyler that "the *Washington* Galley was in such shattered Condition and had so many Men killed and wounded she struck to the Enemy after receiving a few broadsides."[457] The British took the 110 crewmen and officers of the *Washington* as prisoners of war. After repairs were made to the damaged galley, the British navy put it back into service as a transport vessel for the British troops.[458] (The British prisoners' list indicated that most of the crewmen of the *Philadelphia* had been transferred to the galley *Washington* after the loss of their gunboat [gundelo] at Valcour Island.) Just before General David Waterbury's surrender, Captain Benjamin Rue and sixteen of his men from the *Philadelphia* escaped over the side of the galley *Washington* and fled to the shore in a bateau, unmolested by the British troops. Captain Benjamin Rue and his men made their way by foot to Fort Ticonderoga.[459]

The galley *Congress* with Captain Philip Ulmer and his marines on board was about two miles ahead of the galley *Washington*. The *Congress*, following the eastern shoreline, now became the focus of the British warships' heaviest gunfire. The British schooner *Maria*, the fastest and the least damaged vessel, came upon the *Congress* first. The *Maria* fired grapeshot and round shot into the battered galley, and soon several other British vessels entered into the fight as well. The *Congress* was quickly surrounded, but General Arnold and the men on the galley put up a heroic fight. British firepower tore to pieces the galley's rigging and sails, and grapeshot killed many crewmen, gunners, the first lieutenant and several other officers.[460] There was a running gun battle between the British warships, the galley *Congress* and the four remaining gunboats that were locked in mortal combat for two and a half hours.[461] The warship *Inflexible*, which carried eighteen guns and was the largest of the British fleet, and the two armed schooners *Maria* and *Carleton* paid special attention to the galley *Congress*. Two enemy vessels were under its stern and one on its broadside. Rounds of heavy cannon fire and grapeshot were hurled at the *Congress*. Cannonballs crashed through the wooden hull and the sides of the ship, killing many men, and a number of shots hit at the waterline. The sails and rigging were shredded, and the hull was soon shattered from the heavy pounding from the British broadsides. It was a wonder that the *Congress* was still able to remain afloat and was able to fight for hours against such terrible odds. The skill of the ship's captain kept the *Congress* afloat and fighting. Captain Philip Ulmer might have been the acting captain at this time since he was the only experienced maritime officer still unharmed and capable of sailing the row galley. General Arnold knew and trusted Captain Ulmer's sailing abilities and experience under wartime conditions. General Arnold was kept busy aiming the cannons for firing since the surviving crewmen were inexperienced with the guns.[462]

The schooner *Carleton* had been battered and damaged from the fighting on the first day at Valcour Island, but the *Maria* and the *Inflexible* were in decent shape, and their crews were fairly rested and ready to fight. The *Congress*, however, was badly damaged, and the galley's crewmen had endured days of demanding exertion and deprivation with little or no sleep or food. General Arnold reported that all three British vessels were within musket shot or point-blank range of their heavy guns. As the running gun battle continued through "The Narrows" of the lake, the cannons and swivel guns were hotly blazing away. The *Congress* tacked and brought its broadsides into action. The exhausted men on the galley pulled on the ropes and tackles, and they managed to run their guns out of the gun ports that had been chewed up by enemy broadsides. Grapeshot whistled past the men, and solid iron cannonballs slammed into the hull of the *Congress*. British firepower tore the rigging and sails to pieces, and grapeshot killed the first lieutenant and several other ranking officers.[463] The remnants of the American fleet, locked in deadly combat with their guns blazing, continued south along the eastern shore of Lake Champlain and toward Button Mould Bay. Four more armed vessels in the British fleet joined the British warships in the running gun battle against the *Congress*, during which time the acting captain sailed the wounded vessel nearly nine miles, from Split Rock toward Button Mound Bay and Ferris Bay just to the south.[464] Battling their way up the lake, the *Congress* overtook the four American gondolas: the *Boston*, the *Providence*, the *New Haven* and the *Connecticut*. The gunboats (gondolas) were swept up in the running gun battle, and they found themselves hopelessly outgunned and caught up in a disastrous situation. The horrific sights of death and destruction that the crew and officers with General Arnold experienced, the feelings of intense fear, the deafening sounds of cannon fire and the choking smell of gunpowder would remain with these brave men for the rest of their lives.

The little American fleet had sustained such damage during the running gun battle that General Arnold realized further resistance was impossible with his riddled and sinking vessels.[465] Determined that he and his soldiers would not surrender, General Arnold ordered that the fleet should head for the eastern shore and run the vessels ashore at Ferris Bay. While Arnold aimed the cannons for firing, the acting captain directed the men handling the sweeps to prepare for an emergency maneuver to free the galley from the punishing crossfire of the British vessels. On a given order, the oarsmen and those not firing the guns pulled hard on the sweeps in the opposite direction. They were able to clear the galley *Congress* from the punishing British crossfire and enable it to get free. The galley made its turn toward the small, half moon–shaped cove at the southern end of Button Mould Bay near the Ferris farmhouse where there was a small beach area. Arnold knew the area well from earlier visits on Lake Champlain with the Ferris family the year before. The *Congress* and the four remaining gondolas headed for the protection of Ferris's cove. The water was too shallow for the larger British ships to pursue the escaping Americans. The *Congress* brought up the rear of this action, continuing to fire the guns at the British vessels to protect the disembarkation of the men from the smaller American gunboats. Arnold ordered that the cannons were to be dumped overboard and the vessels destroyed.[466]

Captain Philip Ulmer would have remained with General Arnold on the *Congress* until directed to disembark. The remaining crewmen from the battered *Congress* and those from the gunboat *Spitfire* who were working as part of the crew on the *Congress* slipped over the side of the ship, taking their small arms, supplies and wounded crewmen with them. The sails and ropes were cut from the masts and used as slings to lower the wounded men into the arms of the waiting soldiers below in the water. The slings were then used as litters to carry the injured men through the woods with the escaping soldiers and lake residents. The *Spitfire* crewmen (mostly marines) mounted the ridge above the small beach where they had come ashore, and they took defensive action to cover the escaping Americans from the continued gunfire from the British warships. The marines with Officer Nathaniel Cushing and with the sergeant of marines, James Cushing[467] (Nathaniel's younger brother), covered the retreat from the rise above the beach. The Indians with the British forces had been put ashore above Button Mould Bay to pursue, capture or kill the escaping American soldiers and lake settlers. These Indian allies from the Great Lakes region with Mohawk chief Joseph Brant's braves continued to shoot at the exhausted survivors and tried to set a trap for them. The Indians were able to capture a few of the men, whom they tied up, gagged and dragged away. Except in rare cases, the captive Americans were never seen again. Philip Ulmer and the militia marines returned gunfire at the pursuing British and Indian troops while covering the exhausted survivors and settlers in their escape through the woods toward the safety of Crown Point.

The captains of the four gunboats set them on fire. General Arnold was the last to leave the galley *Congress*, setting it on fire as he disembarked. Arnold climbed along the bowsprit and dropped into the water. He waded ashore and scrambled up the sandy rise to the top crest of the hill, where Captain Philip Ulmer and the marines covered his retreat. The burning American ships, with their flags "Appeal to Heaven" and "Don't Tread on Me" still flying, sent flames high into the air.[468] When the magazine with the remaining gunpowder and munitions caught fire, there was a loud explosion that sent shrapnel in all directions. Unfortunately, one of the wounded officers was accidentally left on board the galley. When the fire reached the magazine, the galley exploded, and an officer's body was thrown high into the air, much to the surprise and horror of the fleeing settlers, the American troops and General Arnold. General Arnold ordered that the remains of the officer's body, Lieutenant Ephraim Goldsmith, be collected and buried with honor before continuing the retreat to Crown Point. Squire Ferris, whose family lived in a house near the bay where the American troops reassembled, stated: "To the credit of Arnold, he showed the greatest feeling upon the subject and threatened to run the gunner through on the spot."[469] James Wilkinson wrote of General Arnold during the Canadian campaign and the battle on Lake Champlain, where he described Arnold's landing at Ferris's Bay in his journal:

Arnold set the ships on fire, but ordered the colours [sic] not to be struck, and as they grounded, the marines were directed to jump overboard, with their arms and accoutrements, to ascend a bank about twenty-five feet elevation, and form a line for the defence [sic] of their vessels and flags against the enemy, Arnold being the last who debarked. The enemy did not venture into the cove, but kept a distant cannonade until our vessels were burnt to the water's edge, after which Arnold commenced his march to Crown Point about fifteen mile distant, by a bridle way through an unsettled wilderness.[470]

The British ships continued to fire at the escaping American soldiers and frightened settlers as they took shelter in the forest. The ragged line of survivors gathered at the Ferris farmhouse and quickly started southward through the dense woods following a bridle trail toward Crown Point about ten miles away. The Kelloggs were also lake settlers who lived near the Ferris family, and they had entertained Arnold as a guest previously.[471] The Kellogg family had heard the thundering of the guns and had observed the running gun battle on the lake. They tried to make their escape from Button Mould Bay in a small boat, but unfortunately, they were caught in the crossfire between the opposing enemy forces. The family made a hasty retreat to the nearest point of land and scurried into the woods, taking refuge at the Ferris farm. The American marines, soldiers and crewmen hurried the wounded men from the shore and into the woods for safety as enemy gunfire continued to be hurled at them. The escaping Americans carried and dragged the injured men using their clothing or makeshift cloth litters cut from the ships' sails and bound with rope and cordage from their vessels. They regrouped near the Ferris farmhouse and quickly made their way toward Crown Point, led by the Ferris men. The Indian allies who had been put ashore above Button Mould Bay tracked the fleeing American troops and frightened lake settlers through the woods. They tried to set a trap for the escaping soldiers and settlers, but it was unsuccessful. The Indians continued to pursue, harass and shoot at them all the way to Chimney Point at the southern end of Lake Champlain. They crossed over Wood Creek in ferry boats, small fishing boats and canoes, and they made their way to Crown Point.

The ragged, exhausted soldiers with the lake settlers arrived at Crown Point at four o'clock the morning of October 14. The sloop *Enterprise*, the schooner *Revenge*, the galley *Trumbull* and the *New York*, which had arrived the day before carrying the wounded and some gear from the battle at Valcour Island, were found anchored at Crown Point. It was determined that Crown Point was not going to be able to sufficiently care for the wounded, hungry and exhausted soldiers, nor could it be properly defended by the fleet survivors and lake refugees from the approaching British Royal Navy. It was decided that the fort would have to be abandoned by the defending American troops. The breastworks at Crown Point were by no means formidable, and they were destroyed. The remaining stores and munitions were removed or destroyed, and the fort was set on fire. The exhausted fleet survivors, the American troops stationed at the fort and lake refugees moved southward toward Fort Ticonderoga. It was reported that smoke and the glow from the flames could be seen as far as Fort Ticonderoga, about fifteen miles away.

The general report of the returning fleet survivors read: "Fort Ticonderoga and Fort Independence were awakened to 3 alarm guns fired from the outpost at Crown Point to confirm the British were advancing. The American fleet remnants reached Fort Ticonderoga by evening with more than 100 residents of the Champlain Valley. Thomas Hartley's detachment brought up the rear after destroying the fortifications at Crown Point and carried off all the horses, cattle, and supplies."[472] The orders issued on the morning of October 14, 1776, at Fort Ticonderoga thanked General Arnold and the men of the fleet for their "gallant defence of American liberties." General Gates believed that "such magnanimous behavior would serve to establish the fame of the American army thro [throughout] the globe." The little fleet had done its part by delaying the powerful British and Hessian forces until the winter weather had made its presence known. Now it was the army's turn to prove itself "whorthy [worthy] of the noble cause that they are engag'd to defend."[473]

Dr. Stephen McCrea, surgeon to the American fleet, was so engrossed in caring for the wounded "of our ruined navy" that it was not possible to send Dr. Jonathan Potts, who was located at the Fort George hospital at Lake George, an accounting of the battle except to state that the action was "as bloody as unfortunate." Reverend Ammi Robbins, a Connecticut chaplain who served with the American army in 1776, visited the wounded and was overcome by the "horrible spectacle." It was only with the "greatest reluctance" that he "concented [sic] to accompany the wounded on their journey to Fort George hospital."[474]

An evaluation at the end of the engagement showed that the British forces had captured only the galley *Washington*, the *Lee* and the gunboat *New Jersey*. The American fleet had lost one schooner, two galleys and seven gunboats (gondolas); ten vessels were lost out of a fleet of fifteen ships. The killed and wounded numbered between eighty and ninety men; more than twenty of the casualties were on Arnold's flagship *Congress*. In describing the conduct of General Arnold and the men who fought in the three-day battle on Lake Champlain, General Horatio Gates aptly described the situation as it truly was. In a letter to General Schuyler on October 15, 1776, he wrote, "...few Men ever met with so many hair Breadth Escapes in so short a space of time...and that upwards of 200 with their Officers escaped with Genl Arnold..."[475]

The British acknowledged "that no man ever manoeuvred [*sic*] with more dexterity, fought with more bravery or retreated with more firmness, than Arnold did on both of these occasions."[476]

The British historian Sir George Otto Trevelyan, in his writing *American Revolution*, stated: "His [Arnold's] fellow countrymen repaid his frankness with almost universal approbation (admiration). Arnold's leadership and courage under fire were an inspiration to all of his militia soldiers."[477]

TABLE 2

AMERICAN SHIPS AT THE BATTLE OF VALCOUR ISLAND

SHIP	TYPE	GUNS	CAPTAIN	RESULT
Boston	Gun Boat	3	Job Sumner	Grounded in Ferris Bay; burned October 13, 1776
Congress	Row Galley	8	James Arnold (with General Arnold)	Grounded in Ferris Bay; burned October 13, 1776
Connecticut	Gun Boat	3	Joshua Grant	Grounded in Ferris Bay; burned October 13, 1776
Enterprise	Sloop	12	Reuben Dickinson	Hospital ship, escaped
Lee	Row Galley	6	Robert Davis	Ran aground October 13, 1776; captured by British

SHIP	TYPE	GUNS	CAPTAIN	RESULT
New Haven	Gun Boat	3	Samuel Mansfield	Grounded in Ferris Bay; burned October 13, 1776
New Jersey	Gun Boat	3	Moses Grimes	Captured by British and reused
New York	Gun Boat	3	John Reed	Captured by British
Philadelphia	Gun Boat	3	Benjamin Rue	Damaged and sank near Valcour Island on October 11, 1776; raised in 1935 and on display at the Smithsonian Institution in Washington, D.C.
Providence	Gun Boat	3	Isaiah Simonds (Simmons)	Blown up by the crew on October 12
Revenge	Sloop	8	Isaac Seaman	Escaped
Royal Savage	Schooner	12	David Hawley	Ran aground on Valcour Island and burned October 11, 1776
Spitfire	Gun Boat	3	Philip Ulmer	Badly damaged October 11; sank October 12 near Schuyler Island. Crew members transferred to the galley *Congress*.
Trumbull	Row Galley	10	Seth Warner (with Wigglesworth)	Escaped
Washington	Row Galley	10	John Thacher (Thatcher) (with Waterbury)	Damaged October 11; captured by British October 13, 1776, and reused

After the Battle at Valcour Island on Lake Champlain

The British warships sailed to Crown Point and anchored with the American captives who had been taken during the Lake Champlain engagement on board. While they waited on board the ships, Sir Guy Carleton had the British troops repair some of the fortifications at Crown Point. He moved his headquarters from his flagship *Maria* to Crown Point, where he set up his military headquarters on October 25, 1776.[478] After many days of negotiations between the American and British envoys, the American prisoners, who numbered about 110 men, were released on parole to return to their homes. It was made very clear that if the paroled Americans engaged in any future fighting against the British forces before they were released from their parole by an exchange of prisoners, they would be put to death immediately if recaptured. Officers were generally considered to be valuable pawns of war in the delicate diplomatic dance of political leverage and prisoner arbitration. They were usually held as prisoners of war by their captors until there was a formal agreement and prisoner exchange for British officers. Upon receiving parole at Crown Point from General Carleton, a flag of truce was sent to Fort Ticonderoga that was in the charge of British captain Sir James Craig. With Captain Craig were the paroled American prisoners and General Waterbury. The paroled injured soldiers were sent to the hospital at Fort Independence; however, they were kept separate from the rest of the regular continental and militia soldiers at the fort. There were several officers, like Captain John Thacher, who were held by the British for a later parole and exchange of prisoners. The majority of the paroled soldiers were hurried along toward Skenesboro the same night they were released. The American parolees were sent to their homes by different routes, and they were not reunited with their fellow soldiers at Fort Ticonderoga, whose morale was very low at this time.

There had been sixty-eight men who had come to Fort Ticonderoga as carpenters from the Connecticut militia with Brigadier General Waterbury and Captain John Thacher. They had been aboard the galley *Washington* when it was captured.[479] The rest of the men taken captive aboard the *Washington* had previously been crewmen of the gundelo *Philadelphia*.[480] During the three-day battle on the lake, Captain John Thacher had been severely injured by the fallen center mast aboard the galley *Washington*.[481] Generals Carleton and Burgoyne were so impressed by the courage of Captain John Thacher during the battle that out of respect for his bravery, one of General Burgoyne's personal surgeons was commissioned to attend to Thacher's injuries, and Burgoyne returned Thacher his sword.[482] His legs were badly mangled, leaving him lame for the rest of his life. (He later lost one of his legs.) Captain Thacher remained a British captive and was held as a prisoner of war with several other officers at Mount Royal in Montreal, Canada, until a future prisoner exchange could be arranged. He was later exchanged with other American officers and prisoners of war on Long Island on August 15, 1778.[483]

General Sir Guy Carleton landed a force of British army soldiers at Crown Point and immediately occupied both the east and west shores of Lake Champlain. He had planned to proceed at once against Fort Ticonderoga the next day, but on October 15, a strong wind sprang up and for eight days blew so hard that the British ships were wind-bound, and the fleet had to remain anchored at Crown Point while the British hoped the weather conditions would change. These days were of great value to the American troops at Fort Ticonderoga. General Gates, who was commander of the ground forces in the region, had assembled about twelve thousand men. While Sir Guy Carleton and the British forces were delayed at Crown Point due to bad weather, the American troops surrounded the works at Fort Ticonderoga with strong abatis (felled trees with sharpened branches pointing outward toward the enemy), and they made carriages and mountings for forty-seven cannons. An attack was expected to occur at any time, and the soldiers were kept on ready alert.

General Carleton ordered three of his largest ships to anchor at Chimney Point on the eastern shore of the lake tributary across from Crown Point. Farther to the south at Putnam's Point, not far from Fort Ticonderoga, a body of light infantry, grenadiers and some Canadians and Indians were encamped. The woods were filled with reconnaissance parties of British troops and their allies, who fanned out and scouted as far south as Lake George. On October 20, the captured American galley *Washington* was back in the service of the British fleet on Lake Champlain. It had been taken to Fort St. John, where repairs had been made at the shipyard. The name had not been changed because the British, metaphorically speaking, felt that it was the British way of sticking their finger in the eye of General Washington. Besides, Washington's naval fleet had been a thorn in the side of the British for some time, and the capture of the galley named for Washington was sweet revenge.

The *Washington* galley carried General Burgoyne from Fort St. John to Isle aux Noix, and the next day the *Washington* carried German general

Friedrich Riedesel and General Burgoyne from Isle aux Noix to Crown Point.[484] General Riedesel, commander of the Hessian forces in America, accompanied General Sir Guy Carleton on this expedition into American territory.[485] On the morning of October 27, a few British bateaux crowded with soldiers approached Fort Ticonderoga. Gunfire was exchanged with the shore batteries. General Riedesel recorded in his journal the probing of the British and German advance forces around Fort Ticonderoga and of the American defenses and fortifications there.[486] Five large transports landed with a detachment of soldiers at Three Mile Point, and two armed gunboats approached the eastern shore near Fort Ticonderoga. Another party of British troops was sent into a small bay about four miles below the breastworks of the fort. General Gates ordered American defenses to be manned and directed that the three regiments from Mount Independence should reinforce the main garrison at Fort Ticonderoga.[487] Two of the regiments stationed at Mount Independence were regiments in which Philip Ulmer, his brother, George, and Nathaniel and James Cushing were active soldiers and marines with Colonel Bond's and Colonel Paterson's troops. A great show of American troop strength and military power would give the British and Hessian forces cause to rethink their invasion strategy this late into the year. Colonel John Trumbull of Connecticut wrote of this episode in his journal. The entry stated that "Ticonderoga must have had a very imposing aspect that day when viewed from the lake. The whole summit of cleared land on both sides of the lake, was crowned with redoubts and batteries, all manned with a splendid show of artillery and flags. Our appearance was indeed so formidable, and the season so far advanced, that the enemy withdrew without making any attack...The number of our troops under arms (principally militia) exceeded 12,000."[488]

Having learned to his satisfaction that the Americans were capable of making a spirited defense at Ticonderoga, General Sir Guy Carleton withdrew his forces and returned to Crown Point in the late afternoon. The Americans had not fortified Crown Point, and he estimated that it would require at least 1,100 men working for six weeks to make it ready as an outpost for winter.[489] Sir Guy Carleton made preparations to retire to Canada and prepare for an invasion into the heart of New England the next year. The rear guard of the British army left Crown Point on November 3, and the same day Crown Point was reoccupied by the American forces. General Gates wrote a letter to the Continental Congress on November 5, 1776, informing them of the British withdrawal from Ticonderoga. The statement read:

I have the honor to congratulate Congress upon the retreat of Lieutenant-General Sir Guy Carleton, with the fleet and army under his command, from Crown Point, Saturday last…Your Excellency's most obedient, humble servant,
—Horatio Gates.[490]

With the departure of General Sir Guy Carleton and the British and Hessian forces, General Horatio Gates dismissed the militia and departed for New Jersey with most of the regular troops to join Washington's Continental Army. General Anthony Wayne was left in command of Fort Ticonderoga.[491]

General Riedesel noted in his journal the fact that on passing the bay where Arnold's boats were scuttled and burned, he observed British troops engaging in raising the cannons and other sunken war matériel.[492] Sir Guy

General Sir Guy Carleton. Artist unknown. *Courtesy of the Library of Congress.*

Carleton was criticized for not attacking Fort Ticonderoga at this time. As a result of the British naval triumph over Arnold's little naval fleet on Lake Champlain in October 1776, General Sir Guy Carleton was made a Knight of the Bath, and Captain Douglas of the *Isis* was made a baronet.

IMPORTANCE OF THE NAVAL CAMPAIGN ON LAKE CHAMPLAIN IN OCTOBER 1776

What this American defeat on Lake Champlain really won for the national cause is best told by Admiral Alfred Mahan, a famous American author, naval strategist and naval historian.[493] He wrote in his article "The Naval Campaign of 1776 on Lake Champlain":

That the Americans were strong enough to impose the capitulation of Saratoga was due to the invaluable year of delay, secured to them in 1776

by their little navy on Lake Champlain, created by indomitable energy and handled with indomitable courage of Benedict Arnold and his brave men. That the war spread from America to Europe, from the English Channel to the Baltic, from the Bay of Biscay to the Mediterranean, from the West Indies to the Mississippi…is traceable through Saratoga, to the rude flotilla which in 1776 anticipated the enemy in the possession of Lake Champlain…Considering its raw material and the recency of its organization, words can scarcely exaggerate the heroism of the resistance which undoubtably depended chiefly upon the personal military qualities of the leaders…The little American navy on Lake Champlain was wiped out, but never had such a force, big or small, lived to better purpose or died more gloriously, for it had saved the lake for that year. Whatever deductions may be made for blunders and for circumstances of every character, which made the British campaign in 1777 abortive and disastrous, and so led directly to the American alliance with France in 1778, the delay, with all that it involved, was obtained by the lake campaign of 1776.[494]

SUMMARY OF THE BATTLE ON LAKE CHAMPLAIN

Under General (and Commodore) Arnold's encouragement, the construction of the first American naval fleet was built at Skenesboro, New York, in the summer of 1776 under the supervision of General Waterbury. General Schuyler worked hard to facilitate and provide the supplies and needs of the shipbuilders, artificers and soldiers at Fort Ticonderoga and Skenesboro. General Schuyler and General Arnold were frustrated by Congress's indecisiveness and lack of support—financially, militarily and materially—which jeopardized the mission that the Continental Congress had authorized some months before. Congress's ultimate lack of support and direction at the appropriate time cost the lives of countless soldiers, marines and seamen, as well as the mission that the Congress had previously set forth as being critically important to the success of the United Colonies.

The three-day naval engagement on Lake Champlain, which began with the battle at Valcour Island, occurred on October 11–13. This engagement was the first official naval battle after the Continental Congress declared the country's independence from Great Britain on July 4, 1776. This little-known naval engagement on Lake Champlain has been overlooked in history because of Benedict Arnold's later treachery when he changed his allegiance to the side of the British forces. However, the strategic importance of Lake Champlain as the northern gateway for commerce, trade and transportation from Canada by way of the St. Lawrence River into the heart of the American colonies cannot be overstated. The three-day conflict on Lake Champlain in October 1776 was an important mission because it successfully delayed the British allied forces from invading the American colonies for one crucial year. If General Carleton had continued his southern invasion offensive from Canada with his powerful combined allied forces into the heartland of colonial resistance, the British forces would most likely have been successful in dividing the thirteen colonies in half, and the American Revolution would have been quickly quashed.

General Arnold's small flotilla of brave men bought General Washington and the Continental Congress the time needed to rally support in the public sector, to acquire financial backing for the army, to gather military strength and material resources and to build up an army and naval force that made it possible for a successful engagement at Saratoga the following year. The Battle of Saratoga would become the turning point in America's struggle for freedom from Great Britain. America's success at Saratoga brought about the support and involvement of France, Spain and the Netherlands in America's struggle for independence from the domination and repressiveness of the British Empire. Without the heroic efforts of General Arnold's small naval fleet on Lake Champlain in delaying the combined British allied invasion forces in October 1776, the history of the United States of America would have been very different.

Perhaps one of the most important lessons learned from the Canadian campaign with Arnold's expedition to Canada in 1775 was that it validated General Washington's need for a professional army. Most of the new army recruits after January 1, 1777, agreed to serve for three years or for the duration of the war. This new policy made it possible to create a force of trained soldiers and experienced regiments and to plan long-range objectives and reach designated goals. Congress began to understand that the short-term companies of militiamen would leave the field of engagement as soon as their enlistments of days, weeks or several months were completed. This older method of short enlistments jeopardized any long-term military planning, combat strategy or war effort. Congressional legislators with little or no wartime experience were ineffectual in conducting the war from their desks. The Continental Congress learned that it had to trust and depend upon the decisions of the generals and officers in the field of conflict. The war needed to be conducted in smaller, more concentrated engagements using hit-and-run guerrilla warfare techniques. The enemies' communications routes and military supply lines needed to be stretched to the breaking point. In this way, the much larger, more powerful British forces with their superior arms, firepower and troop strength could be systematically worn down, and their goods and supplies could be confiscated and used by the Continental Army forces. By cutting off needed supplies to the British forces on land and sea and intermittently attacking smaller enemy scouting parties and detached companies, the British and Hessian army's morale and troop strength would be weakened and undermined. Newspaper reports of successful American military engagements, even small ones, would reshape public opinion in England and in other European countries. The disruption of commerce and world trade would cause an added financial strain on the London Exchange and would cause the faltering economy in Great Britain to affect all parts of British society. A European controversy about the validity and the techniques of warfare in North America began to change the attitudes of many people around the world who had once supported England's markets and military dominance. These factors became effective strategy tools that, over time, would help in hastening the end of war in America.

Chapter 5

New York and New Jersey

REASSIGNMENT TO WASHINGTON'S MAIN CONTINENTAL ARMY

At Fort Ticonderoga, the remnants of the companies and regiments were consolidated and reorganized. On October 26, 1776, Arnold's brigade, which had participated in the invasion of Canada and fought on Lake Champlain, was temporarily reassigned as General Poor's New Hampshire brigade for a month. It was then assigned to Colonel Vose's brigade on November 26, 1776, once a part of Colonel Greaton's Massachusetts regiment. This was necessary because of the death of Colonel Bond, the commander of the Twenty-fifth Continental Regiment, on August 31, 1776, at Fort Ticonderoga. The remnants of the regiment, many of whom had been part of General Arnold's brigade in Canada and on Lake Champlain, were again reorganized and reassigned to several other companies. Ensign Philip Ulmer remained with Colonel Joseph Vose's Massachusetts regiment that was formed by combining the remnants of the Sixth, Eighteenth, Fifteenth and Twenty-fourth Continental Regiments.[495] Colonel Vose and Philip Ulmer had become well acquainted with each other during their service at Montreal and at Lake Champlain. Toward the end of November, General Washington ordered General Gates to send military troops from Fort Ticonderoga to join the main Continental Army, which was in retreat in New Jersey in the Middle Department of the Northern Theater of army operations. General John Sullivan brought two brigades of two thousand men on a forced march through northwestern New Jersey to the shores of the Delaware River in Pennsylvania, where a stand would be made against the British and their allied forces. In December, General Washington requested that General Lee and his troops from northwestern New Jersey should join him on the Delaware River near Trenton. General Lee evaded and delayed joining Washington's troops. The two principal commanders of the Continental Army were on the verge of an open break.[496] On the night of December 13, while staying at White's Tavern with his aides, General Lee was captured by a company of British cavalry (dragoons) led by Banastre Tarleton, who had been informed of Lee's location by Loyalists. Lee was taken to Brunswick (also called New Brunswick), where the British cavalry colonel, William Harcourt, interrogated him. Charles Lee was considered a traitor to the king of England and his comrades by his British captors, and he was held in close confinement. General Lee sent word to British general Howe that he was ready to offer information and unsolicited advice on how Washington's Continental Army might be defeated. British leaders were greatly surprised at General Lee's disloyalty and treachery.[497] Americans knew nothing about this treachery and received the news of General Lee's capture as a major setback to the American cause. One British officer wrote of Lee's disloyalty: "He [General Lee] is perfect in treachery as if he were American born…They swallow their oaths of allegiance to the King and Congress alternately…I think nothing but total expiration of the inhabitants of this country will ever make it a desirable object of any Prince or State."[498]

In the meantime, only a small division of about two thousand men remained at Fort Ticonderoga and Mount Independence, with Colonel Anthony Wayne as their commander, to defend the frontier post in the Northern Department. General Washington directed the sick and reserve soldiers to Morristown in western New Jersey, where winter quarters were being prepared for the American army troops. The remnants of the Twenty-fifth Massachusetts Regiment, in which Philip Ulmer had served, were reconfigured and consolidated under Colonel Vose's command. Colonel Vose's regiment marched from Fort Ticonderoga with Poor's, Paterson's and McDougall's regiments, all under the command of General John Sullivan, and in Sullivan's column.[499] In western New Jersey, part of General Sullivan's column split off and went to Morristown and Pluckemin with the sick, feeble and injured. These troops needed to rest and recover from the injuries and ailments received during the

Canadian Expedition and the recent battle on Lake Champlain. The troops of General McDougall's New York Continental regiment, with Colonel Greaton's and Porter's Massachusetts regiments and two New Jersey militia companies under Colonel Ford at Morristown and Colonel Winds at Pluckemin, were not involved in the actions at Trenton and Princeton.[500] They were needed to construct the army troops' barracks and to make preparations for the supplies and provisions needed by General Washington's Continental Army before they would enter winter quarters at Morristown for the winter of 1777.

After a hard march through northwestern New Jersey under General Sullivan's command, the New England and New York troops from Fort Ticonderoga managed to arrive at Washington's encampment along the banks of the Delaware River in Pennsylvania by December 22, 1776, just days before General Washington's famous night crossing of the Delaware River. These newly arrived regiments combined with other New England regiments (approximately thirteen in all) and were assigned to General Arthur St. Clair's brigade in General Sullivan's first division on the right wing of the main Continental Army.[501] General Washington estimated that there were fewer than one hundred men in each regiment. Ensign Philip Ulmer became an active participant in the difficult Delaware crossing on the night of December 25, 1776 (his twenty-fifth birthday), with the combined troops of Colonel Vose's and Colonel John Paterson's First Massachusetts Continental Regiment, which absorbed them into their ranks. These combined New England troops functioned with Colonel Sargent's and Colonel Glover's regiments, all under the command of Brigadier General Arthur St. Clair. On January 1, 1777, Philip Ulmer was advanced in rank as a lieutenant in Colonel Vose's regiment, and he also served as first lieutenant with General Paterson's regiment, Captain Abraham Hunt's company.[502] Colonel Joseph Vose's regiment became designated as the First Massachusetts Continental Regiment and served with General St. Clair at Princeton.[503] Lieutenant Philip Ulmer was officially commissioned on March 27, 1777, as first lieutenant in Colonel John Paterson's regiment as well as Colonel Vose's regiment with Captain Abraham Hunt's company, where Philip appears in "The List of Officers" of the Continental Army. The reorganization of the Continental Army was completed by General Washington and his military command in the spring of 1777.

American Retreat from New York and New Jersey

Some persons condemn me for having endeavoured [sic] *to conciliate His Majesty's rebellious subjects, by taking every means to prevent destruction of the country…I acted in that particular for the benefit of the King's service.*
—*Sir William Howe, 1779*[504]

General Washington felt the weight of the multiple defeats that had taken place in the Canadian and New York campaigns. The Americans' defeat by General Howe's British forces on Long Island, Manhattan Island and the surrounding Westchester County vicinity weighed heavily upon General Washington. The loss of New York City and Fort Washington, where the general observed many of his American troops die in a massacre, was a bitter defeat. Looking through his telescope from the New Jersey Palisades across the Hudson River, General Washington was a witness to the slaughter of his brave troops who had fought valiantly in the face of overwhelming enemy strength to defend Fort Washington on Washington Heights (located in the entrance area of present-day George Washington Bridge). The worst of it was to watch these brave American soldiers put to the sword after they had surrendered to the British army troops.[505] General Washington was devastated and blamed no one but himself. He hung his head, turned away from the gory scene and walked silently into the woods to pray, and there, he wept like a child.[506] In the agony that consumed him at the time, Washington felt that he had lost the American cause and the war, and he had lost his own way as a leader and as a man. In his emotional pain and despair, he was inconsolable.[507] His officers did not know how to comfort him. This was the lowest point of his long military career. Some of his officers began to question his leadership and decision-making abilities. In a letter written to Adjunct Joseph Reed, General Charles Lee wrote, "Oh! General—an indecisive mind is one of the greatest misfortunes that can befall an Army."[508]

General Washington learned from his errors in the New York campaigns and began to develop a new strategy. He began to collect information about British troop movements by developing his intelligence network. Citizens and farmers, deserters, spies and paid informers began to yield information about the British plans, maneuvers and troop strength. Intelligence reached General Washington at his New Jersey headquarters that the British and Hessian forces in the New York City area were moving into New Jersey in an offensive to remove Washington's army forces from New Jersey. General

Greene's assignment had been to guard the New Jersey Palisades, and he had failed to do so. When news of the landing of British and Hessian troops on the western side of the Hudson River was received at Fort Lee, all discipline broke down and near panic set in. General Washington and General Greene arrived on horseback and managed to rally and reorganize the troops. General Washington ordered General Greene and his troops to evacuate Fort Lee and leave nothing behind that the enemy might use against them. At the head of the retreating American column, General Washington and General Greene marched the troops westward toward New Bridge and then continued the march toward Washington's headquarters in Hackensack, New Jersey.

Having captured the New Jersey Palisades, General Charles Cornwallis led the British forces in a quick march to Fort Lee and arrived shortly after the American forces had left the fort. The British successes in occupying Long Island and the New York City vicinity, coupled with the capture of Fort Washington at Washington Heights (on Manhattan Island) and Fort Lee in New Jersey, kept the British and Hessian spirits high. Generals Howe and Cornwallis decided to regroup the combined British and Hessian forces in New Jersey and not to immediately pursue Washington's retreating army. By November 22, General Cornwallis's forces crossed the Hackensack River at New Bridge and proceeded south, where they took over the town of Hackensack. The British and Hessian forces continued to pursue the American army southward through New Jersey. On December 2, the retreating American troops arrived in Trenton. Fortunately, General Washington had sent General William Maxwell ahead to secure all the boats and rafts that he could find on the Delaware River and to have them ready at Trenton upon the army's arrival there.[509] Cornwallis's British troops and the Hessian troops led by Colonels Rall and von Donop relentlessly pursued Washington's army troops. The combined British forces arrived at Trenton as the last boat carrying American troops was leaving the New Jersey riverbank for the Pennsylvania side. They shot at the escaping American troops and yelled obscenities at them.

The intention of the Howe brothers, General William Howe and Admiral Lord Richard Howe, at the end of 1775 and 1776 was to deal with His Majesty's rebellious subjects with moderation and firmness. General Howe's plan was to implement a pacification program to restore order to the American colonies and help the majority of loyal colonists (Loyalists) to return their allegiance to King George III and to England. Instructions from London had directed the Howe brothers to "make peace if possible and…war if peace was out of the question."[510] Many British officers and leaders in the British Parliament felt the pacification program would not work and supported a different, more forceful and violent strategy. Lord George Germain, the secretary of state for the North American colonies, also preferred the deliberate use of extreme violence and terror to break the American will to resist.[511] Loyalists in New Jersey welcomed General Cornwallis's forces as liberators and were astounded when they were plundered by British and German soldiers who could not distinguish a British Loyalist (also called Tories) from an American supporter or sympathizer (Whig).[512] Brutality, plundering, intimidation and gross abuses of New Jersey citizens by British and Hessian soldiers were reported to General Washington and the Continental Congress throughout the New Jersey colony. British and Hessian soldiers in the field were accustomed to the European military viewpoint that "to the victors belonged the spoils," and the use of brute force would surely break the American Revolution. The American cause became more than a conflict of tactics and weapons. It had become a conflict of different ideologies and different choices of governance and institutions. First- and second-generation American citizens rejected the yoke of European feudalism and religious persecution from which their parents and grandparents had fled. The colonial settlers chose to fight against European kings and dictators to secure their own freedom, liberties and the opportunity to pursue their own future interests and build their own fortunes in America.

Following General Howe's moderation plan, General Cornwallis's objective was to keep general Washington's army moving southward, to push them out of New Jersey and not to engage them in battle unless necessary. British general Henry Clinton disagreed with General Howe's pacification agenda with the rebellious colonists. His view was to deal forcefully and decisively with the rebellious colonists. General Henry Clinton, who had been preparing for his Rhode Island expedition to subdue the colony, interrupted his plans and offered to redirect his forces to New Jersey. His plan was to cut off General Washington's retreat southward, destroy the American army and capture the leaders of the rebellion. A second suggestion that General Clinton made to General Howe would be to land his division of troops along the Delaware River and strike at Philadelphia and capture the leadership of the Continental Congress.[513] After listening to General Clinton's strategy plans, General William Howe rejected the plan, and General Clinton was ordered to carry out his own assignment to capture Rhode Island and secure the harbor and town at Newport. Newport would become a major British supply depot and shipping center for the British forces in New England. The capture of Newport and the surrounding towns in Rhode Island cut off the New England privateering and merchant vessels in the Narragansett Bay area. By capturing this vital seaport, General Henry Clinton curtailed and stopped the delivery of crucial military supplies for the American forces that were being brought by trading schooners and cargo vessels from French, Spanish and Dutch ports in the West Indies. Newport had served as General Washington's army supply port where munitions and military goods were unloaded from the ships and moved to the main military supply depot at Springfield, Massachusetts, for military use in the Northern and Highland Departments and in the New England colonies. The American naval effort to keep the American supply lines open and flowing was now in jeopardy.

The logistical problem of supplying a large army with needed munitions, material goods and supplies was difficult for both the American and the British armies. The supply lines for the British forces were especially difficult during the winter and stretched from England, more than three thousand miles away across the Atlantic Ocean, all the way to Halifax, Nova Scotia, Quebec City in Canada; to Boston, Massachusetts; and to New York City. A British plan was developed to maintain the British forces in America during the winter of 1776–77. General William Howe needed housing as well as food and forage for his army in New Jersey. Admiral Richard Howe, his brother, needed a safe haven for the British fleet before winter arrived. Newport had a desirable harbor, and it was closer to the Gulf Stream waters that provided milder, freer conditions from ice than the harbor at New York City. Both locations would provide the British army's needs through the winter months. An occupied Rhode Island would restore to the British Crown another colony and provide a major military base, with General Henry Clinton as commander. This strategy was part of the plan to recover the other New England colonies. The campaign in New Jersey, with General Cornwallis as commander of the British allied forces, would drive the Continental Army troops out of New Jersey and restore yet another colony to the British Crown.[514] Many people, both Tory and Whig, believed that the rebellion would not survive the winter.

Chapter 6

American Covert Activities in France

The balance of power and the events that were transpiring in Europe and England had a definite effect on the direction of the American Revolution. Since the United Colonies had been restricted by Great Britain from producing their own defensive materials and arms (firearms, gunpowder and heavy cannons, etc.) and their own manufactured dry goods (tents, blankets, shoes, cloth, etc.), America remained dependent on Britain and Europe for these needed items. America had great natural resources of raw materials but did not have a way of manufacturing or mass-producing useful products for sale. The potential wealth of the American colonies remained in the hands of wealthy British and European merchants, international commercial traders and business investors and foreign land speculators. The success of the American Revolution was dependent on financial and military aid from countries in Europe that also opposed the dominance and expansionism of the British Empire. Colonial delegates to the Continental Congress first sought to appease and plead with the king of England and the British Parliament to lift the oppressive taxation demands, regulations and controls that had been placed on the American colonies, but Benjamin Franklin's pleas were rebuffed. The British government continued to exploit the dependency of America's colonies for British goods and to utilize the sale of America's natural resources to finance their own wars in Europe as well as enrich their own economy in England. The Continental Congress and the American colonies desperately needed help from France and other European countries if the American Revolution had any hope of being successful.

SILAS DEANE SENT TO PARIS

Silas Deane was sent to Paris, France, in June 1776 by the Secret Committee of the Continental Congress (later called the Committee of Foreign Affairs) to serve as an emissary to the French government. His mission was to acquire financial and military support, as well as desperately needed supplies and military matériel for the American cause. Deane met Pierre-Augustine Caron de Beaumarchais (referred to hereafter as Beaumarchais), who was an arms agent for the French government, and he was willing to help supply needed armaments and military supplies for Washington's Continental Army. In Europe, Silas Deane became reacquainted with Edward Bancroft, who was a Connecticut Yale College colleague, friend and physician. Dr. Edward Bancroft became Deane's personal secretary, his French translator and trusted confidant. (Unfortunately for Deane and other American commissioners, Bancroft turned out to be a double agent for the British foreign minister, Lord Stormont.) Deane, who did not speak French, had become desperate for word and instructions from the Continental Congress after five months of silence. Deane wrote a letter to Congress using invisible ink that John Jay's brother, Dr. James Jay, had provided for him:

> Paris, 9th November, 1776
> Gentlemen,—I have written to you often and particularly of affairs here. The want of intelligence retards everything. As I have not word from you since 5th of June last, I am well-nigh distracted…All Europe have their eyes on the States of America, and are astonished to find month after month rolling away without your applying to them in form. I hope such application is on its way: nothing else is wanting to affect your utmost wishes.
> —Silas Deane[515]

On the evening of November 16, Silas Deane finally received correspondence from the Congress with a copy of the Declaration of Independence, which had been mailed on August 7. Silas Deane quickly wrote to Vergennes requesting a meeting to deliver the official Declaration to King Louis XVI and the French court. In his message to Foreign Minister Charles Gravier, the Comte de Vergennes, Silas Deane proposed a treaty of commerce and alliance with France. Deane also sent a copy to Spain through the ambassador to Spain in which he proposed a treaty of alliance between the United Colonies and the Bourbon rulers of France and Spain. By presenting the ambassadors with the official Declaration of Independence,

Silas Deane gained new importance and authority in the French court as a "de facto" representative of the government in America.[516]

On December 4, 1776, Silas Deane received unexpected news that Benjamin Franklin had landed in a small village in Brittany. Franklin informed Deane in a message that the Continental Congress had recognized the importance of America's relationship with France, and it had appointed Ben Franklin, Thomas Jefferson and Silas Deane as co-commissioners to negotiate a treaty of commerce and an alliance with France. This notice gave Silas Deane an official title and status as an emissary from the United Colonies. In the same message, Franklin had added a postscript that Jefferson had declined Congress's nomination because his wife was very ill in Virginia. Congress appointed Arthur Lee as a co-commissioner to France. Arthur Lee, the brother of congressional delegate Richard Henry Lee, would cause difficulties for the other commissioners, Benjamin Franklin and Silas Deane. Arthur Lee had poor diplomatic judgment, an arrogant and righteous demeanor and desires for money, personal power and political influence. These traits for celebrity would undermine the efforts of Silas Deane and French agent Beaumarchais to provide military arms and supplies for Washington's Continental Army and for European goods for trading with the Indians. Conflicting diplomatic events that were occurring in Europe would have a direct impact on events in the United Colonies and on the officers and soldiers serving in the American armies and state militias. The success or failure of the American Revolution was dependent on the relationships and diplomacy of the American commissioners in Europe and France's financial support and its shipments of military arms and supplies for the Continental Army.

Silas Deane negotiated a secret deal with French foreign minister Charles Gravier, the Count de Vergennes, to subsidize the war needs of the American Continental Army and the Continental Congress in their struggle for independence from England. To keep the one-million-livre subsidy a secret (about $8 million today), a contract was made to import prime Virginia tobacco. Silas Deane and Benjamin Franklin promised to sell about five million pounds of the Virginia tobacco for one million livres, which was greatly discounted in price from the accepted price on the French market at the time.[517] The contract was really a deception to hide the French loan subsidy and France's support for the American Revolution. Co-commissioner Arthur Lee secretly worked to undermine the efforts of Deane and Franklin. Arthur Lee wrote to the "Secret Committee" that Congress had appointed to handle the covert French arms sales and financial dealings for the Continental Army. He complained about his lack of influence and authority over France's foreign aid, and he threatened to expose the covert arms dealings. In a letter to Congress, Arthur Lee related that promises made by Beaumarchais had not been completely fulfilled, and he implicitly stated that Congress had no obligation to pay for the goods by shipping Virginia tobacco to Beaumarchais because the shipments of arms were a gift.[518] What Lee really wanted to do was to act as principal agent and sell the prime tobacco in the European marketplace and reap substantial monetary rewards for the sales himself. As it turned out, Lee's message to the Continental Congress was misleading and untrue. The military arms were not a gift but were sent in exchange payment (barter) for prime Virginia tobacco. Great Britain passed the Navigation Acts, which prohibited the export of tobacco except to England. Strained relations between Arthur Lee and the other commissioners in France festered and grew nasty during 1776 until events finally came to a head in the fall, about the same time that the "Conway Cabal" conspiracy was uncovered against General Washington at Valley Forge.

As Silas Deane moved into a more public role on the diplomatic stage, the front company that he had set up with Robert Morris in Philadelphia and Rodriguez Hortalez in France quietly moved thousands of tons of supplies and equipment from all over France to the port at Le Havre. Three cargo ships—the *Amphitrite*, the *Seine* and the *Romain*—were being prepared to sail to America.[519] The efforts to gather the thousands of tons of supplies, cannons, gunpowder, cannon balls, tents, grenades and muskets had to be carried out secretly, often under the cover of darkness, to avoid detection by the British agents and spies. The *Amphitrite* was prepared to sail to New England in November with newly commissioned French officers led by Colonel Tronson du Coudray, who had been made a general by the insistence of Foreign Minister Count Vergennes. However, the news of Washington's army forces' recent defeats around New York City caused concern among the French officers, and they forced a delay of the sailing of the ship.

By mid-December 1776, General du Coudray had returned to his ship, and Beaumarchais, who acted as the French arms agent, supervised the final details of the massive shipment to the American army forces. For two solid nights, one hundred men worked constantly to load the *Amphitrite* and the *Seine*. The *Amphitrite* was loaded with twelve tons of gunpowder and about five hundred tons of equipment and other supplies.[520] General DeKalb and his military entourage were in La Havre preparing to leave for the American colonies on the French ship *Romain* (which was later renamed the

Amélie.)[521] Many tons of goods ended up on the wrong ships, and the bills of lading listed supplies on one ship that were actually loaded onto another ship. This confusion of bills of lading and the mixed-up supply lists would later complicate the efforts of Beaumarchais to receive compensation from the Continental Congress for military supplies and armaments sent from France. The French officers unexpectedly demanded a full year's pay before they would set sail, which Beaumarchais managed to provide with papers that would not incriminate the crew members or officers in arms smuggling if the British ships should stop them. Beaumarchais made it appear that the ships carried supplies to the French sugar islands in the French West Indies and that any interference with the ship and its cargo would be regarded as an act of war. Deane and Beaumarchais labored for nine months to launch dozens of cargo and supply ships to the American colonies to arm Washington's Continental Army.

Beaumarchais and Commissioner Deane's smuggling activities to arm Washington's Continental Army were discovered through a spy within the American ambassadors' headquarters located at Valentinois, France. British Lord Stormont, ambassador to the French court, was informed by his spy agent, Edward Bancroft (who served as personal secretary, friend, confidant and French translator for Commissioner Silas Deane), that the French businessman Beaumarchais was involved with smuggling military supplies and arms shipments through a front company in support of the American colonies. Lord Stormont angrily went to French foreign minister Charles Gravier, Comte de Vergennes, and he demanded that the shipments to America be immediately stopped from leaving the port at Le Havre. With the huge amount of military guns and supplies gathered at Le Havre, Vergennes could no longer deny that Beaumarchais was supplying Washington's Continental Army in America. Lord Stormont pointed out that France's support of the American colonies was in violation of the expressed terms of the Treaty of 1763 that ended the French and Indian War. This blatant violation of neutrality brought France and Great Britain to the brink of war. French foreign minister Vergennes issued a halt to Beaumarchais' ships to prevent them from leaving the port. The *Amphitrite*, however, had sailed the day before the stop order was given. The *Seine* and the *Romain* were seized along with the *Mercure*. The *Amphitrite's* officers and crewmen soon returned to Brittany due to bad weather and spoiled food. Foreign Minister Vergennes was afraid of the anger of British Lord Stormont, who threatened the French government with war, citing the violation of the neutrality agreement that France had signed with Great Britain. An embargo was temporarily imposed upon the four vessels that were to sail for America. Commissioner Benjamin Franklin, who handled the political and diplomatic aspects of the Continental Congress's mission in France, and Silas Deane, who handled the smuggling aspects for arming the Continental Army, worked together to reverse the embargo. The French efforts to supply military arms and supplies for General Washington's Continental Army and to provide financial support to the Continental Congress seemed doomed, and with it, the American War of Independence.

FRENCH ARMS SENT TO AMERICA

After feverish efforts by Deane and Beaumarchais to persuade the French government to allow Beaumarchais' ships to sail for North America, the embargo was suddenly lifted, and by the end of February, the four cargo ships departed from the French port of Le Havre for America. By April 1777, there were three more cargo ships that had set sail from a small port near Nantes with French troops, armaments and military supplies on their way to America: the *Thérèse*, the *Concorde* and the *Marquis de la Chalotais*. Commissioner Deane and French arms dealer Beaumarchais had labored for many months to have the cargo ships launched for America. These seven French ships carried enough military arms, cannons, bombs, matches, carriages, hardware (shovels, axes, spades etc.), troop supplies (tents, blankets, shoes, etc.) and other needed items to equip an army of thirty thousand men.[522] These were the first of approximately forty supply ships that Beaumarchais sent to the United Colonies during the American Revolution.

Because British and American Loyalist spies and informers had infiltrated into all levels of the government and army structures, the commissioners in France had to rely on newspapers and occasional letters from family and friends in America for updates on the progress of the Revolution and the successes and failures of Washington's Continental Army. Franklin was aware of the failure of the congressional delegates to work together to make rational and impartial decisions for the good of the country. Most delegates had their own self-interest at heart. The commissioners were aware of the inability of Congress to finance an extended war against Great Britain. Ben Franklin knew that General Washington's forces had been driven from New York after a string of defeats and thousands of casualties at White

Plains, New York City; at Fort Washington on Manhattan Island; and at Fort Lee in New Jersey by General Howe's massive army forces on land and by sea. In December, the British naval fleet captured the American naval base at Newport, Rhode Island, and stopped the deliveries of supplies and armaments for the New England state militias and for the Continental Army troops in the Northern and Highland Departments. The commissioners in France knew about Washington's continued retreat southward across New Jersey, Delaware and Pennsylvania. The situation for Washington's army troops was very discouraging. British enemy forces controlled most of New Jersey, and General William Howe's Royal Army and Hessian forces were poised to march on Philadelphia. Congressional delegates, anticipating the capture of the city, were preparing to evacuate Philadelphia and move south to Baltimore, Maryland. The devastated colonial economy and the divided allegiances of the citizens in the country were a miserable state of affairs. Benjamin Franklin knew that the Revolution was not going well in America.

General Washington felt the pressure for an American military victory after so many defeats in New York and New Jersey. Enlistments for soldiers and officers would run out at the end of the year, and General Washington's army would disperse again, as they had at the end of 1775, leaving the Continental Army without a sufficient fighting force to defend the country. Lieutenant James Monroe reported that Washington's forces had dwindled in early December 1776 to about three thousand men. Washington's Continental Army continued to melt away as many companies came to the end of their enlistments. Feeling that the American cause for independence and liberty was almost lost, Washington wrote to his brother, Augustine Washington, in Virginia on December 18, 1776: "If every nerve is not strained to recruit a new Army with all expedition, I think the game is pretty near up."[523] General Washington had to reorganize his plans and military strategy. He needed to make some difficult and decisive choices for the good of the army and the colonies. He desperately needed to have a battlefield success in order to restore the spirit of the troops, encourage new recruitments within the colonies to enlist in the Continental Army and invigorate enthusiasm in the public sector for the American cause of freedom and liberty.

Thomas Paine joined the Continental Army as a "gentleman volunteer" and became an aide-de-camp and personal friend of General Nathanael Greene. General Greene was George Washington's close friend and military advisor. Thomas Paine worked as a war correspondent, the first in American history.[524] He published the pamphlet *Common Sense* in January 1776, which challenged the authority of the British government and the royal monarchy.

The plain language that Paine used spoke to the common people of America and was the first work to openly address the reasons for independence from Great Britain. Thomas Paine joined the Continental Army in July 1776 and shared in the fighting and misery with the soldiers during the war. He shared in the dark times during the retreat from New York and New Jersey to the banks of the Delaware River in Pennsylvania. He shared with the men of the Continental Army a deep devotion to the American cause.

Thomas Paine explained to his friend Samuel Adams some years later: "The black times of Seventy-six were no other than the natural consequence of the military blunders of the campaign."[525] On the retreat through New Jersey, Thomas Paine, who accompanied General Washington during this time, began to write another pamphlet that he called *The American Cause*. It was a call to arms and an attempt to awaken the American people "to some evils in the world which were even worse than war, and one of them was tyranny that British ministers were attempting to fasten on their former colonies."[526] The first publication, which appeared in the *Pennsylvania Journal* on December 19, 1776, was distributed within days and was read in the encampments to the Continental Army troops along the Delaware River. The emotional impact on the American soldiers and the common people throughout the thirteen colonies was enormous. The first sentence of Paine's pamphlet *The American Cause* became the watchword, and later a battle cry, for the American troops: "These are the times that try men's souls…"

Up until this pivotal point, the war for American independence had been largely unsuccessful militarily, and many great issues of the American Revolution hung in the balance. The time for making tough decisions had arrived, and hard choices had to be made.

Chapter 7

Battles of Trenton, Assunpink and Princeton

NEW JERSEY CAMPAIGN: BATTLE OF TRENTON

Washington and his staff officers had been looking for a chance to make a counterattack against the British forces in western New Jersey. The brigades commanded by Generals Gates, Sullivan and Lee from the Northern Department in New York began to arrive in Washington's camps along the Delaware River on December 20, 1776.[527] By December 22, General Sullivan brought in two brigades of two thousand men, mostly from Massachusetts, Connecticut and New York, after a hard march through the hills of northwestern New Jersey.[528] Ensign Philip Ulmer, his brother, George, and friends Nathaniel and James Cushing, who were with Colonel Paterson's Massachusetts regiment, were with these New England troops from Fort Ticonderoga led by General Sullivan. On December 22, 1776, General Washington announced that the American forces had grown strong and that all of the reinforcements had arrived.[529]

Colonel Joseph Reed, Washington's adjutant general, wrote a message to General Washington on December 22, 1776, about the British movements in New Jersey. The most important part of the letter was to move quickly and decisively. Colonel Joseph Reed further wrote:

> *We are of the opinion my dear General that something must be attempted to revive our expiring credit, give our Cause some degree of reputation &*

prevent total depreciation of the Continental money which is coming on very fast…even a Failure cannot be more fatal than to remain in our present situation…some enterprise must be undertaken in our present Circumstances or we must give up the cause…Will it not be possible dear General for our troops to act with advantage to make a diversion or something more at or about Trenton—the greater the alarm the more likely the Success will attend the attacks…Delay is equal to a total defeat…we must not suffer ourselves to be lulled into security and inaction…the Love of my country, a Wife and four Children in the Enemy's Hands, the Respect and Attachment I have for you—the Ruin and Poverty that must attend me & thousands of others will plead my Excuse for so much Freedom.[530]

General Washington and his advisors devised a plan to cross the Delaware River on Christmas night and surround Colonel Johann Rall's Hessian garrison encamped at Trenton. A council of war was called late on Christmas Eve, and plans for an attack upon Trenton were worked out in detail. Major General Sullivan, Brigadier General St. Clair and Colonels John Paterson, John Glover and Henry Knox were among those in attendance with General George Washington at his camp headquarters. These would all be officers with whom Ensign Philip Ulmer would serve during the conflict. To maintain secrecy, General Washington selected a secret password and wrote it on small slips for all the units in the army. The password was "Victory or Death." Officers were under orders to remain "…fixed in their divisions with a white paper in their hats to be distinguished as a sign for the men to follow their leaders, and a signal to the officers that they were to lead from the front."[531] This practice seems to have remained in the U.S. Army since Washington's historic crossing of the Delaware River on the night of December 25, 1776.

THE CONTINENTAL ARMY CROSSES THE DELAWARE RIVER

The force of the current, the sharpness of the frost, the darkness of the night, the ice made during the operation, and a high wind, rendered the passage of the river extremely difficult, but for the stentorian lungs and extraordinary exertions of Colonel Knox.
—*Major James Wilkinson, 1819*[532]

On December 25, 1776, when the soldiers left their camp along the Delaware shore about four o'clock in the late afternoon, the sun was low but shining brightly on the horizon. It was Philip Ulmer's twenty-fifth birthday, and he spent the day with his company in preparation for a mission that would be physically and emotionally challenging. The weather began to change rapidly as the soldiers marched from their camp through the snow toward the river at McConkey's and Johnson's ferry landings. Shortly after sunset, it began to drizzle, and by the time the troops reached the banks of the river, the drizzle had turned to a driving rain. By eleven o'clock at night, a howling nor'easter overtook them with terrific force. "It rained, hailed, snowed and froze. The wind rose so high it blew a perfect hurricane…" as the army gathered at the river, wrote a young soldier named John Greenwood, who served in Colonel Paterson's Massachusetts regiment.[533] Besides the ice and snow storm, the army forces had to face another obstacle. The Delaware River was a tidal river below the falls at Trenton, New Jersey. The ice that floated downstream was trapped by the incoming tide and driven upstream, and it had jammed and compressed the ice against the falls. The massive ice jam was located at the point where the troops were supposed to have crossed. In other locations along the river, similar problems had developed. At another crossing where the Delaware River was about a quarter-mile wide, the water was turbulent, and the wind had caused a dangerous chop on the water. The currents in the swollen, icy river were swift and strong. Above the falls at Trenton, the ice was so thick along the Jersey side of the river that the boats could not reach the land. The soldiers had to get out of the boats about 150 yards from shore, struggle across the ice on foot and climb the icy banks onto the land. Some of the boats with the artillery were carried away with the blocks of ice and could not be brought ashore. Many boats were threatened with complete destruction.

By midnight, the entire expedition was on the verge of collapse. Of the three divisions involved in the attack on Trenton, two were defeated by ice and the turbulence on the river. Only the northern force remained at Johnson's and McConkey's ferries. Officer Philip Ulmer and his fellow soldiers were involved during the Delaware River crossing with Colonels Glover, Sargent and General St. Clair's brigades in General Sullivan's First Division as the right wing of the main Continental Army. They were able to cross the icy river in big Durham boats, which were sturdy boats built to carry heavy cargos for the Durham Iron Works. Their high sides and sharp ends were used by the infantry during the crossing. Flat-bottomed scows were used for the soldiers, too, but they were not as sound as the Durham boats. The big Delaware ferries were built to carry army horses, artillery and ammunition wagons. Most of the men crossed the Delaware River standing up because anyone who sat in the bottom of the boats would have been sitting in ice water. The river ferries and freight boats had few, if any, seats. There were accounts of men who were ordered to jump up and down in several inches of watery slush to clear ice from the boats and keep them from freezing.[534] Once on the New Jersey side of the river, the troops built fires along the shore and tried to warm themselves. The men were shaking with cold and were wet to the skin but in remarkably good spirits.[535]

The First Division was led by General Sullivan and consisted mostly of New England soldiers in the brigades of Glover, Sargent and St. Clair. Colonel Sargent's brigade, where Philip Ulmer had been assigned with Colonel Vose's regiment to serve with McDougall's New York Continental troops, had joined forces and marched with General John Sullivan's First Division to General Washington's encampment.[536] They were assigned to the Continental Army's right wing.[537] The Second Division served as the left wing and was led by General Nathanael Greene. General Greene's Second

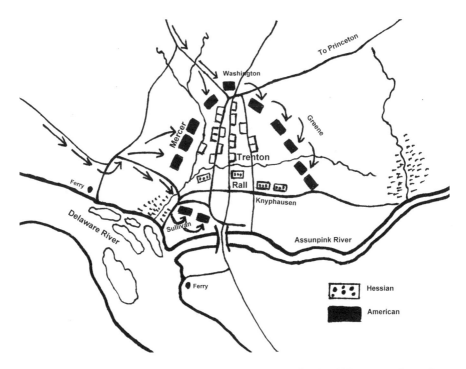

Military actions of the American and Hessian troops at the Battle of Trenton on December 26, 1776. *Courtesy of the author.*

Division included the brigades of Stephens, Mercer and Stirling.[538] They had been ordered to march together from the ferry landings and then divide and enter Trenton by different roads. General Sullivan's division was to advance along the River Road and enter Trenton from the south by Water Street and the southwest. General Greene's division was ordered to move inland and enter the town from the northwest, away from the river.

Brigadier General Glover and Colonel Sargent's brigades were stationed near the River Road and bridge. The American troops advanced on Trenton with seven or eight field artillery cannons deployed for every thousand muskets. The American commanders distributed their guns for maximum effect. The leading American detached units went into action with drag ropes, handspikes and hammers. Their orders were to seize the Hessian cannons and turn them against the enemy, and if that failed, they were to disable the guns by spiking the touch holes. The heavy artillery was to be used as shock weapons against the enemy and as supporting arms for their own infantry. The two divisions headed by Generals Sullivan and Greene struggled through the rain, snow and bitter cold wind to get into position. Timing of the attack was of great importance. General Washington had given orders that "every officer's watch should be set by his, and the moment of the attack fixed." Captain William Hull of the Seventh Connecticut Regiment wrote of this event, "They tugged out their large pocket watches and matched them to the timepiece of the General." This was one of the first recorded instances of synchronized watches in a military campaign.[539]

THE BATTLE OF TRENTON AND PHILIP ULMER'S PARTICIPATION

Massed artillery from the American forces across the Delaware River in Pennsylvania began firing into the town of Trenton. Heavy fire of seven batteries from the banks across the river rained down upon the Hessian positions. Hessian posts near the river were abandoned under the heavy cannonade, and they retreated into the town. General Washington and General Greene's American troops surprised the Hessian picket guards positioned in houses along Pennington Road and took captives. With 1,200 men and ten fieldpieces, General Washington and General Greene's brigade approached the town from the north. Informed along the march by a courier that the storm had made muskets unfit for firing, General

Washington responded, "Tell General Sullivan to use the bayonet. I am resolved to take Trenton."[540]

Almost simultaneously, General Sullivan's division with General St. Clair's brigade (composed of remnants of thirteen New England regiments with fewer than one hundred men per regiment)[541] entered the town by River Road from the south. General Sullivan's troops announced their arrival by the boom of artillery. Generals Washington and Greene advanced their troops to the junction of King and Queen Streets, where six field cannons had been quickly positioned with the line of fire down both streets. Several battalions rushed forward to secure Princeton Road, preventing any escape in that direction. Three Hessian regiments ran out from their quarters and responded quickly to the surprise American attack. Colonel Rall's Hessian regiment in the center of town assembled and moved up King Street. The regiment of von Lossberg formed on King Street, and the regiment of von Knyphausen gathered by the Quaker meetinghouse on lower Queen Street.

A contingent of soldiers from General Sullivan's troops drove General von Knyphausen's Hessian soldiers through town and seized the bridge on the Bordentown Road. As Colonel Rall rallied his Hessian soldiers and prepared to fire their two brass cannons, General St. Clair's brigade, using bayonets because their gunpowder was wet, moved up King Street and engaged the German troops. The New England battery came forward to give support to General St. Clair's combined regiments (which included Philip Ulmer with Colonel Vose's troops and Colonel Paterson's First Massachusetts Regiment). They caught the advancing Hessians in crossfire and captured the two brass cannons. The Hessian infantry fought doggedly and were able to recover the German guns taken by the American troops. General Greene's division approached the town from the north. The enemy made a show of resistance but retreated in the face of the approaching American forces. Colonel Rall rode up and assessed the situation. He often responded to an attack with a counterattack. Colonel Rall decided to attack the American troops directly against their main strength inside Trenton.[542] A hot battle ensued with attacks and counterattacks.

With drums beating and colors flying, two regiments of Hessian infantry marched back toward King Street in the center of town, determined to rescue their guns that had been captured and to rout the American soldiers of General St. Clair's troops. General St. Clair's infantry soldiers joined with Colonel Knox's gunners and worked the cannons so hard that the axle of one of the carriages broke and disabled it. Colonel Knox rode up to them, looked toward the Hessian artillery and said: "My brave lads, go up and take those two held pieces, sword in hand. There is a party going and you must join them."[543]

The battery commander repeated the order to attack. The New England gunners and soldiers charged side by side straight toward the Hessian guns. The Hessians fired at the charging soldiers, injuring several American soldiers. Troops led by Captain William Washington and Lieutenant James Monroe from Colonel Adam Stephen's Virginia brigade (from General Greene's division) rushed forward to help, and they captured some of the Hessian troops. The other Hessian soldiers abandoned their guns and ran away in retreat. American gunners seized the guns and turned one of them toward the German infantry and loaded the guns with grapeshot. The Hessians fled into an orchard outside of town. A fierce fight ensued, and many German troops were killed and wounded. The American light infantry aimed at the Hessian officers and brought down four captains. German Colonel Rall (Rohl, the German spelling) was shot twice in the side. Mortally wounded, Colonel Rall fell from his horse. Rall was carried from the field by several of his men and taken back to his headquarters, where he subsequently died. The close combat, clashing of swords, massed musketry and field cannon at point-blank range created a scene of "horror and distress, blood mingling together, the dying moans, and Garments rolled in blood. The sight was too much to bear," as artilleryman Sergeant Joseph White wrote in his journal.[544]

Under heavy fire, the charge of the Hessian soldiers failed, and slowly the resisting German forces began to give way in retreat. The remnants of Colonels Rall and von Lossburg's broken Hessian regiments retreated to the east of town into an orchard. American infantry and artillery moved forward around them, and several American officers who knew German (such as Philip Ulmer) began to call "in both German and English to stack their weapons and surrender."[545] An unidentified young American German-speaking officer approached the fearful Hessian soldiers and spoke with their senior German officers and offered them surrender terms. The Hessian soldiers talked among themselves, and then they lowered their colors to the snow and grounded their weapons. It was said that the American troops mixed with the captured Hessian soldiers, and "after satisfying their curiosity, they began to converse familiarly in broken English and German."[546]

While these actions were taking place outside the town of Trenton, near the river, part of Sullivan's division, composed of Colonel Sargent's and Colonel Glover's brigades from Connecticut and Massachusetts, were directed to secure the bridge along the Assunpink Creek, a tributary of the

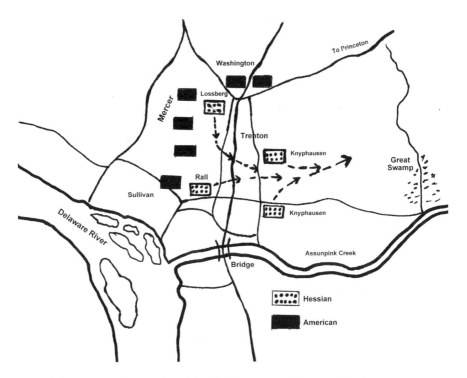

Map of the retreat and surrender of the Hessian troops at Trenton, New Jersey, on December 26, 1776. *Courtesy of the author.*

Delaware River, from escaping enemy troops. Colonel Glover's brigade moved forward swiftly and overwhelmed the Hessian guards and seized the bridge. They took a blocking position on the far side of the Assunpink Creek in order to capture any escaping enemy soldiers. Colonel Sargent's brigade quickly moved up the Assunpink Creek. With help from some troops of General St. Clair's regiment, they were able to surround and capture escaping Hessian soldiers. The last of the Hessian regiments to surrender at Trenton was Knyphausen's regiment, who had unsuccessfully tried to escape over the bridge. The Hessian troops finally laid down their arms in surrender. John Greenwood wrote in his journal, "General Washington, on horseback and alone, came up to our major and said, 'March on, my brave fellows, after me!' and rode off."[547] General Washington, extending his hand, said to Major James Wilkinson, an aide in General St. Clair's brigade, "Major Wilkinson, this is a glorious day for our country."[548]

Most American and British officers could speak only English. When the English-speaking officers met people who spoke a different language, most of the officers would shout at them in English, thinking that if they shouted loud enough, they might be understood. Letters sent between the commanding officers were communicated in three languages.[549] General William Howe issued general orders to his officers in English and French. Colonel Rall spoke neither English nor French but only a rough soldier's German. He spoke to his men in a heavy Hessian dialect. Colonel von Donop did not speak English. He wrote in French to English officers and spoke German to his Hessian men. Colonel Stirling wrote in English to his superiors and spoke Gaelic with his Highlanders. One British officer had difficulty understanding what was said in any language except his own.[550] As a young American officer, Ensign Philip Ulmer spoke and understood German and English fluently. Philip was probably of great assistance to General Washington and his senior officers in being able to translate instructions and to give directions to the German-speaking Hessian officers and soldiers taken captive at Trenton. His bilingual abilities and translation skills would prove to be a valuable resource in later battles and encounters.

General Washington's Continental Army moved back across the Delaware River to their camp in Pennsylvania with great difficulty, taking with them their 760 British and Hessian prisoners as well as captured supplies that included six brass cannons.[551] As the news of the American victory at Trenton began to spread, its greatest initial impact was with the citizens in the United Colonies. Many people received the victory as a vindication of the American Cause and a sign of God's all-powerful Providence and using the Continental Army as an instrument in His divine purpose.

AFTERMATH OF THE SUCCESS AT TRENTON

The chain, I own, is rather too expensive, but…trusting to the general submission of the country to the Southward of this chain, and the strength of the corps placed in the advance posts, I conclude the troops will be in perfect security.
—*Sir William Howe, December 20, 1776*[552]

There was a feeling of confidence that was growing in the American army following its victory at Trenton. The strategy of General Washington and his advisors changed as they learned from their previous mistakes. In the British camp, the feeling was different. The disaster at Trenton had caused the British commanders in New Jersey to rethink their belief that the American rebellion was nearly broken. The number of top-ranking officers in the British and Hessian armies had steadily been depleted by the American troops targeting and killing their officers. Reinforcements for the British and Hessian troops had to come thousands of miles across the Atlantic Ocean. General Howe's forces had lost the initiative in New Jersey, and they had also lost control of the countryside. The British army retained control of only a few fortified cities in New Jersey, and they were on continuous alert for unexpected and random attacks at any time by American detached companies using hit-and-run techniques. In order to regain their momentum, General Howe and General Cornwallis decided to commit all of the British military strength in a direct thrust toward the American encampment.[553]

In General Washington's camp in Pennsylvania, Washington called a council of war with his generals and ranking officers to discuss what future operations might be necessary. Washington's troops were exhausted, and many suffered from various illnesses and injuries. The army's supplies of food, clothing and blankets were running low and needed to be replenished. The weather was becoming unbearable for the poorly supplied American troops, and almost half of the regiments were officially reported "ineffective."[554] Concern was rising that many veteran regiments would be leaving the Continental Army and returning to their homes, having completed their enlistment at the end of the year. This was the case for veteran soldiers with Lieutenant Philip Ulmer and others whose enlistments would end soon.

With his American forces weakening and dwindling, General Washington's officers were concerned that a strong enemy encounter would shatter the Continental Army. If the Delaware River froze, as it often did in the harsh January cold, the enemy could march across the ice and capture Philadelphia, the seat of colonial government. Washington's Continental Army had never been successful in stopping the strong and well-trained British and Hessian forces in open combat. After the successes of the British forces in capturing New York, New Jersey and Rhode Island, the possible attack on Philadelphia and the capture of the leadership in the Continental Congress would certainly become a crushing blow to American independence, liberty and freedom. The American army's success at Trenton might be considered an accidental event and viewed by many as a fluke. The American cause had come to another crisis point. Hard choices had to be made, and great issues hung in the balance.

The first response of the council was not supportive of another conflict with the British forces so soon. However, as the possibilities of another successful engagement began to turn the tide of opinion, the officers came to the determination that a bold and decisive strike might liberate a large portion of western New Jersey and demonstrate that the success at Trenton was not an accident. The council adjourned in unity, high spirits and mutual support.[555] On December 28, 1776, General Washington sent messengers from his headquarters to the generals and officers in the field to prepare the troops to move back across the Delaware River to New Jersey. General Washington sent the following message to John Hancock, president of the Congress: "I am just setting out, to attempt a second crossing over the Delaware…It will be attended with much fatigue and difficulty on account of the ice which will neither allow us to cross on foot, nor give us easy passage with boats."[556]

At first light on December 29, the army began to move out of its camps along the Delaware River and proceeded to the frozen riverbanks. General Greene's troops found that the ice at their crossing at Yardley Ferry was two or three inches thick. The infantry found that they could walk across the Delaware River on the ice. The ice was unable to support the horses and artillery, however. Greene's troops had to leave their artillery guns and the wagons that held their tents and supplies behind, and they proceeded without them. That night in Trenton, the troops slept out in the open and tried to keep themselves warm by the flames of campfires. In the meantime, upstream, General Washington and General Sullivan's division were trying to cross the river at McConkey's Ferry. Ensign Philip Ulmer participated with these troops in the effort to cross to the New Jersey side without success. They were unable to walk across on the ice or to use their boats because of thick ice. The next day, General Washington and General Sullivan's division were able to cross the Delaware River. With assistance from both divisions working together, some of the field guns and wagons were brought over the river on ferry barges. They managed to accomplish the final crossing on New Year's Eve.[557] Henry Knox and his gunners had repaired broken axles and carriages and added captured Hessian field guns. They had found other heavy equipment in Philadelphia as well. Colonel Henry Knox and his Continental artillery brigade brought thirty to forty pieces across the river, which was twice his strength at Trenton.[558]

As the Continental Army gathered on the New Jersey side of the Delaware River on December 31, 1776, General Washington was confronted with another urgent and vitally important dilemma upon which the success of the army depended—supplies and soldiers. The distribution of supplies was the weakest link in the long chain of vital needs of Washington's Continental Army. A sufficient distribution of goods and supplies would enable the men to remain healthy and to function effectively as soldiers. Washington wrote to Robert Morris, "The greatest impediment to our motion is the want of provisions, some of the troops are yet on the other side of the river [in Pennsylvania] only waiting provisions."[559] Commissary officers complained that farmers would not sell produce and meat to the army, and the millers would not grind grain for bread and biscuits. The merchants and businessmen would only accept hard specie (gold and silver coins) and not Continental paper money, which was considered worthless.[560] The staple of the army diet in the winter of 1776 was salt meat, bread or biscuits. Commissary General Joseph Trumbull of Connecticut was able, with difficulty, to provide food supplies to General Washington's army troops. The "eastern states," as New England was called, provided the army's largest supply of provisions, clothing and money.[561] Connecticut became known as the "Provision State." With the renewed efforts of Robert Morris (a wealthy merchant and the leader of the Philadelphia Associates) and the support from Connecticut's Governor Trumbull, the provisions and supplies began to flow to Washington's Continental Army. The American troops were able to resume their work of carrying out their campaigns in New Jersey. By preventing the British from acquiring dominance and control of New Jersey, it kept the British forces from claiming another colony for the British Crown. Washington's winter campaign in New Jersey in 1776–77 prevented the capture of Philadelphia, where the seat of government was located at this time.

The most immediate and urgent problem that faced General Washington was the issue of the expiration of many soldiers' enlistments on December 31, 1776. Many of his most experienced soldiers were determined to depart, having served since the siege of Boston in 1775. One of these regiments was Colonel Glover's Marblehead mariners, who had helped answer the Continental Army's needs for water transportation and maritime defense. Many of the Massachusetts infantry regiments had soldiers and marines from the Province of Maine. They had served with General Arnold in the Canadian and northern New York campaigns, and they wanted to depart for home when their enlistments were completed. Many of these veteran soldiers and mariners from coastal Massachusetts in frontier Maine district planned to leave the army and pursue a career in "privateering." In the fall of 1775 and in the year of 1776, cargo, trading and merchant ships had been outfitted in coastal ports with swivel guns and cannons. Captured British supply vessels and transport and cargo ships had provided the seagoing men with large financial rewards. British goods seized by the privateering vessels were subsequently sold to merchants up and down the eastern seacoast and in the West Indies for huge profits. The profits from the sales were divided in designated percentages among the captain of the armed vessel and the crew, and one half of the financial rewards went to the Continental Congress's treasury. All of the military goods, munitions and troop supplies seized on prize British ships were sent to support the Continental Army troops.[562] Large fortunes were being made in Marblehead, Salem, Boston and other New England seaport towns such as Newburyport and Waldoboro. Many soldiers wanted to become a part of the lucrative ventures. They wanted to sail for the glory of the American cause and enrich themselves with unimaginable fortunes as well.

WASHINGTON'S APPEAL FOR THE SOLDIERS TO REMAIN IN THE CONTINENTAL ARMY

The great and radical Evil which pervades our whole System & like an Ax at the Tree of our safety, Interests and Liberty here again shews [sic] *its baleful influence—Tomorrow the Continental Troops are all at liberty.*
—*General Washington, December 31, 1776*[563]

The Continental Army was in great danger of unraveling and melting away. In an urgent message to Robert Morris on December 31, General Washington wrote: "Tomorrow the Continental Troops are all at Liberty. In order to get their assistance have promised them a bounty of 10 Dollars if they will continue for one Month—But here again a new difficulty presents itself. We have not the money…"[564]

Enlistment requirements in the Continental Army had been changed by the Continental Congress in early January 1777 to service "for three years or the duration of the war." General Washington called together his merchant and entrepreneurial officers from the Philadelphia Associates. General Thomas Mifflin, a persuasive politician and Philadelphia merchant, suggested that a bounty of ten dollars might be offered to men who agreed to remain winter soldiers for a few more weeks. The most difficult test would be to convince the New England regiments, composed of the most experienced and battle-tested soldiers, to remain with the Continental Army through the winter. The New England regiments were eager to return home, but they agreed to listen. Thomas Mifflin mustered the New England regiments and rode on his horse along their lines, firmly pleading with and haranguing the soldiers. He spoke of the American cause, appealed to their conscience and offered ten dollars hard money if they would stay for six more weeks.[565] General Mifflin asked the soldiers to "poise firelocks" if they agreed to stay. To the surprise of everyone, nearly all the firelocks went up in agreement. Two New England soldiers from Rhode Island wrote of the incident: "The poising began by some men of each platoon and was followed by the whole line…We all poised with the rest…Our regiment, with one accord, agreed to stay to a man; as did the others, except a few who made their escape by the enemy at Trenton and was not seen in the army afterwards."[566] The news of General Mifflin's success with the enlistments was carried to General Washington, who was pleased with the results but surprised by the cost to acquire the soldiers. He wrote to Congress that a bounty of ten dollars was "a most extravagant Price, when compared to the time of Service, but the example was set by the State of Pennsylvania with respect to their militia, and I thought it no time to stand upon trifles when a body of firm troops, inured to danger, were absolutely necessary to lead on the raw and undisciplined."[567]

General Washington decided to appeal to the Continental soldiers in General Greene and General Sullivan's divisions. He mustered the New England regiments and personally appealed to the soldiers to serve for six more weeks. One young sergeant wrote, "The general personally addressed us…told us our services were greatly needed, and that we could do more for our country than we ever could at any future date, and in the most affectionate manner entreated us to stay."[568] The drums rolled, waiting for volunteers. The regiment commanders called for men to step forward, but not a man stepped forward. The troops were tired and had suffered many deprivations during the past months. They were determined to return home to their families and resume their lives again. The soldiers watched as General Washington wheeled his horse about, rode in front of the regiment and spoke to them again. He said, "My brave fellows, you have done all I have asked you to do, and more than could be reasonably expected; but your country is at stake, your wives, your houses, and all that you hold dear. You have worn yourselves out with fatigues and hardships, but we know not how to spare you. If you will consent to stay one month longer, you will render that service to the cause of liberty, and to your country, which you probably can never do under any other circumstances."[569] The drums rolled again, and a few soldiers stepped forward, then several others, followed by many more. Their example was followed by nearly all who were fit for duty in the regiments. The soldiers had felt the force of General Washington's personal appeal and responded. Of the soldiers in the three brigades, almost half decided to return home. About two hundred volunteers stepped forward. These veteran soldiers knew what General Washington was asking them to do. They knew what the cost might be upon them. Veteran soldier Ensign Philip Ulmer stepped forward and enlisted in Colonel Vose's regiment. He received a promotion on January 1, 1777, to lieutenant and immediately became involved as an army officer with more responsibilities of leadership within both Colonel Vose's and General Paterson's regiments.[570] His translation skills and assistance as an interpreter became valuable assets to his regiment and to General Washington and his intelligence officers. Lieutenant Philip Ulmer led a number of small detached units on special assignment from Colonel Vose's and General Paterson's regiments in General St. Clair's brigade on the right wing of Washington's Continental Army.

BATTLE OF THE ASSUNPINK CREEK

After the surprisingly successful attack at Trenton on December 26, 1776, British general Howe ordered General Charles Cornwallis to take a trained force of British and Hessian reinforcements from the New York City vicinity and recover Trenton. General Washington had established his headquarters at a large house that had belonged to Loyalist John Barnes on Queen Street at Trenton, New Jersey. General Washington and his council of war expected a strong British counterattack. Washington received a report that the British reinforcements were marching south in a long column from New York City toward New Brunswick and Trenton. Washington and his council decided to meet this attack outside of town. General Cornwallis's British forces moved southward from Princeton along Trenton Road on January 2, 1777, with the order to take back Trenton and to drive the Americans out of New Jersey and across the Delaware River. The last fight at Trenton had taught Washington's commanders that a strong defensive position was located on a high knoll south of Assunpink Creek outside of the town.

Lieutenant Philip Ulmer served an active role in Colonel Vose's and General Paterson's regiments. These combined regiments were part of General Sullivan's division on the Continental Army's right wing located at Phillip's Mill. This location provided an easy ford across the Assunpink

Creek and was the weakest position for the American army to hold near the swamp. There were several fords where the deep creek could be crossed as it flowed southward from Trenton to the Delaware River. The icy water flowed quickly along the steep and swollen banks of the creek near the junction with Delaware River and could be crossed only by a narrow stone bridge. To the south of the creek was a slope of land that rose toward an open field, which was a good location for the infantry, and had broad fields for the artillery. General Washington had conferred with General Knox so that the guns were placed with interlocking sights at the critical crossings along the creek and bridge.[571]

There were two upper fords where General St. Clair's brigade was positioned with twelve guns hidden behind Phillip's and Henry's mills. Washington ordered that fortifications were to be constructed at the fords at both mills. General St. Clair's veteran New England troops were located at the fords to defend the right flank of the Continental Army. These veteran soldiers worked hard with axes and shovels to prepare a defense at the crossings, the weakest link in the rebel defenses. From their position at Phillip's ford, Lieutenant Philip Ulmer and Major Wilkinson (aide to General St. Clair), with other soldiers in St. Clair's brigade, watched what was transpiring along Trenton Road. British infantry and Hessian grenadiers advanced upon the American regiments that had been sent forward to engage the British and slow their approach to Trenton. General Cornwallis deployed his column into a line of battle and brought up the field guns. Volleys of musket fire and artillery guns followed. An artillery duel started and lasted for almost twenty-five minutes. General Cornwallis held the high ground above Trenton, which was fully visible to the American troops on the other side of the Assunpink Creek. He ordered his men into long lines in "battalion order" along the crest of the rise where they were most readily seen. In the town, British infantrymen marched forward in columns toward the creek. The American troops could see the awesome size of the attacking British and Hessian forces that outnumbered them considerably.[572]

Located at Phillip's Mill, Major Wilkinson with General St. Clair's brigade on the American right recorded in his memoirs that "the soldiers had a sense of foreboding, an 'awful moment' deeper than they recalled in any other battle."[573] On the British left wing, Hessian colonel Carl von Donop led his battalion and the remnants of Colonel Rall's brigade to an elevation overlooking Phillip's Mill ford. This maneuver was to prevent a flanking movement on the British left by St. Clair's New England brigade, which was guarding the upper fords of the Assunpink Creek.[574] These American troops were outnumbered five to one by Cornwallis's regiments across the swift Assunpink stream.[575] The order Donop had given to his Hessian soldiers was to grant "no quarter" to American prisoners caught.[576] The journal of a Hessian soldier in the battalion noted that the Americans "withdrew in the most perfect order, being attacked by the Linsing and Black battalions."[577] The American troops, with General St. Clair's brigade, continued to hold the British forces back from their position until sunset. During the day, General St. Clair dispatched several young veteran officers and soldiers on a reconnaissance assignment to discover if there was another way of getting around Cornwallis's superior army forces. Discreetly, the reconnaissance scouts observed and probed the British positions. They reported their findings to General St. Clair. Lieutenant Philip Ulmer, who was fluent in both German and English and who had often led small detachments of reconnaissance scouts from Colonel Vose's regiment, might have been among the scouts who patrolled the country lanes beyond the right flanking position at Phillip's Mill. Lieutenant Philip Ulmer also served as a lieutenant of General Paterson's First Massachusetts Continental Regiment in General St. Clair's brigade with General Sullivan's division at this time.[578]

Toward the end of the day, the American troops on Trenton Road continued their fighting retreat through the town of Trenton and southward toward the stone bridge at the Assunpink Creek. The British picked up the pace and tried to cut off the American troops' flanking move. The Hessians and British light infantry continued their pursuit of the New England brigade, firing at the American soldiers from between the houses and into the flanking troops. Any retreating American soldiers or townspeople who were caught by Colonel von Donop's troops were tortured and killed, following Donop's orders of "granting no quarter." The American troops ran toward the bridge over the creek in an attempt to get across and make their escape. Other retreating soldiers splashed across the icy and swollen stream at the lower fords close to the Delaware River. The American artillery began to cover the routed American soldiers in their attempt to escape from Cornwallis's advancing British and Hessian army forces. Major Wilkinson recorded in his journal that "it was getting dark, the evening was so far advanced that I distinguished the flame from the muzzles of our muskets."[579]

As the American soldiers streamed back across the Assunpink Creek, General Washington directed them to defensive positions. Washington distributed his strength to cover the important crossing places. Washington's military defense greatly depended on the artillery at this time. In the center of his southern defense on the hill, Washington and Knox had placed about eighteen heavy guns, all to cover the little stone bridge under which the swift, swollen and icy creek flowed. Upstream at Phillip's Mill and Henry's Mill, twelve cannons had been placed near the mills with General St. Clair's brigade. Other cannons were positioned to cover the lower fords with General Greene's brigade.[580] The infantry under the command of General Greene was positioned to the American left position, where they could shoot the enemy troops if they forded the lower creek. Some of General Greene's regiments were also positioned near the artillery to protect and lend support if the enemy managed to get across the bridge. In the twilight, the British forces launched probing attacks at the major crossings over the Assunpink Creek. Some of the British troops attempted to make their first attack at the lower fords of the creek on the American left. They were met by a storm of musketry from the American troops from the other side. The artillery joined in and assisted in driving the British attackers back. The attackers suffered many casualties and retreated to the cover of the buildings on the outskirts of town near the upper stream.

The Hessian artillery guns were brought forward and began to fire. The cannonade continued for about fifteen minutes in an attempt to soften up the American position. In the gathering darkness, the British and Hessian commanders drove their densely packed column of soldiers forward in an attempt to storm the bridge. Every American soldier within range fired at the attacking forces. The attackers were driven back over the bridge, leaving behind very heavy casualties. Again the British and Hessian forces regrouped and made another surge for the bridge. As the combined enemy forces approached, Henry Knox prepared his artillerymen for another hot engagement. The American troops waited until the enemies were within range. Suddenly the American army unleashed a terrific barrage of artillery and musket fire upon the approaching enemy troops. To the amazement of the American troops, the British and Hessian forces continued to advance. Wave after wave of men surged forward, where they were cut down by heavy fire. Just as the leading enemy troops were almost over the bridge, the intense gunfire became so destructive that the enemy troops broke ranks and fled.[581] One American wrote about the British and Hessian's second attempt to cross over the Assunpink stone bridge: "The [British] officers reformed the ranks and again they rushed the bridge, and again was the shower of bullets pushed upon them with redoubled fury. This time the column broke before it reached the center of the bridge, and their retreat was again followed by a hardy shout from our line."[582] At that moment, there was a release of emotional triumph, and cheers and shouts of joy filled the air.

Reinforcements were brought up, and the British prepared for a third assault upon the bridge. The British assembled a heavy column of soldiers in an attempt to force their way over the bridge. American troops fired all together and met General Cornwallis's surge of British and Hessian forces with heavy artillery and musket fire. There was a very heavy loss of life among the British and Hessian forces. The bloody bodies of dead and dying soldiers piled up on the bridge, and some fell over the sides into the swiftly flowing creek below. The British and Hessian infantry retreated. American troops moved forward toward the bridge. One artilleryman wrote, "The bridge looked red as blood, with their killed and wounded and red coats."[583] Another American soldier wrote, "It was then that our army raised a shout, and such a shout I never since heard; by what signal or word of command, I know not. The line was more than a mile in length, and from the nature of the ground the extremes were not in sight of each other, yet they shouted as one man."[584] Many of the American troops returned to Trenton for the night, while other exhausted soldiers sank to the ground, and many slept where they lay.

Due to the darkness, the heavy casualties and the exhaustion of the troops, General Cornwallis's forces retreated north and east of Trenton. General Cornwallis decided to wait and finish the battle the next day. A British council of war was called by General Cornwallis, who was encamped to the north of Trenton. The second battle near Trenton at the Assunpink Creek would end the rebellion by breaking the will and the back of the Continental Army. The British and Hessian officers felt certain of victory the next day. The British artillery continued to fire into the American positions across the creek all during the night. General Henry Knox's artillery guns returned fire with a barrage of shells that went north of the town. The cannonballs exploded with flashes of light and corresponding muffled booms in the darkness throughout the night. In his headquarters, General Cornwallis discussed his plans for the morning's surprise attack against Washington's army. He ordered that most of the German troops be pulled back to the north of Trenton in an effort to draw the American troops out of their secure positions. The British Regulars were sent to the east of Trenton into the wooded area along the upper fords of the Assunpink Creek. He deployed about two thousand Hessians into the woods near the ford at Phillip's Mill with the order to attack Washington's right flank at the break of day and overwhelm General St. Clair's brigade.[585] Cornwallis had discovered the weakness of the American position, and under Colonel von Donop's directions, the Hessian soldiers were not to grant quarters to the American troops. Lieutenant Philip Ulmer and his regiment were encamped at Phillip's Mill with Colonel St. Clair's brigade. A massacre of the American troops was anticipated at Phillip's Mill the next morning. Cornwallis's main army forces were ordered to surround Washington's troops at the river with the intent of forcing the Americans to surrender or die.

A council of war was called after dark by General Washington at General St. Clair's headquarters on Queen Street in the southern part of Trenton. A sense of optimistic fatalism, which had appeared before in the American army in the "dark days of seventy-six," seemed to be present in the room.[586] General Washington worked closely with his subordinates and held frequent councils of war in which he encouraged a free exchange of ideas, a lesson learned from earlier mistakes in decision-making during the New York campaign. General Washington learned to work more skillfully with his officers and lieutenants in the field by the construction of a consensus. Washington encouraged his lieutenants to openly discuss their ideas and to join freely in the common decision-making process. Lieutenant Philip Ulmer was present with the other officers and experienced scouts for the reconnaissance report, which had been ordered by General St. Clair earlier during the day. General St. Clair wrote about the open meeting of his officers and local citizens:

> *General Washington summoned a council of the general officers at my headquarters and after stating the difficulties in his way, the possibility of defeat, and the circumstances that would necessarily result if it happened, desired advice; the situation of the two armies were known to all; a battle was certain if he kept his ground until morning, and in case of an action a defeat was to be apprehended; a retreat by the only route thought of, down the river, would be difficult and precarious...the loss of the corps he commanded might be fatal to the country: under these circumstances he asked advice.*[587]

There was an officer's report given to the council regarding the reconnaissance mission by several experienced scouts who General St. Clair had sent out earlier that day. The detached company had scouted the country lanes and pathways beyond their right flank at Phillip's Mill, and they had found a pathway that led north, by a roundabout route, to a crossing called "Quaker Bridge." The bridge was near a Quaker meetinghouse in the woods.

The Quaker road led northward toward the town of Princeton. General St. Clair suggested that "if the army could reach that point unobserved and unopposed, it then could proceed almost due north to Princeton, distant about six miles from the bridge…From Princeton the main roads could be used for turning the left of the enemy, gaining a march upon him, and proceeding with all possible expedition to Brunswick."[588]

It was decided that the American troops should take this roundabout route to the Quaker Bridge crossing and then proceed north to Princeton, which was weakly protected. This plan received general support from those in attendance. Large fires were ordered to be built and maintained during the exceedingly cold dark night. Some troops made a noisy use of picks and shovels, while others made a show of guarding the crossings on the Assunpink Creek. Orders were given to as many as five hundred men that they were to continue working at this activity in the light of the bright campfires at night. While these activities were going on, other soldiers were hard at work in the darkness behind the fires packing their equipment, wrapping the wheels of their cannons in rags and preparing to march.[589]

After midnight, General Washington ordered the baggage wagons to be moved out toward the southeast, and the troops were ordered to fall into line. The officers' orders were given by whispers for the troops to get into line and begin to march as quietly as possible.[590] Because of the darkness of the night, some of the troops under General Greene near the Trenton Bridge became confused, frightened and disoriented. These army units panicked in the darkness and fled toward Bordentown to the southeast. General Washington lost about one thousand men in the panic, a substantial part of his army force at the time.[591] The rest of the army detachments held together and continued to march in a long column. Moving carefully and quietly, General Paterson's First Massachusetts Continental Regiment at the Phillip's Mill location near the Great Bear Swamp filed off by detachments. Lieutenant Ulmer filed off with his detachment of soldiers with Colonel Vose's and General Paterson's troops. They could observe the Hessian soldiers sitting around their campfires warming themselves and smoking their pipes. General St. Clair's troops marched about one mile to the south and another mile to the east through a densely wooded terrain. They continued following the pathway until they were able to join the main body of the Continental Army on a country road heading northeastward around the Great Bear Swamp. The American army divisions with General Sullivan and General Greene, the division commanders, followed the roadway north to the Quaker Bridge, which had to be crossed. Once across the bridge, the road continued northward toward Princeton, about sixteen miles away. Their roundabout escape route took the American troops away from the enemy and clear of the British and Hessian positions.

The Continental Army troops continued to march through the bitter cold night to the Quaker Bridge, but they found it too weak to accommodate the heavy artillery equipment and ammunition wagons. Another bridge had to be hastily built before the American army forces could move forward. A party of axe men and carpenters worked frantically to accomplish this task. While these men worked on the bridge, General Washington reorganized his troops. Washington split his army into two divisions, with General Greene in command of the left wing, with fewer troops, and the right wing led by General Sullivan's reinforced division, which became the main body of the army. Both divisions had Continental Army troops in the lead, with militia troops in the middle and more Continental troops in the rear. Careful thought was given by the officers as to the best method of integrating the veteran regiments with the inexperienced militia troops to ensure stability within the ranks. General Washington planned a surprise attack the next morning on Colonel Mawhood and the few British troops left at Princeton. Having finally crossed over the stream at Quaker Bridge, the Quaker Bridge Road afforded the marching columns an opportunity to move more quickly toward Princeton. As daybreak arrived, the unfortunate delay at Quaker Bridge spoiled Washington's strategy of a surprise attack.

As the American troops picked up the pace and began to approach Princeton, the spirits of the soldiers rose. The two divisions divided into two wings as they approached Princeton. General Greene's smaller left wing division marched on the lower road to the west along Stony Brook and through a ravine that led to the well-traveled Post Road, the main road between Trenton and Princeton. Their orders were to form into a blocking position and stop any traffic on the main road in both directions. The objective was to keep the British garrison at Princeton from escaping from the town and also prevent British and Hessian reinforcements from coming from Trenton. General Sullivan's right wing division with the main army was to deliver the key attack upon Princeton. Leading from the front was the division commander, General John Sullivan, then General Washington's secretaries, followed by Colonel Richard Harrison and Major James Wilkinson. Close behind were General St. Clair's New England brigade, with Lieutenant Philip Ulmer and his regiment, and Mifflin's Pennsylvania brigade of Continentals and militiamen "marching in files without flanking parties."[592] Lieutenant Colonel Sherman's Connecticut infantry, with several large guns and possibly with Alexander Hamilton's New York artillery, marched together toward Princeton. Beyond the Quaker Bridge, General Sullivan's long column turned to the east on Saw Mill Road and picked up their pace. This road went around a small wooded area to the south of the Quaker meetinghouse and turned north toward the back of Princeton College (present-day Princeton University).

BATTLE OF PRINCETON

On the morning of January 3, 1777, General Cornwallis's British troops awoke to discover that the American army had slipped away during the night. Cornwallis at first thought that Washington's army had retreated to Bordentown, but hearing the cannonade coming from the north in the direction of Princeton, he assembled his army forces and made a forced march from Trenton toward Princeton. General Cornwallis and his officers were furious that they had been outwitted by Washington's American army soldiers.[593] Colonel Mawhood had been given the responsibility of defending Princeton by General Cornwallis prior to his leaving with the main British and Hessian army forces to retake Trenton from the Americans. Colonel Mawhood's orders from General Cornwallis were to hold the town of Princeton, guard the British army stores and protect its communications. Following the battle at Assunpink Creek (often referred to as the second battle of Trenton), General Cornwallis sent an urgent dispatch to Princeton asking Colonel Mawhood for assistance. Colonel Mawhood's relief forces (half of his regimental troops) were ordered by General Cornwallis to march at dawn toward Trenton with needed men and supplies for Cornwallis's forces. General Greene was headed north toward Princeton on Post Road with his division of American troops while Colonel Mawhood was marching south with the British relief troops to Trenton on the same road. As fate would have it, an unexpected and bloody battle was imminent in the countryside to the south of Princeton between the opposing army divisions.

Both of General Washington's Continental Army divisions, led by General Greene and General Sullivan, advanced rapidly upon Princeton in the cold early morning hours on January 3, after sunrise. One of Colonel Mawhood's forward reconnaissance scouts spotted the approach of the main American army on the high ground of Saw Mill Road outside the town. There was a

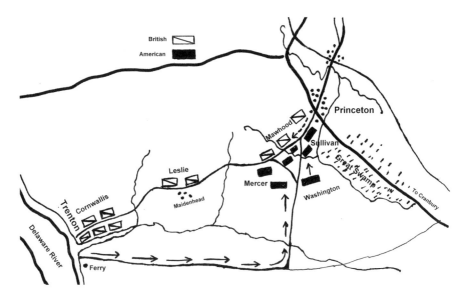

Military actions at the Battle of Princeton on January 3, 1777. *Courtesy of the author.*

moment of indecision as Colonel Mawhood thought about his choices to either retreat back to Princeton or to meet the American troops directly. Colonel Mawhood decided to attack the main Continental Army forces who were marching eastward along Saw Mill Road. He ordered his Fifty-fifth Regiment to take their artillery with eight guns and the supply wagons back to safety in Princeton. Colonel Mawhood led his Seventeenth of Foot Infantry Regiment with two field guns across the snow-covered countryside, straight toward the main body of the American forces in the distance.

General Greene's division was still marching through the deep ravine along Stony Brook toward Post Road and could not see the approaching British forces. The two converging military forces were unaware of each other even though they were very close to each other. In the distance from Saw Mill Road, General Washington, who was with Sullivan's division with St. Clair's brigade, could see from his high ground location what was about to happen. He sent a messenger to warn General Greene about the approaching British forces. Greene would have to deal with the encounter as best as he could while the main army proceeded on to Princeton on its mission. The messenger arrived quickly and delivered Washington's message to General Greene. Greene ordered General Mercer to lead his brigade out of the ravine and engage the British troops. Both forces suddenly became aware of each other and headed for the high ground.

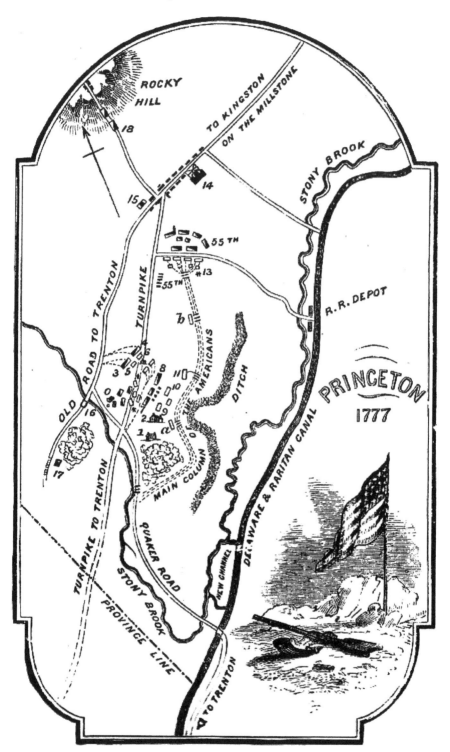

The British forces headed toward the high ground in an orchard nearby, and Colonel Mawhood had his troops form into a line for battle with their two field cannons readily available. General Mercer also headed for the same orchard (now called Mercer Hill), where the opposing enemy regiments engaged each other in gunfire. The American forces with General Greene's division were about three times the size of General Mawhood's regiment. Mercer's troops moved forward and discharged a volley of musket fire. The outnumbered British regiment withdrew under the destructive gunfire of Mercer's regiment. The Americans continued to drive forward and took cover behind a low hill. Mawhood's regiment suffered many casualties and was becoming depleted of soldiers. More relief troops soon arrived for both sides. Mawhood's infantry formed a line and marched forward and discharged a volley of gunfire. Generals Greene and Mercer's troops discharged a withering volley of their own. Volley followed volley from each side. The thick smoke from the gunpowder rose above the field of battle in a hazy cloud. The British forces suffered greatly, with heavy losses of soldiers and officers. The orchard and snow-covered field were red with blood, which flowed on the frozen ground.[594] Mawhood waited and watched for the right time for a final attack. When he saw the proper moment, he ordered his regiment to charge with bayonets. The British infantry came forward in a desperate charge, full of rage and fury, through the clouds of gunfire and musket smoke. Mercer's riflemen, who did not have bayonets, recoiled in confusion and started to flee. Mercer fell to the ground when his horse was hit by musket fire. General Mercer called for his men to retreat. He was caught by some British soldiers and knocked to the ground with a blow from a musket-butt. The British infantry thought that they had caught General Washington. They gathered around him and ordered that he "call for quarters." He refused to surrender and made a lunge at his British captors with his sword. The British soldiers bayoneted him over and over again. One British soldier was said to have exclaimed, "Damn him, he is dead. Let us leave him."[595]

The American infantry had lost many of their leaders in the British attack, and the rebel troops with General Mercer's brigade were sent into a rout by the frightening British bayonet charge. The American troops were in retreat,

Opposite: Map of the village of Princeton, New Jersey, in 1777 from an engraving in 1855. Artist unknown.

Following pages: *The Death of General Mercer at the Battle of Princeton, January 3, 1777*. By John Trumbull. *Courtesy of Library of Congress.*

with the British infantry close behind them. More American troops streamed onto the battlefield. Captain Joseph Moulder, the commander of a small battery of Philadelphia artillery, brought his heavy guns quickly into action. His artillery, with two long-barreled four-pounder field guns, fired deadly rounds of grape and canister into the British infantry and stopped it.[596] Other American troops rallied and took their places on the battlefield. They were joined by other American field guns. One of the guns was commanded by Sergeant Joseph White, who served in General Knox's artillery regiment. He later wrote, "During this time they [the British] discovered our weakness, and brought three pieces of cannon in play to our right with grape and case."[597] The British were so close to the American gunners that the cannon fire went over the heads of the British troops. The Philadelphia volunteers, known as the Philadelphia Associates, had been among the routed soldiers, but they managed to rally their men and form into a line for battle.

At that critical time, General Washington arrived on the field with relief troops and took control of the battlefield. Washington led the relief troops in a direct attack into the center of Colonel Mawhood's troops, who were quickly outnumbered and outflanked. Washington led the American troops forward and ordered them to fire while continuing to march forward. The British line broke, but the British Regulars still continued to fight. The British Regulars regrouped and fought their way through the closing American circle. Some of these British combatants were able to escape and made their way toward Trenton. Other British soldiers were able to escape and headed for the British headquarters at New Brunswick. As other surviving British troops ran westward, Colonel Mawhood went a different way. He ordered his regiment at the orchard (present-day Mercer Hill) to retreat to Princeton, where he resumed the command of his regiment inside the town.

While the battle was going on in the orchard to the south of Princeton, other British troops were preparing to defend the town. General Sullivan's division continued its march toward Princeton. Colonel Mawhood, the commander of the British Fifty-fifth Infantry, decided to meet the oncoming American forces outside of town. Mawhood directed his infantry troops to form a strong defensive position behind a deep, steep ravine called Frog Hollow. The advancing American forces with General Sullivan engaged the enemy in a heated firefight at Frog Hollow. Colonel Mawhood sent a detached infantry unit of heavily equipped soldiers to attack the American flank. General Sullivan deployed two American regiments that broke up the British maneuver. Some of Sullivan's detached companies were able to climb down the steep ravine and crawl their way up the other side of the icy slope beyond the flank of the British soldiers. Other American troops continued to advance on the other flank.[598] The British, finding that they were being surrounded, decided to retreat to a stronger breastwork and continued the fight from a different location. Sullivan's forces used their heavy artillery and guns against the British right flank. Two of the heavy American guns fired on a dam upstream of Frog Hollow. The dam broke, causing water to flow swiftly through the ravine and sweeping the breastworks away.

The British forces retreated to another breastwork near Princeton College. General Sullivan's and St. Clair's troops, which included Lieutenant Ulmer, advanced on Mawhood's troops and prepared to storm their position. Finally, after a brief firefight, a British officer placed a white handkerchief on the point of his sword and offered his surrender to General Sullivan.[599] The surrender was accepted. Some of the American soldiers pursued a small number of fleeing British soldiers onto the grounds of Princeton College, where the British troops took refuge in Nassau Hall. Nassau Hall was the military armory where the British army kept its military stores and supplies. The British troops knocked the windows out of Nassau Hall with their muskets and prepared to defend the armory building. The American artillery was deployed, and the American troops took positions outside of the building at strategic locations.

The American battery commander, Alexander Hamilton, gave the order to open fire on Nassau Hall.[600] The artillery piece recoiled and nearly killed Major Wilkinson, who was with Lieutenant Philip Ulmer in St. Clair's brigade during this encounter. After a heated firefight, the last of the British troops surrendered, ending the battle at Princeton. The British suffered heavy losses in the fighting around Princeton. Ensign George Inman, who served in Colonel Mawhood's Seventeenth Infantry, recorded that his regiment suffered a casualty rate of 45 percent in the conflict. Among the detachments composed of inexperienced recruits and replacements, casualties were even heavier. In one Grenadier company, the casualty loss rate was 53 percent. The Royal Artillery lost ten men, about half of the crew for the field guns that were engaged.[601] Colonel Mawhood lost nearly half of his strength.[602] Many more British and Hessian soldiers were captured in different locations around the town. Lieutenant Philip Ulmer's bilingual skills would again be useful in securing the surrender of the Hessian troops and in directing the captured Hessian soldiers to the prison encampments, where they would be interrogated and their disposition would be determined.

General Cornwallis's troops, who had engaged in a hurried forced march from Trenton, managed to arrive at Princeton soon after General

Washington's army had left the town. General Washington, expecting a British counterattack from General Cornwallis, had formed up his forces and led the army northeast from Princeton toward Kingston, New Jersey, without delay. General Cornwallis feared that the major British depot at New Brunswick, where the British war chest, military stores and magazines were located, would likely be the next place that Washington's army troops would attack. The large British military base was protected only by one regiment of British soldiers. If General Washington had chosen to attack New Brunswick, the major British military stronghold would have easily fallen to the Americans, and the plans of General Cornwallis to subdue and crush the colonial rebellion would have been lost. If the British war chest had been seized, and the most valuable military depot in New Jersey captured, the British commander in America would have had to end the war at this time. These concerns weighed heavily upon General Cornwallis as he hurried his British and Hessian forces toward Princeton in a rapid forced march. The remains of Cornwallis's army continued their force march toward New Brunswick, New Jersey, to defend the city and to secure the vulnerable British military stronghold.

At Kingston, New Jersey, the main road divided. One road went to Somerset, and the other went to New Brunswick. At this intersection, while still on horseback, General Washington called his council of war together to consider the possibilities. One choice was a quick strike at the main military depot at New Brunswick. The other choice was an attack on the Somerset Court House, where the British baggage train with supplies might be seized.[603]*

The American army was exhausted from a long night march and having fought two battles in rapid succession. James Wilkinson wrote that the exclamation from one of his officers was: "O that we had 500 fresh men to beat up their quarters at Brunswick."[604] General Washington decided to march his troops to Somerset, New Jersey, in the hope of capturing the British baggage train. Unfortunately, the British baggage train had left Somerset an hour before the American troops arrived. None of the

---

* *Author's comment*: General Washington was unaware that only one small British regiment was protecting the British depot at this time and that a large number of the military stores, supplies and munitions were kept there. The British war chest with the currency for financing military operations and the army's payroll for General Howe's British forces was located at the fort in New Brunswick. The capture of the depot at New Brunswick would have hastened the end of the American Revolution.

American brigades or regiments had strength left to pursue the wagon train and the British guards. General Washington's army camped at Somerset overnight on January 3. His army troops resumed the march in the morning for Pluckemin, where the exhausted American troops were finally able to enjoy some rest and a good meal, after having had no food for several days. With the Watchung Mountains to the west of his exhausted and battle-worn troops, and the Morristown regiments nearby preparing the winter quarters for the approaching army troops, Washington's army forces proceeded to Morristown, where they arrived at sunset on January 6, 1777. General Washington's Continental Army finally went into winter quarters.[605] Lieutenant Philip Ulmer was with these exhausted troops who had fought for ten days. With the victories at Trenton and Princeton, morale rose in the ranks and more men enlisted in the Continental Army for longer durations of time, primarily for three years or the duration of the war as mandated by the Continental Congress.

General Cornwallis's British and Hessian army forces, having suffered three defeats in ten days, were exhausted and needed to retire to their winter quarters. British general Howe ordered the withdrawal and abandonment of many military forts and outposts in western New Jersey. The British forces retreated toward eastern New Jersey and New York City for their winter quarters. General Cornwallis left a much smaller British force in western New Jersey at Amboy and New Brunswick. The battle at Princeton was the last major action of General Washington's winter campaign in New Jersey.

CONCLUSION OF WASHINGTON'S WINTER CAMPAIGN OF TEN CRITICAL DAYS

General Washington wrote a revealing letter to John Hancock and the Continental Congress on January 5, 1777: "My original plan when I set out from Trenton was to have pushed on to seize the biggest British base in New Jersey, with all their stores and magazines, and a rich military chest."[606]

The bloody fighting at Trenton, Assunpink Creek (the second battle of Trenton) and Princeton had exhausted the American troops and had weakened the American army's ability to defend itself. Many of the soldiers had suffered no rest and little to eat for two nights and a day even before the engagements had begun.[607] The American commanders were concerned for the health and well-being of their soldiers, who had been challenged to the extreme of their endurance. Many soldiers needed clothing, coats, shoes, blankets and other basic supplies in order to stay warm during the harsh and bitterly cold winter weather.

General Cornwallis's British and Hessian army troops were expected to pursue the weary American troops as rapidly as their soldiers could move. However, the British and Hessian forces were exhausted, and many of their troops were depleted. The resistance that Colonel Mawhood's regiments had given at Princeton succeeded in delaying the American forces long enough to disrupt and change a major part of General Washington's planned operation and objectives. The British army had missed a chance to strike a decisive blow to General Washington's Continental Army forces on the night of January 3–4, when the army was exposed and unable to defend itself. One Hessian captain, Johann Ewald, wrote about this missed opportunity in his journal: "Several days later it was learned that after the coup at Princeton, General Washington and his army had camped in the woods at Rocky Hill, two hours from Princeton, until the morning of the 4th—completely exhausted, without ammunition or provisions."[608]

The American successes in the ten critical days between the battles at Trenton and Princeton began to have an impact on the British commanders' fundamental thoughts concerning the American resolve for independence from Great Britain. The British mindset had started to change. The British commanders were more concerned about being attacked instead of being the attackers and conducting aggressive attacks upon the resisting rebel forces. The brutality and abuses on colonial settlers and townspeople in New Jersey at the hands of the occupying British soldiers and Hessian mercenaries turned public opinion against the invaders and began to bond the American people together in a common cause.

REACTION TO THE AMERICAN SUCCESS AT TRENTON AND PRINCETON

The news spread quickly throughout the thirteen colonies about the Continental Army's success over the powerful British Royal Army and the feared German Hessian mercenary soldiers at Trenton and Princeton. There was a major change in public opinion throughout the thirteen colonies and in Europe. Support grew for the American cause and America's struggle for independence from Great Britain. Recruiting parties, which had previously had difficulty recruiting men for military service, suddenly had men joining by companies.[609] The minds of the people had been altered, and a new spirit of hope and commitment had been ignited. In New York, the British leadership had been dismayed by the news. British writers blamed the Hessian troops for the defeat. Hessian officers in the field blamed General Howe for his disposition of the troops in New Jersey.

In Europe, the news of an American success at Trenton and Princeton sparked a controversy about the Hessian presence in America. The controversy questioned the morality of the soldier trade in the same way that the trafficking in the slave trade was being addressed.[610] The successes at Trenton and Princeton enlarged the debate about the American Revolution and the legitimacy of Europe's old regime. The Battles of Trenton and Princeton changed attitudes about the American resolve in the war for independence on both sides of the Atlantic Ocean. A leading European statesman and critic of the soldier trade, Count de Mirabeau, attacked the soldier trade as slave trade and human trafficking. He asked the Hessians to remember the misery that it brought to their own sons: "The Hessian trade was all the more odious because it supported English despotism in a failing struggle against American rights…Cross the seas, hurry to America, but embrace your brothers there, defend these generous people against the arrogant rapacity of their persecutors…Learn from America the art of living free."[611]

Dramatic Turn of Events: Trenton and Princeton

The Battles of Trenton and Princeton gave the Continental Congress a new confidence in 1777 because it proved that American forces could defeat the powerful and feared British Regulars and Hessian mercenary soldiers. The previous defeats of the Continental Army in the Canadian and New York campaigns and the army's forced retreat across New Jersey to the banks of the Delaware River in Pennsylvania in 1776 had caused low American morale in Congress, in the army ranks and throughout the colonies. The Continental Army's successes at Trenton, Assunpink Creek and Princeton boosted the flagging morale of the American colonists and helped to increase enlistments and reenlistments in the American army. The Continental infantry stayed beyond their enlistments. The military supplies, provisions and needed resources were being made available to Washington's army in New Jersey. The colonial privateers along the eastern seacoast and in the West Indies were having great success in capturing British cargo and transport vessels. The American troops greatly needed military supplies such as adequate armaments, uniforms, shoes, blankets and entrenching tools, but most of all gunpowder. Pleas and appeals were made to the colonies for more supplies and support for the soldiers.

The import of gunpowder had been banned in 1774 by the British government. The capture of military goods from British ships helped to supply the American troops with cannons, arms, lead, gunpowder and many needed supplies. The sale of domestic and commercial goods from the British ships, as well as the prize vessels themselves, proved to be financially lucrative. The treasury of the Continental Congress received half of the financial worth of the captured vessels and goods when they were sold, and Washington's Continental Army received all of the military supplies, guns and ammunition. The captains of the privateering vessels and the crewmen shared in the remaining half of the monetary rewards in designated percentages. The merchants made huge profits on speculation, investments and the sale of trade goods in America. The customs agents, who determined the prize status of the captured vessels and their contents, also received a share of the profits. Suppliers in Europe were eager to benefit from some of the bountiful American trade after decades of control by the mercantile houses in Great Britain.

The American military leadership had learned from their mistakes in several unsuccessful campaigns, and they developed different strategies. General Washington's goals remained constant throughout the American Revolution. He believed that independence could be won by maintaining Americans' resolve that freedom, liberty and self-determination were worthy goals to strive for, attain and preserve for all freedom-loving people. Through continued persistence, by preserving an American army for protection and defense and by raising the cost of war to the enemy until it was unsustainable, victory could be won. Washington held to these strategic ends, but he remained flexible about the operation of the war. One evolving strategy was based on limiting the enemy's mobility and its ability to resupply its troops. Another strategy was to move quickly and take the initiative in conducting small unexpected attacks against the stronger enemy forces, then retreating quickly and limiting casualties to their own American soldiers. The new strategic approach of concentrating a large part of the army strength against a small part of the enemy's superior forces and slowly wearing down and severely weakening the larger enemy's troops was very successful. The heavy use of massed firepower led to fewer casualties among the American troops. This "force multiplier" became an important part of American plans for conducting wartime engagements against the enemy.[612]

The attitude of the Continental Congress in conducting the war also began to change. The need for a more permanent and reliable army recruitment procedure for longer periods of time became obvious. General Washington sought soldier enlistments for up to three years or the duration of the war, and this policy was approved by the Continental Congress in the fall of 1776. Congress had previously intervened actively in military affairs. Congress told the generals how to run the war and even tried to make tactical decisions for them. Most congressmen had no experience in conducting a war. Some delegates and representatives thought they knew more about military affairs than the generals who were veteran soldiers and had experienced fighting on the battlefield in numerous conflicts. It became evident after the defeats of 1775–76 that Congress could not efficiently operate in an executive role and was not qualified to manage a war. The Continental Congress and General Washington, with his advisors, worked out a compromise. To satisfy Congress's need for civilian control, General Washington's powers were limited in time and extent, and his major decisions were subject to congressional supervision. Washington and his secondary generals were given the power to run the war, but they were careful to recognize the principle of review and supervision by civilian leaders. This became an example for "the separation of powers and the rule of law."[613]

Chapter 8

Winter Quarters at Morristown

Our affairs at present are in a prosperous way…The country seems to entertain an idea of our Superiority—Our recruiting goes on well—& a Belief prevails that the enemy are afraid of Us. If then you should be drove, which nothing that the Enemy's want of Spirit can prevent—the Tables will be turned, the country get dispirited, & we shall again relapse into our former discredit.
—General Washington's letter to General Sullivan[614]

Winter Quarters in 1776–77

The year 1777 was perhaps the most important for the British War Ministry and for Prime Minister Lord Frederick North's administration in the British Parliament. The British War Ministry was led by Lord George Germain, the British secretary of state for the American colonies. The issue was whether the British forces in North America could score enough success in putting down the American rebellion that the French government would not dare to enter the war openly to aid the American colonists in their struggle for independence. However, it was in this critical year that British plans were the most confused and British military operations were the most disjointed and disorganized. The British campaign of 1777 provided one of the most interesting object lessons in American military history of the dangers of divided command.

The military supplies for the American army forces were shipped to Newport, Rhode Island, and taken overland to the army supply depot in Springfield, Massachusetts. In December 1776, British general Clinton was sent by General Sir William Howe to seize and occupy Newport, Rhode Island. The strategic operation of capturing the town was accomplished without much opposition.[615] The British-held naval base at Newport, Rhode Island, would serve for future raids and British operations against frontier Massachusetts (Maine), at Boston and other Massachusetts coastal seaports and in Connecticut.[616] With New York City and Newport serving the British forces as secure naval and military bases, General Howe had a chance to begin an early campaign against Washington's army forces that he had been denied the previous year at Boston. General Howe submitted a comprehensive plan to Lord Germain for a spring and summer campaign that would have one army force of about ten thousand soldiers invade Massachusetts by going through Rhode Island while a second army force of ten thousand soldiers would invade and seize the main American forts and principle outposts in the upper New York colony through the Lake Champlain and Hudson River Valleys. At the same time, a British army force of seven thousand soldiers would hold the occupied sections of New York City, Long Island and Rhode Island. A final British army force of eight thousand men would hold occupied New Jersey and keep General Washington's army troops tied down in New Jersey. All of these objectives were scheduled for the spring and summer of 1777, with the colonies of Pennsylvania, Delaware, Maryland and Virginia as targets for the fall campaign and the Carolinas and Georgia as the objects for the winter campaign.[617] Lord Germain, however, could only provide about half of the British and Hessian forces required for the plan to be implemented. General Howe drafted a second plan that was sent to Lord Germain in late December 1777. This plan was to seize Philadelphia and the province of Pennsylvania using ten thousand soldiers, with the remainder of his forces divided between Rhode Island (supported by a suitable naval force to control the growing threat of New England's privateers and the Colonial Navy) and New York Island (to guard the strategic harbor, New York City and part of New Jersey). There would also be three thousand soldiers stationed on the Hudson River to protect the British stronghold at New York City from American troops. This second plan by General Howe was approved by Lord Germain, the secretary of state for strategic planning in the American Theater of war operations.

After Burgoyne helped defeat the American invasion forces, he returned to England in December. He began seeking political support for a plan to divide the American colonies by invading America from Canada. General Sir Henry Clinton was also in Great Britain trying to get authority for an independent command of his own. General Burgoyne wrote out his strategy as "Thoughts for Conducting the War on the Side of Canada." He presented his own plan for a northern campaign to Lord Germain on February 20, 1777, while on holiday in London, England. He won approval and surpassed his rival, General Sir Henry Clinton, for independent command. The northern campaign that was proposed and adopted by Lord Germain and his committee would call for a three-pronged assault, with the main force of British and Hessian soldiers commanded personally by British general John Burgoyne. The plan was to invade America by moving southward from Montreal to Lake Champlain. By using the Lake Champlain Valley water corridor, the British allied forces would proceed down the Hudson River Valley corridor to Albany, the American military headquarters of the Northern Command. A second army force, commanded by British colonel Barry St. Leger, was to descend from Montreal through the Mohawk Valley using the Mohawk River to the Hudson River. St. Leger's troops, using the Hudson River, would proceed southward to Albany, New York. A third British force, under General Howe, was to ascend north up the Hudson River and break through the American Highlands defenses at Peekskill and Poughkeepsie, New York, under the command of General Israel Putnam and General William Heath. Once this was accomplished, the combined British forces would rendezvous at Albany, isolating the rebellious New England colonies from the southern colonies. The rebellion could be methodically crushed, ending the war for American independence. General Burgoyne was so confident of his success that he recorded his bet in a betting book in a London "Gentleman's Club": "John Burgoyne wagers...one pony [50 guineas] that he will be home victorious from America by Christmas Day, 1777."[618] King George III and Lord Germain, who served as secretary of state in Lord North's cabinet, approved both General Howe's second plan and General Burgoyne's plan by late March 1777. Lord Germain believed that General Howe's plan to capture Philadelphia would be completed in time to send aid and support to General Burgoyne in his northern New York campaign.

Because of the lag in communications across the Atlantic Ocean, Lord Germain and other senior planners in the War Ministry in London viewed themselves as coordinators and providers of resources, not as operational commanders. Operational decisions and strategic planning needed to be made by the commanders in the field directing the operations. Lord

Germain and his war planners expected that General Howe and General Burgoyne would be able to communicate and work together without direction from London. The British War Ministry believed that General Howe's campaign to capture Philadelphia, the colonial seat of government, would draw out Washington's American troops and direct them away from General Burgoyne's northern campaign into northern New York and the Hudson River Valley. Once King George III and Lord Germain approved the two separate plans, difficulties in timely communication between the British commanders in America caused the two commanders to go their separate ways.

During the winter encampment of General Washington's army at Morristown, New Jersey, General Washington and his advisors developed their own new defensive strategy. Lieutenant Philip Ulmer and other officers were directed to lead small detached military units in an improvised series of surprise attacks on small British foraging companies.[619] These sudden hit-and-run attacks upon unsuspecting British companies were met with great success. Following Washington's new evolving strategy and instructions, the American forces could retain the initiative of their successes and keep the British commanders off balance using this new method of surprise attacks. The material and emotional impact was especially successful when a small company of American soldiers was able to control the time and place of the attack against a much stronger force and a more well-equipped enemy. Smaller Continental and militia troops, such as Lieutenant Ulmer's detached unit, could act with speed and precision, while it took planning and a long time to move an entire regiment or army from place to place. In this way, General Washington's Continental forces were able to outmarch and outmaneuver the British Regulars and Hessian troops and minimize American losses.

American troops did all in their power to reduce the mobility of the British and Hessian forces. With his Continental troops in interlocking positions around the British outposts of Amboy and New Brunswick, New Jersey, daily skirmishes against the British soldiers seeking forage and food supplies took a steady toll upon General Howe's men and their morale. Intelligence reports on enemy movements were delivered to General Washington, supporting the success of his new strategy. Soon General Washington was able to report to the Continental Congress that the British troops could only leave their encampments in small companies for brief periods for fear of sudden attacks from American detached militia soldiers, who had become quite successful in limiting British and Hessian mobility. Washington wrote: "[Intelligence reports] confirm their want for forage…If their Horses are reduced this Winter it will [be] impossible for them to take the Field in the spring…many small engagements could severely reduce the fighting strength of British and German regiments."[620]

THE FORAGE WAR AND THE DISCOVERY OF COUNTERFEIT CONTINENTAL DOLLARS

With the added risk that British supply ships might be attacked by Continental Navy warships and armed privateering vessels from the colonial state navies, the British and Hessian soldiers had to forage for food and supplies to support their army companies and regiment troops in New Jersey. The enemy troops often behaved in extremely cruel and brutal ways toward the New Jersey townspeople, and they took whatever they needed or wanted from the helpless citizens. The Hessian and British soldiers engaged in pillaging, plundering and the physical abuse of the elderly and the helpless women and young girls. Anyone who resisted the aggressive enemy demands was brutalized or killed, and their homes were ransacked and/or burned. These barbarian tactics caused great fear and loathing in the towns, villages and countryside farms throughout New Jersey. The neighboring colonies heard and read about the abuses, and they turned against the invading British and Hessian forces. The townspeople gave their support to the American troops, who were their only hope for protection. The American soldiers took every opportunity to harass and attack the British troops wherever they were found. This gave the American forces the opportunities that they needed to obtain vitally needed supplies of their own such as fresh meat, flour, hay, wood and livestock feed from the grateful residents whose hatred and fear of the British and Hessian army soldiers grew daily. Small military units or corps, led by officers like Lieutenant Philip Ulmer, targeted the British horses, wagons and feed supplies. Without sufficient forage supplies, the British horses would become weakened and unable to pull the heavy supply wagons and field artillery. Without sufficient food, the abusive occupying enemy soldiers would become weakened and sick. The success of this new strategy against the British and Hessian forces strengthened the resolve of the Continental and militia soldiers and developed support for the American cause among the country settlers and townspeople. German captain John Ewald, who fought with the Hessian Jaeger Corps for the British Royal Army during the Revolution, observed, "…the whole province [of New Jersey] was in arms, following us with Washington's army, constantly surrounding us on our marches and besieging our camps…Each step cost human blood."[621]

In one important encounter, when a small company of men were foraging for supplies for their regiment, a horse-drawn wagon driven by a British Loyalist farmer bound from New York City to Philadelphia was surrounded by a small detachment of American soldiers. The wagon was thoroughly examined for goods. Hidden underneath the produce and firewood, the American soldiers discovered many large bags stuffed full of counterfeit Continental dollars. This forage incident and surprising discovery was reported to General Washington and the Continental Congress. There was great surprise expressed about this detection because the government and military leaders had been unaware that counterfeit money, printed by the British aboard the HMS *Phoenix* in New York Harbor, had been flooding the colonial markets.[622] The counterfeit Continental dollars and other worthless printed currency in various denominations flooded the colonial markets and merchant businesses. The value of the currency fell, and inflation of the price of goods increased dramatically. American Continental dollars were considered worthless and were no longer accepted in Canada, Europe, the West Indies or in other trading markets around the world. Merchants and business traders in towns and cities throughout the thirteen colonies would not accept the Continental dollars or other paper currency—only gold and silver coins (specie) would be acceptable.

The counterfeit dollars, it was later disclosed, were first circulated by a distribution network of Loyalists and later by unknowing colonists and soldiers who had received paper currency as payment for their goods or services. The flood of counterfeit dollars into the American marketplace caused high inflation, the devaluation of Continental dollars and other colonial currency, and it threatened to destroy the American economy. The Continental Congress began to realize the impact and severity of this British strategy. Payment for the American soldiers' military services and the ability to transact business became of great concern for General Washington and the Continental Congress. As the price of goods skyrocketed due to high inflation, the Continental dollars became virtually worthless. The British government continued to use counterfeiting as a means for undermining the American economy for many years during and after the Revolutionary War. New Hampshire governor Josiah Bartlett wrote to William Whipple about the British counterfeiting scheme in 1777: "We have lately discovered a most diabolical scheme to ruin the paper currency by counterfeiting it, vast quantities of the Massachusetts bill & ours [in Rhode Island], that are now passing are counterfeit, and so neatly done that it is extremely difficult to discover the difference…by what appears at present, it is a Tory plan and one of the most infernal that was ever hatched."[623]

The American currency system was on the verge of total collapse. Benjamin Franklin experimented in adding mineral flecks to the paper material, and he added intricate leaf designs that were difficult for the British counterfeiters to copy. This was an effort to reestablish confidence in the American economy. The faith that the colonists had in their country's own monetary system was being destroyed by massive counterfeiting efforts and get-rich-quick schemes. American currency was so devalued by 1779 that the Continental Congress decided not to print any more paper currency. The country moved from paper currency to using gold and silver coins (specie) because they were more difficult to counterfeit and easier to detect.

Fortunately for our young, struggling country, Thomas Paine's pamphlets *Common Sense* and *American Crisis* resonated with the American people. "These were the times that tried men's souls," wrote Thomas Paine. To many of the soldiers, the American cause became more important than their military pay, which was issued in paper currency or with land-bounty. This was true for Philip Ulmer, who apparently served for some years as an unpaid soldier and officer for the American cause.

Philip Ulmer appears in the Continental Army with the rank of lieutenant on the "Continental Army Pay Accounts" with Colonel Vose's regiment for military service from January 1, 1777, to January 4, 1778.[624] The American Continental soldiers and various militia troops from many different states remained with General Washington's army in winter quarters at Morristown during the winter of 1777. Philip Ulmer appeared in the "List of Officers of the Massachusetts Militia," renamed the Continental Army, in Colonel John Paterson's regiment, where his service in General Washington's Continental Army was documented in March 1777.[625] On March 27, 1777, Philip Ulmer was commissioned at Morristown, New Jersey, as a first lieutenant in Colonel John Paterson's regiment with Captain Hunt's company.[626] He also continued to serve as a first lieutenant in Colonel Vose's First Massachusetts Regiment as well.

Sometime in April 1777, Lieutenant Philip Ulmer took a leave of absence (furlough) from the Continental Army, and he returned to Waldoboro in the eastern frontier of Massachusetts. Colonel Vose took a leave of absence from the main body of Washington's Continental Army in winter quarters at Morristown at the same time as Lieutenant Philip Ulmer. During his furlough, Lieutenant Philip Ulmer married his longtime sweetheart and childhood friend, Christiana Jung (called Young). They settled down for a short time in Waldoboro with Christiana's widowed mother on their family farm before Philip returned to his army regiment with Colonel Vose. Lieutenant Philip Ulmer continued to recruit new soldiers for his company and regiment from Waldoboro, St. George, Kennebec and the Thomaston vicinity while he was on furlough.[627] Colonel Joseph Vose raised new recruits for the First Massachusetts Regiment from the vicinity south of Boston.[628] These new recruits enlisted for three years in the spring of 1777. Lieutenant Ulmer enlisted his neighbors David Beckler and Peter Lehr, his cousin George Ulmer Jr. and other friends and relatives for his company that served with Colonel Vose's regiment.[629] George Ulmer, Philip's younger brother, enlisted in 1777 as a private in Colonel Vose's First Massachusetts Regiment with Captain Hunt's company for three years, where he planned to serve with his older brother.[630]

TRYON'S RAID ON DANBURY, CONNECTICUT

On April 27, an express rider handed Colonel Joseph Vose orders to proceed in a forced march to the White Plains vicinity near Pound Ridge, New York (in the lower Highlands Department). There was a company of enemy soldiers from the British army who were reported to be encamped outside the village.[631] The message related that on April 26, 1777, a British raiding party led by Brigadier General William Tryon made an attack on Danbury, Connecticut, where General Washington's major military supply depot was located. General William Tryon, the deposed governor of New York, attacked the major American supply depot at Danbury. This was a punitive action against the Americans, and it enabled them to also acquire food supplies and needed dry goods for the British troops stationed in the New York City vicinity. General Tryon and his raiding party marched from their anchorage at Compo Beach in Fairfield County, Connecticut, inland to the town of Danbury unopposed. He ordered his raiding party to destroy the rum stores and other supplies. However, hundreds of soldiers in the raiding party were soon very drunk! The inebriated bands of British soldiers shouted, sang, stumbled about and filled the town with terror just as darkness fell. Before their departure the next morning, the British destroyed four to five thousand barrels of pork, beef and flour; five thousand pairs of shoes; two thousand bushels of grain; and sixteen hundred tents, among other supplies and military stores.[632] Nineteen houses were burned along with twenty-two barns and storage buildings. The destruction of the major supply depot for Washington's army at Danbury was a significant loss since the supplies were to be used during the fall and winter encampments at Saratoga and at Valley Forge for the American troops as well as for the American troops stationed in the Highland Departments in the New York vicinity along the Hudson River Valley.

General Tryon's British raiders met militia and community resistance as the British raiding party made its retreat southward along the swampy and mud-rutted dirt road toward Ridgefield. The town of Danbury was left burning behind them. Some of the British raiders, many of whom had spent the night drunk in Danbury, had loaded casks and barrels of rum and molasses onto confiscated horse-drawn wagons. They intended to keep the casks and barrels as spoils from the supply depot raid and to celebrate when they returned to their anchorage in New York Harbor. Most of the wagons, however, became mired in the deep mud-rutted road just to the south of Danbury. With frustration and harsh words of displeasure, these raiders had to push most of the barrels off the wagons and into the swamp beside the road and abandon the sweet nectar in the swampy hollow. (Note: Today, the area just to the south of Danbury where this incident occurred is called "Sugar Hollow.") General David Wooster quickly rallied his militia troops in the area and led a pursuit after Tryon's raiders out of Danbury along the southern road toward the village of Ridgefield. General Wooster with his militiamen and General Waterbury with his militia troops engaged General Tryon's raiding party in an intense firefight just to the north of Ridgefield village. General Wooster was shot during the skirmish and carried to a safer location where he later died. The combined state militia troops continued to pursue the British raiders through the village of Ridgefield. The militiamen and farmers from the Ridgefield vicinity put up a valiant fight to repel the British raiders from their village. (Note: A cannon ball from the battle at Ridgefield can still be seen lodged in the building structure of the old Keeler Tavern in the village center of Ridgefield.) As General Tryon and his British raiders made their way southward toward the seacoast, they were met by more local farmers, merchants and militiamen all along their retreat route.

General Arnold was on leave with his family at this time. He hastily organized and led a company of militiamen and volunteers from the seaports of New Haven and Stratford along the shoreline road to intercept the British escape route to the Long Island Sound, where Tryon's ship was anchored. General Arnold's militiamen met up with General Wooster's militia soldiers and General Waterbury's militia troops who were hotly pursuing the British raiders toward the sea. There was an intense engagement, a running gun fight, between Tryon's British raiders and the Connecticut militia forces. General Tryon's raiders managed to fight their way toward their waiting transport ship, anchored at Compo Beach near Norwalk on the Long Island Sound. General Tryon's troops were successful, and they made their way to their waiting ship. The British transport ship took General Tryon's raiders back to their anchorage at New York Harbor, where they celebrated the success of their mission with rum and merriment.

Colonel Vose's regiment was ordered to proceed promptly to Danbury and the White Plains vicinity of Bedford and Pound Ridge villages, where his regiment remained for a time with the Second Connecticut Brigade.[633] First Lieutenant Philip Ulmer was still on furlough recruiting soldiers for his company in his hometown and the Lincoln and Cumberland County vicinities when the British raid upon Danbury occurred. By mid-May 1777, Lieutenant Philip Ulmer received an urgent dispatch from Colonel Vose. The dispatch informed Lieutenant Ulmer that the major supply depot located at Danbury had been attacked and the arsenal had been destroyed by General Tryon and his British raiding party. Word of the attack and General Wooster's death was unsettling news to Lieutenant Philip Ulmer since he had served as an officer with both General Wooster and General Arnold during the Canadian campaign in 1776. Colonel Vose's regiment was reassigned by General Washington to defend the southern defensive positions in the Highland Department near New Castle and Peekskill, New York, on the Hudson River.

First Lieutenant Ulmer assembled the newly enlisted soldiers and hastened to join his commanding officer, Colonel Joseph Vose, at the military encampment several miles to the west of Ridgefield, Connecticut, at Pound Ridge near New Castle, New York. Having ended his furlough early, Lieutenant Philip Ulmer and his recruits marched inland through Litchfield and Newtown and past the remains of Danbury. They had been directed to take this inland route to Pound Ridge and New Castle in order to avoid further enemy confrontation. Philip and his company of new recruits rejoined Colonel Vose and his new recruits from south Boston at the militia encampment near Pound Ridge village in the lower Highlands Department, which was commanded by General Israel Putnam.[634] The home and farm of Major Ebenezer Lockwood became the militia headquarters for the southern defensive line in the vicinity of Pound Ridge and New Castle (in present-day Westchester County, New York). A price of forty golden guineas was placed on Major Lockwood's head by British general William Tryon because of his leadership as a rebel militia officer and for providing his home and farm as the headquarters of the American military forces in western Connecticut and the White Plains vicinity.[635] Colonel Sheldon's Connecticut Light Dragoons (cavalry regiment) also encamped at Major Lockwood's farm with the Second Connecticut Brigade in the disputed territory (considered Tryon County by the British), which extended from Long Island Sound as far north as New Castle near Peekskill, New York. Colonel Vose's troops, which included Lieutenant Philip Ulmer and his company of recruits, remained in the vicinity until it was determined that the threat of another forceful British raid was unlikely.

While stationed in the Pound Ridge vicinity, four soldiers from frontier Maine with the First Massachusetts Regiment died and were buried beside a large boulder on the main road between Pound Ridge and New Castle. A marker was placed in front of the boulder to indicate where the four unknown soldiers from frontier Maine were buried.* After a number of weeks, Colonel Vose's Massachusetts regiment was ordered to march to the main headquarters of the Highlands Department at Peekskill, New York, to defend against possible British raids along the Hudson River.[636] Sometime later, British cavalry officer Banastre Tarleton, with his dragoons and Hessian raiding party, returned to Major Lockwood's farm at Pound Ridge, which had served as a militia headquarters. The Hessians confiscated Major Lockwood's "herd of imported cattle and a troop of his brood mares."[637] Tarleton and his dragoons surrounded the farmhouse, terrorized the family and threatened to burn the house down with Major Ebenezer Lockwood's family inside if Hannah (Smith) Lockwood, Major Lockwood's wife, did not reveal where the militia troops had moved their army encampment. After a tense standoff, the Lockwood children, Hannah Lockwood and two black servants were released and made their way through the orchard toward the brook. Tarleton's raiding party set fire to the Lockwood farmhouse, barns, stables, sheds and the new, unfinished barracks and took the horses and cattle. Before leaving the area, Tarleton's raiders set fire to the church and the buildings in Pound Ridge and Bedford, New York.

---

* *Author's comment*: Many decades later, a permanent marker was dedicated at the burial site of the four fallen soldiers who served in the First Massachusetts Regiment during the Revolutionary War.

The main body of Colonel Vose's First Massachusetts Regiment, which remained at Morristown, New Jersey, with Washington's main army in early 1777, was reassigned to the Highlands Department under the command of General Putnam and General Heath.[638] Colonel Vose's regiment was reunited with his troops who had remained in winter quarters at Morristown with Paterson's regiment. Lieutenant Philip Ulmer was reported encamped with Colonel Vose's First Massachusetts Regiment before August 15, 1777.[639] General Putnam commanded the troops in the lower region near Peekskill, and General Heath commanded the troops in the northern region of the Highlands Department guarding West Point. General Washington had given General Heath specific orders to use his division in the Hudson Highlands to protect the critically important ferry crossings located at various places along the Hudson River and to distract the British garrison in New York City. The Continental Congress recognized as early as November 8, 1775, that the Hudson Highlands was the only area between New York City and Albany where the Hudson River could be blockaded against British warships and raiding vessels. The Hudson Highlands, under the command of General Heath, effectively became a "territorial department" of strategic importance that was preserved until the end of the American Revolution.[640] The Highlands Department was responsible for the defense of the lower Hudson River Valley and the counties around White Plains and New York City. The Highlands Department was under the command of General Heath (in the northern area) and General Putnam (in the southern area).[641] Many of the soldiers in Colonel Vose's regiment, including Philip Ulmer, had served with General Heath and General Putnam during the battle at Bunker Hill and during the siege of Boston in 1775–76.

Colonel Vose's First Massachusetts Regiment joined other regiments from New England that had operated with one another during the siege of Boston in 1775–76 and during the retreat from Canada with General Arnold's forces in the spring of 1776. They had also participated in the fleet construction activities at Skenesboro and Ticonderoga during the summer of 1776. Some of the New England troops had participated in the battle at Valcour Island on Lake Champlain in the fall of 1776. These New England militia troops and Continental Army forces were massing in the Highlands Department because of the major British invasion campaign that had begun in June 1777. General Burgoyne's British and Hessian forces were successfully invading the New York Colony from Canada at this time using the major waterways through the Lake Champlain and Lake George regions. Fort Ticonderoga was captured by the allied British invasion forces, and a Hessian raiding party attacked Bennington, Vermont, on August 16, 1777, to provide forage for needed food and other supplies for the invading army. Fortunately, Major General Benjamin Lincoln, who commanded Colonel Simond's militia troops and Brigadier General John Stark's militia troops, was successful in repulsing the Hessian attack upon Bennington and the surrounding community. Their success in depriving Burgoyne's forces of critically needed supplies eventually hastened the surrender of Burgoyne's forces at Saratoga several months later.

Having captured Fort Ticonderoga on Lake Champlain, General Burgoyne's forces moved southward on Wood Creek toward Skenesboro, where General Burgoyne occupied Peter Skene's abandoned palatial home, located high on a hillside above the stream. He dispatched Mohawk Indian scouts to discover a quicker route through the thick woodlands and creeks to the Hudson River. There had to be a better route to the Hudson River to the south that General Burgoyne's army could use through the surrounding mountainous Adirondack region. Mohawk Indian scouts captured several local inhabitants to guide them through the wild mountainous terrain to Fort Edwards, east of Glens Falls, New York. Jenny McCrea, the widow that she attended, a local couple and their six children who lived in the vicinity of Fort Edwards were all taken hostage by the Mohawk Indian scouts. They were forced to guide the Indian scouts through the wilderness area and show them the shortcut through the mountains to the Hudson River. Having completed the task, the Indians mercilessly killed Jenny McCrea and the hostages and scalped them. When news of the massacre reached the general public, there was a great outcry of rage against General Burgoyne's British and Hessian invasion forces and their Indian allies. Thousands of men throughout the colonies rallied to the cries of "Remember Jenny McCrea," and they enlisted to fight against the enemy invasion forces from Canada advancing south through the Hudson River Valley. Militiamen and volunteers massed at the American encampment at Stillwater and Saratoga, New York. Jenny McCrea and the murdered victims would become martyrs of the American Revolution, having been brutally tortured and scalped by the hostile Mohawk Indians under British general Burgoyne's command.

General Howe's British forces stationed in New York City were to join General Burgoyne's advancing British Royal Army and allied forces at Albany by using the Hudson River waterway. The plan was to split the New York Colony in half, thus separating the northern and southern colonies from each other with a "divide and conquer" strategy. New England regiments from the Highlands Department and militia volunteers from other colonies were reassigned to the Northern Department to halt the enemy thrust toward the American stronghold at Albany. The military stronghold controlled the Hudson River and Hudson River Valley region, the heart of the colony. The newly assigned regiments, which included Colonel Vose's regiment, were sent by boat up the Hudson River from Peekskill to the Northern headquarters at Albany, New York. From Albany, regiments were reassigned to the Saratoga and Stillwater vicinity, where General Schuyler and General Gates were determined to make a stand against General Burgoyne's advancing army forces. The British and Hessian forces were successfully making their summer invasion campaign from Canada into the heartland of the American colonies.

The young new enlisted soldiers from New England had rarely traveled outside of their local counties. Since joining the American army, they had seen architectural and mechanical wonders that were amazing to their young minds. Several young soldiers like Ebenezer Wild, who traveled through the Lake Champlain and Hudson River Valleys with Lieutenant Philip Ulmer and Colonel Vose's troops, wrote of some of these wonders: "[We saw] the rapid construction of naval vessels to engage the British navy on Lake Champlain, the mammoth iron gates of Crown Point, the thick iron chain across the Hudson (which stretched about a mile), army wagons turned into sleighs for winter attacks, canoes turned into gunships as blunderbusses were attached to their bows, and an inventive farmer who had constructed a large wooden barn with a retractable roof."[642]

Chapter 9
Battle of Saratoga

Foreign Affairs in France and the Effect on Washington's Army

In Europe, the success at Trenton opened up an international debate on the American Revolution and raised questions about the legitimacy of Europe's old regime. The Battle of Trenton transformed attitudes toward the American Revolution and the American cause on both sides of the Atlantic, as well as attitudes in the Royal Houses in Europe. The news from Trenton stimulated a controversy on the Hessian mercenary presence in America, the morality of the soldier trade which, like slavery, was considered a trade in human flesh by "sellers of souls."[643] It raised questions about the legitimacy of the government that engaged in this trade and added to the sting of defeat and the stain of moral disgrace. The Comte de Mirabeau, a leading European critic of the soldier trade, argued that the soldier trade supported the English despotism in a struggle against American rights. He wrote a pamphlet that supported the moral American cause of freedom and liberty. Comte de Mirabeau wrote that Europeans should be fighting in America as *volunteers*: "Cross the seas, hurry to America, but embrace your brothers there, defend the generous people against the arrogant rapacity of their persecutors...Learn from the Americans the art of living free."[644]

The United Colonies in America were in a desperate state of affairs, and America sought help from France, who shared the same dislike and opposition to Great Britain. The Continental Congress had no ability to finance a war against England and little ability to manage its economy. The Congress had no treasury to pay for a war and possessed neither the legal authority nor the practical means to collect taxes from the colonial states or to mint coins. It could only recommend, request and entreat the states to provide material goods and support for the war effort. The Continental Congress had left the various states with the power to provide for their military soldiers serving in the Continental Army or to let them starve. Many soldiers and officers went without pay because the Continental Congress had no funds for the treasury. All Congress could do by way of finances was to print paper currency, which it did on a massive scale, and then pour the currency into what was an agrarian barter economy. The value of the paper currency fell, prices rose rapidly and merchants refused to accept Continental currency for goods and supplies. With no means to purchase basic necessities, soldiers and their families became desperate, struggling to survive. Rapidly rising inflation eventually forced the Continental Congress to renounce the currency that it had issued and devalue the paper money that had been printed. Soldiers discovered that the pay that they had received for their military service was mostly worthless and was not accepted by merchants for goods. The war caused severe economic hardships for all Americans. Support for the basic needs and supplies of General Washington's Continental Army and the success of the American Revolution hung in the balance.

In December 1776, Benjamin Franklin was sent to France as one of three co-commissioners from the Continental Congress whose goal was to gain recognition for American sovereignty and independence from England and to acquire financial support for the American Revolution. France still held resentment against Great Britain over the terms of the Treaty of Paris in 1763. The three commissioners in France were Benjamin Franklin, Silas Deane and Arthur Lee, who had replaced Thomas Jefferson when he refused the appointment due to his wife's poor health issues. The commissioners were given little financial support by the Continental Congress, which had almost no money in the treasury to finance and support them in their mission to France. The commissioners often had to draw upon their own personal wealth and influence to meet their financial ends. The American headquarters in France was located at the elegant villa Hotel de Valentinois. The villa was owned by one of Benjamin Franklin's merchant friends, the Count de Chaumont, who was sympathetic to the justice of the American cause.[645] In gratitude for the free lodging and generous hospitality extended to Ambassador Franklin by the Comte de Chaumont and his wife, Benjamin Franklin erected a lightning rod over his villa.[646] Neither Franklin nor Deane acknowledged their doubts about the success of the American Revolution in public. Behind the beautiful exterior of Valentinois, the commissioners were deeply worried about the future success of the American Revolution. Ambassador Franklin used his power as a senior diplomat, his acclaim as a famous scientist and his celebrity as the representation of American Enlightenment for his own purposes. While Benjamin Franklin was wined and dined, Silas Deane was kept busy with the covert details of negotiating, financing, equipping and supplying the military needs of Washington's Continental Army. British and French spies were everywhere seeking information. Several British spies reported that between Franklin and Deane, Deane was "the more active and efficient man."[647]

Word of Washington's successes at Trenton and Princeton did not reach the commissioners in Paris until months after the events had taken place. With the many defeats and retreats of Washington's forces, the commissioners began to question if they should make a separate peace with the British government. Franklin and Deane secretly wrote to British foreign minister Stormont, proposing a prisoner exchange. The ambassador returned the unopened letter with the written notation: "The King's Ambassador receives no applications from rebels unless they come to implore his Majesty's mercy."[648] The Foreign Ministry sent a secret envoy to meet with Ambassador Franklin to discuss the possible terms for a settlement. Both Benjamin Franklin and Silas Deane saw the possibility of using the negotiations with the envoy as a way of pressuring the French government into action. Beaumarchais, a French arms dealer, informed Minister Vergennes that unless France acted soon, the American government would be forced to come to terms with England, and France would miss the opportunity to strike a blow against the British Empire.[649]

A deal was negotiated between Ambassadors Franklin, Silas Deane and the French Foreign Ministry (represented by Conrad-Alexandre Gerard) to release the *Amphitrite* and Beaumarchais' other merchant ships that were being held temporarily until arrangements could be worked out. It was decided that the supply ships would be escorted and protected by an armed French convoy. The commissioners agreed that the American Congress would pay for all the ships, men and military supplies provided by the French. These payments to France would come from the sale of prime Virginia tobacco, furs and other desirable American products by Beaumarchais' front company in the European and international marketplace. Ambassador Gerard agreed that France would directly loan the Americans 2 million livres (about 15 million American dollars). In late May 1777, news arrived in France that the first of Beaumarchais' ships, the *Mercure*, had arrived safely in Portsmouth, New Hampshire, on March 17 with twelve thousand muskets, one thousand barrels of powder, thirty-four bales of woolen stockings, two cases of shoes and many more bales of woolen caps, linen, cloth, blankets and other needed items.[650] Two more ships arrived at Falmouth, Massachusetts, and two other ships reached the West Indies with cannons and supplies for the American army troops. The *Amphitrite* reached Portsmouth in April 1777, and tons of military supplies were unloaded, including 32,840 cannon balls, 129 barrels of powder, 52 cannons, about 9,000 grenades and 219 chests of small arms.[651] The news spread that the Continental Army had enough guns, cannon powder and uniforms for thirty thousand men.[652] These were the first of approximately forty ships that French arms agent Beaumarchais and American arms agent Deane smuggled to certain American ports during the Revolution through the Rodriguez and Hortalez shipping company.[653]

The challenge for the militia soldiers in Portsmouth, New Hampshire, and in the Falmouth vicinities in York and Cumberland Counties was to transport the smuggled French military supplies and heavy equipment to the Continental Army troops that were massing at Stillwater near Saratoga (about twenty miles north of Albany) before General Burgoyne and his British and Hessian forces could successfully move south from Montreal, Canada. Moving tons of military supplies and heavy warfare equipment was a monumental challenge, but it was one that had to be met if the British forces were to be stopped before reaching Albany. Failure to stop the British and Hessian allied army at Saratoga, New York, would have resulted in the splitting of the New England colonies from the southern colonies and in the loss of the American Revolution. With the arrival of the military supplies from France, the morale of the New Hampshire and Massachusetts militia troops soared, causing new enlistments in the state militia and in the Continental Army. Many of Lieutenant Philip Ulmer's cousins, relatives, friends and acquaintances enlisted to serve in the anticipated Saratoga engagement with other soldiers from the Waldoboro, St. George and Falmouth areas. Many of these new recruits enlisted to serve in Colonel Vose's and in General Paterson's regiments with Lieutenant Philip Ulmer, who served as a lieutenant in both regiments. Lieutenant Ulmer was well respected, trusted and admired by the local young men who chose to serve under his leadership and command.* Before long, a large number of volunteers from many colonial states flocked to Stillwater near Saratoga, New York. By September 1777, the American troops swelled to more than twelve thousand men. They wanted to be involved in stopping British general Burgoyne's invasion forces and striking back against the repressive British Imperialist Empire.

British Campaign for Philadelphia

General Howe retired his troops from New Jersey and went to Staten Island (New York City), where they spent their winter quarters in comfort. British and Hessian army outposts were manned during the winter of 1776–77 in towns and villages that stretched along the eastern part of New Jersey. In late May 1777, General Washington opened his military campaign with a march from Morristown in the western mountainous region of the New Jersey colony (Watchung Mountains) toward Bound Brook, several miles from the British outpost at New Brunswick. General Howe ordered his military troops in New Jersey into a defensive position and attempted to draw Washington's forces into a full-scale engagement with his superior British and Hessian forces. General Howe kept trying to force a clash, but General Washington wisely avoided becoming drawn into a conflict. General Washington determined that a cautious defensive and retreating approach was the best strategy against the superior strength of the British armed forces. The spring maneuvering around Bound Brook prevented the British general from repairing the damage in public relations with the civilian population that had been brutally and harshly abused by the British and Hessian mercenary soldiers during the winter.

In the summer of 1777, British general William Howe, having secured his hold on New York City in 1776, proceeded to concentrate his efforts on capturing Philadelphia, the largest city in North America. Philadelphia was considered the new American capital and the home of the Continental Congress, the seat of political and governing authority. It was a prosperous major seaport on the eastern seacoast of colonial America, and the city

---

* *Author's comment*: The names of the soldiers from frontier Massachusetts who served with Lieutenant Philip Ulmer in 1777–78 can be found as active participants in the Saratoga National Historical Park records in New York State and in the records of the Valley Forge National Historical Park in Pennsylvania.

could be supplied with goods and military needs from the sea using the Delaware River. Philadelphia was also populated by numerous Loyalists and defenders of the British Crown, as well as supporters of the British armed forces. The British occupation of the city would be similar to that of Boston, Massachusetts, which had been lost the year before in March 1776.

General Howe finally opened his Philadelphia campaign on July 16, 1777, when the British and Hessian troops from New York City boarded a large fleet of 210 ships commanded by Admiral Lord Richard Howe, General William Howe's brother. The British fleet set sail on July 25, but the fleet was plagued with difficulties. There were heavy storms, collisions between ships and shortages of food, fresh water and fodder for the horses. After a month at sea and with the food supplies seriously low, General Howe's fleet landed at Head of Creek, Maryland, in the Chesapeake Bay on August 25. General Washington's army tried to prevent the approaching British forces from capturing the city of Philadelphia by using various blocking maneuvers. The opposing forces fought a number of skirmishes outside of the city. However, on September 26, 1777, General William Howe finally outmaneuvered General Washington's army troops, and the British marched into Philadelphia unopposed. The British Royal Navy forces were able to use their naval superiority against important coastal towns and cities along the eastern seacoast. However, the control of the countryside was an increasingly difficult matter due to the relatively small land army and the constant need for reinforcements, military supplies, munitions and other materials for the British and Hessian troops.

The Continental Congress was forced to abandon the city of Philadelphia, and the congressional delegates hastily retreated into the countryside toward Lancaster, Pennsylvania, where they would be safer from the advancing British and Hessian forces. The Continental Congress was later forced to move to York, Pennsylvania, when General Howe's troops engaged in a number of military forays into the countryside for forage and to probe the American defenses. The Continental Congress finally moved south to Baltimore, Maryland, where the state legislators from the various colonies were not in constant danger and anxiety. The occupation of Philadelphia by British and Hessian forces lasted until June 1778.[654] The capture of Philadelphia and its occupation by the British forces did not bring an end to the rebellion as the British thought it would. In eighteenth-century warfare, normally, the side that captured the other side's capital city won the war. However, the Continental Army and the Continental Congress did not play by the same rule book as those in

Europe. In Europe, there were powerful kings and queens and castles to defend as the seat of political and governmental authority. The capture of the colonial seat of government at Philadelphia, primarily the buildings where the state representatives met, didn't end with an American surrender of the city or government buildings. The seat of American government and political authority rested in the state legislators who were chosen by the American people to represent them. When in danger or under siege, the congressional legislators simply moved to another location, where the government's business continued to be conducted. The British Parliament and the British Crown never seemed to understand this new American concept of government by and for the people.

THE NORTHERN DEPARTMENT CONFRONTS GENERAL BURGOYNE'S ARMY

General John Burgoyne took command of General Sir Guy Carleton's Royal Army in Canada with approximately eight thousand regulars and three thousand Hessian soldiers under the command of Baron Friedrich von Riedesel, as well as Indian and Canadian volunteers. On June 21, 1777, General Burgoyne opened his three-pronged northern campaign by moving his combined British and Hessian army and allied forces southward from Montreal, Canada. General Burgoyne's invasion plan was to lead an attack from Canada using the natural waterways into the heart of the New York colony. The main body of Burgoyne's allied army was to sail south on Lake Champlain and seize control of the American frontier forts on Lake Champlain and Lake George in the Adirondack Mountains north of Albany. The British allied forces would proceed southward on the Hudson River toward Albany and secure that important commercial town and military stronghold. At the same time, part of the British army, under the command of Colonel St. Leger, would travel southward along the Mohawk River and seize Fort Stanwix. The British troops would join forces at Albany, New York. General Clinton's British army forces, under command of General William Howe in New York City, would move northward along the Hudson River, seizing the American forts in the Highlands Department along the river. They would then proceed up the Hudson River and join forces with those of General Burgoyne and Colonel St. Leger at Albany. The New England colonies would be divided from the middle and southern colonies, and the insurrection would be quashed. The American rebellion for sovereignty and independence would come to a decisive end. However, General Burgoyne's plan did not unfold as he expected.

BATTLE OF SARATOGA: THE PIVOTAL BATTLE OF THE REVOLUTIONARY WAR

The foundation of all the Northern success was laid long before Gates' arrival there. Gates appeared just in time to reap the laurels and rewards.
—*General Nathanael Greene*[655]

In July 1777, Colonel Vose's regiment was operating in the lower Highlands Department along the Hudson River. The regiment was reassigned to the Second Massachusetts Brigade, whose commanding officer was General John Glover. General Glover's brigade, which now included Colonel Vose's regiment, was then reassigned to the Northern Department on July 24, 1777.[656] Colonel Vose's regiment, which had three companies by this time, was put on sloops and sailed up the Hudson River in order to save time in its journey to Saratoga.[657] By July 29, the First Massachusetts Regiment, led by Colonel Vose, disembarked from its sloops at Albany. The newly combined troops started their march northward toward Saratoga along the dirt road that ran along the shore of the Hudson River. Colonel Vose's troops arrived at the American encampment at Stillwater, New York, on July 31, 1777, at about five o'clock in the afternoon. Colonel Vose's regiment then proceeded to set up its insufficient supply of tents and prepared its camp for supper with the other American army regiments and militia companies that had already arrived ahead of them.[658]

With the successful advance of General Burgoyne's British invasion forces through the Lake Champlain Valley, General Schuyler ordered the army regiments and militia companies under his leadership to fall back from Stillwater to the islands at the mouth of the Mohawk River (called the Van Schaick's Islands) while awaiting the arrival of more militia troops from the New York, Connecticut and Massachusetts colonies. Unlike many other withdrawals, this was an unhurried and orderly one. General Paterson's brigade led the withdrawal with Colonel Gamaliel Bradford's regiment (the Fourteenth Massachusetts Regiment). These soldiers were followed by the troops under Generals Glover and Poor and Colonel John Nixon's brigade, which were in the rear of the army troops.[659] First Lieutenant Philip Ulmer's detached company with Colonel Vose's First Massachusetts Regiment were divided, and Lieutenant Philip Ulmer and Colonel Vose's soldiers were assigned to General Glover's brigade [660] while other soldiers in their regiment were assigned to Learned's regiment and General Paterson's Regiment. Philip Ulmer served as first lieutenant with both Colonel Vose's regiment and General Paterson's regiment during this time.[661] The detachment of troops with Colonel Vose and Lieutenant Ulmer gave support wherever needed and conducted reconnaissance missions for General Gates's Northern Army.[662] Detachments were posted along the southern bank of the Mohawk River to prevent the British from crossing at that point. General Schuyler wrote to the Committees of Safety informing them about the news of turning back the British forces at Bennington and Fort Stanwix. General Schuyler had won the gift of time by his strategy of stretching out the enemy's lines to the breaking point, by obstructing the enemy's progress wherever possible and by straining the enemy's supply lines and communications. General Schuyler was also able to provide adequate supplies and provisions for his own soldiers, which the growing rebel army forces greatly needed.[663]

On August 10, 1777, General Schuyler received notification by the president of the Continental Congress, John Hancock, that Congress had decided to replace him and that his rival, General Horatio Gates, would be his replacement.[664] Congress had sent instructions to the states of New Hampshire, Massachusetts, Connecticut, New Jersey, New York and Pennsylvania to send as many militia regiments as General Gates thought necessary to defend the Northern and Highland regions of New York from the British incursion.[665] General Gates and the American troops faced a large, well-equipped British allied army that was rapidly advancing in northern New York. General Washington issued a general call to arms "to let all New England rise and crush Burgoyne."[666] General Horatio Gates assumed command at the military headquarters of the Northern Army at Albany on August 19, 1777. He proceeded from Albany to the main camp at Stillwater, New York. General Gates found most of his new command camped on Van Schaick's Islands, where General Schuyler had moved them. A brigade under General Poor was camped up the Mohawk River to protect the American troops from a possible attack by St. Leger's British and Indian forces from Fort Stanwix. Colonel Learned's and General Arnold's troops had gone to Fort Stanwix on the western frontier to hold and turn back the British forces who were to move southward and join Burgoyne's main army at Albany.[667] General Lincoln's troops, who had been sent by General

Washington as reinforcements with Morgan's riflemen from his Pennsylvania campaign, were located with Colonel Stark (in present-day Vermont) to fight the combined British and Hessian forces if they should cross to the eastern side of the Hudson River at that point.

During General Burgoyne's summer campaign in 1777, Crown Point and Fort Ticonderoga on Lake Champlain were easily seized by the superior forces of the British and Hessian allied army moving from Fort St. John southward through the Lake Champlain Valley. The outposts at Skenesboro to the south of Fort Ticonderoga and Fort Anne and Fort Edward near Lake George were soon captured by the British forces. General Burgoyne's invasion forces crossed the Hudson River. Burgoyne sent troops to Bennington (in Vermont) to confiscate supplies, acquire as many horses as possible and find food for their large army.[668] General Burgoyne was concerned about his dwindling food supplies and issued orders that warned: "the fate of the Campaign might depend on provisions."[669] The invading Hessian forces led by Lieutenant Colonel Baum were turned back by General Benjamin Lincoln's Continental troops and a regiment of militiamen led by Colonel John Stark, a veteran of the Battle of Bunker Hill.[670] About the same time as the skirmish at Bennington, a detachment from the Seventh Massachusetts Regiment (part of General Paterson's brigade) was led to Stillwater by Colonel Jeduthan Baldwin, the American army engineer for General Gates. Burgoyne's troops were continuing to advance toward the main American encampment at Stillwater near Saratoga, New York. The detached American troops retrieved as many wooden planks and supplies as their rafts would carry and brought them back to Gates's fortified encampment. They set fire to the remaining supplies left behind at Stillwater so that the enemy British troops couldn't use the materials. The American troops burned bridges and blocked and tore up roads as they headed back to their main camp at Bemis Heights near Saratoga overlooking the western banks of the Hudson River.[671]

General Horatio Gates, now in command of the Northern Department, set up his marquee tent that served as his headquarters at the main camp at Bemis Heights outside of Saratoga. In a letter that was read to Lord North's British Parliament, General Burgoyne expressed his surprise to Lord Germain, secretary of state for the North American colonies, over the rapid mobilization of the militiamen and volunteers and the fierce patriotism exhibited by the American soldiers: "The great bulk of the country is undoubtedly with the Congress in principle and in zeal, and their measures are executed with a secrecy and dispatch that are not to be equaled. Wherever the King's forces point, militia to the amount of three or four thousand, assemble in twenty-four hours. [They are] the most rebellious race…"[672]

As General Burgoyne's detached brigade drew back from Bennington and proceeded toward Burgoyne's main camp, Colonel St. Leger was stalled in the Mohawk Valley. General Arnold, who had been sent to halt Colonel St. Leger's progress from Canada, managed to engineer a mutiny among the Indians, and the Indians departed from the advancing British forces. Colonel St. Leger's army was left with few native Indians who knew the area and could scout the American defenses without being noticed. General Arnold and Learned's detached troops successfully stopped St. Leger's advance, and the British troops retreated back to Montreal. The American troops returned to General Gates's main encampment from Fort Stanwix on August 31 having successfully repulsed Colonel St. Leger's British and Indian forces.

The American forces had many scouts who had been watching the British advance through their spyglasses. The British forces with General Burgoyne were highly visible. Burgoyne often rode and marched with his troops with "his flags unfurled and flying high in the autumn breeze. His bands played British military music loud enough to be heard from some distance."[673] General Burgoyne's column of supply wagons, cannons and about eight thousand troops stretched for several miles along rutted and very difficult roadways. Food and supplies had become a more and more serious problem for Burgoyne's large army. Alienated settlers vehemently resisted the violent tactics of the invading British and Hessian troops who pillaged and plundered their quiet communities. The confiscation of supplies, dry goods and animals, as well as the brutal intimidation of innocent inhabitants by Hessian raiding parties, caused the settlers to give strong support to the American resistance. The need for packhorses to carry the British army's provisions and equipment over the land became a desperate issue.[674] The shortage of horse teams prevented the army from advancing more than a few miles a day. The British and Hessian soldiers struggled along at a slow pace, carrying their tents and heavy provisions on their backs during the long invasion campaign through the New York heartland of the Champlain and Hudson River Valleys. The horses, which were brought from Canada, were needed to pull the heavy artillery and ammunition supplies, haul baggage and serve as cavalry mounts. General Burgoyne's troops became fatigued and weakened as the weeks slowly passed. Supplies and communications with Canada were stretched to the limit and eventually broke down. As more and more British and Hessian soldiers deserted their posts, General

The actions of the opposing American and British armies during the British invasion campaign of the New York colony in the summer and fall of 1777. *Courtesy of the author.*

Burgoyne ordered harsher and more brutal punishments to be used on deserters. This caused fear and intimidation within Burgoyne's army ranks. Indians were offered rewards for capturing deserters, and they were told to scalp any deserters they killed.[675]

The British and Hessian forces continued to move slowly southward with the hope and expectation that General Howe would send General

Clinton northward from New York City with reinforcements and needed supplies as planned. The communications between General Burgoyne and General Howe's army forces had completely broken down. The American troops had made traveling and foraging extremely difficult for General Burgoyne's forces. The American troops wrecked or destroyed nearly all of the bridges on the route south along the Hudson River, wrecked the roads with obstructions and felled many trees, which had to be cleared. Burgoyne's troops were forced to continually stop and reconstruct bridges and clear the roads and pathways before progressing farther south.[676] Sufficient food supplies for the large British and Hessian army became a constant issue of increasing concern for the British troops and for the horses as the invading forces penetrated deeper into the New York colony and into the heart of American resistance.

General Gates had used his troops to block any route down the western side of the Hudson River by building a series of earthworks around the American camp that extended westward past land that was owned by a farmer whose name was Freeman. The earthworks were about three-quarters of a mile in length and formed three sides of a square. The open side on the south had a deep ravine. The area was thickly wooded except for a few areas where farmers had cleared open meadows for farming and grazing. Bemis Heights (named for a tavern-keeper in the area) was located on a ridge of bluffs with a commanding view and overlooking the Hudson River two hundred feet below. Cannons placed on the heights and fortifications on the flood plain below would command the river valley, an excellent position for a defensive battle when General Burgoyne's forces finally made their attack.[677] General Gates had positioned his cannons in places that he felt would be most effective. The field guns were positioned so that they would cover the river, forcing General Burgoyne's troops to come ashore into the waiting American defensive line. General Gates was prepared and waited for the British attack that would come soon.[678]

On September 13, 1777, the British troops began to arrive on the eastern bank of the Hudson River, having been repulsed by the Continental and militia troops at Bennington, Vermont. Two nights after the British forces crossed the Hudson River to the western bank, all of the American troops at Bemis Heights were ordered to be on high alert. Ebenezer Wild, who was a sergeant in Colonel Vose's regiment, wrote in his diary: "We had orders to lay upon arms and not pull off any of our clothes. At two o'clock, the regiment was awakened and ordered to construct even more earthworks in the dark."[679] From September 16 to September 18, more and higher earthworks were constructed in front of the camp by the First Massachusetts Regiment, who were positioned in the center of camp and would face the frontal impact of the British and Hessian attack.[680] The writing and documentation from Ebenezer Wild's diary indicated the location of Colonel Vose's regiment. The enlisted soldiers encamped in the cleared fields on the western side of the river. The John Neilson farmhouse became the headquarters for the mid-level officers, while the Ephraim Woodworth house, one-quarter mile south of the Neilson house, became the main headquarters for the American army troops. About ten miles to the north of this location, British forces crossed the Hudson River to the western side and steadily advanced southward along the Hudson River.

THE BATTLE OF SARATOGA BEGINS

The Battle of Saratoga was actually two engagements fought eighteen days apart on the same ground around Freeman's Farm, nine miles south of Saratoga, New York, along the western side of the Hudson River. The first engagement between the American and British forces was on September 19. General Burgoyne moved his troops in three columns and advanced on General Gates's encampment in an attempt to outflank the American force's left wing position. Scouts for Burgoyne had learned that there were heights, several miles farther to the west, and they were unprotected and unoccupied. Possession of that ridge would be the key for a successful British attack. First Lieutenant Philip Ulmer served with General Paterson's brigade and also with General Glover's brigade, under the personal command of General Horatio Gates. These brigades and Colonel Nixon's brigade made up the right wing of the American army at Bemis Heights.[681] Their orders came directly from General Horatio Gates.

General Gates learned of General Burgoyne's advance, but being a defensive strategist and low on ammunition, he decided to let the enemy come to him.[682] General Benedict Arnold, anticipating Burgoyne's maneuver on the American left wing, appealed to General Gates to send troops forward and conduct an offensive encounter while they had the advantage. Gates gave Arnold permission to lead some American troops forward to meet the enemy; however, Gates remained in his tent and did not participate with his soldiers in the fighting. Arnold placed significant forces in General Burgoyne's way, and he sent Colonel Morgan and three hundred New Hampshire light infantry to track Burgoyne's troops.[683] The advanced guard engaged the British forces a mile north of the American camp at Freeman's Farm. Ebenezer Wild, who served in Colonel Vose's regiment, wrote in his diary: "About one o'clock [after the thick fog had cleared] we were alarmed by the enemy. We marched from our encampment and manned the [earth]works above us. About two o'clock, an engagement ensued between their advanced party and ours which lasted fifteen minutes without cessation. Our people drove them and took some prisoners."[684] Morgan's riflemen, with extraordinary accuracy, were able to kill most of the officers in the advanced British right wing guard at Freeman's Farm. The British forces fled back into the forest behind Freeman's log cabin and were pursued by the American troops, who ran directly into the main British forces led by General Burgoyne. The British counterattacked the American advance guard with bayonets and scattered the American troops. Morgan's riflemen fled and regrouped, joining with other American troops led by General Arnold and the regiments of Poor, Learned, Paterson and Dearborn.

There was a furious, four-hour-long battle with the opposing sides attacking, counterattacking and retreating under a constant volley of gunfire from both sides. Prussian general Riedesel's left wing Hessian forces of nearly one thousand men were positioned along the river with heavy artillery.[685] They had been ordered to attack General Glover's forces along the river road on the west banks of the Hudson River. General Burgoyne counterordered Riedesel to bring his Hessian soldiers and cannons from the river and to join the conflict with the main attack force at Freeman's Farm in support of the commander. General Gates sent more American troops into the foray with Glover's brigade, who had been positioned near the river on the main road opposite General Riedesel's forces.[686] Lieutenant Philip Ulmer and his young recruits in Colonel Vose's detached unit (corps) were with these troops. The fighting was fierce as the two opposing armies were locked in deadly conflict.

General Glover, who was at the scene, wrote in a letter to his friend and fellow patriot Azor Orne in Marblehead, "Both armies seemed determined to conquer or die. [There was] one continual blaze without an intermission 'til dark. The enemy was bold, intrepid, and fought like heroes, and I do assure you, sirs, our men were equally bold and courageous and fought like men fighting for their all."[687] A British soldier described the battle scene between the opposing forces: "The heavy artillery, joining in concert like great peals of thunder, assisted by the echoes of the woods, almost

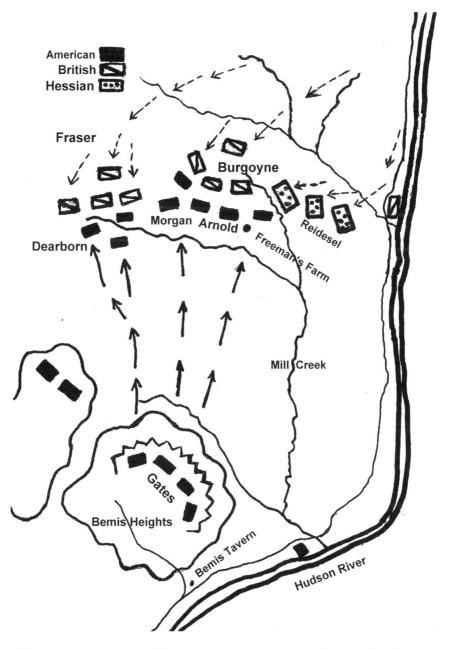

Military actions at the Battle of Freeman's Farm, the first battle at Saratoga, New York, on September 19, 1777. *Courtesy of the author.*

deafened us with the noise. This crash of cannon and musketry never ceased 'til darkness parted us."[688]

The American forces began to run low on ammunition and had to withdraw from Freeman's Farm and the broader areas of conflict. The British forces succeeded in gaining control of the field and claimed victory, but it came at the cost of significant casualties. General Burgoyne withdrew his troops to his main camp near the Hudson River, and the troops remained there for about two weeks. Following that first bloody battle at the Saratoga battlefield, General Burgoyne decided to wait and to hope that reinforcements would arrive from New York City. With reinforcements and supplies available at Albany, it would not take long before Burgoyne's troops would move south to New York City, unite with the British forces of General Clinton and end the American hope of liberty, freedom and independence from Great Britain. General Clinton had written that some of the British troops from New York City would arrive in about ten days. General Howe's army forces were engaged in their own campaign for Philadelphia and would not be of assistance. General Burgoyne expected reinforcements from Colonel St. Leger, who, unknown to General Burgoyne, had left Fort Stanwix and proceeded back toward Canada, having lost many of his Indian scouts and troops. General Burgoyne's invasion forces were in serious trouble with no help or support from other sources. General Gates's American forces at Saratoga continued to grow stronger until he had over eleven thousand armed and angry colonists.[689] The settlers all seemed to feel that Burgoyne's British and Hessian forces had to be stopped before they could reach Albany and capture it. If the American cause was to experience success, this was the time, and Saratoga was the place. The superior British and Hessian forces could be surrounded and defeated by the struggling American Northern Army.

There had been a brewing resentment between General Horatio Gates and General Benedict Arnold, which erupted during the difficulties and conflicts at Saratoga. General Gates, like some other officers, did not like the cavalier way that Arnold conducted himself. Horatio Gates's dislike may have been based on Arnold's loyalty to General Schuyler, General Washington's good friend, whom Arnold liked and respected. Generals Gates and Schuyler disliked each other, and they had written and said uncomplimentary and disrespectful things about each other in letters to influential congressional delegates in Philadelphia and in their personal appearances before the Continental Congress. This feud of jealousy and desire for power and recognition became one of the uglier personal feuds of the Revolutionary War.[690] General Arnold's courageous and bold leadership while under heavy gunfire during the first battle at Freeman's Farm had won the admiration of the American troops in the field. Lieutenant Philip Ulmer, his brother, George, and several cousins from Waldoboro had witnessed Arnold's daring leadership firsthand. General Arnold's brave but reckless efforts to lead the American troops won the day. General Gates spent his time reorganizing troop assignments in the safety of his tent, a considerable distance from the heat of the battle. It

General Benedict Arnold. By H.B. Hall from a John Trumbull portrait. *Courtesy of the National Archives & Records Administration.*

was General Arnold, and not General Gates, who won the admiration and devotion of the American troops who had been engaged in the bloody combat against General Burgoyne's British and Hessian forces.

General Gates waited for three days without telling Arnold about the reorganizing of the troops. He did not tell General Arnold that Morgan's riflemen, the heroes of the conflict, had been reassigned away from his command along with several other companies of veteran soldiers from the New England regiments. Some soldiers in Colonel Vose's regiment had been detached and served with Learned and Paterson's regiments at Freeman's Farm and Bemis Heights. General Horatio Gates had sent a report about the Saratoga battle at Freeman's Farm to the Continental Congress on September 19. In the report, General Gates took credit for stopping the British advance, for pushing the British army back into its main encampment and for having inflicted many hundreds of British casualties. He never mentioned General Arnold's bravery or heroic leadership while under heavy enemy gunfire. There was not a mention that General Arnold was even involved in the conflict! Understandably, General Arnold was furious, and a very heated argument between the two generals ensued. The soldiers who were camped near Bemis Heights, such as Philip Ulmer's company with the

First Massachusetts Regiment, couldn't help but hear about the bitter conflict between the two generals. General Gates's aide, James Wilkinson, was an eyewitness to the altercation.[691] General Gates was relentless in condemning General Arnold, and Gates said that he had discussed Arnold's demotion with members of the Continental Congress. He further told General Arnold that he would not continue to hold a command and that he would be replaced by General Benjamin Lincoln. General Gates issued a common traveling pass to Arnold so that he could leave the army.[692] The hatred between the two generals became so intense that one officer wrote that he "was certain that while Burgoyne sat in his camp pondering defeat, the two leading American generals at Saratoga would kill each other in a duel."[693]

Colonel Joseph Vose's regiment was kept moving throughout the encampment at Bemis Heights. The troops were moved from one location to another, first occupying a hill to the right of the main camp on one day and then a wooded area on the left of camp the next day. This movement of troops was probably done in order to keep the soldiers' minds and bodies busy and to relieve the stress of waiting for the enemy's next maneuver and attack. Attack alarms were sounded often and at various hours of the day and evening. On September 25, Ebenezer Wild, who was with Lieutenant Philip Ulmer in Colonel Vose's scouting party at this time, wrote in his journal that he was almost killed on this day.[694] He had been ordered to join the scouting party shortly before dawn to check on the latest British troop positions. "We marched within a quarter of a mile of [the enemy]. The fog and darkness of the morning prevented our going any further 'til after daylight, when we rushed on the guard and a very hot fire ensued for the space of two or three minutes. The guard ran into their lines as fast as they could. We killed and wounded eight of them and took one prisoner and returned to our camp again about sunrise. Four men in our party were lost in the engagement."[695]

The success of the scouting operation encouraged Colonel Vose's commanding officer, General Gates, to send out another scouting party on a three-day reconnaissance around the British encampment to discover its strength and its access to forage goods and materials. Lieutenant Philip Ulmer, a veteran officer with Colonel Vose's regiment with previous scouting experience, was probably one of the officers who led the long scouting trip through the woods around Lake Saratoga to gather information about the enemy troop positions. On October 1, the scouting party discovered a mill that had been owned by General Schuyler and had been seized by the British.[696] "We marched upon a rising ground above the mill and grounded our arms, and a party of us, with axes, went cutting away Schuyler's bridge.

After we destroyed it with axes as much time would admit of, we set fire to it. We stopped till it got well a-fire and then marched off in a different road."[697] The next day, Ebenezer Wild thought that he might be killed. He related in his diary that the scouting party was under orders to burn buildings that contained grain or other supplies that could help the British army troops. Sergeant Wild, who was with Lieutenant Philip Ulmer and Colonel Vose's troops on the scouting operation, related that a second mill was discovered that had several buildings nearby. British soldiers guarded the buildings that they had taken. To the great relief of Colonel Vose's scouting party, the British guards surrendered without firing a shot.[698] The buildings, which were filled with grain, were set afire, and the American scouting party returned to General Gates's main camp with ten prisoners (three of them were officers), twelve horses and eighteen cattle that could feed the American troops. The three-day scouting operation had been a success.

There was great anxiety behind the British lines as the American forces continued to increase in size daily.[699] The British and Hessian supplies were running out, and foraging was difficult in the sparsely settled area around Saratoga. General Burgoyne finally received a messenger who informed him that Colonel St. Leger had retreated back to Canada. Another messenger informed Burgoyne that none of the couriers who had been sent with desperate requests to General Clinton for reinforcements and military assistance reached the General in New York City, and they had all been arrested. General Burgoyne was left on his own to conduct the incursion against the New England colonies. General John Burgoyne's army forces were being surrounded by the growing American militia troops, and assistance from General Howe, General Clinton or Colonel St. Leger was not forthcoming.

There was anxiety in the main American camp as the soldiers waited for the British forces to make their attack. On October 6, General Gates sent the First Massachusetts Regiment with five hundred men (which included Lieutenant Philip Ulmer and Sergeant Ebenezer Wild) as an advanced guard to discover what General Burgoyne's troops were doing and where the enemy forces were positioning themselves.[700] There was no attack on the American encampment that day. When it was apparent that no troops would arrive from General Clinton or Colonel St. Leger's forces, General Burgoyne again pressed the attack on October 7, two weeks after the first conflict at Freeman's Farm.

General Burgoyne decided that he might be able to outflank the American troops on their left wing and continue to maneuver southward toward Albany. When fighting broke out in the midafternoon, the First Massachusetts

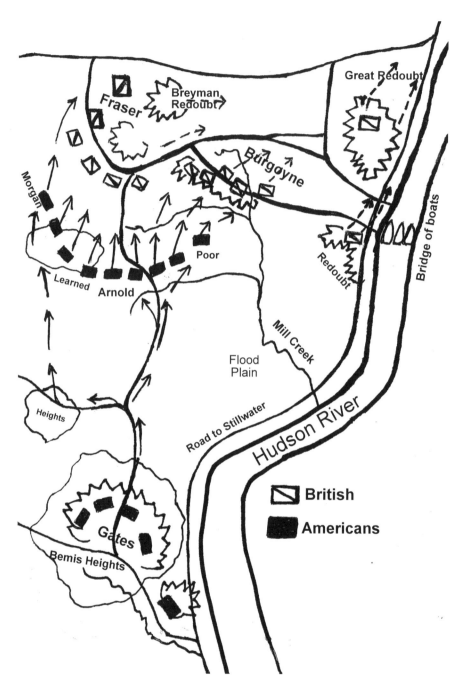

Military actions at the Battle of Bemis Heights, the second battle at Saratoga, New York, on October 7, 1777. *Courtesy of the author.*

Regiment did not engage but remained near the headquarters at Bemis Heights. In very heavy fighting on the American left flank, Benedict Arnold, who had been relieved of his command by General Gates, led a spirited rallying of the American troops in open defiance of General Gates's orders to stay off the battlefield. Arnold reached the battlefield on horseback, arriving between the American left flank and General Burgoyne's troops. He rallied the troops and ordered Morgan to have his sharpshooters fire at General Fraser, who rode a large gray horse. The sharpshooter, perched in a pine tree, took careful aim and killed General Fraser, who fell from his horse, sending his men into panic and confusion. General Arnold ordered the American troops to follow him as he led a charge on the well-fortified redoubt that had been constructed behind the flank of the British lines.[701]

The American forces, which included Colonel Learned's regiment and Colonel Paterson's regiment and had been detached from Glover's brigade, followed General Arnold, firing at the enemy as they ran forward toward the redoubt. General Gates sent relief troops from Glover's brigade (probably with Lieutenant Philip Ulmer and Colonel Vose's detachment of soldiers) to assist in attacking the redoubt with Paterson's and Learned's troops.[702] They were met by a hail of heavy musket fire from the Hessians in and around the Breymann's redoubt. Knowing that they were about to be overrun, the Hessian troops rallied for a final stand. Suddenly, General Arnold's horse was shot and stumbled. At the same time, General Arnold's leg was struck by a musket ball. The horse fell to the ground on top of General Arnold and broke his wounded leg. The firing around Arnold intensified as the American troops captured Breymann's redoubt several minutes later, killing and routing the Hessians inside of it. As darkness fell, the entire Continental Line advanced quickly, forcing the British and Hessian soldiers to flee. General Burgoyne ordered a general retreat, and the British army forces pulled back. Surprisingly, the American forces had apparently suffered few losses.[703] The heavy engagement was again marked by General Gates's absence from the battlefield. General Gates remained in his marquee tent at Bemis Heights charting and directing the action of his forces. Although he did not actively participate in the conflict, he would be given the recognition as the "Hero of Saratoga." General Arnold, who had risked life alongside of the fighting soldiers and had actually led the American troops to victory, would be granted little or no recognition for his heroism.

Forced to retreat after his defeat on October 7, General Burgoyne's allied army troops continued to withdraw northward toward Lake George and Fort Ticonderoga. A small detached scouting patrol from the First

Massachusetts Regiment was ordered to reconnoiter the enemy and report its movements. Colonel Vose's reconnaissance party with Lieutenant Ulmer continued to harass the British troops as the British and Hessian forces retreated northward. At one point, General Burgoyne ordered that the British army forces should halt and regroup. On October 8, General Burgoyne's encampment came under fire from various American cannon batteries that surrounded it. The house where Baron von Riedesel stayed was hit by eleven cannonballs.[704] General Philip Schuyler's country house, which had been used by the British officers, was burned as the British troops left the area. As the reconnaissance party approached, it found that the British forces had moved farther north, leaving some cannon and light infantry behind to protect the retreat. Colonel Vose and Lieutenant Ulmer, with their scouting detachment from the First Massachusetts Regiment, suddenly met the British troops head-on. Sergeant Wild, who was a sergeant with the First Massachusetts Regiment, wrote: "The enemy retreated to some works they had in their rear, where they fired from and did us some damage. As we were marching through their [former] lines they fired a number of cannon at us."[705]

Colonel Joseph Vose ordered that the patrol should disperse. A cannon that was situated in front of Vose suddenly erupted. Colonel Vose's horse was shot from under him, and the cannonball exploded underneath the horse.[706] The British had rigged the cannon with a slow fuse in the hope of killing as many unsuspecting American soldiers as possible. Lieutenant Ulmer would have rushed to assist his commanding officer who had been blown off of his horse and lay stunned and prostrate on the ground. Colonel Vose had narrowly escaped death. The horse had absorbed the brunt of the exploding cannonball, saving the lives of many of the soldiers who were in the scouting party. The startled and frightened soldiers fled toward the woods. The scouting party regrouped under the direction of Lieutenant Philip Ulmer.[707] Colonel Vose's reconnaissance party returned to Bemis Heights, where the incident was reported to General Gates. On another assignment soon afterward, Ulmer's detached company was sent to inspect the Lake Saratoga area and to report any flanking activity of enemy troops who might attempt to escape to the west.[708]

On October 10, the First Massachusetts Regiment encountered and successfully pushed enemy reconnaissance scouts, who were probing the American lines, northward in retreat. Ebenezer Wild wrote in his diary: "We marched within a half mile of the enemy and camped in the woods. There was considerable firing on both sides."[709] On October 11, the First

Massachusetts and other regiments tightened the circle around General Burgoyne's British and Hessian forces at their encampment. Colonel Vose's regiment, with Lieutenant Philip Ulmer, advanced to Schuyler's Creek, where the troops were engaged in another firefight. They were able to capture a British officer and thirty-six men.[710] On October 12, Ebenezer Wild wrote in his diary: "…there was considerable smart cannonading the biggest part of the day on both sides, and we fortified against the enemy considerable on the hills around us." On October 13, there were more firefights, and Sergeant Wild wrote: "There was considerable firing on both sides all day. We continue in the woods."[711] The next day, the British agreed to surrender and accepted a cease-fire. General Burgoyne delayed signing the surrender document, known as the Saratoga Convention, as long as he could in the desperate hope that General Clinton and the British reinforcements might soon arrive and save his army. General Burgoyne finally determined that relief troops were not coming and that it was prudent to accept the advantageous surrender treaty. In spite of the opposition, General Burgoyne realized that many of his best officers were sick, wounded or dead. His army was worn out from fighting. Communications and supply lines had been severed, and they were without sufficient food to feed the troops and horses. Additional American troops and volunteers were rising up and joining the fight against General Burgoyne's British and Hessian invasion forces. A total defeat would be disastrous to Burgoyne's army, and a victory would not gain them anything since they were surrounded and in a hostile country. General Burgoyne was reminded that "the life and property of every Loyalist, Canadian, and noncombatant depended on execution of the treaty."[712]

GENERAL BURGOYNE SURRENDERS THE BRITISH ROYAL FORCES: CONVENTION OF SARATOGA

*All their muskets had bayonets attached to them, and their riflemen had rifles.
There was absolute silence in those regts. [regiments] as can only be demanded
from the best disciplined troops. We were utterly astounded, not one of them
attempted to speak to the man at his side.[713]*
—*Baroness Frederika von Riedesel*

Ten days after the second battle at Freeman's Farm in Saratoga, New York, the mighty British and Hessian allied army forces, under General Burgoyne's command, had no choice but to totally surrender after being surrounded by the much larger and growing American army. The American, British and Hessian commanding officers spent several days negotiating the terms of surrender. First Lieutenant Philip Ulmer, who spoke and wrote fluently in both German and English, would have been very useful in translating and explaining the treaty negotiations to the German generals and officers during this crucial time. Under the generous terms of the Saratoga Convention, General Burgoyne would be allowed to have his troops surrender their weapons "with Honors of War" (which included retaining their colors), and they would march out of the camp with dignity. The British and Hessian troops would be escorted under guard to Boston, where they would be held as prisoners of war until arrangements could be made to send them back to their own countries.

General Gates reaped the laurels of victory and was recognized as the "Hero of Saratoga" even though he had spent most of his time at the encampment headquarters in his marquee tent with his charts instead of leading his troops in battle. General Arnold, who had led the American troops through the heat of two battles and had risked his life numerous times, received little recognition from General Gates. It was General Arnold who had actually led the American troops to victory at Saratoga, and Arnold was held in high esteem by the soldiers in the field. General Gates did not consider General Arnold's bold actions at Saratoga as heroic but as insubordinate actions and a challenge to his authority. The American success at Saratoga and the surrender of the superior British Royal Army and Hessian mercenary forces had a euphoric effect on the morale of the American troops. Henry Sewall of York, Maine (who also served with Lieutenant Ulmer at Saratoga), wrote in his diary about the military triumph: "Perhaps an unprecedented Instance that nearly 6,000 British & foreign Troops, under the command of an accomplish'd General, should surrender themselves Prisoners of War in the field to an Army of raw Continental Troops & Militia!"[714] The victory at Saratoga was considered something of a miracle. Many, if not most, of the American soldiers had an abiding faith in the Almighty and His influence on the affairs of men, and it was through divine Providence that the two bloody engagements at the Saratoga battlefield ended in a victory for the American troops.

Prior to the surrender ceremony, General Burgoyne changed out of the uniform that he had worn for sixteen days and nights. He dressed carefully

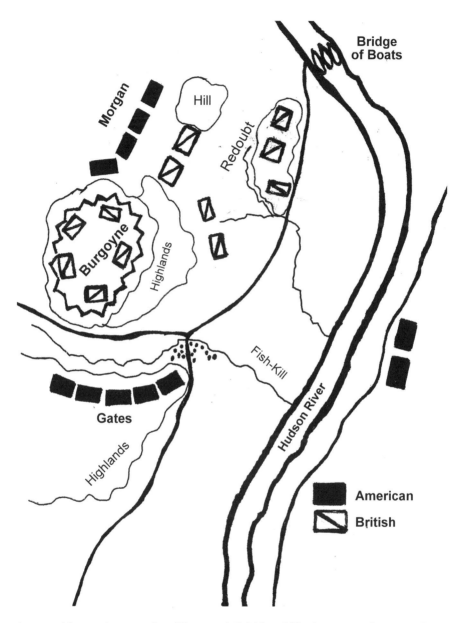

Army positions at the surrender of Burgoyne's British and Hessian army at Saratoga, New York, on October 17, 1777. *Courtesy of the author.*

in his clean scarlet coat with gold braid and his hat, which was adorned with plumes. General Burgoyne and General Horatio Gates rode toward each other, dismounted from their horses and acknowledged each other. General

Burgoyne removed his plumed hat and bowed at the waist to General Gates. Burgoyne withdrew his sword from his scabbard and presented it to Gates. The two commanders spoke briefly to each other, and then General Gates returned General Burgoyne's sword to him.[715]

General Baron von Riedesel met with his Hessian soldiers and artillerymen and assured them that they had fought bravely and courageously. He had the regimental flags brought to him. General Riedesel discretely removed them, and he gave them to his wife, Frederika Charlotte Riedesel. The baroness sewed the regimental flags into her pillow, and they were secretly taken back to Brunswick, in Nova Scotia.[716] The British and Hessian artillery parked the cannons in the field while the infantry men emptied cartridge boxes and stacked their muskets. Some of the angry and defeated British soldiers broke the butts of the muskets, and they threw the broken guns on the arms piles.[717] General Burgoyne's troops, having surrendered their weapons, marched out of camp to the music of the fifers playing "The World Turned Upside Down" and "The Grenadiers' March."[718]

General Horatio Gates had ordered the American troops to line the road that the British would march along into the American camp for the surrender ceremony. The troops were to stand at attention with muskets at their sides and their eyes looking straight forward or lowered in respect for the defeated soldiers.[719] The troops were ordered to assemble in their own regiments. Sergeants gave orders for the ranks to be closed, dressed and to stand at attention with their muskets and attached bayonets for their final parade. Soldiers in General Burgoyne's mighty British Royal Army began to parade by. The defeated Hessian and British army soldiers, regiment after regiment, brigade after brigade, marched in a long parade through the gauntlet of American troops along the road toward Albany.

Ebenezer Wild, a sergeant in Colonel Vose's First Massachusetts Regiment, wrote in his diary about the surrender event. Since Lieutenant Philip Ulmer was also in Colonel Vose's First Massachusetts Regiment with a detached company of soldiers, one can assume that the details of the events that were described in Ebenezer Wild's journal would have likewise involved Lieutenant Ulmer with the same detachment. Ebenezer Wild wrote:

> *We marched around the meeting house and came to a halt…we had an unobstructed view of the place of the surrender. We had an unobstructed view of the size of the British army with its thousands of soldiers, cannon, camp followers, bands, and wagons. General Burgoyne and his chief officers rode by us there, and then we marched further down the road and*

grounded our arms and rested there. At half after three o'clock, General
Burgoyne's army began to pass us, and they continued passing 'til sunset.

The parade into the camp for the historic surrender event, which the
soldiers in the First Massachusetts Regiment thought would take an hour
or so, actually took all afternoon. Company after company of British and
Hessian soldiers and camp followers marched past the American victors, who
looked straight ahead or at the ground and did not speak a word in response.
Private Daniel Granger, a militia volunteer who enlisted in General Enoch
Poor's New Hampshire regiment, described the surrender event at Saratoga.
He wrote in his diary:

We saw the American courier race away from the English camp with
the surrender and watched over the river as the American celebration
began…Soon we saw them coming. General Gates's troops were arranged
on both sides of the road, drums and fifes playing "Yankee Doodle," cannon
roaring in all quarters and the whole world seemed to be in motion. Officers
lost command over the soldiers. I got as near to General Gates's marquee
tent as I could for the crowd, and saw General Burgoyne and his suite ride
up, and dismount and go into General Gates's marquee, and soon the van
of the prisoners made their appearances. The Hessian troops came first
with their luggage on horses that were mere skeletons, not able apparently
to bear the weight of their own carcasses. These troops had some women,
who wore petticoats, bare-footed and bare-legged, with huge packs on their
backs, some carrying children and leading another of two. They were
silent, civil, and looked quite subdued. The English troops followed and
were cross and impudent enough. Having seen a large and well-equipped
British army of about eight thousand surrender as prisoners of war and
leaving on the field the finest and largest park of artillery that ever was seen
in America, with all their carts, timbrels, and vehicles for the conveyance of
their ammunition, was a great and pleasing novelty indeed.[720]

The British and Hessian troops could not believe that they had been
outmaneuvered and defeated by the ragtag American soldiers. Lieutenant
William Digby explained the demoralized feelings of the British soldiers at
the surrender. Digby wrote in his memoirs about the British Royal Army
band's most famous military song "The Grenadiers' March": "We marched
out with our drums beating…but the drums seemed to have lost their
inspiring sound."[721] American fifers suddenly started playing the shrill notes

of the tune "Yankee Doodle," which was a melody first introduced by a British doctor during the French and Indian War to make fun of and mock the American recruits, who were considered peasants or country folk, not professional soldiers.[722] It was surprising and even embarrassing to the British officers to hear the fifers play the song when the British army assembled to be witnesses to the surrender.[723]

German baroness Frederika von Riedesel, an eyewitness of the Saratoga battle, kept a personal journal in which she wrote her observations of the American troops, as did her husband: "Each soldier had on clothes which he was accustomed to wear in the field, in the tavern, the church, and in everyday life…they stood in an erect and soldierly attitude…[The appearance of the American men] they were so slender, fine-looking, and sinewy, that it was a pleasure to look at them…that Dame Nature had created such a handsome race!"[724]

The standards in Europe, which had been set by the Prussian Army, required that the men in the military had to be five feet to five feet five inches tall; however, the majority of the American soldiers were five feet eight to five feet ten inches tall, "…far ahead of those in the greater portion of Europe," observed the Baroness Riedesel and other German officers like Brigadier General Specht.[725] Almost all of the American soldiers carried powder horns and haversacks over their shoulders, stood with the right foot slightly forward, their right hand on their musket and the left arm hanging by their side.[726]

Following the surrender ceremony, General Gates invited General Burgoyne and all of General Burgoyne's brigadiers and regiment commanders to join in a reception feast inside his marquee tent, where ham, goose, beef and boiled mutton were served at a table. Liquor was offered; however, there were only glasses for General Gates and General Burgoyne.[727] The German officers with General von Riedesel and Brigadier General Specht were delighted to discover that a few of General Gates's officers, such as First Lieutenant Philip Ulmer, spoke German fluently, while some others spoke French.[728] There was a feeling of cordialness and congeniality inside the tent, which was noted by Lord Francis Napier: "Not a single man gave any evidence or the slightest impression of feeling hatred, mockery, malicious pleasure or pride in our miserable fate…it seemed rather as though they desired to do us honor. They behaved with the greatest decency and propriety, not even a Smile appearing in any of their Countenances, which circumstance I really believe would not have happened had the case been reversed."[729]

After the cordial and congenial time in the marquee tent, the occasion came to offer toasts. General Burgoyne raised a glass to George Washington, and General Gates responded by offering a toast to the health of the king. The officers left the tables and went outside the tent to watch the British and Hessian soldiers as they continued to file past the double lines of the American troops. After Burgoyne's defeated soldiers filed past, there were almost 300 women—215 were British, and 82 were German.[730] They were followed by the women of the officers and soldiers. Toward the end of the procession, there was a collection of camp followers, and they were accompanied by a number of deer, raccoons and other wildlife animals that had been turned into pets by some of the lonely soldiers. The line of prisoners continued through the afternoon and well past sunset.[731] Baroness Frederika von Riedesel received a message from her husband that she and the children were to join him in the American camp. In her journal, she noted that "nobody glanced at us insultingly, that they bowed to me, and some of them even looked with pity to see a woman with small children there."[732] Upon arrival at the marquee tent in the carriage, Baroness Riedesel realized that the officers were about to have the dinner. This was an inappropriate time for a woman and little children to be present. Major General Philip Schuyler, who had traveled from Albany to witness the surrender that he had tried so hard to facilitate, came forward and invited the baroness and her children to enjoy their meal in his tent. After the Baroness and the children had eaten, General Philip Schuyler invited her to stay with his family in Albany. With the approval of her husband, Baron von Riedesel, she and the children departed in their carriage for the Schuyler home with an American military escort.

At sunset, Generals Burgoyne, Phillips and Riedesel rode away from General Gates's marquee tent toward Stillwater, escorted by a detachment of impressively uniformed Connecticut dragoons and accompanied by Richard Varick, General Schuyler's personal aide and secretary. Comfortable lodging was found for the defeated generals at the home of General Schuyler and his family in Albany. The German and British officers and soldiers, as well as their families and entourage, camped overnight and proceeded the next day to Boston, where they remained prisoners until their war status and disposition would be determined by the Continental Congress. General Burgoyne remained as a prisoner houseguest of General and Mrs. Schuyler for five days before proceeding on to Boston. It was during his time at General Schuyler's home in Albany that General Burgoyne wrote a letter to Lord George Germain at the Ministry of War in London summarizing the events at Saratoga from early September until the final surrender of the British and Hessian forces in mid-October. Burgoyne's invasion expedition of 1777 that was expected to bring an end to the rebellion in the American colonies had caused a heavy loss in countless lives and a great cost in British treasure. On October 17, the number of British and Hessian soldiers who lay down their arms was reported to have been 5,895 on the day of surrender. That was approximately two-thirds of the force that had left Canada and moved down Lake Champlain toward Fort Ticonderoga on July 1. While several British regiments remained at Fort Ticonderoga to maintain control of Lake Champlain, General Burgoyne had lost almost nine out of ten soldiers during his invasion campaign to reach Albany.[733]

On October 18, the day after General Burgoyne's surrender at Saratoga, General Gates received an alarming express message that General Clinton was sailing north up the Hudson River with a large army and was going to attack Albany.[734] Colonel Vose's First Massachusetts Regiment received orders from General Gates to pack up and move out. Soldiers in Colonel Vose's regiment were sent on a grueling, fast-paced, forty-mile forced march to Albany to defend the city.[735] Even before the morning fog had lifted, the troops had packed their tents and were marching on the road south to Albany. By late morning, Colonel Vose's regiment reached Stillwater, where it passed the German prisoners who had been encamped while the British were ferried by bateaux across to the eastern shore of the Hudson River. Brigadier General Johann Specht, a disciplined German officer of the Second Brigade under General Riedesel's command, watched as the Americans marched past. He observed, "The whole day as well as night, very many American regiments filed past us from Saratoga in the strictest order with considerable trains of artillery and continued their march toward Albany."[736]

When Vose's troops arrived at Albany at about nine o'clock the next morning, they found that the alarm information was only a rumor. The British troops were not making an attack on Albany but were attacking towns farther south on the Hudson River. British major general John Vaughan and a small fleet of enemy transport vessels had sailed up the Hudson River from New York Harbor past the Highland forts that had been abandoned by the Americans who had been ordered to Saratoga. They paused long enough to shell and set fire to the shipyards at Poughkeepsie.[737] British general Vaughan awaited news and orders from General Burgoyne, who was, at this time, engaged at Saratoga. He decided to cause some damage to the towns along the Hudson River that were undefended. General Vaughan gave orders to fire upon and burn Kingston (Esopus), where the New York legislature and Governor Morris were meeting in an emergency session.[738] While Kingston was still burning, information was finally received by General Vaughan and the British fleet that Burgoyne's army had been defeated and would be forced to surrender to the American forces. The information caused great anger among the British army troops, and they felt a great need to vent their frustrations. General Vaughan landed his British troops at Rhinebeck, New York, and gave orders to march north toward Clermont—destroying, plundering and looting American citizens' homes and property—and rejoin the transports at Robert Livingston's Clermont mansion along the shores of the Hudson River. Before leaving the Hudson Highlands area and returning to New York Harbor, General Vaughan torched Livingston's brick house as well as Chancellor Livingston's Belvedere home.[739] Ironically, there had been eight men from the Livingston family who had fought against General Burgoyne's army at Freeman's Farm at Saratoga during this time. The American troops at Albany were relieved that the British transports to the south of Albany had decided to retreat back to the harbor at New York City.

General Glover's brigade, part of General Benjamin Lincoln's division, was given the honor and the responsibility of guarding the 5,700 British and Hessian prisoners on their march to the prisoner-of-war camp near Cambridge, Massachusetts. Lieutenant Philip Ulmer played an important part during the surrender ceremony, and he was assigned to escort the Hessian officers and soldiers back to Boston. By October 22, Brigadier General John Glover was prepared to leave Albany for Boston. Glover and his American troops had been given the honor and responsibility of escorting and guarding the prisoners of war on the march to Boston. On that day, about 2,400 British troops were sent by way of Northampton, and almost 2,200 German troops and hundreds of camp followers were sent by way of Springfield, Massachusetts.[740] The next day, General Glover left with General Burgoyne for Worcester, Massachusetts, where they were expected to arrive in ten days. Lieutenant Philip Ulmer and the detached company of German-speaking soldiers were assigned as escorts and guards for the prisoners during this time. German-speaking officers and aides were needed to give directions, deliver orders and interrogate the Hessian prisoners of war. Lieutenant Philip Ulmer probably met German officer Johann Specht, who served in General Riedesel's brigade, and he likely became acquainted with General Riedesel and his family during the journey from Saratoga to the Boston area. During the long journey, the German American soldiers and the Hessian captives became friendly and intermingled with one another, sharing experiences and stories about life in America and life in Germany and Europe.

Under the terms of the Saratoga Convention agreement between Generals Gates and Burgoyne, the prisoners of war would depart on transport ships for England. General Burgoyne's soldiers should have been paroled and returned to Britain on the condition that they engage in no further conflict with America, a common military practice in the eighteenth century. However, when the British and Hessian prisoners of war reached Boston, the terms of the Saratoga Convention were not honored. Instead, General Washington and the Continental Congress believed that the British Parliament would simply replace the defeated troops with more soldiers from Great Britain and Germany and then send the new replacements to America. The Continental Congress refused to ratify the generous Saratoga Convention of surrender agreed to by Generals Gates and Burgoyne.[741] Though some of the British and Hessian officers were eventually exchanged for captured American officers, most of the enlisted soldiers in the "Convention Army," as it became known, were held captive in prisoner-of-war camps in New England, Virginia and Pennsylvania, awaiting final disposition that did not come until the end of the Revolutionary War.

Some captive Hessian soldiers at the prison retention camp at Prospect Hill near Cambridge requested asylum in America.[742] The terrible stories of violence and barbarism that the British authorities had told the Hessian soldiers about the uncivilized colonists in America proved to be untrue. After becoming acquainted with ordinary German American soldiers and learning about the opportunities, freedoms and liberties that were enjoyed in the colonies, many Hessian soldiers who did not have family responsibilities or business opportunities in Europe became interested in remaining in America. A number of these Hessian soldiers eventually settled in frontier areas where other German-speaking Americans had settled. America was beginning to be viewed by many of the Hessian soldiers as the land of freedom, liberty, opportunity and prosperity. This was a very different view than the propaganda that they had been led to believe from the British and German rulers, politicians and military authorities.

After delivering the prisoners of war to the detention camp at Prospect Hill near Cambridge, Lieutenant Ulmer and his company of soldiers from Colonel Paterson's and Colonel Vose's regiments marched to Valley Forge and rejoined their regular regiments at General Washington's encampment.[743] Some of the soldiers in Ulmer's detached company whose enlistments were due to expire soon remained as prison guards at Prospect

Hill until they were discharged from further service and they could return to their homes to frontier Maine. A number of the captured Hessians made friends with several Lincoln County militiamen and officers who were to be discharged at Boston after completing their enlistments. A number of those Hessian soldiers desired to stay in America and to seek better opportunities for themselves and a better way of life. Through the German-speaking American guards at Prospect Hill, several communities in the Waldo County vicinity, which included Waldoboro, Union and St. George, heard the stories of the Hessian prisoners' predicament, and they offered to welcome a number of the Hessian prisoners of war into their community and to give them material support, lodging and jobs.

After agreements were made with their supporters and the sponsoring communities, a number of the Hessian prisoners were released and placed on parole under the sponsorship of several Lincoln County militia officers and soldiers who had served with Lieutenant Philip Ulmer at Saratoga. On October 25, 1777, John M. Schaeffer petitioned for three Hessian prisoners—one for himself and one each for Waterman Thomas and Andrew Schenck of Waldoboro.[744] One of the first Hessian prisoners to arrive in the town was Heinrich Isence (Ince), born in Hanover, Germany, who had been caught during the Hessian raid at Bennington (Vermont) by General Stark and his militia soldiers. He was brought to Waldoboro by Andrew Schenck and resided in the settlement for a brief time before joining his fellow German countryman Andreas Suchfort (Sukeforth), who was brought from the prisoner-of-war camp by Philip Robbins of Union (located in the backcountry area to the north of Waldoboro).[745] Andreas Suchfort later moved to Waldoboro, where he soon owned a farm (later known as the Merle Castner farm) and raised a large family. He became friends with the Ulmer family in Waldoboro. Andreas Suchfort married Catherine Newbert of Waldoboro in 1778.[746*] Other Hessian prisoners who sought political asylum also became residents of Waldoboro. Some of these men were Peter Walther (paroled to General McCobb), Doctor Theobald (a surgeon and chaplain) and Doctor John G. Bornemann. These German parolees became quickly assimilated into the town of Waldoboro and became productive members of the community as landowners and businessmen.[747]

---

* *Author's comment*: Catherine was the sister of Christopher Newbert, whose life Captain Philip Ulmer would save the following year during the Penobscot Expedition in 1779.

Reaction to the Surrender of
General Burgoyne's British Royal Army Forces

The British Parliament's reaction to General Burgoyne's surrender at Saratoga and the defeat of the British army during the spring campaign of 1777 was expressed simply: "The English Ministry were most displeased with the unfruitful termination of the campaign."[748] The defeat further weakened the British government under Lord North. As a result of the success of the Continental Army over the British Royal Army and Hessian mercenary forces at Saratoga, the French King, Louis XVI, recognized America's sovereignty from Great Britain. The French government decided to declare war on England and join forces with the American colonies. Spain soon followed France's lead and declared war on England as well.[749] The major victory at Saratoga dramatically improved America's prospects for winning the Revolutionary War. The New York campaign on Lake Champlain in October 1776, which delayed the invading British forces for a crucial year, and the two battles fought at Saratoga that led to the surrender of General Burgoyne's entire army of British and Hessian forces are commonly seen as the turning points for American independence and liberty from England's repressive control over the thirteen American colonies.

The capture of General Burgoyne's British allied army forces secured the New England colonies from separation from the rest of the country and halted future invasion campaigns from Canada (at least until the War of 1812). Baroness Riedesel observed that there was a certain quality in the American people that gave them something of an edge against the British. She noted in her memoirs that every inhabitant in the region "is a born soldier and a good marksman. The thought of fighting for their country and for freedom made them braver than ever."[750]

Aftermath of the Battle of Saratoga

Perhaps an unprecedented Instance that near 6,000 British & foreign Troops, under the command of an accomplish'd General, should surrender themselves Prisoners of War in the field to an Army of raw Continental Troops & Militia![751]
—Henry Sewall of York (Maine), October 17–18, 1777

James Wilkinson, General Gates's aide, was given the honor of delivering the news of General Burgoyne's surrender of the British and Hessian army invasion forces to the Continental Congress. Major Wilkinson took fifteen days to report the momentous event to the members of the Continental Congress. He apparently stopped off and did some courting en route to Congress. When the joyful news was finally delivered, a member of the Continental Congress suggested that a pair of spurs should be given to General Gates as a reward for the brilliant success.[752] The news of General Burgoyne's surrender was received on the East Coast on October 23, 1777. There was great rejoicing and "a general discharge of cannon at Boston, Marblehead, Salem, Beverly, Cape Ann, Newbury, and Portsmouth, and all ships and vessels of force in all those harbors."[753] General Washington did not learn the information about the American victory at Saratoga until October 25, when he received a letter from General Israel Putnam stationed in the Highlands Department. General Gates did not write to General Washington to inform him of the Saratoga success until November 2, two weeks after the event.[754] This was considered a snub or an insubordinate action by many officials since the commander in chief of the Continental Army, George Washington, should have been the first person informed of the success of his soldiers. Resent continued simmering below the surface between the generals.

The total surrender of General Burgoyne's army forces at Saratoga became a dramatic turning point in the American Revolution. The British defeat was made possible by the delaying strategy of the small American naval fleet on Lake Champlain in the fall of 1776. Although the battle on Lake Champlain was considered a tactical defeat, the engagement enabled the Continental Congress to rally support to fight for sovereignty and independence from England, and it gave General Washington's army the precious time that was needed to become organized and ready to fight General Burgoyne's allied invading forces the following year. With the British defeat at Saratoga in 1777, General Sir Guy Carleton's entire northern front in Canada was at risk of collapse. General Carleton found himself shorthanded of defensive forces in Canada, and he ordered the isolated British troops at Fort Ticonderoga and Diamond Point on Lake George to retreat back to the safety of Montreal and Quebec. In addition to the return of the British prisoners of war, the Saratoga Convention provided for volunteer sailors, bateau men and artificers to return to Montreal. On November 8, General Henry Powell evacuated Fort Ticonderoga and Mount Independence, and by December 1776, the remainder of the British troops had cleared the inland waterways from northern New York to Canada, completing the retreat beyond the Canadian border.[755]

The outcome of the surrender at Saratoga was different for General Burgoyne's Royal Army troops. Instead of being released at Boston to return to Europe, as agreed upon by Generals Gates and Burgoyne, the Continental Congress decided that it was more advantageous to keep the prisoners from the Saratoga battle and prevent their replacement by more European troops.[756] Official word of the total surrender of Burgoyne's army forces was received from General Carleton in Parliament on December 2, 1777. The king and many in the British Parliament blamed General Howe for the Saratoga defeat because he pursued his own strategy to capture Philadelphia and certain southern seaports, and he did not properly support Burgoyne's 1777 campaign to divide the New England colonies and end the rebellion. General Howe had sent his second-in-command, General Clinton, with troops to capture Newport, Rhode Island, instead of supporting General Burgoyne and his invading troops from Canada. However, the British capture of Newport by General Clinton's forces in late 1777 sealed off Narragansett Bay. It abruptly severed Providence's route to transatlantic trading with Europe, trading with the southern coastal colonies of America and trading with the island seaports in the West Indies. The British forces were stretched too thin in many directions, which endangered the mission of recapturing the rebellious colonies. British general Sir Henry Clinton was ordered to replace General Howe as commander in chief of British forces in North America.[757] General Howe was accused of "having cost Great Britain America."[758] Lord George Germain came under attack by the House of Commons and was accused of being unfit to serve as secretary of state for the American colonies and incapable of conducting a war.[759]

General Burgoyne was allowed to return to England after the Saratoga defeat to answer charges before the House of Commons in early 1780. Testifying on the decisive battle, General Burgoyne attributed the results directly to the actions of Benedict Arnold:

> *I have reason to believe my disappointment on that day* [October 7, 1777] *proceeded from an uncommon circumstance in conduct of the enemy. Mr. Gates, as I have been informed, had determined to receive the attack in his line; Mr. Arnold, who commanded the left, foreseeing the danger of being turned, advanced without consultation with his general, and gave instead of receiving battle. The stroke might have been fatal on his part if*

he failed. But…had the other idea been pursued, I should in a few hours have gained a position, that in spite of the enemy's numbers, would have put them in my power.

FRANCE JOINS THE AMERICAN FORCES AGAINST GREAT BRITAIN

Europe, and not England, is the parent country of America. This new world hath been the asylum for the persecuted lover of civil and religious liberty from every Part of Europe…The same tyranny which drove the first emigrants from home pursues their descendants still.
—Thomas Paine

On October 18, the Continental Congress's Foreign Affairs Committee sent a copy of General Gates's letter describing his victory over General Burgoyne's British and Hessian forces at Saratoga to Congress's three foreign agents in France—Benjamin Franklin, Silas Deane and Arthur Lee. Two weeks later, the Foreign Affairs Committee sent a letter announcing the joyful news of Burgoyne's defeat and the surrender of the entire army. The message further directed the three agents in France: "We rely on your wisdom and care to make the best and most immediate use of this intelligence to depress our enemies and produce essential aid to our cause in Europe [with] public acknowledgement of the Independence of these United States."[760]

Once the news reached King Louis XVI of France at Versailles, everyone in France rejoiced that the American army had forced the surrender of General Burgoyne. The invincible and feared image of Great Britain's Royal Army and Prussian mercenaries had been tarnished. On December 12, Comte de Vergennes, the French foreign minister of King Louis XVI, asked the French Court for permission to send a courier to Madrid, Spain, with a request for the Spanish king's agreement, and a proposed treaty, for assistance to the American colonies. Within five days, the Spanish king's council had approved the alliance. On December 17, 1777, the Comte de Vergennes informed the three American commissioners that His Majesty, King Louis XVI, "was determined to acknowledge [America's] Independence and make a Treaty with us of Amity and Commerce [and support America's insurrection and its independence] by every means in his power."[761]

Return to the Philadelphia Campaign

There had been friction building between British general Howe and General Clinton, his second-in-command. The management of the war had reached a decisive point for the British commanders. General Clinton considered Washington's army as the heart of the rebellion; however, he had been ordered by General Howe to maintain control of New York City, Long Island and Rhode Island while General Howe sought another strategy to weaken Washington's army. General Howe wanted to keep General Washington's troops off balance and on the move so that Gates's troops in the north and Washington's troops to the south would be diverted by other actions and would not be able to join forces and attack New York City, a major British stronghold. General Howe had decided to capture the American capital of Philadelphia, a major prosperous seaport and the governing seat of the Continental Congress. The occupation of Philadelphia would undermine the will of the American people to continue the rebellion and would serve as a major victory for the British army.

During the summer of 1777, General William Howe, who was interested in receiving recognition from the British Parliament for his own success in a military campaign, took a force of fifteen thousand troops from New York City and sailed south in about three hundred vessels to the Chesapeake Bay.[762] They landed along the shores of the Elk River. General Howe's invading army marched along the colonial highway, which ran from Virginia to Pennsylvania. The British troops camped at the little town of Elkton, Maryland, which was several days' march from Philadelphia. In anticipation of the enemy's arrival, the townspeople of Elkton hid their horses, cattle and valuables in the woods so that the soldiers couldn't confiscate them. The British troops stayed for several days in the vicinity, during which time General Howe made his final plans to capture the city. General Howe's army marched north toward Philadelphia, where they engaged General Washington's main Continental Army at Brandywine and Germantown outside the city. Having outmaneuvered Washington's army troops, on September 26, 1777, General Howe and the British forces entered the city, where they remained comfortably in winter quarters for about six months.[763] No assistance was given to General Burgoyne's campaign to split the colonies, and General Howe's actions in Pennsylvania and his orders to General Clinton to capture and secure Newport, Rhode Island, sealed the fate of General Burgoyne's army forces at Saratoga, New York.

Chapter 10

Valley Forge

GENERAL WASHINGTON ORDERS GENERAL GATES'S ARMY TO VALLEY FORGE

With Burgoyne's captured British army on its way to Boston, General Washington sent orders directing the military troops (which had been sent as reinforcements to General Gates at Saratoga) to march to Valley Forge and rejoin the main Continental Army that would be in winter quarters about twenty miles northwest of Philadelphia. Colonel Vose's First Massachusetts Regiment began its 250-mile march from Albany on October 30, 1777, to join Washington's main Continental Army.[764] The march to Washington's main encampment at Valley Forge, Pennsylvania, began about thirteen days after the surrender of General Burgoyne's British and Hessian troops at Saratoga. The journey of Colonel Vose's regiment (described in Ebenezer Wild's diary and in other diaries and letters of American soldiers) served as an example of the tangle of problems that plagued the American army encampment at Valley Forge. There were jumbled orders; poor intelligence; mismanagement; overly long marches; court-martials; snowstorms; rain deluges; bitterly cold and unsettled weather; lack of proper clothing, boots and blankets; and lack of food, axes, cooking pots and other needed supplies for survival in the winter environment at Valley Forge. Colonel Vose's troops learned that the clothes, which they had expected and had been promised by the Continental Congress, were not there.[765] The soldiers were given secondhand shirts and basic supplies by the Pennsylvania troops. The wagons with the needed supplies for the American troops arrived late. After a brief rest, the troops with Colonel Vose's First Massachusetts Regiment and several other regiments (all associated with General Paterson's brigade) continued their push south toward Morristown in the Watchung Mountains of northwestern New Jersey. The next day, there were heavy rains that thoroughly soaked the troops.[766]

On November 21, the First Massachusetts Regiment camped at Morristown for several weeks before moving south along a narrow dirt highway toward the small village of Basking Ridge.[767] This gave the time necessary for the troops that had accompanied the captured Hessian troops to the prisoner-of-war camps at Cambridge and Prospect Hill an opportunity to rejoin Colonel Vose's regiment. (This would have included soldiers with Lieutenant Ulmer.) Two days later, the First Massachusetts Regiment camped outside of Princeton, where the army troops, ten months earlier, had achieved a surprising victory over General Cornwallis's British and Hessian forces. Sergeant Ebenezer Wild, with Colonel Vose's regiment, wrote in his diary that the field where the American troops set up their camp was uncomfortable and "very full of briers."[768] The brigade did not resume its march on November 24, according to Wild's journal, because of a court-martial that was held so that Colonel Vose could give out discipline to his regiment.[769] The soldiers formed a large circle for the judicial proceedings where the men would serve as witnesses. Two privates and two sergeants were tried for leaving the company without permission. The court-martial board found all four men guilty. One sergeant was demoted, and the other was reprimanded before the entire company. The two privates were to be whipped, but the colonel gave leniency after they repented, and they were not whipped after all.[770] The court-martial proceedings kept the company of soldiers occupied, and they did not arrive at Mount Holly until the next day. The regiment made camp and slept in the thick woods on the outskirts of the town.

Intelligence reached Colonel Vose's First Massachusetts Regiment that a British scouting party was moving out of Philadelphia. In order to take the enemy scouting party by surprise, the American troops were awakened at three o'clock in the morning and marched ten miles in the dark before arriving at Moorestown. Unfortunately, the intelligence was incorrect, and the British troops had already returned to Philadelphia.[771] After resting for a while, Vose's troops resumed their march to the ferry crossing over the Delaware River, arriving at about nine o'clock at night. Once on the other side of the Delaware River, they proceeded to a place where two main roads came together, and the troops quickly set up their camp and spent the rest of the night. The next day, a severe storm covered the region, and the troops stayed in their tents the whole day trying to keep dry as sheets of cold rain fell upon their camp.[772] The next few days were cold and windy, and the temperatures rose and fell as the men continued their routine camp chores.

THE SKIRMISH AT WHITE MARSH

General Washington spent several weeks after his defeat at Germantown encamped with the Continental Army in various locations throughout Montgomery County, just north of British-occupied Philadelphia. In November, the Americans had established an entrenched position about sixteen miles north of Philadelphia where the British troop movements could be monitored and General Washington could evaluate his options. On December 4, General Howe, the commander in chief of the British forces in North America, led a sizable force of troops out of Philadelphia in one last attempt to destroy General Washington's Continental Army before the onset of winter. The British and American troops encountered each other near White Marsh, Pennsylvania. Confrontations between the two opposing forces occurred over several days from December 5 to December 8 just to the area north of Philadelphia. It took the form of a series of skirmishes as the two forces maneuvered around each other in a military probing action. General Howe returned to Philadelphia without engaging General Washington's army troops in a decisive conflict. This served as the last military encounter of 1777 between the British and American forces. With the British back in Philadelphia, Washington felt that he could finally take his troops into winter quarters at Valley Forge.

On December 5, Sergeant Ebenezer Wild noted in his diary that the company's food supplies were vanishing: "We drew some fresh meat and flour, but had nothing to cook in. Was obliged to boil our meat on the fire and bake our bread in the ashes."[773] Several days after Ebenezer Wild wrote of his concerns about the dwindling food supplies within Colonel Vose's regiment, many other soldiers complained that their supplies had not been replenished either. Blankets and warm woolen coats had not arrived on schedule, and the usual shipments of food were nowhere to be found. None of the officers knew why winter coats, shoes, blankets and other clothing that had been on order for months in advance had not been delivered. These issues would have to be addressed when the troops arrived at the Valley Forge encampment.

On December 12, the First Massachusetts Regiment, with Lieutenant Philip Ulmer and his detached company of soldiers who had recently rejoined Colonel Vose's regiment, crossed the Schuylkill River, and they camped in a wooded area just as a snowstorm began to descend upon them. As the storm became worse, the soldiers were told to either pitch their tents or cut down trees and construct lean-tos for cover. Some of the men were told to gather firewood from the forest trees for warmth and for cooking. Ebenezer Wild wrote in his diary, "We had no tents nor axes to cut wood to make fires. The tools which were needed were missing. It was a very bad storm."[774] Some of the men were able to construct makeshift lean-tos and make fires. However, the winds increased, causing flames from the campfires to ignite two lean-tos. The men whose structures had been destroyed by the fires ended up with no protection from the storm and slept out in the open in the snow. As the snowstorm came to an end, several days of steady rain followed. The men of the First Massachusetts Regiment were kept in their camp in the middle of the forest and were unable to proceed toward Washington's encampment at Valley Forge.

On December 18, in spite of another snowfall, Colonel Vose's troops celebrated Thanksgiving, which had been proposed by the Continental Congress.[775] Ebenezer Wild wrote: "We had but a poor Thanksgiving. Nothing but fresh beef and flour to eat without any salt and but very scant of [beef.]"[776] There were no pots for cooking the lean, unsalted beef, so it was thrown on the coals and broiled or cooked in that way. The water that was used by the soldiers to drink and to mix with flour to make fire-cakes or biscuits came from a brook that ran along the camp. So many men were dipping and washing in the stream that the water became dirty, muddy and unhealthy.[777] With poor sanitation habits, some of the soldiers had relieved themselves upstream of the camp, and other men downstream, and dipped the water out to drink. Many of the men became ill, and many soldiers died of infections, viruses and various diseases.

ENCAMPMENT AT VALLEY FORGE

For some days past, there has been little less than a famine in camp. A part of the army has been a week, without any kind of flesh, and the rest for three or four days. Naked and starving as they are, we cannot enough admire the incomparable patience and fidelity of the soldiery…
—*General Washington, February 16, 1778*[778]

General Washington, his Continental Army and various militia troops from many colonial states encamped at Valley Forge, where they stayed for the next six months. Washington's troops were exhausted, famished and in need of winter shelter after the battles at Brandywine and Germantown and after several other skirmishes against General Howe's British forces outside of Philadelphia. The brigades that had fought at Saratoga, under the command of General Horatio Gates, had endured a long march from Albany, and they were equally exhausted and needed shelter. General Washington's gathering troops brought their supply wagons and General Henry Knox brought his field guns to Valley Forge. On December 19, the weather had changed and was clear, cold and windy. The regiments from various colonial states arrived and proceeded to set up their winter quarters along the Schuylkill River, northwest of British-held Philadelphia. Lieutenant Philip Ulmer and the soldiers of the First Massachusetts Regiment marched to Valley Forge and were assimilated into the Continental Army. Four days after arriving at Valley Forge, nearly three thousand men from Washington's army were reported nearly naked and sick, and many were unfit for duty.[779]

General Washington faced critical problems when he first arrived at Valley Forge. Among the problems Washington faced were the lack of dry goods (clothing, blankets, shoes, coats, etc.) and sufficient food supplies, and there was no housing or shelter for the army troops in the cold winter weather. George Washington had been given dictatorial powers in 1776 by the Continental Congress when he became commander in chief of the Continental Army. The special dictatorial powers gave Washington authority to seize clothing and needed supplies from American citizens whenever and wherever he found them. (However, these powers were later rescinded.) In September 1777, the Pennsylvania State Assembly had authorized him to take whatever clothing supplies he needed from the inhabitants living in the southern part of the state.[780] General Washington refused to assert this dictatorial power over the residents, and he reminded the state assembly and Continental Congress that martial law was unthinkable to him and that he would find another way to resolve the problems. Washington ordered a search to be made to procure the needed meat supplies for his starving troops. Foraging expeditions were sent out into New Jersey and throughout the mid-Atlantic colonies to find cattle and bring them to Valley Forge. The scouts located a considerable amount of cattle on farms as far away as Massachusetts and Maryland that were herded and driven several hundred miles to Valley Forge to feed the hungry army.[781]

The soldiers were faced with the immediate challenge of building a log city that could house all of the fourteen thousand troops and about two thousand horses, with stables and wagon barns, cattle pins, parade grounds, granaries, blacksmith shops, privies and several hospitals to care for the sick and injured. Cabins were built along planned dirt lanes with soldiers from each state grouped together in their own neighborhoods.[782] Each cabin held twelve soldiers and had bunk beds and a small fireplace in the back of the structure for cooking and for keeping warm. The officers' cabins were similar, but they held half the amount of men. Lieutenant Philip Ulmer was housed with other officers from his First Massachusetts Regiment in the rustic, wet and drafty officers' cabin.

While the cabins for the soldiers were being built, the men lived in tents and were exposed to the extreme weather and climate conditions for many weeks. Because of the frigid weather conditions, digging privies was difficult in the frozen ground, so proper sanitation soon became a great issue. Soldiers drank dirty water from the nearby streams and urinated wherever they desired throughout the camp. Garbage was left outside of the building structures to rot. Vermin quickly took over the area, carrying diseases. Horses died and were left wherever they collapsed. The decaying remains brought more sickness to the camp. Disease from close quarters and sickness (smallpox, camp fever, dysentery, pneumonia, infections) caused severe problems. Lack of proper clothing, shoes, blankets, warm coats and food supplies, as well as the lack of insulation between the logs of the cabins, caused misery inside the American encampment, and this led to more sickness and death.[783] From the day that the troops first arrived at Valley Forge, the hut city was plagued with problems. The misery, sickness and death that the troops endured at Valley Forge would test the endurance and courage of the American Patriots like no other time in American history.

On December 23, the soldiers who had recently arrived at Washington's encampment were put to work constructing a "hut city." The hut city was built of logs cut from the forests in the surrounding area. The officers had hoped to use the local sawmills around Philadelphia to cut planks and boards to be used for roofs and doors. The cold weather, however, had caused the streams to freeze, making the mills inoperable.[784] The different regiments were directed by their officers to the locations where their small "communities" were to be built, depending on their particular state and divisions. Philip Ulmer had spent his twenty-fifth birthday the year before (1776) with Washington's army troops at the Delaware crossing and the raid on Trenton. On December 25, 1777, Philip Ulmer spent his twenty-sixth birthday huddled outside a tent, trying to keep warm beside a campfire in the frigid, cold and snowy conditions at Valley Forge, Pennsylvania.[785]

The dissention, deceit and rumors within the army ranks were already having a serious effect on the morale of the officers. Complaints were heard within the camp questioning General Washington's decision to remain at Valley Forge. On December 26, Dr. Albigence Waldo, a surgeon from Connecticut, wrote in his journal entitled *Life at Valley Forge (1777–1778)*:

> *The Enemy has been some Days the west of Schuylkill from Opposite the City to Derby, there intentions not yet known. The City* [Philadelphia] *is at present pretty Clear of them. Why don't his Excellency rush in & retake the City, in which he will doubtless find much Plunder? Because he knows better than to leave his Post and be catch'd like a fool cooped up in the City. He has always acted wisely hitherto, His conduct when closely scrutinized is uncensurable. Were his Inferior Generals as skillful as himself, we should have the grandest Choir of Officers ever God made…*[786]

On December 27, about fifty officers in General Greene's division resigned their commissions. Other officers in other regiments soon followed those in General Greene's division. Lieutenant Philip Ulmer, like other officers in General Sullivan's division, resigned in January 1778. Dr. Albigence Waldo wrote in his journal:

> *Dec.28, Yesterday upwards of fifty Officers in Gen. Green's Division resigned their Commissions, Six or Seven of our Regiment are doing the like to-day. All this is occation'd by Officers Families being so much neglected at home on account of Provisions, their Wages will not by considerable, purchase a few trifling Comfortables here in Camp, & maintain their families at home, while such extravagant prices are demanded for the common necessaries of Life, What then have they to purchase Cloaths* [sic] *and other necessaries with? It is a Melancholly*

reflection that what is of most universal importance, is most universally neglected, I mean keeping up the Credit of Money…The present Circumstances of the Soldier is better by far than the Officer, for the family of the Soldier is provided for at the public expence if the Articles they want are above the common price, but the Officer's family, are obliged not only to beg in the most humble manner for necessaries of Life, but also to pay for them afterwards at the most exhorbitant rates, and even in this manner, many of them who depend entirely on their Money, cannot procure half the material comforts that are wanted in a family, this produces continual letters of complaint from home…[787]

First Lieutenant Philip Ulmer remained in the Continental Army pay accounts for service from January 1, 1777, to January 4, 1778.[788] He served as first lieutenant in both Colonel Vose's regiment and in Colonel Paterson's regiment with Captain Hunt's company. He appeared in the Valley Forge muster rolls from December 1777 through March 1778 in Colonel Vose's regiment.[789] In early January, at the Valley Forge encampment, First Lieutenant Philip Ulmer requested permission to resign from the Continental Army over a disagreement about a promotion to army captain and about long-overdue payments for military service that were both due him.[790] (The Congressional Treasury Department had apparently not paid or had only sporadically paid many of the officers and soldiers who had been in service to the United Colonies since the siege of Boston in 1775.) Philip Ulmer's service records appeared with the Second Massachusetts Brigade, in the First Massachusetts Regiment with Captain Abraham Hunt's company and in the Fourth Division of General Benjamin Lincoln's division with General Glover as commander at the Maine encampment at Valley Forge from January through March 1778.[791]

Among the Waldoboro recruits in the Maine encampment who were with First Lieutenant Philip Ulmer in winter quarters at Valley Forge were: George Ulmer (Philip's brother), George Ulmer Jr. (son of Philip's uncle, John Ulmer, of Marblehead and Waldoboro), George Leissner, Ezekiel Winslow, Conrad Heyer, Isaiah Cole, Daniel Beckler, Frederick Schwartz (died at Valley Forge), Charles Heavener and others.[792] This small corps of Patriots from Waldoboro, with a few thousand other soldiers, represented the real blossoming of the American spirit in the Revolutionary War struggle. The deprivations, the sicknesses, the diseases and the extreme suffering that the soldiers at Valley Forge endured were beyond the comprehension of most American citizens.

The shortage of provisions led to a "fatal crisis," as General Washington called it, and endangered the continued survival of the Continental Army. The procurement and transportation of supplies of all kinds was not administered by the army but was under the incompetent federal administrators in York and later Lancaster, Pennsylvania, where the Continental Congress had taken refuge after the British forces captured Philadelphia. There was little congressional oversight of the supply departments, and theft became rampant. The poor management of the commissary department and bad weather conditions caused the breakdown of the transportation of dry goods, provisions and military supplies. The commissary mismanagement and insufficient wagons and carts all combined to cause a logistical collapse that brought the army provisions and supplies almost to a halt. The defective organization and administration of the quartermaster general's department had been, from the beginning of the war, a source of embarrassment to the Continental Army. The quartermaster general, Thomas Mifflin, quit in October 1777; however, the Continental Congress did not replace him until March 1778, causing the commissary department to be in complete disarray and confusion.[793]

Soldiers threatened mutiny because they did not have proper clothing, shoes and warm coats for the harsh weather conditions. Many soldiers were in rags because of the incompetence of the clothier general, James Mease, who had decided to go on vacation instead of completing the sewing and tailoring work in a timely manner.[794] The American colonies did not have textile mills that could produce clothes for the hundreds and thousands of soldiers like those in England. Shipments of clothing from the colonial state of New York were lost en route to the troops at Valley Forge. A large clothing warehouse and depot at Danbury, Connecticut, had been burned by a British raiding party. Officers from other camps in New York and New Jersey halted shipments for Valley Forge and removed many uniforms and blankets, and they gave the dry goods and supplies to their own soldiers.[795] The lack of clothing caused the troops at Valley Forge to be unable to participate in work crews or in needed camp drills. General Paterson, with whom Colonel Vose's regiment functioned closely, told his superior commanders that three-quarters of his men could not report for parade because they had no clothes, warm coats or shoes. General Paterson wrote in a letter to Thomas Marshall in February 1777, "They [the troops] are naked from the crowns of their heads to the soles of their feet."[796]

A fellow officer with Lieutenant Philip Ulmer in Colonel Vose's First Massachusetts Regiment, Lieutenant Archelaus Lewis, wrote to a friend,

Jesse Partridge, "There is two-thirds of our regiment barefooted and bare-backed, not a second shirt to put on not breeches to cover their nakedness... this is the case with the greatest part of our army. By your conduct, you as good as say why should we trouble or concern ourselves about them? They are tied fast and let them look out for themselves."[797] Unable to obtain the needed clothing at Valley Forge, many soldiers begged their friends, family and even their neighbors to send them needed clothing and supplies. Many soldiers saw their lack of clothing, shoes and other basic needs as a lack of patriotism and support by their own states and by the Continental Congress. Colonel William Shepard, one of the regiment commanders who served with Lieutenant Ulmer in Glover's brigade at Valley Forge, wrote a desperate plea to the Massachusetts legislature complaining that his "destitute men lived barely above a state of want...due to the inaction of clothing procurements back home."[798] The Massachusetts legislature ruled that the procurers were negligent and ordered the immediate production of new clothing for their regiments in the winter camp.

Over the winter months at Valley Forge, 2,500 men (out of 10,000) died from disease and exposure. With so little protection from the cold, rainy and harsh weather conditions, bad colds turned into various infections like bronchitis and pneumonia, and the soldiers were sent to the dreaded hospitals, where many died in wretched conditions. Benjamin Rush wrote to General Gates that citizens were not willing to enlist in the Continental Army because of its terrible medical conditions, lack of proper supplies, wretched care and insufficient provisions. Rush wrote: "The common people are too much shocked with spectacles of Continental misery ever to become Continental soldiers."[799] General Washington was dismayed with the medical tragedy unfolding at the winter encampment. Washington took steps to enforce proper hygiene, garbage disposal and ventilation in the log huts. He made visits to his sick soldiers and risked his own health when he made regular visits to hospitals and offered words of encouragement to the suffering troops. As new soldiers arrived at the encampment, General Washington ordered that those not already inoculated from smallpox should be inoculated.[800] The inoculated men were sent to a separate hospital to recover so as not to expose the other sick soldiers suffering from other illnesses to additional complications.

Starvation continued to be a serious threat that could not be ignored. General Washington wrote to his friend Governor Jonathan Trumbull Sr. of Connecticut for help at this desperate time.[801] Governor Trumbull and the citizens of Connecticut responded with food and supplies that strained the resources of the citizens. Connecticut became known as the "Provision State," and the citizens in Connecticut were willing to sacrifice their own comfort in order to help Washington's Continental Army in its time of greatest need. General Washington wrote to the new president of Congress, Henry Laurens, that the supply departments of Congress obstructed him at every turn and that local farmers would not or could not help him. He related that he and his soldiers felt that the government had abandoned them. General Washington further related that he feared a revolt by the general public when they found out how badly the soldiers were being treated. He firmly stated to the president of the Continental Congress that he felt that "within days, the army would starve, dissolve, or disperse."[802]

It is from the writings of General Washington's own pen that an adequate idea of the miseries at Valley Forge can best be described: "To see men without clothes to cover their nakedness, without blankets to lie on, without shoes (for want of which their marches might be traced by the blood from their feet)…is a proof of patience and obedience, which in my opinion can scarce be paralleled."[803]

Finally, at the earnest request of General Washington in March 1778, General Greene accepted the office of quartermaster general but reserved his right to command on the field of battle. The job of commissary general was given to Jeremiah Wadsworth, who carried out the assignment with efficiency. The letters written to the governing bodies of the different colonial states by General Greene and Jeremiah Wadsworth appealing for help and support for the suffering soldiers at Valley Forge began to show some results.[804] The problems of acquiring food and needed supplies for the army soldiers, which had plagued the army from the beginning of the encampment in mid-December 1777, began to change and improve.

The turning point of the Valley Forge encampment came when General Washington's priority was no longer to fight General Howe and the British forces. Washington's concern was to preserve his own army and prepare it for the next campaign in the late spring, when the Continental Army would leave winter quarters at Valley Forge. Attrition and ineffective recruitment had left the army dangerously weak, and the greatly increasing number of officer resignations made it obvious that equitable pay and pension benefits needed to be recognized.[805] The battle losses of the summer and fall of 1777 had exposed the need for more recruits, reorganization, discipline and skillful training for the American troops. European adventurers and volunteers offered their services for profit, for recognition and what became known as the American cause. French noblemen, foreign officers and European countrymen came to America for many reasons. Some men were looking for romantic adventure, while others had the desire to strike a blow against England in revenge for events during the Seven Years' War. Some European volunteers held sentiments of liberty, equality and freedom expressed in the American cause.

The Marquis de Lafayette of France and German-born Baron Johann DeKalb (who were introduced by a mutual friend) were given a commission and letters of introduction to the Continental Congress by the American emissary, Silas Deane. He wrote that the Marquis de Lafayette's wealth and his family's political influence in France might be useful to America's needs, and Deane further suggested that Lafayette and DeKalb (a former German officer seeking adventure in America) should be given the rank of major general in the American army. The Marquis de Lafayette and his older companion, Baron DeKalb, were commissioned as generals by the Continental Congress at the end of July 1777. They served as foreign volunteer aides and were officers on General Washington's staff during the Continental Army's stay in its winter quarters at Valley Forge in 1777–78. General Lafayette, General DeKalb and German-born Baron von Steuben (who joined Washington's staff at Valley Forge in March 1778) played important leadership roles in the operation of the Continental Army. Young European noblemen, adventurers and volunteers with little or no experience in military warfare were elevated by Congress to the rank of general. These unmerited appointments caused veteran American officers and soldiers to become disgruntled and resentful of the foreign opportunists. Some of the officers on General Washington's staff and in the field began to scheme and plot a way to remove General Washington from his role as commander in chief of the Continental Army.

Chapter 11

Political Unrest

POLITICAL UNDERCURRENTS IN EUROPE AND IN THE CONTINENTAL CONGRESS

There were other international and politically covert activities going on in France, the West Indies and in the United Colonies. Silas Deane had been sent to France by the Continental Congress in early 1776 to seek monetary and military support from the French government for the American cause of freedom, liberty and independence from Great Britain. Silas Deane served as the sole emissary representative of the Continental Congress until Benjamin Franklin was commissioned to serve in Paris as well. Silas Deane, who did not speak French, had to mediate his way through the foreign politics of the French court at Versailles while seeking financial assistance from other European governments.[806] He was charged with the responsibility of purchasing needed supplies for Washington's Continental Army such as tents, pot and pans, blankets, shoes and socks, flints, shovels, handkerchiefs, etc. Deane was also charged by the Secret Committee of Congress with buying goods for trade with the Indian tribes to appease or attain cooperation from them.[807] Deane also had his own trading business with Robert Morris (his benefactor) to manage. On the same day that Silas Deane purchased and shipped saltpeter and sulfur to Washington's Continental Army, the records in his account books showed the export of flour to Portugal, the exporting of cloth for the Indians and the sending of large orders of oil, claret, olives, capers and other items to Robert Morris's customers in Philadelphia. All of the exchanges were recorded in the same account book in order to disguise Deane's secret mission, as he had been instructed to do by the Secret Committee of Congress.[808]

Ambassador Franklin was sent to Paris by the Continental Congress in December 1776. However, Benjamin Franklin had enemies in Congress who sought to undermine his efforts as a delegate, as a businessman and as a commissioner. The animosity between some of the delegates had begun several years before the American Revolution. France's influence and control effectively ended in North America after the French and Indian War with the signing of the Treaty of Paris in 1763. In order to avoid future tension with the Indian tribes in Canada and those west of the Allegheny Mountains, at the end of the war, King George III issued the Royal Proclamation of 1763, which annulled all of the American colonies' western land claims, reserved all of the land west of the Allegheny Mountains for the Indian tribes and prohibited colonial settlements or land purchases in the Ohio River Valley. The king's proclamation effectively called a halt to colonial westward expansion. However, almost immediately, the Board of Trade agreed to grant some limited licenses for western settlement. The licenses were granted mostly to wealthy merchants, financial investors and land speculators who sought to make great fortunes in the undeveloped and resource-rich lands in the Ohio and Mississippi Valley regions. Benjamin Franklin and his investors in the Grand Ohio Company, and the Lee families and their investors in the Mississippi Company, had become bitter rivals over land speculation, business investment and financial wealth, which later erupted into full-scale conflict within the Continental Congress.[809] The bitter disputes and rivalries among some of the delegates in the Continental Congress posed a threat for the survival of Washington's Continental Army and for the survival of the United Colonies.

Ambassador Franklin and the American agent Silas Deane worked hard behind the scenes to gain military and financial support from France for the American Revolution. Richard Henry Lee, a legislative delegate in the Continental Congress, tried to undermine his rival Benjamin Franklin and Silas Deane's efforts in France by revealing their efforts to supply arms to the Continental Army and to issue American privateering commissions abroad. Richard Henry Lee and Arthur Lee (who was appointed as one of the three commissioners in France) threatened to expose Deane's secret efforts with France's agent, Comte Beaumarchais, to smuggle arms and military ordnance through Roderigue Hortalez & Company (a bogus shipping firm) and funnel covert aid and military supplies to General Washington's army through the French port of Martinique in the West Indies.[810] The Lee brothers and other detractors of George Washington in the Continental Congress further threatened to expose the covert support and smuggling activities of Spain and the Netherlands at their ports in the West Indies as well. Silas Deane harbored the hope of expanding the role of American privateering activities to undermine the superior military and economic strength of Great Britain and provide the military arms and supplies that General Washington needed for the Continental Army which the Congress was unable to supply. Silas Deane, like Benjamin Franklin and other wealthy merchants, speculators and congressional delegates, became an investor in several privateering vessels, including one with Robert Morris, who was a wealthy Philadelphia merchant and investment banker. Robert Morris was a strong supporter of General Washington and the American cause. Robert Morris was later referred to as the "financier of the American Revolution."

The French government supported the American principles of freedom, liberty, justice and equality. France, however, wanted to maintain an appearance of neutrality in the struggle between the American colonies and Great Britain. Silas Deane enlisted the support of Count de Vergennes, France's foreign minister. Deane needed access to French ports (and ports in the West Indies) to be used in making evasion measures easier for American privateers from the Royal Navy warships and prevent the prosecution of American privateers by British courts harder in their neutral countries.[811] The king of France and the king of England (and their respective governments) were constantly resentful of each other and sought every chance to exploit each other's weaknesses. The cat-and-mouse game between the British government and the neutral French government that was smuggling arms and supplies to the Continental Army intensified during the American Revolution. The charade continued for some time until British spies infiltrated the French court and the government agencies and discovered the truth about the arms-dealing business going on between French agents and American agents.

THE CONWAY CABAL AND ITS EFFECTS ON THE CONGRESS AND THE CONTINENTAL ARMY

General Washington had his detractors, especially when the American army was suffering from the lack of supplies, lack of public support and the events of war were unsuccessful. The outlook for American success both economically and militarily was uncertain throughout the Revolutionary War. Sickness and disease continued to undermine the ability of the army to function efficiently. Three ambitious detractors came together to form a "cabal," or plot, to remove General Washington from his leadership role and replace him with General Gates as the commander in chief of the Continental Army. This plot became known in American history as the "Conway Cabal." Thomas Conway was an ambitious Irish-born foreign officer from France who constantly criticized General Washington within the officers' ranks of the American army. Dr. Benjamin Rush was a respected doctor and close friend of John Adams who served in the Continental Congress. Benjamin Rush was a divisive congressional signer of the Declaration of Independence, and he was able to influence other Washington detractors such as Thomas Mifflin, who was a former legislative delegate from Pennsylvania and former quartermaster of the Continental Army. Mifflin had been accused of incompetence and embezzlement from the Continental Army, and he was removed from his duties.[812]

General Horatio Gates, an ambitious retired British army soldier, had become an American general in the Continental Army and served on General Washington's staff. He was held in high regard following the success at Saratoga in the fall of 1777. Horatio Gates constantly wrote to members of Continental Congress, glorifying himself and undermining other army generals with whom he interacted. General Gates sometimes appeared in Congress, or sent his surrogates, to berate General Arnold as insubordinate, and he accused General Washington of incompetence. These prominent leaders in the Continental Congress and in the military establishment led the opposition and generated disapproval of General Washington's handling of the war. They plotted to remove General Washington from his role as the commander in chief of the Continental Army. George Washington became so frustrated and embittered by the deceptions in the Continental Congress and among some of the military officers within his staff that he threatened to resign from the army if his leadership and performance continued to be questioned and undermined.

General Washington learned about the secret plot to have him replaced by the Continental Congress in a roundabout way. Major James Wilkinson, an aide to General Gates, was visiting the headquarters of American officer Lord Stirling. James Wilkinson, while drunk, revealed to Major McWilliams, an officer in Stirling's regiment, the anti-Washington sentiment and the desire to have General Washington replaced. Written in late October 1777, the contents of a letter from General Thomas Conway to General Gates were relayed to Lord Stirling by Major McWilliams. Lord Stirling was greatly alarmed by "such wicked duplicity of conduct,"[813] and he felt obliged to report the letter's contents to General Washington. In the letter, General Conway wrote to General Gates that: "Heaven has been determined to save your Country; or a weak General and bad Councellors would have ruint it."[814] Other derogatory comments followed in the letter that undermined Washington's decision-making and his leadership abilities. When confronted with this revelation, General Washington wrote a letter to General Conway to let him know that his letter to General Gates had been exposed.

On January 2, 1778, General Washington forwarded General Conway's denunciation to the Continental Congress along with a cover letter in which he expressed his personal dislike and distrust of Thomas Conway. Washington made it clear to the Congress that it never affected the professional manner in which business and support was conducted. General Gates wrote a letter concurrently to General Washington and Congress seeking to learn how Washington came in possession of Conway's secret and confidential letter to him and demanded to know who the person was who betrayed his trust. General Conway found out that it was James Wilkinson who had revealed the contents of his letter to General Gates. Conway reported this information to Thomas Mifflin, who strongly chastised General Gates for being careless with his letters. General Washington revealed that no one outside his family knew about the Conway Cabal and the disparaging correspondence going on behind his back except the Marquis de Lafayette, who gave an oath of secrecy. Washington stated in his letter to Horatio Gates, with a copy to the Continental Congress, that he desired to "conceal every matter that could, in its consequences give the smallest Interruption to the Tranquility of this Army, or afford a gleam of hope to the enemy by dissentions therein…"[815]

About this same time, the Continental Congress authorized the establishment of a Board of War. The congressional legislators began to make their own preferential decisions about advancement of officers. They gave to the Board of War unusual powers that should have belonged to General Washington. The Continental Congress appointed General Horatio Gates, credited with the victory at Saratoga, president of the Board of War on November 27, 1777. As president of the Board of War, Horatio Gates exercised congressional control over Washington's Continental Army and authority over General Washington. General Horatio Gates's aide, James Wilkinson, was made a brigadier general and given the position as secretary of the Board of War. Thomas Mifflin served on the Board of War from 1777 to 1778.[816] General Conway offered his resignation to the Continental Congress and enumerated his reasons for his resignation. Conway's resignation was referred to the Board of War.

Congress reconstituted the Board of War with Mifflin, Wilkinson and Gates as members, and it rejected the resignation of General Conway. Political foes of General Washington in Congress gave Conway a promotion to major general and assigned him to a new post, the army inspector general. Conway's new job was to prepare a training manual and to assemble and implement a guide to military maneuvers, which General Washington and his troops were required to follow. He would work alongside General Washington, who was at Valley Forge, but was responsible only to the Board of War. Generals and other officers protested Thomas Conway's promotion to inspector general. Colonels wrote letters to Congress about General Wilkinson's behavior and lack of confidence from the troops. Letters were written in support of Washington by the officers at Valley Forge, which included Alexander Hamilton, who wrote a series of letters chastising the plotters of the Conway Cabal. In receipt of letters of support from the majority of Washington's officers, Congress was forced to fully support General Washington.

As president of the Board of War, Horatio Gates suggested that plans should be developed to invade Canada and try to eliminate the British threat that remained to the Northern Department. Congress agreed to the campaign to invade Canada and gave Gates authority to work out the details. General Gates sought to draw the distinguished and wealthy General Lafayette into his sphere of influence. He urged that General Lafayette be appointed as commander of the Canadian Expedition. With the aid from General Stark's New Hampshire militiamen and the Green Mountain militia boys, it was hoped that once Generals Lafayette and DeKalb arrived in Canada with a small army of about four thousand American soldiers, the French Canadian people would rise up against the British occupation forces and greet Generals Lafayette and DeKalb's forces as liberators.[817] General Gates moved quickly to advance his plans forward with General Lafayette's Canadian Expedition in January 1778.

General Washington, however, was not told about this invasion plan. Washington learned of the plan when the Board of War sent him a letter with the proposed appointment of General Lafayette. Lafayette told Washington that he did not want the commission and that he would rather stay at Valley Forge and serve on Washington's staff. General Washington told Lafayette to accept the commission and said that he believed the expedition would not become a reality.[818] General Lafayette received his appointment from the Board of War on January 23, 1778, to command the spring expedition to invade Canada.[819] After pledging his loyalty to General Washington, Lafayette rode to York, Pennsylvania, where the Continental Congress was located at the time, and he spoke on Washington's behalf. General Lafayette, who delegated himself as spokesman for the French court, did his best to convey to Congress the confidence with which the French government regarded General Washington, who was considered the ultimate leader of the American cause. General Lafayette implied that the French court could not even conceive of another commander. General Lafayette spoke firmly on Washington's behalf, making it clear that he respected General Washington and his leadership of the Continental Army. General DeKalb, at General Lafayette's insistence, was to be made second-in-command, followed by General Conway as third-in-command. Observing the proceedings and the animosity and resentment within the Continental Congress, Lafayette was dismayed and stated that "there was open dissention in Congress [with] parties who hate one another as much as the common enemy."[820] General DeKalb wrote about the dissention and deceit that he found among the foreign officers who were in the American army:

> *On the whole, I have annoyances to bear, of which you can hardly form a conception. One of them is the mutual jealousy of almost all the French officers, particularly against those of higher rank than the rest. These people think of nothing but their incessant intrigues and backbitings. They hate each other like the bitterest enemies, and endeavor to injure each other wherever an opportunity offers. I have given up their society, and very seldom see them. La Fayette is the sole exception; I always meet him with the same cordiality and the same pleasure. He is an excellent young man, and we are good friends...La Fayette is much liked, he is on the best of terms with Washington.*[821]

Generals Lafayette and DeKalb Introduced to General Washington's Officers

The Continental Army was reorganized by General Washington in January 1778. Washington introduced General Lafayette and General Johann DeKalb, Lafayette's older Germany companion, to the officers assembled at his headquarters at Valley Forge. First Lieutenant Philip Ulmer was present at the meeting at Washington's headquarters and was introduced to these two foreign generals. Lieutenant Philip Ulmer met General DeKalb and General

Lafayette both through the military chain of command and through the Masonic fraternity. He likely was able to converse freely with General DeKalb in his own language, which was, without a doubt, pleasing to General DeKalb, who spoke only German. General Washington, General Greene, General Paterson, General St. Clair, General Glover, Colonel Vose and other chosen officers were members of the Masonic fraternity with Generals Lafayette and DeKalb, who were both Master Masons prior to their arrival in America.[822] General Washington's officers and staff met at council meetings, but only Washington's close staff and chosen officers were members in the Masonic military lodge during the encampment at Valley Forge.[823] Philip's connection with the Masonic lodge and fraternity would have secured the trust and confidence of both Generals Lafayette and DeKalb and helped to establish a personal relationship with his commanding officers. Lieutenant Ulmer continued to serve with both Colonel Vose's First Massachusetts Regiment and General Paterson's regiment in General Glover's brigade.[824] Glover's brigade became part of DeKalb's Fourth Division at Valley Forge.[825]

General Lafayette spoke French, English and very little German, while General DeKalb spoke German, a little French and no English. Most of the American troops under Generals Lafayette and DeKalb's command spoke only English, having come from English-speaking colonies. Lieutenant Philip Ulmer was one of a few officers who were fluent in both spoken and written English and German. An experienced officer with bilingual translation abilities was necessary for the foreign officers to help them communicate with the American troops under their command. Therefore it is very likely that First Lieutenant Philip Ulmer served as a German-English interpreter and translator for General DeKalb and other German-speaking officers in Washington's army who held command over English-speaking troops. With his bilingual skills, Lieutenant Ulmer could gather important information and translate captured German military documents, letters, maps, charts and other vital material from German into English for General Washington and his inner command. As an experienced American officer during the Canadian Expedition and on Lake Champlain in 1776, as well as his involvement in the two engagements at Saratoga in 1777, Lieutenant Philip Ulmer had proven his courage, integrity and leadership skills. His translation and communication skills would have been most valuable to General Washington's command and to General Lafayette and General DeKalb during the second Canadian Expedition in early March 1778. Ulmer's considerable reconnaissance experience, his advice and his knowledgeable council would have been vital in determining if a second invasion of Canada in early 1778 had a viable possibility for success or would likely end in failure.[*]

LIEUTENANT PHILIP ULMER RESIGNS
FROM THE CONTINENTAL ARMY

First Lieutenant Philip Ulmer endured the suffering and hardships with the other young soldiers in his company and regiments during the difficult winter months at Valley Forge. During the reorganization of the troops at Valley Forge, for some political reason, First Lieutenant Philip Ulmer did not receive his anticipated advancement in rank to captain. Lieutenant Ulmer and other veteran officers knew that Philip had earned and deserved the advancement in rank to captain, having honorably and actively served in the Massachusetts militia and the Continental Army since 1775. Philip was the most senior officer with extensive wartime experience and was the most qualified person. However, the company's junior officer, Second Lieutenant Oliver Hunt (son of Captain Abraham Hunt, the company commander) was appointed to lead the company of soldiers that Lieutenant Ulmer had recruited in early 1777 from Waldoboro, St. George and the Lincoln County vicinity.[826] Ulmer's recruits had enlisted to serve under his leadership, and they had bravely fought beside him during the battles at Saratoga. Lieutenant

---

* *Author's comment*: The relationship that developed between First Lieutenant Philip Ulmer, General Lafayette and General DeKalb must have been a very positive one. After the Revolutionary War, General Lafayette made a brief visit to frontier Maine to meet with Philip Ulmer, who was a major in the Lincoln County state militia at the end of the war. Unfortunately, during the southern campaign, General Johann DeKalb was mortally wounded at the battle at Camden, South Carolina, in August 1780. After suffering for three days from his injuries, he died and was buried at Camden. General DeKalb had been in command of Philip Ulmer's division with General Paterson's brigade at Valley Forge. This visit took place during General Lafayette's tour in 1784, when Lafayette was visiting in nearby New Hampshire.[827] General Lafayette wanted to see frontier Massachusetts (Maine) for possible land investment opportunities, and he wanted to thank the New England officers and soldiers for their personal service to him and to General DeKalb during the Revolution. He sought out Philip and George Ulmer in frontier Maine at the end of the Revolution before his return to France.[828]

Ulmer was brushed aside and no longer had the leadership or command of his own recruits, which included his brother, George, and several cousins from Waldoboro. The enlisted soldiers from frontier Maine were angered by Captain Hunt's unjust and devious behavior toward their senior lieutenant, whom they held in high esteem. The injustice of the assignment surprised Lieutenant Ulmer and greatly angered him as well as his company.

Nepotism, cronyism and family favoritism seem to have been the primary reasons why First Lieutenant Philip Ulmer did not receive his expected and well-deserved rank advancement. (Note: The same nepotism used by Captain Hunt to advance his family members in rank was also used by Colonel Vose, as records show. Several of Colonel Vose's family members also appear in high leadership positions under his personal command on the Valley Forge muster and pay rolls in spite of minimal wartime service or experience.) Second Lieutenant Oliver Hunt had remained with Captain Abraham Hunt's company while Lieutenant Philip Ulmer was fulfilling his assignment and responsibilities with General Glover's detachment of German-speaking soldiers who were directed to escort the Hessian prisoners of war to the prison camps located at Cambridge and Prospect Hill near Boston. Feeling betrayed by his company commander and disrespected for his devotion to duty, Lieutenant Philip Ulmer asked for an immediate discharge from the Continental Army in early January 1778. Ulmer's paperwork and the actual acceptance of his resignation were delayed for many weeks while colleagues tried to dissuade him from resigning. Although he was given other assignments to perform, Lieutenant Philip Ulmer felt deeply disappointed by the nepotism, cronyism and deception that he observed in the federal government among the state delegates, the federal authorities, the wealthy and influential leaders and in the military establishment among the officers and volunteer opportunists. Lieutenant Philip Ulmer's military discharge was finally granted on February 8 or February 14 (military records vary).[829] However, he remained on the muster roll at Valley Forge through the month of March 1778 on assignment in General DeKalb's division under the command of General Lafayette.[830]

In the fall of 1777 and early 1778, the use of political influence, unethical behavior and monetary manipulations often led to the abuse of power and authority in the Continental Congress and within the military establishment. This was distasteful to many officers like Lieutenant Philip Ulmer, who believed deeply in merit, honesty and the American cause. Many officers resigned and left Valley Forge in disgust and in disillusionment over the Conway Cabal scandal, the lack of support given by the Continental

Congress (some of whose members were involved in the cabal) and the lack of basic military supplies, food, clothing and shelter for the troops. Many of the officers and soldiers, such as First Lieutenant Philip Ulmer, had not received payment for their military services from the treasury of the Continental Congress for many months, and some Patriots received no payments at all for their service and sacrifice to the country.[831] Many veterans had to seek redress through the state and federal court system, which took many years to be resolved. Some veterans never lived long enough to receive justice and proper compensation for their service to the nation. Philip had not been paid for his military service since the beginning of the Revolution, and he had not been home for many, many months. He had concerns about the safety and survival circumstances of his new wife, Christiana, and his family back in Waldoboro. Two of Lieutenant Ulmer's respected senior officers who knew him well, Colonel Joseph Vose and Colonel William Shepard, wrote to General Washington on Philip's behalf for an honorable discharge from the army. The requests read:

Joseph Vose and William Shepard to General Washington
Valley Forge 13ᵗʰ Feb'y 1778

Upon the Application of Lieut. Ulmer of my Reg't for a discharge from the Service he having settled off all his Accounts, I hereby Recommend him to your Excellency for the Same.

Joseph Vose Col.
Camp Valley Forge Feb'y 13ᵗʰ 1778

May it please your Excellency

Upon the Request of Lieu't Ulmer of Col. Voses Reg't for A Discharge from the Service, I would humbly Recommend him to your Excellency for the same, tho with great Reluctance he having Done honour to the Corps as an officer.

I am your Excellencys most Hum'l Serv't

W. Shepard Colo. Commdr.

"Philip Ulmer, of the First Massachusetts Regiment, was allowed to resign effective February 14, 1778."[832]

Lieutenant Philip Ulmer remained on the muster rolls at Valley Forge through the end of March 1778, which indicates his extended volunteer service during this time.[833] General Washington had other plans for Philip Ulmer, whose bilingual abilities and military experience in the Northern Theater were still needed.

Political Wrangling Threatens to Derail the American Cause

The dissension in the military leadership and deep divisions among the leadership of the Continental Congress threatened to undermine the American cause. General Washington held to the truth of his convictions in spite of vicious personal attacks upon his character and military leadership abilities. The Conway Cabal took place in the late fall of 1777 and early 1778. By early 1778, the plot began to fall apart, and it finally collapsed, leaving behind bitter feelings and distrust in the Continental Congress and among the military officers. Since the British forces under General Howe had seized Philadelphia, the Continental Congress met and conducted government business at York, Pennsylvania, at this time. On January 19, 1778, Generals Conway and Gates appeared before the Continental Congress to try and clear their names. They would not reveal the "weak General" who was referred to in their derogatory letter.[834] The conspirators' derogatory claims against General Washington were eventually dismissed in light of the strong support given to General Washington by others in the army and in Congress. In light of the duplicity and foolishness of Generals Gates and Conway, the movement to unseat General Washington as commander in chief lost steam and fizzled out. Thomas Mifflin resigned from the Board of War in 1778 as a result of his involvement in the plot, and he left the military service under a cloud of embezzlement suspicions. However, the Continental Congress continued to seek his advice. Thomas Conway was transferred to a subordinate command in the Hudson Heights, which he protested, and he resigned from the Continental Army. Congress accepted his resignation in 1778, but Conway remained a problem for General Washington. General Conway continued to badmouth Washington at every opportunity. James Wilkinson resigned as secretary of the Board of War. General Horatio Gates returned to his troops a chastened general.[835]

In the Continental Congress, the issue of personal gain from private speculation and public service positions continued to be debated and to cause divisive problems until a referendum was called. The referendum was on the right of officials to combine public service and private speculation for personal gain. One result of this fundamental argument about the role of capitalism in a democracy was sharply defined.[836] This was the beginning of early political parties which favored on one side "the loyalist and power-weakening emphasis in the Revolution" and on the other "stability, nationalism, and a centralized authority."[837] The bitter divisions in Congress that were caused by the Conway Cabal might have been better addressed on their own individual virtues. The rancor in all areas of the leadership of the new, struggling nation threatened to undo the very principles, objectives and goals that had brought the men together in the first place and for which many thousands of soldiers had suffered and died. These values were expressed in the Declaration of Independence and would become the basic noble concept upon which their new nation would be born…the United States of America.

GENERAL LAFAYETTE AND THE EXPEDITION TO INVADE CANADA IN 1778

Among the schemes of the Conway Cabal was a plan by General Gates, president of the Board of War, for an invasion of Canada. General Washington disapproved of this plan and knew it would be a failure. General Gates overrode Washington's objections and, with Congress's approval, continued with his plans for the Canadian Expedition in early 1778. General Gates believed that with the combined forces of Generals Lafayette and DeKalb's brigades, General Stark's small force of regulars stationed at Albany in the Northern Department and forces from the Green Mountain militiamen who could be enlisted to join, an invading army of four thousand men might be formed. The command of this army was offered by the Board of War to General Lafayette. It was hoped that on General Lafayette's arrival in Canada, the French population would hail him as their deliverer, rise up against the British forces in Canada and expel them.[838] If the invasion of Canada were successful, Canada would be able to become the fourteenth colony in the United Colonies, and General Gates and his supporters would become the heroes of American freedom and independence. General Gates's place in history would have been secured as the founding father of the American republic instead of General George Washington.

General Lafayette was appointed to lead the American invasion forces on January 23, 1778. General Washington's detractor, General Thomas Conway, was made second-in-command by General Gates, president of the Board of War. General Lafayette appealed this decision to the Continental Congress, citing General DeKalb's seniority and his own desire to have General DeKalb as second-in-command.[839] The Continental Congress agreed to General Lafayette's request, and General Conway was made third-in-command of the Canadian Expedition. The information about General Lafayette's appointment was sent in a letter to General Washington from General Gates, president of the Board of War, on January 24, 1778. General Lafayette did not accept the command until he had consulted with General Washington. Washington expressed his belief that General Lafayette should accept the appointment, and he believed that the second invasion of Canada would not materialize. General Washington felt that there were not enough troops, supplies or money from Congress to support the Canadian Expedition.

General Johann DeKalb became the commanding officer of the Fourth Division, which included Generals Paterson's and Learned's Massachusetts regiments with other detached New England companies from General Glover's brigade (that would include First Lieutenant Ulmer)[840] who were assigned to General Lafayette's and General DeKalb's brigades.[841] Much of the direct evidence from this period is vague; however, the circumstantial evidence suggests the following: Lieutenant Philip Ulmer was located at Valley Forge in Colonel Vose's First Massachusetts Regiment and with Paterson's regiment in General Glover's brigade.[842] General Washington, during the reorganization of his army, assigned General DeKalb to become the division commander of Brigadier General Glover's brigade.[843] There were four regiments, including Colonel Joseph Vose's First Massachusetts Regiment, where Philip Ulmer served as a first lieutenant in Glover's brigade.[844] Other regiments with General Glover's brigade included Colonel William Shephard's Fourth Massachusetts, Colonel Edward Wigglesworth's Thirteenth Massachusetts and Colonel Timothy Bigelow's Fifteenth Massachusetts Regiments.[845] First Lieutenant Philip Ulmer was among the detached companies of officers and soldiers who went to Albany, the center of military operations in the Northern Department, with General Lafayette and General DeKalb in the proposed invasion of Canada in early March

1778. (Note: A probable time when General Lafayette, General DeKalb and First Lieutenant Philip Ulmer would have developed a close friendship was during the second Canadian Expedition in early March 1778.[846] He would have served as a German-English translator for DeKalb and interpreter for his English-speaking troops. He would have served as an experienced reconnaissance officer and advisor for Lafayette, an assignment he had successfully performed during his military service in 1776 and 1777 in the operations in Canada, in the Northern Department and at the Battles of Trenton, Princeton and Saratoga. It would have been the only known time when a strong relationship could have been formed between the two generals and First Lieutenant Philip Ulmer.)

General Lafayette left for Albany, New York, with a small detached party of intelligence and reconnaissance officers to investigate the preparations for a second Canadian invasion. General Lafayette's advance party, which probably included Lieutenant Philip Ulmer, arrived on February 17, 1778, eight days earlier than the rest of the small army of expeditionary troops. The authorities in Albany had expected the army troops on February 28, so they were quite taken by surprise when the advance reconnaissance company arrived ahead of time. General Lafayette wanted to determine how much preparation had actually been done and how much more preparation still needed to be done. New York governor George Clinton, who was a strong supporter of General Washington, met General Lafayette and expressed his dissatisfaction with the proposed Canadian Expedition during the winter weather. After consulting with Generals Schuyler and Arnold and with his intelligence officers, Lafayette decided to make a careful study of the supplies and essential needs for the expedition. General Lafayette and his intelligence officers found that there were too many things lacking to make the expedition a success. Generals Schuyler, Lincoln and Arnold were opposed to the expedition because of the lack of soldiers, food and money. They counseled against the early spring invasion of Canada.[847]

As the investigation continued, General Lafayette and his intelligence officers found that the American citizens were disgusted that the Board of War wanted to carry on an invasion without sufficient supplies, clothing or men during the winter weather. It was determined that the small army of soldiers from Valley Forge, about 1,200 men, lacked sufficient supplies of all kinds for a successful winter campaign. The soldiers had not arrived that General Gates had promised to supplement the army expedition to Canada. There was every indication that the additional soldiers would not arrive at all. General Lafayette further discovered that in the Northern Department, the Continental Congress owed officers, soldiers and others more than $800,000, a sizable sum of money at that time. Money was still owed to soldiers and others who had served in the first Canadian Expedition in 1775–76 and in the New York campaign in the Northern Department in 1776–77. General Lafayette was able to finally recover half of the amount owed to the men, but that would not meet the present needs of the situation. Lafayette received specific information that the British forces in Canada were aware of his expedition and that the British troops were waiting for them. The British forces in Canada were well prepared for the invasion, and they knew the details of the campaign through their British spy network centered in Quebec City. The situation was very serious, and there were no prospects for improvement since the operation had been compromised. Generals Lafayette and DeKalb found debt, dissatisfaction and deceit everywhere.[848]

In a letter to General Washington dated February 23, 1778, General Lafayette wrote: "I am sent, with great noise, at the head of the army to do great things. The whole continent, France, and what is the worst, the British army will be in expectation."[849] Finally, at the end of March 1778, it was determined that the Canadian Expedition should be delayed indefinitely. Congress passed a resolution regarding General Lafayette's service: "That Congress entertain [sic] a high sense of his prudence, activity, and zeal and that they are fully persuaded nothing has or would have been wanting on his part, or on the part of the officers who accompanied him, to give the expedition the utmost possible effect."[850]

In early April 1778, General Lafayette returned to Valley Forge with his small army that included First Lieutenant Philip Ulmer. General Lafayette was greeted warmly by General Washington. Washington had learned that he could give important responsibilities to General Lafayette, and he could place his confidence in Lafayette's decisions. Upon his return to the Valley Forge encampment, General Lafayette learned that the conspiracy to remove General Washington as commander in chief of the Continental Army had run its course with the rout of the conspirators and detractors in Congress.

General Baron von Steuben, an experienced Prussian officer from the vicinity of Baden-Württemberg, Germany, had been made a general by Congress and had become a foreign volunteer on General Washington's staff with the challenge of training the soldiers at Valley Forge and of transforming the Continental Army into a formidable fighting force.[851] General von Steuben, who spoke German and some simple French but no English,[852] arrived in the encampment at Valley Forge on February 23, 1778. He started to reassemble, train and drill the new recruits and regiments in military skills and procedures. Orders were given to the troops by General von Steuben in German or simple French. General von Steuben had a thick German accent, and he needed to have his orders and directions translated into English for the American troops. The few American officers and soldiers who were bilingual translated the general's orders into English for the other soldiers to follow. General von Steuben condensed his set of commands into about ten words for battlefield repositioning and firing. The simplified commands were easily understood and could be quickly implemented. General von Steuben turned the drills into contests between the companies and regiments. The soldiers and officers welcomed the competition. It funneled the soldiers' frustrations and vented their anger with the British and Hessian troops into a force for discipline and skill. The contests between the men escalated until, within a few weeks, the soldiers were practicing their drills and marching maneuvers on their own, without supervision. Each regiment was determined to do better than the other regiments.[853] Through the translator's directions, the American soldiers responded positively to General von Steuben's leadership. The Continental soldiers were patiently trained and repeatedly drilled by the Prussian general.

Lieutenant Philip Ulmer had trained and drilled Captain Hunt's company of soldiers in the same German style of military order and discipline that he had received as a young enlisted soldier from Lincoln County. With Ulmer's expected discharge from the Continental Army, Philip prepared his brother, Private George Ulmer, to assume his assignment as translator and interpreter for Colonels Paterson and Vose's regiments in General DeKalb's division. George Ulmer was advanced in rank to sergeant and became a drill sergeant in Captain Hunt's company with Colonel Vose's regiment in March 1778.[854] Sergeant George Ulmer's bilingual abilities would be valuable in translating and communicating orders to the non-German-speaking troops.

At Valley Forge, General von Steuben wrote his own manual, *The Army Blue Book*, for drills and maneuvering techniques for the battlefield. The field actions were altered, by his direction, and used throughout the American Revolution. General von Steuben's army manual was written in German. The manual was translated into French (probably by General DeKalb or another foreign officer) and then re-translated from French into English by General Greene and Alexander Hamilton.[855] The orders were given in short, concise words and were easily understood. The soldiers were able to react quickly and to conduct the appropriate maneuvers. Regiments drilled and competed against one another for skill and recognition.[856] By June 1778, the overall conditions at Valley Forge had improved greatly, and the American army had learned the classic European battlefield maneuvers that would enable them to defeat the British troops in a direct confrontation. General Washington's desperate efforts to save his suffering army demonstrated one of the most important heroic times in his military career. When Washington's army troops left Valley Forge in June 1778, they had become a fighting force that was able to confront and be successful against the well-trained British forces of General Howe. Due to General Howe's inability to handle the growing threat of American privateering in the colonies and in the West Indies, there was a change in the British command. Sir Henry Clinton was ordered to replace General William Howe, who had resigned as commander in chief of the British Royal Army forces in America.

LIEUTENANT PHILIP ULMER LEAVES THE CONTINENTAL ARMY

Having completed his special assignment with General Lafayette and General DeKalb on their aborted Canadian Expedition, Philip Ulmer was granted his delayed discharge by General Washington in early April 1778. Lieutenant Philip Ulmer settled his personal accounts before leaving Valley Forge. Ulmer appeared on a list of men whose gratuity had not been paid by the federal government for his military services as a lieutenant with Colonel Vose's regiment in the Continental Army.[857] Lieutenant Ulmer's departure from General Washington's Continental Army was greatly regretted by his commanding officer, Colonel Joseph Vose; General John Paterson; and other officers like General William Shepard. The soldiers from Philip's company and officers with Vose's and Paterson's regiments were greatly saddened to see their respected friend and trusted officer leave the army. Some of the soldiers and officers at Valley Forge had served with Philip Ulmer since the call to arms in April 1775. They admired Lieutenant Philip Ulmer's integrity, faithfulness and strength of character in the performance of his duties. They respected his courage while under enemy fire and his leadership skills throughout the war. George Ulmer (Philip's younger brother), some of the Ulmer cousins and their friends from Lincoln County had enlisted in 1777 to serve under Lieutenant Philip Ulmer's leadership for three years in the Continental Army. They unhappily remained in Captain Hunt's company with Colonel Vose's regiment after Philip's departure from Valley Forge.

Lieutenant Ulmer, however, prepared the way for his brother to assume his role as a German-American translator and interpreter for Generals Lafayette, DeKalb and Baron Von Steuben and for the troops in Captain Hunt's company who served with the First Massachusetts Regiment at the Valley Forge encampment.

Before leaving Valley Forge in early April 1778, Lieutenant Philip Ulmer was called before the Masonic traveling lodge, where General Washington served as the worshipful master at Valley Forge.[858] The generals and military officers with whom Philip served were in attendance. Lieutenant Ulmer was presented with a sword from the surrender at Saratoga, where he had been an active participant and served as a bilingual translator for the American and Hessian officers. General Washington and the officers thanked Major Ulmer for his extensive service to the Continental Army; to the Massachusetts regiments of Colonels Gardner, Bond, Vose and General Paterson; and to the American cause. Lieutenant Philip Ulmer had actively participated in almost all of the major battles of the American Revolution since the beginning of war in 1775 until this time. Ulmer family lore indicated that the ceremonial sword or sabre had been taken from the battlefield at the surrender of the British and Hessian forces at Saratoga and was presented to Lieutenant Ulmer (most likely by General Washington) at Valley Forge. This was undoubtedly the most meaningful event in Philip Ulmer's life and an honorable recognition for his faithful military service to the United Colonies.*

---

* *Author's comment*: The Revolutionary War sword remains with one of the Ulmer family descendants, and it has been passed down in the family through many generations, although the sword's present location and ownership is unknown. It is certain that Philip Ulmer's grandson, Horatio Gates Stevens (child of Philip's eldest daughter, Christiana Ulmer Stevens) was named for General Horatio Gates, the Continental Army general whom Philip Ulmer had served under during the Revolutionary War.[859] Another grandson, Captain John Bennett, was given Philip Ulmer's original military commissioning document, signed by John Hancock, president of the Continental Congress, on April 20, 1776, that has been passed down through his Bennett family.[860] Philip Ulmer's commissioning document with the rank of major was given to another family member. A copy of this commissioning document of Philip Martin Ulmer as a major is presently held in the Maine State Archives in Augusta, Maine, and a copy of the document can be found in a history book about Maine.[861] Different descendants and relatives of Major Philip Ulmer and his brother, General George Ulmer, have received mementos of their Revolutionary War Patriots, and they have continued to be passed down through the generations.

Some of the soldiers whose enlistments had expired at Valley Forge returned to their homes from the war, and they chose to become privateers and sailed for fortune and glory. Other soldiers chose to remain in the state militia and defend the eastern coastline of Massachusetts and New Hampshire against the British naval attacks on seaport towns and coastal villages. Since the Massachusetts state militia had naval warships and armed sailing merchant vessels, some militia companies went to sea to defend the New England coastline from sporadic British raiding parties, from the enemy naval bombardment of coastal communities and from further economic destruction. Lieutenant Philip Ulmer left Valley Forge and returned to his wife, Christiana, and the Ulmer family in Waldoboro in April 1778. He enlisted in the state militia in Lincoln County and was quickly advanced in rank to captain by Colonel McCobb, who knew his military service and leadership abilities. He was assigned to serve in Colonel McCobb and Colonel Prime's regiments. Philip requested and was given the assignment of supervising the construction of coastal forts and defenses with his own detachment of soldiers from the three frontier counties of York, Cumberland and Lincoln. He served under the command of Generals Solomon Lovell and Charles Cushing at Pownalboro (present-day Wiscasset, Maine). Captain Philip Ulmer supervised the construction of forts, barracks and defenses all along coastline of frontier Maine.[862] Ulmer had recognized early on that the frontier seacoast was vulnerable to British raids and sea attacks. He utilized his military experience, technical knowledge and strategies in the building of the coastal defenses. Captain Philip Ulmer's company of soldiers built forts, barracks, breastworks and other fortifications all along the vulnerable rivers and coastal areas of frontier Maine. He had determined that neither the General Court of Massachusetts nor the federal government had the needed funds, military troops, necessary provisions or military supplies to defend the eastern frontier. The settlers in frontier Maine would have to find a way of defending themselves through their own resourcefulness. Defending the frontier coastline, the seaports and the towns from enemy attack became a passion for Philip Ulmer that would follow him for the rest of his life.

While these events were occurring back home in Massachusetts, George Ulmer was advanced in rank to sergeant at Valley Forge. This advancement was likely an effort by Captain Abraham Hunt to calm the discontented young recruits from Lincoln County who had enlisted to serve with Lieutenant Philip Ulmer. They were disillusioned and disheartened by the unjust treatment of Lieutenant Ulmer, whom they held in high esteem and affection. Sergeant George Ulmer continued to serve with Colonel Vose's regiment, following in his elder brother's footsteps. He was able to translate and deliver orders and directions for Generals DeKalb and Baron von Steuben during the training and company drills of the Continental troops. He was able to express the needs of the army troops in German to the commanding officers. Philip Ulmer's former company, part of Colonel Vose's and Paterson's regiments, later participated with Generals Lafayette and DeKalb in the battles that took place at Germantown and Brandywine in Pennsylvania and at Monmouth, New Jersey.[863] Philip's brother, Sergeant George Ulmer, was involved in these battles with General Lafayette and General DeKalb's army troops. The successful military actions against the British and Hessian army forces following the battle at Monmouth on June 28, 1778, shifted to the Southern Theater of operations.

The battle at Monmouth signified the end of major conflicts in the Middle Department of the Northern Theater. The engagements between the British forces and the Continental Army moved dramatically to the Southern Theater. The soldiers whose enlistments were still in effect remained with the Continental Army and moved into the Southern Theater of military engagement against the British and Hessian forces under the command of General Sir Henry Clinton and General Cornwallis. Soldiers from frontier Maine became part of General DeKalb and Benjamin Lincoln's command in General Lafayette's division on the right wing of Washington's Continental Army. They participated in a number of famous battles in the southern colonies. Some of the soldiers from frontier Maine who had been recruited by Lieutenant Philip Ulmer in the early spring of 1777, at their request, were reassigned from Valley Forge to the Eastern Department in the "Defense of the Eastern Frontier" (also called the Sea Coast Defense). British naval forces stationed at Halifax, Nova Scotia, continued to raid, harass and burn ports and villages in the eastern frontier of Massachusetts and along the eastern seacoast of New England. The Continental Army troops, under General Sullivan's command, were stationed at Providence, Rhode Island, where they participated in the unsuccessful combined attack on Newport on August 29, 1778, with French admiral d'Estaing's naval fleet. The British later abandoned Newport, Rhode Island, and by the spring of 1780, American and French forces were stationed there. Soldiers who had been recruited for three years from Lincoln County in the spring of 1777 by Philip Ulmer, like Sergeant George Ulmer and his cousin Private George Ulmer Jr., completed their military enlistments and were discharged from military service. They returned to their homes in Massachusetts and frontier Maine, where they tried to resume their normal lives.

The Franco-American Alliance
Changes the War Strategy

France's entry into the American Revolution after the victory at Saratoga had changed the British war strategy with the signing in Paris of the Treaty of Alliance and the Franco-American Amity and Commerce Treaty on February 6, 1778.[864] Spain and the Netherlands followed France's lead and joined the conflict by supporting America's Revolutionary War against Great Britain. General Clinton was ordered by the British ministry of war to abandon Philadelphia and defend New York City, Florida and British interests in the West Indies. British vessels were now vulnerable to French naval attacks, as well as scores of American privateering vessels. The aggressive activities of the American privateers against the British shipping industry and upon the military supplies for the British Royal Army and Hessian forces were having a devastating effect on British trading, British society and the British economy. The London Stock Exchange and the investment speculators were greatly stressed over the wild fluctuations of the financial markets. Pressure was placed on the British government by the London merchants, business speculators and financial investors to respond to the growing threat that the American privateers posed. Vice Admiral Graves was called back to England in disgrace because of his failure to stop "those pirating rascals from taking British supply ships…and adequately blockade port towns to starve the Rebels into submission."[865] His replacement by Admiral Richard Howe did not improve the situation.

Word was received that a French naval fleet, commanded by Admiral d'Estaing, had been sent to aid the American forces and that the French king had sent a personal envoy to America. To avoid being trapped by the approaching French fleet and American forces, on June 18, 1778, the British and Hessian forces began to evacuate Philadelphia, leaving it in ruins, and they made their way across New Jersey on their retreat to New York City with a baggage train twelve miles long. Philadelphia was quickly reoccupied by displaced American supporters and members of the Continental Congress. General Lee was freed in a prisoner exchange around this time. Benedict Arnold, the valiant leader of the battles at Saratoga, was posted to Philadelphia as military governor. General Washington's Continental Army, state militia regiments and volunteers moved northeast from Valley Forge to attack the rear of the long retreating British column. As the British forces retreated toward New York City, the American army forces made it as difficult as possible for them to proceed. The troops burned bridges, muddied wells and cut trees and left them crisscrossed on the main travel roads. General Washington's detached army companies shadowed and harassed General Sir Clinton's British forces during their difficult withdrawal from Philadelphia, across eastern New Jersey and toward the British stronghold at New York City. General Washington was able to force several skirmishes and battles in New Jersey, culminating with a battle at Monmouth on June 28, which became the last major battle in the Northern Theater.[866] Washington's second-in-command, General Charles Lee, ordered a controversial retreat during the Monmouth engagement, allowing General Clinton's British forces to escape under cover of night. The Battle of Monmouth was declared a victory for General Washington's Continental Army since it held the field of battle the next day. General Lee faced charges of cowardice for his lack of leadership during the battle at Monmouth. Lee was found guilty by a review board and was court-martialed.

In July 1778, the French declared war against England, and within the year, Spain entered the war as well. Great Britain declared war on the Netherlands for supporting the French and Americans. Soon thereafter, the British were involved in fighting in the West Indies, India, Africa and the Mediterranean. In a space of two years, the American Revolution became a world war, with British forces fighting on many fronts, and victory for Great Britain was no longer assured. By the middle of July, the French naval fleet sailed into the Delaware Bay below Philadelphia with the flag of France flying from the sixteen warships. Admiral d'Estaing, Commissioner Deane and the French minister plenipotentiary, Conrad-Alexander Gerard, arrived on the *Langue-doc*, the flagship of the French fleet. The American delegation that met Deane and the French dignitaries had never seen ships as large as those of the magnificent French fleet, carrying so many powerful guns. On board the vessels were four thousand French troops, a number equal to almost half of the entire Continental Army at that time.[867] Admiral d'Estang's French fleet and French Minister Gerard's arrival revived a feeling of dignity and hope in the citizens of Philadelphia after so much suffering and hardship at the hands of occupying British troops. A newspaper correspondent from one of the local papers wrote: "Who would have thought that the American colonies, claimed by every pettyfoging [*sic*] lawyer in the house of Commons, and every cobbler in the beer houses of London, as part of their property, [would] receive an Ambassador from the most powerful monarchy in Europe."[868]

The focus of the war quickly shifted from the northern colonies to the Southern Theater, as well as to conflicts in the West Indies, on coastal Europe and in other places of the world. Charleston, South Carolina, was attacked in April 1780 by a British army of 1,400 troops commanded by General Henry Clinton. American general Benjamin Lincoln, General Washington's second-in-command, was trapped at Charleston and surrendered his entire army of 5,400 soldiers after a long fight. It was the greatest American defeat of the Revolutionary War. Some of the American troops, however, were able to escape and joined up with several militias, including those of Francis Marion, the "Swamp Fox," and Andrew Pickens in South Carolina. General Lincoln was later returned in an exchange of prisoners of war. The British forces maintained control of the town of Charleston until December 1782.

On August 16, 1780, the British forces of General Charles Cornwallis routed the American forces of General Horatio Gates near Camden, South Carolina. General Gates had 4,000 men, of which 1,500 were regular Continental troops and the others were militia soldiers. The British had 2,000 men, of which 1,500 were regular troops. The British opened the battle with a dense volley into the American militia regiments, causing heavy casualties. The volley was followed by a bayonet charge. The American militia soldiers, lacking bayonets, panicked and fled as the British forces advanced. The panic spread to other militia troops, who broke rank and also fled. General Gates, seeing the left flank of his army collapsing, also fled with the first militia from the battlefield. Gates mounted a swift horse and, leaving his struggling army troops still fighting on the field, rode northward to Charlotte, North Carolina, sixty miles away, where he took refuge. General DeKalb, who commanded the Continental right flank, attacked the British left flank, causing Rawdon's British line to retreat. Cornwallis rode to his left flank to steady Colonel Francis Rawdon's men instead of pursuing the fleeing American militia. The British wheeled around to help their left flank and launched a bayonet attack on General DeKalb's left flank and center of the Continental regiment, which numbered about 800 men who now faced 2,000 British troops. General Gates never rallied the troops in his division and did not come to the defense of DeKalb's exposed division. There was stiff resistance for some time by General DeKalb's troops until General Cornwallis ordered Colonel Banastre Tarleton to charge the rear of the Continental line with his cavalry. The cavalry charge broke the Continental line, which fled from the battlefield. General DeKalb tried to rally his fleeing troops but was shot numerous times by musket fire. After one hour, the American forces were completely defeated. Colonel Tarleton's cavalry pursued the fleeing American troops for about twenty miles before reining in his company at dusk. General DeKalb was killed at the Battle of Camden in South Carolina due in part to General Horatio Gates's cowardice, his lack of planning and his hasty retreat from the engagement. General Washington called for a court of inquiry to be conducted into Gates's dereliction of duty, with Baron von Steuben to reside at the court.[869] General Gates's strong political connections in the Continental Congress later helped him successfully avoid inquiries into the defeat at Camden.

General Nathanael Greene replaced General Horatio Gates as the commander of the Southern Army. General Greene engaged in a strategy of avoidance and attrition against General Charles Cornwallis's British forces in the Carolinas. Although the British forces had a string of successes, they were mostly tactical victories. The Continental Army forces strategically sought to weaken the British army by overextending their supply lines, exhausting the British troops and causing high casualties, while American army troops remained intact and continued to fight. The American troops shadowed Cornwallis's British army forces throughout the Carolinas attempting to engage them in costly skirmishes. In early January 1781, the Battle of Cowpens in South Carolina became a defeat for the British army troops in the South. Angered and frustrated, General Cornwallis was determined to destroy General Greene's Continental Army forces in the south. However, the American victory at the battle of Cowpens in January 1781 was followed by other successes. These American victories brought great fighting spirit to the American soldiers in the war-torn Carolinas, who had been struggling for a success in the Loyalist-dominated southern colonies. The series of American victories became a turning point for the reclaiming of South Carolina from British influence and control.

The Battle of Guilford Court House was a battle fought on March 15, 1781, in Greensboro, the county seat of Guilford County, North Carolina, during the American Revolutionary War. A force of 1,900 British troops under the command of General Lord Cornwallis defeated an American force of 4,000 under General Nathanael Greene, a Rhode Island native. Despite the relatively small numbers of troops involved, the battle is considered decisive. Before the battle, the British appeared to have successfully re-conquered Georgia and South Carolina with the aid of strong Loyalist factions, and the British general thought that North Carolina might be within their grasp. In the wake of the battle, General Greene moved into South Carolina, while General Cornwallis chose to invade Virginia. These decisions allowed General Greene to unravel British control of the South while leading Cornwallis northeastward to Yorktown, Virginia. General Cornwallis, who was in command of the British land forces, was given confusing orders by General Henry Clinton. Cornwallis was directed to retreat and to take a defensive position at a deep-water port where the British naval forces could assist and evacuate the British troops if needed at Yorktown, Virginia. Cornwallis's troop movements were shadowed by a division of Continental Army troops, led by General Lafayette.

As a result of the Franco-American Alliance that was signed after the American victory at Saratoga, the Count de Rochambeau, who was in command of the French army forces, and the Count de Grasse, who was in command of the French naval fleet, were sent as a French expeditionary force to the United Colonies by the king to assist and support the Continental Army in its struggle against Great Britain. The French and American armies united north of New York City during the summer of 1781 where General Washington was preparing his troops to lay siege to the city of New York. Word was received by General Rochambeau that Admiral de Grasse and his French fleet were in the West Indies, and they would sail to the Chesapeake Bay to join forces with the combined French and American forces near Yorktown who were laying siege to Cornwallis's British troops inside the town. The Franco-American allied forces near New York City began moving south toward Virginia, engaging in deceptive tactics to mislead the British in New York City that a siege was planned by Washington's troops outside the city.

Admiral de Grasse's fleet sailed from the West Indies and arrived in the Chesapeake Bay area around the end of August, bringing additional French reinforcement troops and providing a naval blockade of Cornwallis's troops at Yorktown. The Admiral Count de Grasse transported with him 500,000 silver pesos collected from the citizens of Havana, Cuba, to fund the supplies for the Yorktown siege and payroll the Continental Army. At the end of August, off of the Virginia Capes, the French fleet became engaged in an intense battle with the British fleet, led by Sir Thomas Graves, that had come to rescue Cornwallis's army troops at Yorktown. As a result of the French fleet's victory at sea, Admiral de Grasse was able to block escape of Cornwallis's troops by sea.

On September 14, General Washington and his troops arrived in Williamsburg, Virginia. The combined allied forces under General Washington and General Rochambeau continued to arrive for several days. Communications and plans were made to coordinate a siege on Yorktown, where General Lafayette and the Franco-American forces began to surround the British troops. On September 26, transports with artillery, siege tools and some French infantry and shock troops from the Head of

Elk at the northern end of the Chesapeake Bay arrived and gave General Washington command of an army of 7,800 Frenchmen, 3,100 militia and 8,000 Continentals. Early on September 28, Washington and Rochambeau led the allied army out of Williamsburg to surround Yorktown. The French took the positions on the left, while the Americans took the position of honor on the right. The American soldiers from the Maine district who were with Lafayette's troops fought bravely at Yorktown. They successfully attacked, captured and held redoubt number ten near the York River. The cannon and gunfire unleashed on Yorktown from the French and American allied positions became heavier than ever as new artillery pieces joined the line and bombarded the British positions. After a long and bloody siege at Yorktown that lasted several days, General Cornwallis called a council of war with his British and Hessian officers and informed them that British naval and relief forces, which they had been expecting to arrive, would not be coming to their defense. The French naval fleet, commanded by Admiral de Grasse, had engaged the British fleet at sea, causing great damage to the British fleet. The British fleet was forced to retreat to New York City for repairs and supplies, leaving Cornwallis in a precarious defensive situation. The British council of war agreed that their situation was hopeless and surrender was the only option.

On the morning of October 17, a drummer appeared, followed by an officer waving a white handkerchief. The American bombardment of Cornwallis's troops ceased, and the officer was blindfolded and led behind the allied lines. Soldiers from frontier Maine were present at the surrender of General Cornwallis's troops at Yorktown on October 17, four years to the day after General Burgoyne's surrender at Saratoga, New York. Negotiations began on October 18 between British lieutenant colonel Thomas Dundas and British major Alexander Ross and American colonel John Laurens and the French Marquis de Noailles, who was the envoy to the United Colonies and General Lafayette's father-in-law. To make sure that nothing fell apart between the Franco-American allies at the last minute, General Washington ordered that the French be given an equal share in every step of the surrender process.

The Articles of Capitulation were signed on October 19, 1781, after two days of negotiations. General Cornwallis surrendered his entire British and Hessian army, resulting in the capture of approximately eight thousand troops, 214 artillery pieces, thousands of muskets, twenty-four transport ships, wagons and horses. General Cornwallis's British forces were declared prisoners of war and promised good treatment in American camps. The officers were permitted to return home after taking their parole. General Cornwallis refused to meet formally with Washington, and he refused to come to the ceremony of surrender, claiming illness. Instead, Brigadier General Charles O'Hara presented the sword of surrender to General Rochambeau. Rochambeau shook his head and pointed to General Washington, who remained on horseback. O'Hara offered it to Washington, but he refused to accept it. He motioned to his second-in-command, Benjamin Lincoln, who had been humiliated by the British at Charleston, to accept the sword in the surrender ceremony. The British soldiers marched out and laid down their arms in between the French and American army troops while many civilians watched. General Cornwallis's surrender ended the disastrous southern campaign for the British Royal Army. News of the surrender reached England on November 25, sending shock waves through the British government. Although King George III wanted to continue the battle, the surrender forced Prime Minister Lord North to resign in March 1782. His replacement began the peace process that culminated in the signing of the Treaty of Paris in September 1783, granting sovereignty and independence to the American colonies and essentially marking the end of British power in the colonies. This was the final turning point of the American Revolution.

The fighting and skirmishes along the eastern seacoast of America would continue for some time after the official peace treaty was signed in Europe. Peace did not come to the Province of Maine until April 1784, when the remaining British troops at Castine finally abandoned Fort George and returned to the British stronghold at Halifax, leaving the fort in ruins. Major Philip Ulmer and a small detachment of men were sent to make certain that the British troops had actually left Castine and to determine the condition of the fort.

Following the American victory at Yorktown, Virginia, General Lafayette sailed to France in 1782, where he attended to American interests in the French Court and to personal issues at home. Lafayette was devoted to the American cause and the principles of liberty and freedom for all men. He was a strong antislavery advocate and often spoke strongly for the end to slavery. This did not endear him to many southern officers, soldiers and businessmen. Slavery was an abomination in his view and should be eliminated everywhere. Lafayette had the conviction that he, like his mentor General George Washington, ought to have a central role in bringing political liberty to France. In the hallway of his Paris mansion, he hung a framed copy of the American Declaration of Independence, and next to it was a conspicuously empty frame, which he said was for a French Declaration of Rights.[870]

Chapter 12

Privateering During the Revolution

PRIVATEERING BECOMES A VALUABLE RESOURCE FOR AMERICA

The British trade embargo and blockade of American seacoast communities by British warships was having a disastrous affect on the colonial states' economy and on American merchant trading enterprises. In response, hundreds of refitted American merchant transports and converted cargo vessels were armed with cannons, mortars and swivel guns to prey upon and capture British supply and transport vessels. The Continental Congress and agents appointed by the Congress issued commissions and "letters of marque." The letter of marque was a license granted by a state or government agent to a private citizen granting permission to arm a ship and seize enemy merchant vessels of rival nations. The captured enemy ships and their contents, considered as prizes or entitled goods, could then be sold, making large profits for the holder of the letter of marque and the crew of the ship. Only vessels of the enemy were fair game. Privateers sailed on two types of vessels. One type was a well-armed ship for attacking and capturing the enemy's vessel, and the other type was primarily a vessel with an assigned "prize crew" that sailed the captured vessel to an approved port for verification. An appointed state or government agent would determine if the vessel was a true prize capture. Pirates were regarded quite differently than privateers. Pirates were persons who robbed, plundered and committed illegal violence at sea, in seaports or in coastal towns. A pirate owed allegiance to no one but himself and his crew. Pirates considered vessels of all nations as fair game. During times of war, pirates could become privateers by selling themselves to the highest bidder. Today's ally might well become tomorrow's enemy.

There were fortunes to be made in privateering by enterprising and adventurous sailors, merchants and ship owners. The sailors aboard the privateering vessels were guaranteed a portion of the booty captured on enemy ships. The ship's owner and sailing captain received the largest share of the prize booty from captured enemy vessels, and the crew was rewarded in percentages according to rank or position. The American government received a percentage (about half) of the financial reward of the goods sold or auctioned, half of the hard specie (gold and silver coins) and all of the military supplies and munitions for the American military forces. Each seaman, who sailed on a single privateering voyage of a few months, was rewarded a certain share of the prize as well. If the captured enemy ship was laden with expensive goods, a seaman could receive enough income for a year or more from the single voyage.[871] Many New England men were able to improve their personal conditions and become merchants and ship owners. They were able to become wealthy and added a new class of prosperity to the region. As privateering enterprises became more popular, thousands of mariners and former soldiers became involved in the fighting that extended the naval conflicts along the coastlines of England, Ireland, Scotland and the West Indies, as well as some conflicts in the Mediterranean and Indian Ocean (with the Bombay and China trade). American vessels used French ports for shelter, supplies and repair services as well as for prize ports where enemy goods could be sold and traded.

Neutral nations such as Holland, Spain and France (until 1778, when the Franco-American Alliance was signed) were willing to covertly trade with the American colonies. American ships, such as the Ulmer trading vessels, would sail to a Caribbean island, such as Dutch-held St. Eustatius or Spanish-held Puerto Rico, and trade their cargos of wood products, corn, lime, dried fish, marble, rye and other grains for goods. The returning vessels brought such mercantile goods as salt, sugar, molasses, spices, tropical fruit and gunpowder that was essential for the military troops in New England. French cannons and firearms were traded for American goods at the French port of Martinique. Privateering was successful in the West Indies, as far south as the Spanish and Portuguese seaports of Brazil, Venezuela and other ports in South America, as well as seaports along the eastern coast of America from Florida to as far north as Halifax, Nova Scotia, in Canada.[872] In the West Indies, where British subjects lived on Antigua, Anguilla and other British-owned islands, New England privateers captured one out of every four enemy vessels trading or cruising in the Caribbean Sea.[873] The activities of the American privateering vessels were so successful that America's food problems slowly began to be solved. In Great Britain, the impact on the marketplace was being increasingly felt. The British merchants, who had been irritated at first with the privateers' activities, became publicly alarmed. In a letter to Parliament, the British ambassador to Spain wrote: "A fleet of our vessels came from Ireland a few days ago. From sixty vessels that departed, not above twenty-eight arrived here, the others, it is thought, being all taken by American privateers...If this American War continues, we shall all die of hunger..."[874]

The value of privateering for the governments lay in the fact that privately owned vessels could be rented or leased by the government for the purpose of privateering. The owners paid the crews an agreed-upon share of the profits, and the government received a "free navy" that also received a percentage of the capture. Governments could interrupt the enemy supply lines and sea commerce at no cost to the government agency except to issue a piece of paper, a letter of marque. The government did not have to buy, build or outfit any vessel or train, maintain and pay a crew. There were drawbacks for a government that was composed of a large number of privateers. If the government also had a navy, like the Continental Navy, there was competition between the two. The government paid the crews of the naval vessels less than they could make working on armed privateering vessels since they were considered as part of the Continental Navy and were paid accordingly. Officers and crews opted for the possibilities of riches versus low government pay and preferred slack discipline instead of rigid military discipline. Ship chandlers and other suppliers greatly preferred casks for their supplies instead of IOUs from the government agencies. Privateering thrived in the United Colonies during this time, and most of the privateers were from the New England region.

Maritime historians reported that nearly eleven thousand American seamen were engaged in privateering.[875] Privateering had a mixed impact during the American Revolution. On one side, many war materials that were destined for the British army in North America ended up in the hands of the American Patriots, including thousands of pounds of sterling. In one such incident, the annual pay for the British troops in North America was captured and ended up in the United States Treasury.[876] On the negative side, there was a great drain on the Continental Navy for sailors. The need for seamen and sailing masters became so critical that at one point, the navy could not man its warships. The merchant suppliers preferred the cash from the privateers for their goods rather than credit from the government. Throughout the war, approximately 70,000-plus men served aboard privateers that carried approximately 20,000-plus guns. In comparison, the Continental Navy, which never had more than 8 warships at sea at one time during the war, had a total of 53 armed vessels, 340 officers and 3,000 seamen and carried an estimated 2,770 guns. Privateers had hundreds of armed vessels at sea and captured an estimated 3,087 prize vessels, including 89 British privateers. The British forces, however, only accounted for 1,135 American merchantmen and 216 privateers. The Continental Navy and the American privateers captured about 16,000 seamen compared with 22,000 British soldiers and Loyalists who were captured on land. The estimated total value of captured privateers' prizes ranged from approximately $15 to $60 million. The British government estimated that 10 percent of the troops and cargo ships sent to America during the American Revolution never made it.[877*]

---

* *Author's comment*: It had been previously thought by historians that there had only been about two thousand American privateers that actively participated during the Revolutionary War. However, new data that has been recently published in *The Letters of Delegates to Congress, 1774–1789* indicates that Congress alone issued 1,697 letters of marque.[878] Many privateers who operated in European or West Indian waters harassing the British vessels received their letters of marque from American agents, like Benjamin Franklin and Silas Deane, who were stationed in the region. Since the publication of the congressional documents, we now know that there were many more privateering vessels actively involved during the Revolutionary War than had previously been estimated.

PHILIP ULMER RETURNS TO WALDOBORO

The grand Privateer ship DEANE*…will hail on a cruise against the Enemies
of the United States of America…This therefore is to invite all those Jolly
Fellows, who love their Country and want to make their Fortunes at one Stroke,
to repair immediately to the Rendezvous at the Head of His Excellency Governor
Hancock's Wharf, where they will be received with a hearty Welcome by a
Number of Brave Fellows there assembled...*
—*The* Boston Gazette[879]

In early April 1778, Philip Ulmer returned home to Waldoboro where
he resumed his life with his wife after many years of military service and
began to pursue civil avocations.[880] His civilian interests would again
include sailing and developing his business prospects. Philip Ulmer had
resigned from the Continental Army for personal and political reasons.
Some of these reasons were primarily due to the nepotism, deception and
in-fighting that he had witnessed among the colonels and generals that
he respected. He was disappointed in the unfairness that he experienced
in the military service with rank advancement of unqualified individuals
(often young family members of his commanding officers) and of foreign
adventurers over more qualified and experienced American officers.
In spite of his disappointment about being passed over for military
advancement at Valley Forge, Philip Ulmer still deeply believed in the
American cause of freedom, liberty and justice.

Fortunately, Philip's uncle Captain John Ulmer Jr. (hereafter referred to
as John Ulmer since he had a son also named John Ulmer Jr. at this time),
and his extended Ulmer family in Waldoboro and at Salem/Marblehead
would be able to help him with his adjustment back into the community.
Captain John Ulmer served locally in the defense of the eastern frontier
of Massachusetts by converting transports and trading ships into armed
vessels for state militia use. John Ulmer, who had a large family to support,
also assisted in supplying the Massachusetts state troops with needed goods
and supplies. Philip's uncle John was one of several men in the community
who appeared on the "roll of honor" for supplying meat and goods to the
Massachusetts state militia troops.[881] Philip Ulmer likely became involved
in converting fishing boats, sloops and small schooners into armed vessels
and became involved in merchant trading and possibly some privateering
activities in the coastal vicinity. Privateering offered a way to acquire financial
security quickly for hundreds of returning soldiers and seamen on furlough,

men between enlistments or men who had left the military service to resume private business enterprises. For the New England privateers, especially those who lived in frontier Maine, the most popular hunting area for British cargo and supply ships and for troop transports was located at the Gulf of St. Lawrence, the Penobscot Bay region and along the coastal area of Maine Province. Any British supply transports from England that were destined for the troops in Canada or in the eastern states of America were easy prey for American privateers. Of course, caution had to be exercised since the British had a major naval stronghold at Halifax, Nova Scotia. The Gulf of St. Lawrence became so popular as a hunting area that privateering vessels often got in one another's way. On a number of occasions, privateering captains went to battle stations only to discover that their prey was a fellow privateer or an American merchant vessel. Philip Ulmer could have been among those who sailed aboard private- or state-owned armed vessels like so many returning veteran soldiers and sailors whose enlistments had been completed. But it is more likely that he became active in the community and in the militia. He had learned from his experiences in the military service that advancement by nepotism and cronyism was a common procedure. Success and opportunity seemed to be based on a person's influential friends and political associations or on a person's wealthy status, relatives and benefactors. Philip had earned his military advancements through years of hard work, sacrifice and dedication to duty, but those qualities would only take him so far based on merit. He decided that he would use the knowledge and influence that he had gained in the military and help his younger brother to advance in position and to become successful. Their parents had died when the brothers were young, and they had only each other to rely on as immediate family. The uncles and cousins had their own families to support, although they were supportive and helpful.

What we do know of Philip Ulmer's activities after his return from military service with General Washington's Continental Army indicates that he became active in the Massachusetts state militia. In the records of *The Sea Coastal Defense of the Eastern Frontier*, Philip Ulmer appears on the list of officers serving in the frontier region. Lieutenant Ulmer enlisted in the Massachusetts state militia, and he was advanced in rank to captain. He served with Colonel Samuel McCobb's regiment in Lincoln County under the command of General Charles Cushing at the militia headquarters at Pownalboro in Lincoln County. Philip continued to recruit young soldiers for the state militia and for the Revolutionary War effort. He remained supportive and active with the Massachusetts state militia and with the local Broad Bay Guards (sometimes referred to as Rangers), serving in the coastal defense with the state militia regiment, commanded by Colonel Joseph Prime.[882] Captain Philip Ulmer sought special assignment to defend exposed places[883] from the commanding officer at the state militia headquarters. The defense of the seacoast and the exposed coastal ports and towns were of great interest and concern to Philip Ulmer. He recognized the vulnerability of the situation in the District of Maine and lack of sufficient fortifications and appropriate defenses along the frontier coastline against British attack. Captain Philip Ulmer, who served in Colonel Prime's regiment at this time, was ordered to command a detached militia company to build forts and defenses to protect the strategic points and vulnerable communities in the vicinity of the York, Cumberland and Lincoln districts. His duty was to construct defensive forts to protect the crucial river ports, seaports and the other strategic points in the frontier coastal region. The Massachusetts Provisional Congress (and the Continental Congress) had few resources, supplies and finances to defend the frontier District of Maine. Captain Ulmer's company of Massachusetts state militiamen gave the seaport and river communities the best protection that they could with limited resources.

Captain Philip Ulmer was given responsibility over a detached company made up of militiamen from the three counties of York, Cumberland and Lincoln. His assignment was to supervise the construction of a fort at the entrance of the Penobscot Bay in Camden Township to defend against the incursions of the British troops who often raided the seacoast and river settlements. This fort was called Fort Pine Hill and was located near Clam Cove. [Note: Clam Cove is located at present-day Rockland, a section of Thomaston, Maine. The location of the fort was referred to as Camden (Cambden, old spelling) because it was situated in Camden Township.][884] Captain Philip Ulmer directed the construction of breastworks to protect the fort, and he had an eighteen-pounder cannon mounted to defend the fort and harbor area against the British warships that patrolled the Penobscot Bay region from Halifax. The soldiers' barracks were situated a half mile back from the fort in the barn at the Gregory Farm. Mr. Gregory acted as the commissary for the militia soldiers stationed near the fort at Clam Cove and at Lermond's Cove (at present-day Rockland). Lieutenant Kelloch of Warren and Captain Blunt served with Captain Philip Ulmer's company at Fort Pine Hill.[885] Fort Pine Hill became the headquarters for the defense of Penobscot Bay and the easternmost region of Massachusetts.

The eastern coastline of frontier Massachusetts prior to the statehood of Maine in 1820. *Courtesy of the author.*

Captain Philip Ulmer's detached company continued to be involved in the construction of outposts throughout the coastal areas of York and Cumberland Counties, as well as strategic locations in the Penobscot Bay region. Several of the soldiers in Captain Ulmer's company stated in their Revolutionary War pension petitions that they had sailed aboard a privateer and on a state-owned armed sloop commanded by Captain Curtis.[886] In other Revolutionary War pension petitions, several soldiers with Captain Philip Ulmer's company further stated that Ulmer's detached company marched to Damariscotta, Sheepscot and Towns End (at present-day Boothbay) in May and June 1779, where the troops built forts and barracks.[887] The battery that was built at Towns End (also called Townsend) had five cannons, the largest of which was a twelve-pounder.[888] They built a fort at Cox's Head (located at the mouth of the Kennebec River), where barracks were also erected; however, soon afterward, a British warship fired on the fort and barracks, trying to destroy the structures.[889] Several militia companies were sent by General Charles Cushing from the state militia headquarters at Pownalboro to assist in further fortification and repair of the damaged fort.[890] There were rumors that another British raid was being planned in the area, but this did not occur. The inhabitants of easternmost Massachusetts in Maine Province were in constant fear for their lives and safety from sudden attacks by enemy warship and British raiding parties on their villages and seaports.

LAND GRAB IN FRONTIER MASSACHUSETTS IN THE DISTRICT OF MAINE

Before the end of 1778, the only three counties in the Province of Maine at the time—York, Cumberland and Lincoln—were created by Massachusetts Congress into a maritime district called the "District of Maine."[891] The General Court of Massachusetts passed a law with the terms that many Tory or Loyalist settlers would have their land confiscated because they had become "absentees" or had moved to other British strongholds or to England. Two of these "absentees" were from Waldoboro. They were Francis Waldo (son of General Samuel Waldo) and General Waldo's son-in-law, Thomas Flucker (the father of Lucy Flucker Knox, who married General Henry Knox in 1774).[892] Under the law, the judges of probate were authorized to appoint agents to administer the Waldo/Flucker estates. The only male heir to General Samuel Waldo's estate was his grandson, Samuel, who was a British Loyalist and had relocated to England, where he later died. The property of Thomas Flucker, who was the royal secretary of the Province of Massachusetts and proprietor of Old Broad Bay, was declared confiscated. The inhabitants of the town and surrounding counties scrambled to seize the land, have their surveys made and then have the surveys recorded as their respective land claims.[893]

This land grab procedure led to conflicts after the Revolutionary War with General Henry Knox and his wife, Lucy (Flucker) Knox, who was the

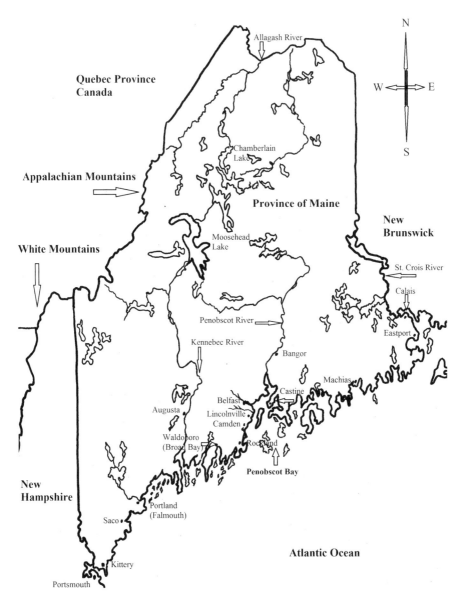

Map of the eastern frontier region of Massachusetts in the Province of Maine during the American Revolution. *Courtesy of the author.*

granddaughter of General Samuel Waldo and owner of the Waldo Patent. She was the only heir and beneficiary of the old Waldo estate and land patent still living in America. The inhabitants of Waldoboro and other neighboring settlements within the Waldo Patent became "squatters," and they claimed land that was part of Lucy Knox's inheritance from her grandfather General Waldo.[894] This land grab in 1778 caused serious problems when Henry and Lucy Knox attempted to reclaim the Waldo/Flucker inheritance property, part of the original Waldo Patent. General Henry Knox and his wife were absent from their property for many years. Eventually, General Henry Knox retired from government service, and Henry, Lucy and their family moved to their newly constructed estate at Thomaston, Maine. They became involved with the difficulties of reclaiming Lucy Knox's inherited Waldo Patent property from the angry squatters who had claimed the property as their own during the war. This led to heated encounters between the proprietors and the settlers throughout the area.

Prior to the Revolution, Philip's uncle John Ulmer had been well known in the merchant trading business that had originally been developed by his father, Captain John Ulmer Sr., one of the Broad Bay settlement founders. Uncle John had also developed his own interests in business investments, money lending, land speculation and shipbuilding in the Waldoboro area. He had acquired large landholdings, which he later sold off prudently, over many years, to support his large growing family and to finance other business enterprises.[895] Philip Ulmer, his uncle John and his relative Matthias Remilly made a land deal in 1772 to have a huge tract of land surveyed for themselves by William Farnsworth. The tract of land extended on the west side of the river "above the head of Broad Bay and some miles up the river [Medomak River] above any present settlers."[896] This was basically land appropriation in the Medomak River watershed, which they disposed of in small lots to future settlers. This proved to be a wise investment and very lucrative. Philip was encouraged by his uncle John to acquire desirable and useful land along the rivers and streams where dams could be built for a power source and could be used to power their various businesses such as sawmills and gristmills. The river waterways were used for transportation, and the coves were considered desirable to establish shipyards to construct various types of fishing boats and sailing vessels. These various businesses would finance other opportunities as well. In 1779, John Ulmer sold his one-third ownership in the huge tract of land to Remilly for a sum that was pure profit.[897] Philip Ulmer was eventually able to accumulate enough money to purchase the Slaigo stream, the cove and the surrounding land, which was a very desirable property in the Waldoboro area.[898]

John Ulmer, Philip's uncle, had been elected to become a selectman for the town of Waldoboro in March 1778.[899] By the vote of the town, he was also to serve on its Committee of Correspondence, Inspection and Safety.[900] He had become a wealthy businessman and a strong leader in the community. During the Revolutionary War period, there were about twenty-five mills in the town, and they were devoted to every type of work in which power was essential. Those lands on the upper Medomak River in the watershed vicinity were the most valuable properties since there was sufficient water to operate the mills in all seasons. These sites were under the control of John Ulmer and the extended Ulmer family relatives. He also acquired all the sites on the east side of the lower falls, which included a dam and the primary mill site.[901]

The Ulmer family, through timely land acquisitions and business investments, owned a shipyard at Broad Cove, several gristmills and sawmills and several pieces of valuable property along the Medomak River, deep into the backcountry of Waldoboro and along the seacoast. Sites along the river were gradually sold to developers or settlers, and the Ulmer family became prosperous and well established in the Waldoboro area. Philip's uncle John Ulmer became the major real estate agent and business broker in the Medomak watershed and Waldoboro vicinity. His investment holdings and land acquisitions ran deep into the wilderness backcountry of the watershed. His property embraced most of the present-day village of Waldoboro and the built-up sections east of the river to Willett Hill.[902] His vast land interests, which were acquired from Lucy and Henry Knox, extended eastward to the Penobscot Bay and the backcountry regions of the Waldo Patent. He likely served as Henry Knox's land agent and sold land to new inhabitants for settlement in the Maine frontier. John Ulmer and his large family were able to prosper in spite of the deprivations caused by the Revolutionary War, and he became a contributor of goods and supplies for the state militia troops. The house of Philip's grandfather had been greatly enlarged by his uncle John, and it had become an inn (called The Ulmer). The Ulmer provided another source of income for the large Ulmer family and became a center for social gatherings.[903] As a sailing captain and merchant shipowner, John Ulmer's influence rose in the Lincoln County vicinity. He was elected as a selectman and town leader in Waldoboro. These pursuits caused him to give up his earlier interests as a shipbuilder, Lutheran lay minister and a schoolmaster for the community, which were interests of his father, John Ulmer Sr., one of the early founders of the Broad Bay (Waldoboro) settlement in 1743.[904]

EXTENT OF REVOLUTIONARY PRIVATEERING

The immense naval force of Great Britain was rendered incompetent to fully protect her own shipping. They were rendered incompetent by the privateers of a country that possessed not a single sail of the line, and that had been only a year in existence as a nation.[905]
—*Thomas Clark, British historian*

Typical of the era, Philip Ulmer, with his uncles and longtime associates, combined self-interest and investment opportunities with significant contributions to the Revolutionary War and the American cause. The Ulmer family in Waldoboro was involved with shipbuilding and ship conversions to armed privateering vessels. They sailed on coastal voyages for various types of goods and merchandise as far south as the West Indies. They were also involved with lumbering and lime production in the District of Maine. The ability to combine merchant commerce with cargo vessels supplying the army soldiers with needed goods had an impact on trading in seaport towns on the eastern coast of America. American privateering remained a growing industry, with applications for letters of marque and sailing warrants quadrupling between 1778 and 1781.[906] By this period of time, there were about 500 privateering warships at sea and fewer than 10 Continental ones. The total of privateering ships would eventually increase to 1,697 vessels with approximately 64 Continental Navy ships during the Revolutionary War.[907] The competition for seamen (especially experienced New England sailors) to sail aboard Continental vessels and the privateering vessels became contentious during the war years. General Washington praised the New England community for "the valuable prizes that have been lately brought into your port. We stand in need of all your activity to increase our supplies by these means."[908] In order to promote privateering, Washington directed in one of his letters that "ammunition from the Continental magazine" should be made available to the public so that "they should not be suffered to want so essential an article."[909]

James Tracy, captain of the *Yankee Hero* (which Philip Ulmer helped to build with his uncle John and relatives at Broad Bay Cove in 1770), was captured with 170 American crewmen by the British warship HMS *Lively*.[910] This was the same warship that had captured Philip's brother, George Ulmer, near Marblehead Harbor in 1775.[911] John and Patrick Tracy of Newburyport, who were shipbuilding clients and Ulmer family friends, lost not only money during the first several years of the war but also forty-one privateers, either captured by the British or destroyed in battle.[912] Hundreds of men from the New England coastline communities, as well as soldiers on furlough or between enlistments, were involved in privateering.[913] Hundreds of privately owned armed privateering vessels, as well as state-sponsored armed ships-of-war, went to sea during this time. The men sailed for the glory of the American cause and also to quickly build their own financial fortunes. By 1779, the Tracy brothers had recuperated their financial losses with their privateering vessels, bringing 120 enemy prizes into port with cargos valued at about $3,950,000. The Tracy brothers donated $167,000 of their profits to George Washington's Continental Army.[914] This was a sizable sum of money during the Revolutionary War period. Seamen and sailing masters from Waldoboro, St. George and the surrounding towns were among the hundreds of privateers who served on board some of these privateering ships or aboard armed state naval vessels.

Chapter 13

British Attempt to Annex Maine

BRITISH PLAN TO INVADE AND ANNEX FRONTIER MASSACHUSETTS (MAINE)

Before the French and Indian War, England had attempted to claim territory along the eastern coast of Massachusetts (now the state of Maine) and establish a territorial hold on it. The British war planners looked for ways to gain control over the rebellious New England colonies while most of their effort was directed at other campaign operations that targeted the southern colonies. The ultimate goal of Lord Germain, the secretary of state for colonial affairs in North America, and his secretary, William Knox, was to establish a military presence on the Bagaduce Peninsula of the Penobscot Bay and begin to build a new colony in the Maine Province to be known as New Ireland, with Maja-bagaduce (the Bagaduce Peninsula) as its military and naval fortress along the Maine coastline and Castine as the capital.[915]

The British threat to conquer or annex the District of Maine was part of a larger scheme of conquest. The establishment of the military fort at Bagaduce became a haven for Loyalists and Tories from all parts of Massachusetts and New England. Castine became a point of entry for contraband goods and illegal smuggling activities in the frontier District of Maine. One of many inducements for Loyalists and Tories to settle in the district of Maine Province was that the capital of a new province would be composed of territory between the Penobscot River and the St. Croix River (at New Brunswick in Canada) and was to be called New Ireland. The project of creating the colony of New Ireland was sanctioned by King George III and his ministry, which saw the new colony as a refuge and resort for banned and displaced British citizens who would have their own colony. A constitution was written for the new colony: "With the absolute power of the British government; to make this power secure for all coming time, every landlord on acquired land, whether by grant, from the Crown, by purchase, or by inheritance, was bound to make a test declaration of Allegiance to the King in his parliament, as the supreme legislature of the province…"[916] To combat the prevailing disposition of the people to Republicanism, "there was to be by the side of the Governor & Council no elective assembly until the circumstances of the province permitted it, but a middle branch of legislature, of which every one of the members was to be named by the Crown, to be distinguished by title or emoluments, or both; and though otherwise appointed for life, to remain ever liable to be suspended or removed by royal authority."[917]

The early settlers of the Massachusetts frontier region had every indication that the British had the intention of overrunning their communities, displacing them to other locations and forcing them to make a Declaration of Allegiance to the king of England. The feudal system with its inequalities and repressive rule by European monarchs, rulers and the privileged and elite class was a major reason why many immigrants from Europe and Great Britain had come to America in the first place. The colonial settlers and new immigrants in America risked everything they possessed for a chance at a new life and a new future for themselves, their children and for future generations. They were determined to fight for freedom from servitude and the repressive bonds of the feudal system that they had left behind in Europe and England, thousands of miles across the Atlantic Ocean.

THE AMERICAN REVOLUTION
BECOMES A GLOBAL CONFLICT

Oceangoing sailing vessels had to follow the strong ocean and wind currents when crossing the Atlantic Ocean on their trade routes to Europe due to the strong North Atlantic ocean currents (part of the equatorial current of the Gulf Stream) that flow along the eastern coast of North America from south to north. The deep ocean Labrador currents from Canada brought trans-ocean sailing vessels close to Nova Scotia and along the seacoast of frontier Maine. With major fortresses and naval shipyards at New York City, Bagaduce (later called Castine) and Halifax, the commercial shipping and merchant trading could be monitored by the British Royal Navy and strictly controlled in the New England colonies. An embargo placed on coastal ports, the closing of harbors and a disruption of the commercial trade routes would eventually collapse the American economy. The New England settlers, who depended greatly on trading to survive in their harsh winter environment, would be forced into submission through starvation, intimidation, violence and fear; or they would be forced to move elsewhere, enabling Tories and Loyalists to move into the area, plunder the homes and villages and claim the vacated land for themselves; or the frontier citizens in Maine Province could just die from deprivation, sickness and disease. Loyalist settlers were encouraged and were given strong incentives to move into New Ireland territory, to push out the defiant American families from the area and to take over the frontier settlers' property. These Loyalists would become the residents of the newly formed Province of New Ireland. By exploiting the natural resources of the Maine Province (lumbering, lime-burning and abundant fishing and hunting), the new Loyalist settlers of New Ireland would become prosperous producers of needed goods, supplies, wood products and maritime needs (such as tall timber for masts and lumber for ships) for Great Britain, Europe and the West Indies.

As the Revolutionary War shifted to the Southern Theater, the British military forces operating on the New England seacoast were directed by Lord Germain to secure and protect their British possessions in eastern Canada and New England. Prior to the summer of 1778, the British Royal Navy was engaged in the support, supplying and transportation of the British forces employed against the rebellious American colonies along the coasts, rivers and lakes of North America. The Royal Navy tried to protect British commerce against the attacks of the American privateers. On February 6, 1778, the Franco-American Alliance was signed with the successive support of Spain and the Netherlands.[918] Word of the alliance took many weeks to be communicated to those involved in the fighting in the field and especially to vessels at sea in various parts of the world. The American naval and privateering encounters with Great Britain's armed vessels extended beyond the range of the American colonies to the coastline of Europe, the islands in the West Indies, to Brazil in South America, to the Mediterranean and to the Bay of Bengal in India with its lucrative China trade business. This next phase of the Revolutionary War evolved from primarily a land-focused conflict into a naval conflict that began in the summer of 1778 and continued until the end of the war in 1783. The American Revolution soon became a more global conflict. The war strategy had included operations already underway to protect American commerce and to support campaigns on the land, but the fighting changed to include naval campaigns on a grand scale, carried out by fleets of diverse maritime powers displaying flags from many countries.

Since the beginning of the American Revolution, it had been a common practice of both the British Royal Navy and Royal Army to plunder American towns and villages and then put them to the torch. This was especially true of the British Royal Navy. The British navy made a practice of invading coastal seaports and burning the towns and destroying their ships, causing great deprivation to the defenseless townspeople in frontier Massachusetts. Destroying British commerce was a mission of the Continental Navy, but not the burning of towns. Burning or scuttling the merchant fleet in its harbor would cause more damage to British shipping in one night than had been done by the privateers and naval ships over several years. Economically, it was considered a success since shipping rates and maritime insurance rose to prohibitive levels on the London Exchange. Wealthy American merchants and important state and town leaders were captured by British raiding parties, and they were held as bargaining chips for ransom or used as leverage for the release of British prisoners held in American jails.[919] The British troops invaded the homes of community leaders, government officials and state militia generals or officers. The raiders demanded prize money for the release of prisoners. The American privateers, the state navy and the Continental Navy did not inflict the British Loyalists, Tories or sympathizers with the devastation that the British Royal Army and Royal Navy routinely inflicted on the American citizens.

In the Province of Maine, privateering vessels were operated by local Patriots in the Penobscot Bay region as well as by other sailors and adventurers along the eastern seacoast. The New England privateers (carrying letters of marque) and other Americans sailing armed vessels had been harassing British shipping on the trade routes along the New England seacoast as far north as Halifax, Nova Scotia. Because of the Massachusetts sailors' knowledge of the rocky coastline of New England, the attacks on the British commerce were made quite effectively with speed, ease and safety. The local sailors and seamen knew the coastal islands, the hidden coves and the rivers in the region. The privateers could strike the British vessels quickly, capturing the enemy ships with their cargo, military supplies and munitions with success. The British forces at the naval shipyard at Halifax and at the military fortress at Louisbourg decided that a substantial fort should be built at Bagaduce on the eastern shore of the Penobscot Bay. The new fortress would protect British shipping and commerce in New England and would command the harbors and coastline of Massachusetts, New Hampshire and the frontier Province of Maine.[920] British presence in the Penobscot Bay would hinder the privateering and smuggling activities along the coastal frontier region of Massachusetts (in Maine Province) and would enable the further British exploitation of the rich natural resources of the Penobscot Bay and Passamaquoddy Bay region.

The large territorial region in frontier Massachusetts had abundant forests with trees for lumbering and for ships' timber that could be harvested to supply the naval shipyard at Halifax and in Great Britain. To carry out the British plan, a force of nine hundred soldiers, convoyed by seven or eight naval vessels, was sent from Halifax to Maja-bagaduce (hereafter Bagaduce or Castine) under the command of General Francis McLean.[921] General McLean's expedition left Halifax on May 30, and they arrived at Bagaduce unopposed on June 12, 1779.[922] The British Royal Navy transports, escorted by three sloops-of-war, landed approximately seven hundred Royal Artillery and engineers in addition to two regiments of trained foot soldiers (more than nine hundred men) at Bagaduce, which was on a peninsula near the strategic mouth of the Penobscot River and Bay.[923] On the peninsula, the British intended to construct breastworks, several batteries and a "citadel," or fortress. The next day, General McLean and Andrew Barkley, the captain of the naval convoy, decided on an appropriate site to construct the new fort. The fort was to be named Fort George in honor of King George III of England. Fort George would be able to control ship movements along the New England seacoast from the St. Lawrence River to the New York Harbor. From this location, the British forces would be able to raid the New England coastal shipping and ports, and they could launch forays against cities and towns along the New England coastline.

By June 16, the British support troops and three warships arrived at Bagaduce.[924] Trees and undergrowth were cleared for the site, and the area was prepared for the erection of the fortress. Defensive works in the center of the peninsula were built with two batteries outside the fort to provide cover for the *Albany*, which was the only ship that was expected to remain in the Penobscot Bay area. A third battery was built on an island south of the bay near the mouth of the Penobscot River, where British captain Mowat's flagship, *Albany*, was anchored. The construction of the works occupied the troops for a month. Local residents who lived on the western shore of the

Portrait of King George III in 1762. By artist William Pether after a painting by Thomas Frye. *Courtesy of the Library of Congress.*

Penobscot Bay were pressed into hard labor to help construct the fort for the British commander. There was great alarm among the residents about the British forces building a permanent fort to control the shipping and commerce along the New England seacoast. Frantic appeals for state militia troops and defensive armaments were made to the Massachusetts Provincial

Congress in Boston to protect the Massachusetts citizens in the frontier coastal towns in Maine. Having built most of Fort George, the barracks, storage structures and defensive fortifications, the British fleet left the harbor at Bagaduce and returned to Halifax, Nova Scotia, leaving three sloops-of-war—the *Albany*, the *North* and the *Nautilus*—assigned to the station under the command of Captain Henry Mowat.[925] (Captain Mowat was the same commander whose fleet of British warships had destroyed the harbor and unarmed town of Falmouth in October 1775, destroying the ships anchored at the docks and leaving the town in flames.)

FRONTIER MAINE STRIKES BACK AGAINST BRITISH INCURSIONS

A great alarm was spread throughout the Province of Maine about the British fortress under construction at Bagaduce. General Charles Cushing, who was the state militia commander at Pownalboro, where the militia headquarters for the eastern frontier was located, sent an urgent letter to the Massachusetts Provincial Congress with a request for an immediate expedition to be organized and sent to dislodge the enemy on Bagaduce before the British forces could become entrenched in the fortress under construction.[926] (The town of Pownalboro was located about six miles westward of Waldoboro, where Philip Ulmer's family lived.) When the Massachusetts General Court in Boston learned of the extent and purpose of the incursion from General Cushing and the fear of the residents in the Penobscot region, it petitioned the Continental Congress, seeking immediate assistance from three Continental Navy warships: the twelve-gun sloop *Providence*, the fourteen-gun brig *Diligent* and the thirty-two-gun frigate *Warren*, all of which were anchored in Boston Harbor.[927] The Continental Congress authorized an expedition to destroy the British military base under construction at Bagaduce. Commodore Dudley Saltonstall (the brother-in-law of Silas Deane) was designated the commander of the squadron, and he was to lead the naval portion of the expedition.[928] General Lovell was chosen to lead the land attack on Bagaduce, assisted by Brigadier General Wadsworth, second-in-command.[929] Commodore Saltonstall assigned Lieutenant Colonel Paul Revere to be in charge of the artillery support. Colonel Revere went aboard the ordnance brig with all the artillery and the munitions for the expedition.[930]

The Massachusetts General Court approved the request for an expedition and directed that a force of 1,200 to 1,500 men should be raised from the counties of Cumberland, York and Lincoln to dislodge the British forces at Bagaduce.[931] However, only 873 militiamen and volunteers actually participated in the expedition. There were an additional 227 Continental and Massachusetts Marines who participated in the Penobscot Expedition. On June 24, 1779, armed ships for the expedition departed from Boston, and the fleet arrived in the Penobscot Bay area on the same day. The American fleet rendezvoused at Towns End (present-day Boothbay), which was part of the town of Waldoboro at the time. The fleet consisted of the flagship *Warren*, a frigate of thirty-two guns, accompanied by nine ships, six brigs and three sloops, all carrying a combined total of 344 guns. These vessels were joined by twenty-four transports, many privately owned.[932] Rumors were received by the British forces on Bagaduce that an American expedition was being raised to oppose the construction of the British fortress and strategic British stronghold.

Philip Ulmer, who served in the Massachusetts state militia in Colonel McCobb's regiment, was called for special service in the Penobscot Expedition from July 8, 1779, to September 24, 1779. Philip was a captain in Colonel McCobb's regiment, and he recruited soldiers for his company in the local communities and as far eastward as Camden (near Rockland and Thomaston) on the Penobscot Bay.[933] He participated on the Penobscot Expedition as the commanding officer of a detached company from the three frontier counties of Maine Province under the command of General Wadsworth and General Lovell.[934] Captain Philip Ulmer commanded his detached corps of soldiers with Colonel McCobb's regiment.[935] Colonel McCobb was advanced to the rank of brigadier general during this time. Reverend John Murray of Towns End (Townsend) was induced to join the expedition as the chaplain of Colonel McCobb's regiment. He volunteered to carry dispatches from General Lovell to the Massachusetts General Court (the governing body) in Boston.[936]

Captain Philip Ulmer appeared on the list of officers with General Cushing, General Peleg Wadsworth, General Solomon Lovell and Brigadier General Samuel McCobb, who were all involved in the defense of Massachusetts and the eastern frontier of the Province of Maine.[937] The volunteers who served in Captain Philip Ulmer's company with General McCobb's regiment were Sergeant Joshua Howard and the following privates who appeared on the payroll of this company: three Achorn brothers (Jacob, John and Michael); the two Mink brothers, Paul and Valentine; the two Hoch brothers; Martin, George and John Ulmer Jr. (three cousins of Captain Philip Ulmer); John

Varner (Werner), another Ulmer cousin; Joseph Simmons; John Welt; Peter Wichenbach; (Frank) Henry Oberlock (Oberlach); John Benner; John Hunt; Christopher Newbit (Newbert, lost an arm during the attack on the fort on Bagaduce); Jacob Genthner; Peter Orff (Off); Christopher Walk; James Kaler; George Hoffses; Isaac Sargus; Peter Lehr; and Charles Hebner (who was sick during much of his enlistment).[938] There were others in this company from St. George as well. Waldoboro became the primary source of supplies and distribution for the Penobscot Expedition.[939] Colonel Waterman Thomas of Waldoboro "advanced large sums of money to procure provisions for the troops at the Eastward [and] to procure provisions for the soldiers now doing duty at Cambden [*sic*]." Colonel Waterman Thomas, (nephew of General John Thomas,[940] who died of smallpox in the Canadian Expedition in 1776) became the "Quartermaster and Commissary for the whole Eastern Department."[941]*

Penobscot Expedition

It is the Expression of the Council [of Massachusetts]…*that you will push your Operations with all possible Vigor and dispatch and accomplish the business of the Expedition before any reinforcement can get to the enemy at Penobscot. It is also reported here and believed by many that a Forty Gun ship and the Delaware Frigate sailed from Sandy Hook on Sixteenth Current and Stood to the Eastward; their destination was not known.*
—*Letter excerpt from the Massachusetts Council to Brigadier General Solomon Lovell, July 23, 1779*

Ordered that the Board of War be and they are hereby directed to furnish the two Indians of the Penobscot Tribe, now in the Town of Boston with Two Hats, one of them laced, two Blankets and two Shirts.
—*Excerpt of an order given by the Massachusetts Bay Council dated July 27, 1779*

---

* *Author's comment*: Following General John Thomas's death in Canada, the town of Thomaston (Maine) was named in his honor. Philip Ulmer's family in Waldoboro had known the Thomas family prior to the war, and Philip had served with General John Thomas in Canada in May 1776.

Armed vessels from Massachusetts and New Hampshire state navies joined Commodore Saltonstall's naval forces at Towns End (a section of Waldoboro). Twelve privateers were cajoled into state service for the expedition as well. The task force eventually had nineteen armed ships mounting 344 guns and twenty-four transports for troops and supplies.[942] The transport vessels carried a landing force of about 1,200 men under the command of Brigadier General Solomon Lovell. The bulk of the troops were Massachusetts state militiamen, joined by about 300 U.S. Continental Marines.[943] Ultimately, the Penobscot Expedition turned into the largest American naval expedition of the Revolutionary War. Commodore Saltonstall's orders were to completely eliminate the British presence in the Penobscot Bay area. Saltonstall's superiors in the Massachusetts Council of War emphasized that he would have to "preserve the greatest harmony with the commander of the land forces, so that the navy and army may cooperate and assist each other, and at all times Study and promote the Greatest Harmony…between land and sea Forces."[944] It was advice that Commodore Saltonstall would discount, to the detriment of the entire mission.

The general orders were to assemble at Towns End in Lincoln County, where the officers and primary division leaders boarded Commodore Saltonstall's flagship, *Warren*.[945] On board were Commodore Saltonstall, General Solomon Lovell, General Peleg Wadsworth (General Lovell's second-in-command), Lieutenant Colonel Paul Revere (in charge of artillery) with other officers and approximately three hundred U.S. Continental Marines, about one hundred Massachusetts state artillerymen and the two Penobscot Indian chiefs who had been in Boston to negotiate the terms of Indian involvement.[946]

A council of war was called by General Lovell, who had quartered himself at the parsonage of Reverend Jonathan Murray, to discuss the plans for the attack on the British fort at Bagaduce. Colonel Lovell introduced Wadsworth and Commodore Saltonstall and the three colonels of the militia regiments. Major Jeremiah Hill, the expedition's adjutant general, was introduced with the two brigade majors, William Todd and Gawen Brown. The quartermaster, Colonel Tyler, and Dr. Eliphalet Downer, the surgeon general, were introduced. Captain Philip Ulmer and Colonel McCobb met Captain John Welsh, the U.S. Continental Marine commander who was with his troops on board the *Centurion*. Captain Welsh and his lieutenant, William Hamilton, would lead the U.S. Marines in the first wave of the amphibious assault upon the cliffs at Dyce's Head with Captain Philip Ulmer's company of Lincoln County militiamen from Colonel McCobb's regiment. Colonel

Paul Revere's artillery troops, with the help of some Continental Marines, were to capture Cross Island (later called Nautilus Island) to the south of the Bagaduce Peninsula near the entrance of the harbor to the east, where the British warships were first anchored. The artillery troops were to turn the cannons on the British fleet and keep the British marines occupied while the American ground forces made their attack upon the partially built fort. Colonel Revere was to leave a small company of soldiers to man the battery at Cross Island and keep the British fleet occupied in the harbor. If all went well, Revere's men would rejoin the main forces attacking Fort George.

General McLean had knowledge of this expedition four days before the arrival of the American flotilla from Tory informants.[947] He made every effort to make his position defensible. Batteries were set up in strategic locations to protect Fort George, "The Neck" (a marshy isthmus that connected the main island to the Bagaduce Peninsula) and the narrow Bagaduce Harbor from the approaching American flotilla from the west. Neither the British general McLean nor Captain Archibald Campbell, who was second-in-command at Fort George, believed that the American forces would make their attack upon the steep cliffs of Dyce's Head since they were too dangerous and formidable. Dyce's Head was an almost sheer cliff that rose from a narrow, rocky shore in a near-perpendicular direction from the Penobscot Bay. The steep cliffs angled to a lesser degree about two-thirds of the way to the top of the heavily brushy and treed ridge at the top. The British expected the attack to come from the marshy isthmus to the north or on the lower slopes to the east near the harbor. There was much to be done to fortify the breastworks and trenches, and the British general knew that he was poorly prepared for a major encounter with the American forces. The British forces had partially completed breastworks and a fortification on the heights of the Bagaduce Peninsula. Three Royal Navy sloops—*Albany*, *North* and *Nautilus*—each mounted eighteen guns.[948] They remained anchored in the Bagaduce Harbor, protected by a small gun battery at Cross Island near the entrance of the harbor. British batteries had been strategically set up in Jacob Dyce's corn field on the peninsula at Half Moon near the partially constructed fort to protect the harbor area and the Penobscot River below. An unfinished battery to protect the fort from the north was located at The Neck connecting the peninsula to the mainland.

The American warships and transport vessels set sail from Towns End on July 24 and entered the Penobscot Bay on July 25, 1779.[949] Fort Pine Hill, located at the entrance to the Penobscot Bay, had been built to defend the frontier settlers against British raiding parties from Halifax and to defend against enemy incursions on the Penobscot River and bay regions. The *Warren*, *Hunter*, *Sky Rocket*, *Centurion* and other transport vessels sailed toward Fort Pine Hill, where they were met by a large party of about forty Penobscot Indians, other militia officers, soldiers and New England volunteers. At the fort at Camden, Captain Mitchell and his state militiamen from Cumberland County boarded the *Sky Rocket*. A company of approximately forty armed Penobscot Indians in canoes joined the expedition. The flotilla sailed eastward toward the Penobscot Bay and their fateful encounter with the British forces at Bagaduce (present-day Castine).

As soon as the American flotilla appeared, General McLean dispatched a messenger to Halifax requesting reinforcements.[950] British gunners on land and on board the warships were able to engage in a firefight with the American task force as it entered the Penobscot River and harbor area. However, for two days after arriving in the Penobscot Bay, bad weather and turbulent seas made it unsafe to land the American troops. There was a skirmish on July 26, during which John Welsh's Continental Marines and Colonel Revere's

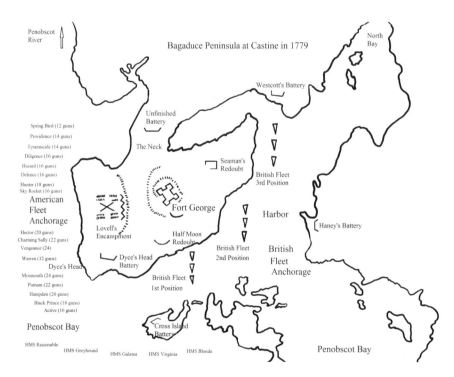

American and British fleet and army positions on the Bagaduce Peninsula during the Battle of Penobscot Bay in July–August 1779. *Courtesy of the author.*

artillery company, while under covering fire from the American warships, captured the British battery at Cross Island at the entrance to the harbor where the British fleet was anchored. They captured the British cannons and raised the American flag at the island.[951] Paul Revere, who was General Lovell's commander of artillery, turned the captured British cannon on the three British warships defending the harbor entrance. Captain Mowat, who commanded the three British warships, withdrew up the river to a position nearer Fort George and the other defensive batteries. On July 27, the seas were again too turbulent for landing the troops. The landing party of Continental Marines and state militia soldiers were kept on board their transport ships until weather conditions improved. The soldiers and marines had to remain in a standing position, without a place to rest, all night. This first invasion force included Captain Philip Ulmer and his company of soldiers from Lincoln County. By early morning, weather conditions had finally changed. Peleg Wadsworth and the Continental Marines and Colonel McCobb's Lincoln County militiamen were given the signal to climb down into the longboats and make their way to the narrow rocky beach area at the foot of the cliffs. They were followed by Mitchell's militia troops from Cumberland County, who were on board the *Sky Rocket*. It was necessary to land on the western side of the peninsula due to the positioning of the British fleet anchored on the eastern side of the peninsula near the fort. A triage area was set up on the rocky beach where the boats landed.

THE ASSAULT ON DYCE'S HEAD

When I returned to the shore it struck me with admiration to see what a precipice we had ascended, not being able to take such a scrutinous [sic] view of it at the time of the battle; it is at least, where we landed, 300 feet high and almost perpendicular, and the men were obliged to pull themselves up by twigs and trees. I don't think such a landing has been made since Wolfe.[952]
—*General Solomon Lovell*

William Williamson, a sergeant with Captain Philip Ulmer's company, in his accounting of the tortuous ascent at Dyce's Head (Dyce's Point), wrote:

Considering the obstacles faced, this assault was one of the most distinguished feats in American military history, calling for rare skill, determination, and

individual heroism. From the standpoint of sheer "guts," it outranks the better known feat of Wolfe's men scaling the cliffs at Quebec, which were no higher, where the men followed a well-beaten path which they were not forced to climb under heavy fire…Certainly no one in the world other than backwoodsmen could have accomplished such a miracle…there was not a more brilliant exploit of itself during the [Revolutionary] *war than this.*[953]
—*Governor William D. Williamson*

The soldiers and marines who served in Captain Philip Ulmer's company with Colonel McCobb's militia regiment commenced their military service on July 8 and ended their enlistment on September 24, 1779, at the conclusion of the Penobscot Expedition. These courageous men climbed the heights of Dyce's Head and laid siege to the British fort (Fort George) on Bagaduce. In Captain Philip Ulmer's company were the following men:

Philip M. Ulmer,	Captain
John Matthews and Alexander Kelloch,	Lieutenants
Joshua Howard, William Robbinson, Joseph Coombs, Abraham Jones,	Sergeants
Elisha Bradford, Francis Young, Eben Jameson, Matthew Watson,	Corporals

Privates:
John Ulmer (Philip's cousin), Christopher Newbit, Jonathan Crockett, John Miller, Charles Jameson, John Blackington, Ephram Snow, Richard Kating, Ichabod Barrows, Jacob Keen, Joseph Ingraham, James Heard, Stephen Peabody, Paul Mink, Ephram Stimson, Joseph Simmons, Peter Ott (Camden), Andrew Wells (Camden), Leonard Metcalf (Camden), Nathan Knight, Martin Hiesler, Peter Wincheboo, Valentine Mink, Jacob Gentner, Daniel Gardner, John Tuck, Robert Hawes, Silvester Prince, Samuel Marshall, John Carver, Andrew Robbinson, John Gordon, John Brison, William Gregory, Dennis Connary, Jacob Acorn, John Acorn, Michael Acorn, John Wisk (or Wissle), Baltus Stilke, Cornelius Morton, John Hunt, Paul Jameson, George Condon, Luke Jones, Charles Kayler, John Libby, Henry Oberlock, James Eustice, Martin Brodman, William Palfry, Christopher Walk, John Cornmouth, John Benner, Samuel Crane, George Hoch, Joseph Jameson, Isacc Sargent, Levi Loring, George Hofses, Charles Demorse, Thomas Adams, James Warner, Thomas Morton, Francis Vinal, Charles Conner and Martin Hoch.[954]

There were Penobscot Indians who were also involved with Captain Philip Ulmer's troops who climbed Dyce's Head and gave substantial support during the entire Penobscot Expedition.

On July 28, the American landing assault force, with General Wadsworth leading the way, stormed ashore on the southwest end of the Bagaduce Peninsula after several armed vessels—the *Tyannicide*, the *Hunter* and the *Sky Rocket*—shelled the cliffs and the heavily wooded area above the landing beach to cover the landing parties' assault.[955] The initial troops landed in three divisions: about two hundred state militiamen on the left and in the center with the company of Indians, and two hundred Continental Marines on the right.[956] The young fifer-boy named Israel Trask (from the Waldoboro area) was with General Wadsworth's division. He was directed by General Wadsworth to remain sheltered behind the large granite boulder on the shore at the beach (later called Trask's Rock). Young Israel Trask played the jaunty tune of the "Rogue's March" on his fife continuously during the ascent upon the steep cliffs.[957]

Initially, the expedition went well for the American forces. Captain John Welsh and Lieutenant William Hamilton led their Continental Marine company, and Captain Philip Ulmer led his detached militia company from General McCobb's regiment. These first landing forces were assisted by a company of Penobscot Indians. The combined assault troops began scaling the hazardous precipice at Dyce's Head. The cliffs were an extremely difficult climb of approximately two hundred feet. The seemingly perpendicular cliffs on Bagaduce were hazardous under the best of conditions.[958] Once ashore, the assault troops were met by a heavy barrage of picket gunfire from Captain Campbell's troops from the cliffs above. Reuel Robinson, whose predecessor, William Robinson, was a sergeant in Captain Ulmer's company, recorded the storming of the cliffs at Bagaduce: "Captain Philip Ulmer's company of Marines was among the first to ascend the heights in the face of an opposing body of troops, the precipice being so steep that it could only be climbed by breaking ranks and each man clinging as he could to the bushes. They formed again on the summit and drove the enemy to the fort which might have been captured but for the mismanagement of those who were chief in command."[959]

Captain Philip Ulmer's state militia company and marine volunteers faced stiff resistance from Captain Campbell's British picket troops that were posted on top of the steep cliff overlooking their landing point. Captain Welsh was killed almost immediately in the assault, and Lieutenant William Hamilton soon fell mortally wounded.[960] Captain John Hinkley of Georgetown, who served with Captain Philip Ulmer in Colonel McCobb's regiment, was killed by a British sniper while he was standing on the large boulder near fifer Israel Trask while urging on his men.[961] Captain Philip Ulmer, while under intense gunfire from above, helped lead the combined assault troops on their mission to reach the top of the cliffs and to capture Fort George. The cliffs were very steep, and the men had to pull themselves up the surface of the cliff by holding onto tree branches, bushes and rock crevasses. Captain Ulmer "instructed his men to fire twice during the ascent, then to reload and make the top."[962] The British troops at the top of the cliff kept up continuous gunfire on the advancing Marines and state militiamen.[963] It was reported that "the musket balls rained down upon the American soldiers like hailstones."[964] The climb became less difficult toward the top of the heights as the slope became less angled and more navigable. Nonetheless, they cleared the bluff in less than twenty minutes, suffering thirty to thirty-five dead and many more wounded. In the overall assault, General Wadsworth reported that the Americans lost more than 25 percent of the initial landing forces.[965] Captain Philip Ulmer's company and the Continental Marines had spearheaded the initial assault upon Bagaduce, and they had suffered heavy casualties. Of the four hundred men who participated in the initial assault, the Americans suffered more than one hundred men dead, with many more men suffering various other injuries.[966] General Peleg Wadsworth's account of the climb upon Dyce's Head was that "they had lost 100 men within 20 minutes time..." General Wadsworth further compared the exploit upon Dyce's Point to "General Wolfe's heroic ascent to the Plains of Abraham at Quebec."[967]

When the British soldiers saw the Penobscot Indians, the Continental Marines and Captain Philip Ulmer's militia company clearing the top of the cliff, they quickly retreated back to their reinforced fortress. Joseph Coombs, who served with Captain Ulmer in Colonel McCobb's regiment, wrote of his observation of Captain Philip Ulmer during the landing at Dyce's Head on July 28, 1779: "I observed at the landing of the troops Capt. Ulmer behaved himself as a brave officer, and was much applauded by the Spectators."[968] Captain Ulmer's bravery and leadership were noticed, written about and commented on by officers and soldiers alike. However, Captain Philip Ulmer's name was unfortunately lacking when credit for the difficult ascent and the near success in capturing Fort George was given. Multiple notations in the ships' log books and soldiers' journals noted the difficulty and heroic ascent upon the cliffs of Bagaduce; however, the mysterious state militia captain who took initial control of the ascent at

Dyce's Head after the Continental Marine captain and his lieutenant were killed remained unknown. There was no other state militia company captain involved with the initial assault troops from General McCobb's regiment at Dyce's Head except Captain Philip Ulmer. This mysterious captain who heroically assumed command and leadership of the combined marine and militia assault troops was undoubtedly Captain Philip Ulmer.

Once ashore, the American forces under General Lovell's command moved Colonel Revere's artillery to a position only six hundred feet from Fort George.[969] General Lovell ordered the Massachusetts militiamen and Continental Marines to build entrenchments for protection on the hilltop at Bagaduce. The land at the top of peninsula had heavy tree growth except for a cleared area in the middle of the peninsula, in the vicinity of the fort and the several battery sites. The cleared section had been the farmland and corn field belonging to Jacob Dyce that had been taken over by the British troops. Instead of attacking the fort right away, General Lovell decided to build a battery at "a hundred rods" from the British lines and bombard the British into surrendering.[970] Captain Philip Ulmer's troops continued to build zigzag entrenchments as they worked their way closer to the British fort. One of the young soldiers with Captain Philip Ulmer, Christopher Neubert (also appears as Newbit and Newbirt) from Waldoboro, was severely injured when a cannon ball from a six-pounder cannon from the fort was deflected from its trajectory by a tree and his right arm was shattered and left hanging by a piece of skin from his side. In an eyewitness account, Paul Mink, who was in Captain Philip Ulmer's company from Waldoboro, stated in his Revolutionary War documents that:

> *While digging the trenches, one Christopher Newbirt* [sic] *who was with us, he was just raising himself up with a shovel full of dirt, when a 6#* [sic] *shot from the fort of the enemies, struck one of his arms, just above the elbow and shattering it so much that nothing but the skin held it on…and remember hearing him say as he fell, "I am dead!" One of the marines cut the skin which held his arm and buried it and then the captain* [Captain Ulmer] *bound up his arm and we carried him to the* [Penobscot] *river, from thence he was taken to the hospital on Fort Point, so-called…this was the second or third day after we landed in Baggaduce* [sic].[971]

General Solomon Lovell, militia commander of the land forces, sought volunteers for the purpose of making a feint upon Fort George. General Lovell was intent on drawing the enemy out of his defensive works where he could be ambushed and captured, or the British soldiers could be killed when they retreated. Eyewitness Adjutant General Jeremiah Hill wrote in his testimony to the Massachusetts General Court about the American attack on the British forces at Bagaduce: "[Captain] Philip Ulmer performed with great courage and continued to lead his men forwards inspite of his leg injury from grapeshot, brandishing his sword, and encouraging his men forward."[972]

Two soldiers in Captain Philip Ulmer's company, Alexander Kelloch of Warren and Joseph Coombs of Thomaston, volunteered to serve with Captain Philip Ulmer and other Continental Marine volunteers in this daring mission. Joseph Coombs related:

> *Captain Ulmer with his officers and upward of fifty men tendered their services in the* [enterprise] *in which Captain Ulmer received a severe wound in his thigh* [possibly the right] *which knocked him down. He was taken from the field by two marines…I was within six feet of him when he fell…before we left this field, he resumed the command tho' extremely lame, he showed me the wound, the effect was a large contusion which gave great alarm to the company, as they were warmly attached to him for his bravery.*[973]

Alexander Kelloch, a lieutenant in Captain Philip Ulmer's company, wrote in his testimony to the General Court about Captain Ulmer's injury:

> *In early August Captain Ulmer received a severe wound to his thigh which knocked him down & he was carried from the field by Lieut. Mathews & one of his soldiers. I was near him when he fell & immediately took the command of his troops* [illegible]*…before we left the field Capt Ulmer returned & assumed the command but was extremely lame & scarcely able to walk, he showed me the wound on his thigh, which was a large contusion. The thigh was very much swollen & turned blackish & discolored. This wound gave great alarm to the company who were very attached to him…I further say that I have since been acquainted with Maj. Ulmer & believe that his debilitation by* [illegible]*…& unable to perform manual labor.*[974]

Captain Philip Ulmer's soldiers highly respected him as a person and trusted his judgment in life-and-death situations. He had shown himself to be a wise and courageous leader and caring friend even under the most extreme circumstances. His company of soldiers held him in high esteem and felt great affection for him as their commanding officer. They trusted his leadership and judgment to the extent that they followed him repeatedly into the face of heavy enemy gunfire.

General Lovell ordered the next attack on August 1, and it was made at night. The object was to seize a part of the British breastworks closest to the bay where the British Royal frigates had taken shelter. This maneuver would cut off Fort George's garrison from communication with the naval support, allowing the Americans to defeat each force individually. The assault on the British breastworks at two o'clock in the morning by Colonel Samuel McCobb's center column, which included Captain Philip Ulmer's company, was successful. However, the British warships opened fire on the position, causing the American forces to retreat to their entrenchments.[975] The left column with Captain Thomas Carnes's men with a detachment of marines, and the right column composed of sailors from the fleet, continued to advance and stormed the Half Moon battery overlooking the harbor area. As dawn arrived, the guns from Fort George opened up on the captured battery. A detachment of British soldiers made a charge, routing the American troops, who took eighteen prisoners with them as they retreated. There were four American casualties and twelve wounded as a result of the engagement.[976] The result of the nighttime action caused General Lovell to be reluctant about conducting another attack on Fort George while exposed to potentially heavy land- and sea-based cannon fire. General Lovell urged Commodore Saltonstall to attack the sloops (which his naval fleet outgunned) and remove the threat to his land forces. Once the threat was removed, the American fleet's guns would be able to suppress artillery fire from Fort George during another attack by the combined state militia and Continental Marine forces on the ground.

Commodore Saltonstall decided that this action was too risky, and he continued his overly cautious behavior and delay tactics. He ordered that more batteries were needed, and he directed that Captains Haney and Westcott should build batteries up the Bagaduce River and at the isthmus to the north of the British stronghold. In the following days, General Lovell and his militia commanders, and even some of Commodore Saltonstall's own officers, pleaded with the commodore to attack the British sloops, but he ignored their pleas. Cooperation between the American land and sea forces deteriorated. Dispatching two whale boats, General Lovell sent messages back to the General Court in Boston, the Massachusetts governor and the Council of Safety about the difficulties in dealing with Commodore Saltonstall. He requested reinforcements be sent promptly while they held their positions at Bagaduce.[977] While General Lovell and his officers waited for a response, General Wadsworth wrote:

> *In the meantime we reduced our out Posts & Batteries, destroyed a considerable Quantity of Guns, spiked their cannon in all their out works & gave them fair opportunity of Sallying if they chose it. In the meantime we were employed daily, or rather Nightly in advancing upon their Fort by Zigzag intrenchments till within a fair gunshot of their Fort so that a man seldom shew* [showed] *his head above their Works. Whilst thus lying upon our Arms almost inactive 14 days, it was urged upon Genl* [General] *Lovell to erect some Place of resort up the river at the Narrows, in Case of Retreat so that the Troops might have a place of resort in case of necessity & also to have some place of Opposition to the Enemy should He push us that far—but the Genl would hear nothing of the kind; alleging that would dishearten our Army & Shew* [show] *them that we did not expect to succeed—& forgetting the good old Maxim "to keep open a good Retreat."*[978]

The Navy Board of the Eastern District ordered Commodore Saltonstall to attack the British sloops and complete the action before the British Royal Navy relief forces could arrive in the area. Reluctantly, on August 13, Commodore Saltonstall made plans to take some sort of action. By then, it was too late. There were reports that a British Royal Navy fleet from New York Harbor and from Halifax would arrive with relief forces soon. At midnight on August 13, two American warships acting as pickets spotted a British task force from New York Harbor approaching the Penobscot Bay. British commodore Sir George Collier, aboard his flagship, HMS *Raisonable*, was in command of the British Royal Navy fleet. Commodore Collier's naval forces consisted of six warships, including the sixty-four-gun ship-of-the-line *Raisonable* and four heavily armed frigates.[979] The British fleet consisted of seven armed sailing ships, one two-deck ship-of-war, two frigates, two sloops-of-war and two smaller vessels, totaling 204 guns and approximately 1,530 men.[980] Commodore Saltonstall's warships still outnumbered the British naval fleet and carried more and heavier guns than did the British vessels. The British commander at the naval shipyard at Halifax sent several naval vessels with British troops southward along the coastline of frontier Massachusetts in an effort to trap the American forces between the two converging British Royal Navy forces at Penobscot.

As the morning dawned on August 14, the American forces discovered that they were indeed trapped between the approaching British naval reinforcements. Commodore Saltonstall, having received intelligence shortly after midnight that the British fleet of ships was approaching, gave orders for an immediate retreat.[981] General Lovell wrote in his journal that the batteries were dismantled, and the artillery embarked on the transports. The fatigue parties with the entrenching tools and every other article of value were onboard by daylight, and the troops were taken aboard by sunrise. The only articles not brought aboard were two eighteen-pounders and one twelve-pounder on an island at the entrance of the harbor under the care of the officers of the U.S. Navy.[982] Orders were given to proceed up the Penobscot River under the command of General Wadsworth. General Lovell wrote in his report to the Massachusetts Committee (Court) of Inquiry that "every effort was made to secure these pieces [the cannons on the island], but time was too short, and the covering ships had withdrawn."[983] General Lovell waited for Commodore Saltonstall to try to offer resistance to the British naval fleet and enable the transports with the troops and stores to escape up the river. General Wadsworth sought information on a location up the river where a stand could be made and the American fleet could be saved.[984]

General Lovell, fearing the destruction of the fleet, tried to secure its defense by urging Commodore Saltonstall to make a line across the river and make a stand with the remaining troops.[985] Commodore Saltonstall apparently had not made contingency plans if the expedition was unsuccessful. General Lovell wrote in his journal that he "found the Commodore to be undetermined & resolute—completely unmanned."[986] Instead of making a stand against the British naval fleet, Commodore Saltonstall, whose heavily armed ships had their guns bearing broadside on the advancing British, surprisingly ordered that the American fleet (except for two armed transports) should turn about and retreat up the Penobscot River, to the astonishment of American general Lovell and British commodore Collier. Commodore Collier made no delay and attacked the American fleet boldly. The sudden attack of the British fleet had the desired effect—panic that resulted in the total retreat of Commodore Saltonstall's entire American naval fleet. The *Hunter, Hampden* and *Defence* [*sic*], in attempting to reach the sea by the western passage around Long Island, were intercepted by the British Royal Navy relief forces from Halifax.[987] The *Hunter* and *Hampden* were captured, and the *Defence* ran into an inlet and was set on fire.[988]

Commodore Saltonstall's heavily armed warship *Warren* overtook the slower troop transports that were in retreat up the Penobscot River.[989] General Wadsworth received orders from General Lovell to make a "retreat with all possible dispatch."[990] With the warship *Warren* already under sail

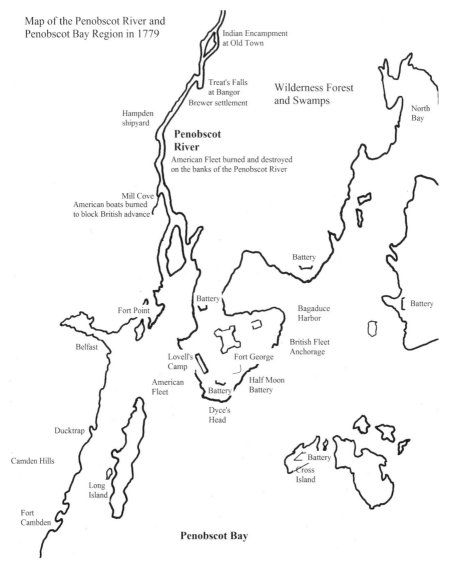

Map of the Penobscot River and
Penobscot Bay Region in 1779

Indian Encampment
at Old Town

Treat's Falls
at Bangor
Brewer settlement

Wilderness Forest
and Swamps

North
Bay

Hampden
shipyard

**Penobscot
River**

American Fleet burned and destroyed
on the banks of the Penobscot River

Mill Cove
American boats burned
to block British advance

Battery

Battery

Fort Point

Battery

Bagaduce
Harbor

Battery

Belfast

Lovell's
Camp

Fort George

British Fleet
Anchorage

American
Fleet

Battery

Half Moon
Battery

Dyce's
Head

Ducktrap

Camden Hills

Battery
Cross
Island

Long
Island

Fort
Cambden

Penobscot Bay

Map showing the Penobscot River and the Penobscot Bay region in 1779. *Courtesy of the author.*

and in full retreat, General Wadsworth evaluated their division's position. He ordered the last of his ground troops to make their retreat in whatever vessels or canoes were available. The few transport vessels that had not already fled with Commodore Saltonstall when the British fleet first made its appearance ultimately joined their counterparts in the retreat up the

Penobscot River. Eventually, the entire American fleet met its destruction on the banks of the river, some ships grounded and others set on fire. Captain Philip Ulmer, injured in his thigh by grapeshot during the siege on Fort George, had originally arrived at Bagaduce with Colonel McCobb, General Wadsworth and General Lovell.[991] During the expedition, Commodore Saltonstall and General Lovell had developed irreconcilable differences in the operation of the mission. Their deep dislike of each other had a disastrous effect on the soldiers and the mission. With the *Warren* underway with Commodore Saltonstall, General Lovell was taken aboard the *Hazard*, and the transport got underway following the retreating American naval fleet.[992] Major Todd reported: "From this point on—there was a scene of consternation and confusion. Finding there was no support from the armed vessels the transports proceeded to get underway—with the enemy closing in quickly. Nothing was thought of the crew [or soldiers] but a speedy escape on to shore. No attempt was made to save anything. Some vessels were run on shore, some anchored with all sails set…"[993]

Dr. Downer, who was the expedition's surgeon general, had complained since the initial assault on July 28 that keeping the badly wounded men in makeshift shelters of branches and sailcloth was unhealthy. As a result of his complaints, a hospital for wounded American soldiers was established at Fort Point on the remains of buildings at Fort Pownal (later called Cape Jellison) at the entrance of the Penobscot River. It was located about five miles upriver and on the opposite shore from Bagaduce. As the British continued to pursue the American fleet that was in retreat up the Penobscot River, Peleg Wadsworth took forty men to evacuate the wounded patients to the sloop *Sparrow*, which lay offshore. Among these forty men was Philip Ulmer's company of soldiers that included his cousin, Paul Mink, who recorded the event. The soldiers, most with bandaged stumps (including Christopher Neubert from Captain Ulmer's company), either walked or were carried on stretchers made from oars and coats to the Brewer and Treat houses farther up the Penobscot River near Treat's Falls (present-day Bangor).

The small boats, transports and naval vessels encountered great difficulty during their retreat up the Penobscot River because of strong tides. General Wadsworth related the difficulties that were encountered in a letter to Maine historian and governor William Williamson:

> *Our Fleet soon persued* [sic] *the Course of the transports, but soon went theirs, forcing their way through the Narrows against a strong tide with Oars & Studen* [sic] *sails all sett,* [sic] *whilst part of our Transports*

had run on shore just at the foot of the Narrows. The troops landed, the flames bursting forth from the midst of them, set by their own Crews. The Enemy persuing [sic] to within Cannon Shot but unable to persue farther against a strong tide, left those that would be persuaded to enter the Transports & rescue a small Quantity of provisions for the retreat & collect and embody themselves for their own safety. Three of four Companies were thus kept together with which I marched the next morning for Camden, where they arrived the second day & made a stand. The rest of the Troops went up the River in the Vessels of War & Transports landing as they saw fit & Genl [sic] Lovell under the guidance and Assistance of the Indians made his way to the head of the Tide in the Penobscot...In about a fortnite [sic] arrived at Townsend when was the first that I had seen or heard from him since ordering the Retreat...That part of the Fleet that got up the River ahead of the Enemy were either burnt or destroyed by their own crews making their way thro [sic] the woods in a starving condition.[994]

Many of the retreating troops went ashore at Fort Pownal (Pownall), located at the entrance of the Penobscot River.[995] The fleeing and panic-stricken men, in a dozen or more transports that were caught in the receding river tide, ran their vessels aground at Mill Cove to escape the approaching British warships that continued to fire upon them. Many men jumped overboard from the boats and ran in terror into the dense forest, while other soldiers set the boats on fire so that the British could not capture them. Several vessels of the British fleet pursued the escaping American forces for many miles up the Penobscot River with continuous gunfire. As the retreating American vessels were run aground and set on fire, the powder kegs onboard the vessels began to explode in all directions. Many frightened soldiers were hit by the exploding material, and many suffered severe burns from fires that ignited all around them. The dry August woods erupted in flames, trapping and consuming many terrified, wounded and disoriented soldiers and sailors. The British warships continued to shoot at the fleeing American militiamen and Continental Marines in the forest. Paul Mink, a soldier in Captain Philip Ulmer's company, wrote in his journal that "a British fleet came from Halifax [and] drove our vessels up the river as far as Sanders Point, where the Transport we went from Boothbay on, was burnt by us to prevent the enemy from getting hold of us, also the ship *Warren* was burnt about the same time, as was the hospital, after first taking out the wounded and sick. We slept in the woods all night and the next day marched thro [sic] the woods [to] Camden."[996]

Lieutenant Colonel Paul Revere was the commander of the artillery on the American ordnance brig that had all the artillery and ammunition on board. The ordnance brig was the sole defense of the army in case a stand should be made. The floating artillery barge had gotten clear of the transports, and not wanting the precious contents to fall into British hands, a small number of the crewmen made their way several miles up the river, where the artillery barge was deserted. The heavily armed ordnance brig was boarded by soldiers, set on fire and all of the contents were burned, with very explosive and dramatic results.[997] Shrapnel, gunpowder and wooden pieces from the flaming vessel were blown in all directions. At Mill Cove, fire quickly consumed the transports and sails. Fire spread through the undergrowth and climbed up the pine tree bark, setting the branches and tops of the trees ablaze. Flames and billowing smoke reached high into the sky as the fire spread through the forest treetops and underbrush. In the panic and confusion, the frightened militiamen, Continental Marines and citizen volunteers dispersed in all directions. Most of the soldiers and marines from the Boston and lower Massachusetts area had no idea in which direction they should go to find safety and protection from the pursuing British forces.

Officers were dispatched by General Lovell to collect and take charge of the dispersing troops. Captain Philip Ulmer made his way through the chaos and led his company in retreat to the shore near Cape Jellison. The militia hospital was located at Fort Point (present-day Cape Jellison), and the injured and burned soldiers from the expedition were being treated there. The retreating militiamen helped to evacuate their injured comrades up the river by canoes, small boats and through the woods to safety at the Brewer and Treat families' homesteads near Treat's Falls. Captain Mowat and his British warship kept up continuous gunfire as they proceeded up the Penobscot River in pursuit of the escaping soldiers. Mowat briefly anchored his armed warship near the Brewer house. Captain Mowat threatened to destroy the family settlement because they had given protection and aid to the wounded and burned American soldiers. There was a tense encounter between the Brewers and Captain Mowat on the riverbank. The British captain eventually relented and moved on, firing upon the retreating American soldiers who were trying to escape into the forest woodlands. Captain Mowat and his troops patrolled the river for several days, terrorizing the settlers on the river. Mowat eventually tired of his patrolling and left the river, satisfied that he and his troops had caused enough terror and fear to the river inhabitants, and his warship returned to its anchorage at Bagaduce.

Captain Philip Ulmer knew the Penobscot Bay well, having lived, sailed and fished in the area all his life. He successfully kept his company of soldiers from entirely dispersing during the Penobscot retreat.[998] Captain Ulmer led his men back into the woods behind the Brewer homestead and away from the enemy gunfire on the river shore. The hungry, frightened and exhausted soldiers and marines with Captain Philip Ulmer's company slept in the woods the first night. Philip, limping from his painful leg injury, attached his militia company flag to the end of a wooden pole and used it to assist him in walking. Using the pole as a standard, he led the remains of his militia company and other volunteers westward through the dense woodlands along an old Indian trail toward the safety of Fort Pine Hill. General Peleg Wadsworth and a number of the Continental Marines who were also unfamiliar with the Maine wilderness followed Captain Ulmer's leadership to the fort at Camden.[999] Captain Philip Ulmer saved the lives of numerous soldiers who would have died in the unfamiliar wilderness without his quick thinking, guidance and knowledge of the area.

General Wadsworth wrote: "…the three or four companies were thus kept together with which I marched the next morning for Camden, where they arrived the second day & made a stand."[1000] On Sunday, August 15, Colonel Jonathan Mitchell wrote in his diary that he and his troops:

> who had been lost [in the woods] *came across our Regt…of sailors and marines.* [We] *Went across a large meadow; struck a road in the woods and kept on…and proceeded on to Belfast where we arrived at 12 o'clock… Came across a river and crossed in canoes…Arrived at a fine plantation and had a good dish of tea. Genl* [Peleg] *Wadsworth and Capt.* [Ebenezer] *Buck supped with us. Had a fine barn to sleep in and rested comfortably.* [The next day, the troops] *Marched early through marches, beaches and thick woods, over mountains and valleys to Ducktrap where we arrived, the sun an hour high. One of our* [four] *prisoners deserted this morning.* [The next day, August 17,] *Set off early and traveled by the shore. Halted by Gen. Wadsworth's orders.* [We] *Arrived at the westerly part of Camden at 1 o'clock. The place called Clam Cove.* [Went to] *Headquarters and drew an allowance of fresh beef. Turned out a Sergeant's Guard and took possession of a large barn for our barracks…* [August 18] *Heard that Gen. Lovell and Admiral Saltonstall were taken by the enemy.*[1001]

The surviving soldiers began to arrive singly or in small groups to the frontier settlements after nearly a week in the wilderness, suffering from exposure and extreme hunger.[1002] A party of the troops made its way through the wilderness to Kennebec, while another party with Captain Philip Ulmer's company made its way toward the Penobscot shoreline, using a well-traveled trail, to Fort Pine Hill at Camden.[1003] Desperate for food, the soldiers consumed any edible substances that they could find. A local resident that lived near Fort Pine Hill reported: "They came into the settlement [Camden] worn out, hungry, and ravenously devoured raw green peas & whatever came to their hands—a churn of buttermilk standing at the door of Mr. Richard's house. After rest and refreshment, this party, which had 40 men, most lived in the vicinity, departed for their homes."[1004]

Upon arriving at the fort at Camden (located near Clam Cove), Captain Philip Ulmer, who was in command of the fortification at Camden in 1779–80, discussed what had happened at Bagaduce and what they should do next with his officers. They discussed the chaotic retreat up the Penobscot River; the many vessels being destroyed at the Narrows near Fort Point (the remnants of Fort Pownal and present-day Cape Jellison), which was the location of the expedition's hospital at the mouth of the Penobscot River; and the destruction of transports along the banks of the Penobscot River from Mill Cove as far north as Treat's Falls (Bangor). Captain Philip Ulmer and his company of soldiers became actively involved in guarding the local seacoast from further British attack.[1005]

Continental Army troops had been dispatched from Rhode Island to the Penobscot Bay to aid the expeditionary forces that were laying siege to Fort George at Bagaduce. Their assignment was to assist General Lovell and Commodore Saltonstall with the unexpected change of events that had occurred when British relief forces sailed from New York Harbor and from Halifax and had arrived in the Penobscot Bay region. The British fleet had trapped in the bay and routed the American forces, which made a hasty and disorganized retreat up the Penobscot River. The Continental relief troops arrived too late in the vicinity to actually participate as reinforcements for the expedition. The relief mission was abandoned, and the Continental troops were ordered to protect Falmouth (Portland) in Cumberland County from a further attack by the British warships. These relief troops (about four hundred Continental regulars) had previously participated in the Battles of Monmouth and Quaker Hill. The dispatched Continental troops with Colonel Jackson and Vose's regiment eventually returned to their duty station at Providence, Rhode Island.[1006] Sergeant

George Ulmer (Philip's brother) was with these troops with Colonel Henry Jackson's regiment at this time.

When the British threat of naval attack had passed and it was finally safe to take action, Captain Philip Ulmer took a small detached company of militiamen up the Penobscot River to evacuate any river settlers who needed assistance getting to the safety of Fort Pine Hill.[1007] The Brewer family's log house was located many miles up the Penobscot River, and it was used as a shelter for the injured and burned troops from the Penobscot Expedition. About twenty-two burned and injured men were cared for by the Brewer family. The Treat family (who lived on the river near Treat's Falls, at present-day Bangor) took care of about twenty or more burned and injured survivors. Captain Ulmer and his troops brought many of the burned and injured men back to Camden, where a house (probably the Gregory or Tolman farmhouse) had been prepared to receive and care for them. The Gregory barn served as a military barracks, and it was filled with weary soldiers. The Brewer family and about thirty other river settlers in the immediate river vicinity were move to safety in whaleboats (dories) manned by Captain Philip Ulmer's and Major Lithgow's militiamen from Fort Pine Hill. As a result of Captain Ulmer's actions during the Penobscot Expedition, he was recommended by General Wadsworth to receive advancement in rank to major.

Many militia soldiers, Continental Marines and volunteers who had participated in the Penobscot Expedition were abandoned by their officers and commanders and were left on their own in unfamiliar territory to find their way back home (many as far away as Boston) by whatever means they might find. Soldiers, marines and militiamen who were unacquainted with the wilderness frontier of eastern Massachusetts ended up lost in the dense forest and swamps, where many died of their burns and wounds or from starvation and exposure to the cold night temperatures. Unidentified human remains were found for years after the disastrous expedition, scattered for miles throughout the wilderness frontier. Many of the young soldiers left behind only bones, buckles, knives and pieces of their muskets as a testimony to their heroic service to the Continental Congress, to their state and to their new, struggling nation during the Revolutionary War.

General Solomon Lovell had not been captured by the enemy as rumored. He had been taken by some of the Penobscot Indian braves over Treat's Falls, up the river and to their Penobscot Indian village, called Indian Old Town (near present day Old Town, Maine).[1008] General Lovell remained at the Penobscot Indian village for about a fortnight before being brought back

DAR memorial to the American fleet that fought at the Battle of Valcour Island, New York, on October 11, 1776. *Courtesy of the author.*

Signing of the Declaration of Independence on July 4, 1776. By artist John Trumbull. *Courtesy of the Architect of the Capitol.*

Driving off the HMS *Carleton* at Valcour Island on Lake Champlain, October 11, 1776.
Courtesy of Ernest Haas; Lake Champlain Maritime Museum, Vergennes, Vermont.

Painting of the discovery of the gunboat *Spitfire* on the bottom of Lake Champlain. *Courtesy of artist Ernest Haas; Lake Champlain Maritime Museum, Vergennes, Vermont.*

General Horatio Gates. By Charles W. Peale. *Courtesy of the National Portrait Gallery.*

Surrender of General Burgoyne at Saratoga, New York, October 17, 1777. By John Trumbull. *Courtesy of the Architect of the Capitol and the Library of Congress.*

Cannon explosion onboard the gunboat *New York* at Valcour Island on October 11, 1776.
Courtesy of Ernest Haas; Lake Champlain Maritime Museum, Vergennes, Vermont.

The Spirit of '76. The original painting was named *Yankee Doodle* and was painted for the first Centennial Exposition held in Philadelphia. After several showings, it was suggested that the name should be changed to *The Spirit of '76.* By Archibald M. Willard. A copy of the painting hangs in Abbott Hall, Marblehead, Massachusetts. *Courtesy of the Library of Congress.*

General Washington Crossing the Delaware. By artist Emanuel Leutze. *Courtesy of the Metropolitan Museum of Art.*

Above: *General Washington Rallying His Troops at the Battle of Princeton, January 3, 1777.* By William T. Ranney. *Courtesy of the Princeton University Art Museum.*

Following pages: General Arnold's fleet coming ashore at Ferris Bay on Lake Champlain, October 13, 1776. *Courtesy of Ernest Haas; Lake Champlain Maritime Museum, Vergennes, Vermont.*

The *Philadelphia* sinking and being assisted by the galley *Washington*, Battle of Valcour Island, Lake Champlain, October 11, 1776. *Courtesy of Ernest Haas; Lake Champlain Maritime Museum, Vergennes, Vermont.*

Cannons mounted on Mount Defiance overlooking Fort Ticonderoga, New York. The La Chute River from Lake George (to the left or west of the fort) and the Little Wood Creek from Skenesboro (to the south of the fort) combine together at Fort Ticonderoga and flow northward past Crown Point and into Lake Champlain. *Courtesy of the author.*

General Burgoyne's Surrender at Saratoga. By Percy Moran. *Courtesy of the Library of Congress and the Architect of the Capitol.*

Painting of Washington and Lafayette at Valley Forge. By artist John W. Dunsmore. *Courtesy of the Library of Congress.*

Evacuation of the gunboat *Spitfire* near Schuyler Island, New York, on October 12, 1776. *Courtesy of artist Ernest Haas, Lake Champlain Maritime Museum, Vergennes, Vermont.*

General Henry Knox's mansion, Montpelier, at Thomaston, Maine. *Courtesy of the Library of Congress.*

Left: Picture of the Lincolnville harbor as seen from Ducktrap cove at low tide. The Revolutionary War and War of 1812 cemetery where Major Philip Ulmer is buried is located to the left of the picture at "The Point." *Courtesy of the author.*

Right: A salvaged cannon used in the defense of Lincolnville (Maine) during the British invasion campaign from Halifax, Canada, in August–September 1814 in frontier Maine District. *Courtesy of the author.*

The landing area where the American Continental marines and Captain Philip Ulmer with his militia company from McCobb's regiment began their treacherous climb up Dyce's Head on the Bagaduce Peninsula during the Battle of Penobscot Bay in 1779. *Courtesy of David Van Horn.*

Grave of Major Philip Ulmer and his wife, Christiana, at the Revolutionary War and War of 1812 cemetery at Ducktrap harbor-cove in Lincolnville, Maine. *Courtesy of the author.*

to a nearby port settlement by the Indians. After settling his arrangements for military reinforcements and other matters, General Lovell was taken by boat to Boston on September 20.[1009] General Lovell returned to Boston to face a Committee of Inquiry (also called the Court of Inquiry) appointed by the Massachusetts General Assembly to investigate the failure of the Penobscot Expedition.

Colonel Jackson's Continental Army regiment from Rhode Island, which had been dispatched to the Penobscot River to assist in the expedition, arrived too late. Admiral Collier's British naval forces arrived ahead of Jackson's troops. Jackson's troops withdrew and did not participate in the Penobscot campaign. Instead the troops were redirected to Falmouth (present-day Portland), where they remained briefly before returning to their station at Rhode Island. General Lovell later joined Colonel Jackson's troops at the Kennebec outpost.[1010] Sergeant George Ulmer, Philip's brother, was with Colonel Jackson's troops at this time. Jackson's troops returned to Providence, Rhode Island, and George Ulmer remained with Colonel Vose's regiment at Rhode Island with the Continental Army until his three-year enlistment was completed on March 15, 1780.[1011]

The Abenaki-Penobscot Indians remained faithful to the American side even under the pressure of British commander General McLean, who tried to turn the Indians against the American settlers, troops and volunteers.[1012] To their credit, the Abenaki Indians in the Penobscot region remained true to their promise made to General Washington at the beginning of the Revolutionary War in 1775. Lieutenant Andrew Gilman, who commanded the Indians who operated with Captain Philip Ulmer's company, stated that the Penobscot Indians who served in the Penobscot Expedition "acted with fidelity and friendship towards the Americans."[1013] Approximately forty-one Indians from the Penobscot tribe lost their lives in the Penobscot campaign. The Indians who were killed during the Penobscot Expedition were recovered and buried according to the Indian tradition and rituals. The brave militia soldiers, Continental Marines and volunteers still lie in silence, many unidentified and in unmarked graves at Bagaduce (later called Castine).

Of the utter confusion and chaos that followed the retreat, General Lovell wrote in his official report that "an attempt to give a description of this terrible Day is out of my Power. It would be fit Subject for some masterly hand to describe it in its true colours [sic], to see four Ships persuing [sic] seventeen Sail of Armed Vessells [sic] nine of which were stout Ships, Transports on fire, Men of War blowing up, Provision of all kinds

& every kind of Stores on Shore throwing about, and as much confusion as can possibly by conceived."[1014] The destruction of the American fleet was complete, with only two vessels falling into enemy hands. At the time, Secretary of State Timothy Pickering of Salem understated: "Our Naval affairs are shocking and our Commanders are shamefully bad."[1015] Brigadier General Peleg Wadsworth wrote on September 29, 1779, that "the Failure of the Expedition under Enquiry seems to me to be owing principally to the Lateness of our Arrival before the Enemy, the Smallness of our Land Forces, & the uniform Backwardness of the Commander of the Fleet."[1016]

The American fleet that participated in the Penobscot Expedition included sixteen armed ships and privateering vessels from New Hampshire and Massachusetts, as well as three Continental Navy men-of-war, totaling 344 guns in all. This was the largest fleet assembled by the Americans during the Revolutionary War.[1017] The three British armed sloops at Bagaduce totaled 56 guns. If proper action had been taken in a timely fashion before the arrival of British naval reinforcements from Halifax and New York City, the American naval squadron commanded by Commodore Saltonstall could have achieved a successful outcome. Casualty estimates ran as high as five hundred men lost and presumed dead.[1018]

The captain of the warship *Warren*, flagship of Commodore Saltonstall, noted in the ship's logbook the bravery of Captain Welsh, who led his company of Continental Marines; the unknown militia captain (Captain Philip Ulmer), who led his company of soldiers from Colonel McCobb's Lincoln County regiment; and the Penobscot Indians on the initial assault at Bagaduce. The observers on the many transports involved in the Penobscot Expedition later wrote in their journals and testimonials about the brave soldiers, who were less than one hundred men, and their amazing climb up the dangerous cliffs at Dyce's Head. The official reports noted that Captain John Welsh was killed at the start of the assault on the steep slope at Bagaduce, and his lieutenant, William Hamilton, also fell mortally wounded. Another fourteen marines and militiamen were killed initially, and twenty more were wounded by the British snipers shooting down at them from the cliffs above.[1019] The heroic actions of Captain Philip Ulmer and his men were noted in the logs and journals during the initial scaling of the cliffs at Dyce's Head and also when he assumed the leadership role of the marines when their commanding officer and first lieutenant were killed by enemy musket fire. The observers did not know Captain Ulmer's name but simply noted his actions and leadership during the steep climb while under heavy enemy gunfire from above. As daring and heroic as Philip Ulmer's actions were during the Penobscot Expedition, Captain Philip Ulmer was one of the many unknown combatants whose valor and dedication to duty has gone unrecognized and unrecorded in history.

The heavy casualties from the initial surge were later buried upon the more level ground above Trask's Rock (later called Hinkley's Rock). The remains of the dead, almost one-third of the initial assault troops, included casualties from Captain Philip Ulmer's company. Approximately five hundred American marines, state militiamen and volunteers were eventually listed as killed or missing as a result of the Penobscot Expedition.[1020] The Penobscot Indians insisted on conducting their own burial rights, according to their native tradition, for the Indian warriors who died at Bagaduce. Unfortunately, the Indians who died in the Penobscot Expedition were not accounted for in the final reports. The land surface at Duce's field has been changed with time, and the exact locations of the soldiers' bodies has been difficult to designate; however, more than one hundred men who were with the initial assault troops under General Lovell's command and Peleg Wadsworth's command were buried above the cliffs at Dyce's Head.[1021] The fragments of the destroyed American naval fleet, remnants of old cannons and human remains were the only testament left behind of the struggle to expel the invading British forces from their stronghold at Bagaduce.

Considering the obstacles faced and the intense British gunfire from enemy snipers from above, according to Maine historians, the assault on Dyce's Head was "one of the most distinguished feats in American military history, calling for rare skill, determination, and individual heroism. From the standpoint of sheer 'guts', it outranks the better known feat of General Wolfe's men scaling the cliffs at Quebec, which were no higher, where a well-beaten path which they were not forced to climb under heavy [enemy] fire. Certainly no one in the world other than backwoodsmen could have accomplished such a miracle."[1022]

Governor William D. Williamson, in 1839, wrote: "It was afterwards fully ascertained that General McLean [who held the British military command of Fort George on Bagaduce] was prepared to capitulate, if surrender had been demanded… There was not a more brilliant exploit of itself during the war than this."[1023]

The outcome of the Penobscot Expedition would have likely been successful if the initial attacking American land forces had been permitted by General Lovell to continue to press their assault on Fort George with sufficient support from additional land and naval forces, commanded by Commodore Saltonstall. The surrender of the partially built and scarcely defensible British fort at Bagaduce would likely have been tendered to Captain Philip Ulmer with the fifty surviving soldiers and Continental Marines. British general Francis McLean stated later in a meeting at the fort with Colonel Brewer, an officer in General Lovell's staff: "I believe the commanders were a pack of cowards or they would have taken me. I was in no situation to defend myself, I only meant to give them one or two guns, so as not to be called a coward, and then have struck my colours [sic], which I stood for some time to do, as I did not wish to throw away the lives of my men for nothing."[1024]

The Massachusetts General Court appointed a Committee of Inquiry to investigate and determine the cause of the failed expedition. General Artemas Ward was the president of the Committee of Inquiry.[1025] The court-martial hearings were held on board the Continental frigate *Deane* on October 25, 1779. There was an extensive court-martial investigation into the cowardice charges against Colonel Paul Revere and incompetence charges against Commodore Saltonstall. Commodore Dudley Saltonstall, who was in command of the Penobscot Expedition, would not attack Captain Mowat's three Royal Navy ships and marine forces that were anchored in the Bagaduce Harbor and disable them. Fearing a great loss of life from the cannon fire of the enemy ships and the fort, General Lovell would not give permission for the ground troops to assault Fort George and capture it until the enemy ships were destroyed. General Lovell and General Wadsworth were acquitted of wrongdoing, and they did not face a court-martial for their actions in the failed Penobscot Expedition. Commodore Saltonstall and Colonel Paul Revere did face court-martial charges for their cowardly behavior and failed leadership. Commodore Saltonstall was found guilty of his charges and subsequently left the military service; however, he later became a successful privateer and a wealthy businessman. Colonel Paul Revere was found guilty of cowardice and failed leadership but appealed the charges, and he was eventually exonerated. These high-profile court-martial cases overshadowed the bravery of Captain Philip Ulmer's company of state militiamen, the Continental Marines and the Penobscot Indians in the expedition. Their story was one of success in accomplishing their nearly impossible mission in the initial ground assault. Those brave men led the initial climb on the steep cliffs at Dyce's Head while under heavy gunfire, they routed and forced the retreat of the British soldiers into Fort George, and they would have captured General McLean and the British forces at Bagaduce if they had been given the order to do so.[1026]

The Penobscot Expedition was viewed as a spectacular failure, mostly due to poor cooperation among the commanders of the land and sea forces and Commodore Saltonstall's failure to engage the British Royal Navy forces in a timely manner. Colonel Mitchell testified before the Committee of Inquiry that "if the British shipping had been destroyed and the land forces had been aided by men of the fleet, armed with [sufficient] muskets, they could have destroyed the enemy… The British fleet could have been crushed a day before they were reinforced."[1027]

Adjutant General Jeremiah Hill, who served on General Lovell's staff, testified that: "[The] soldiers were very poorly equipped, the chief of them had arms but many of them were out of repair and very little or no ammunition…"[1028] The General Court of Massachusetts determined "that Commodore Saltonstall being incompetent ever after to hold a commission in the service of the State, and that Generals Lovell and Wadsworth be honorably acquitted."[1029]

CAPTAIN PHILIP ULMER'S CONTINUED DEDICATION TO THE MILITARY SERVICE

Evidence of Captain Philip Ulmer's continued military service and his concern and compassion for the safety of the Penobscot Bay inhabitants are best described in the following communication to Brigadier General Charles Cushing following the Penobscot naval disaster:

Penobscot, Oct. 4, 1779

SIR:—By order of Major Lithgow I proceeded to Penobscot River. I have the pleasure to inform you the inhabitants appear very friendly to the American cause, but are in a most deplorable condition; they are ordered by Gen. McLean to repair immediately to Maja-Bagaduce to work on the fort erected there: in case of failure Gen. McLean is determined to turn and destroy their interests and deem the inhabitants rebels. It is impossible for so many families to get all through the woods and there is no carriage by water. They had determined to carry on their places, if they can have a guard sufficient to protect them. I am fully convinced it is my duty to recommend to you in the strongest terms in their behalf, that you will take into consideration their distress and send them immediate relief—either boats to remove them, or men sufficient to guard them here which cannot be less than two or three hundred: as to provisions, may be had here sufficient to supply them.

I am Sir,
Philip Ulmer, Captain[1030]
Brig. Cushing
Communicated by Joseph Williamson, Esq.

Two months after the Penobscot Expedition, Captain Philip Ulmer was ordered by General Cushing to proceed to his assignment at Fort Halifax on the Kennebec River with his scouting party of sixteen soldiers. His orders were to protect the inhabitants in the best manner possible until Major William Lithgow could send more soldiers from Fort Pine Hill to assist Captain Ulmer's company. The report written by General Charles Cushing on October 18, 1779, from the militia headquarters in Pownalborough stated:

Inclosed [sic] *is a Letter sent express by two men from Penobscot through the woods by way of Fort-Halifax from Capt Ulmer who is there with a Scouting party of about sixteen Men—In consequence of which I have ordered a Company of Men to March from Fort-Halifax to Penobscot & there Protect the Inhabitants in the best manner in their Power until the time for which they were detach'd shall expire which will be the first of next month…have also directed Major Lithgow to send a Company from Cambden to Co-operate with them at certain seasons as he can spare the men from that Quarter… Have also appointed Mr Jedediah Prebble of Penobscot to Supply the men that may be sent there with provisions…I have stationed some troops at the mouth of Kennebeck River where it will be needful to Continue them & in several other places, but principally at Cambden—where it is likely the greatest number of Men may be stationed…*[1031]

THE OUTCOME OF THE PENOBSCOT CAMPAIGN

The initiative for the Penobscot Expedition was mostly undertaken by the State of Massachusetts and almost wholly funded by the state. The Massachusetts government insured all of the private transport vessels; paid the crews; supplied the state militia; provided the weapons, ammunition and stores; and bore the heavy loss of the expedition. The huge financial loss effectively bankrupted the state. The financial loss in U.S. dollars today could be conservatively estimated at about $300 million.[1032] The Penobscot Expedition in 1779 had been approved, but lightly supported, by the Continental Congress, which sent only three naval warships—the *Warren*, the *Diligent* and the *Providence*—with their Continental Marine detachments from Boston Harbor. Permission to deploy the Continental Navy warships had been sought and received by the Continental Navy Board. This meant that a small portion of the defeated forces had been federally sanctioned. Since the naval disaster was blamed on Saltonstall's incompetence, the other colonies would be made to recompense Massachusetts for the financial loss of the expedition. Commodore Saltonstall was found guilty of gross negligence and for betraying the whole expedition with his obstinate and indecisive behavior. It was not until 1793 that the federal government of the United States largely reimbursed Massachusetts for its financial loss in the 1779 Penobscot Expedition. Future proposals by the Massachusetts General Court to mount an expedition to dislodge the British forces from the fort at Castine (formerly Bagaduce) would be abandoned due to the lack of money and the need for additional troops, military supplies and provisions. The American citizens in the Province of Maine felt more and more isolated and defenseless against the pillaging, plundering and incursions of the British troops and their Tory and Loyalist associates. The colony of Massachusetts did not have the currency or resources to supply the growing needs of the frontier Province of Maine, which was under increasing attack from enemy invasion. Cumberland, York and Lincoln Counties in the frontier region of Massachusetts would have to find a means to provide for their own basic needs of survival.

The disastrous American retreat up the Penobscot River, and total defeat, had resulted from the poor leadership and lack of cooperation among the top commanding officers of the Penobscot Bay operation. The American forces lost approximately forty-three vessels of various types that were sunk, scuttled or burned by the American troops along the banks of the Penobscot River to keep the vessels out of the hands of the British forces. The tragic naval disaster along the shores of the Penobscot Bay and River composed most of the American naval fleet. In the initial assault on the British stronghold on Castine (Bagaduce), the American forces lost approximately 35 percent of the Continental Marines and Massachusetts militia volunteers from Colonel McCobb's regiment, as well as a number of Penobscot Indians who climbed the cliffs at Dyce's Head.[1033]

The Penobscot Expedition has never been acknowledged for its true importance in the planned strategy of British conquest and dominance in America. The incursion was the first step in England's larger plan to establish the new colony of New Ireland in the Maine Province and expand its imperialism throughout the North American continent. This was an important naval battle disaster that was part of the American Revolution, but American history is silent about its significance. The struggle for dominance in the Penobscot region and the final determination of the American-Canadian border in North America would not be decided until the final signing of the treaty that ended the War of 1812. Other Revolutionary War battles and battlefields have been recognized, and the sacrifices of the many thousands of American servicemen and volunteers who fought and died for American freedom have been recognized. Naval historians have stated that in terms of the number of ships lost as a result of the Penobscot Expedition, it was the largest naval disaster in American history until the surprise attack on Pearl Harbor on December 7, 1941.[1034]

PHILIP ULMER'S HEROIC LEADERSHIP

[Captain] *Philip Ulmer performed with great courage and continued to lead his men forwards inspite of his leg injury from grapeshot, brandishing his sword, and encouraging his men forward.*
—Adjutant General Jeremiah Hill[1035]

While under heavy enemy fire from above, Captain Philip Ulmer bravely led his company of militia volunteers in climbing the high cliffs at Dyce's Head with the first assault troops of the Continental Marines that landed on Bagaduce. Once the heights were scaled, he led his men in an attack on the British snipers in Captain Archibald Campbell's picket guard, forcing them to retreat to Fort George. Captain Philip Ulmer led his company in a charge upon Fort George, where General McLean and his regiment of British soldiers were held under siege. General McLean and his officers were prepared to surrender to the American troops after firing several shots.[1036] The final attack on the fort was called off due to a disagreement in procedure, tactics and strategy between the land and sea commanders, General Lovell and Commodore Saltonstall. With the arrival of Admiral Collier's fleet and British reinforcements, Saltonstall ordered the American fleet to retreat up the Penobscot River. Captain Philip Ulmer was successfully able to keep his frightened men together during the chaotic retreat up the Penobscot and the fiery destruction of the transports and Continental Navy vessels on the banks of the river. He and his company assisted General Wadsworth in the evacuation of the injured troops at Fort Point (at Cape Jellison) to safety up the river. He led his company and other displaced Continental Marines with General Wadsworth through the forest wilderness to Fort Pine Hill at Camden. Captain Philip Ulmer earned the respect of General Peleg Wadsworth through his leadership, courage and devotion to duty while in severe pain with an injury to his thigh from enemy grapeshot. A strong friendship was forged between Captain Philip Ulmer and General Wadsworth during the heat of enemy gunfire and flaming destruction of the fleet on the banks of the river during the Penobscot Expedition.

General Solomon Lovell was not charged with dereliction of duty, nor was Colonel McCobb or Colonel Peleg Wadsworth. After the Penobscot court-martial hearing, Wadsworth was advanced in rank to brigadier general. He was appointed as the commander of the Defense of the Eastern Frontier of Massachusetts in March 1780.

General McLean feared a second attack on Fort George to remove the British forces from their outpost at Castine.[1037] Following the defeat of the American naval fleet up the Penobscot River, he redoubled his efforts to complete the fortress, the barracks and the batteries on the strategic peninsula and surrounding islands. Captain Mowat patrolled and forcefully threatened the residents of the Penobscot Bay region. General McLean sent British raiding parties to coastal towns and villages along the local rivers, where they sought to capture the isolated and defenseless settlers to impress them into British service as laborers to build the British barracks, forts and other defensive structures. Appeals for protection were made to General Charles Cushing by the local residents along the river settlements for state militia soldiers and assistance since they were easy prey to the British harassment and raiding parties. On October 18, 1779, General Charles Cushing wrote a letter from the state militia headquarters at Pownalboro in frontier Maine to the president of the Massachusetts Bay Congress that he had sent Captain Philip Ulmer and his company of sixteen militiamen to reconnoiter the situation in the area of Fort Halifax on the upper Kennebec River. (Fort Halifax was the fort from which Arnold's expedition to Canada had departed in the fall of 1775.)

Families along the Kennebec River and Penobscot River received help from Captain Philip Ulmer and his militia company. Captain Ulmer and his soldiers evacuated the residents to the protection of Fort Pine Hill at Camden. (Cambden, the original spelling, was located in Camden Township.) Captain Philip Ulmer wrote to General Cushing again on October 28, 1779, about the conditions at the Penobscot:

> *Sir: by order of Majr* [sic] *Lithgow I proceeded to penobscott* [sic] *river to have the pleasure to inform you the inhabitants there appear to be very friendly to the American Cause but are in a most Deplorable Condition...they are ordered by Genl Mclain* [sic] *to repair immediately to magerbagaduce* [sic] *to work on the fort erected there in Case of failure. Genl Mclain is Determind* [sic] *to burn & destroy their Interests & Deem the inhabitants Rebels. It is impossible for so many families to git* [sic] *off through the woods & there is no Carrage* [sic] *by water...& they have Determind* [sic] *to tarry on their places if they can have a gaurd* [sic] *Sufficient to protect them...I am fully Convine'd* [sic] *it is my Incumbent Duty to you Sir...in the most Strongest terms in their behalf that you will take into your Consideration their Distress & Send them Emmediate* [sic] *Relief... either Boats to remove them off or men Sufficient to guard them here which Cannot be less than twp* [two] *or three Hundred...as to provisions may be had here Sufficient to Supply them...*
>
> *I am Sir your most obedt* [sic] *Humble Serv't.*
> —*Philip Ulmer Capt* [1038]

Since his first letter of October 4 to General Cushing did not see results, Philip Ulmer wrote a similar letter about the distressing conditions of the small settlements on the Kennebec and Penobscot Rivers, again bringing to the general's attention the need for immediate relief in evacuating the families and militia assistance and protection from British raiding parties at Castine. Inhabitants of the Kennebec River and Penobscot River settlements were evacuated primarily through the woods or by small boat when available by Captain Philip Ulmer's company of militiamen. The inhabitants were taken to the protection of the fort at Camden or to other settlements where they might have relatives who could support and assist them in their distress. The British warships continued to patrol the Penobscot Bay and Passamaquoddy Bay region and kept tight control of the Massachusetts frontier region from Eastport to Falmouth.

By December 1779, Fort George was in a state of good defense. Bomb-proof apartments were built in three of the bastions, and batteries were erected at various strategic points around the peninsula.[1039] Barracks were built for officers and soldiers, and before winter set in, the British troops were well housed, well clothed and well fed, which was a striking contrast to the harsh conditions that General Washington's army faced in tents, without proper clothing and few provisions at Morristown, New Jersey, during the bitter cold winter of 1780–81. After several months, General McLean was ordered to Halifax in 1781, where he soon died. Colonel Archibald Campbell, General McLean's successor at Castine, remained as commandant at Fort George for several years until the end of the war.[1040]

The actions of Captain Philip Ulmer and his detached company, the Penobscot Indians and the Continental Marines appear in the writings of General Solomon Lovell and Colonel Peleg Wadsworth. Their testimonies before the Committee of Inquiry of the General Court of Massachusetts have been recorded and are on file in the statehouse in Boston and appear in the Massachusetts Archives, the National Archives and Records Administration and the records of the Congressional House of Representatives. In support of Major Philip Ulmer's petition for a government pension as an injured Revolutionary War officer, soldiers who had served under his command gave eyewitness accounts of his heroic leadership at Bagaduce and his ability to keep his company together during the chaotic aftermath of the disastrous retreat up the Penobscot River. The pension petition was introduced by Representative Benjamin Brown to the Continental Congress and referred to the Honorable Mr. Chappell, chairman of the Committee on Pensions and Revolutionary Claims.[1041] Philip Ulmer was examined by two doctors from the District of Maine—Ezekiel G. Dodge and Isaac Bernard of Thomaston—who were approved physicians and surgeons. They wrote statements concerning Philip Ulmer's injured leg and a description of the disability that he incurred during the Revolutionary War. Judge David Sewall wrote a verification of the examination, and Jonathan Hall, justice of the peace, also verified the examination by the two doctors. Major Philip Ulmer's petitions were later approved by the Fourteenth U.S. Congress in Session One on January 11, 1816.[1042]

Confusion About the Ulmers

Some historical accounts are unclear as to which of the Ulmer brothers, Philip or George, was in the Penobscot Bay region in early 1778 to early 1780. Popular accounts from past historians cite George Ulmer, Philip's brother, as being the "Captain Ulmer" involved in the construction of militia fortifications at Fort Pine Hill and mounting of the eighteen-pounder cannon on the Penobscot Bay prior to the Penobscot Expedition in 1779. Some accounts cite George Ulmer as having been actively involved in the Penobscot Expedition, but this is not the case. George Ulmer was an enlisted soldier with the rank of sergeant at this time with the Continental Army at Providence, Rhode Island, from January 18, 1779, to January 18, 1780, in Colonel Vose's regiment, according to his military records.[1043] Because of supply issues in Boston, the Continental Army's relief forces were delayed. Sergeant George Ulmer's Vose's regiment was among the relief troops with Colonel Jackson's brigade that arrived in the frontier region at the end of the Penobscot Expedition. Colonel Henry Jackson's brigade was not involved with the American forces during the attack on Fort George at Castine or the retreat up the Penobscot River. The relief naval ships did not arrive in time to assist Saltonstall's retreating American fleet but sailed instead to Portsmouth, New Hampshire, where they stayed briefly before returning to their assignment at Providence, Rhode Island. According to George Ulmer's official military records with the secretary of the Commonwealth of Massachusetts in Boston and in the official government book *Massachusetts Soldiers and Sailors in the Revolutionary War*, Volume XVI, he was not in frontier Maine until the end of March 1780 after the winter thaw. He returned to Waldoboro with his bride, Mary Tanner, whom he married while stationed at Providence, Rhode Island.

George Ulmer has also been erroneously credited by some early historians and writers in Maine as the Ulmer brother who rescued the inhabitants on the Kennebec and Penobscot Rivers from British raiding parties and harassment after the Penobscot Expedition. This could not be the case since he was with Colonel Vose's regiment that was stationed at Providence at this time. It was actually Captain Philip Ulmer and his small company of men that successfully evacuated the inhabitants of the river settlements. George's elder brother, Captain Philip Ulmer, was actually the "Captain Ulmer" referred to in the old historical accounts and noted incidents that took place in frontier Maine in 1778 through 1780. He was in command of Fort Pine Hill at Camden (Cambden, old spelling) in 1779–80, prior to and after the Penobscot Expedition in the summer of 1779. Philip Ulmer was promoted to the rank of major on March 25, 1780, as a result of his leadership and courageous actions during the Penobscot Expedition. Major Philip Ulmer was in direct service to General Peleg Wadsworth and appears in the military records in command at Fort Pine Hill at Camden from March 25 to November 25.[1044]

The brave actions of Captain Philip Ulmer during the Penobscot Expedition are proven in the writings of Adjutant General Jeremiah Hill, who was on General Lovell's staff, and in communications with General Charles Cushing at his state militia headquarters in Pownalboro. Further support is found in eyewitness accounts of several state militiamen who served in Philip Ulmer's company, as well as in Philip's own account of the engagements in his government petition for pension to the U.S. Congress. General Cushing's letter to the Honorable Jeremiah Powell, president of the Massachusetts Provincial Congress, on October 18, 1779, and Captain Philip Ulmer's report to General Cushing on October 4 and October 28, 1779, about the situation of the inhabitants in the Kennebec and Penobscot areas clearly prove that Philip Ulmer was the officer involved in these activities in the frontier region in the fall of 1779 and the winter of 1780 and not his brother, George Ulmer. Confirming evidence can be found in the book *Documentary History of the State of Maine*, Volume XVII, by James P. Baxter and in the *Collections of the Maine Historical Society*, Second Series.

References citing George Ulmer in the Waldoboro and in the Penobscot region prior to March 1780 are not correct, according to the official government records. From the above references, it is clear that Captain Philip Ulmer participated in the Penobscot Bay encounters and was the rescuer of distressed inhabitants living along the Kennebec and Penobscot Rivers. George Ulmer left the Continental Army in Rhode Island in late January 1780 when his three-year enlistment was completed. George Ulmer stayed with his wife's family in Rhode Island before visiting with Ulmer relatives in the Marblehead/Salem vicinity. George did not return to Waldoboro in frontier Maine until late March 1780. Upon George's return to Waldoboro, he enlisted as an adjutant in the state militia in Colonel Prime's regiment. Major Philip Ulmer and his detached company were on special assignment with Colonel Prime's regiment. They were involved in building forts and barracks and preparing armed defenses in order to fortify vulnerable coastal seaports and towns along the Massachusetts frontier of Maine Province.[1045] Major Ulmer's brother, George, became a part of this effort to defend the seacoast.

Chapter 14

The War Ends in Maine

Devastating Effect on the Economy in the Eastern Frontier

The complete disaster of the Penobscot campaign had many effects on the frontier Province of Maine and on Massachusetts as a whole. Since Massachusetts had financed the expedition, the cost of fifty thousand British pounds was added to the state's debt. That meant that more taxes would be levied on the citizens of Massachusetts and the Province of Maine. The inflation of currency, which was already high because of the ongoing war, had now become about forty to one. In Falmouth, a bushel of corn was thirty-five dollars; of wheat meal, seventy-five dollars; of molasses, sixteen dollars per gallon; and nineteen dollars bought a pound of tea.[1046] Debts and overextended credit were causing serious problems for people throughout the state of Massachusetts. The heavy taxes and the demands for more soldiers and supplies for the Continental Army were crushing for the citizens. Most of the merchant transports and cargo vessels in the frontier region were destroyed or greatly damaged. Coastal trade was blocked by vessels of the British fleet, and an embargo on shipping was in effect that caused Massachusetts businesses to become paralyzed. Food was scarce because of severe droughts, and people throughout the state of Massachusetts, especially in the frontier District of Maine, were sick and dying from disease, malnutrition and the extreme weather conditions.

The British enemy had secured its stronghold on Bagaduce and continued its tight blockade along the New England seacoast. There was an influx of Tories and Loyalists moving into the Province of Maine from other parts of New England to enjoy the protection of the British forces in the Penobscot region.[1047] Small raiding parties from the British regiments at Bagaduce (hereafter Castine) joined with local Loyalists who had been displaced during the war and with Tory settlers who moved to the Province of Maine to enjoy the protection of the British forces at Castine. They started small-scale raids of plunder and retaliation against the American sympathizers and Patriots in the three counties of Maine Province.[1048] These enemy raids continued until the end of the war and beyond. The new state constitution for Massachusetts, which had been under discussion for many months and written as a draft, was finally completed in January 1780.[1049] It was printed and sent to all the plantations, settlements and towns in the Province of Maine for ratification, which required a majority vote of two-thirds from each town. Approval was finally achieved, and the document went into effect at the end of October 1780.*

British troops from Castine continued to stir unrest in the frontier region of easternmost Massachusetts. Raiding parties were sent out to the coastal communities in an attempt to capture prominent citizens and military officers, who were brought to the fort and imprisoned. This was an effort to undermine the leadership of the towns and cripple the ability of the militia command to operate. There seems to have been an attempt to negotiate the release of prisoners who were prominent military officers or community leaders and had been captured or kidnapped from local coastal towns and villages. The winter, from December 1779 until mid-March of 1780 in Lincoln County, was particularly cold and severe. The snow was many feet deep, and the coast of frontier Maine Province along the Penobscot Bay was frozen to its mouth and some distance out to sea (some sources indicated several miles out to sea).[1050] People were able to pass over the rivers and over the Penobscot Bay to the opposite shore on the ice. Philip Ulmer was in command of a company of state militiamen stationed at Fort Pine Hill in Camden (present-day Rockland, Maine) during this

---

* *Author's comment*: The Massachusetts state constitution remained unchanged until March 15, 1820, when the Province of Maine separated from Massachusetts and became the twenty-third state. The first governor of Maine was John Hancock, who was actively involved throughout the American Revolution.[1051]

time. In February, Ulmer sent Lieutenant Benjamin Burton under a flag of truce to obtain the release of a prisoner at Castine by walking across the frozen Penobscot Bay.[1052] Eliakim Libbey had been captured a number of weeks before on a schooner cut out of the ice on the Westkeag River that was loaded with lumber for the West Indies. Lieutenant Burton passed from Camden over the ice to Bagaduce. The picket guards who patrolled the peninsula regularly and the sentinels who manned the walls of Fort George day and night were very alarmed and suspicious as Lieutenant Burton approached Castine to speak with the commanding officer at Fort George and deliver a message from his commanding officer, Philip Ulmer. Ulmer's message to the British commander was successful. Lieutenant Burton was returned to his outpost at Fort Pine Hill on the opposite shore over the ice with the released American prisoner.[1053]

In March 1780, General Wadsworth was appointed to command the Eastern Department for the whole District of Maine, and he had been empowered to raise a company of volunteers in Lincoln County to serve under his command.[1054] Among the first acts of General Wadsworth when he arrived at his new duty station was the promotion of Captain Philip Ulmer to the rank of major. He remembered Philip Ulmer from earlier encounters to be an honorable, trustworthy and energetic soldier. Philip Ulmer enlisted in Colonel Joseph Prime's state militia regiment from March 25, 1780, to November 25, 1780. Philip Ulmer was advanced in rank to first major before the end of November 1780 with Colonel Prime's regiment.[1055] Philip Ulmer received his commission as a second major on March 27, 1780.[1056] He was thanked by General Wadsworth and other state militia officers for his faithfulness to duty during the Penobscot Expedition and his contributions of military service to the American cause during the ongoing Revolutionary War. Brigadier General Peleg Wadsworth appointed Philip to serve on his staff in defense of Eastern Massachusetts at Thomaston, where his military headquarters was located.[1057] Major Philip Ulmer was given a horse to facilitate his duties while in service to General Wadsworth.[1058] Major Ulmer was appointed by General Wadsworth to command a company of state militiamen at Fort Pine Hill in Camden for the frontier defense of the Eastern Department.[1059]

Major Philip Ulmer appeared on General Wadsworth's list of officers appointed to a special command of detached soldiers. Major Ulmer's company was made up of chosen men from the three militias of York, Cumberland and Lincoln Counties, and it was detached from Colonel Prime's regiment for special operations in the defense of

Massachusetts.[1060] His assignment was to construct forts and barracks as well as to build defenses in strategic locations to defend against attacks by British troops and British warships stationed at Castine and Halifax.[1061] In mid-April, the ice had melted in the rivers of frontier Maine, and General Wadsworth proceeded to establish his military headquarters at Thomaston on the eastern side of the Medomak River near St. George village.[1062] One of his first acts was to impose martial law throughout the District of Maine in an attempt to stem the smuggling and illegal trading among some of the inhabitants in the Maine District and the British enemy.[1063] General Wadsworth issued a proclamation that forbade communication and support to the enemy with serious consequences for those who ignored his orders.

General Wadsworth had been promised six hundred troops by the Massachusetts General Court to enforce martial law and blunt the enemy attacks in the eastern frontier of Massachusetts.[1064] He received about half of the number of troops that were promised, and he received no logistical support. Massachusetts was impoverished after the unsuccessful Penobscot Expedition and the many years that the country had been at war. In April 1780, General Wadsworth notified the General Court that fifty men had arrived in spite of the repeated requests to the county brigadier generals to raise the quota of enlisted soldiers. By the end of May, General Wadsworth reported that two hundred men had trickled into his headquarters over a two-month period.[1065] He reported that he had camping supplies for one hundred men, a supply of meat for only ten days and enough bread to last two days. When provisions ran out, the general proposed to send the soldiers out fishing so that they wouldn't starve, but it would be at the expense of their military troops' effectiveness to guard the coastline.[1066]

In April 1780, the General Court of Massachusetts proposed another expedition to repel the British forces from Fort George at Castine (Bagaduce). Aid and support was sought from General Washington, the commander in chief of the Continental Army.[1067] They were told that the Continental Army soldiers were unpaid and that every department was without money and credit. General Washington showed that the project far exceeded the resources and the ability of the army to carry out successfully. In deference to General Washington's advice and the lack of soldiers and monetary resources themselves, a second Penobscot Expedition was abandoned.

Although the British held Castine until the end of the war, they were not entirely unmolested. The American defeat was in a slight way alleviated, according to the following account of a small but successful expedition that appeared in the July 10, 1780 *Boston Gazette*:

> *A few days ago a detachment from the troops under General Wadsworth went up Penobscot-river* [sic] *having pass'd* [sic] *the fort* [at Bagaduce] *in whale-boats in the night, and took two* [British] *sloops which had weighed up some of the cannon lately belonging to our privateers which were burnt there. They had got 8 cannon on board and were coming down the river, little expecting to be conducted by our people* [Americans]*; but Capt. Mowat had the mortification to see them passing down by the fort, out of reach however, in triumph. They fired at the fort to vex the enemy and got safe away. Mowat followed them to Cambden, but General Wadsworth having drawn up his men and made a breastwork to frighten the enemy, he and his ship were obliged to meach* [sic] *back again, and we are in full possession of the vessels which were intended to infest our coasts. General Wadsworth has taken 40 prisoners, including the men who were on board these vessels.*[1068]

General Wadsworth's detachment of special operations soldiers mentioned in the newspaper article was probably led by Major Philip Ulmer, who was on the general's staff and in the personal service of General Wadsworth. Major Ulmer was also in command of the fort at Camden (Cambden, the old spelling) at this time. His detached company of men had ready access to the Penobscot River and to the boats necessary to carry out this successful raid.[1069]

In July 1780, there were distressing occurrences and attempted abductions of prominent residents and Patriots in the seaport communities of "Downeast" Maine. Pillaging and plundering of undefended families by British raiding parties and by displaced Tories occurred frequently. In mid-July 1780, a displaced Tory named John Jones, who acted in defiance of the martial law imposed by General Wadsworth, led a detachment of raiders to Pownalboro at night and kidnapped Charles Cushing, the high sheriff and brigadier general of the state militia in Lincoln County.[1070] John Jones and his raiders took Charles Cushing as prisoner in his nightshirt and marched him four miles through the woods, where he was taken by boat to Fort George on Castine and was put into prison. General Charles Cushing was later paroled and exchanged.[1071] General Cushing resigned his various offices and permanently left Pownalboro and the Province of Maine. Colonel Samuel McCobb was advanced in rank to general and assumed the leadership role vacated by General Cushing's capture and the resignation of his militia leadership for Lincoln County.[1072] Raids by British troops along the seacoast towns continued to be made at night in an attempt to capture and imprison leading citizens and militia generals and senior officers. Some generals hired guards to protect themselves and their families while they slept. Many of the displaced Tories in the district became prowlers and raiders by land and by sea. Fear, anxiety and suspicion filled the lives of the settlers during this time. General Wadsworth issued a proclamation prescribing the death penalty for anyone who was found aiding and abetting the enemy.[1073]

General Wadsworth received a warning during July that the British stationed at Fort George were going to attack the town of Falmouth (Portland) again. Colonel Joseph Prime's regiment was called out for service, and officers were appointed to lead the defense of Falmouth Neck. Colonel Prime's appointed officers included Major James Johnson, Major Philip Ulmer, Quartermaster Josiah Chase, Sergeant Enoch Knight and Adjutants Nate Lord and Moses Atkinson.[1074] The headquarters of this regiment was located at Falmouth, with five regiments stationed at Falmouth Neck and another at Cape Elizabeth with Captain Ethan Moore. Fortunately, the British raid did not come to pass. General Wadsworth sailed back with his detached regiment to his military headquarters on July 25. Major Ulmer was sent back to Fort Pine Hill to defend along the Penobscot Bay coastline at Camden. Other regiments were sent to support his defensive efforts there.[1075] Major Philip Ulmer's detached troops apparently were also involved in sailing armed state sloops in defense of the Maine seacoast, according to men who served in his company.[1076]

Major Philip Ulmer remained in service to General Wadsworth, and he served in a leadership and supervisory role with the building of strategic forts and outposts along the Penobscot Bay. The soldiers in Philip Ulmer's militia company recorded their movements from location to location, where they built forts and barracks in defense of the seacoast of frontier Maine Province.[1077] Since his leg injury left him with a permanent limp, Major Ulmer's horse made it possible for him to cover a broader area of the frontier outposts along the seacoast while in the special service of General Wadsworth.[1078] Wadsworth's outpost assignments had been extended along the Penobscot Bay region from the Kennebec River to the St. Croix River, which was the dividing boundary between the eastern frontier of Massachusetts and Nova Scotia (at New Brunswick), Canada.[1079] People termed the less-developed territory between the Penobscot River and the St. Croix Rivers "to the Eastward."[1080] Since colonial times, the Province of Maine had been referred to as "Downeast" due to the prevailing winds from the west. Ships sailing from Boston to Halifax had to sail downwind, or down east. Sailors who were unfamiliar with the prevailing winds and the shifting currents along the coastline of Maine could quickly find themselves in serious trouble with the possibility of a ship disaster on the rocks and shoals, a loss of valuable cargo and a loss of life.

GEORGE ULMER RETURNS TO WALDOBORO AND THE STATE MILITIA

George Ulmer, Philip's brother, married Mary (Polly) Tanner of Providence, Rhode Island, on June 24, 1779, when he was in the Continental Army with Colonel Vose's regiment stationed at Providence.[1081] Sergeant George Ulmer remained with Colonel Vose's regiment in the Continental Army until his three-year enlistment was completed. On January 18, 1780, Sergeant George Ulmer was discharged from the Continental Army.[1082] After two months of rest and relaxation in Providence, Rhode Island, probably staying with his wife's family and with Ulmer relatives in Salem, the Continental Army offered George Ulmer the rank of second lieutenant if he would reenlist.[1083] George Ulmer reenlisted on March 25, 1780, and served until November 25, 1780.[1084]*

Upon his return to Waldoboro, George Ulmer reenlisted in the state militia. With his older brother's help, George was appointed to serve as an adjutant in Colonel Prime's regiment. He was assigned to serve with Major Philip Ulmer's detached troops at the military outpost at Camden, where the fort was being fortified and defenses improved.[1085] Major Philip Ulmer served as a liaison between General Wadsworth and Colonel Prime's regiment, whose assignment was to build defensive outposts, fortify and improve forts and breastworks along the vulnerable frontier coastline. When a position of lieutenant was available with the local militia, Major Philip Ulmer enabled his brother to fill the position in Lieutenant Colonel Joseph Prime's regiment

---

* *Author's comment*: There is a discrepancy between the government records and the reports given by George Ulmer's descendant Wendell E. Wilson concerning George Ulmer's service at this time. George was either serving in the Continental Army with his regiment or was with the state militia in frontier Maine, but he couldn't have been in two places at once.

on June 1, 1780.[1086] George Ulmer was discharged on December 24, 1780, after serving for six months and twenty-four days in Major Prime's regiment with Major Philip Ulmer.[1087] The roll was certified at the Lincoln County militia headquarters at Thomaston.

During the Revolutionary War, Indian support was greatly needed to keep the British from overrunning the coastal settlements on the eastern Massachusetts frontier. The Abenaki-Penobscot and Passamaquoddy Indians who lived in the Penobscot Bay region were impressed with the British success against the American fleet in the summer of 1779. They were also unhappy about the interruption in their supply of dry goods and provisions from Boston that the Massachusetts General Court had promised to them. After the failure of the Penobscot Expedition, the colony of Massachusetts Bay lacked funds to obtain the needed provisions and lacked the means to transport them. Most of the colony's ships-of-war, merchant schooners, sloops and various transport vessels had been destroyed during the retreat up the Penobscot River. Few towns had any vessels available to transport goods of any kind. British privateers at Bagaduce (hereafter Castine) made the supply routes between Boston to Machias extremely dangerous, and the supplies that did get through were not nearly enough to meet the needed requirements. Indian agent John Allen worked hard to restore the Indians' confidence in the American cause. He had to extend his personal credit, and he was reduced to gathering goods and supplies from settlers and from seaport communities who might help him with the provisions for the Indians.[1088]

On May 10, 1781, George Ulmer enlisted with his brother's regiment at Camden as a first lieutenant in Captain Jordan Parker's company and in General McCobb's regiment.[1089] He was sent on an important mission to deliver provisions to Georgetown, located in the Kennebec River Valley of Lincoln County in the Penobscot-Abenaki Indian tribal region. The friendship and goodwill between the Americans and the Indian tribes depended upon the goods, supplies and provisions that were given and traded between the militia troops and the native Indians. The trading houses set up near the frontier forts at Machias (where there was a garrison of three hundred militia soldiers), Georgetown (located in the Indian tribal area) and Fort Pownal (located on the Penobscot River) prior to the Revolution were under constant threat by the British raiding parties from Halifax, Nova Scotia. The British plan was to starve the frontier settlers into submission and woo the native Indians away from the American side by disrupting the supply lines of provisions to outlying frontier settlements and to restrict trade with the Indian tribes. Fort Pownal, which had served as a trading post with the Indians and settlers, as well as a defensive fort, was destroyed as a result of the defeat of the American forces during the Penobscot Expedition. It was necessary to continue to supply provisions to the other frontier trading outposts. The continued American support and cooperation with the Indians and settlement traders was most important to maintain peace in the frontier area of Maine.

Lieutenant George Ulmer was sent to deliver provisions to the militia soldiers at the garrison at Cox's Head (near present-day Phippsburg), located on a bluff at the mouth of the Kennebec River.[1090]* Lieutenant George Ulmer continued to serve in the Eastern Department with his older brother, Major Philip Ulmer, until he was discharged on December 1, 1781.[1091] George delivered supplies and provisions from the state militia headquarters to the garrisons and camps at Cox's Head, Georgetown, Owl's Head and Camden, as well as to other coastal outposts. George Ulmer generally spent the winter months, December through late March, with his family in Waldoboro. After wintering over at his home for several months, George Ulmer enlisted again in the Lincoln County militia in the frontier defense of eastern Massachusetts. Each time George was discharged, having served for six to eight months in the militia at one rank, he reenlisted at another rank higher than he had just served.

Philip Ulmer was able to expedite his younger brother's remarkably rapid advancements through the militia ranks by using his own position as major and liaison on the staff of General Wadsworth and later with General McCobb at the military headquarters in Thomaston. As opportunities opened for advancement in the militia, Philip assisted his brother in filling new vacancies and more desirable posts. Major Philip Ulmer enabled his brother, George, to become an adjutant on the staff of Colonel McCobb just ten days after reenlisting in the state militia. Second Lieutenant George Ulmer enlisted in the state militia on March 13, 1782, and he served until November 20, 1782, and was discharged after eight months. He reenlisted as a captain in Colonel James Hunter's (also appears as Hunt) company

---

* *Author's comment*: This was the location of the original and unsuccessful Popham Colony, one of the earliest English settlements in the new world that was established a few months after the Jamestown Colony in Virginia in 1607 and before the Plymouth Colony in 1620. This was also the location of the fort and barracks that Major Philip Ulmer had directed his company of militiamen to build in 1779 prior to the Penobscot Expedition.

at the fort at Camden, where he served for about eight months.[1092] Major Philip Ulmer served off and on with his brother at Fort Pine Hill in Camden, where they were attached to Captain McAllister's company, a detachment of Colonel Prime's regiment. Major Philip Ulmer served as commanding officer of a detached company that often included his brother, George. As part of his duties, Major Ulmer constantly sought to improve and fortify Fort Pine Hill's breastworks and defenses after persistent efforts by the British forces at Castine to destroy the fort.

On Major Ulmer's recommendation, George Ulmer was advanced in rank to captain and offered the command of Fort Pine Hill, which was composed of two hundred militiamen. Major Philip Ulmer and Captain George Ulmer supervised the building of stronger and improved entrenchments at the defensive outpost. Fort Pine Hill eventually became the headquarters and main defensive military stronghold of the Penobscot Bay region for the defense of the eastern frontier of Massachusetts. While in service to General Peleg Wadsworth in the eastern frontier, Major Philip Ulmer was assigned to command militia troops at Fort Pine Hill to stop the smuggling and illegal trade going on between the Loyalists and other settlers in the seaport towns with the enemy troops located at Fort George on Castine. The British naval warships in the Penobscot Bay were constantly cruising in the coastal region. Armed merchant ships and privateers with their prize vessels made the harbor at Fort George a busy place.[1093]

The defensive outpost at Camden was strategically located at the mouth of the Penobscot River and the Penobscot Bay. Fort Pine Hill, with its eighteen-pounder cannon, controlled the shipping, navigation and commerce along the coastal region from Boston and Cape Ann to Machias on the Penobscot Bay. The militia troops were housed in the barn at the Gregory farm a half mile inland from Lermond Cove (later called Clam Cove, and presently Glen Cove in Rockland), while the officers were invited to stay in the main farmhouse. There was an eyewitness account found in a soldier's journal about the Penobscot Indians who were camped with them. The soldier garrisoned at the barn described the Indians playing a game of lacrosse, a game that they had never seen before. The journal went on to describe how pleased the Indians were to be sharing the food of the soldiers and being invited to camp with the soldiers at the Gregory barn. The journal described how, during the night, several Loyalist men tried to sneak up on the sleeping soldiers and set the Gregory house on fire. Fortunately, the Penobscot Indians heard the men and alerted the soldiers in the barn, and the Penobscot Indian braves and militiamen chased the Loyalist men away. These were some of the same Penobscot Indians who had joined Captain Philip Ulmer's company in climbing the cliffs at Dyce's Head at Bagaduce. The Indians had remained faithful to the American side throughout the Revolutionary War in spite of the British efforts to convert, seduce and intimidate them. The British raiding parties would not bother the American troops at Machias if the Indians were present and were serving to protect the American troops and outposts along the coast.

The British privateers at Castine and British warships cruising off of the coastline of frontier Massachusetts continued to fire upon the outposts, villages and towns at will, and they disrupted the transport of goods and provisions to the seaport settlements and militia outposts. Provisions and other essential supplies from Boston and other trading seaports to the south could not be shipped to the towns of the eastern frontier because there were so few vessels available and so few supplies obtainable that could be spared. These were desperate times for Massachusetts and especially in the Province of Maine, which relied primarily on navigation and trading for its provisions and goods from Boston for the survival of the frontier inhabitants. There was little relief in sight. Repeated pleas for help to the Massachusetts General Court were left unanswered or denied. By July, the troops at Camden with Colonel Prime's regiment had gone without pay, provisions and food long enough. They were ready to leave their post. With great difficulty and pleading, General Wadsworth persuaded them to remain on duty.

All of the coastal and backcountry towns and plantations in the Province of Maine were in great economic distress from the lack of food, trading and commerce. Seaborne commerce was the lifeblood of the economy in the Province of Maine. Without trade, the commercial and agricultural towns in York County were faced with stagnation. The destruction of the coastal and overseas trade was devastating since the communities of Cumberland and Lincoln Counties depended on fishing, imported goods and imported food to survive.[1094] Taxes in the local towns and villages continued to increase. A tax on beef was imposed, and wages were continuously needed to pay the militia soldiers for their protection and services on land and sea. The Massachusetts General Court continued to call on the towns and backcountry villages for their quotas of soldiers for the Continental Army and for particular provisions that were needed for the troops such as shoes, shirts, blankets, coats and food supplies. By the fall, the town of Waldoboro "voted unanimously not to pay any more taxes until further notice," and by the end of the year, the townspeople "voted that the town is not able to pay the beef tax."[1095]

By the end of the year, the troops at Camden still lacked bread and adequate clothing for the cold and harsh weather of frontier Maine. In December 1780, the militia troops who had been called out for military service in the spring with Major Philip Ulmer, his brother and the rest of his company in Colonel Prime's regiment were dismissed early by the General Peleg Wadsworth. The militia company went into winter quarters in their various homes. General Wadsworth was left at his headquarters at Thomaston with a small detail of militiamen from the local towns to serve as guards to protect the Wadsworth family. General Wadsworth was frustrated with the lack of support from the Massachusetts General Court in spite of repeated and urgent pleas for necessary supplies and provisions. He requested a discharge from his command, stating that he found himself "quite unequal to the Task, where there are some Intricacies, more perplexities & much Service to be done & but little to do with…the whole Country on either Side [of] Bagaduce from this Place to Machias, but for the Inhabitants, lays open to the Enemy."[1096]

The plundering and pillaging committed by the British raiding parties, and the acts of vengeance and retribution by displaced Tories with their lawless acquaintances, finally reached a culmination during the year of 1781. The British troops at Castine had set up their own intelligence service with the Loyalists and Tories in the Lincoln County area, who kept the commanding officer at Fort George, Colonel Campbell, informed of General Wadsworth's plans and military status. On February 18, 1781, before General Wadsworth could leave his command, a British raiding party commanded by Lieutenant Stockton was led by a local Tory through the darkness of the cold winter night to the house where General Wadsworth and his family were sleeping.[1097] The raiding party surrounded the house and fired their guns through the windows, injuring several militia guards, who made a hasty escape into the woods. At least two of the guards were men from Waldoboro, Privates Sechrist and Private Hickey (who received a musket ball in the thigh), and they killed or wounded several of the British raiders before fleeing into the woods. General Wadsworth made a stand against the British raiders, but he was injured in the arm by gunfire and taken prisoner. The general's wife put a blanket around his shoulders as he was taken out into the cold and snowy night in his nightshirt and was forced to walk a considerable distance to a rendezvous location (near Belfast). He was taken across the Penobscot Bay to Fort George, where British colonel John Campbell, who was in command of the fort, was pleased to have Wadsworth captured. General Wadsworth's wound was cleaned and dressed by the British doctor, and he was imprisoned.[1098] Following General Wadsworth's capture, the military command of the Eastern Department in Boston assigned Colonel Samuel McCobb to replace him in the eastern frontier of Massachusetts. Samuel McCobb was promoted to brigadier general and took command of the Lincoln County militia forces at their headquarters in Thomaston.[1099]

The night attacks by the British raiding parties stationed at Fort George continued. On February 24, 1781, a raiding party from a British privateer vessel of eighteen guns, the *Allegiance*, was sent from Bagaduce to capture Captain Daniel Sullivan, who lived near Frenchman's Bay, about halfway between Machias and Fort Pine Hill. He was the brother of American general John Sullivan, who served on General Washington's staff in the Continental Army.[1100] The raiding party surrounded Captain Daniel Sullivan's house overlooking Sullivan's harbor on Frenchman's Bay (near present-day Bar Harbor, Maine).[1101] After a brief struggle in the house, he was taken captive in his nightshirt. Captain Sullivan and Mr. Beans (Sullivan's neighbor) were taken as captives and dragged out into the bitter-cold winter night without proper clothing. In an effort to escape, Captain Sullivan tried to bribe the British guard, but his offers were rejected. He was forced to watch his house and his neighbor's house set on fire. Mr. and Mrs. Beans were an elderly couple who had housed Colonel John Allen during his visit to the county seat. The British raiders had narrowly missed capturing John Allen, Maine's Provincial Indian agent for the Penobscot and Passamaquoddy Indian tribes, by several hours.[1102] Captain Sullivan was taken to Fort George on Castine (Bagaduce), where he was ordered to take an oath of allegiance to the British Crown. He refused to take the oath, and he was imprisoned at Castine. Patriots continued to be targeted, captured or killed. Property of the local inhabitants and their sailing vessels were confiscated or destroyed.

In April 1781, Major Benjamin Burton was taken prisoner on the St. George River during his passage from Boston to his home at St. George (also appears as St. George's) near Thomaston. He was taken to Castine and put into prison with General Wadsworth.[1103] The prisoners learned that they were to be sent to England aboard a privateer, where they would remain as prisoners or be killed. On June 18, after several months as prisoners, the two captives escaped by cutting a hole through the ceiling. They climbed over the walls of the fort, and they made their way safely overland to their homes near Thomaston.[1104] Major Burton soon departed for Boston, and General Wadsworth, who had already resigned from his command prior to being captured, left the Province of Maine with his family and went to Boston as well.[1105] Following the escape of General Wadsworth and Major

Burton, Captain Sullivan was transported to Halifax and then to New York, where he was imprisoned in the infamous prison ship HMS *Jersey* in New York Harbor. He later, having been exchanged, died on his passage home.[1106]

The only thing preventing the British from taking over the Province of Maine was their fear of alienating the Indians. Major John Allen's diplomacy was crucial to the continued support of the Indians for the American towns and settlements in the frontier region. Fortunately for John Allen and the struggling residents of Lincoln County, the powerful French presence in America provided a means of countering the British influence. The eastern Indians had drawn heavily on French culture and support against the English over many decades prior to the American Revolution. Driven by the brutal treatment and abuses of the British upon the citizens of coastal Maine, the French admiral at Newport dispatched a three-masted frigate of thirty-two guns, the *Hermione*, to the eastern waters of Massachusetts as a visual deterrent to the British forces at Bagaduce and Halifax and to show French support to the beleaguered inhabitants of coastal Lincoln County.[1107] The French warship *Hermione* had carried General Lafayette and the French infantry forces to Boston and then to Newport, where they debarked.

General Heath wrote the following to General Washington on May 31, 1780: "Captain La Touche, of his most Christian Majesty's frigate, the *Hermione*, on her late cruise, ran into Penobscot Bay, where he lay some time, and took a plan of the works, which he has forwarded to the Minister [Chevalier de la Luzerne] at Philadelphia."[1108]

One can only imagine the excitement and elation that must have electrified the gathering of militia soldiers at Fort Pine Hill and at the military headquarters at Thomaston. One can imagine the exhilaration and cheers of the residents of the beleaguered coastal towns and villages as they witnessed the impressive French warship sailing toward the Penobscot Bay and its cruise along the coastline of the eastern frontier region with the American flag and the French tricolor flags flying from the tall masts. The British picket guards and soldiers at Fort George on Castine must have felt fear and anxiety as they beheld the awesome presence of the French fleet passing so closely by their location. The French three-masted warship *Hermione* sailed close enough to the British fort and breastworks at Castine to make a detailed plan for a possible invasion of the peninsula. The French frigate, having made its presence known, then sailed back to Newport, Rhode Island. The drawings and the plan were forwarded to the French minister, Chevalier de la Luzerne, at Philadelphia.[1109] The plan to remove the British forces from the Penobscot region was introduced by General Rochambeau in April 1780, and he sought the consent of General Washington to move forward with the plan.[1110] Washington gave General de Choise, the officer who proposed the expedition, a letter of introduction to the Massachusetts General Court.[1111] General Rochambeau did not approve of General de Choise's plan, and the proposed expedition was abandoned due to the disagreement between the generals.

In the spring of 1781, the General Court of Massachusetts requested that the French admiral de Barras in command of the French fleet at Newport, Rhode Island, permit the warship *Mars* to cruise along the eastern coast of frontier Maine Province. The General Court of Massachusetts also requested that Admiral de Barras send a frigate as soon as one could be spared to the same waters to defend the frontier region.[1112] On July 21, the French warship *Hermione*, with several other French warships that included the *Astrée*, commanded by Captain Jean-Francois de Galaup, engaged in a sea battle against six British warships from Halifax, Nova Scotia. The British frigate *Iris* (formerly the USS *Hancock*) under Captain James Hawker was among the British vessels that fought the French warships through most of the day and into the night near the British military fortress at Louisbourg, Nova Scotia. The sea battle ended indecisively, and the warships disappeared into the night to return to their ports for repairs. The French frigate *Hermione* reported firing more than 509 cannonballs during the encounter.[1113] Word of the mighty sea battle that had taken place off the coastline of Lincoln County energized the spirits of the local inhabitants and brought hope to the eastern frontier region. The French naval presence and fighting ability was impressive to the Indians in the Penobscot region, and it was most encouraging to the war-weary, intimidated and deprived residents of "Downeast" Maine Province. After a brief stay in Newport to repair and resupply the ships, the French artillery and troops at Newport boarded the *Hermione* and other transport vessels and sailed toward the Chesapeake Bay under command of Admiral de Barras and their meeting with destiny at the battle of Yorktown. French sea power eventually played a crucial role in the surrender of General Cornwallis's British Royal Army at Yorktown, Virginia, in October 1781, almost four years to the day after General Burgoyne's surrender at Saratoga, New York.

Since France now supported the American Revolution and the presence of the French fleet was made known to the inhabitants of Maine Province, many of the Indian tribes in the frontier region viewed with favor the American cause for freedom and liberty from Great Britain. The Indians did not generally support the Revolution actively, but they chose to remain neutral in the conflict. However, there is evidence that hundreds of Indians did indeed take an active role throughout the Revolution in many capacities. One Indian chief assured agent John Allen that "Our Language to the Britains [sic] is from our Lips only, but when we address the Americans and French its [sic] from our Hearts."[1114]

A wampum belt was sent to the Massachusetts General Court by the Penobscot-Abenaki Indians who were under Colonel Allen's jurisdiction in frontier Maine Province. The wampum belt represented their pledge of friendship and fidelity to the United Colonies and King Louis XVI of France. The belt was presented to the leaders of the Massachusetts General Court to manage on behalf of the Continental Congress in Philadelphia. The wampum belt was thirteen rows wide and represented the thirteen United Colonies, with a cross at the end that represented their attachment to the French.[1115] The other white places represented the different villages of the Indians.[1116] The wampum belt was to be returned to the Indians with medals attached at each end as tokens of accepting their alliance and friendship. One end was to represent the United Colonies of America, and the other was to represent France's King Louis XVI, whose representative was Monsieur Velnais on behalf of France.[1117] The Indians held this matter as sacred, and having the procedure conducted properly was necessary in securing the friendship of the Indian tribes in the province's frontier region. The Indians were true to their word and remained loyal to the Americans and to the settlers in Maine Province. They continued to provide protection for the frontier settlement at Machias, while the rest of frontier Maine Province was left mostly open to the British and their sympathizers. In spite of the Indians' indecisiveness with the British efforts to corrupt them and to woo them away from their support of the American Revolution, the eastern Indian tribes of frontier New England remained neutral and nonbelligerent throughout the entire war.[1118]

SMUGGLING AND CONTRABAND TRADE DEVELOPED ALONG COASTAL MAINE

During the years of 1781 to 1783, the condition of towns and settlements in the Province of Maine (referred hereafter as frontier Maine) became increasingly desperate for food, provisions and other needed supplies to survive. The frontier Maine settlements continued to feel more vulnerable and more isolated from the rest of Massachusetts. The British stronghold at Castine had seized 80 to 90 percent of the vessels owned by Lincoln County inhabitants. The county seat at Pownalboro had only one coasting vessel for the town. The enemy warships that patrolled the coastline of New England had captured almost all the sailing vessels that attempted to pass through the British blockade in frontier Maine. Sailing ships from other seaports in Massachusetts or farther to the south gave little hope of relieving frontier Maine's suffering by exchanging firewood and lumber products for cash or desperately needed supplies, necessities and provisions. The Massachusetts General Court extended some relief to certain individuals and, less directly, to coastal towns by permitting limited and temporary trading with the enemy at Castine and Halifax. Before long, a flourishing contraband merchant trade developed in some of the coastal towns in frontier Maine. Illicit trading between some frontier settlers and the British enemy at Fort George was going on in many coastal towns, including Waldoboro. In order to avoid detection, a trail was made through the woods north of the town of Waldoboro. The trail then turned northeast behind the mountains (near present-day Camden Hills) and turned east to the Penobscot Bay.[1119] Herds of cattle were driven along this trail and were received by the British soldiers at a designated location for their use at Castine. This caused indignation among many Patriots in the town and surrounding areas.

The flourishing contraband trade disturbed both the American and British authorities. Nova Scotia's lieutenant governor complained that the contraband activities were carried on like "fair trade" in London. He stated, "I have found all manner of Goods brought here from the old Country [England] constantly purchas'd [sic] and sent to the Rebellious Colonies."[1120] On the American side, Major General Peleg Wadsworth complained that "small craft constantly passing between Maine and Nova Scotia, producing old permits from [the General] Court, which somewhat embossed me…" In the vicinity of Bagaduce, the situation was much worse. General Wadsworth went on to relate that "despite martial law, 'clandestine Traders' continued their activity pretending to be captured by the British and then getting released to repeat their 'treasonable practices'…"[1121] The Cumberland County Court substantiated Wadsworth's claims of the frequency with which people traversed between Fort George on Castine "without leave of any proper authority within this Commonwealth, some with Permits from persons who have no right to grant them to ransom Vessels that have been taken from them—some to trade with the Enemy—and others with an

Express design of working for them."[1122] Efforts were made to stop the illicit trading with the enemy; however, they were not very successful.

By mid-March 1781, a proposal was circulated among some eastern Lincoln County towns to plead with the Massachusetts General Court for a status of neutrality, which was considered the only means of survival in a war in which the government provided no security and the enemy was brutal and merciless to the innocent civilians. The proposal was raised in a conversation between John Hancock, the new governor of Massachusetts, and Colonel Francis Shaw Jr., who served as chairman of Gouldsboro's Committee of Inspection, Correspondence and Safety. He quoted the governor, John Hancock, as saying: "…Since the state was unable to protect the eastern communities, the inhabitants [of the District of Maine] had an 'undoubted Right' to make the best terms possible for the protection of life, family, and property."[1123]

The committees of several neighboring towns of Gouldsboro met to draft a petition requesting that both the British and the Massachusetts Congress recognize a condition of neutrality from Penobscot Bay to the St. Croix River near New Brunswick, Nova Scotia. The neutrality petition was based on the familiar Whig premise that the government was contractual and conditional and that "Alliance and Protection are Reciprocal" and inseparable.[1124] Machias responded to this petition with defiance. Machias was the easternmost settlement in Maine and had become the most fortified and well-supplied town in the district. Colonel Ludwig's militia regiment from Waldoboro had marched on many occasions during the war to Machias, where they spent many months as militia guards against British raids. Machias had become a haven for refugees from Nova Scotia and a staging area for invading British territory and for privateering activities against British cargo transports. Primarily, it was the stronghold against further British invasion from the north and protected by the friendly Penobscot and Passamaquoddy Indian tribal communities.

Protection and friendship with the Indians was largely dependent upon provisions and the diplomacy of John Allen at Machias. The town of Machias was so strategically important that both Massachusetts and the Continental Congress contributed to its defense.[1125] The town of Machias had a defensive stronghold and an active trading-house. It had become as important a town for business and trade as the county seat at Pownalboro. As long as Machias was able to hold out, the smaller settlements and towns in the District of Maine took courage that the British forces at Halifax and Castine could not control the region. The Massachusetts General Court, because of fraud and counterfeiting of documents, voided all existing permit passes. The General Court required merchants to petition the court again for trading licenses.[1126] The merchant traders were put under more stringent regulations to prevent abuse of their trading conditions and covert activities in their dealings with the enemy. This neutrality petition caused dissension throughout the towns and settlements of Maine district. The Revolution had become a civil war by inciting emotional responses and actions and by polarizing and dividing families, friends, neighbors and communities from one another.

THE FRANCO-AMERICAN CAMPAIGN OF 1781

We are at the end of our tether, and...now or never our deliverance must come.
—General George Washington, April 9, 1781[1127]

The population in most of the colonial states had been ravaged by illness and a terrible smallpox epidemic, killing many thousands of soldiers in the American army camps and people throughout the colonies. Continental currency continued to hyper-inflate and finally collapsed in May 1781 prior to the Battle of Yorktown. In America, paper currency to specie (hard-minted coins of gold and silver) had the ratio of 175 to 1 officially, or by the informal calculations of the public, 525 to 1.[1128] To mark the collapse of American currency, there was a spirited procession held in Philadelphia, with people marching with dollars in their hats like paper plumes. There was a very unhappy dog that trotted along in the parade tarred and pasted with the worthless dollars.[1129] General Washington wrote to Robert Morris in Philadelphia to send hard specie to pay the troops under his command. A large number of the Continental Army soldiers had not been paid for a very long time, and there was great discontent among the troops. Congress was not able to provide for the many needs of General Washington's army or provide sufficient recruits to reinforce the American troops, which numbered about six thousand poorly equipped men.[1130]

In the spring of 1781, the Continental Army was almost unable to function. The rebellion was in its seventh year, and the crushing strains of conflict continued to devastate the trading- and agrarian-based economy. The French allies, who included the elite Royal Deux-Ponts of Baron von Closey, were under the command of the Count de Rochambeau. They were still encamped in Newport, Rhode Island, due to the British naval vessels that blocked the harbor and kept them bottled up. The British forces occupied strategic parts of New England and all of Manhattan Island at the mouth of the Hudson River. In the Southern Theater of operations, General Cornwallis's British army marched, raided and plundered almost at will across the southern colonies. The British Royal Navy totally controlled the seas. The British naval forces had destroyed the American naval fleet, the Massachusetts militia flotillas and the armed merchant vessels and transports in New England following the disaster of the Penobscot Expedition in October 1779. The southern colonies had little sea protection and remained open to the destructive whims of General Cornwallis.

In late March 1781, King Louis XVI sent Admiral Comte de Grasse from France back to the West Indies with 20 French ships-of-the-line, 3 frigates and 156 transport vessels. The flagship of the French fleet, the *Ville de Paris*, was the largest warship at the time.[1131] It was an imposing vessel of about 110 guns on three gun decks. Admiral de Grasse's orders from the French Court were stated in a message to Count de Rochambeau: "His Majesty has entrusted me with the command of the naval force destined for North America. The force which I command is sufficient to fulfill the offensive plans...of the Allied powers to secure an honorable peace."[1132]

Admiral de Grasse's mission was to reinforce the French possessions in the West Indies and then turn his attention and actions to the North American Theater. It was not until early July in White Plains, New York, that Rochambeau's French forces first met their American allies. General Rochambeau shared half of the French war chest with General Washington to pay the disgruntled American troops who were long overdue for their payment allowance and wanted to leave the army. The American troops were given French silver and gold specie for their services and decided to stay with Washington's army. General Washington used the French specie to purchase needed provisions and supplies for the Continental Army troops that the Congress had not supplied. General Washington and General Rochambeau had originally planned to combine their troops and attack the British forces stationed on Manhattan Island. However, upon further examination of the fortifications around Manhattan Island, General Rochambeau declared New York City impregnable.

General Washington had sent General Lafayette to the Southern Department with a small force to harass General Cornwallis's troops who were rampaging through Virginia and the Carolinas. The British forces with General Cornwallis overplayed their pillaging, plundering and brutal behavior with the residents and frontier settlers in the southern colonies.

The local militia troops throughout the southern colonies used guerrilla warfare tactics against the British invading forces and were led by such men as Francis Marion and Thomas Sumter, who became very successful in hit-and-run techniques. These were the same tactics that had been used with success by General Washington's troops against the British forces while in winter quarters in Morristown, New Jersey, several years before. General Nathanael Greene, Washington's trusted officer and friend, challenged Cornwallis's British troops using his combined American army and militia forces. With the combined forces of Generals Greene and Lafayette and with the local militia troops that helped in the Virginia and Carolina campaigns, the weakened British army of General Cornwallis retreated to the small port village of Yorktown (also called Little York). They expected Admiral Graves's naval fleet to rescue them by sea. General Rochambeau urged a campaign against General Cornwallis's British army, which had begun erecting fortifications at Yorktown near the mouth of the Chesapeake Bay in Virginia.

By the summer of 1781, the French war chest, which General Rochambeau had shared with General Washington to pay the disgruntled American troops, was dramatically depleted.[1133] Although a shipment of gold and silver specie was due to arrive in Boston in the early fall, Rochambeau knew that he could not depend on these funds for the Virginia campaign. He wrote to Admiral de Grasse stating that his funds were insufficient to maintain the army through the summer and appealed to him to bring more funds when he came from the West Indies to meet the allied army at Elk River landing (Maryland) at the northern end of the Chesapeake Bay.[1134] In America, he felt that it was impossible to secure the needed gold and silver specie to further conduct the war against the British forces. Rochambeau sent a dispatch to Admiral de Grasse apprising him of the Franco-American plans and also communicated to Count de Grasse the condition of the Continental Army: "I should not conceal from you, M. l'Amiral, [sic] that these people are at the very end of the resources… that Washington will not have at his disposal half of the number of troops he counted upon having. While he is secretive on this subject I believe that at present he has not more than 6,000 men all told."[1135]

Admiral de Grasse turned to the Spanish for assistance. The Spanish had been aiding the French with financing their battles against the British in the West Indies. Francisco de Saavedra became the central person who assisted Admiral de Grasse in raising the needed funds through a last-minute collection of gold and silver specie from Spanish officials in Havana,

Cuba.[1136] In a dispatch from the Chevalier de la Luzerne, French minister to America and French aide to General Washington, it was impressed upon Admiral de Grasse that "it is you alone who can deliver the invaded states from that crisis which is so alarming that it appears to me there is no time to lose."[1137] After receiving the needed funds, Admiral de Grasse sailed his naval fleet with all possible speed toward Virginia.

In the meantime, General Washington and General Rochambeau learned in mid-August that Admiral de Grasse was sailing for the Chesapeake Bay with all the French ships and troops that he had collected. General Washington left behind a small party of militiamen at White Plains to make British general Henry Clinton think that the allies were still planning for a siege of New York City. Washington wrote a letter to General Lafayette outlining a fictitious plan to attack New York City. British intelligence intercepted the letter, and it had the desired effect, which worked to Washington's advantage. In August, General Clinton prepared for an assault on British forts on Manhattan Island. Generals Washington and Rochambeau proceeded with the combined allied troops in a forced march of 450 miles from White Plains, New York, to Williamsburg, Virginia. Heeding General Rochambeau's request, Admiral de Barras sailed from the Franco-American headquarters at Newport, Rhode Island, with nine warships loaded with allied troops, supplies and the siege artillery. The fleet headed for a rendezvous at Chesapeake Bay with Admiral de Grasse's fleet, which had sailed from the West Indies.

It was at this very crucial time that the French fleet of twenty-eight ships under Admiral de Grasse arrived off the shores of the Virginia Capes near the Chesapeake Bay on August 30. General Cornwallis was unaware that Generals Washington and Rochambeau and Admiral de Barras were on their way toward Yorktown, Virginia, and the Chesapeake Bay. British admiral Graves, with five ships from New York Harbor, headed south to join with Admiral Hood's fifteen ships to confront the French fleet of Admiral de Grasse. However, Admiral de Grasse and his fleet of twenty-eight to thirty warships were already in the Chesapeake Bay. Admiral de Grasse sent a number of transports and frigates to the Elk River landing in Maryland, where the allied troops boarded and were taken down the bay to Virginia.[1138] The allied soldiers, heavy artillery and military material were unloaded in preparation for the siege of Cornwallis's Royal Army troops at Yorktown.[1139] General Washington had instructed General Lafayette to position his troops in a manner that prevented Cornwallis's retreat to North Carolina.[1140]

The Franco-American army marched through Philadelphia in a parade before Congress. The *Freeman's Journal* of September 5, 1781, reported: "The appearance of these troops far exceeds anything of the kind seen on this continent, and presages the happiest success to the cause of America."[1141] Later that same day, General Washington learned that Admiral de Grasse and the French fleet had arrived at the Chesapeake Bay. It was reported that the usually stoic American general ran to greet Rochambeau, hat in one hand and handkerchief in the other, and embraced Rochambeau over and over again, shouting, "He's here! He's arrived!"[1142] The bemused General Rochambeau further described Washington's excitement: "[Washington was] waving his hat at me with demonstrative gestures of greatest joy. When I rode up to him, he explained that he had just received a dispatch… informing him that de Grasse had arrived."[1143] The reaction of the normally reserved General Washington to Admiral de Grasse's arrival underscores the importance with which the American commander in chief viewed the French naval reinforcements.

There was an intense battle waged between the British and French fleets off the Virginia Capes on September 5, 1781.[1144] The battle at sea raged throughout the day and night. Finally, both sides halted and disengaged to count their casualties and attend to the wounded. Having repaired their ships on September 6, the fighting at sea resumed the next day. The dueling navies had moved from the Chesapeake southward to Cape Hatteras, North Carolina. By September 9, Admiral de Grasse turned back to the Chesapeake Bay, fearing that British reinforcements might arrive there before they could take their blocking position. When Admiral de Grasse's fleet arrived, they were greeted by the reinforcements of Admiral de Barras. The admiral, at this time, had thirty-five warships and would be able to hold the Chesapeake Bay and the major rivers for the siege and land battle at Yorktown that was to soon unfold.

Admiral Graves and Admiral Hood called a council of war and concluded that with the condition of the British fleet and the position and strength of the French fleet, little could be done to give assistance to General Cornwallis and his troops at Yorktown. The British ships withdrew, leaving General Cornwallis and his army to defend themselves against the Franco-American forces. Generals Washington and Rochambeau arrived at Williamsburg on September 14 ahead of their troops. On September 17, Admiral de Grasse invited General Washington aboard his flagship, the *Ville de Paris*, where they enjoyed a meal together and conferred in a council of war. Much to the amusement of the guests, Admiral de Grasse, who was six foot two, kept referring to General Washington, who was six foot four, as "mon petit general."[1145] News of the defeat of Admiral Graves's Royal Navy fleet at sea off the Virginia Capes shocked King George III and the Parliament in London. The king confided to the Earl of Sandwich: "I nearly think the empire ruined…this cruel event is too recent for me to be as yet able to say more…"[1146]

Some of the soldiers from frontier Maine who had enlisted and served with Lieutenant Philip Ulmer at Saratoga and Valley Forge remained with the main body of the Continental Army when the war shifted to the Southern Theater. Washington's army forces fought against Generals Clinton and Cornwallis's British army forces in numerous southern battles. The British Royal Army, supported by the Royal Navy, raided and devastated towns and villages throughout the southern colonies. General Washington and his Continental Army fought bravely to defend the southern towns against the successes of the strong British forces and their southern Loyalists. General Benjamin Lincoln and his entire American army of approximately five thousand regulars and militiamen were surrounded at Charleston, South Carolina, and taken captive by British general Clinton and his army and naval forces on May 12, 1780. General Lincoln was later released in a prisoner exchange. He returned to the service of General Washington and was involved at the battle at Yorktown the following year.

In 1781, Washington's American troops and Rochambeau's French army troops bypassed the anticipated attack upon New York City to reclaim the British-held stronghold. The combined allied army troops made a forced march to Williamsburg, Virginia, in order to trap General Cornwallis's army troops at Yorktown, where they had retreated to await their rescue by the British warships sent from New York City. The French naval fleet, commanded by Admiral de Grasse, was able to engage the British naval fleet that was attempting to reach Yorktown to evacuate Cornwallis's troops. The British fleet was turned away and returned to New York City, leaving Cornwallis's army surrounded by the allied forces with their backs to the York River and with no means of escape. On September 28, 1781, the combined Franco-American armies left their encampment at Williamsburg and marched to Yorktown, Virginia, and laid siege to the seaport town. An intense allied siege of Yorktown began, and it lasted for several weeks. When the American attack upon Cornwallis's British forces commenced with the roar of the cannons, the American soldiers from the frontier District of Maine were actively involved with General Lafayette's soldiers attacking the British troops at redoubt number nine, and General Lincoln's troops were attacking the enemy at redoubt number ten near the York River. The battle at Yorktown was eventually an American success, and British general Charles Cornwallis was forced into surrendering his entire allied British army. On October 19, 1781, General Washington wrote a message to Congress praising the efforts of the Franco-American forces: "The combined Army on this occasion…I wish it was in my Power to express to Congress how much I feel indebted to the Count de Grasse and his fleet…"[1147]

General Cornwallis was so humiliated about losing the battle at Yorktown that he made up the excuse that he was too ill to participate in the surrender ceremony. He appointed General O'Hara to surrender his sword to General Washington. Washington was angered by Cornwallis's flimsy excuse and refused to accept his sword. He gave the honor to his second-in-command, General Benjamin Lincoln, who accepted the sword signifying the surrender of the British army. At the conclusion of the surrender ceremony at Yorktown, the American Continental soldiers whistled the tune "Yankee Doodle," accompanied by their fifers, as the British Royal Army forces left the field of battle—just as they had done at the surrender of General Burgoyne's British and Hessian forces at Saratoga, New York, four years earlier in October 1777. What had begun as a derogatory British joke against the American colonists as "Yankee Doodles" (morons and idiots) became a theme song that would come to haunt the British troops in their defeat. The musical tune "The World Turned Upside Down" was ordered to be played by the British general.[1148] The powerful British Royal Army and Royal Navy forces, whose superiority and strength had been feared all over the world, had been set back upon their heels.

TREATY OF PARIS ENDS THE REVOLUTION

The incursions by the British privateers and raiders continued in the Province of Maine and along the eastern seacoast even after the British surrender at Yorktown, Virginia, on October 19, 1781. This was a hard-earned victory for General Washington's Continental Army forces with support from Count Rochambeau's French army troops and the French Royal Navy fleet of Admiral Count de Grasse. Soldiers from the District of Maine, some of whom had served as recruits with Major Philip Ulmer earlier during the Revolution, wrote home to their families about the successful victory at Yorktown and the surrender of General Cornwallis and the British army. A provisional agreement of peace between Great Britain and the American Congress did not occur until November 30, 1782, and it took almost another year until a formal treaty followed on September 3, 1783.[1149]

In frontier Maine, the end of the Revolution came in a tentative manner. In the spring of 1783, the war was virtually over in most colonial states except in "Downeast" Massachusetts in the District of Maine, where raids upon the local settlers and conflict over the frontier territorial borders remained active. Until the end of the war, Massachusetts felt obliged to provide funds to maintain a garrison during the summer months for the safety and security of the Maine coastline. Coastal towns felt vulnerable to enemy attacks from the British raiding parties at Fort George on Castine. The town of Machias did not have sufficient defenses, and a convention of towns from Cumberland County expressed concern that Lincoln County might not be able to keep the enemy under control in the Penobscot Bay. A letter was written to the General Court from the convention of assembled towns expressing their hope that "a part of the Continental Forces may be spared to defend this northern State to which the attention of the Enemy now seems to be directed."[1150] However, no help arrived, and the predicament in which Maine found itself brought little sympathy from other states and towns that were no longer in conflict with British raiders and Tories. Maine found itself more and more isolated from Massachusetts and the other states in the union.

In 1782, General Washington himself discouraged the French from undertaking another attack on the British troops at Castine. The risk, Washington felt, was simply too great for an objective so "insignificant" so late in the war.[1151] The British troops at Castine continued their raids and deprivations upon the seacoast communities. On May 28, 1782, the British brig *Observer*, commanded by Lieutenant John Crymes, was returning to the harbor at Halifax at night when the warship discovered and engaged the American privateer ship *Jack*, commanded by Captain John Ropes of Salem. The American vessel tried to escape, but a long and severe sea battle ensued. The *Observer* chased the American vessel *Jack* for several hours before catching it off the coast of frontier Maine. Captain John Ropes was killed as a result of British cannon fire. Both vessels suffered from numerous holes shot through their sails. The British marines tried to board the American privateer but were initially repulsed several times. However, the British boarding party was eventually successful. The *Jack* struck its colors around afternoon on May 29. The surviving crewmen were taken prisoner and transported to the British military stronghold at Halifax.

The following month, the American privateers raided British ports again in Nova Scotia and continued to be a threat to British commerce, navigation and troop supplies for the rest of the war.[1152] The optimistic occurrence for the coastal inhabitants of Maine was when Lieutenant Preble and several militiamen aboard an armed state sloop from Massachusetts slipped into the harbor at Castine during the night and, under the guns of Fort George, successfully sailed off with a British privateer as a prize.[1153] This bold action infuriated the British soldiers, and they vowed to avenge this outrageous rebel act upon the coastal towns and settlements in frontier Maine. In March 1783, British privateers took their toll of what little shipping survived. Jonathan Sayward of York County (Maine) wrote that "the Little Privateers are still taking a number of our vessels…"[1154] George Washington stated: "The thing that sets Americans apart from all others is that they will die fighting before they accept surrender on their knees."

The Treaty of Paris was eventually signed on September 3, 1783, officially ending the Revolutionary War. This agreement was followed by the cession of hostilities in most colonial states. There was a general withdrawal of the British forces from the colonies except in Maine and in the South, where territorial borders were still disputed, and the American army disbanded on October 18, 1783. The news did not arrive at the British fort on Castine until December and was met with great joy and celebration. The fort at Camden fired its cannon over and over again until the British troops at Fort George on Castine fired their cannon back in acknowledgement. The last ship with Loyalists and Tories did not leave Castine for Halifax, Nova Scotia, until January 15, 1784.[1155] The British garrison was finally broken up, storage buildings were burned and Fort George was finally abandoned. The Massachusetts Bay state did not acknowledge the abandoned post until an officer, probably Major Philip Ulmer, who served as an aid and reconnaissance officer for the general at military headquarters at Thomaston, was sent by General McCobb with his company to investigate Fort George. They arrived in the spring of 1784 to make an inventory of what little remained at the British fortress.[1156] Lincoln County, which extended from the Kennebec River northeastward to Eastport in frontier Maine, seems to hold the claim that the Revolutionary War was waged longer there than in any other part of the country.[1157]

PEACE BRINGS NEW PROBLEMS TO WALDOBORO

It is incumbent on every generation to pay its own debts as it goes. A principle
which if acted on would save one-half the wars of the world.
—Thomas Jefferson

The economic difficulties brought about by the Revolution upon the coastal
and overseas commercial trading business had caused untold suffering in the
towns throughout the District of Maine. The people of Waldoboro faced
many problems rebuilding their community like so many other colonial towns
and settlements after eight years of war. The Revolutionary War had caused
many deprivations to the United Colonies. Due to prolonged drought, severe
winters and erratic weather conditions, sufficient food and provisions were
unavailable for the Maine Province. The British blockade along the coastal
areas of frontier Maine prevented trading that was essential for the towns,
villages and settlements to survive. The coastal towns' merchant trading,
lumbering and shipbuilding businesses were mostly destroyed. British raiding
parties and illicit trafficking of cattle and scarce food supplies by some town
Loyalists and opportunists further strained the town's resources. An active
business in contraband items and illicit trading with the enemy was carried
on behind the scenes. Animals for meat and other provisions for the British
troops at Castine and Halifax were smuggled past the militia soldiers in
Lincoln County whose job it was to stop this type of activity. There were
heavy taxes from the bankrupt state of Massachusetts levied on the citizens
to pay for the war. Inflation skyrocketed, and paper currency was essentially
worthless.

However, by the end of the war, there was fraternization among the
American settlers, Loyalists and the British soldiers in some Penobscot-
area communities. The split in Waldoboro between the Patriots and the
Loyalists was never characterized by outrage and violence but mostly by
strain, suspicion and silent social pressures exerted upon the community. In
a relatively short time, the split between neighbors and even family members
was healed, leaving a united community facing the problems of peace.[1158]
In 1783, Philip Ulmer was voted by the town of Waldoboro to serve as a
first selectman with Jacob Ludwig and Joshua Howard, both soldiers who
had served during the war in Philip's Lincoln County militia company.[1159]
In petitioning the Massachusetts legislature for relief from taxation,
agricultural backcountry settlements pleaded their geographical isolation,
their unproductive soil and recent development of settlements in the

wilderness frontier. Coastal communities were vocal in pleading for tax relief due to the wartime toll suffered by them in British raids, the dislocation of their lumber trade and the collapse of the fishing industry.[1160] Philip Ulmer, as first selectman, wrote to the Senate and House of Representatives in the Massachusetts General Court about the conditions in their community in the spring of 1783. The community of Waldoboro found itself in a very distressing condition. The worst consideration was the huge burden of debt that was bound to cripple the economy and greatly reduce the standard of living for many years to come.

Follow-up of Philip Ulmer's Military Information

Major Philip Ulmer's original Twenty-fifth Massachusetts Regiment (Gardner/Bond's regiment), which had been reassigned and reorganized many times and finally designated the First Massachusetts Regiment, was eventually disbanded on November 3, 1783, near West Point, New York.[1161] The young soldiers who had served with Philip Ulmer in Colonel Vose's First Massachusetts Regiment during the war began to find their way home to Maine from the Middle and the Southern Departments. Major Philip Ulmer continued to serve in the Massachusetts state militia like many other soldiers in the Province of Maine after the conclusion of the Revolutionary War. In 1797, years after the Penobscot Expedition, Philip Ulmer, with four other Revolutionary War veterans who had also served in the conflicts with him, sent a petition to the Massachusetts General Court for the rights to salvage the remains of the vessels from the Penobscot Expedition.[1162] Philip Ulmer was greatly concerned that there could be future enemy conflict in the frontier region of Maine district, and the state government of Massachusetts might be unable to defend the frontier region of the state from enemy attack. The Massachusetts General Court granted permission based on the petition that Philip Ulmer had spearheaded for salvage operations on the Penobscot River. The five Revolutionary War veterans began salvaging the remains of cannons and armaments at Cape Jellison (also called Fort Point and Fort Pownal), located at the mouth of the Penobscot River and the junction with the Penobscot Bay near Mill Cove. This was the location where about twelve or more armed transport vessels had been run ashore during the disastrous retreat of American troops up the Penobscot River in 1779. Philip Ulmer and his fellow Patriots decided that the only way their seaport towns and coastal settlements in the frontier Penobscot Bay region were going to be able to defend themselves from further danger from British raiding parties was to salvage whatever they could from the remains of the abandoned and destroyed vessels from the Penobscot Expedition in 1779.

With the colony of Massachusetts so deeply in debt, the isolated towns in Maine had to depend on the local and county militias to defend them against attack from foreign or domestic enemies. The reconditioning of the salvaged cannons and munitions took years to accomplish and proved to be the only way that the communities were able to have protection from further coastal attacks as hostilities again began to ignite between France and England. Some cannons and artifacts were brought to seaport villages such as Camden and Ducktrap (Lincolnville). Other munitions and cannons were sent to other coastal towns and vulnerable river communities. The salvaged cannons were helpful in defending against British raids and hostilities in the northern seaport towns of "Downeast" Maine during the War of 1812. The remains from Philip Ulmer's salvaging efforts of the vessels from the Penobscot Expedition with his fellow veteran militiamen are still in evidence today. One old cannon can still be found on the beach in Lincolnville with a plaque memorializing the War of 1812.

SUMMARY

There were several important events that changed history for the American forces early in the Revolutionary War. The American forces involved in the Canada Expedition with Benedict Arnold were considered a part of the "secret mission" to invade Canada, and their names had been ordered removed from the military records by General Washington's orders. The American retreat from Canada was considered successful; however, the Canadian Expedition turned out to be a failure due to the lack of congressional support and money (hard specie—gold and silver coins) to fund the mission, lack of food provisions and supplies for the men and enough soldiers to conduct the campaign.

In October 1776, just three months after the Continental Congress declared American independence from England, the battle at Valcour Island occurred on Lake Champlain (in present-day northern New York State). Benedict Arnold commanded the small American naval fleet on a suicidal mission that successfully delayed the combined forces of the powerful British Royal Navy, Royal Army and the Hessian mercenary forces on Lake Champlain long enough for the cold weather to set in. The British forces retreated to winter quarters in Canada until the following year. By this delaying tactic on Lake Champlain, the Continental Congress was able to come together, form a united front and make responsible decisions for the United Colonies as a whole instead of their own self-interests. General Washington was given a year in which he was able to receive greatly needed arms and munitions from France and to assemble the Continental Army, an army that was strong enough and ready to take on the British forces at Saratoga and defeat them. With the British and Hessian defeat at the Battle of Saratoga in October 1777, the French were encouraged to enter the war on the American side and signed an alliance. Spain and the Netherlands soon followed suit. The French provided volunteer military forces, money to support the war effort against England and the assistance of several fleets of French naval warships. The Penobscot Expedition in the fall of 1779 at Bagaduce in the eastern frontier of Maine District had ended in a terrible defeat that devastated the American naval forces along the New England seacoast. The British blockade along the eastern coast of New England was causing devastation and hardship on navigation, commercial trade and transportation and threatened the very survival of the American citizens in many areas of New England. The war was a roller coaster of successes and failures and affected the economy and livelihood of all the American colonies.

The most momentous and emotionally stressing period in the American Revolution came in September 1780. General Washington had concluded his conference with French general Rochambeau at Hartford, Connecticut (called the Hartford Convention), and he had planned to return to the Continental Army, where General Greene, his second-in-command, was in charge of his army forces. Information had been sent by way of General Washington's Culper Spy Ring that the British allied forces were planning a major campaign in 1781. The Continental Army was quite weak at this time, and it was struggling to survive from a long shortage of supplies and funds. Morale had sunk to low depths of uncertainty, and militiamen and new recruits were staying at home. The Congress had been unable to settle upon its support of the Continental Army and its size for the 1781 campaign. General Washington was uncertain how to maintain the present strength of his forces and worried about the heavy loss of the soldiers as their enlistments ran out at the end of the year. He had endorsed General

Rochambeau's plan to build the French troop strength at Newport, Rhode Island, to fifteen thousand soldiers over the winter and spring of 1781, but Washington could only hope that the United States would be able to match those numbers by a new recruitment effort.

Sir Henry Clinton had concentrated mobile forces in New York City, where transports were being prepared to receive them. West Point, the principal American headquarters in the Hudson Highlands Department, was weak, and unknown to General Washington and his staff, was being weakened and undermined from within by General Benedict Arnold, who was in command of West Point at the time and was preparing to defect to the British side. The third week of September 1780 was a critical week in American history and had a dramatic impact on the very founding of the nation. It was during the week of September 8 to September 15 that General Benedict Arnold and the British spymaster, John André, met at the farm of Joshua Hett Smith of Haverhill, where Arnold and André plotted the capture of General George Washington, General Lafayette, General Knox and other close aides who were traveling together and were involved in the Hartford Convention. General Arnold and Major André coordinated arrangements for the assault on West Point and the timing of the capitulation of the fortress complex. Critical papers were exchanged indicating the vulnerabilities of the fortress at West Point and the attack plan. Confirming details of Arnold's compensation for his defection were exchanged. General Arnold's and John André's escape was to be made aboard the British warship *Vulture*, which was at anchor near Teller's Point in Haverhill Bay on the Hudson River. The stage was set, and the plans for General Washington and his aides' capture, the capitulation of West Point and the anticipated surrender of the American forces to the British forces was in the last stages of preparedness.

Fortunately for the American cause, Major Benjamin Tallmadge, one of Washington's intelligence officers and one of the central agents in the Culper Spy Ring, learned through an informant of the sinister kidnapping plan. He suspected right away that Benedict Arnold was a traitor who was preparing to defect to the British side. He alerted General Washington, who took prompt action. Major John André was captured by three picket guards from a Westchester militia regiment company near Tarrytown, New York. André was held for trial and later hanged as an enemy spy. General Benedict Arnold was able to escape capture by ordering several bargemen to take him downstream to the HMS *Vulture*. Arnold boarded the British vessels and sailed down the Hudson River to the British stronghold at New York

City. He made his escape and boarded a British ship to England, where he was rewarded for his defection. Benedict Arnold later returned to America aboard a British warship and led several brutal British sea attacks upon the American coastline, killing thousands of his former American countrymen. Arnold was banned from ever returning to America by the Continental Congress under penalty of death.

Although the immediate threat to West Point was averted, General Washington and the Continental Congress feared that the news of Benedict Arnold's defection would cause the further deterioration of America's determination to continue the long war for American independence. However, the betrayal had the opposite impact on Patriot morale. Instead, it gave new life and determination to the American colonies. The Americans experienced what can best be described as a religious revival with the saving hand of "Providence," a heavenly intervention, in favor of the successful outcome of their American cause. The Continental Congress announced a day of prayer and thanksgiving to mark the role of "Almighty God" in saving the nation "at the moment when treason was ripened for execution."[1163] Thomas Paine wrote that the most important event was the "providence evident in the discovery"[1164] of Arnold's plot before it could succeed. General Washington addressed the national emotion of thanksgiving: "In no instance since the commencement of the war has the interposition of Providence appeared more conspicuous than in the rescue of the post and garrison at West Point from Arnold's villainous perfidity."[1165]

Arnold had not only betrayed his trusting friends, officers and soldiers, but he had betrayed his country! The soldiers who had fought with such bravery and devotion with General Arnold for many years did not want to be known as having been associated with Benedict Arnold, the traitor. In the military records of 1775–76, in soldiers' and sailors' pension petitions and in individual military records, the soldiers disassociated themselves with expeditions and campaigns in which they had served with the hated traitor. None of the volunteer militiamen and Continental Army soldiers wanted to be associated with the stigma attached to General Arnold's treachery. Petition claims were later sent to the War Department for Revolutionary War pensions and financial support for soldiers and sailors who were considered invalids due to their war injuries, maiming and amputation or other medical reasons. These military records and testimonies are silent about any association or military service with Benedict Arnold. The mention of Benedict Arnold in the soldiers' applications could have caused rejection of their petitions, and a stigma would have been placed upon them by association. Benedict Arnold became the most reviled and hated figure in American history because of his defection. The loathing of Benedict Arnold as a traitor was universal. The Continental Congress, in order to protect the innocent soldiers and seamen who had served with General Arnold during the Revolutionary War, resolved "to erase from the register, the names of the officers of the army of the United States, [associated with] the name of Benedict Arnold."[1166]

The American economy had been badly crippled as a result of the American Revolution. France and Great Britain both saw an opportunity to benefit from trade with United States. However, the economies of England and France had suffered too as a result of the revolution in America. France had overextended itself in supporting the American Revolution and brought great stress and hardship upon its own economy and French citizens. The citizens in Paris later rose up against King Louis XVI, his advisors, the aristocracy and the nobility who had bankrupted their nation. The consequence was the French Revolution. England and the other European allies intervened to quell the chaos in Paris, and finally the allies restored order to France. However, there was a Reign of Terror that followed as France tried to establish a new form of governing power.

Napoleon Bonaparte eventually came to power and established a dictatorial rule and strong military force. Napoleon's ambitions of European rule led to France and England warring against each other again. Both countries sought to lure (or coerce, if necessary) the American government into joining their particular side in the ongoing conflict in Europe. Both France and England recognized the vast amount of land, diverse resources and manpower that could be exploited in America for their own purposes if America entered the conflict on their own particular side. America had become a pawn in a large international game of chess between the bickering and warring European countries. The American president and the Congress struggled to remain neutral in the conflicts in Europe. The president tried to avoid becoming a part of France and England's high-stakes game. The president's Embargo Acts and the tight government restrictions on navigation and commercial trading stifled the lifeblood of the American economy.

Chapter 15

Changes in Massachusetts after the War

CONDITIONS IN MASSACHUSETTS AFTER THE REVOLUTIONARY WAR

After the signing of the Treaty of Paris in 1783, many thousands of Loyalists and Tories realized that Britain was not going to give them protection from their American neighbors in the colonial settlements. Thousands of displaced and fearful British subjects fled on ships to London, which caused a great influx of mostly penniless and needy refugees. The strain on the British citizens in London and the surrounding villages, as well as the merchant businesses and related trading agencies in London, caused a huge strain on the British government. A resettlement scheme was proposed by the British Parliament for the refugees from America to be resettled in Canada.[1167] Five hundred acres of land were offered to the heads of families (bachelors were offered three hundred acres) to relocate to Nova Scotia and the eastern frontier in Maine between the Kennebec River and the St. Croix River in New Brunswick, Nova Scotia. In addition to the land offered, the refugees would be given three weeks' allowance of rations, a year's worth of supplies, clothing, medicine and arms.[1168] It was only after the end of the fighting that the displaced refugees were willing to claim the resettlement offer from the Parliament.

Benedict Arnold returned from London, England, in 1785. He and his son, Richard, settled in St. John, New Brunswick, near the St. Croix River as part of the resettlement offer. He established a store and a merchant trading business with the West Indies.[1169] Arnold returned to London in 1786 and brought his family back to St. John in 1787. His mercantile store conducted business with the towns in the Passamaquoddy region of frontier Massachusetts. In the late 1790s, Arnold outfitted a privateer, and he continued to do business during the quasi-war (undeclared war) conflicts in the West Indies against French interests. The British eventually granted Arnold and his sons a land grant of fifteen thousand acres in Upper Canada.[1170] Philip and George Ulmer's business interests in merchant trading and shipping in the West Indies came into conflict and competition with Benedict Arnold's shipping and trading businesses during this time. Their mercantile store and financial interests in the Penobscot region came into conflict as well. Once military officers and friends during the early part of the Revolution in 1776, the merchant businessmen became adversaries and competitors in the District of Maine in the late 1790s.

Even after the signing of the Treaty of Paris, King George III and the British Ministry in London maintained the desire to continue holding on to the Northwest Territories in North America. The British Parliament sought to acquire or annex the northern frontier territory in the District of Maine and create the colony of New Ireland encompassing lands along the Penobscot and Passamaquoddy Bays. The Canadian-American border issues had been a problem in reaching an end to the Revolutionary War, and border issues would again become a contentious issue in reaching a settlement at the end of the War of 1812. Peace would not come to America until land claims and border issues with Canada and Mexico were finally settled between the United States and the European powers of France, Spain and England.

The British government needed to address the tricky problem of the many thousands of black people freed by the British during the war whose former and unforgiving colonial masters were determined to reclaim them as property and return them to slavery. General Carleton wrote, "I had no right to deprive them of that liberty I found them possessed of…"[1171] Carleton decided to allow the black people to embark upon the Canada-bound vessels, but he compiled a registry in case their former owners sued the British government for compensation.[1172] General Washington, at the urging of Congress, complained greatly about the transport of black people from American shores and told Governor Carleton that it was theft of valuable property and resources. Sir Guy Carleton referred George Washington to the British Registry that he kept and related that should his policy be found later to violate the peace treaty, the Crown would compensate the masters of the freed blacks who were transported to Canada, New Brunswick (on the Maine-Canadian border) and Nova Scotia.[1173] Many of the freed black people settled in the border region of Canada on unclaimed land, and others settled into the Passamaquoddy Bay area and married into the Passamaquoddy Indian tribe. These mixed races and their children were referred to as "Black Indians."

As the British troops left New York City, Castine and other colonial coastal towns, the British secret service also relocated to Canada with thousands of Loyalist and displaced Tory refugees. Many former secret agents went underground, poised for reactivation if needed. Although the war was basically over, the struggle was not. The American government was weak and suffered from economic and diplomatic difficulties. The dominant countries in Europe considered a thriving and independent America as a challenge and a possible threat to their own countries' wealth and powerful position in the world. The American monetary system was in shambles, thanks to the success of British counterfeiting during the war that made Continental paper dollars issued by Congress virtually worthless. The Spanish and English hard specie of gold and silver coins, which were minted in Europe, were the accepted monetary standard worldwide. Since America did not have the ability to mint their coinage, the European hard specie was difficult to acquire.

After the cessation of hostilities, Britain expected to resume its former relationship with the American colonies. The merchant trade, shipping and business dealings soon resumed with Great Britain. However, England expected that the new American republican experiment would eventually collapse. Great Britain was poised to intervene if the new American government called upon British arms to save them from themselves. Sir Guy Carleton was elevated in peerage to Lord Dorchester, and he continued to run intelligence operations in America from his location in Quebec.[1174] The French and the Spanish were also expecting that the American experiment would collapse and that they might be able to divide up the colonies amongst themselves.[1175] French and Spanish espionage became a greater concern to the new American government in the ensuing years as well. George Washington stressed to the Congress that a "competent fund" was needed to pay for covert activities to secure the safety of the citizens and gather vital information for military operations and defense. In 1790, Congress created a contingency fund to be used for espionage services to ensure the security of the nation.[1176]

America became overrun with spies from many countries that conducted their espionage battles on American soil. France began plotting against Spain, which was Britain's ally at the time, and attempted to lure the Americans into supporting the French side. Covert attacks were made on Spanish territories in Florida, Florida's island keys and the Louisiana coastal towns by French privateering vessels. The French and the British wanted to block and control the rich American shipping trade conducted from the mouth of the Mississippi River, in the islands of the West Indies and along the eastern coast of South America to Brazil. Two of Philip and George Ulmer's trading vessels from Ducktrap, carrying rich cargos from the West Indies to the Penobscot Bay, were captured by French privateers in 1797.[1177] The American crewmen on the Ulmer-owned ships were captured, imprisoned or killed. The cargos on board their merchant ships were confiscated and sold by the French privateers to markets in Europe and other French sailing masters in the West Indies for a sizable profit. Other Ulmer cargo transports met similar fates. One of the Ulmer brothers' trading vessels was listed simply as "lost at sea," perhaps in a hurricane or some other event. Another trading vessel, believed to be the *Hiram*, was later recaptured and survived to sail again. In 1800, John Wilson, son-in-law of George Ulmer, was sailing master of the sloop *Hiram* that departed from New York for St. Thomas.[1178] The *Hiram* was seized by a French privateer in September 1800 and taken to San Juan, Puerto Rico. The sloop was taken to Guadeloupe, a main customs port for the French, and the vessel was "condemned" (confiscated) on October 4, 1800.[1179] This meant that the rich cargo and ship were a "legal prize," and the goods and supplies that were meant for its home seaport in the Penobscot Bay were confiscated and sold.

In another incident, captured documents by the British vessel *Cerberus* taken from a French privateering vessel indicated that a bribe was being solicited by Edmund Randolph, American secretary of state, to undermine the signing of the Jay Treaty with England.[1180] Randolph denied being involved in the bribe attempt. American suspicions of France's motives increased with the arrival of twenty-five thousand French Jacobin refugees, who had fled after the execution of Robespierre.[1181] It was feared that some of these refugees were also espionage agents sent from France to capture vital information from the American government. The American government passed the Alien and Sedition Act of 1798, which allowed the legal prosecution of suspects on a vague and wide-ranging set of charges in order to guard and protect the government and the American citizens from foreign threat and interference.

Spain's main objective after the American Revolution was to separate the western territories from the rest of the United Colonies (hereafter United States) and attach them to its possessions in the Louisiana Territory. James

Wilkinson, who served in the same regiment with Lieutenant Philip Ulmer as an aide-de-camp to Generals Gates, Arnold and St. Clair, was a former brigadier general in the Continental Army. He was hired by the Spanish at an annual salary of two thousand dollars to facilitate and move the Spanish plan forward.[1182] James Wilkinson settled in Kentucky, which had previously been a part of Virginia, and he stirred up the inhabitants and attempted to persuade his fellow settlers to secede from the United States and become part of the Spanish Empire. Once Kentucky was given statehood, James Wilkinson's subversive activities ended, but he continued to take Spanish gold payments. Wilkinson sought to regain his commission as a brigadier general in the United States Army since his finances were depleted. In 1796, James Wilkinson was appointed as commander in chief of the United States Army, which meant that, for a brief time, an undercover Spanish agent was commanding the United States military service.[1183]

EFFECTS OF THE REVOLUTION IN MASSACHUSETTS AND THE EASTERN FRONTIER (MAINE)

After eight years of war, colonial states such as Massachusetts were deeply in debt and were mostly destitute. The shock of postwar reality in Maine, and throughout New England in general, bordered on disillusionment and despair. American paper currency was considered worthless, inflation rates for food provisions and basic supplies were exorbitant and the merchant trade had collapsed due to the British embargo on seaport cities and towns. Many soldiers and officers had remained unpaid for their military service during the war, and many were given land-bounties instead of virtually worthless government currency. Philip Ulmer remained one of the unpaid Continental Army officers who finally had to sue the United States government for three years of military service, yet unpaid as late as September 1787.[1184] Mainers felt the financial legacy of the Revolutionary War as the most immediate threat. Many communities were swamped with debts for military bounties and support of their soldiers and their families. The state debt in Massachusetts was staggering, as was the backlog of unpaid wartime taxes. Inland and backcountry settlements were isolated from commercial markets and were without surplus agricultural goods to sell and convert into taxes. Aggravating the problem of heavy taxes was a lack of money. Part of the reason was British exclusion of American trading from the West Indies islands, causing Maine to lose markets for its lumbering and fishing industries. An independent United States could not enjoy the profits of its goods and natural resources due to the efforts of England to undermine access to European and West Indian ports. England wanted the new American republic and the independence movement to fail so the colonial states would again submit to British rule and control. The French wanted the American republic to fail so that France, Spain and other European countries could incorporate land in the colonial states for their own countries' use and exploit the natural resources for their own purposes.

For poverty-stricken Massachusetts, the lure of land in postwar Maine Province attracted immigrants from Europe who hoped for a better future by owning property. Property ownership held the promise of liberty from poverty and security for the future. Property also attracted men of wealth and political influence. Property also gave settlers and less wealthy citizens an opportunity to vote and have their opinions heard by the state representatives and government. The old speculative land companies, such as the Kennebec Proprietors and the Pejepscot (Penobscot) Company, were reorganized under new leadership, and together with the Waldo heirs, they undertook vigorous measures to reassert their control over their respective and overlapping claims to land in "Downeast" Massachusetts (Maine).[1185] Changes in society after the Revolution caused a new elite social class to emerge. Former generals, officers and soldiers who received land-bounties in payment for military service began to descend upon Maine and the southern colonies to claim lands that they thought belonged to them. Men with land were able to vote and become political leaders and wealthy merchants.

Henry Knox Tries to Reclaim His Land in the Waldo Patent Territory

My objective is to fill the county with industrious settlers and to make it flourish in all aspects. A few wretches may from the darkness of ignorance oppose my views but they cannot be many.
—Henry Knox[1186]

After the American Revolution, General Henry Knox, proprietor of the Waldo Patent territory, was determined to collect payment from all of the settlers or squatters living on "his" property. Land that had lain vacant during the war years or had been confiscated from British settlers who were known Loyalists or British sympathizers became part of a massive land grab.[1187] Illegal claims were often made on owned land in the Waldo Patent that legally belonged to Lucy and Henry Knox. Knox had become the patent proprietor by his marriage to Lucy Flucker, heir to the huge Waldo estate prior to the Revolution. Following Henry Knox's service to America as secretary of war from 1785 to 1794, Knox turned his attention to consolidating the Waldo Patent territory again under one owner. Henry Knox's political position, business dealings and purchases of state land following the war increased his holdings to several million acres.

Former generals Henry Knox, Benjamin Lincoln and Peleg Wadsworth acquired large tracts of land on which to base their political and business ambitions. General Wadsworth returned to Maine after the war and purchased eight thousand acres near Hiram (Maine) for speculation, but he settled in Falmouth as a merchant.[1188] Generals Knox and Lincoln were more ambitious in their plans. Benjamin Lincoln obtained fifty thousand acres of land in the District of Maine, but his real importance was in helping to finance his friend Henry Knox in his grand schemes of land development and venture capitalism.[1189] Henry Knox, by marriage, deception and manipulation, acquired the old Waldo Patent territory from the Waldo/Flucker heirs and creditors, which was about 1 million acres between the Kennebec and Penobscot Rivers.[1190] After the war, Henry Knox went into partnership with William Duer of New York, whom he had known during the Revolution and who was an ambitious land speculator. Together they attempted to corner the entire market for public lands in the Eastern Country of frontier Maine. Henry Knox expanded his land holdings by purchasing over 2 million additional acres of land from the state of Massachusetts. Not content with this amount of land for speculation, the partners contracted for another 1 million acres of state land extending to the east of the Penobscot.[1191] Schemes of land speculation and commercial development were not always successful, but it showed the exciting hopes and visions generated by the available land in Maine for those powerful enough to obtain it. Henry Knox stated on several occasions to wealthy investors and speculators that "no part of the U.S. affords such solid grounds of profit to capitalists, as the District of Maine."[1192]

The quest for land was revived after the war, and the old tensions between those (like Henry Knox) who claimed vast acres of land by virtue of a formal government grant or inheritance and those who claimed it simply by right of occupation and improvement erupted in the ensuing years. Proprietors, squatters and settlers who leased land from the owners had come into conflict with one another even before the Revolution, and the contest for land was renewed after the war in the courts and in the woods. Soldiers who received land-bounties for their military service flooded onto the state lands to make their claims after the war. These veteran soldiers and squatters justified their informal possession of land with the conviction that those who had fought and suffered in the common cause of freedom should all benefit from the unoccupied land acquired from the British Crown. This was an essential attribute of liberty and republicanism.[1193] Squatters on state-owned land would ignore the government's threats of eviction, and eventually, after several years of agitation and resistance, they were offered one hundred acres of state land at a nominal cost to resolve the conflict.[1194]

However, with private landowners, things were different. Businessmen viewed their lands as a means of investment and profit. Squatters were considered interlopers and uncivilized intruders who were denying the landowners their just profits. Squatters were considered a threat to the very fabric of orderly society. The rightful proprietors of the property threatened squatters with legal action and forced eviction and removal, or they were offered leases to continue living on the claimed land which they had improved. Those who accepted leases or mortgages frequently discovered that they were obliged to pay for land that had no clear title and left them vulnerable to other claimants or investors who took over their business enterprises. Philip and George Ulmer discovered themselves in this same situation after years of land improvement and business development at Ducktrap Harbor and Cove, where they had built several business enterprises. They had invested years of their lives, labor and finances in developing their land and businesses ventures. They had to accept whatever the proprietor dictated in order to keep their property and investments. The threat of losing property for taxes or of being jailed for debt struck at the very concept of liberty in a society where property ownership conveyed dignity and personal autonomy. The American society was becoming sharply polarized, causing fear and anxiety at every level.

The proprietors, wealthy land speculators, educated businessmen and lawyers skillfully manipulated the court system for their own gains. It was difficult to have delegates from Maine represented in the Massachusetts General Court at Boston to defend the interests and needs of Mainers (settlers in the Province of Maine). Since overland travel was difficult, the primary means of transportation for delegates and representatives from the districts in Maine was by sailing vessel, which was seasonal and weather-dependent. The Massachusetts General Court in Boston was a long way from the frontier towns in Maine, and it was expensive for congressional delegates to remain for an extended period of time in Boston while their business interests suffered at home. At first, the frontier settlers did not resort to violence against the proprietors in the District of Maine, but before long, resistance and frustration gave in to defiance—and eventually violence—against the perceived injustice of the proprietors and the agents who were hired to work for them. This tension and unrest between the land owners and the settlers who "squatted" on their claimed land took another direction.

This new direction took the form of a movement to found a separate state of Maine with a government that was more responsive to the needs of the frontier settlers and squatters. A separate state of Maine would enable local founders and leaders of the frontier towns to satisfy their political ambitions in a state of their own without competition from prestigious Massachusetts competitors such as John Hancock, John Adams and Samuel Adams and other wealthy merchants, politicians and lawyers. Statehood would enhance the importance of a government and judicial system that was more responsive to the claims and the needs of settlers in frontier Maine. The town of Falmouth was expected to become the capital of the new state of Maine. Falmouth was also expected to become the leading seaport in the western region of Maine, and this would benefit the settlers in the coastal region. In spite of the efforts of "separatists" to present their plan for separation and simple self-governing by men who lived in Maine, the issue underwent an abrupt change and became more controversial.

The postwar depression caused unrest and hardships for war veterans, farmers and inhabitants who were poor and unable to pay the inflated and oppressive taxes. Postwar idealism confronted postwar reality, causing disillusionment bordering on despair throughout New England. Settlers' land and homes were confiscated, and their families were turned away with no means of support or way to survive. The courts were generally unsympathetic to the plight of the poor and homeless. Wealthy Boston merchants and venture capitalists were poised to take advantage of the desperate conditions in frontier Maine. Veterans from the war who had received land-bounties in lieu of payments for services began to flock to the frontier of Maine to claim state-owned land and build their "American dream" of property ownership, a home, a livelihood and prosperity for themselves and their future generations. For those unable to make a living in Maine Province's harsh environment, the frontier territories in western Pennsylvania, the Ohio Territory and the Northwest Territory (which included the Indiana Territory) held the hope for a future for adventurous pioneers and settlers. These western territories offered land speculation, land ownership and business opportunities for those who were hardworking, industrious and enterprising. The great migration westward to the Mississippi River and the Great Lakes region had begun.

After the war, General Peleg and Elizabeth Wadsworth returned to Maine in 1784, and they built the first brick house in Falmouth (Portland) for their growing family. At this time, Philip Ulmer was the selectman of the town of Waldoboro. General Wadsworth renewed his friendship with Philip Ulmer and the successful Ulmer families at Waldoboro. He had learned from his years as an officer in the military service that it was not necessarily *what* you knew that could make you successful but *who* you knew politically, socially and businesswise that could provide opportunities, contacts and support to help you become successful. Like Philip's financially successful uncle, John Ulmer, who lived at Waldoboro, Peleg Wadsworth was able to build a prosperous life as a land agent and surveyor near Falmouth. He acquired large tracts of land (the Wadsworth Grant of 7,800 acres), some of which was the confiscated land of frontier settlers who were unable to pay their state and local taxes or who had been British Loyalists. Lumber was milled at Wadsworth's double (up-and-down) mill, located on the Great Falls Brook on his property.

General Peleg Wadsworth built a large mansion for his large family (with ten children) on the tract of land between the Saco River in Maine and the Ossipee River in New Hampshire. He later incorporated the town of Hiram on this tract, serving as selectman, treasurer and magistrate. Peleg Wadsworth became actively involved in politics and served as the chairman of the first convention to address the issue of Maine statehood in 1785. He was elected to the Massachusetts Senate, and later he became the legislator in the third U.S. Congress. General Wadsworth respected Philip Ulmer's leadership in the state militia in 1780–81 and his personal service to the general when Wadsworth was the commanding officer of the Eastern Defense of Frontier Massachusetts. Peleg Wadsworth and the Ulmer brothers, Philip and George, established a business relationship in their lumbering and commercial trading enterprises at Falmouth, Waldoboro and Ducktrap Harbor. The personal and business relationship between Peleg

Wadsworth and the Ulmer brothers continued to deepen as their political aspirations in the Massachusetts Senate and the House of Representatives developed prior to the War of 1812.

In the fall of 1784, General Henry Knox took General Lafayette and his entourages on a sailing tour of coastal Maine to show off his vast landholdings and the proposed homesite for his summer estate in Thomaston (Maine), near the St. George River. General Knox had acquired by inheritance vast holdings of land from his wife, heir to the Waldo Patent territory. Knox used his status as a general and his political position to maneuver and manipulate the legal system to acquire millions more acres of state land after the war.[1195] General Knox's coastal sailing tour was given to General Lafayette, General Benjamin Lincoln, Colonel Henry Jackson and others to show the potential for the great wealth that they might also acquire through land speculation and investment in business development ventures (venture capitalism). At this time, Philip and George Ulmer were actively involved in developing their land claim at the Ducktrap watershed and cove. With advice, guidance and financial backing from their uncle John Ulmer, who had become quite wealthy through land speculation and business investments by this time, the brothers were able to build a milldam on the Ducktrap stream, a sawmill, several gristmills and a shipyard at the cove, as well as trade and shipping businesses at Ducktrap Harbor and cove. The brothers cleared land and began to build log houses for their families since Ducktrap would become their new home.

The Ulmer sawmill and dam, which was destroyed and rebuilt a number of times during the years that the Ulmer brothers owned it. *Courtesy of the Lincolnville Historical Society.*

At some point during General Lafayette's tour of frontier Maine, Henry Knox and his touring companions apparently sought out the Ulmer brothers, who still lived in the nearby coastal town of Waldoboro, formerly Broad Bay settlement. Generals Knox, Lafayette, Lincoln and their other companions apparently visited with the Ulmer family at the Ulmer home in Waldoboro (most likely the large Ulmer Inn, which had once been the home of Philip and George Ulmer's grandfather and later their uncle John and his family).[1196] General Wadsworth might have also been present at the gathering since he lived only a short distance away in Falmouth (Portland) and had served with these same Patriots during the Revolution. In later years, one of General Peleg Wadsworth's sons and one of General Samuel McCobb's sons moved to Lincolnville and built their homes at Ducktrap near Philip Ulmer's family.

Meanwhile, on the national scene, George Washington realized that the new nation, under its Articles of Confederation, was not functioning well. In 1787, he strongly advocated for a Constitutional Convention to be held at Philadelphia to discuss the issue. Washington presided over the Constitutional Convention that drafted the United States Constitution. When the new Constitution was ratified, the Electoral College unanimously elected George Washington to become the first American president. George Washington took the oath of office on April 30, 1789, standing on the balcony of Federal Hall on Wall Street in New York City. He attempted to bring rival social and political factions together to unify the nation. He supported Alexander Hamilton's programs to pay off all state and national debt, to implement an effective tax system and to create a national bank, despite opposition from Thomas Jefferson. Washington was careful not to infringe upon the policy-making powers of the Congress, although this became of great concern to him. Washington proclaimed the United States neutral in the wars raging in Europe after 1793. When the French Revolution led to a major war between France and England, President Washington insisted on a neutral course of diplomacy, ignoring the recommendations of Secretary of State Thomas Jefferson and Secretary of Treasury Alexander Hamilton. The new nation of America needed time to heal and become strong and united. President Washington became increasingly disappointed as two opposing political parties began to emerge at the end of his second term of office. In his Farewell Address, he urged his countrymen to reject excessive party spirit and geographical distinctions that could lead to state and national discontent. In foreign affairs, he warned against long-term alliances that could drag the nation into foreign conflicts. In his letter to "Friends and Citizens," Washington warned that the forces of geographical sectionalism, political factionalism and interference by foreign powers in the nation's domestic affairs threatened the stability of the republic. He urged Americans to subordinate sectional jealousies to common national interests.

Chapter 16

Philip Ulmer after the War

PHILIP ULMER'S FAMILY LIFE
AFTER THE REVOLUTIONARY WAR

Philip Ulmer married Christiana Jung (Young) in the spring of 1777 at Waldoboro (Broad Bay settlement) while he was on furlough from the Continental Army. Christiana Jung (hereafter Young) was born on March 5, 1753, and was the daughter of Valentine and Dolly Young (Jung, the old German spelling), who were immigrants from Germany.[1197] In 1773, Dolly Young was listed as the widow of Valentine Young (a Dutch Ranger and Broad Bay militiaman) with a farm on the east side of Waldoboro.[1198] Philip and Christiana met as children in Broad Bay (Waldoboro), and they married years later. Typical of most weddings at this time, the marriage celebration was a multi-day party.[1199] Neighbors would bring "pot luck" entrees and other food staples, breads, pies and desserts. The various food items were laid out on tables for everyone to share. Gravies, pot pies and streusels in both deep and shallow dishes of various kinds were served. Clams, oysters, shrimp, codfish, eels, salmon, mackerel and trout were often caught fresh and cooked, and the feast was served to the assembled guests. Rum from the West Indies added to the festivities and spirit of the wedding celebration.

Philip Ulmer returned to the eastern frontier of Massachusetts in April 1778, where he continued to serve with the Massachusetts state militia in Lincoln County. He turned his attention to civil and domestic issues like raising a family in Waldoboro. Philip lived with his wife, Christiana, in a small house, possibly on the Young farm with Christiana's widowed mother on the eastern side of Waldoboro. In time, Philip and Christiana Ulmer had three children who were born in Waldoboro, and six children were born later in Lincolnville (Ducktrap). All nine children reached adulthood, but only eight were raised in Philip's house.[1200]

TABLE 3

CHILDREN OF PHILIP AND CHRISTIANA ULMER

NAME	BORN	VILLAGE	MARRIED
Jacob	December 30, 1778	Waldoborough (or Lincolnville)	Eleanor Thomas
Charles	January 20, 1781	Waldoborough	Mary Holden
Christiana	April 16, 1783	Waldoborough	Paul H. Stevens
Dolly	May 18, 1786	Lincolnville	James W. Merrill
Margaret	July 18, 1788	Lincolnville	Bezelen P. Dalman
Susanna	February 19, 1791	Lincolnville	Samuel Berkmar
Philip	June 19, 1793	Lincolnville	Mary W. Thomas
George	May 5, 1795	Lincolnville	unknown
Grace	June 5, 1797	Lincolnville	Job White

The Broad Bay settlement, part of the Waldo Patent, had been incorporated in 1773 into the town of Waldoboro (Waldoborough). There were many Ulmer family members and extended families that lived and raised their children in the towns of Waldoboro and nearby St. George on the eastern side of the Medomak River. In early times, Mrs. Young served as a midwife for the communities of St. George and Waldoboro.[1201] Around 1777 or 1778, Mrs. Young (believed to be of English extraction) moved with her husband (possibly a descendant of Deacon Young from the upper town of St. George) and their family to the settlement in Ducktrap Plantation, where they became early settlers of the area. Philip and Christiana's first child, Jacob Ulmer, was likely born in Ducktrap (Lincolnville) and delivered by Mrs. Young, who had delivered other Ulmer family babies at Waldoboro. Philip and Christiana actually lived in Waldoboro at the time of Jacob's birth, but they might have traveled to Ducktrap, where baby Jacob was delivered by Mrs. Young.* After Mrs. Young moved away from the area, Mrs. Kelloch of St. George took over the midwife responsibilities for the St. George and Waldoboro communities. Later, Mrs. Peabody and Mrs. James acted as midwives for the St. George and Waldoboro vicinity. The midwives responded to the medical and birthing needs of the local communities in all kinds of weather. They occasionally had to swim their horses across the Medomak River to attend to a woman in labor if the ferry was not available for service. Some of the sons of the Young and Kelloch families served in Philip and George Ulmer's militia companies during the Revolutionary War.

Prior to the Revolution, Philip Ulmer, his uncle John Ulmer and his relative Matthias Remilly acquired a large tract of land on the west side of the Medomak River "above the head of Broad Bay and several miles up the river above any present settler."[1202] Philip had retained his holdings in the land partnership during the war with the help of his uncle John, who was a major real estate broker, banker (money lender) and sea captain with his own trading vessel by this time. Fortunately, Philip had property to return to after the war. In 1783, Philip purchased a prime piece of property at Slaigo Cove, where he planned to establish a shipbuilding and commercial business.[1203] Philip had become a respected community leader, military officer and landowner in the Waldoboro community where he was born. It was during April 1783 that Philip and Christiana's third child was born, also named Christiana. In 1783, Philip Ulmer was elected to serve the community as a first selectman with two other respected Patriots, Jacob Ludwig and Joshua Howard, who had served as soldiers in Philip's state militia company during the Revolution.[1204] The town started an ambitious program of highway building. It was voted to establish a road "between William Farnsworth Jr. and Philip Ulmer's land from the main road in South Waldoboro at the meetinghouse corner easterly to the upper waters of the Goose River."[1205] Other major roads and minor roads were built that made travel and the transportation of goods and services faster and more convenient in the Waldoboro community and the shoreline areas. The development of roads and building schools and a library in the Waldoboro community became an important interest for Philip Ulmer.

---

* *Author's comment*: This could explain why Jacob Ulmer, who was named for Philip's deceased father, appears in the birth records of both Lincolnville and Waldoboro in the Massachusetts Vital Statistics Records and the Maine Vital Records Index.

As Waldoboro was trying to recover from the devastating war, the Massachusetts Congress imposed heavier taxes on the Massachusetts citizens in order to pay for the war debts and rebuild its economy. Philip Ulmer wrote a petition to the General Court of Massachusetts appealing for tax relief for the town's residents. The following is the transcribed petition written by Philip Ulmer and signed by the selectmen of the town of Waldoboro:

To the Honorable the Senate and House of Representatives in General Court Assembled.

The Petition of the town of Waldoborough in the County of Lincoln Humbly Sheweth [sic] *that by Reason of the Late War, this town has been Reduced to Great Distress, and though now by the Blessing of Providence Peace is Restorer unto us: yet we shall sorely feele* [sic] *the Effects of the War. By our Enemies taking Post at Penobscot and Continually infesting this Coast with their Privateers and small Boatts* [sic] *our Lumber and fishing Trade in which alone we had any Concern Has been almost totally Suppressed, almost Every Vesel* [vessel] *we owned in the Beginning of the War, fell into their hands: and tho* [sic] *from time to time Vesels havd* [sic] *been purchased, Money borrowed for this purpose, whereby a debt has been Contracted, as the Inhabitants Could not possibly subsist without Some to convey their lumber to Market, yet of this we have been stript* [sic] *of our Lumber and fish on Boord* [sic], *or the Returns of it in Provision for the Support of our families, so that by a Late Computation our Losses by water amounts to 3160 pounds, Besides the Arms, Ammunition Provisions and Apparels that have been taken by Plundering Refugees. The Season for a Number of years Past have been Verry* [sic] *unfavourable* [sic], *and the Drought so severe that the Peoples Attention has been more than Ever to Cultivate their farms; yet they have not been able to Raise above half enough of Bread for their Consumption, and the risqué* [sic]*of Importation being so Great and many Dispos'd* [sic] *to take advantage of the necessities of others, there by the Price of the Necessities of Life has been raised so high People were in the Greatest Difficultys* [sic] *and obliged to part with every Commodity they had to Dispose at the Buyers Price, so that Corn has been sold for four Dollars and more, and other articles in Proportion. Our hay has also been Cut off with the Drought for several years, so that our Stoks* [stocks] *has greatly Diminished by what they were at the Beginning of the War, and at Present there is such a Scarcity of Bread that hardly all the Lumber we have on hand can procure us bread for the Season, a Cord of Wood not fetching above a half a Bushel of Corn Besides the Debt contracted by Individuals thro [sic] the occasions by the War, the most part of the State Taxes for some years have not been Discharged and the town is utterly unable to Discharge the same, and if your Honours [sic] should now exact from us these taxes it would utterly Ruin the town, and Give such a Crush to the town, as it Could not for many years Recover of, and Put it out of Power for the future to pay Such a Proportion of taxes for Defraying the Expences [sic] of Government as otherwise it might. We would therefore beg your Honours would take our Distressing Situation under your serious Consideration and Discharge us of these taxes that were Due before Peace was made, and your Petitioners as in Duty bound shall ever Pray*

Philip M. Ulmer
Joshua Howard
Jacob Ludwig
Waldoborough, May: 13: 1783.
Selectmen of Waldoborough[1206]

Philip Ulmer served his Waldoboro community well as a public servant and representative of the town as a selectman. From this letter to the General Court of Massachusetts, it is obvious that the town was in a very stressful condition and that the standard of living was reduced to subsistence level. The burden of debt that was placed upon the town inhabitants was one that would cripple the economy and reduce the standard of living for many years to come. Somehow, Waldoboro and the surrounding towns would have to find a way to revive their lumbering, shipbuilding, fishing and merchant and commercial trading enterprises in order to breathe new life into Lincoln County.

BACKGROUND ABOUT DUCKTRAP

Until June 23, 1802, Lincolnville had been known only as Duck Trap. Duck Trap, located on the Penobscot Bay several miles northeast of Fort Pine Hill, had received its name originally from the Penobscot-Abenaki Indians who lived in the area. The migratory Indian hunters had known of the quiet harbor and cove for many generations and referred to the cove only as "Duck Trap." The game birds would seek out the quiet hidden cove for breeding, nesting and protection from harsh seas, variable weather and predators. The area surrounding the cove was covered with tall forest trees and tall grasses. When the game birds entered the narrow neck of the cove to feed on small fish and to nest, they had difficulty taking flight when danger threatened. The fish and game birds were "trapped," thus the name "Duck Trap" (referred to hereafter as Ducktrap).[1207] The Indians could easily kill as many birds as they needed to feed their families, and they could catch as many fish as they wanted by blocking the narrow neck of the protected cove from the harbor. The mud collected along the banks of the cove made good Indian pottery, which was used for cooking or storage. The sweetgrass, which was collected from the gently sloping banks along the eastern side of the Ducktrap stream that flowed into the cove from the nearby hills, could be made into desirable baskets of all kinds, sleeping mats, storage containers, nets and rope for various needs, and many other products as well. Eggs could be collected from the nests of the Canadian geese and ducks. Ducktrap cove was a most desirable hunting ground for the local migratory Indian tribes.[1208]

PHILIP AND GEORGE ULMER'S BUSINESS LIFE

George and Philip Ulmer had grown up in Waldoboro, where their grandfather Captain John Ulmer Sr. had been a respected military officer, community leader and merchant tradesman. Their uncle John Ulmer had helped to raise Philip and George after their father, Jacob, and their grandfather Captain John Ulmer Sr. died in the early 1760s. Uncle John Ulmer was also a ship owner, sailing captain, business owner and financial investor, as well as a successful land speculator and real estate developer in the Waldoboro vicinity. As the Revolutionary War slowly came to a close in frontier Maine, George and Philip Ulmer sought to stake out a strategic economic position in frontier Maine where they could develop their own prospects and business enterprises. They sought to become successful businessmen and political leaders like the merchants and officers whom they admired and sought to emulate.

In 1784, with advice and support from their uncle John in Waldoboro, George and Philip searched for a tract of land along the western shore of the Penobscot Bay that might be a possible site that would enable them to develop a multifaceted business complex and become entrepreneurs. Having served with the Massachusetts state militia during the American Revolution, the Ulmer brothers had often served at Fort Pine Hill at Camden (Rockland, Maine) with Colonel Prime's regiment, and they knew the Penobscot Bay coastal area well. Several miles north of Fort Pine Hill, they had discovered the small settlement of Ducktrap, which had a small, protected cove and a sufficient watershed area that might be an appropriate choice for their business ventures. The brothers saw an opportunity to acquire a large tract of land where they might combine several promising mill sites along the Ducktrap River, and the watershed stretched back into a rich virgin forest region. The river emptied into a protected harbor-cove that might be ideal for building sloops and schooners for trading and shipping purposes. The proposed tract of land in the Ducktrap watershed seemed to provide an adequate forest for lumbering, waterpower from the river, access to the sea and settlers who might be hired as laborers for their business venture.

James Getchal, an illiterate squatter, had already occupied the land beside the quiet harbor-cove, a favorite hunting and fishing location of the local Indians.[1209] Fortunately for the Ulmer brothers, James Getchal lacked the capital to be able to develop the site and readily sold his land claim to Philip and George for thirty pounds in September 1784.[1210] Getchal moved farther down the coastline to "squat" in another location. The Ulmer brothers greatly enlarged the land claim by running survey lines around the entire Ducktrap River basin and watershed, which was several hundred acres.[1211] In the Ulmer brothers' visionary development plan, the watershed's lumber could be harvested from their land, floated to a mill-seat dam and cut in their own mills. The wood and other products could be shipped from their own wharves, on their own trading vessels, to seaports along the eastern coast of America and as far south as the West Indies. Some oceangoing vessels could open up a merchant trade with Europe and other places in the outside world. Goods from Europe, the Mediterranean, India, China and the West Indies could be brought back to Ducktrap and sold in their own stores. Since the Ducktrap watershed and mill-seat property was originally purchased from a squatter with an illegal claim, the title to the property that the Ulmer brothers purchased and developed, unfortunately, was not valid. The Ulmer brothers did not find out about the illegal land claim problem for a number of years, long after they had invested years of their labor and large amounts of money to develop their business enterprises at Ducktrap Harbor and cove.

TAKING A LEAP OF FAITH

After much discussion about the possibilities of a business partnership with his brother at the Ducktrap harbor and cove mill seat, Philip decided to take a leap of faith. With encouragement, and probably financial support, from their uncle John, the Ulmer brothers ventured into the shipbuilding, cargo shipping and merchant trading businesses. Like his brother, George, Philip probably went ahead of his wife, Christiana, and their three young children to prepare a place for his family to live at Ducktrap (in present-day Lincolnville, Maine). Philip and George cleared a wooded site near the Ducktrap Harbor-cove, where they proceeded to build modest log cabins for their families. Once the log cabins were built and preparations were completed, the two young families moved to the sparsely settled coastal settlement at Ducktrap Harbor-cove. Philip and Christiana Ulmer moved with their three children from Waldoboro to their new rustic log home at "the Trap" in 1786. Philip had settled down on a piece of property on the western side of the Ducktrap River, while his brother, George, and his wife, Mary (hereafter called by her preferred nickname, Polly), settled on land to the eastern side of the river. Philip and Christiana Ulmer eventually had more children who were born in their rustic home at "the Trap." Christiana's widowed mother, Dolly Young (Anglicanized from Jung), moved from Waldoboro with Philip's family and took up residence with them at Ducktrap.

George Ulmer and his wife, Polly, had several children, but only the two eldest daughters, Mary and Sarah, survived to become adults. It is believed that their young son, George Ulmer Jr. (called by his nickname, Sudley), died as a young child at Ducktrap in 1787 since there are no other records of his presence having been recorded except in the private Ulmer cemetery at Ducktrap Harbor-cove. A daughter, Susanna (called by her nickname, Sukey), was born on November 25, 1785, in Ducktrap. Unfortunately, she accidentally drowned at Ducktrap Harbor-cove in June 1789 when she was about four years old. Sukey had been wading in the water at the neck of Ducktrap cove near "the Point," within sight of George Ulmer's house, when her legs were suddenly swept out from under her in the strong receding tide, and she drowned. She was buried on the small point of land at the entrance to the cove near where she drowned.[1212] Polly Ulmer was so distraught with the death of her small child, Sukey, that she went into early labor and suffered a miscarriage of her unborn son, who was also to be named George Ulmer Jr. Susanna

(Sukey) and her brother, George Ulmer Jr. (Sudley), are believed to have been the earliest known residents to have been buried at Ducktrap Harbor-cove in Lincolnville. There were no other children born to Polly and George Ulmer after this final tragic loss of their youngest children. George and Polly desperately wanted another child to replace the young children that they had recently lost. They wanted a namesake to carry on George Ulmer's name and the Ulmer family legacy.

Christiana Ulmer gave birth to a male child in May 1795, and the baby was named George Ulmer in honor of Philip's brother, George. Philip and Christiana's youngest son, George Ulmer, once he was weaned as a toddler, was probably raised in the home of Philip's brother and sister-in-law, George and Polly Ulmer. Philip and Christiana already had seven children (three boys and four girls) in their large family at Ducktrap at this time. The record of a young child named George disappeared from Philip and Christiana's family records about the time that the young toddler would have been weaned. A young male toddler suddenly appeared in the town records as an adopted child of Polly and George Ulmer, and he was named George Ulmer Jr. It is reasonable to speculate that the young child named George Ulmer, who was born to Philip and Christiana, was probably given to George and Polly to be raised as their own adopted child. There are no town records that indicate that Philip and Christiana's young toddler son, George Ulmer, ever passed away. He simply disappears from the immediate family, and a child of the same name appears in George and Polly Ulmer's family as an adopted son. Adoptions within a family were commonplace in the eighteenth and nineteenth centuries. Childless relatives or lonely grandparents (as in George and Martha Washington's case) often reared relatives' children, especially those from large families. With or without legal action or change of surnames, the adopted children lived with and were accepted as heirs of their adoptive family without giving up a loving relationship with their birth parents.[1213] Philip and Christiana soon had another child who was born not long after their young child, George, disappeared from Philip Ulmer's family records. Her name was Grace. The eight children living in Philip and Christiana Ulmer's home on the western side of the Ducktrap cove grew up at "the Trap" with their cousins, Sarah (Sally) and Mary, who were Polly and George Ulmer's two surviving daughters, and with the adopted child named George Ulmer Jr.

Building the Ulmer Brothers'
Business Ventures

After the Revolutionary War, veteran soldiers, sailors and marines, along with many new and displaced settlers in New England, sought a chance to work, to become successful in business and possibly become wealthy from the rich and abundant resources in the eastern frontier of Massachusetts (Maine). Many veteran soldiers of the Revolutionary War had received land-bounties from the government in payment for their military services in the Continental Army. The land claims in dispute in many parts of frontier Maine (unknown to the settlers) were not over available state land but over already owned land belonging to the heirs of the Waldo Patent and other land company investors (Kennebec/Plymouth Patent and Penobscot Patent Proprietors) in the Massachusetts Bay Colony.[1214] The small Ducktrap settlement, several miles to the northeast of Fort Pine Hill, had been sparsely settled prior to the Revolutionary War. Militia soldiers from Waldoboro, St. George and other settlements had marched through Ducktrap on a number of occasions during their militia duty assignments to protect Machias from British attacks. With the land-bounties promised by the Congress for military service during the war, some of the war veterans who were familiar with the Penobscot area moved to settlements like Ducktrap. The unsuspecting war veterans settled or "squatted" on plots of land that they illegally claimed for themselves. Like many other new Ducktrap settlers, the Ulmer brothers were also squatters on the land that was actually part of the Waldo Patent properties prior to the war.

Revolutionary War veterans like Major Philip Ulmer and his brother, George Ulmer, who was a captain in the local militia by the end of the Revolutionary War,[1215] moved to frontier Maine seeking land to settle upon and a chance to build a better future. The war veterans who had received government land-bounties believed that they had a legitimate claim to the frontier lands on which they had settled. Philip and George Ulmer believed that they had paid for a rightful claim for the Ducktrap watershed property at "the Trap" from James Getchal in September 1784.[1216] James Getchal, an opportunist and squatter, seems to have also duped other unsuspecting war veterans and other New England settlers with illegal land claims along the coastal frontier. Several war veterans and militia soldiers who had served with Major Philip Ulmer during the Revolution and on the Penobscot Expedition moved to Ducktrap near the log cabin of Philip Ulmer, whom they greatly respected.

The first thing that George and Philip developed when they committed to their business venture at Ducktrap cove were plans to build a milldam across the Ducktrap River and a sawmill that could be powered by the water flowing over the dam. These were two prerequisites to supply water power and access to their developing lumbering and shipbuilding businesses. The Ulmer family business associations at Salem and in Boston enabled Philip and George to obtain credit from wealthy Boston merchants and bankers. The land claim that Philip and George Ulmer purchased from James Getchal was greatly expanded into the watershed area, and a dam and bridge were constructed over the Ducktrap River.[1217] The Ulmer sawmill cut logs into planks and boards, and the brothers had vessels built in the quiet cove at "the Trap" with the timber cut from the surrounding hills. The cargo vessels anchored in the nearby harbor sailed from the loading docks constructed along Lincolnville beach and carried the wood products to markets in Boston, Philadelphia and other southern seaports as far away as the West Indies.

The Ulmer brothers continued to expand their trading business to include a shipyard in the harbor where many coastal sloops and schooners were built, some of which made commercial transatlantic voyages. The Ulmer brothers were the biggest employers in the local area and the first entrepreneurs

Picture of the Ulmer sawmill and lumbering operations on the Ducktrap River. *Courtesy of the Lincolnville Historical Society.*

in Ducktrap (later Lincolnville). The Ulmer brothers employed the local townspeople and some local Penobscot Indians to clear the land for crops and for harvesting timber. George and Philip eventually owned or held interests in five mills of various types built on the Ducktrap stream. These business enterprises extended into the backcountry of the Ducktrap watershed for the lumbering of the dense virgin forest and further extended into the Greene Plantation (present-day Belmont) vicinity.[1218] The sawmills provided for the numerous shipping needs and building purposes. The "King Pine" trees that were about two feet in diameter were used for masts that were harvested for the sailing ships. Wood was hauled by oxen or by horses to the banks above the millpond and rolled into the water. The wood was cut into appropriate sizes depending upon the particular needs. Shipbuilding took place on the gentle slope on the east side of the harbor-cove.

A carding mill and flour mill were built on the east side of the Ducktrap stream. The flour mill was later moved to the west side. After the grain was ground using waterpower, it was bolted through silk, and it was considered at that time to be the best in the state. Casks made from barrel staves and barrel

A sloop built at the location of Philip Ulmer's shipyard in Ducktrap cove. Philip Ulmer's house appears on the hill between the two masts. *Courtesy of the Lincolnville Historical Society.*

heads were assembled at the cooper shop near the road. Wooden casks, as many as 1,500 at a time in the late 1790s, were later shipped by Philip and George to their uncle John and cousin George Ulmer Jr.'s lime-burning facility at Glen Cove (Rockland) to supply the lime kilns located there. Wood for the kilns was rolled down the bank to vessels tied to the wharves on the western side of "the Trap." Lime for the Ulmer lime-burning facility at Ducktrap came from the quarry near Coleman Pond, and it was considered the finest lime to be found. In the winter, ice was cut from the millpond and shipped to Boston and other southern ports, and some of the ice was stored locally in wooden structures layered beneath sawdust from the sawmill. Ice could be kept packed in saw dust as an insulation for many months at a time, right through the summer and into early fall. It was a commodity that was in great demand and was financially lucrative, just like the firewood and lime used to make mortar for building and other purposes.

On the point of land that made a part of the Ducktrap cove, there was a hayshed that stored the pressed hay until it was shipped. A short distance to the west of the cove toward the town beach, there was a red brick house that was used as a general store on the first floor. On the second floor, there was a hall where special meetings could be held. Next to the store was another small building with a windmill on top that was used to grind corn and other grains.[1219] Fishing was conducted outside the small harbor near the cove and extended all along the seacoast. Wharves were built along the west side of the Ducktrap River and the town beach vicinity where vessels were loaded with cargo that would be shipped to many places in the world. During the construction of the wharves in Ducktrap cove, Indian pottery from a small local migratory Penobscot-Abenaki Indian tribe was found.[1220] Pottery continued to be discovered for many generations after the Ulmer brothers first established their dam, mills and wharves along the shore of the Penobscot Bay, in the cove and along the beach at Ducktrap Harbor (present-day Lincolnville Beach). The Ulmer brothers were the first entrepreneurs to hire and support the local migratory Indians tribes living in the wooded backcountry and Penobscot Bay area. Some of these Indians had served with the Ulmer brothers earlier during the Revolutionary War, at the military headquarters at Thomaston and at Fort Pine Hill in Camden.[*] Some of these same Indian braves had served with Captain Philip Ulmer in the Penobscot Expedition in 1779 against the British forces at Fort George on Castine.[1221]

---

[*] *Author's comment*: Present-day Penobscot Bay Medical Center in Rockland is located on the grounds of the old fort.

As the nephews of Captain John Ulmer, a respected and wealthy merchant trader, real estate speculator and landowner in the Waldoboro vicinity, Philip and George Ulmer were able to secure trade goods on credit from merchants in Boston to stock their newly built store and shipping chandlery at Ducktrap Harbor. The Ulmer store, located near Philip's house, carried goods for sale from the West Indies, England, France, the Netherlands and southern coastal towns that the returning trading vessels brought back to Ducktrap. With commodities and profits made from the Ducktrap watershed, Philip and George were able to pay back their creditors and were able to secure new capital (mostly for dry goods, basic necessities and supplies) to continue expanding their businesses. In time, the Ulmer brothers developed the largest frontier trading and mercantile enterprise in the Penobscot Bay region.[1222]

Many settlers in the surrounding area were eager for dry goods, supplies and provisions from the Ulmer general store. Tempted by easy credit, many settlers became the Ulmers' debtors. Settlers sustained their credit by delivering mill logs, cordwood, staves, shingles, spars, clapboards and ship's timber to the Ulmer brothers' wharf. The poor settlers who were barely able to make a living farming were extended credit by the Ulmers for needed supplies and provisions for their families. Through a barter system, the debtors could make payments for credit by exchanging cordwood and other products they might produce (such as fur pelts, candles and handmade items) that the Ulmers could use in their shipbuilding and trading business. The settlers were eager to work at the Ulmers' various businesses in exchange for goods (such as rum, molasses, cloth, spices, food and other provisions) that came back on the lumber ships from other southern seacoast towns, from Europe and Great Britain or from the West Indies and other foreign ports.

General Henry Knox had one of his agents investigate the mill seat, the shipyard and the related business developments of the industrious Ulmer brothers at "the Trap." He decided to exploit the brothers' lumbering, shipbuilding, shipping and mercantile ventures. Philip and George Ulmer had invested their lives and fortunes in the settlement community and in their Ducktrap business enterprises. They had developed the lumbering business at the Ducktrap watershed and the mill seat at the harbor-cove. They had built their prosperous shipbuilding, cargo shipping and mercantile businesses at Ducktrap that employed and supported the town and provided a comfortable livelihood for their families. It would be a rude awakening for the Ulmer brothers when they later discovered that their purchased land claim and their business developments and investments were not valid. Henry Knox, who obtained the Waldo Patent territory through his marriage to Waldo's heir, Lucy, could legally take over their various businesses and evict them from their land and homes if his terms were not met.

In 1788, John Hancock was the governor of Massachusetts. Benjamin Lincoln was the lieutenant governor and had served with Henry Knox during the Revolution. The Ulmer brothers had gambled in making extensive land purchases from Henry Knox in 1788 on the Ducktrap watershed property. If General Knox was patient about collecting on the Ulmer brothers' promissory notes, and if their shipping business went well, they would enhance their prospects for success, and all would prosper. Philip Ulmer supervised the Ulmer brothers' shipbuilding business and commercial shipping operations while George acted as land agent for the Penobscot region's original Waldo Patent holder, General Henry Knox. George's surveying and land sales for Henry Knox netted the brothers commissions in the form of special price breaks by which they could obtain their large landholdings.[1223] These landholdings provided the lumber for the sawmills that produced the wood products for the shipbuilding and related businesses. The successful development of the Ducktrap watershed and harbor helped the small settlement to grow and develop into a busy and productive village. Many sailing and coastal vessels were built and sailed from Ducktrap Harbor and cove on the Penobscot Bay.

Philip and George had no choice but to accept whatever terms they could make with Henry Knox since his power and political influence extended high into the state government. The Ulmer brothers again had to purchase the Ducktrap property with a legal deed and legal land claim from Knox

Ducktrap bridge and millseat at Ducktrap harbor-cove in Lincolnville, Maine. Major Philip Ulmer and other Patriot soldiers of the Revolutionary War and War of 1812 are buried in the small Ducktrap cemetery at the point to the left of the schooner. *Courtesy of the Lincolnville Historical Society.*

and his lawyers.[1224] They were too heavily invested at Ducktrap Harbor and cove to risk losing everything that they had worked so hard to develop at the watershed since the end of the war. They encouraged their neighbors and influential friends to make the same deal with Knox that they had made. Within a short time, most of the coastal settlements, including almost all of the leading men in the area, submitted to Knox's terms in August and September 1788.[1225] Henry Knox gave his financial, political and business patronage to George and Philip's commercial developments at Ducktrap Harbor and Ducktrap watershed. General Knox used his political influence to advance George Ulmer's personal and political standing in the county and state; however, this benevolence, in turn, kept George dependent and submissive to Henry Knox's desires, whims and personal requests for twenty years. As General Knox's principal land agent, surveyor and tax collector, George was resented and unpopular with the settlers and squatters in the Waldo Patent territory with whom he had to deal as the proprietor's representative and Knox's legal rights enforcer.

HENRY KNOX AND HIS WALDO PATENT LAND

Before the Revolution, the Waldo heirs would have quickly stopped the Ulmer brothers from occupying and developing such a valuable tract of land as the Ducktrap watershed and millseat. The confusion of the war caused the suspension of proprietary control and created new opportunities that enabled people like the Ulmer brothers to take advantage of the situation. During the colonial times, the wealthy proprietors tried to establish mercantile empires by monopolizing the profits of the middleman who stood between the settlers that produced goods from the natural resources and the outside markets. The proprietors sought to control the harvesting of the forest's resources in order to keep commodities passing through their hands and to fix the prices for imported trade goods and provisions that were sold at their own stores. For this reason, powerful proprietors usually refused to sell millseats, but chose to run the sites themselves, or they leased out a few sites to trusted subordinates for a profit.

After the war, in the mid 1780s, the returning wealthy proprietors (company landowners) and the displaced property landowners of frontier Maine found that entrepreneurial newcomers had taken over their commercial monopolies on illegally claimed land. Some of the settlers had made improvements to their claimed land and had developed businesses. They were unwilling to be uprooted and displaced by the returning proprietors. This caused a dilemma that positioned the legal landowners against the most influential settlers (squatters). Failure to restore the prewar mercantile and land monopolies in the Waldo Patent would have given some of the most valuable property to illegal settlers in the coastal seaport settlements and squatters in the backcountry regions. After reassessing the postwar situation in frontier Maine, Henry Knox decided that obtaining land payments from "the people" (squatters and settlers on illegally claimed land) would enable him to regain control over the Waldo Patent's coastal areas and the unsettled backcountry districts and was a more achievable goal.

In 1785, an agent of Henry Knox, Major William Molineux, Esquire of Camden Township, observed the Ulmer brothers' development of the Ducktrap River watershed and millseat at "the Trap" and advised Henry Knox to break up the business monopoly at the Ducktrap watershed and reassume his proprietary authority. Instead, Henry Knox decided that he might be able to acquire the influence of Philip and George Ulmer, who were quickly becoming leading men in their growing settlement. Henry Knox felt that he could manipulate the Ulmer brothers into his service by offering them his business and political patronage and the purchase of the watershed land that they were developing from his estate. By submitting to Knox's business terms, the brothers could receive a proper land title to "the Trap." The residents of Ducktrap and New Canaan plantations (as they were known at the time) had been the Waldo Patent's most resistant and hostile settlers.[1226]

It was important for Henry Knox to find a way to reclaim control of his Waldo Patent territory and to bring the settlers and squatters living on his property to his financial terms. They needed to either purchase the land from him and receive a clear land title or lease his land and pay him a land tax (rent) for living on his property. Many people who lived on illegal land claims (result of a land grab) or who temporarily "squatted" on his land did not want to do either. Veterans of the American Revolution had received land bounties in lieu of payment for military service, and they felt entitled to claim land seemingly not owned and unoccupied in the Maine frontier without knowing the clear ownership of the land. When Henry Knox tried to reassert his authority and control of his Waldo Patent property, this caused stress, anxiety and confrontation with many disgruntled settlers and squatters. Knox's plan was to enlist the Ulmer brothers' influence and respected position in the plantation settlements and pressure them to bring the squatters on his Waldo Patent land to Knox's terms to pay taxes for land-lease plots; or the squatters could purchase the real estate they settled and developed; or they could move to another place so that the land could be sold to someone else. Through the efforts of the Ulmer brothers, the squatters and settlers on the Waldo Patent land began to accept Knox's terms. They used leverage as creditors and employers to influence the townspeople into paying the taxes that were owed to Henry Knox for living on his land. With Philip and George Ulmer's help, half of the six hundred squatter families who lived in the Waldo Patent's coastal settlements, including almost all of the leading men in the county, submitted to Knox's terms by September 24, 1788.[1227] Those who objected to settling with Henry Knox continued to resist Knox's efforts to tax or seize their land, sometimes resorting to threats of violence. The settlers of Islesboro on Long Island, some of whom predated the Revolution, petitioned the General Court of Massachusetts to examine the claim of Henry Knox to the ownership of the island property located in the Penobscot Bay. A commission was eventually appointed in 1797 to settle and declare the rights of ownership on the island. The islanders requested incorporation as a separate and independent town. The act of incorporation as a town was passed by the Massachusetts General Court on January 28, 1789. An agreement was eventually made between Henry Knox and the settlers of Long Island (present-day Islesboro, Maine) on August 3, 1799, at the house of Major Philip Ulmer in Ducktrap.[1228] The results of the meeting were recorded on May 24, 1800, and printed in the *Proceedings of the Boston Society at the Annual Meeting, January 10, 1893.* Philip Ulmer's role as a leader, community organizer and councilor for the poorly educated and powerless frontier settlers was demonstrated throughout his life.

In August 1788, through very favorable terms framed by General Knox and his financial backers, the Ulmer brothers were able to secure for themselves a commission in the form of special price breaks for the large landholdings of the whole Ducktrap watershed and the millseat that they had built at Ducktrap Harbor with a secure title to the land. Henry Knox readily sold them the entire harborfront in 1788.[1229] The Ulmer brothers eventually owned as much as 2,668 acres of virgin forest in the surrounding area.[1230] Henry Knox agreed to sell the brothers their lime quarries, millseats and harbor lots for four shillings (or sixty-seven cents) per acre. Knox also renounced the Waldo heirs' prewar practice of forbidding construction of any sawmills or limekiln facilities on the premises sold. The purchaser of Henry Knox's deed became the complete owner of his piece of property.[1231] For the Ulmer brothers, the only payment demanded for the land by Henry

Knox was a series of promissory notes secured by two mortgages, one from each brother. In return for Henry Knox's financial help and patronage in the Ulmer business enterprises at Ducktrap Harbor and mill seat at "the Trap," George and Philip Ulmer were required to pay investment dividends to Henry Knox from profits made in their businesses.[1232] By conceding a small part of his vast wilderness holdings to the coastal settlements' leading men at bargain prices, Henry Knox was able to receive substantial payments from the settlers who had illegal claims and from squatters who couldn't afford to purchase land. Henry Knox was able to regain control over the Waldo Patent's unsettled coastal and backcountry lands in the frontier region of eastern Massachusetts in present-day Maine.

In January 1789, General Henry Knox, as partner and financial backer in the developing Ulmer business enterprises at Ducktrap, gave a challenging assignment to George Ulmer, Knox's newly appointed tax and real estate agent. The assignment would test his abilities to deal with the many disgruntled settlers and squatters who were living illegally on his patent property in the Waldoboro coastal area. George rode into his hometown of Waldoboro, and he was promptly met by an angry crowd of townspeople. The Waldoboro settlers did not approve of the decision that George and his brother, Philip, had made in supporting Henry Knox's reassertion of ownership to the Waldo Patent land claims. They did not approve of George and Philip's purchase of their own land claims in Ducktrap from Henry Knox because it undermined their own position on their own illegally claimed land in Waldoboro. George's life was threatened, but fortunately he was able to explain and defend his stand concerning the land purchases as a business endeavor and not an effort to undermine anyone. Major William Molineux, Henry Knox's agent, observed the confrontation in Waldoboro and reported back to Henry Knox that "[George] acted an artful part [and] rendered us more service than any man on the patent."[1233] George was able to escape without harm, "dissipating the remaining doubts among Knox's minions," as Knox's agent would later report. Henry Knox wrote back to his agent: "I am glad to hear from you of the firmness of Capt. [George] Ulmer. We must cultivate the two brothers."[1234]

As the Ulmer brothers' business patron, Henry Knox appointed George Ulmer as his principal land surveyor and tax agent to supervise the development of the new settlements and backcountry villages. For his services, Henry Knox obtained two coveted positions as justices of the peace for both Philip and George Ulmer from the Massachusetts Governor's Council.[1235] In return, Henry Knox expected their loyalty to him for the political favors that he had given to the Ulmer brothers. General Knox used his influence in getting an act of incorporation passed in the Massachusetts General Court for a toll bridge to be erected over the Ducktrap River to facilitate transportation along the important east–west coastal road along the Penobscot Bay. George Ulmer and his associates were expected to collect the tolls from those using the bridge. Money from the tolls was meant to maintain and improve the bridge structure and to replace the bridge if it were damaged or destroyed in spring floods and in harsh storms during the year. The toll collector would be paid for his services. Henry Knox was able to obtain an appointment for George Ulmer as the collector of the Federal Direct Taxes of 1798 in Ducktrap, Northport and Belfast.[1236] In the early 1800s, General Knox was able to intervene to obtain a government pension for a supposed war wound received by George Ulmer by exempting him from the medical examination legally needed to obtain the government pension. George later admitted the injury was caused by an accident and not received as a result of the war.[1237] George Ulmer became heavily indebted to General Knox as his business and political patron.

For the next twenty-plus years, the fortunes of the Ulmer brothers were to a great extent tied to the whims and desires of Henry Knox, politically, financially and business-wise. Capitalizing on Henry Knox's patronage, the Ulmer brothers were able to develop the largest mercantile business on the western shore of the Penobscot Bay.[1238] Henry Knox was able to supervise the development of all phases of the Ulmer business enterprises, and he reaped financial rewards in profits and dividends from the labors and successes of the Ulmer brothers.[1239] George received a commission for serving as Henry Knox's land surveyor, real estate agent and tax collector on leased land and sale of land to the frontier settlers. The Ulmer brothers shared in handling the lumbering and the mill seat operations, and they owned or had interests in five mills of various types that were operated by business associates.[1240] Philip served as business executive and administrator for the shipbuilding, commercial shipping, mercantile and trading enterprises. The operations of the Ducktrap stores associated with their businesses were shared responsibilities.

In 1779, John Ulmer, uncle of Philip and George, sold his one-third ownership in the huge tract of property on the west side of the Medomak River in Waldoboro to Matthias Remilly (a family relative). The original shared tract of property that John had owned with Philip Ulmer and Matthias Remilly stretched back many miles into the backcountry watershed above the head of the river and extended eastward to the Penobscot Bay.[1241]

In 1794, John Ulmer sold 264 acres on the east side of Waldoboro to David Doane of Barnstable County, Massachusetts, that included a gristmill, a sawmill below the county road and the bridge that he had previously given to the town of Waldoboro for public land.[1242] In the mid-1780s and early 1790s, John Ulmer sold most of his other landholdings in Waldoboro and the backcountry area in order to help finance the new business ventures for himself and his sons at Camden Harbor (present-day Rockland). John Ulmer purchased a valuable parcel of land from Henry Knox in 1794. In 1795, John and his son, named George (also referred to as George Ulmer Jr. during the Revolution), built a large lime-burning and shipping business at Lermond's Cove, about eighteen miles from Philip and George Ulmer's successful lumbering, shipbuilding, cargo shipping and merchant trading enterprises at Ducktrap Harbor-cove. Captain John Ulmer built and navigated some of his own merchant ships that were built at his shipyard at Clam Cove for his shipping and lime-burning businesses at the harbor (present-day Rockland, Maine). The Ulmer lime-burning facility, operated by Philip's uncle John, his cousin George Ulmer Jr. and several other cousins, eventually became the largest mercantile and shipping enterprise of its kind on the eastern coast.[1243] Henry Knox sought to exploit John Ulmer's shipbuilding, shipping, quarrying and lime-burning businesses at the harbor since he needed to maintain his control over entrepreneurial business developments in his Waldo Patent holdings. Knox sought to also receive financial dividends and profits for himself from his business investments.[1244]

RADICAL ACTIVISM ERUPTS IN THE WALDO PATENT TERRITORY

[I am] *the best friend of the industrious and moral part of the settlers. The idle and wicked cannot benefit any new country, and the sooner they depart the better for the settlement.*
—*Henry Knox*[1245]

The radical itinerant preacher Samuel Ely, who had fought at the Battle of Bennington and had been tried by court-martial for collecting booty on the battlefield during the Revolution, was again causing problems and stirring up rebellion in western Massachusetts and northeastern Connecticut in 1781–

1782.[1246] In January 1782, Samuel Ely led an insurrection in Hampshire County, a precursor to Shay's Rebellion by four years. In April 1782, Ely led a rebellion of farmers against the new land tax in Northampton and forced the closure of the Court of General Sessions prior to the end of the American Revolution.[1247] The county judges in Massachusetts ordered Samuel Ely arrested. He was tried and convicted of "treasonable practices" and held in the county jail. In June, a gang of armed men broke into the jail in Springfield, Massachusetts, and liberated Samuel Ely, who fled to Vermont and continued his radical and violent activities. In September 1782, the Vermont courts tried and convicted Ely of sedition, and he was handed over to the Hampshire County court to stand trial there.[1248] Preacher Ely pitifully petitioned the Supreme Judicial Court for his release because of poor health. In March 1783, Ely was released on bond by the court with the stipulation that he would leave the state of Massachusetts and not return.[1249] Instead, he moved eastward, where he squatted on land in the Waldo Patent of frontier Maine (present-day Saturday Cove, Northport). Preacher Ely continued fomenting unrest among the poor settlers and backcountry farmers, encouraging defiance and rebellious activities against wealthy land owners, judicial courts and successful authority figures. Preacher Ely's radical ideology and fiery speeches incited unrest and rebellion among the backcountry settlers and poor farmers in the frontier areas of New Canaan and Greene plantations. The activities of these radicalized activists would later cause problems for Philip and George Ulmer's personal lives and businesses at Ducktrap several miles to the south.

Between 1786 and 1787, the Massachusetts General Court moved to make justice more accessible to the isolated residents of Lincoln County.[1250] The Probate Court and Registry of Deeds was extended to Machias; the Court of Common Pleas and Sessions was established at Waldoboro and Hallowell. The Massachusetts legislature set extra terms of the regular courts and a term of the Superior Court at the county seat at Pownalboro, and in addition, the General Court separated Lincoln County into two additional jurisdictions of Hancock and Washington Counties.[1251] Henry Knox used his influence to have George Ulmer appointed as sheriff of Hancock County. Knox also appointed George Ulmer as his principal land agent and surveyor to supervise the development of his backcountry property. As men with "genteel aspirations," orderly principles and commercial relationships with businessmen in the wider world, the Ulmer brothers received the status of "Esquire," the recognition as "respected gentlemen" in court cases and land deeds.[1252] George Ulmer also served as the postmaster in the Lincolnville and Camden Township vicinity in 1796 and in the following years.[1253] As postmaster, George Ulmer was kept informed and in touch with other frontier coastal towns, knowledgeable about the interior village settlements and the important leaders and merchants in the frontier communities. He was able to keep informed about the latest political and business news, and he made valuable contacts with wealthy leaders in the state government of Massachusetts. As justice of the peace in the Hancock County vicinity, it was George Ulmer's job to "maintain the Peace" in the coastal and interior settlements, to arrest those individuals who stirred rebellion against the state or disregarded the laws of the state and county and to hold offenders in the town jail or county prison at Castine for trial. George Ulmer remained with the local militia and served as major at the fort and county prison at Castine. Henry Knox used his influence in the Massachusetts General Court to obtain the appointment of George Ulmer as the Collector of the Federal Direct Taxes of 1789 in Ducktrap, Northport and Belfast.[1254]

Philip Ulmer, being a humble and principled person, rarely used his social and political status of Esquire in any of his official business papers or to obtain social status recognition. Philip focused his attention and service on his community and the needs of his large family. Philip co-authored a code of bylaws for the town of Ducktrap, and he wrote a petition requesting permission from the General Court of Massachusetts for the settlement to be incorporated on June 23, 1802, as the town of Lincolnville.[1255] He represented Lincolnville in other petitions to the General Court of Massachusetts and to the House of Representatives, listing the town's deprivations and its needs for relief from burdensome state taxes. Philip co-authored a petition written to the president of the United States about Lincolnville's economic concerns for the new nation and the deprivations caused by the imposed U.S. embargo on Maine's seaport trading communities. Philip was elected to represent Lincolnville in the General Court of Massachusetts as a legislative representative to the House of Representatives in 1807 for two terms.[1256] As the justice of the peace, Philip Ulmer performed legal ceremonies in the local towns and county vicinity that included the marriages of several of his children in Lincolnville.[1257] Philip Ulmer remained active in the administrative concerns of the town of Lincolnville, as well as its business and political life, until days before his death in October 1816.

George Ulmer was very conscious of sustaining the external recognition of his political standing as a reputable gentleman within the state and the community, and he used the influential Esquire designation frequently. George Ulmer, like many men who became influential leaders in frontier

Maine, was a person who was keenly aware of the usefulness of influential political contacts and the patronage of wealthy Maine proprietors and merchants to advance his own personal goals of authority, social recognition and political status. Because of George and Philip Ulmer's help in bringing the squatters and settlers to terms with Knox's land tax and claim settlements, General Knox used his influence to secure an act in the General Court of Massachusetts for the incorporation of a toll bridge across the Ducktrap River.[1258] Prior to this government act, the Ulmer brothers erected, repaired and replaced the Ducktrap Bridge many times over the years, at their expense, in order to facilitate easier passage from one side of the Ducktrap River to the other. Once the toll bridge was built according to the directions of the state and the toll was instituted, many people tried to wade across the river above and below the bridge in order to avoid paying the toll.

In 1790, the federal census indicated that Samuel Ely had taken up residence at Pownalboro (near Waldoboro), where he continued to stir up unrest in the community against Henry Knox, the proprietor of the Waldo Patent.[1259] In June 1792, having been ousted from Pownalboro, Samuel Ely moved farther eastward and squatted on land in the Waldo Patent at Saturday Point (in Northport), several miles north of "the Trap," where the Ulmer brothers lived and had their lumbering, shipbuilding and merchant trading businesses. Samuel Ely resumed his rebellious activities by encouraging the settlers in the Ducktrap, New Canaan and Greene Plantation areas to drive off Henry Knox's land surveyors and tax agents (often by intimidation and violence) and to "discipline" those who supported or represented the Great Proprietors, owners of the Waldo Patent and the two large holding companies in Lincoln County and the Penobscot region. Ely forcefully challenged the legality of the grants to Henry Knox on the grounds that great proprietary tracts, backed by the legal authority of the state, elevated the few above the many and was contrary to republican liberty.[1260] The rebellious squatters in the backcountry resorted to physical violence and sometimes murder of those who did not agree with their ideology. Samuel Ely and his armed supporters justified their violence by concluding that the Massachusetts state government, namely the Massachusetts General Court, must suspend its particular oppressive and unconstitutional laws and taxes. They felt that the political fathers in the Massachusetts General Court could be forced into correcting their mistakes by causing widespread unrest and armed rebellion among the farmers and poor settlers. By humbling the powerful proprietors, like Henry Knox, and their supporters with acts of violence to their personal property and businesses, they could eventually force successful leaders in government to submit to the pressures of the rebelling crowd.

Samuel Ely continued to agitate and stir up resentment against General Knox and his surveyors, agents and supporters. The squatters on Knox's patent property feared eviction from their homes for non-payment of taxes on their squatted land. Some settlers in the Ducktrap and New Canaan area held illegal land claims on which improvements had been built, and they had not paid taxes, nor did they intend to pay taxes, to Knox, the rightful owner of the land. The squatters and settlers opposed Henry Knox's real estate development plans and his imposed land-lease taxes on property that Knox legally owned in Ducktrap, Northport and the surrounding backcountry area of Greene Plantation. Most of the settlers in the backcountry plantation areas delayed paying Henry Knox the taxes that were due to him. They hoped that the General Court of Massachusetts would intervene to quiet the agitated and rebellious settlers with one-hundred-acre homesteads for five dollars.[1261]

Threats were made against Henry Knox's land agents (such as George Ulmer) and supporters (such as Philip Ulmer) that erupted into violent actions. Land surveyors and agents of Henry Knox were harassed, ambushed, assaulted and shot at by disgruntled squatters in the backcountry, who called themselves Liberty Men.[1262] Settlers who supported Henry Knox in his land claim or had come to terms and had purchased their own land from Knox were often threatened and sometimes had their milldams and sawmills destroyed, their barns and houses burned down and their cattle mutilated. This violence was eventually focused upon George and Philip Ulmer at Ducktrap because they had come to terms with Henry Knox for the purchase of their watershed land in 1788 and had accepted Henry Knox's business patronage and political influence in the state legislature. George Ulmer, who was in the employ of Henry Knox as his principal land surveyor and real estate agent, became a primary focus for Ely and his Liberty Men. George, while fulfilling his duty as Knox's agent and tax collector, was taken captive on at least one occasion by Samuel Ely's radical supporters. He was threatened with bodily harm, with the destruction of his business ventures with Philip at "the Trap" and with death by a gang of Samuel Ely's followers.[1263]

In February 1793, during a particularly tense altercation, George Ulmer publicly struck Samuel Ely and challenged him to a duel.[1264] In April 1793, Samuel Ely and his supporters obtained their vengeance with axes and crowbars, tearing down the Ulmer milldam on the Ducktrap

River[1265] and causing the Ulmer brothers a great financial loss. The logs that were held in the booms above the dam for sawing were washed away into the bay, causing a danger to shipping. The bridge across the river was washed out by the broken dam, and the sawmill could not be used during the important spring sawing and shipbuilding season since the dam provided the power to run the mill.[1266] Philip Ulmer's shipbuilding, cargo shipping and trading businesses sustained huge financial losses. The workers at the sawmill and the shipyard, as well as carpenters and the sailors who sailed the cargo transports and trading vessels in the import and export business, had to be laid off until the milldam could be rebuilt and more lumber was able to be harvested, cut and brought to the mill. The dry goods remaining in the Ulmer chandlery and merchant stores were quickly depleted. The Ulmer brothers, their families and the Ducktrap community suffered for these acts of unprovoked destruction and violence. The milldam was destroyed twice during Samuel Ely's efforts to incite violence and destruction against the Ulmer brothers, who were known supporters of Henry Knox. Other destructive actions against the Ulmer brothers and their patron, Henry Knox, continued in the effort to cripple their businesses and destroy their economic wealth. The violence impacted everyone in the town in one way or another.

Even though Philip was not directly involved in any of the activities of the detested land surveyors or tax collectors for Henry Knox, he and his family suffered great business losses from the violent activities incited and carried out by Samuel Ely and his radical supporters against George Ulmer and Henry Knox's other surveyors and agents. On at least two occasions, logs that had been brought to the Ulmer sawmill by poorer neighbors to obtain goods from the Ulmer stores to pay their credit debts (barter system) or to pay Henry Knox's taxes for land use (paid "in kind" for lease or rent) were sabotaged. Preacher Ely had the booms cut by his activist supporters during the night, and the next morning, hundreds of spars were discovered floating in the Ducktrap Harbor, piled up in disarray in the cove and floating in Penobscot Bay.[1267] This action of vandalism hurt the Ulmer brothers' businesses financially as well as hurt the poor farmers and neighbors who needed goods from the Ulmer stores or who were trying to pay their credit debts and land taxes. George Ulmer wrote a letter to Henry Knox describing the events. In 1793, Samuel Ely was charged in the Hancock County Court of Common Pleas with the destruction of the Ulmer brothers' milldam at Ducktrap Harbor. Twice Ely was charged in 1796 with destruction of the log booms at the Ducktrap milldam and with the loss of hundreds of valuable spars that were dispersed in the Penobscot Bay. The destructive actions at Ducktrap Harbor-cove caused a great danger to merchant navigation and commercial shipping in the harbor and to those who fished and sailed on the Penobscot Bay.

HENRY KNOX'S HUNGER FOR LAND AND A GRAND LIFESTYLE

In spite of Henry Knox's leadership and recognition as a respected and accomplished general during the Revolutionary War and his service to the country as the secretary of war during George Washington's presidency, he had an inner driving need to demonstrate his wealth and power through his successes as a land speculator and in multifaceted business enterprises. Eventually, Henry Knox's hunger to acquire more land and businesses caused him to plunge deeper into debt. His financial overextension in multiple directions without sufficient capital would eventually lead to his downfall. In 1791–92, Henry Knox and his ambitious New York agent, William Duer, undertook a huge speculative gamble in which they attempted to corner the entire market for public lands in frontier Maine.[1268] William Duer had been a member of New York's Committee for Detecting and Defeating Conspiracies, the enforcement arm of the political revolutionaries.[1269] Duer had been involved during the Revolution with the early formation of the Culper Ring (Washington's first spies) by recommending Nathaniel Sackett to General Washington as an undercover agent for espionage operations against the British forces stationed across Long Island Sound in the New York City and harbor vicinity.[1270] On occasion, Duer also carried secret messages from the spies in the Culper Ring to General Washington wherever he was located in the Highlands Department outside of New York City.

Henry Knox was a very shrewd and astute person at keeping and using his military, political and business contacts throughout his life. He knew how to manipulate and curry favor with people for his own personal gain. General Knox had served as commander of General Washington's artillery, and he had cultivated influential men who had also served as officers during the war. Henry Knox had developed numerous business contacts with wealthy merchants and politicians in the federal and state Congresses during his service as secretary of war in President

Washington's administration. A number of well-known businessmen, politicians, military officers and French diplomats and emissaries again reappeared in Henry Knox's life in the 1790s in frontier Maine.

General Knox was able to use his considerable political capital, military reputation and government position as a retired secretary of war to persuade the Massachusetts General Court to waive its 1.0-million-acre limit on land sale and permit the purchase of 3.5 million acres for him and for his partner, William Duer.[1271] Henry Knox's good friend General David Cobb was the Massachusetts General Court's speaker of the house. David Cobb, using his position and influence in the state government, enabled the restrictions to be waived in Henry Knox's case.[1272] There were two intermediaries who helped Henry Knox acquire millions of acres of state land in the Province of Maine. They were Henry Jackson and Royal Flint, who served as Knox's agents or "front men."[1273] Through these intermediaries, General Henry Jackson and Royal Flint, Henry Knox and William Duer made the huge land purchases in two parcels—one in eastern Maine and the other at the head of the Kennebec—for less than twenty cents an acre.[1274] The land speculators hid from the Massachusetts General Court their inability to pay for the land. They planned on future land sales to the influx of veterans and settlers to finance their monopoly of land pricing in frontier Maine Province.

Henry Jackson and Benjamin Lincoln, who had both served as officers with General Knox during the war, also served as intermediaries and financial backers for Henry Knox's land dealings. Henry Jackson served as Henry Knox's lawyer. Through devious financial and political manipulation, through manipulation of land prices and by receiving dividends through business patronage, Henry Knox and William Duer planned to meet all subsequent payments to the commonwealth.[1275] Henry Knox had finally been successful in rejoining the divided parts of the original Waldo Patent territory under his single ownership by inheritance through his marriage to Lucy, granddaughter of General Samuel Waldo.[1276]

The two venture capitalists, Henry Knox and William Duer, soon found that they were financially overextended, and by March 1792, Duer was bankrupt and taken to debtors' prison.[1277] Henry Knox, who was almost as insolvent, did not have the financial capital to make the upcoming payments to the Commonwealth of Massachusetts for the vast acreage of state land that he had purchased. Henry Knox contacted his friend William Bingham, a wealthy capitalist in Philadelphia and a former American arms agent during the Revolution. Bingham had been the American arms agent stationed on the island of Martinique (West Indies) to supply Washington's Continental Army with military goods, cannons and munitions from France through Robert Morris's company in Philadelphia. It was William Bingham whose assignment was to procure money and military supplies from France (and later from Spain and the Netherlands) for the Continental Army's Artillery Corps, led by General Henry Knox. William Bingham bought out William Duer's partnership with Henry Knox, and he took over all future loans and management of the vast landholdings of state land.[1278] Bingham advanced Henry Knox a large loan and promised Knox one-third of the eventual profits from land sales. Henry Knox never repaid the loan to William Bingham, and Knox faded from the land speculation enterprise. The vast land acquisition became known as the Bingham Purchase.[1279] David Cobb, a former army officer and state politician, became the land sales agent for William Bingham.[1280]

Although General Knox had been an able military leader during the American Revolution and in his tenure in public service as secretary of war, his abilities did not extend into peacetime business investments or land speculation. As a visionary and venture capitalist, Henry Knox had invested his patronage and financial backing in a variety of business ventures such as sawmills, dams for power production, limekilns, brickyards and shipbuilding. Since 1788, Henry Knox had developed not only a close friendship with the Ulmer brothers on a personal, military and Masonic level, but he had also developed a close business relationship as a patron in the Ulmer brothers' various business enterprises at Ducktrap Harbor and cove. Knox continued to receive dividends from the Ulmer brothers' business enterprises at Ducktrap even when his other business ventures failed.[1281] Henry Knox often would bring prospective land speculators or possible venture capitalists to observe the Ulmer business enterprises at Ducktrap Harbor.

With William Bingham's timely loan, in the years 1793–94, Henry Knox proceeded to have his lavish summer retirement home constructed at Thomaston (Maine). Knox contracted to have a magnificent Federal-style summer mansion built on his property along the St. George River and overlooking the Atlantic Ocean. As Henry Knox's principal surveyor, George Ulmer surveyed the land for Knox's Thomaston estate and the homesite for the new residence.[1282] Henry and Lucy Knox planned to entertain visitors and foreign diplomats in a grand style at their palatial summer estate. From Thomaston, Henry Knox would be able to oversee his land development enterprises and his investments in various speculative businesses on his vast landholdings. Knox would often bring influential politicians, wealthy merchants and foreign diplomats from France (whom he had befriended during his political and military careers) to the District of Maine, where he would give them a coastal tour of his vast landholdings and business ventures in the eastern frontier. The business complex that Philip and George Ulmer had built at Ducktrap Harbor and cove was Henry Knox's primary destination on the frontier tour. Henry Knox tried to encourage the wealthy Europeans and wealthy American politicians and businessmen to also become land speculators and business investors in the Maine frontier that he mostly owned. On one such tour of the Penobscot Bay region in 1794, General Henry Knox and the French Duke de la Rochefoucauld-Liancourt visited Philip and George Ulmer to see their shipyard and business complex at Ducktrap Harbor. In the course of the tour of the Penobscot Bay, the Duke observed that:

> *Save the brothers, Almer* [Ulmer], *we found none who could be said to be even moderately intelligent...They are universally poor, or at least live as if they were so in extreme degree. The habitations are everywhere poor, low huts. Everywhere, you find a dirty dark-coloured* [sic] *rye-meal, and that not in sufficient quantity...In short, of all America, the province of Maine is the place that afforded me the worst accommodations of many other places; what I have now said of Maine must be regarded as an affirmation that the condition of human life in that place is exceedingly wretched...*[1283]

The living conditions and lifestyle of George and Philip Ulmer disappointed the duke, although during his entire tour of Penobscot Bay, only the business enterprises of the Ulmer brothers seemed to have impressed him. In his memoirs about his travels through the United States, the Duke de la Rochefoucauld-Liancourt recorded the living conditions and the meal that was served during his visit in 1794 by Mary (Tanner) Ulmer, Captain George Ulmer's wife. The duke wrote that he "partook of a poor supper, and an indifferent night's lodging with Captain Almer [Ulmer], who however opulent, continues to live in a miserable log-house without suitable supplies of bread, rum, sugar, or even flesh [meat]."[1284]

The Duke de la Rochefoucauld-Liancourt, who was in exile during the French Revolution, was a houseguest of Henry Knox for a period of time. During his two years in exile from France, the duke had ample time to visit the Ulmer brothers' successful business complex at Ducktrap Harbor and cove. The Duke probably observed Philip's uncle John and the Ulmer cousins building their mansion house and the large shipyard and lime-burning business at Lermond's Cove (present-day Rockland) in 1795.[1285] The duke also had time to acquaint himself with Waldoboro and other area communities close to Knox's Montpelier mansion at Thomaston. If the Duke de Liancourt had visited the Ulmer brothers two years later, he would have experienced a dramatic improvement in Philip and George Ulmers' living conditions in their new residences at Ducktrap cove.

On another occasion in 1794, Henry Knox brought Charles Maurice Talleyrand de Périgord on a tour of the Penobscot Bay to see frontier Maine's land development potential. Talleyrand, the Prince de Benevent, was a French foreign minister, statesman and diplomat. He was among many citizens of the aristocracy in France who were in exile during the French Revolution, when the nobility in France were being executed in a violent rebellion. Knox and Talleyrand stopped at Ducktrap Harbor during the tour, where Talleyrand was introduced to Philip and George Ulmer and observed the various business enterprises that they had developed at the Ducktrap settlement. He later wrote in his journal: "The strategically-placed squatters [the Ulmer brothers] draw unto himself all the lumber business of the vicinity and his mills [five operating mills on the Ducktrap stream] are the nucleus of a small settlement."[1286]

Philip Ulmer managed the shipbuilding business from their protected harbor-cove at "the Trap," the chandlery store and the navigation and shipping operations, as well as the financial responsibilities of the business partnership.[1287] George Ulmer managed the lumbering operations and the mills in the Ulmer brothers' partnership, and he served primarily as land agent and tax collector for Henry Knox. They jointly supported each other in the lime-burning operation and the general and mercantile stores, which sold local produce as well as basic necessities, dry goods, furniture, supplies and various other products that were brought back on board the cargo ships from other southern states, Europe and the West Indies. All the lumber harvested from the virgin forest was cut at the sawmills owned by the Ulmer brothers and shipped from the wharves at the cove and at Ducktrap beach. By monopolizing an economically strategic location at the Ducktrap watershed, the Ulmer entrepreneurs were able to secure the local timber for laborers at their mills and provide opportunities for the settlers to earn a steady wage at their businesses and stores in the growing village. Ducktrap attracted mariners, carpenters, a tailor, a cooper, a blacksmith, a shoemaker and other artisans to the shipbuilding and shipping trade business center along the mid-coastal area. Henry Knox took pride in showing off the Ulmer brothers' business developments and the growing village at Ducktrap to other potential venture capitalists and land speculators, both American and French.

Having submitted his resignation from government service as secretary of war under President George Washington on December 28, 1794, Henry Knox left Philadelphia in the spring of 1795 with his wife, his six children and a number of servants. They sailed by ship to their new home in Thomaston in frontier Maine. George Ulmer had been employed by Knox to survey the land for General Knox's family estate compound prior to the construction of the main house, guest houses, servants' quarters, carriage house, barns, the small church and other outbuildings.[1288] Lucy Knox first saw their new mansion while she sat on the deck of a sloop commanded by Captain Andrew Malcolm of Warren in Lincoln County (Maine). In her delight, she named the new summer home Montpelier, which meant "Mount of the Pilgrim."[1289] The imposing mansion was built upon the ruins of the old fort that had provided safety to the early frontier settlers in General Samuel Waldo's Broad Bay settlement on the original Waldo Patent.[1290] The grounds around the mansion were terraced with arbors, trees and colorful gardens artistically arranged. A skillfully carved American eagle was mounted on the top of the large gate, which had flowing vines trailing around it and opened into Knox's spacious palatial compound.[1291] Winding walkways through gardens, orchards and forest openings added to the beauty of the grounds. Vine-covered summerhouses were available for invited guests to stay. Twenty saddle horses and carriages were kept in separate quarters to accommodate visitors and sojourners.

In a prominent place within the mansion, Henry Knox had a full-length portrait of his wife's grandfather General Samuel Waldo.[1292] The aristocratic parents of his wife, Lucy Flucker, had opposed their daughter's marriage to a social inferior like Henry Knox.[1293] However, Henry felt that his present wealth, his military and government service to the country and his extravagant lifestyle had elevated him to a different class in society. He now lived "in the style of an English nobleman"[1294] or a prince in his elaborate white mansion (the French guests called it a "grand Château") on the extensive Waldo estate. Not far from the summer residence, a small, white church was built for family worship on a hill overlooking the ocean. The bell in the church tower was cast by Paul Revere.[1295] In later years, the churchyard became a private family burial ground for the Knox family. Of the twelve children whom Henry and Lucy Knox had, only three reached adulthood.

A public announcement was distributed to the settlements in the Waldo Patent inviting them to a celebration on July 4, 1795, at the new family estate of General Henry Knox at Thomaston. Henry and Lucy Knox opened the gates and the doors of their palatial home to the people of the Waldo Patent who had gathered outside his main gates at dawn.[1296] Philip and George Ulmer were business partners of Henry Knox at Ducktrap Harbor and cove, and they were veteran officers and soldiers of the Revolution with General Knox. They were certainly among the many invited and visiting guests at Henry Knox's impressive gala at his new summer mansion in Thomaston on July 4, 1795. Some of the Ulmer sailing vessels could have been involved in transporting and providing supplies for Knox and the furnishings for some of the buildings on the large palatial estate, Montpelier. The Knoxes had large temporary tables, which sat one hundred people at a time, distributed around the piazzas and terraces outside of their elevated three-story home topped with a large cupola.[1297] General Knox had an ox roasted along with twenty sheep to provide meat for the guests. The sheep were some of the coarse-wool breeding stock that Knox had imported from England for his large sheep range on nearby Brigadier Island.[1298] There were abundant amounts of foods, desserts and drinks offered for all to enjoy. People from every settlement in the Waldo Patent were invited to the Knox estate for the great celebration. The Penobscot Indians, whose braves had participated during the Revolution, were invited and camped upon the grounds of the estate for over a week before being politely asked to leave and return to their village. Everyone was awed by the grandeur of Henry Knox's mansion and family estate. One of the Knox's daughters commented later: "The house was so much larger than anything they [the public] had seen, that everything was a subject of wonder. Every object around had all the attraction of novelty."[1299]

The large white mansion, built by Ebenezer Dunton, a Boston housewright, was three stories high with 3,025 square feet per floor. It had nineteen rooms and twenty-four fireplaces.[1300] The Federal-style design for the mansion might have been inspired by designs of Charles Bulfinch, an accomplished architect from Boston. Henry Knox's correspondence with Ebenezer Dunton indicated that the mansion's design was to be an oval-on-axis design: "That there shall be two stair cases in the rear of the oval room lighted by two large sky lights from the top of the house—that the steps of the stairs shall be six inches high, one foot wide & three feet eight inches long…the windows on the front of the house [shall] go down to the floor, allowing [a person] to step from the inside of the house onto the porch when the windows were open."[1301]

Inside the mansion, the central entrance opened into a sky-lit oval room with a large crystal chandelier that hung from the ceiling four stories above. To the left of the oval room was a large portrait of George Washington, the father of his country, and to the right was an equally large portrait of Henry Knox, the father of the people on the Waldo Patent.[1302] Beside the portraits stood matching globes, one of the earth (terrestrial globe) and the other of the heavens (celestial globe)—the universe was depicted on the walls in Henry Knox's parlor. Two flying staircases, one on each side in the back of the oval room, led to the upper rooms.[1303] Furnishings of the French nobility came into Henry Knox's possession from a shipment of furniture that had been bound for America when the nobility was immigrating but had been caught in the net of the French Revolution and the guillotine. Captain Steven Clough of Wiscasset (near Waldoboro) was an eyewitness to the beheading of the French queen, Marie Antoinette.[1304] He hurriedly made his way to where his ships were anchored and, without delay, set sail on his heavily laden cargo and transport ships for his home port in America with the royal furnishing on board. Colonel James Swan's family claimed the furniture for his mansion, while some of the goods went to Henry Knox for furnishings in his mansion at Thomaston.[1305]

Henry Knox's mansion had balconies, piazzas, numerous gardens, an orchard, several guest houses and nine outbuildings—cook houses, stables and carriage houses—set back from the mansion in two matching crescents or semicircles to the east and west of the mansion and stretching inland toward the woodlands. Knox tried to buy deer and other animals to stock a game park on the property.[1306] The commanding view from the top of the hill on which the mansion stood was inspiring, as the onlooker could view down the St. George River to the ocean and inland over Thomaston's small settlement cabins and newly cleared land. Although the mansion was originally conceived as a summer home, the Knox family lived in Thomaston year-round by the time of his death in 1806.

In the winter of 1795–96, while George Ulmer was away on business in Boston, Henry Knox's other agents reported that some people in Ducktrap, New Canaan and Greene Plantations planned to burn down Henry Knox's new summer mansion, Montpelier, and they also threatened to destroy the buildings belonging to Henry Knox's supporters,[1307] which included the businesses of the Ulmer brothers in Ducktrap. In March 1796, George Ulmer, serving as a justice of the peace, returned from the judicial court in Boston with a warrant for Samuel Ely's arrest.[1308] When the news of George Ulmer's warrant was received by Samuel Ely, he fled the vicinity and went into hiding, and his supporters quickly dispersed. By the next month, the grumblings of discontent stirred up by Samuel Ely and his squatter activists melted away, and the Ducktrap and New Canaan backcountry plantation areas appeared to return to normal. However, resentment continued to fester against Henry Knox and his agent, George Ulmer. Later, in March 1796, after Henry Knox's agents had sent Samuel Ely into hiding, a group of Ely supporters visited Philip and George Ulmer's community store and, after drinking freely, hinted that "Knox would be stricken and die soon."[1309] When told of this incident, George Ulmer, Knox's principal agent, hastily wrote to Henry Knox, who was in Boston, to warn him of an attempt to poison him.[1310]

In early April 1796, Samuel Ely and several of his supporters, under cover of darkness, made an attack upon the milldam at Ducktrap with axes and crowbars and caused great damage to the dam.[1311] The loss of the dam and the use of the sawmill in the spring season (the most productive time for shipbuilding) were financially devastating to Philip Ulmer's shipbuilding and shipping trade businesses and to his stores.[1312] In July and September 1796, Philip and George were attacked again during the night, and they discovered the next morning that hundreds of spars intended as land-tax payments to Henry Knox had been released from the log booms above the milldam and were scattered far and wide throughout the Penobscot Bay.[1313] The floating spars and logs in the Penobscot Bay became a danger to fishermen in small boats and to sailing and transport vessels that used and depended on the waterway for travel and their livelihood throughout the bay area. This was a devastating financial loss to Philip Ulmer's shipbuilding, cargo shipping and merchant trading businesses and to the Ulmer brothers' milling business. In a letter sent to Henry Knox, George Ulmer reported that Harris Ransom had confessed that during Samuel Ely's return in September 1796, eighty-two men joined the preacher in written bonds "to burn yours and many other people's houses, rob the stores, and burn the goods before the owners' faces, poison their cattle by mixing poison with salt, and putting in their fodder, and many other matters were to be done."[1314]

In 1796, George and Philip Ulmer were finally financially able to move their families out of their old and drafty log houses, which were too small for their growing families, and they moved into newly built two-story Federal-style houses. The two-story Federal-style colonial houses were located on a hill to the east and west of the Ducktrap stream that overlooked the small protected harbor-cove on the Penobscot Bay. The two Ulmer family houses were almost identical in style and design. George's house was a larger, natural

Philip and Christiana Ulmer's house was located on the western side of the Ducktrap River overlooking Ducktrap cove and Lincolnville harbor on the Penobscot Bay. The original house burned to the ground in the 1930s. *Courtesy of the Lincolnville Historical Society.*

brown wood structure, and it was located on the east side of the Ducktrap stream. Philip's house was somewhat smaller, had a large front porch and was situated on a hill overlooking the bay. Philip's house was painted white and was located on the west side of the Ducktrap River-stream. Philip and Christiana Ulmer's eight children kept their house busy with activity. They planted several gardens to feed their family. One garden was planted for vegetables, one for herbs and another for medical plants. Cows, sheep, chickens and other animals were raised on the property as well, and the children were expected to help on the farm.

In March 1797, George Ulmer arrested Harris Ransom, who had boarded with Samuel Ely's family at Saturday Point (Northport). Ransom was held over for trial for his involvement in the destructive activities led by Samuel Ely.[1315] The following year, in November 1798, George Ulmer's large, new Federal-style house that was located on the eastern side of the Ducktrap River was burned to the ground.[1316] All of the Ulmer brothers' business books and ledgers, accounts, promissory notes from debtors, winter stock of provisions for the chandlery and general store, furniture and clothing went up in flames.[1317] According to George Ulmer in a letter written to Henry Knox the day after the fire:

The house was burnt to ashes leaving us with nothing except what we had on our backs and one bed, and that all of [the] *business records and south-bound mail, which was in the house, were destroyed. As my Situation my dear Sir requires my greatest exertion, if you have anything I can do to earn a trifle, or if it is in your Power to be the means of helping me to Business, it will be received as a fresh mark of friend Ship* [sic] *from one whose bounty I am already So much in debt that it will I fear never be in my power to make any kind of Compensation.*[1318]

PHILIP ULMER'S COMMUNITY INVOLVEMENT

Philip Ulmer was focused primarily on his shipbuilding, shipping and merchant trading businesses in the Ducktrap Plantation community. Philip eventually developed the commercial mercantile business at Ducktrap (later Lincolnville) into the largest establishment on the western shores of the Penobscot Bay.[1319] Philip provided financially for his wife and large family with his successful business enterprises, trade goods sold at his store and excess produce from his farm at Lincolnville. He was a respected community leader, first serving as town selectman, and for many years he served as moderator for town meetings (essentially chairman of the town council).[1320] On several occasions, Philip Ulmer served as chairman of the Board of Selectmen and as an elected representative of the town to the Massachusetts House of Representatives in Boston. He wrote petitions on behalf of the town of Ducktrap to the General Court of Massachusetts putting forth the grievances of the townspeople and expressing their needs for state assistance or for tax relief from heavy Massachusetts state taxes. He was elected to the House of Representatives in the General Court of Massachusetts in 1810.[1321] He was involved in developing schools and roads in the town of Ducktrap as well as maintaining the lumbering harvest at the sawmill and at their other local mills that provided employment for the people of the community. With a family of eight active children living at home, Philip and Christiana were kept busy providing for their family's needs and for the needs of their town.

Eager for store goods and supplies, many settlers in the Ducktrap area became debtors to the Ulmer brothers.[1322] Settlers sustained their credit by delivering to the Ulmer wharves at the harbor many cords of fireplace wood, mill logs, ship's timber and other wood products that were carried to markets in Boston, the West Indies and other American coastal ports along their "coaster" route in the southern colonial states. In addition to his shipbuilding business, Philip managed a shipping chandlery with supplies of all kinds for boats and fishing needs, as well as a store that sold American, European and West Indian goods and provisions that returned on board his trading vessels to the Ducktrap Harbor wharves on the Penobscot Bay. With an abundance of natural forest products harvested from the Ducktrap watershed, the Ulmer brothers could pay back their creditors in Salem, Boston and the West Indies. They secured new capital to purchase more goods, supplies and merchandise for their stores at Ducktrap Harbor and cove, and they continued to expand their commercial businesses.[1323] Developing the millseat on the Ducktrap River was ideal for managing the timber supplied by the abundant forest that stretched deep into the interior hills. The protected harbor-cove at "the Trap" was ideal for building a small shipyard for wooden sloops and sailing schooners at the shore of the bay. The rising tide was used to launch the boats when they were built and equipped to sail.

Philip was a deeply religious man, a devoted husband and father, a community leader, a successful businessman, a respected military officer, a Master Mason and a Worshipful Past Master of Freemasons in frontier Maine. He served as the Worshipful Past Master of the Masonic lodges at Hancock Lodge No. 4, A & F.M. at Castine, and he was the founding member of Amity Lodge, No. 6, A & F.M. (present-day town of Camden), where he served as the first Worshipful Master while under dispensation.[1324] (Camden was formerly known by its Indian name, Megunticook, and later as Camden village before becoming a town.) Like his brother, Philip Ulmer could best be described as a man of "extraordinary vigor of intellect which under all the discouragements of early poverty [he was able to] arrive at a point of such distinction."[1325] He was well known for treating all people with respect and dignity in spite of their social position, the color of their skin or their status in life. Having been raised as boys in Marblehead, Salem and Waldoboro, Philip and George Ulmer were brought up with a wide diversity of people from many cultures. Having been taught from youth about the evils of slavery and human trafficking, they strongly disapproved of slavery. They had learned from their grandfather that one of their Ulmer ancestors in Germany had been captured, sold and made a slave for fifteen years in Egypt before gaining his freedom and returning to his former country, a lesson that they never forgot. Black people, Indians, rich men, poor men, merchants and laborers were accepted and treated equally unless they proved themselves otherwise untrustworthy.

Philip Ulmer continued to demonstrate concern and devotion to his community of Lincolnville (part of Ducktrap Plantation) and his hometown of Waldoboro throughout his adult life. Philip had a profound interest in the education of the children and the adults in his community. Both Philip and George Ulmer donated financially to the town of Waldoboro for the purchase of books to be placed in the newly dedicated town library for everyone in the community to use. Education, public service and a strong religious background had always been of importance in the Ulmer families. Their involvement in Freemasonry became a religious base for their lives.

Philip did not always agree with certain political positions or actions that were taken by his brother in a number of situations, but he respected George's right to have his own opinions. He questioned certain unwise and unconvincing decisions that his brother had made while in service to Henry Knox as his land agent and tax collector. He disagreed with George's obstinate behavior while in command of military troops at Eastport in 1813 that resulted in George's removal from his command and being placed under arrest for his confrontational actions. Philip respected his brother's efforts in carrying out his assigned duties and responsibilities, but George's hot temper and heated overreactions often caused problems for Philip as well. The Ulmer brothers trusted and supported each other through many difficult times. They protected each other, and they kept a careful watch over the well-being of each other's families.

SHIPBUILDING AT DUCKTRAP HARBOR

From Ducktrap settlement's earliest launchings until 1801, some twenty vessels slid down the stocks and were launched at Ducktrap Harbor on the Penobscot Bay.[1326] In addition to those twenty that are on the town register, the Searsport Historical Society records there were three earlier launchings. In 1792, the sloop *Friendship*, which was 83 tons and sixty-eight feet long, was built for an Islesboro/Boston team. The sloop *Industry*, which was over 90 tons and sixty-seven and a half feet long, was built for Yarmouth people. In 1793, *Catherine*, a schooner that was 85 tons and sixty-eight feet long, was built for John Horton of Boston and had Lemuel Drinkwater as captain. *Covemere*, the only brigantine recorded, was over 154 tons and seventy-one and a half feet long and was built for a Boston party. In 1794, another schooner of 47 tons, the *Industry*, was built for and owned by Leonard Dunn. The 29-ton schooner *Lively* was built for and owned by Nathaniel Pendleton.[1327] Many "coasters" that were launched and sailed from the Penobscot Bay region became victims of French and British armed privateering vessels in the West Indies, along the coastline of Europe and in the Mediterranean Sea. Many captured American sailing and trading vessels from the Penobscot and their reported losses were recorded between 1793 and 1813 during the assault on American shipping and foraging by the French and British privateers.[1328] The "coasters" launched from the Penobscot mostly carried dried, salted fish and other meat; whale oil; candles; corn; flour; ice (which had been cut from frozen pond in the winter and packed in sawdust); lumber; staves; shingles; various wood products; lime; marble; and other raw materials that were plentiful in frontier Maine. The foraged goods from the American trading and supply vessels were used by the French and British to feed their own men aboard their armed ships. Other useful products were sold for profit at their own ports in the West Indies or taken to Europe and sold there. The records of the vessels built at Ducktrap Harbor were burned in a fire, and only partial records for other ships built and launched in the Penobscot Bay were found at the Searsport Historical Society in Maine. Unfortunately, the construction records at Waldoboro were also lost in a fire during British raids on the coastal seaport communities.

Philip Ulmer's Ducktrap Harbor shipping enterprises were part of the triangle of trade that prevailed during the late eighteenth and early nineteenth centuries.[1329] Shipping manifests recorded that milled forest products, staves, timber, shingles, lime (produced at the limekiln at the harbor and used for plaster and mortar), bricks, granite and salted codfish were shipped to the West Indies to be exchanged for sugar, rum, molasses, spices, salt, fruit and other needed food products. The third leg of the triangle was the transatlantic run to England for cotton cloth, ribbons, silk, lace, buttons and other European products. These products were sold to the townspeople and settlers in the Penobscot Bay area at the Ulmer mercantile and dry goods store. Although there were a few ocean-crossing ships built at Philip's Ducktrap Harbor-cove, most of the vessels were "coasters" that hugged the seacoast on the north–south run from New England to the West Indies. There might have been as many as twenty sloops and small schooners built at the Ducktrap Harbor before the first ones were recorded in 1792.[1330] From these first recorded vessels until the last vessel of any size was recorded in 1867, about fifty-three sloops, schooners, brigs, barks and "coasters" were built at the Ducktrap Harbor shipyard and launched on the Penobscot Bay.

In 1796, Philip Ulmer built the 342-ton sailing vessel *Hiram* at his shipyard at Ducktrap Harbor with Samuel Whitney Sr. as captain of the vessel.[1331] A few years later, this same ship was owned by Samuel A. Whitney Sr., who gradually bought out Philip's partnership in the Ulmer shipbuilding and shipping businesses at Ducktrap Harbor.[1332] The lucrative "coaster" merchant trading business had made Philip and George Ulmer the wealthiest men in the Ducktrap settlement.[1333] In the Federal Direct Tax list of 1798, George Ulmer was the wealthiest man in Lincolnville and was the wealthiest taxpayer.[1334] Philip Ulmer was second to his brother in every accounting list. By the end of the War of 1812, the Federal Direct Tax list of 1815 for Hancock County indicated that Samuel A. Whitney Sr. was the town's wealthiest man, with valuable holdings that once had belonged to Philip Ulmer. John Wilson, George Ulmer's son-in-law, was ranked as third-wealthiest man in the town. Philip Ulmer was ranked as fifty-third on the list with modest holdings in Lincolnville. George Ulmer no longer possessed any assessable property in Lincolnville and had only two small parcels of land in adjoining towns.[1335]

Chapter 17

The Years After the War

CHANGES IN RELATIONS BETWEEN AMERICA AND THE EUROPEAN COUNTRIES

A general dissolution of principles and manners will more surely overthrow the liberties of America than the whole force of the common enemy. While the people are virtuous they cannot be subdued; but when once they lose their virtue, then they will be ready to surrender their liberties to the first external or internal invader.
—*Samuel Adams, 1779*

In the decades following the Revolutionary War, American merchantmen struggled with a variety of old and new problems. European countries expected America's new government and experimental democratic republic to fail. If the new American republic did indeed fail, the young country could be reabsorbed back into the British Empire or divided up among the European powers, namely the French and Spanish empires that had large land claims in America. On land, England refused to honor its pledge in the Treaty of Paris to remove its military presence in the Northwest Territory. The British military continued to stir up the American Indian attacks upon frontier settlers moving westward and also continued to threaten and conduct sporadic raids against the coastal towns and villages along the eastern frontier of Maine in Massachusetts. The British Ministry still maintained the objective of forming the colony of New Ireland, extending from the

Penobscot River to the Canadian border at New Brunswick and the St. Croix River, as a British settlement. Determining the national borders had been, and continued to be, an issue of contention between the American government and the British, French and Spanish empires in North America.

While American merchant trade with Great Britain resumed quickly after the war, America still had to deal with British protectionist mercantile policies. The British policies had been restrictive prior to the war; however, as an independent nation, America was seen as a competitor and a threat to British commercial interests in the world trading arena. Britain welcomed shipments of raw materials from America, and Americans greatly wanted British goods since they did not have a manufacturing or industrial-based economy. Britain, however, closed its West Indian colonies to American merchant trading ships and declared that American exports to the Caribbean Islands had to be carried on British ships. The British government imposed import duties that made American goods much less competitive in Great Britain.

France took protective measures to deny American trading vessels access to its ports. As some American leaders had feared, France began to involve itself in America's merchant trading businesses and to strongly influence the new American government. Spain refused to negotiate a commercial treaty with American merchant traders that would allow Americans along the western frontier to have access to the Mississippi River. In the Mediterranean Sea, pirates from Algerian and Barbary states preyed on American trading vessels that sought to conduct business in the Mediterranean and in the Middle Eastern countries. America's merchant marine trade was restricted, constrained and harassed constantly by competing European powers around the world.

While France had given invaluable assistance to the United States during the American Revolution, its intervention was primarily prompted by the desire to harm England, its old European rival, rather than concern for the well-being of America. France desired the same freedom, liberty and equality for its citizens that America had managed to achieve through its American Revolution. The king of France and his advisors had strongly supported and financed the American Revolution, and now the country's own economy was greatly depleted and on the brink of collapse. The constant warring with Great Britain on land and sea had led to the citizens being overtaxed, out of work and unable to afford food, clothing or housing. The citizenry of France rose up in rebellion against the French king and their government. In 1789, the French Revolution wrought horrors on the

French monarchy and the ruling class that were astounding and brutal to the civilized world. The resulting dramatic changes and reforms in France caused great alarm in countries throughout Europe, especially those that had monarchies or dictatorships. One can certainly understand why George Washington refused to be designated "King" in the new United States of America. He felt that an elected president with a limited term of office was the best choice to lead the new nation. The American citizens wanted to disassociate themselves from the monarchies, dictatorships and the feudal system in Europe and in other parts of the world. The citizens of the United Colonies wanted to form a more perfect union, a new republic of sovereign and independent states represented by elected representatives who were chosen by the consent of the governed. The Founding Fathers, visionaries of their time, strove to form a new, uniquely American government that had never been seen before anywhere in the world.

Following the turbulent French Revolution, France declared war on England in February 1793. President George Washington attempted to maintain a position of strict neutrality between the warring countries of England and France. Each side attempted to draw America into the conflict. President Washington was determined that the United States would remain neutral during the conflict. Conditions for American sailors, merchant tradesmen and fishing mariners became increasingly more dangerous. Both Britain and France began to intercept, board and inspect American trading vessels for suspected contraband. Great Britain claimed the right to force sailors on American vessels into maritime service on British armed privateering vessels, and American sailors were forced to fight against their own native countrymen. The new American government had insisted on the principle of "free ships make free goods."[1336] This meant that as a neutral country, America felt that it could transport goods to and from either France or England without being subject to capture by either country.

Britain had declared in June 1793 that shipments of food and produce were considered contraband. In November 1793, the British government signed a "secret decree" that empowered the British naval captains to seize any American ship sailing to a French port or carrying French goods. British warships captured more than three hundred American trading vessels before the order became known.[1337] England furthermore claimed the right to impress American seamen on board merchant sailing vessels for service in the British Royal Navy or be sent to prison or killed. These actions infuriated all Americans and turned them against the British Royal Navy to the point that war was again considered likely. President George Washington and many delegates and senators in the Continental Congress bristled at European interference with America's merchant trade and the new nation's struggle to form a functioning government. America needed to rebuild its economy and recover from the devastating depression and high inflation that was the result of the Revolutionary War.

President Washington took a firm stand of neutrality. He persuaded Congress to increase American defenses and approved a month-long embargo in late March 1794. This was not accepted well in the District of Maine since the livelihoods and very survival of the settlers in the easternmost frontier depended on commercial fishing, shipping and trading. President Washington pushed Congress to build an American navy to defend the country from its enemies and to protect against those who might prey on its American citizens and merchant transport vessels, the lifeblood of the struggling nation. He dispatched Chief Justice John Jay as a special envoy to England to negotiate an agreement to resolve the increasingly difficult situation. John Jay's brother, Sir James Jay, had provided General Washington and his Culper Spy Ring with invisible ink during the Revolution.[1338] The Jay Treaty of 1794 made some progress in defusing the mounting conflict between Great Britain and the United States. The result was the affirmation of the rights of neutral ships while stating that French vessels could not use American ports. Britain agreed to withdraw from the Northwest Territory, but questions of the Revolutionary War debts and impressments were left unsettled. The Jay Treaty did secure better terms for American shipping, and it did avert a new war with Great Britain, which was President Washington's objective.

The French government, called the Directory after the French Revolution, was angry with the Jay Treaty. The agreement was seen as a thaw in the relationship between Great Britain and the United States, England's former enemy. France felt that America had abandoned its obligations under the Franco-American Alliance Treaty of 1778, and it had now formed a new alliance with Great Britain. In July 1796, the French Directory retaliated by decreeing that France had the right to search and seize neutral American vessels carrying cargos that it deemed as contraband British goods. The French believed that they would have their way with the new American government under President John Adams since Holland and Spain were allied with France. In an attempt to hinder the political power of the pro-British Federalists with strong support for pro-French Thomas Jefferson for president of the United States, France attempted to influence the presidential election of 1796. However, John Adams succeeded George Washington as president of the United States on March 4, 1797.

George Washington Leaves Office
as the First American President

Of all the habits and dispositions which lead to political prosperity, Religion and
Morality are Indispensable Supports. In vain would that man claim the tribute of
Patriotism who should labor to subvert these great Pillars.[1339]
—*George Washington's Farewell Address*

Accolades and expressions of gratitude were expressed by the military officers and soldiers with whom George Washington had served for many years and from American citizens throughout the eastern United States. President Washington had managed to lead the new nation through a tumultuous time in its history. He had managed to see the country through its birth as a new nation, and he helped to establish a government system that was more responsive to the American people whom it was established to support and defend. Many of the ideas for the new governing structure and representation of the American people by public officials came from the American Indians.[1340]* President Washington was able to keep the struggling new nation out of the conflicts in Europe by upholding America's neutrality, independence and sovereignty in spite of the efforts of France and England to entangle the United States in their countries' constant squabbling and conflicts.

In April 1797, the Massachusetts Grand Lodge of Masons met in Boston under the leadership of Paul Revere, the retiring Grand Master. Masonic brothers and officers from counties and districts throughout Massachusetts (which included the District of Maine) gathered for the Grand Lodge Session to receive a special address by President George Washington and to observe the installation of the new Grand Master, Josiah Bartlett of Charlestown, as Grand Master of Masons in Massachusetts for 1797–98. Since the Masonic fraternity was of such great importance in his life, Philip Ulmer was present at this important meeting of the Grand Lodge of Massachusetts in 1797. Philip had served as an officer at Valley Forge with General Washington, and he was most likely in the traveling military lodge where Washington often presided over Masonic rituals and ceremonies.[1341] Philip served as the grand treasurer for the Grand Lodge of Massachusetts at the constitution of Hancock Lodge No. 4 in 1794 in the District of Maine.[1342] In President

---

* *Author's comment*: It was quite informative to compare the Constitution of the United States with The Iroquois Book of the Great Law and study the similarities between the two governing documents.

Washington's address to the Massachusetts Grand Lodge of Masons, he expressed his profound esteem for their Masonic Principles:

> *My attachment to the Society of which we are all members, will dispose me always to contribute my best endeavors to promote the Honour* [sic] *and Prosperity of the Craft. The Masonic institution was one whose liberal Principles were founded on the immutable laws of Truth and Justice and whose grand Object was to promote happiness of the human race…so far as I am acquainted with the Doctrines and Principles of Freemasonry, I conceive them to be founded in benevolence, and to be exercised only for the good of Mankind…In that retirement, which declining years induced me to seek, and which repose, to a mind long employed in public concerns, rendered necessary, my wishes that bounteous providence will continue to Bless & Preserve our country in Peace, & in the prosperity it has enjoyed, will be warm & sincere, and my attachment to the Society of which we are members will dispose me always, to contribute my best endeavors to promote the Honour* [sic] *and interest of the Craft.*[1343]

George Washington, after about forty years of service to America, retired from public service and returned to his estate at Mount Vernon, Virginia, where he resumed his private life with his family.

CONFLICTS IN EUROPE AFFECT THE ULMER BROTHERS' SHIPPING AND TRADING BUSINESS

The British and French governments were again at war with each other in Europe, the West Indies and other places in the world. Realizing the vulnerability and helplessness of their Penobscot settlement of Ducktrap to defend themselves and the inability of the Commonwealth of Massachusetts to protect and defend the frontier settlers from the predatory attacks by British and French raiders, Philip Ulmer took matters into his own hands and led an effort to salvage cannons and defensive military equipment from the wreckage of American vessels that had belonged to the unfortunate Penobscot fleet in 1779. He wrote a petition to the General Court of Massachusetts requesting permission to raise the wreckage of a vessel that had been sunk in the harbor of Cape Jellison near the mouth of the Penobscot River. The General Court of Massachusetts resolved:

March 10, 1797

Resolved on the Petition of Philip Ulmer and others, allowing them to raise a wreck at their own expense, on Penobscot River.

On the petition of Phillip Ulmer & others, praying for leave to raise the wreck of a vessel, which was sunk in the Harbour [sic] *of Cape Jellison at the time of the attack upon Penobscot in the late war.*

Resolved; That Phillip Ulmer, John Pendleton, Hezekiah French, George Ulmer and Adam Rogers, he & they hereby are permitted & allowed, at their own expence [sic]*, to raise the wreck of the vessel which belonged to the Penobscott* [sic] *Fleet and was sunk in the harbour* [sic] *of Cape Jellison near the mouth of the Penobscott* [sic] *River—and that all the right & title of the Commonwealth in the said Vessell* [sic] *be relinquished to the said Phillip, John, Hezekiah, George, & Adam in case they succeed in attempting to raise the same—Provided they effect the purpose aforesaid within one year from passing this Resolve.*[1344*]

The French government issued a decree that French naval vessels could capture any neutral sloops and schooners carrying British goods, and they could hang American seamen serving on British vessels as "pirates" even if they had been impressed into the British service. Any American vessel lacking a list of crew and passengers would be considered a legal prize. This decree, along with other parts of the document, voided the principle of neutrality and was considered an undeclared proclamation of war with America.[1345]

As a result of John Adams's election to succeed George Washington as the next president of the United States, France recalled its ambassador, and President Adams recalled America's envoy, James Monroe. In retaliation for John Adams's election as president of the United States, the French Directory refused to receive Charles C. Pinckney as Monroe's replacement.[1346] The new American ambassador, Charles Pinckney, was

* *Author's comment*: Sunken and damaged cannons from the destruction of the American fleet in 1779 were salvaged from the Penobscot River and put into service by British troops. Some of the cannons that Philip and his associates raised from the Penobscot River can still be found in several seaport towns and outposts in the Penobscot Bay region, including Lincolnville Beach. Commemorative gun barrels bearing the Massachusetts state seal are found today in places such as Canada, Great Britain and Australia.[1347]

subjected to abuse by the Directory before being expelled from the country. Ambassador Pinckney traveled to Amsterdam (in the Netherlands) and remained there, waiting for instructions. This rebuke was a national disgrace for the United States. Hostilities between the French government and the American government continued to simmer and boil with resentment. President Adams appeared before a special session of Congress on May 15, 1797, to support strong defensive measures and to announce his attempts at a peaceful resolution of differences between the two countries. He pointed out that the French Directory had concluded that America was so politically divided between pro-French and pro-British factions that it would be unable to defend itself, and the political infighting in Congress would soon render it unable to govern. President Adams urged the Congress to dispel the divisive infighting that was splitting the country and unite in a common cause to defend the new nation from destructive influences from Europe. In the address, he stated:

> *We shall convince France and the world that we are not a degraded people, humiliated under a colonial spirit of fear and a sense of inferiority, fitted to be the miserable instruments of foreign influence, and regardless of national honor, character, and interest…The country must be prepared to defend its commerce and its coasts against French* [or British] *depredations by building coastal defense and a naval power…*[1348]

President John Adams, like George Washington before him, recommended the immediate arming of merchant vessels and expressed his firm belief that America should stay out of Europe's quarrels but be prepared to defend America's neutrality. Jefferson and others viewed Adams's defensive program as provocative and thought it was impossible to negotiate and prepare for war at the same time.

By 1798, the French Directory decreed that contraband, including anything on board American trading and merchant ships of British origin, could lead to seizure of the American vessel.[1349] Any American vessel that landed at a British port, except in an emergency, was prohibited to enter any French port. A warning was issued by the French government that any American ship lacking a *role d'equipage* (a list of crew and passengers) was a lawful prize of the quasi-war that was being waged upon the high seas. Soon thereafter, French privateers along the American coastline and in the West Indies stopped and seized American "coasters" (sailing sloops and schooners that conducted trading business with American seacoast ports and towns). Between October 1796 and June 1797, French privateers seized 316 American ships.[1350] Most captured American vessels were relinquished in prize courts in the West Indies, and the goods and cargo were sold at great profit by the captors to European, Mediterranean and West Indian markets. Philip and George Ulmer's commercial shipping and trading businesses became victims of French privateering with the seizures of several of their vessels during the quasi-war with France and England in 1797–1801.[1351]

In May 1797, President Adams appointed Ambassador Pinckney, John Marshall and Elbridge Gerry to serve as a commission of three to negotiate with the French government to end the attacks on American shipping, recognize the principle of "free ships, free goods" and terminate the 1778 Treaty of Alliance that obligated America to fight on France's side in any conflict.[1352] The French Directory wanted America's John Jay Treaty with Britain voided. France felt that the United States had abandoned its obligations as set out in the 1778 Treaty of Alliance and had formed an alliance with Great Britain that was unacceptable to France.

The warring of France and Great Britain had its effects on Philip and George Ulmer's shipping and merchant trade business in the Penobscot Bay region. In 1797, the Ulmer brothers suffered the loss of at least two commercial trading ships to French privateers.[1353] These seized cargo shipping and trading vessels owned by the Ulmer brothers were returning separately from the West Indies with rich cargos valued in excess of 1,600 British pounds.[1354] The loss of the commercial trading vessels and their cargos was devastating to the Ulmer cargo shipping, mercantile and trading businesses.[1355] The sailing vessels were not insured due to the lack of insurers (underwriters) who were willing to insure commercial sailing vessels because of the undeclared war between the British and French privateering vessels that infested the American trade routes during this time. Philip Ulmer suffered additional losses to French privateers with other trading vessels from the Penobscot region in which he had shared financial interests as well. The loss of these wholly owned or jointly shared vessels was a great personal loss to the Ulmer brothers, especially to Philip Ulmer, since his livelihood depended solely on his businesses at Ducktrap Harbor and cove. Philip was heavily invested in the shipbuilding, cargo shipping and merchant trading aspects of the business partnership with his brother. Philip's shipbuilding, cargo shipping and trading businesses were still expected to pay dividends to Henry Knox for his patronage at Ducktrap Harbor-cove.[1356]

George Ulmer received financial support from his personal and business relationships with Henry Knox as his principal land agent, surveyor and tax collector in the region, for which he received lucrative payments separately from his business partnership with Philip. During this dangerous time of conflict on the high seas, the capture of richly loaded cargo vessels belonging to the Ulmer brothers caused the slow reversal of fortune for the Ulmer business enterprises at Ducktrap Harbor and cove. All the next year, Philip and George struggled to recuperate from the financial business losses suffered from the enemy privateers that infested the American coastal waters and preyed on American cargo transports and trading vessels in the West Indies, Europe and other locations in the world.

In 1798, the French Directory declared that France would seize any vessel carrying any kind of British goods, which included items on board the vessel whose origin was England. Any ship that landed at a British port, except in an emergency, was forbidden to enter any French port. Since Spain and Holland were allied with France, the Directory believed that the declaration would cause America to submit to the French demands. At this time, Napoleon Bonaparte and his allies were marching their military forces through Europe, and they were threatening to cross the English Channel and attack England. Federalists in the American Congress feared that France's aggressive policy toward America might be aimed at crippling England. It was feared that if England fell, then America would be next to surrender to Napoleon's powerful French military and naval forces.

In an attempt to defuse the tense international situation, President Adams sent three commissioners to France. Ambassador Pinckney, John Marshall and Elbridge Gerry arrived in France, but the French foreign minister, Charles Talleyrand de Périgord, would not receive them officially. Instead, an intermediary informed them in October 1797 that they must pay a bribe and also guarantee a huge loan to France before Talleyrand would meet with them and discussions could begin.* The three commissioners refused to pay the bribe. French secret agents, on behalf of Talleyrand and the French Directory, tried numerous times to fashion a backdoor deal for the bribe and the loan.[1357] When the commissioners' report about the bribe was received by President John Adams, his Cabinet and the Congress in the spring of

---

* *Author's comment*: This was the same French foreign minister who had been the houseguest of Henry Knox at Montpelier during Talleyrand's two-year stay in America during the French Revolution.[1358] French foreign minister Talleyrand and Henry Knox had paid a visit to Philip and George Ulmer's shipyard and business enclave at Ducktrap Harbor to demonstrate the prospects for investment opportunities in venture capitalism in the District of Maine.)

1798, President Adams angrily demanded that the French bribe should be made public. It caused great outrage throughout America.

When news of the bribe was made public in America, it was called the XYZ Affair because the three agents were identified only by those letters. It caused a major scandal in France as well. The scandal forced Talleyrand to cover up his involvement in the affair and deny any knowledge about the bribe. The Directory and Foreign Minister Talleyrand had misjudged the public reaction to the attempted bribe in America. They seemed to think that America's political, regional and class divisions would prevent the country from uniting against French corruption, demands and intimidating behavior. The French hoped to delay a resolution of the French and American conflict until after the election of 1800. They believed Thomas Jefferson would be elected as the next United States president, and the sympathetic Republicans would replace the Federalists in the Congress. Hoping to keep relations with America from deteriorating any further, the Directory decided to revoke the French privateers' commissions, endorse the rights of neutral vessels and lift the embargo on American trading and cargo ships.[1359] In spite of the French government's declarations toward American shipping, the deprivation and intimidation continued as before. John Marshall returned to the United States, while Ambassador Pinckney remained in France. Talleyrand had warned that if Elbridge Gerry left Paris and returned to America, war between France and the United States would follow. John Marshall told President Adams that Commissioner Gerry felt he was preventing the outbreak of war by staying in Paris.

Congress passed the Alien and Sedition Acts in 1798 that severely restricted the right of free speech and the ability to voice opposition to government policies. This act seemed to affirm Republican charges that the Federalists were determined to destroy the freedoms that had been won in the American Revolution. The controversy that swirled around the XYZ Affair enabled President Adams to secure more funding to expand the small U.S. Navy, and Congress authorized the president to purchase, build or convert ten vessels into warships. On April 30, Adams signed a law creating a U.S. Navy Department, which gave the naval service prestige and power within the government. Opponents of the law were concerned that a separate U.S. Navy Department might grow out of control. Although Adams recognized that the U.S. Navy had to be organized separately, with a single official responsible to the president, he had not learned the lesson from the Revolution that it might be more effective if the U.S. Navy and U.S. Army worked together under the same supreme department head. Since the quasi-war was fought mostly at sea, President Adams's organization of the military command was not questioned. In June, Congress permitted the arming of American merchantmen and authorized the president to accept twenty-four armed vessels offered as gifts or on loan from private persons. The East Coast shipyards used their experience with the Continental Navy and proved their value in building a U.S. Navy for the national defense.

In July 1798, President Adams nullified all treaties with France, and French ships were banned from American ports. The three frigates *Chesapeake*, *Congress* and *President*, which the U.S. Navy had at the time, were sent to sea to accompany cargo vessels in the Caribbean and to patrol the eastern coast of America. In August 1798, Admiral Horatio Nelson defeated the French forces in the Mediterranean off the Egyptian coast, calming fears of a French invasion of either America or England. The U.S. Navy had increased successes against the French warships in the Caribbean. Elbridge Gerry, whom Philip Ulmer knew from living in Marblehead and Salem with his family prior to the Revolution, returned to America in November 1798. Commissioner Gerry convinced President Adams that France did not want war with the United States and that it would negotiate a settlement.

Napoleon Bonaparte successfully staged a coup in November 1799 and dismissed the Directory, the governing body in France. Napoleon assumed power as the first consul of France. President Adams sent a commission of three agents to France in March 1800. The American agents—Chief Justice Oliver Ellsworth, Governor William Davie and William Vans Murray—were received in Paris by Napoleon Bonaparte and treated to a lavish reception. Negotiations were begun promptly; however, it took six months to create the Convention of Montefontaine, which was signed on October 3, 1800. The news of the peace agreement between America and France didn't reach the American public until early November. President Adams and the Federalists were swept out of office in the 1800 election, and the Democratic-Republicans with their more liberal ideology took over control of the federal government.

The Convention of Montefontaine between France and America was almost a treaty since it voided the 1778 Treaty of Alliance. It restored the principle of neutrality for "free ships, free goods"; however, it did not address the matter of American claims for ships and cargos that French privateers had seized. This was a vital issue to the merchantmen, businessmen and sailors whose commercial livelihoods were located along the eastern seacoast of the United States. This issue greatly affected Americans living in the cold environments of New England, especially in the Maine Province, whose lives depended on fishing, shipping, trading and access to foreign and domestic markets for survival. The American international commercial shipping and trading vessels still had to deal with the deprivations caused by the Barbary pirates in the Mediterranean Sea who preyed on them. It would take some time before the American naval forces could eliminate the threat of the Barbary pirates. President Adams had succeeded in avoiding war with France and was able to disentangle America from the European war between France and Great Britain.

During the French Revolution and Napoleonic period, France was plagued by war and desperately needed supplies and wood products of all kinds. French privateers and cruisers took cargo from merchant vessels both legally and illegally, preying on the United States more than any other country. At least 6,479 American claims involving more than 2,300 vessels were filed. These claims give a close approximation of American goods lost to the French warships and armed vessels.[1360] Philip Ulmer's navigation, cargo shipping and commercial trading businesses in the Penobscot Bay suffered great losses to French and English privateers preying on his sailing vessels along America's eastern seacoast, in the West Indies and in the Gulf of Mexico. Transatlantic commercial shipping and trading was suspended by the Ulmer brothers during this period of time because of the dangers to maritime vessels abroad. By the end of 1798, the U.S. Navy had twenty-one warships, which soon grew to fifty-four by 1800.[1361] However, it was too late for armed U.S. Navy escort vessels to be of assistance to Philip Ulmer's cargo and trading shipments that were lost in the Caribbean in 1797–1801. Philip Ulmer's shipping losses to armed French privateering vessels finally caused his business investments to falter and fail. Although Philip tried hard for several years to recover from his financial losses, he was finally forced to sell out his partnership in the Ulmer business enterprises in Ducktrap Harbor and cove. Philip Ulmer sold his half of the Ulmer brothers' business partnership to a new Ducktrap (Lincolnville) resident, Samuel A. Whitney Sr. from Castine, who had been a sailing master on some of his transport and cargo vessels.

While Philip Ulmer was dealing with the international, national and coastal shipping and trading issues, the settlers in the Penobscot Bay region were dealing with dramatic events closer to home. George Ulmer, at this time, was primarily involved with Henry Knox as his principal surveyor, tax collector and land agent. Henry Knox increased his efforts to gain control over the remaining squatters and illegal settlers who had not complied with his previous terms to inhabit his land in the Waldo Patent plantation territories. George Ulmer was also active with the local militia, who were frequently called upon to protect the towns and villages from enemy raiding parties. The state militia continued to monitor the hostile activities in the Penobscot region on land and sea.

UNREST SMOLDERS IN THE BACKCOUNTRY AND ERUPTS IN VIOLENCE

The backcountry squatters in the Ducktrap, New Canaan and Greene Plantation areas were still causing unrest and violence in the Penobscot Bay region. As justice of the peace, it was George Ulmer's responsibility to keep the peace in the disputed county regions. The Liberty Men (known locally as "White Indians" because of the disguises that they wore) had vowed vengeance against Henry Knox's agents, George Ulmer and Samuel Houston, and they stated that the agents would be "executed when opportunity afforded."[1362] Anonymous letters were delivered at night to the homes of land agents, sheriffs, lawyers and court officials with threats to destroy their personal property and inflict bloody violence. Henry Knox's son-in-law and the Lincoln County sheriff, Colonel Samuel Thacher, discovered one morning that an open coffin had been left overnight on his doorstep in Warren.[1363] To add drama and shock to their threats of violence, some "White Indians" killed, roasted and ate the horses of persistent law enforcement deputies.[1364] George Ulmer and other agents who worked for Henry Knox came under increasing threats and active violence from the noncompliant squatters. Twice in the year 1796, in the spring and fall, the most important times for cutting and processing lumber, the Liberty Men made a visit at night to Ducktrap cove. They cast loose the boom holding many logs that were ready to be cut at the Ulmer-owned sawmill.[1365] The resentment that the squatters and illegal settlers felt for George Ulmer as the tax collector and land agent for Knox had an overflow effect on Philip Ulmer, who also felt the financial loss to his shipbuilding and shipping businesses located at the harbor-cove. The Ulmer families became more fearful of the increasing violence and night activities of the Liberty Men.

In November 1798, a carpenter at work inside George Ulmer's new, two-story, Federal-style house carelessly left a fire unattended.[1366] The fire spread to the loose wood chips and then to other parts of the room. The house quickly became fully engulfed in flames, and it was burned to the ground within an hour. George, his wife, Polly, and the young children escaped from the burning house with only the clothes that they were wearing and one bed.[1367] The results of an investigation revealed that the fire, first thought to be an accident, had actually been arson. All of George and Philip Ulmer's business record books, accounts, promissory notes of creditors, all the winter stock of provisions, furniture and clothing were burned to ashes and could never be recovered or replaced.[1368] The business losses were devastating for the Ulmer brothers and their families. Without the business account books, ledgers and other records, Philip and George were unable to recover the financial debts that were owed to them. A new house was hastily built for George, Polly and their two daughters, who had been living temporarily with Philip Ulmer's family. The threats of the Liberty Men continued to be carried out against the supporters and employees of Henry Knox throughout the Lincoln County area.

George Ulmer's efforts to bring the backcountry settlers and squatters into compliance with Henry Knox's terms for land payments on illegally claimed land continued to stir up resentment among the residents of the New Canaan and Greene Plantations through the year 1801. On June 7, 1801, an armed party of Liberty Men in the Davistown area seized George Ulmer, who was on a surveying assignment for Henry Knox. The hostile captors threatened George with death, and they threatened to murder other agents of Henry Knox as well. Fortunately, the armed party of Liberty Men allowed George Ulmer to flee back to Ducktrap. He was greatly alarmed and frightened for his life and the lives of his family members.[1369] When Henry Knox wanted to send out another survey party on June 20, George Ulmer wrote to Knox that he would not lead the dangerous survey party into the backcountry. Knox had to get another agent to lead the survey party. The survey party was sent out by Knox on June 22, and it was ambushed by the Liberty Men, who left one of the surveyors severely wounded.[1370] Other incidents like these continued throughout the year. George, Philip and their families lived in constant fear for their lives.

In 1801, General Henry Knox attempted to use his position as a respected Revolutionary War veteran to quell the violence on his Waldo Patent property. General Henry Knox appealed to the governor of Massachusetts and the Governor's Council in Boston to send state militia troops to end the unrest in the backcountry areas of Greene and New Canaan Plantations, where Knox's surveyors and land agents were under increasing threat of violence and death from radical activist squatters. Henry Knox was unable to persuade the governor and General Court of Massachusetts that an actual insurrection existed in mid-Maine that *required* the use of military force. The Governor's Council determined that the plantation settlers' unrest was more of a personal and domestic issue than a Massachusetts state issue, so state troops were not necessary to handle General Knox's personal business issues. Knox would have to deal with the attacks on his land agents and surveyors in his own way. Unhappy with this decision, General Knox directed Captain George Ulmer, who was in command of a local militia company and still in Knox's service as an agent and surveyor, to organize a militia party and proceed into the backcountry to arrest the rebellious squatters and supporters suspected of being Liberty Men and imprison them in the county jail at Castine.

Since only the State of Massachusetts had the right to order the state militia into action to suppress rebellious activities of insurrection, Henry Knox had overstepped his authority. Knox planned to acquire and pay for the provisions and supplies for the militia operation himself; however, he did not want his involvement known to others, especially the governor and the Governor's Council. The operation was organized under false identities, as Henry Knox directed, to protect his involvement in the local militia raid to get rid of the rebellious Liberty Men. The militia operation was paid for by Knox, but the planning for the operation was done by Captain George Ulmer, and the operation was led by Lieutenant Colonel Thomas Knowlton.[1371] State funds for provisions for the militia activities were appropriated at General Henry Knox's request, under a false identity, for the militia company. Provisions and expenses for the operation were given under George Ulmer's son-in-law's name, John Russ, who served as an officer in the local Belfast militia.

The military operation against the Liberty Men was conducted by George Ulmer and the local militia troops. Many suspected activists (about twenty in number) were arrested and held as prisoners in Belfast. In retaliation, the Liberty Men, who were "dressed in Indian stile[sic] and perfectly black,"[1372] appeared on the outskirts of Belfast (Maine). They captured an unsuspecting resident and threatened to kill him if their demands were not followed. The Liberty Men sent the terrified Belfast resident back into the settlement with the demand that if the prisoners taken in the militia raid were not released immediately, the small Belfast settlement would be burned to the ground. The authorities, led by Captain (and justice of the peace) George Ulmer, quickly removed the prisoners across Penobscot Bay to the county prison at Castine. The presence of the heavily armed militia company at Belfast caused the Liberty Men to disperse.[1373] This illegal militia action ordered by retired General Henry Knox would come back five years later to cause problems for George Ulmer when he was involved in seeking political office as a senator in the General Court of Massachusetts in 1806.

In the fall of 1801, General Knox became angry with several decisions that George Ulmer had made involving land as Knox's land agent and tax negotiations with local settlers and squatters. In October 1801, George appealed to Henry Knox to be lenient with a particular influential settler, Daniel Dollof, who lived in Greene Plantation and was having serious financial difficulties.[1374] Henry Knox chastised George Ulmer harshly, and Knox insisted that leniency was not to be given to any of the settlers. Knox rejected terms that George Ulmer had made with other destitute settlers in the area as well. Knox's unrelenting attitude in spite of George's appeals (which the destitute settlers were unaware of) made the resistance to the proprietor and his agents solidify and harden in the Greene Plantation backcountry.[1375] George Ulmer was humiliated by Henry Knox, who desired to keep George in a subordinate status as a grateful client and not as a junior partner.[1376] George angrily resigned as Henry Knox's tax collector, surveyor and land agent on November 13, 1801. By resigning, George Ulmer lost not only his commissions as land agent and the benefits of Knox's political state patronage in the state government, but his actions threatened the loss of his cherished esquire status that was given as the local court justice.[1377] George Ulmer expressed his long-held resentment of his subordinate status, and he heatedly told Henry Knox, "[My] service sprang from the pure principles of friendship, and not slavish fear. I therefore had not ought to expect contempt in return."[1378]

By the end of 1801, almost all of the settlers and squatters in the Ducktrap and New Canaan plantation settlements had come to terms with Henry Knox's land taxes, and the land surveys were completed.[1379] Finally, with the land surveying completed, the opportunity to have the plantation settlements of Ducktrap and New Canaan incorporated into a town was possible. The repercussions of the very heated exchange between George Ulmer and Henry Knox had serious effects on his unsuspecting brother, Philip; on both of their families; and on the Ulmer brothers' business enterprises at Ducktrap Harbor. Even though Philip was not involved in the heated dispute or the surveying and land-sales activities that George was involved with as Knox's land and tax agent, Philip and his family also felt the loss of Henry Knox's patronage and political support indirectly. Although George Ulmer severed his business connections with Henry Knox, he did receive a letter of recommendation for his state militia service and his personal service to Knox. General David Cobb, who had served with General Knox during the Revolution and in the Massachusetts General Court after the war, was hired by Henry Knox's friend and financial business partner William Bingham of Philadelphia to serve as the first land agent for the Kennebec and Penobscot tracts of land in frontier Maine.[1380]

William Bingham had been active during the American Revolution as an American arms supply agent for Robert Morris's Philadelphia-based trading company at Martinique in the West Indies. The Rodriguez and Hortalez Company was the front company in France that had smuggled French goods, armaments and military supplies for General Washington's Continental Army through the port of Martinique, where Bingham served as the intermediary agent. William Bingham was a wealthy Philadelphia businessman with connections to the European banking houses in London and Amsterdam. Bingham had become General Knox's financial backer, principal creditor and land investor in Knox's frontier territories in Maine. Henry Knox had greatly overextended himself financially in failed business investments, in large tracts of state land bought on speculation and in personal loans that he could not pay back to Bingham. William Bingham became the owner of the state land investments made by Knox and the owner of parts of the Waldo Patent in what became known as the Bingham Purchase.[1381] The Bingham Purchase properties, for which David Cobb was assigned to serve as land agent, encompassed Hancock and Lincoln Counties and the backcountry areas that George Ulmer had overseen previously for Henry Knox. This was the vicinity where the Ulmer brothers lived with their families in Lincolnville.

REVERSAL OF FORTUNE

Henry Knox had become very difficult to get along with due to his large mounting debt to creditors, who constantly sought payment for goods and services rendered to him and to his family. Knox's financial situation was a result of his poor judgment with excessive land investments, his business speculation and his continued indulgence of his wife's lavish lifestyle. Henry and Lucy Knox had obsessively squandered their funds and resources to demonstrate their wealth, power, extravagant European taste and liberal benevolence to rich and poor alike. They found themselves borrowing money from friends and taking out large loans that they could not pay back. Henry Knox still insisted upon his financial dividends from the Ulmer brothers' businesses in spite of the huge financial losses that the brothers had suffered. Philip, who was heavily invested in this part of the business partnership, continued to struggle financially to keep his family and his commercial businesses afloat. The Ulmer brothers' diversified milling interests, the shipbuilding business at the Ducktrap cove and the ship chandlery and mercantile businesses kept their lives and families functioning for a while. When the Ducktrap dam continued to be damaged by the Liberty Men or destroyed by heavy storms, spring flooding from melting mountain snows or by other natural or manmade disasters, the results were financially devastating to the Ducktrap businesses, especially to Philip. The replacement of the Ducktrap Bridge after many unexpected washouts was also another financial drain on the Ulmer family and their business finances. Like the pendulum of a clock, Philip Ulmer's family lived in wealth during prosperous times or on the verge of deep financial loss. It was a delicate balance for Philip to provide for his large, growing family's needs in such an uncertain environment and politically volatile time period.

Henry Knox's extensive land purchases and business speculation came to a sudden halt about this time, and he suffered a dramatic reversal of fortune as well. In 1798, as a result of the devastating effects of the quasi-war upon commerce and his overextension in venture capitalist investments and speculation, Henry Knox was forced to mortgage his lavish white mansion and family estate in frontier Maine to General Benjamin Lincoln and Colonel Henry Jackson.[1382] General Knox also had to mortgage a part of his large landholdings in Waldo County (which included the Ducktrap watershed) to Lincoln and Jackson, who acted as his intermediaries and sureties, in order to pay his creditors.[1383] Henry Jackson acted as his attorney.[1384] In 1802, the Waldo County mortgage was assigned to Israel Thorndike, David Sears and William Prescott of Boston, and they foreclosed on the land.[1385] It is not known what price was paid by the three Boston land investors for the mortgage on the Waldo Patent lands. The three proprietors established a land agency in Belfast (Maine) near Ducktrap in 1809, and many acres of foreclosed land were sold off to interested buyers.[1386] Many of the land titles in Waldo County are derived from the sale of land through these three men. Henry Knox, who was in financially stressed conditions at this time, sold the two mortgages for the Ducktrap watershed to the Bank of the United States and to Abiel Wood,[1387] a Pownalboro merchant who was known to the Ulmer family. Since Philip and George Ulmer's personal lives and business ventures at Ducktrap Harbor-cove were so dependent on Henry Knox's business and political patronage, Henry Knox's financial difficulties and financial decline affected the Ulmer brothers, and the Ulmer brothers' business difficulties affected Henry Knox. For about twenty years, Philip and George Ulmer's lives had been intertwined and dependent on the whims and desires of Henry and Lucy Knox.

PHILIP AND GEORGE STRUGGLE TO RECOVER THEIR FORTUNES

Philip Ulmer struggled to recoup the deteriorating business situation from all of the misfortunes that had occurred during the years 1797–1801. The sloop *Hiram*, of 342 tons, was built at the Ulmer shipyard in 1796 on the Penobscot Bay.[1388] In late 1797, French privateers in the West Indies captured several of Philip Ulmer's heavily laden trading ships. The vessels were not insured because of the high cost of insurance, so the shipments were a total loss to the cargo shipping, trading and mercantile businesses. In 1798, fire consumed George Ulmer's house, causing the loss of the valuable business records, promissory notes and ledger books kept there. In the spring of 1800, another cargo and trading vessel from Ducktrap Harbor, with John Wilson (later son-in-law of George Ulmer) as captain, sailed from New York for St. Thomas.[1389] The sloop and its crew were captured by an armed French privateering vessel in the West Indies in September.[1390] The sloop and the crew, including Captain John Wilson and the valuable cargo for the Ulmer stores at "the Trap," were taken to San Juan, Puerto Rico, and the cargo was sold. Captain John Wilson later returned to Ducktrap Harbor, where he married Mary, George Ulmer's daughter. The sloop *Hiram* was sent to Guadeloupe, where the customs agent confiscated the sloop and valuable cargo as a prize, and the cargo was sold off to the highest bidders. On January 27, 1800, the cargo vessel *Adventure*, with James Holmes of Lincolnville as sailing master, was seized by the French privateer *L'Union*, and the cargo vessel was brought to Guadeloupe, where its contents were confiscated and sold. In 1801, a merchant vessel of 250 tons that was named the *Joseph and Phoebe*, on which David Dunbar served as captain, was built for Joseph and Ebenezer Perkins of Castine. In November 1802, Samuel A. Whitney Sr., a newly arrived merchant mariner from Castine, formerly of Concord, Massachusetts, was voted by the townspeople as an inhabitant of the town.[1391] In a short time, Samuel A. Whitney Sr. would take over most of Philip Ulmer's holdings and his position in the Lincolnville community due to Philip's unfortunate financial circumstances.

While the reversal of fortune of the Ulmer businesses at Ducktrap Harbor-cove affected George Ulmer as well, he managed to survive with his ownership in the general store and his investments in the Ducktrap mills and lumber business. However, there were further setbacks financially for him. When times were prosperous, the Ulmer brothers were loved and respected for what they did for the community and the jobs and merchandise that they brought to the town stores with their businesses. The Ulmer brothers apparently received little help or support when they suffered their reversal in fortune. The perfect storm of unfortunate events meant that Philip Ulmer could no longer bear the cost of the overextended business expenses. He dissolved his partnership with his brother, and he sold out his half-ownership in the various business enterprises to Samuel A. Whitney Sr.[1392] Samuel Whitney Sr. not only bought Philip Ulmer's partnership in the shipbuilding and the cargo shipping businesses, but he also bought his chandlery store and other business investments. In time, Samuel A. Whitney Sr. bought Philip Ulmer's house on the western side of the Ducktrap stream at Ducktrap cove. Philip built a smaller house for his family next door to his brother on the eastern side of the Ducktrap stream. (Note: This house was later owned by Philip's son, Jacob Ulmer, and eventually John Wilson, George's son-in-law.) Two years after his arrival in the town of Lincolnville, Samuel A. Whitney Sr. was listed as the owner and sailing master of the armed sloop of twelve guns, *Hiram*.[1393] The *Hiram* received some fame because it was later captured by French privateers in the West Indies while Samuel Whitney Jr. was its captain.[1394] The vessel was later recaptured by an American armed ship, and the sloop *Hiram* sailed again from the Penobscot Bay with Samuel A. Whitney Jr. as captain.[1395] Samuel Whitney Sr. formed a partnership with George Ulmer that succeeded for a short time.

Political Involvement in the Town of Lincolnville

In January 1802, George Ulmer wrote a petition that was sent to the House of Representatives for the Commonwealth of Massachusetts requesting that a bridge be built across the Ducktrap River to facilitate transportation and commerce in the town and in the region. General Knox exercised his influence in the General Court of Massachusetts to secure an Act of Incorporation that provided for a toll bridge. George Ulmer and his brother, Philip, who jointly owned the local sawmill where the bridge was to be built, would be responsible for the construction and maintenance of the new bridge over the Ducktrap River for public and commercial use. The Ducktrap Bridge provided the main road over the river, connecting the eastern and western parts of the town, and it became a major public thoroughfare for the frontier coastal bay region. The commonwealth granted permission for the bridge to be built under certain conditions.[1396] The conditions spelled out the height, construction and cost for maintaining the bridge. A certain price was placed on everything that might pass over the bridge. The order stated that a toll taker was to collect the tolls, and if that person was absent, the passengers or carriage may pass for free. George Ulmer was assigned the task of implementing the order of the General Court of Massachusetts. With several other investors, the Ulmer brothers constructed the toll bridge across the Ducktrap River.

The Ulmer brothers had previously built and rebuilt the Ducktrap Bridge many times at their own expense, but the continuous need for maintenance and replacement had become prohibitive in view of their financial and business situation at "the Trap." The new toll road continued to be a volatile issue for the local townspeople and travelers in the area who wanted free use of the bridge. The settlers and travelers wanted the improved main road from Megunticook settlement (present-day Camden village) to Belfast, but they wanted the toll bridge to be free. (The settlement village of Megunticook had once been a part of the Ducktrap Plantation that also included present-day Lincolnville.) The travelers didn't want to pay a toll for the continuous repairs or the replacement of the bridge if it should get washed out or damaged from storms and floods or for its deterioration over the years. Destruction or damage to the bridge structure was usually caused by ice jams, spring flooding (freshets), heavy storms, unusually high tides and from heavy use. The responsibility of collecting tolls for maintaining the main road over the toll bridge and the administration of the important bridge structure often caused George Ulmer to be at odds with the community. Great firmness was sometimes necessary to maintain the chartered rights granted by the Massachusetts Commonwealth.[1397] George continued to receive an income as the toll collector from the bridge tolls for a number of years.

In early 1802, a petition was sent to the General Court of the Commonwealth of Massachusetts stating that several village settlements desired to incorporate into a town. On June 23, 1802, the General Court granted the act of incorporation with a directive that Justice of the Peace George Ulmer, Esquire "[is] hereby authorized to issue a warrant, directed to direct some suitable person, an inhabitant of the said town…to notify and warn the inhabitants thereof to assemble… for the choice of such officers, as towns are by Law empowered to choose…"[1398]

The town of Lincolnville was to be incorporated by combining the parts of the two settlements of Ducktrap and New Canaan (near present-day Northport). The settlements were to become a township and a part of the county of Hancock as directed by the General Court of Massachusetts. General Benjamin Lincoln served as Henry Knox's business agent after the war. Henry Knox used his personal influence in the General Court of Massachusetts and inspired the naming of the designated Ducktrap and New Canaan Plantation vicinity as the town of Lincolnville for his friend and colleague.

The two plantations (scattered settlements within a designated regional area) lay partly in Lincoln County and partly in Hancock County. The incorporation of the settlements into the town of Lincolnville would make the town "entitled to all of the powers, privileges, rights, and immunities to which other towns are entitled by the Constitution and laws of this Commonwealth."[1399] George Ulmer, justice of the peace, issued a warrant to his brother, Philip, directing him to assemble the residents of the settlements and notify freeholders and other inhabitants who were qualified to vote to attend a meeting about the incorporation of the town of Lincolnville. "Philip Ulmer Esq., one of the Inhabitants of the Town of Lincolnville, Greetings: You are hearby required in the name of the Commonwealth of Massachusetts to call for the first town meeting to consider the incorporation of the Town of Lincolnville."[1400]

On September 20, 1802, the meeting was called to assemble at the house of John Calderwood. Philip Ulmer was chosen to serve as moderator of the first meeting of incorporation for the town of Lincolnville.[1401] Philip and George Ulmer were elected to serve on a committee to write a petition to the General Court of the Commonwealth of Massachusetts for permission to officially name the town Lincolnville in honor of General Benjamin Lincoln of Massachusetts, a veteran of the American Revolution.[1402] Philip Ulmer was elected as the first selectman of the town of Lincolnville in 1802 after its incorporation, with two other town residents to assist and advise as co-selectmen. The selectmen were voted to act as the town assessors and to be the overseers of the poor as well. Philip Ulmer's eldest son, Jacob, was elected as the first town clerk at age twenty-four.[1403] Philip Ulmer, his brother, George, and Abner Milliken were chosen by the townspeople at the town meeting and were directed to frame a code of bylaws for the newly incorporated town that would determine the governing and the responsibilities for officers who were chosen to lead the town.[1404] Philip and other respected residents were also chosen as the first municipal officers for the new town of Lincolnville. Philip Ulmer and Charles Mathews were voted as surveyors of lumber, an important task in a lumbering community. Philip appears many times in the town records as serving on this committee.

Philip was particularly interested in building Lincolnville's infrastructure by developing schools to educate the youth, creating local job opportunities and providing for the welfare and development of the town. With the incorporation of the town of Lincolnville, Philip Ulmer, as a community leader and frequently elected selectman and moderator of the town, sought a livelihood of public service to provide for the needs of his large family and to serve the community as a whole. Philip felt so strongly about education that he even appeared in the records of the town of Waldoboro, the hometown of his youth, as a patron who donated money to purchase books for the local schools and library there.[1405] His support of education and for many town improvements (road construction, lumber surveying and defense and safety issues) in Lincolnville has been well documented in the history of the town.

On November 7, 1802, another town meeting was held at the house of Noah Miller. A vote was passed during the meeting that "Samuel Austin Whitney be accepted as an inhabitant of this town."[1406] It was, at the time, impossible to know what a profound effect this vote would have on Philip Ulmer personally, and to the town of Lincolnville as a whole, in the years to come. This relatively unknown merchant sailor, a newcomer in the town and county, would eventually displace Philip Ulmer completely at Ducktrap. Samuel Whitney Sr. eventually assumed the position on the tax rolls of the town as the wealthiest man in the county.

By the end of 1802, the petition for incorporation was granted by the General Court of Massachusetts, and Lincolnville finally became incorporated as a town.[1407] For the next couple years, town meetings concerned the building of district schools, the building and repairing of the county and town roads and the building of a toll road over the Ducktrap River.[1408] Philip and George Ulmer served in various capacities of responsibility in helping to establish the governing structure of the town. Philip served in various capacities as a moderator, selectman and municipal officer in Lincolnville for many years. He maintained his standing as a magistrate, served as a justice of the peace and performed marriage ceremonies in the local communities, including those of three of his daughters. George Ulmer served as a court official, justice of the peace and as the sheriff of Hancock County before the county of Waldo was established. George also turned to public service at the state level, where the wealthy and elite men in the state exercised their leadership and governing authority. Philip turned to public service at the local level since his advancing age, family obligations and complications from his leg injury that he received during the Revolutionary War made it more difficult for him to perform more strenuous labor.

Henry Knox used his political influence in the General Court of Massachusetts on behalf of George Ulmer and his associates who had petitioned the court for financial relief in replacing the bridge across the Ducktrap River. In 1803, the wooden Ducktrap Bridge, which was a major crossing on the shore road in the mid-Penobscot region, was again carried away in several storms and floods. It was rebuilt with the money collected from the bridge tolls. On June 18, 1804, the Ducktrap Bridge replacement began, as directed by the "Charter of Incorporation," and it was completed by the beginning of October. As time went by, the inhabitants of the area took out their frustration and resentment about the imposed bridge tolls (ordered by the General Court of Massachusetts) on George Ulmer and his associates who were responsible for the collection of the tolls for bridge maintenance. Philip Ulmer supported George in fulfilling his obligations under the charter issued by the Massachusetts General Court. As the community grew and prospered, the local residents began to complain more loudly about the tolls for the Ducktrap Bridge and the road improvements since they now used the road and bridge more frequently for travel and business. In carrying out the directives and the requirements of the General Court of Massachusetts for maintenance fees (tolls) for upkeep of the Ducktrap Bridge and road, George Ulmer and his associates received the displeasure of the community, who wanted the bridge to have free passage. The dissatisfaction became so great that one day the toll keeper's house (with the toll keeper inside) was pushed into the Ducktrap River! Retribution for the town road and bridge tolls was twice inflicted by vandals upon the log booms that the Ulmer brothers had built for their lumbering, shipbuilding and sawmill businesses with investment money from Henry Knox. The vandalism resulted in the loss of valuable lumber and business income to the two brothers.[1409] The vandals were not caught or punished for their unacceptable behavior, and there was no reimbursement for the financial loss of the lumber or the lost income to the Ulmer businesses at "the Trap."

After several years, Philip sent a petition request to the General Court of Massachusetts to have the bridge tolls revoked, but his petition on behalf of the Lincolnville town's inhabitants was ignored. This bridge request must have offended George since it caused Philip to take a stand against him and in support of the local citizens. George must have felt that collecting the bridge tolls and keeping the records of the cost for maintenance and replacement of the bridge should also yield him a profit for his services. As a public servant of the town, Philip Ulmer's responsibilities as a selectman were to uphold the best interests of the citizens of the town, even if he had to take a stand against his own brother's financial self-interests. On a number of occasions during his lifetime, Philip was called upon to make difficult decisions that would affect the lives of other people whom he had promised to protect, even if it would cause impairment or financial loss to himself and his family members.

THE LOUISIANA PURCHASE
OPENS OPPORTUNITIES IN THE WEST

Spain had signed a secret treaty that ceded the Louisiana Territory to France in 1800; however, European privateering vessels continued to harass American shippers and merchant traders in New Orleans's shipping houses and in the Caribbean. New Orleans was the most important seaport on the Gulf of Mexico. New Orleans was at the mouth of the Mississippi River and served as the gateway into the interior of the country. France had posed a larger threat to American shipping during this time since the Mississippi River and its tributaries were essential for water transportation and for the trading of goods and natural resources from the heartland of America to outside markets of the world. President Jefferson sent an envoy to France for the purpose of negotiating a peaceful solution to the conflicts between the two countries and sent a proposal to purchase the New Orleans area for $10 million. Napoleon needed money to continue to finance his Napoleonic War in Europe against England. Napoleon countered with an offer for the purchase of the entire territory of Louisiana for just $15 million. The negotiators, without further authority, quickly accepted the offer.[1410]

Thomas Jefferson, a strict Constitutional constructionist, had serious reservations about the Louisiana Treaty; however, when Napoleon almost withdrew the offer, Jefferson quickly sent the treaty to Congress for ratification. It might have been the greatest achievement of Thomas Jefferson's presidency. America didn't have the money to purchase the territory outright, but it borrowed the money from Great Britain to be paid back with interest. Great Britain felt that the French treaty with the United States would remove the French threat in America for its natural resources and potential wealth through land settlement and development. The British government thought that in time, the United States would economically collapse under the heavy blockades and imposed embargos on trade and navigation. The British government felt that the disunity among the different states and bitter unrest between the two emerging political parties would cause the collapse of the new republic of the United States and the democratic experiment in America.

In April 1803, the United States bought the huge piece of land from France in what became known as the Louisiana Purchase. It was one of the largest land transfers in American history. The Treaty of Paris, signed on April 30, 1803, transferred sovereignty of the Louisiana Territory (the lands west of the Mississippi River and its tributaries) from France to the United States. The new territory extended from the Gulf of Mexico to Canada and from the Rocky Mountains to the Mississippi River. The land purchase came to about four cents an acre for 828,000 acres, and it secured the heartland of America for exploration and settlement for future American generations.[141] The purchase of the new territory nearly doubled the land area of the United States. The borders in the far western territory would have to be worked out with Spain at another time.

The president dispatched Meriwether Lewis and William Clark to lead a small expeditionary troop called the Corps of Discovery into the Northwest Territory in search of a passage to the Pacific Ocean and to map the new territory. This large purchase of land opened up the western frontier and the Northwestern Territory for exploration and eventual settlement by frontier settlers and venture capitalists. The new frontier drew Americans seeking adventure, land to settle upon and raise a family and the opportunity to explore new lands and business ventures and reap rich financial rewards for their efforts.

LIFESTYLE CHANGES FOR THE ULMER BROTHERS

While these events were taking place on the international scene, the Ulmer brothers, whose personal lives and business successes were interdependent, struggled to recoup their deteriorating situation at Ducktrap. By 1805, both the Bank of the United States and Abiel Wood foreclosed on George Ulmer and Samuel Whitney Sr.'s business partnership at Ducktrap Harbor. They were forced to take out a new mortgage.[1412] Whitney Sr. encouraged George to take out a new mortgage with him. Samuel Whitney Sr. and George Ulmer became new business partners for a short time at Lincolnville and Ducktrap cove. Competitive egos and business disagreements eventually caused the partnership to dissolve. John Wilson bought out George Ulmer's partial ownership with Samuel A. Whitney Sr., and they became business partners at Ducktrap. The business partnership was divided between the men. John Wilson became a successful businessman and a challenging competitor of Samuel A. Whitney Sr. at the Ducktrap Harbor and cove, as well as in the politics of the town.

Philip Ulmer's finances were so depleted by 1806 that he was unable to pay his taxes. In June, Philip Ulmer was convicted and fined for presenting a loaded gun to the chest of a deputy sheriff who had come to seize some of his remaining property to meet his unpaid debts.[1413] Philip was literally dragged from his home by the sheriff and his deputies while protesting loudly. Philip Ulmer's house was sold to Samuel A. Whitney Sr. to pay his debts. Philip had a small house and barn built for his wife and growing family next to his brother's house on the main road from Northport to Lincolnville. This house was sold to Philip's eldest son, Jacob Ulmer, and later sold to John Wilson. Philip moved his family again to another house and barn that he had built in the backcountry of the Ducktrap watershed on Cobbtown Road near Pitcher Pond, where he lived out the rest of his life. (All that is presently left of his homesite are two large impressions in the ground where his house and barn once stood.)

In the spring of 1807 and in December of that same year, a flood destroyed the Ducktrap Bridge, shipyard, wharves, boats and buildings at the cove. The flood carried away the bridge, the sawmill and the lumber at the mill-seat site. Samuel Whitney Sr. weathered the crisis, but George Ulmer had to sell out his remaining partnership in the business to his son-in-law, John Wilson.[1414] Wilson took over George's partnership at Ducktrap Harbor. Samuel Whitney and John Wilson divided the commercial shipping and trading businesses at Ducktrap Harbor and cove and became competitors.[1415] Whitney's businesses were located on the west side of the Ducktrap River (stream), and Wilson's businesses were located on the eastern side of the Ducktrap stream.[1416] Samuel Whitney Sr. and John Wilson became strong business competitors at Ducktrap Harbor and cove at Lincolnville. Both men did well for a number of years.

As George Ulmer's financial situation continued to deteriorate, John Wilson purchased his father-in-law's house in 1811 on the eastern side of the Ducktrap stream.[1417] Polly and George Ulmer Sr. lived with their daughter Mary (also called Polly) and their son-in-law. John Wilson acquired large tracts of land in the backcountry of Lincolnville, Belmont and Belfast vicinity in the Greene Plantation. Samuel A. Whitney Sr. and his son, Samuel Whitney Jr., became so successful in the trading and shipping business competition at "the Trap" that John Wilson's business at Lincolnville eventually failed.[1418] Wilson sold his business at Ducktrap cove but maintained his comfortable lifestyle through real estate sales and various investments that he and his father-in-law, George Ulmer, had made over the years. George Ulmer Jr., who had been adopted by George Ulmer as a very young child from Philip's large family, would later settle in the Belmont section of the Greene Plantation and become an early founder of the town of Belmont.[1419]

In 1815, Philip Ulmer owned three parcels of land in Lincolnville, and he appeared as number fifty-three on the Federal Direct Tax List for Hancock County. George Ulmer no longer held assessable property in Lincolnville at this time. John Wilson, like his father-in-law George Ulmer and like Philip Ulmer, became more involved with politics, land sales and the state militia for financial support. Wilson, who had come to America from Tattenhall, England, just ten years earlier, served actively with the Massachusetts frontier militia during the War of 1812 against his own British countrymen. Since the U.S. government was financially unable to pay many of the soldiers for their service after the war, land-bounties were issued in the Ohio and Indiana Territories, which were part of the Western Reserve. Like so many other veterans, John Wilson and the descendants of George and Philip Ulmer would later seek to claim the land-bounty promised by the federal government in the Western Reserve of Ohio and the Northwest Territories.

POLITICAL CHANGES IN FRONTIER MAINE

How little do my countrymen know what precious blessings they are in possession of, and which no other people on earth enjoy.
—Thomas Jefferson

On the Massachusetts state level in 1804, George Ulmer, an active self-promoter, was elected senator in the General Court of Massachusetts with the political help and influence of General Knox. George enjoyed the political arena, the social status and the recognition that it brought him. He was able to meet other state legislators who held authority and power in the state government. George Ulmer applied for a state government pension as an injured military officer to further his political standing. General Knox used his influence with the General Court and intervened to exempt George Ulmer from the required medical examinations legally needed to obtain a state military pension for a supposed Revolutionary War wound.[1420] The Massachusetts General Court ruled that the limp which George demonstrated was the product of his Revolutionary War service, and he obtained a military pension from the state government for the rest of his life. He later conceded that his limp was not the result of any battle wound but from an accident and that his injury was only temporary.[1421]

In 1805, George Ulmer shifted his prior political affiliation as a Federalist with influential men like Henry Knox and David Cobb. George ran for the Massachusetts State Senate on the new Jeffersonian platform led by Thomas Jefferson and James Madison. The Jeffersonian platform had an agenda that was directly counter to the Federalist agenda led by General Henry Knox and his proprietary supporters. George Ulmer's shift to the Jeffersonian platform and the Jeffersonian political network not only preserved his former political position but also greatly extended it to provide a substitute for his floundering sawmill and mercantile businesses.[1422] George Ulmer and David Cobb became strong political competitors. George was able to defeat Henry Knox's chosen candidate, David Cobb, who had replaced George as Knox's principal agent and business patron in November 1801. Henry Knox and David Cobb were furious about George Ulmer's success in the election and were determined to undermine and sabotage his political career.

George Ulmer ran for governor of the state of Massachusetts in 1806. Henry Knox and David Cobb encouraged the treasurer of the Massachusetts Commonwealth to investigate George Ulmer for fraud.[1423] During the campaign for governor of Massachusetts, the incident of 1801 surfaced, which derailed George Ulmer's campaign for Massachusetts governor. The incident, mentioned earlier, took place while George Ulmer was a militia captain and was in the service of Henry Knox as his land agent, surveyor and tax collector. Upon General Knox's orders, George Ulmer had organized a militia party that marched into the backcountry of New Canaan and Greene Plantations to arrest suspected Liberty Men who were actively disruptive and threatening to Henry Knox's surveyors and land agents. Some of the arrested Liberty Men had threatened the lives of Henry Knox and his family, and they had also intimidated and threatened Knox's agents and supporters with death. Among those threatened by the violent activists were the Ulmer families and the Ulmer businesses at Ducktrap Harbor-cove in Lincolnville.

In April 1806, George Ulmer sent a letter reminding General Knox about the incident, writing, "You advised me…to represent some [other] person as having advanced the provisions observing [that] you did not wish to have your name mentioned."[1424] Dutifully, George Ulmer had accommodated General Knox's desire for secrecy, making out the account for provisions in the name of his son-in-law, John Russ of Belfast. When the commonwealth compensated John Russ for the provisions, he turned the funds over to George Ulmer, who, at General Knox's insistence, kept the money in payment for his services. George's letter to General Knox stated: "My dear sir, What can it mean? Am I at last to be destroyed for having been your faithful servant? I know you do not approve of it but it is verry [sic] strange that those who appeared to be my best friends while I was in your service have become inveterate enemies."[1425]

Having successfully gotten George Ulmer's attention by exposing the questionable militia incident in 1801, Henry Knox once again exerted his political power of intervention in the Massachusetts General Court. General Knox took aside the state treasurer, a fellow gentleman Federalist, and forcefully convinced him that the matter of the arrest of the Liberty Men by the Massachusetts state militia in the summer of 1801 did not require further investigation. George Ulmer had felt Knox's great displeasure for having defeated Knox's chosen candidate, David Cobb, in the election for state senate in 1805. He was relieved to have the investigation of his duplicity in the matter dropped. George Ulmer did not win the senate seat in 1806, losing it to his Federalist rival General David Cobb, William Bingham's land agent and Henry Knox's military friend, agent and supporter.[1426] George Ulmer quickly learned that there were limits to which one could challenge the influence and authority of General Henry Knox and his chosen political agents.

DEATH OF GENERAL HENRY KNOX
AND THE IMPACT ON THE ULMERS

Political unrest continued to simmer in frontier Maine. The threats of vandalism and violence that had been received from Preacher Samuel Ely and his activist supporters at Northport (part of the Greene Plantation) continued to be focused on the Ulmer brothers' businesses at Lincolnville and the personal destruction of George and Philip's wealth and standing in the community. Threats continued to be received by Henry Knox and his surveyors and land agents whose lifestyles offended and enraged Samuel Ely and his activist supporters. The Ulmer brothers' business losses at Ducktrap Harbor impacted Henry Knox's life and lifestyle as well. As Henry Knox's entrepreneurial business ventures in frontier Maine ended in failure, he became more desperate for money. His attitude and how he treated people became more aggressive and offensive to the settlers, who were struggling to survive as well. Knox borrowed money from some of his wealthy friends and took out loans that he had no way of paying back. After moving to Thomaston eleven years before, Henry Knox was soon bankrupt. Violent threats by Ely's followers continued to be sent to Henry Knox and his supporters. Knox was recognized as a Revolutionary War hero who had served as the secretary of war during President Washington's administration and founded the Order of Cincinnati (later called the Society of the Cincinnati). Henry Knox had become a wealthy landowner and entrepreneur after the war, and he had become a powerful and influential politician on the state and national levels. However, Knox had enemies who resented his success and fame. Few people were aware of his financial and business failures, his flamboyant lifestyle or how he exploited and treated people in frontier Maine and made resentful and vengeful enemies. The activist supporters of Samuel Ely apparently carried out some of their threats of defiance and revenge. Henry Knox died unexpectedly on October 25, 1806, of unspecified causes at the age of fifty-six.[1427]

Major Philip Ulmer and his brother, Captain George Ulmer, attended General Henry Knox's funeral, which was conducted on October 28, 1806, at the Knox family estate in Thomaston. Military officers and soldiers who had served with General Knox during the Revolutionary War, political leaders who had served with him in the state and federal government, businessmen, merchants who had business contacts with him, his relatives and friends, the local townspeople and domestics would have attended Henry Knox's funeral in frontier Maine. General Knox, dressed in his full military uniform, lay inside his coffin in the parlor of his impressive Thomaston mansion. An imposing procession was formed at the grounds in front of the mansion. The procession was preceded by a uniformed company of Lincoln County militiamen marching with their muskets reversed. Next came a company of artillery, followed by a company of cavalry, and then came General Knox's coffin, on which lay his hat and sword. Behind the coffin was the general's favorite horse with the general's boots reversed in the stirrups.[1428] The long procession was commanded by Captain Fales, who served as marshal of the day. The whole procession marched to the music of a solemn dirge, accompanied by muffled drums, up the hill to the white church that Knox had constructed on his estate. The tolling bell in the tower had been cast by Paul Revere.[1429] Henry's widow, Lucy Knox, with their two daughters and son, were followed by other relatives, domestics, citizens and strangers.

All of the Knox family members (nine of the twelve Knox children) up to this time were buried in a little cemetery near the white church. The eulogy was given by the Honorable Samuel Thacher of Warren. Following the funeral ceremony, the procession proceeded to the cemetery to the sound of the tolling of the church bell and the artillery firing their guns in salute from the top of the hill. Major Philip Ulmer and Captain George Ulmer, whose lives had been intricately entwined with those of Lucy and Henry Knox, would have been deeply affected by the death of their personal friend, their military general during the Revolutionary War and their business patron for twenty years at Ducktrap (Lincolnville, Maine).

Some claims speculate that Henry Knox swallowed a chicken bone and died from internal complications at his home in Thomaston. However, those close to Henry Knox's family and friends believed that he was actually poisoned while he was eating a chicken dinner. The cause of Knox's untimely death is still being debated today. Silas Deane, who served as a commissioner with Benjamin Franklin in France during the Revolution, died mysteriously from someone putting poison into his food in the same manner as Henry Knox.[1430] We will probably never discover the actual causes of Henry Knox's and Silas Deane's untimely deaths or who might have poisoned these Revolutionary War Patriots. Poisoning seemed to have been a popular method of disposing of wealthy men whose ideology, opinions or business successes were considered offensive to activists or political rivals during this period of time.

Political Ideology Differences
Between the Parties in Massachusetts

The shifting political tide of change and legal reform was led by the Jeffersonian liberal ideology within the Democratic-Republican Party in Massachusetts. George Ulmer united with like-minded leading men throughout the commonwealth in the emerging Jeffersonian political network to replace the Federalist platform of President John Adams's administration. In the frontier counties of eastern Massachusetts (Maine), the former proprietary servants or agents of Henry Knox, like Thurston Whiting, Ezekiel Dodge and George Ulmer, all became leading supporters of Thomas Jefferson's liberal platform of reform.[1431] These former agents had benefited from General Knox's patronage and political support after the American Revolution. They turned against the Federalist political agenda and embraced the Jeffersonian liberal reform platform, which offered further opportunities and political rewards. Colonel James Sullivan, whom George Ulmer strongly supported and rallied for in various counties throughout frontier Maine, was voted as governor of Massachusetts on the Jeffersonian political platform of the Democratic-Republican Party.

The Federalists' platform was based upon the ideology of elitist paternalism that promised stability shaped by a hierarchical society.[1432] The Jeffersonian platform was based upon the ideology of liberal individualism that promised an impartial, minimal government that would provide equal opportunity for all and permit the marketplace to reward the industrious poor rather than the dominating and parasitic rich in society. This would, in their view, steadily eliminate the dominating hierarchy of the rich elite from American society and from American culture. Freed from elite privilege, the marketplace would produce a classless society with prosperity and esteem for all men of industry and merit. Most Americans shared in the Jeffersonian ideology and confidence that the marketplace could be freed of political manipulation by the powerful and wealthy and could promote (instead of corrode) a democratic society of independent producers. While some people preferred the Federalists' promised stability created by an elite hierarchical society, the Jeffersonian liberals appealed to common citizens and to Americans who were ambitious individuals with sufficient interest, connections and attitude to win the acceptance of the Federalists of high social standing.

Prior to his election as the fifth governor of Massachusetts, James Sullivan had been a principal landowner in Limerick (Maine), and he was a lawyer for both Henry Knox and the Massachusetts Bay-Plymouth Company investors. Recognizing James Sullivan's legal talents and political influence in the early 1790s, Henry Knox's agent, Joseph Pierce, had given Sullivan a retainer fee in 1791 to represent Henry Knox in any part of the state government where his assistance was needed.[1433] Times had changed, and the entrenched Federalist state government in Massachusetts was ousted from power and influence. Upon securing the election in 1807 as the Massachusetts Commonwealth's first Jeffersonian governor, James Sullivan rewarded George Ulmer with the county's richest patronage for his strong support in the election: a commission as the Hancock County sheriff and a political advancement to major general in the Massachusetts state militia, Tenth Division.[1434] Thereafter, George was entitled and used the titles of militia general and esquire in recognition of his commission as a state law enforcement official. Since the rank of major general had been given for his political support during the 1807 election, George Ulmer would later resign his rank as militia general when its validity was questioned in a later election when he ran for political office in Massachusetts. George Ulmer sold his properties in the Ducktrap area to his son-in-law, John Wilson, around this time. However, he did not sell his financial interest in the Ducktrap toll bridge to his son-in-law. George continued to extract an income from the local travelers who continuously used the bridge. Eventually the townspeople again raised an outcry in the state court, and another petition was submitted to the General Court by John Wilson in 1816 that was co-signed by seventy-six other citizens of Lincolnville demanding revocation of the tolls that George Ulmer charged for crossing the Ducktrap Bridge. Finally, after considerable political pressure, George Ulmer rescinded the tolls for local residents, and the townspeople withdrew their petitions against him.[1435] He begrudgingly eliminated the bridge toll after having collected more than $2,000 in tolls, which he kept.

In 1807, George Ulmer was elected to the General Court of Massachusetts as a Democratic-Republican senator. Philip Ulmer was elected as a congressman to the Massachusetts House of Representatives to represent the interests and grievances of the townspeople of Lincolnville and the local county areas.[1436]

Senator George Ulmer was described by associates in the General Court of Massachusetts:

> *He was not an educated man, considered in the strict line of scholarship, but a man of great self-reliance and remarkable colloquial gifts; this gave*

him an advantage and a prominence, in many cases, over his superiors in educational acquirements…In any group or assembly of man General Ulmer was personally conspicuous—tall, broad shouldered, and somewhat corpulent; always having the air of a military man. His holiday dress was always military style as long as he lived.[1437]

Dr. Ezekiel Dodge of Thomaston, who was an educated and highly respected professional, once gave Senator George Ulmer a sharp response in the General Court of Massachusetts, where they were both members. On this occasion, they were antagonists on some controversial matter under consideration. George Ulmer led off in one of his offhanded bombastic speeches, in which he attacked Dr. Dodge's position considerably. When George Ulmer sat down, Dr. Dodge rose to reply. He said that he had seen a great many men in his day who could not tell as much as they knew, but he had never before seen one who could tell so much more than he knew as General Ulmer.[1438] This verbal exchange was an example of the confrontational nature of George Ulmer; however, there were many other occasions when George took offense to people who questioned his ideas and authority which ended in threats of a duel or physical or verbal confrontation.

It was during his tenure that the vote for Maine's separation from the state of Massachusetts was raised before the residents of Lincolnville by their congressional representative, Philip Ulmer. The Massachusetts General Court became alarmed that the inhabitants in the Province of Maine might secede from Massachusetts and become an independent state. The state taxes, the natural resources and the general revenue generated for the state's economy would be lost if frontier Maine seceded. Increased efforts were made to give state aid and attention to the grievances of citizens in frontier Maine. The British impressment of Massachusetts seamen and raids on the frontier seaport towns caused the issue of Maine statehood to be delayed for a number of years until the timing was more appropriate.

INTERNATIONAL EVENTS IMPACT THE STATE AND THE TOWN OF LINCOLNVILLE

The U.S. Congress had passed the Non-importation Act of 1806 that prohibited the importation of English goods in order to stop the harsh treatment of American seamen on ships caught running the blockade.

Congress soon passed the Embargo Act in 1807, at the request of President Thomas Jefferson, which banned trade between the U.S. ports and European nations, and it also expanded the prohibition against international trade to all nations. The Embargo Act had been intended to provide pressure upon England and France to remove restrictions on commercial trading with neutral nations that opposed warfare between the European countries. The United States did not wish to be entangled in the European conflicts between France and Great Britain. Napoleon Bonaparte, the ruler of France at this time, decreed under his Continental system that no ally of France or any neutral nation could trade with Great Britain in an effort to destroy the English economy. These vindictive measures hurt neutral American merchant traders as well, prompting Congress to take action to safeguard the economic interests of the United States.

The unpopular 1807 Embargo Act, enacted in December 1807 by President Thomas Jefferson to prevent American involvement in the Napoleonic Wars in Europe, barred trade between the United States and other nations. The point of the Embargo Act was to punish the British and French until they would recognize and respect American authority and sovereignty. In actuality, American merchants were punished because they were prohibited from exporting and importing needed European goods and supplies. The embargo confined all American shipping to port. The Democratic-Republicans in New England were placed in an impossible position of defending a presidential decree that would undermine the New England region's economy and their own business livelihoods and political futures. The embargo brought a deep depression in Massachusetts and in frontier Maine's coastal regions. It also brought a resurgence of the local Federalists in Lincolnville, led by George Ulmer's former business partner, Samuel A. Whitney Sr.[1439] The town of Lincolnville, in September 1808, elected a committee to send a petition to the president of the United States to suspend the trade embargo completely or partially. The committee, consisting of John Wilson, Samuel Whitney Sr. and Abner Heal, appealed to President Thomas Jefferson to consider the dire circumstances of their extremely cold and unpredictable frontier environment, the difficulty of farming the densely forested and rocky soil and the region's dependence upon lumbering, fishing and navigation to survive. The Lincolnville townspeople pleaded for a remedy to their grievances. The federal government in Washington, D.C., took no immediate satisfactory action.

At a meeting held at Philip Ulmer's house on February 8, 1809, another committee was chosen to write a petition of grievances to the Massachusetts

State Congress and was to express the sentiments of the people in relation to the alarming situation in the country and the lack of responsiveness of the state and federal governments to the grievances of the general population. The committee consisted of seven men: Philip Ulmer, Samuel Whitney Sr., Abner Milliken, Hezekiah French, Daniel Decrow, William Kidder and Westbrook Knight. Both the petition and resolves were expressed in "rather harsh and censurable language against the general government."[1440] The economy of the New England states, and particularly of frontier Maine, depended greatly on commercial navigation and trade shipping of cargo such as lumber and multiple wood products, fishing and lime products (such as mortar) for its existence. Smuggling of contraband goods became necessary in order for their town to survive and exist. The general population of frontier Maine clamored for business trade to resume and for relief from the high taxation and overtaxation. The general economy had floundered, and growth from business and trade were at a standstill. These were desperate times in frontier Maine, and people were sick and dying.

Despite the unpopular nature of the Embargo Act, there were some limited and unintended benefits which resulted. It drove capital and labor into the New England textile and manufacturing industries, and it lessened America's reliance on the British manufacturing businesses in England. There was a heavy dependence on Canadian outlets for New England's market production of goods and produce. The Embargo Act was a failure in Vermont and New York State. The Hudson River, Lake Champlain and the Richelieu River water routes north to Canadian ports on the St. Lawrence River offered a way for American goods to be smuggled by water and across the Canadian border land routes to the rest of the world. Using the old northern water transportation routes enabled shipping and trading activities to continue. The illegal smuggling was not restricted to water routes since herds of cattle, sheep and other farm animals were readily driven over the uncontrolled land borders to Canada.

In 1809, Congress enacted an amendment to the ineffective Embargo Act of 1807 that extended the ban from American ports to inland waters and overland transactions—thereby stopping trade with Canada—and mandated strict enforcement of its provisions. Customs officials maintained firm enforcement of the seaport embargo, but the Enforcement Act of 1809 became a political issue that was hotly debated. The Enforcement Act of 1809, also called the Giles Enforcement Act, allowed customs officials to call out the militia to help enforce the embargo. As more restrictions were added, many communities and towns throughout New England seemed to enjoy the hide-and-seek game of revenue and customs agents versus smugglers and the high-profit versus low-profit normal trade game.[1441] In frontier Maine, Eastport had become the primary border town for smuggling with the British agents in New Brunswick, St. John and Halifax, Nova Scotia. Corruption of revenue and customs agents, merchants and even some of the militia soldiers stationed at Fort Sullivan made law enforcement almost impossible. It became a cat-and-mouse game of competition for high stakes.

THE PRESIDENT'S EMBARGO AFFECTS MAINE PROVINCE

The American public strongly opposed the restrictive Embargo Acts of 1807 and of 1809, particularly those citizens who were dependent on navigation, commercial exchange and international trade for their livelihood. The survival of the citizens of the seaport cities, towns and communities in the frontier Maine district depended solely on commercial trading and navigation. In Lincolnville and the surrounding settlement villages in the Penobscot region, the inhabitants were suffering greatly from the Embargo Acts. Many people in the community were so deprived of basic provisions that illness and starvation became a constant threat. Local sailing vessels attempted to break through the seaport blockades in order to provide the provisions and basic supplies for the survival of their families and communities in frontier Maine.

The town of Lincolnville called the inhabitants and freeholders together under the leadership of Major Philip Ulmer, who had been chosen by the townspeople to be moderator of the meeting. It was voted that a committee of seven should be chosen to draft a petition to the Massachusetts State Legislature and to draw up certain resolutions describing the alarming situation in the country and in their community. Philip Ulmer, Samuel A. Whitney Sr., Abner Millikin, Hezikiah French, Daniel Decrow, William Kidder and Westbrook Knight were voted to write the petition and resolutions for the town. The petition and resolves read:

> To the honorable Senate and House of Representatives of the Commonwealth of Massachusetts in General Court assembled, the inhabitants of the town of Lincolnville in legal town meeting assembled at the house of Major Philip Ulmer on Wednesday the eighth day of February a.d. 1809 by leave respectfully to Repoisent [sic] that we live in a section of the state

where newness of the country and sterility of the soil obliges us to rely principally on our forests and navigation for support, the Ocean is that place which the finger of God himself has pointed out to us as the only avenue through which we can realize any advantages from our lumber and fisheries. It is with the deepest regret that we have [been] informed that the federal government has by the several acts laying an embargo on all ships and vessels in the ports and harbors of the United States closed the only avenue through which we can realize the emoluments of our industry and perseverance, the exertion of the farmer, the mechanic and laborer are now paralyzed by the acts of an administration that it had heretofore been our pride and pleasure to support and defend. We must now withstand our confidence, patience is criminal submission, having in vain petitioned for redress, we now look with confidence to one more immediate guardian to save us from destruction, we therefore implore your honorable body to take such measures as you in your wisdom may deem expedient for removing the grievances of which we complain and in duty bound, we ever pray.

Attest, Philip Ulmer, Moderator,
Samuel A. Whitney, Town Clerk.

Resolved *that the alarming and deplorable situation of our country which calls us together at this time is the offspring of unnecessary, impolitude [sic], unconstitutional, oppressive, and arbitrary acts of the general government laying an embargo on all ships and vessels in the ports and harbors of the United States, and the produce of our farmers by land viewing them in this light, we do not conceive they are binding for the people, therefore resolved at the time of this meeting that we will not voluntarily and or assist in carrying them into effect and will consider all those who do as enemies to the prosperity of their country,*

Resolved *that having in vain petitioned the President of the United States for a redress of grievances under which we suffer in consequence of those acts that we will address ourselves. The more immediate guardians of our rights for that redress which we sought of the General Government,*

Resolved *that as the federal administration have abandoned the interests of the people and abused that confidence which we have heretofore with pride and pleasure placed in them, that we will now transfer it to that source from which we look for redress,*

Resolved *that the self-styled* [sic] *county of Hancock meeting held at Frankfort on the 9th day of January last, Hon. George Ulmer in the chair as set forth in the Portland Argosy of the 19th of last month, is an insult to the county and ought to be held up to the complaint and ridicule of the public in as much as there was not one town in the county notified and inasmuch as their numbers did not exceed twenty persons convened in a private manner…*

The foregoing resolves were signed by:

Philip Ulmer	Samuel A. Whitney	William Kidder
Hezikiah French	Daniel Decrow	Joseph Collemer
Ephraim Miller	David Brooks	Abner Millikin
Thomas Spring	Peleg Decrow	Samuel [?]
Chris Dalie	Isaac Heal	Chesley Heal
John Dean Jun.	Westbrook Knight	George W. Shepard
Seth Hunt	John [?]	David Reardon
Steven Young	Reuben Higgins	Caleb Brooks
William McFarland	Isaiah Decrow	Elijah Wentworth Jun
Noah Mason	Martin Brooks	William Dickey
Amon Dalie	Isaac Decrow	John Calderwood
William Stone	John Decrow	Jebidiah Gilman
William Moody	Enoch Knight	Jonas Knight
Gideon Young	Hushai Thomas	John Mahoney
Isaiah Dean	Silas Varney	Moses Young
Richmond Daggett	Hezikiah Batchelder	Elijah Smith
Joseph Pottle	Benjamin Lamb	Solomon Brooks
John Wilson	Nathaniel Knight	Horace Miller
Charles Thomas	Samuel Angier	John Studley
Jonathan Fletcher	Elijah Wentworth	Nathan Knight
Joseph Butterfield		

Voted that each man present that approves of the resolves sign thereof which was unanimously done excepting one person.
Voted that the proceedings of this meeting be made published by inserting them in the public papers. The meeting was dissolved.

—Attest, Samuel A. Whitney, Town Clerk [1442]

The petition and resolves from the town meeting at Philip Ulmer's house were sent to the General Court of the Commonwealth of Massachusetts. This was a declaration that the citizens of the town of Lincolnville and the county of Hancock would not respect or enforce the Embargo Acts ordered by the Congress and the president of the United States. Repeated pleas for help and assistance were sent to the state of Massachusetts and the federal government, but the pleas were mostly ignored. If any kind of assistance was sent, it seldom arrived in a timely manner. The inhabitants of the eastern frontier of Massachusetts would have to defend themselves against enemy incursions and find a way to survive on their own. The separation of the Province of Maine from the rest of Massachusetts was discussed often during the turbulent war years of 1812–15. However, the final decision for statehood would not be achieved until 1820, when the inhabitants of frontier Maine finally decided that they had suffered enough and had been deprived of protection and assistance long enough. The former citizens of Massachusetts decided to become a separate state that was independent from the commonwealth.

Philip Takes a Fateful Stand

Major Philip Ulmer had to make a difficult decision about his allegiance and loyalties. Philip Ulmer had been called back into the military service by the United States government on February 6, 1809, and was appointed a sailing master in the U.S. Navy on a warship.[1443] This was a position in the naval service that he had always desired and hoped to achieve. This was the opportunity to serve in the U.S. Navy, in command of a naval warship, and it was a dream-come-true for Philip Ulmer. Philip left his blossoming political life as a politician in the Massachusetts House of Representatives, and he accepted the opportunity to become the sailing master of a naval warship in the U.S. Navy.[1444]

Major Philip Ulmer and his U.S. Navy seamen assumed their assignment of protecting the coastal shipping and defenses. All of the states were suffering from the intolerable Embargo Acts imposed by the federal government, but the New England states, and especially frontier Maine, suffered the most. It was during this period of time that it was discovered that Philip Ulmer's brother, George, was involved in covert business activities along the New England coastal region with men like William King, a fellow Massachusetts congressman, real estate investor and merchant shipping owner. George had inside information as to his brother's sailing schedule and where Philip's naval warship would be cruising at any given time. Knowing this information made it possible for local sailing vessels to avoid being seized during covert operations. However, George Ulmer's activities were eventually made known to the authorities, and he was arrested and held for court trial (apparently in Portsmouth, New Hampshire). He was found to be involved with covert smuggling and other illicit activities in the frontier region, like many other politicians, merchants and businessmen in New England.[1445] George was able to use his political connections with William King and other Massachusetts state politicians to avoid punishment, and he was released from jail. It was part of doing business and ensuring economic survival. Covert smuggling and shipping activities continued in spite of futile efforts to stop it. The inhabitants needed some way of surviving, maintaining a living for their families and keeping their businesses alive.

Major Philip Ulmer's duties as a naval officer and captain of a U.S. Navy warship included the responsibilities of upholding the detested federal Embargo Acts and arresting and prosecuting smugglers who defied the federal government's orders. It became apparent during the court trial concerning rampant smuggling in the Passamaquoddy Bay and Penobscot Bay region that Major Philip Ulmer had not been as zealous as he might have been in his efforts to suppress navigation of coastal vessels, to capture contraband goods and to prosecute the traffickers in the smuggling and illicit trading that transpired in the frontier region and along the coastal areas. Philip Ulmer's petition to the General Court of Massachusetts that strongly pleaded the case of the townspeople in Lincolnville and other frontier towns clearly indicated his lack of support for the embargo decrees of the federal government. Trying to stop the smuggling of needed goods and supplies in eastern New England was an impossible task since it was so rampant and involved wealthy and powerful men in the state and federal government who gave only lip service to the federal Embargo Acts. Major Ulmer's personal concern had been to prevent British and French privateers, loyalists and foreign agents from taking advantage of the vulnerability of the crippled navigation and commercial trading industry that formed New England's fragile economy and the livelihood of the inhabitants of frontier Maine. He was greatly concerned about the deprivations and suffering of the citizens of frontier Maine and the American people as a whole and the economic impact of the Embargo Acts upon the fragile U.S. economy.

As a navy officer, he had sworn allegiance to the United States and had promised to protect it from all enemies both foreign and domestic. The actions of the president and the federal government with their intolerable embargo acts were hurting the American people and crippling the nation's economy to the point of near collapse, leaving the nation vulnerable for foreign takeover. Major Philip Ulmer had made the fateful decision to stand, to support and to defend the districts and communities in frontier Maine and New Hampshire against the deprivations and hardships imposed by the federal government's Embargo Acts. Ulmer's actions indicated that he had basically given a "wink and a nod" to the covert smuggling and covert navigation activities along the northern New England coastline. It was a decision to support the greater good that would provide for the basic provisions and needed supplies of the frontier inhabitants while he and his naval crew defended the coastal frontier towns against foreign raiding parties and enemy privateers. It was a bitter decision to be forced to make, especially having faithfully served the country as a respected officer on land and sea for almost forty years. It was during this difficult time that Philip and George's beloved uncle, John Ulmer, who lived in Thomaston with George Ulmer Jr.'s family, passed away, causing more hardship for the entire Ulmer family. The whole Ulmer clan gathered at the funeral to honor and mourn the passing of John Ulmer. They laid him to rest in the local cemetery with other relatives, family friends and Revolutionary War soldiers.

Philip Ulmer had made his values, principles and opinions known in a letter concerning the intolerable Embargo Acts that he sent to the Massachusetts General Court on behalf of the citizens of Lincolnville in February 1809. Philip, as a principal leader in the community, strongly expressed the concerns and desperate circumstances of the townspeople of Lincolnville. The letter alarmed the federal government officials and led to a quick reaction since Major Ulmer had just been recalled into the military service as a sailing master in the U.S. Navy. The letter and Philip's expressed views of President Jefferson's Embargo Acts short-circuited his naval career. Three months after being recalled to active duty in the U.S. Navy, by a circular order of the Department of the Navy, Major Philip Ulmer's position as sailing master was rescinded and his warrant revoked.[1446] Philip's life-changing choice to express his concerns to the federal government for the survival of citizens in the state and to protect the needs of his family and the people of frontier Maine were responsible for ending his career as a U.S. Navy officer. Shortly after Major Philip Ulmer left the service of the U.S. Navy, the Non-Intercourse

Act of 1809 was passed by Congress, lifting all embargos on American shipping. Foreign trade was opened to all countries except France and England.[1447] The Embargo Act of 1809, which had cost Philip Ulmer his navy career, was repealed three days before Thomas Jefferson left the presidential office on March 4, 1809. The repeal of the Embargo Acts came several weeks too late for Philip Ulmer. The Non-Intercourse Act of 1809 proved unenforceable, too, and it was replaced in 1810 by Macon's Bill Number 2. This bill lifted all embargos, but it offered that if either France or Great Britain were to cease their interference in American shipping, the United States would reinstate an embargo on the other country. Napoleon Bonaparte, seeing an opportunity to make trouble for Great Britain, decreed that American shipping was to be left alone. The United States reinstated the embargo only against Great Britain. This action moved America closer to declaring war on England.

Major Philip Ulmer continued to serve his country in the Massachusetts state militia with a company of older war veterans who assembled and drilled at Camden village overlooking the harbor. The coastal communities were under constant threat of British foraging activities and attacks on poorly defended local villages and settlements by raiding parties in the Penobscot Bay region. In the fall of 1812, Major Jacob Ulmer, Philip's eldest son, was directed to lead two detached companies from General Blake's brigade on a special assignment to the fort at Eastport (Maine), the easternmost outpost on the disputed Canadian-American border.[1448] Major Ulmer commanded the detached militia troops stationed at Fort Sullivan until Colonel Commandant George Ulmer assumed the command with his company of regular U.S. Volunteers in December 1812.[1449] Eyewitnesses at Eastport clearly reported that Major Philip Ulmer was in command of the militia troops at Fort Sullivan at this time, and he and his troops were relieved "within a year by regular troops" commanded by Colonel George Ulmer.[1450] In any case, Major Ulmer (either Philip or his son Jacob, who both held the same military rank at this time) commanded the detached militia troops at Fort Sullivan until Colonel George Ulmer assumed the command. Major Ulmer returned to his prior responsibilities having completed his military assignment. Major Philip Ulmer continued to serve his country in the Massachusetts state militia with the veterans' corps at the small seaport town of Camden (once a part of Ducktrap Plantation) through 1813. According to the town records of Lincolnville, Philip Ulmer also continued to serve as a selectman and community leader for Lincolnville during the war years of

1812–15. He served the community well and executed his responsibilities faithfully and honorably during the turbulent and violent British invasion of the Passamaquoddy and Penobscot Bay region in the summer and fall of 1814.

In 1814, Philip Ulmer was appointed as a deputy customs official and assigned to the Penobscot Bay region, where he also served as a coastal pilot from his location at Lincolnville and Camden. As a federal law enforcement officer, he worked to enforce the customs laws and other federal laws for every person who entered or left the United States territory in frontier Maine. Among the many functions that he performed were detecting and confiscating contraband, making sure that import duties were paid and preventing those without legal authorization from entering the United States. Since 1789, a customs official's job had been connected with the U.S. Treasury. The U.S. Customs Department became the second-highest revenue collector in the United States though fines, collection of duties and illegal money and contraband seized. Since the federal government did not have the power to tax the different states or the citizens directly, the Madison administration became increasingly dependent on tax revenue and taxes from duties on goods and services to sustain the national economy. Philip Ulmer, in the fulfillment of his responsibilities as a deputy customs officer, would become involved in an incident with a seized British cargo vessel, *Mary*, in November 1814 that threatened to unleash the vengeance and destruction of the British navy warships on the towns of Lincolnville and Camden in the Penobscot Bay.

Chapter 18

The War of 1812

BACKGROUND FOR THE WAR OF 1812 (1812–15)

During the late 1790s and early 1800s, American ships had been caught in the middle of the power struggle between France and England and their constant warring in Europe, the West Indies and South America, the Mediterranean Sea and all along the eastern seacoast of America from Florida and the Gulf of Mexico to the district of Lincoln County in frontier Maine and the disputed border at the St. Croix River at New Brunswick, Canada. The British naval vessels seized approximately 1,000 American sailing vessels, and the French seized approximately 500 along the coast of Europe in the undeclared war (quasi-war) being waged on the high seas.[1451] The French assault on American shipping (1793–1813) involved more than 2,300 vessels that were seized in the twenty-year period, and the vessels were later recorded and the incidents filed.[1452] Between the years 1803 and 1812, the British naval captains captured over ten thousand American citizens on the high seas.[1453] In 1810, Napoleon Bonaparte revoked his former decrees concerning American shipping, and he agreed that France would respect American sovereignty, independence and neutrality in France's war with Great Britain. Great Britain would not revoke its decrees regarding America's sovereignty nor the neutrality of ships and the rights of sailors from neutral countries. As a result, President James Madison suspended American trade with England. England continued to impose its will upon American seaports and upon coastal trading and shipping globally. The British Royal Navy continued to impress American citizens on land and sea.

The War of 1812 in North America has been characterized as a spillover of the Napoleonic Wars in Europe between France and England. The War of 1812, America's second Revolutionary War, has also been considered a "forgotten war" since it was eclipsed by the American Revolution (1775–83) on one side and the Civil War (1861–65) on the other side. However, if the outcome of the War of 1812 had been different, it would have resulted in a different geopolitical balance with a dramatically weakened United States facing disunion and a much stronger Canada, supported by the assimilation of the territorial states of New England into British-held Canada.[1454] Again the rivalry for American resources and trade between France and England contributed to the outbreak of hostilities in America, Europe and the West Indies. England coveted France's valuable sugar plantations in the West Indies, which caused Napoleon Bonaparte's French army and French navy to respond by cutting off Great Britain's access to valuable resources in the West Indies and trading markets in continental Europe. Deprived of the forest resources of the Baltic countries that were needed for shipbuilding, Great Britain turned increasingly to America, where natural forest resources and minerals in frontier Maine and in the Lake Champlain Valley were abundant with lumber, lime, potash, iron and other needed products for England's domestic and world markets.

Napoleon Bonaparte further sought a means of stemming the flow of goods and resources from the Great Lakes and the St. Lawrence River regions in Canada to the markets in England. Napoleon found an ally among the merchants and industrialists in frontier Maine and other New England colonial states who were greatly stressed by the competition from British-made manufactured goods pouring into the United States from Montreal through the Lake Champlain Valley region. American protectionism in the form of high tariffs and President Jefferson's Embargo Acts did little to stop the level of cross-border smuggling. Just as Napoleon's plan was to prevent the flow of goods from Canada, England planned to stop the flow of American goods toward France's war efforts in Europe. The United States sought to remain neutral in the conflict between the rival European countries. America was caught in the tug-of-war between England and France.

British war hawks argued that abundant resources available in British-held North America could not be denied to Great Britain, which needed them.[1455] These voices in the British Parliament felt that the time had come to recover the colonies lost during the American Revolution. It was thought that the separate and independent states in America were so divided by political strife that they would not be able to unite together when faced with an outside threat to the country. The political divisiveness between the Federalists and the Democratic-Republican ideologies at this time had stagnated the federal government and the individual state governments to such an extent that they could scarcely function. States' governments that had received federal directives from an administration of a different political party affiliation were slow to respond or ignored the orders and declarations given by the federal government. Even the states' local community governments had difficulty functioning for the same political reasons. The bitter divisions between the two American political parties were so great that Great Britain felt that America was vulnerable and that the new national government could be easily overthrown.

British Royal Navy warships continued to harass the coastline of the United States by stopping and boarding American ships at will and impressing American citizens into the British naval service. In June 1807, the American frigate *Chesapeake* was fired upon by the British warship *Leopard* after refusing to be boarded off the coast of Norfolk, Virginia. The British forced the *Chesapeake* to surrender, and the British boarding party removed the naturalized American citizens, whom the British claimed were traitors and deserters, from the neutral American vessel. The British naval vessels, in spite of American protests and Jefferson's Embargo Acts, continued for years to stop and impress anyone suspected of having been a deserter or being a naturalized American citizen. More dramatic sea encounters between neutral American sailing vessels and British armed warships led to the attempt by President Jefferson to use peaceful coercion. President Jefferson issued several Embargo Acts ordering all ports to be closed to British commerce both into and out of American ports. The Embargo Acts were a public disaster for American commerce, and they undermined the economy of all the New England states, especially the Province of Maine with its harsh environmental conditions.

In 1810, the liberal party of the Democratic-Republicans assumed the majority in Congress from the Federalists. The spirit of political unrest in America continued to be stirred by England and France's constant antagonism for each other. The war hawks in Congress exerted pressure upon the president to declare war on Great Britain. British agents and military forces were stirring up problems in the Ohio River Valley with the Native Americans. These problems were hindering American expansion and settlement in the western frontier. England continued to defy America's sovereignty and neutrality. The seizure of American vessels on the high seas and the impressments of naturalized citizens and American-born citizens caused a loud outcry of injustice throughout the country. These actions provided the necessary spark for President James Madison to issue a declaration of war against England on June 18, 1812.

With the cessation of hostilities between America and France, the naval warships and armed merchant vessels could concentrate on the issues that it had with Great Britain. Napoleon Bonaparte offered to keep Great Britain so occupied in Europe that England could not send reinforcements in response to an American invasion of Canada, with the goal of expelling the British Royal Army and Royal Navy presence from the North American continent.[1456] With the British preoccupied with Napoleon's French army forces that were sweeping through Europe, the American war hawks in Congress thought the time had come when the British forces in Canada could be expelled from the Great Lakes and the St. Lawrence River Valley. It was thought that once the British forces were expelled from Canada, the Canadian and the French inhabitants might be encouraged to become part of the United States of America. (Note: This was the same plan that Benedict Arnold and General Montgomery's American forces tried to accomplish by invading Canada in the fall of 1775, at the beginning of the American Revolution.) British forces in Canada continuously sought to stir up discontent among the Native Americans in the midwestern Ohio River Valley and the Great Lakes regions. England made land claims in the Northwestern (Rocky Mountain) territory. The French goal was to shut down the busy ports of Montreal and Quebec City and deprive Great Britain of the goods and resources that it needed from North America, thus undermining its economy. American forces could be used for that purpose.

DECLARATION OF WAR, JUNE 18, 1812

Then, warriors on shore, be brave, Your wives and homes defend;
Those precious boons be true to save, And hearts and sinews bend;
Oh, think upon your fathers' fame, For glory marked the way;
And this foe aimed the blow, But victory crowned the day;
Then emulate the deeds of yore, Let victory crown the day.
—old song from the War of 1812[1457]

A declaration of war was declared by President James Madison and the United States Congress. The warships of the U.S. Navy went to sea to avoid being blockaded in port by the British Royal Navy. The American frigate *Constitution* (called Old Ironsides) sailed northward out of the Chesapeake Bay with Captain Isaac Hull commanding. Although it was rated for forty-four guns, it sailed with fifty-six guns since it was thought that the added weight of the armaments and the warship's heavy design would give it an edge over any British frigates it might encounter. The *Constitution* managed to avoid being captured by a British naval fleet stationed off of the New Jersey coast by heading farther out to sea. The American frigate then continued its voyage to Boston to resupply. The *Constitution*, having taken on supplies and provisions, then headed northeast toward the Maine coastline, and it patrolled off of the coast of Eastport (Maine) and Halifax, Nova Scotia. On August 19, 1812, the sentinels aboard the *Constitution* spotted the British warship HMS *Guerriere* approaching them. The warship was headed for the British stronghold and naval shipyard at Halifax, Nova Scotia. The *Constitution* intercepted the HMS *Guerriere* (with thirty-eight guns) captained by James R. Dacres.* American troops who were stationed at Fort Sullivan in Eastport at this time were probably quite aware of the deadly naval engagement that was about to play itself out before their eyes off their coastline.

As the frigates approached each other, Captain Hull ordered the crewmen to hold their fire until the two vessels were about twenty-five yards apart. The two frigates exchanged heavy broadsides for nearly thirty minutes until the *Constitution* closed on the HMS *Guerriere*'s starboard beam, causing the British ship's mizzenmast to collapse. The *Constitution* was able to rake the decks of the HMS *Guerriere* with heavy cannon fire. As the battle continued, the two ships collided twice in the attempts to board. The attempts were beaten off by determined musket fire from the marine detachments. When the frigates collided for a third time, the *Constitution* became caught in the bowsprit of the HMS *Guerriere*. As the two vessels pulled apart, the bowsprit snapped, damaging the rigging and causing the HMS *Guerriere*'s mainmast and foremast to go over the side. British captain Dacres, who was injured in the fighting, convened his officers. It was decided to strike the colors to prevent any further loss of life. After boarding and assessing the damage to the British frigate, Captain Hull determined that the frigate was beyond

---

* *Author's comment*: Captain James Dacres was the son of the commander of the British warship *Carleton* that fought in the Battle of Valcour Island against the small American naval fleet on Lake Champlain in 1776.[1458]

salvaging. The wounded were transferred to the *Constitution*, and the HMS *Guerriere* was set on fire and left to sink.[1459] Alexander Wadsworth, the son of General Peleg Wadsworth, was awarded a silver medal for heroism for his actions while serving aboard the *Constitution* in its battle with the HMS *Guerriere* during the War of 1812.

One can imagine the reaction of the American troops stationed at Eastport who heard the booming broadsides being delivered during the fierce sea battle and observed the smoke rising from the burning British vessel at sea.[1460] Major Philip Ulmer, who had been appointed as a U.S. Volunteer to command a battalion of three companies from the local area, was ordered into the service of the government of the United States pursuant to the law and at the request of the American president. The U.S. Volunteers were subject to the orders of the president from the time of their march from their respective locations to Eastport until they were discharged according to their assignment. References to Major Ulmer's assignment at Eastport are found in the letters of General John Blake. Major General Henry Sewall wrote to General John Blake from Augusta (Maine) on October 30, 1812:

Dear General,

Your favour of the 20 inst. [sic] *has been duly received. With respect to the supplies of provisions, &c for the troops at Eastport, I have for some time rested easy, for two reasons—1. Because the Governor considers those troops in the service and pay of the United States, and on the 26 Sept. last, signified this opinion in writing to B. Gen. John P. Boyd at Boston, who commands all the troops in the service of the United States in the eastern military district, a copy of which communication under date of 3. inst* [sic] *has some time since been transmitted to me, & Major Ulmer informed of this decision. 2. Because I have recently received a letter from B. Gen. Brewer of Robbinstown, dated the 4 inst.* [sic] *In which he writes, that "Major Ulmer & the troops under him have conducted with great propriety, & have given the inhabitants full satisfaction—they are well supplied with good rations & good quarters. They have obtained some powder from the United States Forts but no arms to supply deficiencies have been delivered, although there are several chests deposited in the Fort. Capt. Chamberlain's and George's companies are at Eastport, & Capt. Vose's at Robbinstown." These troops must therefore look to the Government in whose service they are employed, for all necessary supplies. Having myself complied with the orders for marching them to the place of rendezvous, &*

organizing them into a battalion, I consider my task performed.

I am, Dear Sir, with respect and esteem,
Your most obedient H'ble [sic] *Servant,*
H. Sewall[1461]

One can imagine the intense excitement of Colonel George Ulmer's small company of soldiers stationed at the militia battery at Fort Madison (formerly Fort George) on Castine, and also imagine the reactions and cheers of the militia troops at Fort Pine Hill. The militia and U.S. Volunteers at these forts must have been overcome with emotions when the damaged American frigate *Constitution* sailed slowly by the coastal outposts on its way back to Boston for repairs on August 30 with its British prisoners and crewmen on board. With the capture of the British frigate HMS *Guerriere*, American morale received an early boost in the war. This was the first in a series of ship-to-ship victories for the small U.S. Navy fleet. As a result of the success of the frigate *Constitution* and additional American victories, the British Royal Navy forbade its commanders from engaging the American frigates in single-ship combat. The British Royal Navy imposed a strong blockade along the American seacoast that prevented armed merchant and trading vessels, as well as the heavily armed U.S. Navy warships, from leaving port and getting out to sea. In spite of the quality and strength of the American naval vessels, there were too few of them to be effective against the heavily armed British frigates and warships.

On June 1, 1813, the harassment of American vessels came to a head off the Marblehead and Salem shoreline, where Philip and George Ulmer's cousins and extended family lived and where they had their merchant trading businesses. The American frigate *Chesapeake*, which had set sail from Boston Harbor, came under fire from the British frigate HMS *Shannon*, which was reconnoitering the Boston Harbor with the frigate HMS *Tenedos*. The HMS *Shannon* was under the command of Captain Philip Bowes Vere Broke. The *Chesapeake* was commanded by Captain James Lawrence. The brief ensuing sea battle was observed from the shoreline by local townspeople who had heard the loud cannons roaring just off their coast. The townspeople of Salem and Marblehead assembled along the shore to observe the brutal encounter and explosive actions between the two enemy frigates that were locked in deadly combat. The two frigates inflicted heavy damage with broadsides, causing heavy damage to both vessels and the crews. As the two vessels came together, British captain Broke ordered the two vessels lashed together. There was mass confusion aboard the *Chesapeake.* Captain Lawrence, while giving orders to his crew, was shot down and carried below decks, exclaiming, "Don't give up the ship!"[1462]

As the British captain Philip Broke and twenty of the crewmen boarded the *Chesapeake,* the American crewmen left their heavy guns, ran below deck and called for quarter (surrender). Only Chaplain Livermore and the marines on board continued to fight against the British boarding party. Of the forty-four marines, fourteen were dead and twenty were wounded, while Chaplain Livermore was cut down by Captain Broke's sword. Fifteen minutes after the British marines boarded the *Chesapeake,* the American flag was taken down and replaced by the British Union Jack. The surrendered American frigate was sailed, under the command of Captain Alexander Gordon, to the naval shipyards in Halifax, Nova Scotia, for repair. Captain James Lawrence and Lieutenant Ludlow were buried side by side with military honors. This action still remains one of the bloodiest of the War of 1812, and the numbers of casualties on both warships remain to this day the worst for any single ship action in the history of either the United States or the British Royal Navy.[1463] Following the capture of the *Chesapeake* off the coast of Marblehead, Massachusetts, and the removal of its naturalized American citizens, President Madison issued an American proclamation forbidding British ships from entering any harbors of the United States. The proclamation would remain in effect until satisfaction for the attack against the *Chesapeake* was made by the British government and security given against future aggression. This incident had been an insult to the national sovereignty and independence of the United States.

England, having defeated Napoleon Bonaparte's French army in Europe, began to transfer large numbers of its British warships and experienced regular troops to America. The plan was to attack the United States in multiple campaigns. The strategy was to render the country helpless to respond while sequentially attacking from several directions. The ultimate British goal of reabsorbing the rebellious colonies in the United States back into the British Empire would be complete. Again the inhabitants in America would become subservient to the British Parliament and the king of England.

THE BRITISH PLAN TO INVADE THE UNITED STATES

After the defeat of the French army in Europe and the abdication of Napoleon Bonaparte in 1814, Great Britain was able to deploy its veteran Royal Army and Royal Navy forces to the United States. At sea, the superior British Royal Navy blockaded much of the coastline of America, although it did permit substantial exports from New England to be traded with Great Britain and Canada in defiance of the American Embargo Acts. A war strategy was developed in the British Ministry of War for a four-pronged attack on the United States. British vice admiral Sir Alexander Cochrane served as commander in chief of the North American Theater at their military headquarters in Quebec, Canada. Admiral Cochrane was an experienced British naval officer who had served in the American Revolution, during which time his brother, Charles Cochrane, was killed at the Battle of Yorktown. The death of his brother left a bitter resentment and a deep hatred in Admiral Cochrane toward the United States and all Americans. Vice Admiral Cochrane had previously served as the commander of British forces in the Leeward Islands, and he was knighted for his services against the French and Spanish forces in 1806 in the West Indies. He had successfully led an expedition against the Danish Islands in the West Indies and commanded the British naval forces in the seizure of the major French port of Martinique.[1464] In January 1814, Vice Admiral Cochrane was placed in command of the Atlantic and Gulf Coast stations in America by the Ministry of War, replacing Admiral Warren.[1465] The Great Lakes station, which included the Lake Champlain to Lake Superior regions, was considered a separate command by the British Ministry.

The first prong of the British operational plan to invade the United States was initially focused on securing the support of the Native Americans in the American west and in the Great Lakes regions. Once the alliance was made with the Native American war parties, British forces could defeat the American army's sparsely manned outposts in the Great Lakes and western frontier regions. The British and Indian forces were then directed to execute an assault southward from Canada by way of the Great Lakes region and move southward through the Mississippi River Valley, the heartland of the United States. By navigating down the major river tributaries of the Ohio and Missouri Rivers to the Mississippi River, the large British and Indian invasion forces would proceed southward through the Mississippi River Valley and unite with British forces north of New Orleans. British forces stationed on the Gulf Coast and in the West Indies had been ordered to invade the city of New

Orleans on the southern Mississippi delta. Once New Orleans was captured, the British forces were to move northward up the Mississippi River to unite with the British and Indian forces advancing southward from the Great Lakes region in Canada. The heartland of America would be divided in half by the pincher maneuvers of the superior British forces, and the United States military forces would be forced to unconditionally surrender to England.

The second prong of the attack was to thrust southward from the British naval stronghold of Halifax, Nova Scotia, with a large, well-armed British fleet of experienced soldiers and marines to overwhelm the weak Massachusetts state militia forces in the eastern frontier outposts of Maine. Major militia outposts, forts and shipyards were to be seized and held by British troops as the larger fleet continued to move southward along the coastline to capture Boston and New York City. If successful, the British naval forces under Admiral Cochrane, commander in chief of the North American Theater, would attack Philadelphia and destroy this highly important port city on their way to Baltimore, where a major naval shipyard on the eastern coast of the United States was located. Shortly thereafter, the British plan of operations was to follow the attack on frontier Maine with a large British force from Montreal and Quebec. Some reports estimate as many as ten thousand men under the command of Sir George Prevost would march by way of the Richelieu River route to Fort St. John on the northern end of Lake Champlain, where British ships were being constructed for the second phase of the invasion of the United States of America.[1466]

Using General Burgoyne's planned invasion route of 1777, the British invasion forces would proceed down Lake Champlain, destroying any military posts, shipyards and towns that might pose a threat, like Plattsburgh, New York. The British forces were to continue their thrust southward through the Lake George region and down the Hudson River to Albany, New York. From Albany, the invasion forces would proceed south along the Hudson River to New York City, where they would unite with the British fleet moving southward along the New England coastline from Halifax, causing death and destruction along the way. The New England states would be severed from the rest of the United States and defeated by the large combined British army forces from Canada. The New England states, the center and the spirit of the American resistance, had been a thorn in the side of the king of England and the British government since the 1770s. The troublesome New England colonies would finally be crushed completely. The rebellious New England resisters would have to submit and surrender to British rule or die!

Fortunately, the weak American militia forces in New York and in the New Hampshire grant (present-day Vermont) that were defending the Lake Champlain region had Connecticut captain Thomas MacDonough to lead the combined militia forces. He was a young U.S. Navy officer who had seen military service during America's war against the Barbary Pirates in Tripoli (1801–05). Captain MacDonough and his brigade hastily built a naval fleet at Vergennes (Vermont) to engage the British fleet that was invading from Canada. Captain MacDonough's combined militia and marine troops fought a decisive naval battle at Plattsburgh Bay. They stopped the advancing British fleet moving southward from Montreal, whose plan was to divide the New England states from the southern states. Once divided, the individual states could be conquered one by one. Fearing the possibility of severing the line of communication and supplies (as General Burgoyne had done at Fort Ticonderoga and at Saratoga in 1777), the British forces retreated back into Canada and never finished their part of the British operational plan.

The third prong of the British invasion operation plan in America was designed to lay waste to the naval shipyard in Baltimore and to burn the government buildings that were under construction in Washington, the new capital city of the federal government of the United States. The mission of the British invasion forces was to proceed up the Potomac River to the city of Washington and destroy the new government buildings that were under construction. British troops were to pillage, plunder and burn the public buildings in the capital city and destroy the presidential White House, where the president of the United States and his family lived. They were to capture any government leaders and officials as hostages, including President James Madison and his family, and this would force the United States to surrender unconditionally to Great Britain. Fortunately, President Madison and his family were able to escape capture. Having succeeded in their mission to lay waste to the city of Washington and destroy the government buildings, the British troops turned their focus on destroying the shipyard and defenses at Baltimore, Maryland. The British were met with stiff resistance from the American militia troops at Fort McHenry, and they were forced to retreat after the heroic and successful American defense of the harbor fort. This event inspired Francis Scott Key to write the words of the "Star-Spangled Banner," which were later put to music and became America's national anthem.

The fourth prong of the British invasion plan would be focused on New Orleans, the principal port city in the southern part of the country at the mouth of the Mississippi River and the Gulf of Mexico. This important major seaport would be blockaded, the city would be seized and then British forces would move northward up the Mississippi River and lay waste to the river ports and major settlements along the river. The British plan was to finally unite with the British forces moving southward from the Great Lakes by way of the Mississippi River. The final goal was to divide the center of the United States from north to south, all the way from the Great Lakes to New Orleans, and seize control of the center of the country and the heartland of America. The British then hoped to obtain territorial concessions in a major peace treaty.

The British Implement Their Invasion Plan

Since the declaration of war was announced on June 18, 1812, the invasion and conquest of Canada was a major objective of the United States in the War of 1812. Among the significant causes of the war were the disruption of American commerce and trade around the world by the powerful British navy and the impressments of American citizens and naturalized citizens into the service of Great Britain. England refused to honor America's sovereignty and neutrality in the fighting between France and Great Britain, and it did not respect the right of the United States to remain free of involvement in the conflicts between competing European countries. Other causes of the war included the continuing clash of British and American land and border claims in the unsettled western territories (part of the Louisiana Purchase by the U.S. government in April 1803) and the northeast border region of Maine Province and the important fishing rights in the Grand Banks region near Newfoundland and Labrador, Canada. The conflict over control of the mouth of the St. Lawrence River for trade and navigation, the commercial interests and navigation in the Great Lakes region and the vast resources in the Northwest Territories continued to be of prime importance. The desire of frontier expansionists to seize Canada while Great Britain was preoccupied with the Napoleonic Wars in Europe was another motivating factor for the declaration of war in June 1812. Napoleon Bonaparte's Grand Army kept the British army and navy occupied in Europe for several years. After the death of the Russian ruler, Napoleon Bonaparte seized the opportunity to conquer Russia in the winter of 1812. His French army forces were badly defeated by the harsh weather, and much of his army died in the retreat back to France. Napoleon's army was no longer considered a great threat to England, and his total defeat was expected within a reasonable time. British forces were redeployed to America for a second invasion attempt to reclaim the American colonies once and for all. The rebellious and competitive American states were a thorn in the side of England, and they had to be subdued.

In the first phase of the war along the northern border of the United States, the American forces suffered a series of military reverses. The border outposts of Fort Michilimackinac, Fort Dearborn and Fort Detroit (in present-day Michigan) were either evacuated or surrendered when the British forces launched their attack on the small and poorly supplied American outposts. American attempts to invade Canada across the Niagara (in northern New York State) and to press troops on toward Montreal failed completely. Efforts by General William Henry Harrison's American troops to recapture Detroit were repulsed by the British. However, Harrison's forces were able to check the British efforts to move deeper into the region at the western end of Lake Erie in the summer of 1813. In April 1813, General Henry Dearborn's expedition captured Fort Toronto, and the American troops partially burned the British Parliament building and other government offices in York, the capital of Upper Canada. Numerous other conflicts erupted along the northern border between Canada and the United States in 1813–14. The British siege of Fort Erie (August 2 to September 21, 1814) failed to drive the Americans from that outpost on Canadian soil. The American troops later withdrew voluntarily. American forces in the Great Lakes region were able to block the British forces from executing their desired plan to move from the Great Lakes down the Mississippi River toward the British forces who were attempting to capture New Orleans and move northward up the Mississippi River to meet them. The British invasion plan of dividing the United States in half from north to south, if successful, would have forced the American government to surrender to the British forces. The British invasion of the United States would have been wildly successful, and the American colonies would have once again become subservient to the British Empire. In 1814, the United States was faced with the possibility of complete defeat on many fronts.

While these conflicts were occurring along the northern border of the United States in the Great Lakes region, the second phase of the British invasion plan was beginning to unfold. In the Province of Maine, the War of 1812 was fought between the United States' regular and state militia forces and Great Britain's combined forces of the North American colonies of Upper Canada (Ontario), Lower Canada (Quebec), New Brunswick, Newfoundland, Nova Scotia, Prince Edward Island and Cape Breton Island (a separate colony from Nova Scotia). The British had a major military supply depot and a Royal Naval dockyard at Bermuda. Admiral Alexander Cochrane, British commander in chief of the North American Theater, supervised the attacks upon the American defenses and state militia outposts along the coastline in frontier Maine. Admiral Cochrane conducted the initial invasion operation against New England from the British fortress at Louisbourg and the Royal Navy shipyards in Halifax, Nova Scotia. Admiral Cochrane's orders to the British naval forces were "To Destroy the coastal towns and Shipping, and ravage the Country…"[1467]

The British naval fleet captured and burned many of the poorly defended towns on the Penobscot Bay and on the Penobscot River at Bangor and Hampden, where there were American shipyards. The British forces quickly seized the fort at Castine at the mouth of the Penobscot Bay. Castine was planned to eventually become a British point of entry into the colony of New Ireland in the frontier Province of Maine. The fort on Castine, Fort Madison, would serve as a base of operations to monitor and control the New England states and commerce from Halifax to New York City.

A pivotal point in the conflict between the United States and Great Britain came in the fall of 1814, when British invasion forces led by Sir George Provost entered the United States in upper New York State using the Lake Champlain Valley and Hudson River Valley waterways. In conjunction with the British naval fleet's invasion of the Province of Maine, Admiral Alexander Cochrane was to coordinate his invasion attacks in New England with those of Sir George Provost, who was leading a large British force from Montreal and Quebec, Canada. This massive British invasion force, with as many as ten to fifteen thousand infantry and naval troops, pushed southward from Montreal, Canada, on to Lake Champlain.[1468] The British invasion forces under command of Sir George Provost met strong resistance from the American militia forces on Lake Champlain. The British fought a brisk naval battle against the defending American forces at Plattsburgh, New York. The British fleet included the largest warship ever to sail on Lake Champlain, the HMS *Confiance* (flagship of Captain Downie). This warship was captured and passed into American hands.[1469] General Provost determined that the infantry would not be successful without the support of naval forces, so he ordered a retreat back to Canada.[1470] The strategic importance of the Lake Champlain/Richelieu River corridor as an important trade route to trading markets in Montreal and Quebec on the St. Lawrence River cannot be

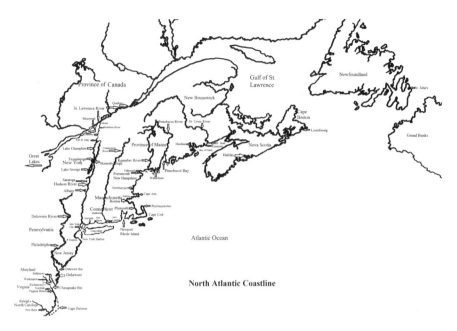

Map of the North Atlantic coastline. *Courtesy of the author.*

overlooked or understated. Trading vessels carried goods, various products, furs and other natural resources to the rest of the world from the Great Lakes region and from Montreal and Quebec, Canada. Commerce and trading by sea and land was the lifeblood of the American, Canadian and European economies. A successful invasion mission in North America was of paramount importance.

With the retreat of the British forces back to Montreal and Quebec, Admiral Cochrane and the British naval forces remained with the invasion mission as they sailed southward along the coastline of the United States toward Boston, New York City, Philadelphia and Baltimore. The powerful British fleet continued to fire upon the coastal port cities, towns and harbors at will. British troops left behind fire, death and destruction wherever they went. Admiral Cochrane's British fleet sailed to Bermuda to resupply and coordinate the next actions and the next phase of the British invasion plans. Bermuda was used as the staging area for the attack on the cities of Washington and Baltimore. This was in retaliation for American troops' attacking and burning of the British government center at York, the capital of Upper Canada, earlier in the year. The European ideology of the "rules of engagement" was that whoever captured the governmental and political center (generally the place where the ruler or dictator of a country lived) would win the war. The British Royal Marines were landed far up the Potomac River near Benedict, Maryland, in mid-August, and they marched toward the city of Washington, meeting little resistance from militia troops along the way. The Royal Marines surrounded the city of Washington and made their attack on August 19, 1814. The British troops burned the Library of Congress, the Capitol building and the White House, as well as other buildings. They pillaged, plundered and laid waste to the city. Dolley Madison, wife of President James Madison, and several of the house servants saved the famous portrait of George Washington, the Declaration of Independence, the Constitution and Bill of Rights and other valuable documents before fleeing to safety in her carriage with the White House in flames behind her. The British Royal Marines reembarked on their warships on August 30, at which point they sailed for Baltimore to participate in the raid with the rest of the Royal Navy fleet. The combined British forces converged on the city of Baltimore and harbor dockyards with the intent of burning them.

The city of Baltimore had become a major industrial, trading and shipbuilding port. It was considered by the British as "the Prize of the Chesapeake." Fort McHenry was strategically located at the harbor entrance to protect the city of Baltimore. The Americans had expected that the British would attack their port city and harbor, so they had strategically sunk a chain of twenty-two vessels in the harbor to prevent the British forces from approaching and destroying the city. The large cannons at the fort helped to keep the British fleet about a mile and a half from the harbor entrance. The British attack on Fort McHenry began on September 13, 1814, with heavy British cannon fire and aerial bombardments that kept up an unrelenting attack on the small fort for about twenty-five hours. The militia soldiers at Fort McHenry, however, refused to surrender the fort to the British Royal Navy fleet.

Francis Scott Key, a Washington lawyer, had come to Baltimore to negotiate the release of Dr. William Beanes and other prisoners of war following the attack on Washington the month before. He became an eyewitness to the extended, heavy bombardment on Fort McHenry from his truce ship that was anchored out in Baltimore Harbor. Before daylight on September 14, the British stopped firing on the fort, and there was a sudden silence. When the clouds of smoke cleared and the rising sun gave light to the scene, the eyewitnesses to the attack were amazed. Miraculously, the large American flag was still flying over Fort McHenry! The soldiers at Fort McHenry, under the command of Lieutenant Colonel George Armistead, had not surrendered to the heavy bombardment of the British Royal Navy fleet. The British assault on Baltimore was repulsed, and a further naval attack was abandoned. The British fleet withdrew. Francis Scott Key was so inspired by this event that he began to write his famous poem, "The Defense of Fort McHenry," which later became known as the "Star-Spangled Banner." Francis Scott Key's poem was set to music to the tune of "To Anacreon in Heaven," and it later became America's national anthem.

While some British ships returned to the harbor at Bermuda, the rest of the British fleet sailed southward toward the British-held islands in the West Indies. The next phase of the British operational plan was for Admiral Cochrane's British forces to resupply the fleet and prepare for the attack on New Orleans. New Orleans was a major American commercial trading, shipping, navigation and shipbuilding port located at the delta of the Mississippi River on the Gulf of Mexico. Once New Orleans was captured and the British forces were united with invading British allied troops from the Great Lakes region, the United States government would be forced to surrender unconditionally to the powerful forces of the British Empire.

Lincolnville Politics in the War of 1812

While the British government approved the plan for a major invasion of the United States to reclaim the colonies in North America, political and economic problems were brewing and coming to a head in frontier Maine. On July 12, 1812, fearing an imminent attack along the eastern frontier in Maine, the townspeople in Lincolnville called a town meeting to determine how to defend themselves. It was voted that the selectmen be directed to obtain "by purchase or otherwise" fifty guns for the use of the town. Among the persons chosen to serve on the "Committee of Safety" were Philip Ulmer, Westbrook and Nathan Knight (brothers) and several other active militia war veterans and concerned citizens of the community.[1471] Political party lines had been rigidly drawn at this time between the Democratic-Republicans and the Federalists on the federal, state and local levels. The Democratic-Republicans supported the national administration in prosecuting the war, and the Federalists opposed the war with Great Britain. There were more Democratic-Republicans in the town of Lincolnville than Federalists when war was declared with Great Britain. The Democratic-Republicans steadily grew in number as the conflict and feelings about the war grew more intense.

Following the declaration of war in 1812 against Great Britain, the first town meeting in Lincolnville was held at Philip Ulmer's house, and the meeting was characterized by much bitterness and violence. There was a good deal of heated discussion and sharp talk on each side. The town meeting ended in a fistfight between the two political sides, and there were many hard blows and blackened eyes.[1472] The whole town was in an uproar. In two or three months, the excitement abated, and a comparative calm prevailed.

There were many settlers in the frontier communities who were loyal Patriots to the American cause, but there were others who were either politically sympathetic to the British or pragmatically inclined to keep trading with the enemy (smuggling) so that their quality of life would remain intact. Politically, one had to be either a Federalist or a Democratic-Republican. The political party differences between the Federalists and the Democratic-Republicans (referred to hereafter as Republicans) were similar to the divisions found in the political and emotional period during the Revolutionary War and during President Abraham Lincoln's administration, which erupted into the Civil War. Like the Civil War that followed several decades later, families were divided in their political inclination and by cultural loyalties. These divisions were manifested between neighbors, communities and states as well. It was a politically charged, emotional and over-reactive period in our early American history.

The towns and settlements along the frontier coastline of Maine felt vulnerable and desperately in need of protection by the State of Massachusetts. British raiding parties increased in frequency due to the need to forage for supplies and provisions, and the enemy raiders continued to harass American citizens and communities at will. Sailors and mariners in the District of Maine were impressed into British service as seamen on the enemy ships and forced to fight against their own countrymen. The British raiding parties used intrusive and brutal methods of pillaging, plundering and killing resisters to get whatever they wanted. Armed enemy privateering vessels, British warships and smugglers infested the waters of the Penobscot Bay and the Massachusetts coastline. The militia companies and regiments in frontier Maine were small and not well armed. The defensive forts and seaports were vulnerable to constant attacks by the enemy warships. Fort Pine Hill, the primary defensive fortification on the Penobscot Bay, frequently came under enemy fire from the British warships that patrolled the coastal region.

The commanding officers at the state militia headquarters in the District of Maine pleaded for assistance for their troops. Food provisions and other needed supplies, both military (such as cannon, guns, ammunition and gunpowder) and personal items (such as warm coats, clothes, shoes and blankets), and military pay for the soldiers were requested from the Massachusetts State General Court and federal government. These essential necessities seldom arrived when needed, if at all. Repeated appeals for assistance to the Massachusetts General Court went unanswered. Appeals to the United States Congress and the president of the United States, James Madison, went unanswered. The inhabitants of frontier Maine would have to defend themselves by using any means that they could, and they would have to fight the British raiders and enemy invasion forces on their own.

The seaport communities on the eastern coast of New England suffered greatly since their livelihood depended on commercial fishing, lumbering, shipping, navigation, lime and commercial mercantile trading. New England inhabitants, trading and shipping merchants and commercial fishermen— out of desperation—ignored the Embargo Acts imposed by the federal government. Smuggling became important for survival, especially in frontier Maine, when every other request for government and state assistance was ignored. Eastport was the northeastern-most village in the disputed northern frontier border between Canada and Massachusetts's easternmost frontier part of Maine Province. The British naval forces continued to capture American supply vessels, and they disrupted commerce along the eastern seacoast. The British raiding parties and armed enemy vessels harassed the local coastal towns with unprovoked attacks. They raided the defenseless communities, and they pillaged, plundered and abused the residents, taking their private property at will. The British, through intimidation and the use of fear, were a constant threat to northern frontier settlements such as Eastport, Machias, Belfast, Lincolnville, Megunticook (present-day Camden village), Waldoboro, Thomaston and Falmouth (present-day Portland). Many settlers moved away from the dangerous northeastern seaport communities and settled in frontier territories of the New Hampshire Grant (part of which later became Vermont), western Pennsylvania and New York, as well as Ohio and the Carolinas. Others held firmly to their convictions of ownership and private property, and they fought against the brutal activities and intimidation of the British troops in their communities. Some others succumbed to fear and persistent threats from the marauding British raiding parties in the Penobscot Bay and were intimidated and abused.

The British (Again) Attempt to Establish the Colony of New Ireland

Great Britain decided to make one last attempt to reclaim its hold on the northeastern-most territory in frontier Massachusetts and one last effort to establish the colony of New Ireland in the Penobscot and Passamaquoddy Bay region. The British attack on the Penobscot Bay region was part of a larger plan by the British government to crush the American resistance and reclaim the frontier colonies in America. In frontier Maine, British harassment of northeastern coastal communities by British warships and privateers had continued during the 1790s, and the attacks increased along the New England coastline in 1813–14. American merchant trading, shipping and commercial vessels were stopped and searched for naturalized American citizens. Great Britain decreed that anyone born in England was considered always to be an Englishman and a subject of the British Crown. British subjects who claimed American citizenship through naturalization were considered to be traitors and subject to harsh punishment.

The coastal communities in the Province of Maine had divided loyalties between the new American republic of the United States and Great Britain. The little town of Eastport, located on the disputed Canadian-American border, had become the center of extensive two-way smuggling in the years 1807–09. Fort Sullivan had been erected on a hilltop at Eastport in 1809 in an attempt to curb smuggling activities with the enemy in this remote frontier area of Massachusetts. Eastport became a base for smuggling and illegal trade between the frontier seaport towns and the British troops at Halifax and later extended to Castine. The losses of American shipping vessels, commercial fishing grounds on the Grand Banks and commercial and mercantile trading was difficult for the residents in frontier Maine. On one side, the residents in frontier Maine were desperately in need of British products, provisions, dry goods and basic supplies to survive in the harsh Maine environment. On the other side, many of the residents were state militia Patriots who were defending the frontier from the British intrusion into their state. National loyalties and the struggle to survive in frontier Maine's harsh environment tore at the hearts and minds of the inhabitants.

DECLARATION OF WAR AND ITS EFFECTS ON THE ULMER BROTHERS

War against Great Britain was finally declared on June 18, 1812, by the president of the United States, James Madison. He called out the Massachusetts state militia to temporarily defend frontier Maine's long, exposed New England coastline. Massachusetts governor Caleb Strong made only a half-hearted response to the U.S. president's request. Governor Strong, a Federalist, used every effort to hinder the federal government's war program in his New England state. Governor Strong ignored the request of the federal government on June 22, 1812, for the Massachusetts militia to man coastal forts, including the three companies designated for the Castine battery at Fort Madison. After several heated exchanges between Governor Strong and President Madison, militia soldiers were sent out to defend the frontier outposts. It was not until August 5 that Governor Strong ordered out the detached militia companies, almost two months after the declaration of war. Governor Strong called up three companies, all of which were from Hancock County.

Colonel George Ulmer was stationed at Fort Madison, a newly reconstructed outpost on Castine, with a company of militia troops to defend the Penobscot Bay region against British raiding parties and smuggling activities. Colonel George Ulmer personally recruited his regiment from Hancock and Washington Counties, making sure that most of his officers were Republicans.[1473] Colonel George Ulmer recruited his brother, Major Philip Ulmer, to serve as a U.S. Volunteer under his command. Colonel Ulmer's recruitment of mostly Republican officers proved to be offensive to the Federalists who lived in the area of Castine. The mission of Colonel George Ulmer's small regiment was to stop the huge smuggling trade in the Penobscot Bay region. This law enforcement mission was offensive to area inhabitants involved in the smuggling trade. Federalist officers made every effort to discourage men from enlisting in Colonel Ulmer's regiment. At a public hearing at Castine, the citizens were discouraged from enlisting in the U.S. Volunteer army.[1474] In response to the public uproar, Governor Caleb Strong replaced Colonel George Ulmer with an officer who was a Federalist and did not ardently support the war.[1475]

Every man of legal age who could serve in the state militia as a privateer or as a veteran soldier defending the town was involved in some way in the defense of the easternmost frontier of Massachusetts. Major Jacob Ulmer, Philip's eldest son, was sent to Eastport as the commander of three detached militia companies from the local districts that served with General Blake's brigade. Major Ulmer and his three companies of soldiers were stationed at Fort Sullivan in Eastport from September 1812 until late December 1812.[1476] There is evidence that the Major Ulmer who responded to the assignment at Eastport in the fall of 1812 was actually Major Philip Ulmer instead of Jacob. Major Jacob Ulmer was serving in the Fort Western vicinity on the Kennebec River at this time. Captain Charles Ulmer, Philip's second son, was stationed at the naval shipyard at Hampden at this time building and repairing armed sailing vessels.

Philip Ulmer served as a selectman and leader of the town of Lincolnville. He was given the government assignment as the deputy inspector of customs for the Penobscot Bay region and was assigned to the Camden/Lincolnville area.[1477] Philip Ulmer enjoyed this assignment in his elder years since he worked close to his home in Lincolnville, where he could be with his wife, Christiana, and the young Ulmer children. Philip was able to oversee the needs, the care and the security of his own family at Lincolnville but also those of his older sons, Jacob and Charles, who were in the militia, as well as George's family. Philip was a wise and stabilizing influence in the family and a man who inspired confidence and trust in those around him. He was a trustworthy man of integrity and high moral character. While Colonel George Ulmer was away at Fort Sullivan, his wife, Polly, suffered a series of strokes that left her completely paralyzed on the right side, and she was going blind.[1478] Philip and Christiana took on more responsibility for the care of their sister-in-law, Polly, and young George Ulmer Jr. Polly Ulmer needed special personal care since her stroke, and the caregiving was provided by Christiana Ulmer and Mary Wilson, who were also caring for their own families. At this time, Mary Wilson and her family owned and lived in George and Polly Ulmer's house on the eastern side of the Ducktrap stream.

The American command at Fort Sullivan in Eastport was necessary to slow the swelling flow of illegal commerce back and forth across the Canadian border, a commerce that greatly benefited the British forces at Halifax, who had difficulty with resupply and provision issues. Unable to trade legally and directly with the British at Halifax and other Canadian settlements, many American merchants shipped their flour and wheat to Eastport, while their British counterparts forwarded the British textiles, dry goods, supplies and hardware to adjoining St. Andrews in New Brunswick. A local flotilla of boats traveled both ways across the passage of water to exchange cargos almost every night. While the American Embargo Acts, followed by the War of 1812, meant a depression in the mercantile, dry goods, supplies and provisions elsewhere in the United States, it provided lucrative opportunities for the settlers in Eastport. Since the customs officials were required to live in the Eastport community, they quickly learned the advantages of personal safety and extra income that could be acquired by those who ignored the lucrative smuggling business being conducted at Eastport. Eastport became the most notorious smuggling seaport in the nation.[1479]

George Ulmer had been made a major general in the Massachusetts state militia and the sheriff of Hancock County by Massachusetts governor James Sullivan, the first Jeffersonian governor. These desired designations were political rewards for his strong support in getting Sullivan elected during the state government election in 1807–08.[1480] In April 1812, the Federalists returned to political power in Massachusetts, and Governor Caleb Strong, who served as the sixth and tenth Massachusetts governor, was George Ulmer's political adversary in the Senate of the Massachusetts General Court. George Ulmer was faced with an embarrassing situation. Governor Caleb Strong forced George Ulmer to resign his political appointment as a militia major general, which was given by former governor James Sullivan. It was not an earned position but given as a political favor. George Ulmer was succeeded in his former military position by David Cobb, who had been lieutenant governor of Massachusetts and had led the fraud inquiry into Ulmer's handling of the state militia arrests of "Liberty Men" in a militia raid near Belfast, Maine, on General Knox's orders. The situation became so intense that, to forestall the imminent embarrassment of discharge from the state militia and the investigation into his misuse of the sheriff's office in October 1812, George Ulmer resigned his posts as sheriff and militia major general.[1481] In a letter to General William King, a fellow Maine Republican with close ties to the national administration, George Ulmer wrote: "I am now really under the necessity of going into the army or navy to keep out of prison or something worse."[1482]

President Madison's administration advocated national military patronage to displaced New England Republicans and war veterans. But the number of available commissions was limited, while the pool of interested politicians was large. George Ulmer's claim was weak compared to other more qualified candidates for several prestigious military positions. Ulmer's claim in receiving a commission was solely based on his past military service with the Continental Army, the plight of his present circumstances and his continued loyalty to a locally unpopular war.[1483] Former Massachusetts senator William King, George Ulmer's political mentor and patron in the Massachusetts General Court, lobbied to have George return to the army or navy to keep him out of prison. General William King lobbied President Madison on George Ulmer's behalf for an appointment as colonel in charge of his own militia volunteers in frontier Maine.[1484] George Ulmer was commissioned by President James Madison as colonel commandant for a force of regular U.S. Volunteers, consisting of one hundred men, to be stationed at Fort Sullivan in Eastport.[1485] President Madison's appointment to the command at Eastport, Maine, was considered the least desirable post in the entire war.[1486] On receiving the appointment of colonel commandant by President Madison, George Ulmer resigned the office of major general of the Tenth Militia Division, which he held at the time.[1487] It was Colonel George Ulmer's assignment and duty to prevent all smuggling and illegal interaction with the British enemy at Halifax and uphold President Jefferson's unpopular Embargo Acts.

Colonel Commandant George Ulmer was ordered to relieve the commander of Fort Sullivan at Eastport with some of his fresh U.S. regular troops from the Penobscot Bay vicinity.[1488] Major Ulmer (probably Philip) was relieved of his duties in a brief change-of-command ceremony at Fort Sullivan in December 1812.[1489] Colonel Commandant George Ulmer apparently was zealous in his efforts to stop the illegal activities at Eastport, which caused the residents to become agitated and rebellious. Eastport had become a center of covert smuggling activities between trading merchants and businessmen in New England and the British traders in the Passamaquoddy Bay region and the towns of New Brunswick and Halifax, Nova Scotia.

When Colonel George Ulmer arrived at Eastport to assume the command of the militia troops at Fort Sullivan, the conditions that he found there could best be described as a military nightmare. Uncertain how long the militia company would be staying at Eastport, barracks had not been built for the soldiers, and the men were housed in two tenements that were described by Colonel George Ulmer as "scarcely fit to shelter cattle, and rented at an exorbitant from a local landlord…the soldiers [were very young like] children that ought to have nurses come with them to take care of them and cannot with prudence be suffered to be out in the night."[1490] One Eastport resident summed up the militia troops as "old men and boys who do government but little service for one year except eat the government provisions and stay by the fire."[1491]

The provisions provided by the Massachusetts government for the troops stationed at Fort Sullivan were characterized by Colonel George Ulmer as spoiled "refuse." The local commissary who was paid to ship provisions to the militia troops at Eastport was a smuggler named Bartlett. He provoked the military troops to near mutiny by telling them "that the government don't allow them good provisions—and will allow them but bad."[1492] Sometimes there were no provisions supplied to the troops at all. The civilian suppliers for the militia troops figured out that they could make double profits by accepting U.S. government pay to transport troop provisions to Eastport, but instead, the provisions were taken directly to New Brunswick for sale to the British troops. Colonel George Ulmer was so angry when he discovered this sinister plot that he wrote a furious letter to William King exposing the discovery. He wrote: "Thus the troops must suffer, while the enemy are furnished with their provisions by traitors!"[1493]

On January 8, 1813, Fort Madison at Castine was permanently manned by a company of Colonel George Ulmer's regular U.S. Volunteers who were commanded by Captain Joseph Westcott of Penobscot. Fort Madison, a newly rebuilt fort, received only eight militia soldiers and one officer, Ensign Preble. Captain Westcott's company of militia soldiers consisted of mostly untrained recruits, and they had severe supply problems as well as a hostile settlement of Federalists who strongly opposed the war. The militiamen were not provided with uniforms or weapons for defense. There were no bunks or straw for mattresses or blankets for Westcott's men. Local merchants refused to extend credit to Westcott so he could feed his troops, and no one seemed to have the authority to supply them. In February, Captain Westcott made the difficult trip to Eastport to report to Colonel Ulmer the extreme conditions of his troops at Castine. Captain Westcott was having the same problems that Colonel George Ulmer was having at Eastport; however, he hoped that Colonel Ulmer might be able to solve his supply problems. Unfortunately, Ulmer was faced with the same desperate conditions. The supply situation remained dismal through the first half of 1813. The Hancock County Federalists remained firm in their opposition to the war and offered no assistance to the deprived militia troops at Castine or at Eastport, who were both commanded by Colonel Commandant George Ulmer.

The small number of Massachusetts state soldiers stationed at Fort Madison was insufficient to defend the battery outpost at Castine. Captain Westcott was lacking enough manpower to guard the prisoners of war who were brought to the prison by American privateers. Prisoners frequently were able to escape from the few militia soldiers at Fort Madison, and they resumed their former activities of smuggling in the Penobscot region. The presence of prisoners of war at the Fort Madison outpost indicated the lack of cooperation that the Hancock County officials gave to the federal government during the War of 1812. In other Maine towns, the local deputy

U.S. marshal often kept prisoners of war in county jails at federal expense. In Castine, only a few prisoner of war soldiers were reported at the Fort Madison battery. Prisoners of war never appeared in the Hancock County "Register of Prisoners," and the government authorities were banned from using the county jail.[1494]

Colonel George Ulmer's malnourished and poorly supplied army troops futilely remained garrisoned at Eastport. Eastport had become a haven for smuggling and was overflowing with American troop provisions bound for profit-minded countrymen across the border who sold them to the British enemy.[1495] Desperately needed clothing, food and other provisions for the state troops were not forthcoming from the government for Colonel George Ulmer's soldiers. Infuriated by the lack of necessary supplies and provisions, Colonel George Ulmer threatened to resign, stating, "I cannot consent to tarry to see the sufferings and distresses of men who are sent here [Eastport], as defenders of their country…"[1496] Having no other source of funding and no one to help with the severe situation in which the garrison found itself, Colonel Ulmer did what he had so often done before: He overextended himself financially to salvage his military position. He obtained firewood, hospital stores, bedding straw, camp kettles, coats and blankets, all on his own personal credit.[1497] Irregular pay for Colonel Ulmer's U.S. Volunteers at Eastport and at Castine infuriated Colonel Ulmer to the point that he wrote a harsh letter to General William King about the unacceptable treatment of his troops. He wrote: "If troops on the frontier, exposed to all the severities of weather, naked, and fed on the meanest foods, must be kept out of their hard-earned pay, how are we to expect success?[1498]

Colonel George Ulmer was obliged to disband one company of soldiers and send them home because the pay for the soldiers and the commissions of the officers were more than three months overdue. Colonel Ulmer became bitter from the realization that the neglect of his command meant it was regarded as a makeshift guard by the high command and his company of U.S. Volunteers would fall into the hands of the British forces. In a letter to one of his superior officers, Colonel Ulmer wrote that the state militia command shouldn't worry about providing regimental flags for his regiment at Eastport: "If we don't have them [the regimental flags], we shall not loose [*sic*] them."[1499]

The local merchants and townspeople were cleverly adept at frustrating Colonel George Ulmer's attempts to suppress the smuggling activities at Eastport and in the surrounding vicinity. In early March 1813, some of the soldiers from Colonel Ulmer's regiment seized the schooner *Polly*, which was carrying a valuable cargo worth approximately $40,000, a huge sum at this time. The collector named Trescott and the militia commissary named Bartlett interceded to claim the prize vessel for the Customs House and to prevent Colonel George Ulmer's U.S. Volunteers from receiving any financial prize money.[1500] In April 1813, the local smugglers fabricated a number of debt charges and other charges of mismanagement against Colonel Ulmer, which resulted in the local sheriff arresting Ulmer and taking him to jail in Machias.[1501] George was humiliated and enraged with the injustice of these covert maneuverings and the disregard for his efforts to carry out his command responsibilities.

Like so many other desperate citizens in frontier Maine, it was during this crisis period that Philip Ulmer became involved in smuggling basic goods and supplies for his and George's family to survive. Philip and other frontier citizens felt that they had no other choice but to engage in smuggling activities. The necessary state aid for essential supplies, which had been promised to them, and the defensive assistance from the state and federal governments were not forthcoming. The citizens of frontier Maine had to find a way to survive and defend themselves on their own. Smuggling and bartering for essential goods and supplies was a logical and necessary way to survive the crisis that was devastating to the state and national economies during the unpopular war.

While Colonel George Ulmer was held in jail during the month of May, Philip Ulmer took George's wife, (Mary) Polly Ulmer, and two daughters, Sarah and Mary (and possibly others), in a small sloop to visit George at Machias. The second objective of the trip was to shop for essential food and necessary supplies at the border villages of Eastport or Lubec and to bring the goods (some might have been banned items) back to their families at Ducktrap. Polly Ulmer's health was not good. She had recently suffered a stroke that had paralyzed one side of her body, and she was losing her eyesight.[1502] On the sailing trip to Machias, Philip sailed the boat close to the shore, where they would be safer in case of bad weather on the Penobscot Bay and would be less conspicuous to any British armed vessels that frequently patrolled the coastline. The small sailing boat was sighted and confronted by the armed British brig HMS *Boxer*, whose captain was Captain Blyth.[1503] The brig was coming from New Brunswick (Canada) and cruising off the coast of Lubec (Maine) when Captain Blyth's seamen sighted and seized the small boat crewed by Philip with the Ulmer family, who appeared to be out for an afternoon sail. The seaport village of Lubec, located at the mouth of the St. Croix River, had become one of the smuggling centers in the Passamaquoddy Bay region.

As the fourteen-gun brig came closer, Philip threw anything over the side of the boat that might cast suspicion that the small sailing sloop was connected to the local state militia or was carrying contraband. Captain Blyth ordered that the women should be taken on board the brig and interrogated below decks to determine the purpose of their sailing trip and if they were actually innocent settlers who were out for a Sunday afternoon sailing cruise as Philip had told them. Philip, who piloted the sloop, was detained by an armed British officer and guards. Polly Ulmer and George's daughters were taken below decks, where Captain Blyth invited them to share tea with him while he questioned them.[1504] Fortunately, after more than an hour and a half, the Ulmer women and Philip were released to continue their sailing cruise. Philip piloted the boat to Machias, where the family was able to visit with George Ulmer, who remained behind bars in the jail.

There was great concern felt for George's circumstances in the jail. George was greatly concerned about the safety of his family at Ducktrap and stressed over his wife's deteriorating health issues. He was angry and distressed about his tarnished reputation and the situation of his authority being disrespected and challenged by his troops at Eastport. His troops at Eastport and his troops stationed at the small battery on Castine had not been paid by the government for their military service for more than four months. George was faced with the accumulated concerns and humiliations about his arrest for nonpayment of his personal and financial debts. Colonel Ulmer, like many other officers, had attempted to provide for his soldiers' needs using his own personal credit since the state and federal government agencies were unable to provide for the soldiers. He continued to be frustrated by his inability to suppress the smuggling trade at Eastport, the goal of his assignment. These factors and other concerns caused George Ulmer to become deeply depressed and mentally unhinged. He continued his alarming rants and talking irrationally. George spoke with great emotion about dying with honor like General Zebulon Pike in the April invasion of York, Canada, in 1813.[1505] He seemed to be obsessed with having his authority respected, clearing his tainted reputation and dying honorably. Philip and George's family became increasingly concerned about his emotional stability and his mental well-being. Having completed their visit, Philip sailed Polly and her two daughters safely back to Lincolnville after their exhausting visit with George and their stressful encounter with the British warship HMS *Boxer*. Polly Ulmer was so impressed by Captain Blyth's courtesy to her and the other women that she placed a brief article in the local newspaper praising his kindness and chivalry.[1506]

George Ulmer was released from jail in late May 1813 and returned to his command at Fort Sullivan. He was appalled to find that Eastport was again "filled with speculators, spies, and smugglers"[1507] and operated without frustration from his leaderless U.S. Volunteers, whose discipline had vanished in their commander's absence. Colonel George Ulmer ordered that all communication with the British was strictly forbidden except under a flag of truce unless otherwise authorized by the colonel. Ulmer received no support from his superiors at the central command headquarters. Secretary of War John Armstrong rescinded Colonel Ulmer's orders forbidding communication with the British enemy.[1508] Although Colonel Ulmer had been sent to Eastport with firm directions to suppress the smuggling at Eastport, his superiors did not give him the authority to stop the illegal trading. The Federalist press, who opposed the war, made every effort to publicize any news item that might suggest the onset of martial law.[1509] Unknown to Ulmer, there was an alternative commercial system used by prosperous merchants as far south as Philadelphia to trade with Great Britain. The Eastport trade had a strong citizenry that opposed any efforts to stop their lucrative system of illicit trading. Also unknown to Colonel Ulmer, his political patron and Maine's leading Republican, General William King, was secretly and heavily involved in illegal commerce (smuggling) with the British in Halifax and New Brunswick, Canada.[1510] This was also true of other wealthy businessmen and politicians associated with the state and federal government. This was crony capitalism and greed that had gone awry with corruption at the highest levels of the state and federal government.

Another interesting piece of intrigue in the illegal commercial trading network that few people knew was that as America's "keystone state," Pennsylvania's allegiance was critical to the continued political viability of James Madison's administration. Pennsylvania's economy relied upon a continued British market for its flour and other commercial goods and products. The Republicans in the federal government were slow to risk their political positions by voting for the taxes necessary to finance the war with Great Britain. The only way to finance the war meant that the Madison administration would become more dependent upon customs revenue. This meant that commerce, however illegal, had to continue the alternative trading system and to pay duties upon goods and other commerce if the nation was to avoid bankruptcy. For many reasons, Colonel George Ulmer was placed in the illogical position of having to simultaneously suppress and permit the illegal commerce at Eastport (Maine) that was so beneficial to the nation's viability.[1511]

COLONEL GEORGE ULMER IS REMOVED
FROM HIS COMMAND

Frustrated, depressed and dispirited, Colonel George Ulmer began to drink heavily and act erratically. Colonel George Ulmer's accounting practices for his regiment grew more and more careless and negligent. This behavior left him vulnerable to charges of embezzlement.[1512] However, the most serious difficulty for George Ulmer was that he had lost control of the soldiers in his regiment while he had been in jail in Machias. The soldiers no longer respected their commanding officer, and they would not follow his orders. On July 4, 1813, the soldiers in Colonel Ulmer's regiment at Fort Sullivan disregarded their commander's direct orders, and they fired their weapons wildly into the air in celebration of the Independence Day commemorative event. Colonel George Ulmer, enraged, stormed onto the parade ground and ordered his shocked officers to level a cannon charged with deadly grapeshot at the soldiers celebrating. As the parade ground fell silent, Colonel Ulmer issued his direct order again, threatening to discharge the loaded cannon if another musket was fired.[1513] The celebrating soldiers called his bluff and resumed their firing into the air. Furious with the insubordination of his soldiers, Colonel George Ulmer stormed off of the parade ground.

George Ulmer's mental state did not improve with the secretary of war's thinly veiled scheme to let Colonel Ulmer's command fail and fall apart. Three of Ulmer's officers were commissioned by John Armstrong, the secretary of war, into a new regular militia regiment. They were instructed to recruit men from Colonel Ulmer's soldiers for the new unit. When Colonel Ulmer discovered what was happening, he had Captain Simmons arrested as an example, and he sent a message to the other two officers to stop recruiting soldiers from his regiment.[1514] The disgruntled officers in Colonel Ulmer's regiment plotted to have the colonel removed from command and his position as colonel commandant. Led by Captain Sherman Leland, the officers drew up a list of complaints that they forwarded to the district commander, Brigadier General Thomas H. Cushing, in Boston. In the complaint, the officers alleged of Colonel George Ulmer (former militia general): "He drinks so hard and there is such wildness and inconsistency in his orders and conduct that he has become perfectly contemptible in the sight of his troops, and the consequence is insubordination and all the train of evils which naturally follow."[1515]

There were reports from about eighty British subjects living in Eastport that Colonel Ulmer used abusive methods in uncovering suspected smugglers in the area. In a bold move, Colonel George Ulmer had used his soldiers to beat down the doors of the British citizens in search of contraband goods. He also made all aliens register and swear an oath of allegiance to the United States or leave Eastport within seventy-two hours. Colonel Ulmer was threatened with being tarred and feathered, probably by those engaged in smuggling.[1516] General Cushing dispatched an aide to Eastport, who, after a hasty investigation, ordered that Colonel George Ulmer be relieved of his duty and placed under house arrest.[1517] Denied a copy of the charges against him, Colonel Ulmer remained under house arrest until after military review, when he was discharged from the military service on December 17, 1813. The government replaced Colonel George Ulmer with Major Perley Putnam of Salem, Massachusetts, in the spring of 1814.[1518]

George Ulmer's deepening depression over his personal life, his concerns over Polly's deteriorating health and the failures in his different careers—in business, in politics and in the military service—caused great concern for Philip Ulmer as George spoke more and more about dying and his wish to die with honor and dignity. George began to lament over the loss of his honor and the twists of fate that had caused his present unfortunate circumstances. On August 28, 1813, George Ulmer wrote to his friend and colleague, Major General William King, recalling the death of General Zebulon Pike at York, Canada, during the American invasion of Canada in the spring of 1813: "…would to God I had been a companion to General Pike and have shared his fate. I am it seems about to receive the rewards of my patriotism and satisfaction for my exertions while on the lines."[1519]

Upon George Ulmer's return to Lincolnville after the conclusion of his court-martial trial, he became obsessed with clearing his name and obtaining his back pay owed for his military service and compensation for his personal debts incurred in his efforts to provide for the men of his regiment at Eastport. George Ulmer appealed to Congressman William King and General Charles Cushing in Boston, and he was rebuffed.[1520] He appealed to John Armstrong, the secretary of war in Washington, who, after twelve days, begrudgingly agreed to see George Ulmer and discuss his military situation. After threatening to take his embarrassing case to the U.S. Congress, John Armstrong agreed to have George Ulmer's complaints heard in the Massachusetts State Supreme Court in Portland (Falmouth), Maine. Secretary of War Armstrong ordered General Cushing to convene a Court of Inquiry that would give George Ulmer the chance to clear his name and restore his honor.[1521]

A Court of Inquiry was held on May 30, 1814, for George Ulmer's trial. The court eventually cleared George Ulmer on the six counts of embezzling pay, rations and weapons. The court found him "literally guilty" of arresting Captain Simmons and mishandling the incident on the Fourth of July at the parade ground, but no criminal charges could be made against the soldiers in the incident.[1522] George Ulmer wrote to President Madison in March 1814 about the injustice that he had experienced while serving at Fort Sullivan in Eastport (Maine).[1523] The Massachusetts State Board of War in Boston and the secretary of war in Washington ignored his grievances and appeals. George Ulmer made a trip to Washington, where he was kept waiting for about a week before the secretary of the War Department finally released his back pay and refunded the expenses that he had incurred in personal debt for provisions and supplies for his U.S. regiment of regular soldiers at Eastport during the winter of 1812–13.[1524] Determined to have justice properly given and to restore his honor, George Ulmer continued to relentlessly pursue legal damages against Sherman Leland and others for malicious libel.[1525] George felt that Leland's libelous actions had destroyed his military career and any hopes that he had of restoring his military or political career after the war. All of George Ulmer's attempts to obtain satisfaction failed in the courts. George Ulmer held a deep resentment for Leland, and he continued to pursue personal retribution from Sherman Leland all the rest of his life. George never fully recovered emotionally or psychologically from the events that had destroyed his military and political careers. He had collapsed under the pressures that had undermined his honor, authority and integrity. Again Philip and Christiana Ulmer helped to support George and his family during these most difficult times in George's life. They cared not only for the needs of their own children and young George Jr. (George and Polly's adopted son) but also the deteriorating physical needs of Polly and the emotional and psychological needs of Philip's brother, George.

Before James Madison left the office of the presidency, George Ulmer sought an opportunity for an audience with him to clear his name and restore his honor. He wanted to clear his tarnished military career and restore his reputation by convincing President Madison of the injustice that had been done to him during his unfortunate assignment at Eastport in 1813 that had led to his removal as the colonel commandant at Eastport, his military trial and court-martial and his imprisonment. By using his political connections as a Massachusetts congressman, George Ulmer was able to receive the help of President Madison's brother-in-law, Richard Cutts, who was also a congressman from frontier Maine.[1526] Richard Cutts was married to Dolley

Madison's younger sister, Anna Payne Cutts. Anna was able to convince her sister, Dolley Madison, to arrange a meeting between George Ulmer and the president. George Ulmer traveled to Washington again. Since the White House had been burned by the British on August 24, 1814, George Ulmer met with James Madison at the Octagon House on F Street, where he was living at the time. George Ulmer strongly appealed to President Madison as a former politician and Massachusetts state congressman and as a fellow Revolutionary War veteran to restore his rank as a Massachusetts state militia general (a political appointment by Governor Sullivan for his support in the governor's election).

George Ulmer's eloquence and earnest appeals were successful with President Madison, who was very sympathetic to the hardships of Revolutionary War veterans, especially those with whom he had served. The president was made aware of the impossible assignment that had been given to Colonel Ulmer in Eastport, which was to prevent smuggling and illegal trade along the frontier border of Maine Province and Canada. George Ulmer's former rank as a general in the Massachusetts state militia was restored, if in name only. George felt that he had been vindicated and his honor restored. He returned home to Lincolnville with a sense of great relief that his honor, his tarnished military reputation and his self-esteem had been successfully restored. George became a self-promoter to restore his status and the recognition of his military service in frontier Maine. On all occasions after this time, George Ulmer made every effort to dress and conduct himself in a military style. Anyone who might question his authority or was thought to be disrespectful to him was quickly confronted and firmly addressed.[1527] It is this perception of George Ulmer as a military officer that remained in the minds of the local inhabitants who referred to him for years as "the General."

The British Invasion of Maine

Meanwhile, in the international arena, the British War Ministry in London claimed that the disputed area of Eastport (Maine) and the surrounding islands were located on the British side of the international border near Nova Scotia, Canada. The Ministry of War viewed the war with the United States as a secondary defensive war and the Napoleonic War in Europe as the primary war. With the conclusion of the war in Europe, with Napoleon's

French army forces defeated, Great Britain's attention turned from Europe to the defeat of America's interests in world markets and to the resistance to England's authority and territorial land claims in North America. The ultimate British goal was to bring the United States to its knees in unconditional surrender using the superior strength and power of the British Royal Navy and Royal Army forces to crush American defensive resistance. The British also wanted to destroy the American government center in Washington and close the major commercial trading and shipbuilding ports in the United States, thus destroying the American economy and the dream of the American people for freedom, liberty, sovereignty and independence from Great Britain. Once a declaration of war was made, the initial British invasion plan of the United States was to be followed by a series of other expeditions in various parts of the United States and in the Great Lakes region over a period of months.

One of the primary goals of the British invasion plan was to destroy the rebellious American colonial states once and for all and bring them under the authority and control of England. The failed American attempt to invade Canada in the spring of 1813 from military outposts in the Great Lakes frontier region (present-day Michigan, Illinois and Ohio) opened the floodgates for a methodical counter-invasion of America by British Royal Army and Royal Navy forces, veterans of the Napoleonic War in Europe. The four-pronged British invasion of the United States began in earnest in early 1813. Since the beginning of the American Revolution and during the War of 1812, it had been the common practice of the British Royal Navy and Royal Army to send raiding parties to plunder American towns and villages and then put them to the torch. This was especially true of the Royal Navy, which made a practice of invading coastal and river port towns and burning both the towns and their shipping facilities. Burning or scuttling the merchant fleet in a town's harbor caused more damage to the inhabitants in one attack than had been done by numerous privateers and naval warships at sea. British attacks increased along the coastal defensive outposts in frontier Massachusetts and in the Great Lakes region.

While the American army forces in western frontier outposts in the Great Lakes region were fighting the British and Indian invasion forces sweeping down from Canada along the Ohio River and Missouri River to the Mississippi River Valley, frontier Massachusetts was having its own problems with the British Royal Navy/Marine invasion forces from the military stronghold at Halifax. The HMS *Boxer*, a British brig with fourteen guns, had been preying on the coastal towns and villages in the frontier region of Massachusetts (Maine District). Numerous bombardments were made upon Fort Pine Hill and its fortifications in an effort to destroy the principal defensive headquarters at the mouth of the Penobscot Bay. The British forces were eventually successful in attacking and finally destroying Fort Pine Hill, leaving behind only the skeleton of the once-vital defensive fort.

On June 6, 1813, Captain Samuel Blyth, aboard the HMS *Boxer*, captured two transport vessels bound for Eastport. The two Penobscot transport vessels were the schooner *Two Brothers* and the sloop *Friendship*, bringing greatly needed supplies and goods for the militia soldiers at Fort Sullivan. (Perhaps they were the same vessels that the Ulmer brothers had built at their shipyard in the 1790s. The sloop *Friendship* was built at Ducktrap [Lincolnville] by the Ulmer brothers in 1792.)[1528] The HMS *Boxer* captured the schooner *Fairplay* on July 25, and the British brig captured the schooner *Rebecca* on August 3 bound for Boston from the town of Townsend, the neighboring town of Waldoboro. On August 31, the HMS *Boxer* captured the American schooner *Fortune*, which carried desperately needed supplies and goods for the town. The seaport residents were dismayed by the continued success that the HMS *Boxer* was having on their coastal communities.

On September 5, the HMS *Boxer* engaged the American brig *Enterprise*, under the command of Captain William Burrows, off the coastline of Waldoboro and Townsend (located at Boothbay). Although the engagement between the two brigs was brief, the battle was a bloody one. Captain Blyth on the HMS *Boxer* and Captain Burrows on the American warship *Enterprise* were each determined to win the conflict. As the two brigs closed in on each other, the large broadside guns opened fire with a deafening roar. The first broadside killed Captain Blyth with a cannonball hitting him in the side, and moments later, Captain Burrows suffered a mortal injury. Lieutenant Edward McCall assumed the command of the *Enterprise*, and Lieutenant David McGrery assumed command of the HMS *Boxer*. The fierce battle continued for thirty minutes, as volley after volley of broadsides pounded into each vessel. The HMS *Boxer* had its mast destroyed, which left the warship vulnerable to attack. The *Enterprise* was able to maneuver around the HMS *Boxer* and rake it over and over again. Both vessels were badly damaged, but the HMS *Boxer* was in ruins. The British crew, who had nailed the British colors to the mast, finally surrendered. The dying Captain Burrows declined to accept Captain Blyth's sword, directing that the sword should be given to the family of the dead British captain. Lieutenant McCall took both vessels to Portland with the survivors and the casualties.

After two days of planning, the military authorities conducted an impressive state funeral for the two commanders. Major Philip Ulmer and other state militia officers in the District of Maine attended the funeral service for the brave sea captains. British captain Blyth and U.S. Navy captain Burrows were buried with full military honors at the same time. (They lie side by side in the Eastern Cemetery in Portland, Maine.) It was a striking and an emotional sight for those who were present at the funeral to see these two brave commanders, who had been enemies engaged in deadly combat, laid to rest together in one quiet grave. The officers placed a tombstone over Burrows and Blyth's grave in honor of their service to their countries. The newspapers in the United States rejoiced in "another brilliant naval victory," one of the few American successes during the third summer of the War of 1812. This sea battle was referred to by Henry Wadsworth Longfellow (grandson of General Peleg Wadsworth) in his poem "My Lost Youth":

"My Lost Youth"

I remember the sea-fight far away,
How it thunder'd o'er the tide!
And the dead captains, as they lay
In their graves
o'erlooking the tranquil bay
Where they in battle died.
And the sound of that mournful song
Goes through me with a thrill:
"A boy's will is the wind's will,
And the thoughts of youth are long, long thoughts."

THE BRITISH ATTACK
ON FRONTIER MASSACHUSETTS (MAINE)

In early 1814, Major Perley Putnam from Salem, Massachusetts, replaced Colonel George Ulmer at Fort Sullivan. Soon after Major Perley Putnam's arrival at Eastport to take command of the fifty soldiers and six artillery pieces at Fort Sullivan, a British expedition was secretly launched from Halifax on July 5, 1814. Sir Thomas M. Hardy sailed with the British squadron consisting of the flagship *Ramillies*, the sloop *Martin*, the brigs *Borer* and *Bream*, the bombship

Terror and several other transports under Colonel Thomas Pilkington.[1529] The British fleet with approximately three thousand marines was met by another fleet from Bermuda with other heavily armed warships, and they all sailed toward Eastport in frontier Maine. By July 11, the British forces entered the Eastport harbor, and Sir Thomas Hardy demanded the surrender of the seaport.[1530] After considerable debate between Major Putnam and the soldiers in the fort, and with the appeals of the townspeople, it was decided that the fort and village would be surrendered. After negotiations, the American flag was lowered at Fort Sullivan, and it was replaced by the British flag. The small militia squad with about twenty men stationed on the small islands off the coast of Eastport observed what was happening, and they destroyed whatever military material they could and fled to safety at Machias. The British landed one thousand armed men with women and children and a battery of artillery with fifty to sixty heavy pieces.[1531] The town, the fort and all islands and villages in and around the Passamaquoddy Bay were taken and occupied. Sixty cannons were mounted by the British troops, and civil rule was established under British officials. The British forces kept firm possession of the region until the end of the war.[1532]

To supply the troops at Halifax and the occupied seaports, Captain Barrie was sent from the Chesapeake Bay with food, provisions and munitions for the British invasion forces in the Penobscot Bay region. Upon his arrival, a larger expedition was planned that included the capture of Machias and other coastal towns on the Penobscot Bay from the Kennebec River to the St. Croix River. Rear Admiral Edward Griffith, commander of the naval squadron, assembled a powerful fleet of ships with massive firepower. Lieutenant General Gosselin was in command of the land forces, which numbered about 3,500 well-equipped army troops.[1533] The British display of naval power was terrifying to the small companies of poorly equipped militia soldiers. When the awesome power of the British invasion naval forces was unleashed upon the small settlement villages along the Penobscot Bay and Kennebec River, there was little that could be done by the militiamen to defend the area. Surrender was their only choice. Flags of truce were sent to the targeted villages with orders not to resist. If the villagers surrendered, innocent lives would be spared. If they resisted, many lives would be lost, and their villages would be destroyed. In twenty-six days, the British forces swept through Hampden, Bangor and Machias, looting, pillaging, plundering and destroying or capturing seventeen American vessels in the area. The militia regiments and older war veteran troops (Revolutionary

War Patriots) throughout the Penobscot region were called to defend against the superior British invasion forces. The militia companies were overwhelmed by the firepower and numbers of armed fighting men that the British forces had. Although the militia troops fought bravely in numerous skirmishes against the advancing British troops, time and again, the defending militiamen and volunteers had to retreat and relinquish more and more towns and villages along the Penobscot Bay to the heavily armed invading forces.

The small company of militiamen stationed on Castine under Lieutenant Andrew Lewis saw the formidable fleet approaching. They fired the two field guns at half-moon redoubt as an alarm and a warning to the militiamen at Fort Pine Hill across the Penobscot Bay of the advancing British fleet. Before leaving Castine, Lieutenant Lewis spiked the two field guns, spiked the four twenty-pounder cannons and lit a long fuse that exploded the battery's magazine and destroyed the military munitions.[1534] Taking their packs, the soldiers (part of Colonel George Ulmer's U.S. Volunteers) quickly abandoned the fort and made their way by boat to the safety of Fort Pine Hill on the mainland, the principal defensive fort on the Penobscot Bay. Fort Madison's purpose as a U.S. military outpost came to an end with the huge explosion and fireball as the magazine exploded. Castine soon fell to the same fate as the rest of the targeted seaport villages and towns. The British forces burned many towns and villages on the Penobscot River, especially the shipyard towns at Bangor and Hampden. The invasion forces were successful in capturing the fortification at Castine (Fort Madison). The British troops occupied the town, dug a canal at "the Neck," threw up defensive batteries and secured the British stronghold. The capture of Castine, the proposed capital for the new British colony of New Ireland, enabled the British to establish a strategic port of entry in the Penobscot Bay region. Castine served as the capital for commerce and became a British stronghold until the end of the war. An active trade was soon developed in the Penobscot Bay that included smuggling in defiance of the president's Embargo Act. A British expedition in the Penobscot region had been successful in capturing and occupying the territory between the Kennebec River and the St. Croix River (near New Brunswick), which had been the British plan all along for the establishment of the British colony of New Ireland.

Lincolnville and Camden
during the War of 1812

When the specter of war with Great Britain became a reality, the citizens living in the District of Maine felt increasingly vulnerable to British attack, and they repeatedly appealed to the Massachusetts General Court and the federal government in Washington for more troops and arms to defend their frontier region. Neither the Massachusetts state government nor the federal government were able to defend frontier Maine since there was no standing army or navy, and there was little or no money in either treasury to support one. The inhabitants of frontier Maine were left on their own to provide for their own defense against enemy raiding parties and invading British military forces. Philip Ulmer had anticipated future conflicts with the British forces at Halifax. Prior to the War of 1812, Philip and a small company of men (which included his brother, George) had petitioned the Massachusetts government for permission to salvage cannons and other military equipment and armaments from the wreckage of the American fleet that had been destroyed in the American retreat up the Penobscot River in 1779. Philip's foresight and planning came into play in the defense of the Lincolnville and Camden village communities several years after the Massachusetts General Court granted his petition for salvage rights of the destroyed American fleet. His military strategy and defensive planning would save their towns from enemy destruction.

Major Jacob Ulmer, Philip Ulmer's eldest son, became the colonel of a battalion of militiamen in the Lincoln County area. There was also a company of cavalry composed of men from Camden and Thomaston (a section of Rockland) led by Dr. Isaac Barnard of Thomaston, who was appointed as captain. He was succeeded by Major Philip Ulmer, the son of John Ulmer of Thomaston.[1535] This particular cavalry company was led by the cousin of Philip Martin Ulmer of Lincolnville, who was also a militia major at the same time. This younger Major Philip Ulmer (son of Philip's uncle John) was the same child who was born in 1775 near the American encampment at Plymouth, Massachusetts, when Philip was involved in refitting and arming the American schooners *Spitfire* and *Washington* for Washington's navy. The older citizens of the local towns organized a volunteer "Alarm List" composed of men between the ages of forty-five and sixty-five. Some of these veteran soldiers had seen military service in the Revolutionary War, and all were exempt, by law, from military duty. This veteran company of about forty men, Revolutionary War Patriots that included Major Philip Ulmer, elected John Pendleton as their militia captain.[1536]

With the large British invasion forces having captured Eastport, the British Royal Marines proceeded to the naval shipyard at Hampden on the Penobscot River, where the major shipyard was located. The American warship *Adams*, the captured British transport HMS *Victory* and other armed American vessels were repaired and kept hidden. The HMS *Victory*, which had sailed under letters of marque and reprisal, had been captured in March 1814 and brought to the wharf in Camden, where it was declared a prize by Customs Inspector Joseph Farley of Waldoboro.[1537] Philip Ulmer knew Joseph Farley from his hometown of Waldoboro, and he worked with Farley as a deputy customs inspector in 1814 in the Penobscot Bay area. The cargo aboard the HMS *Victory* contained mostly coffee, cocoa and logwood and also had on board ten cannonades. The vessel was believed to be sailing from Jamaica with supplies for Castine. Farley issued a permit to land the cargo on March 26 at Camden village, where the cargo was offloaded and stored in the cellar of the Masonic lodge, the same Masonic lodge (Amity Lodge in Camden) where Philip and George Ulmer served as lodge officers. The cargo was sold at a public venue with many merchants from Boston who came to purchase the confiscated goods. The *Victory* was taken to the Hampden shipyard, where the U.S. Navy corvette, the *Adams*, was under repairs, up the Penobscot River near Bangor.[1538]

The militia companies from many counties in General Blake's brigade responded to the call to arms, and they hurried to Bangor and Hampden to stop the approach of the invading British troops. Philip Ulmer's second son, Charles Ulmer, served as an aide to General John Blake at this time, and he was located at the Hampden shipyard near Bangor.[1539] These troops were involved in building, arming and repairing American vessels for naval service in the defense of the Massachusetts seacoast. Major Jacob Ulmer was among the state militia officers in General Blake's brigade who were called for service and hurried to Bangor and Hampden to defend the towns and shipyards from British attack. The fighting was intense as the state militia troops tried to block the advancing British forces, but they were forced to retreat time and again. Philip Ulmer served as the wartime selectman for the town of Lincolnville during the War of 1812. His duties included the evacuation of the women and children inland and to other safer towns where they could receive protection and preparation of the remaining elderly men and militia veterans to make a stand against the advancing British forces at the outskirts of the town. Belfast soon fell to the powerful forces of the

British Royal Marines, who left the town in flames. The small settlement at Northport and the towns of Lincolnville and Camden were the next coastal towns in line for British naval attack.

Philip Ulmer's two eldest sons, Jacob and Charles, were involved in the heated firefight and the chaotic retreat from Bangor, the Hampden shipyards and Belfast. The British fleet and raiding parties descended upon the poorly defended small towns and coastal villages and burned them to the ground. After losing the skirmishes at Hampden, Bangor and Belfast to the British forces, the state militia troops with General Blake's brigade retreated toward Ducktrap Harbor at Lincolnville to make a defensive stand.[1540] If every effort to defend Lincolnville failed, the volunteers and militia troops would have to make a hasty retreat toward the defenses set up at Camden village, about four miles away to the southwest. Between Lincolnville and Camden village, a cannon battery had been mounted on Mount Battie in the Camden Hills to protect Camden's strategic harbor. Major Philip Ulmer continued to fight with the veterans' militia company and with the retreating state militiamen to protect the towns of Lincolnville and Camden village from the invading British forces.

After attacking Belfast and leaving the town in flames, British admiral Cochrane sent out reconnaissance scouts to determine the next objective in their tactical plan to subdue the Penobscot Bay region. Philip Ulmer was familiar with the brutality and tactics of the British invasion forces during the American Revolution. His major concern was to protect and defend his family and community from enemy plundering and devastation. As the town's selectman and an experienced military advisor and strategist, Philip evacuated nonessential townspeople to safer locations in the backcountry and to safer towns to the southwest. He prepared a military strategy with General Blake to defend the towns of Lincolnville and Camden village. The plan was to have military defenses, batteries and barricades built along the Penobscot shoreline and along the ridgeline of the Ducktrap and Camden hills, which overlooked the narrow three-mile channel between the Lincolnville mainland and Long Island (hereafter referred to as Islesboro). Philip's son Charles and his company manned the artillery battery on the island of Islesboro across from Lincolnville Harbor. The objective was to trap the British ships in a crossfire if they entered the narrow channel between the island and Lincolnville Harbor. The enemy warships would have great difficulty maneuvering, and the British forces would receive a mighty blow in their plans of conquest in the frontier region. The tactical plan for the defending American militia forces was to make a stand somewhere along the mid-Atlantic mainland and to discourage the invading British forces from completely ravaging and destroying the shipping and shoreline towns in frontier Maine.

Philip Ulmer had the older veteran militiamen and the remaining town volunteers set up a clever ruse of fake and real artillery batteries on the ridgeline of the hills near Ducktrap Harbor-cove. Philip's first responsibility as a leader was to defend the town. The clever ruse was to convince the invading British naval fleet that the town was heavily occupied, well-armed and ready to fight. Barricades were strategically placed along the shoreline road by militia soldiers from the vicinity south of Northport to the south of Camden village. Logs resembling cannons were placed upon stacked wood and mounted on rocks. These fake cannons were interspersed with several real cannons that had been salvaged earlier from the Penobscot River. The refurbished cannons were distributed among the forest trees on the hills surrounding Ducktrap cove and Lincolnville beach. Scarecrows resembling people, with sticks resembling muskets, were placed near the fake cannons. At night, campfires were lit along the shore road and in the hills to try and convince the invading British forces that the town was heavily defended. Seen from a distance by the reconnaissance scouts, the Lincolnville hills and shoreline appeared heavily armed and bristling with guns and troops. Philip Ulmer had remembered from his service during the Revolutionary War that this ruse had been successfully used a number of times to mislead the British troops. It was hoped that it would work again.

Through their telescopes, the British scouts saw the barricades being built along the Penobscot shoreline and the supposed heavy defenses and troops on the ridgeline of the forest hills near the harbor. The scouts reported their observations to Admiral Cochrane, who decided that it was probably a trap for the unsuspecting British fleet. Admiral Cochrane changed his attack plans to destroy Lincolnville and Camden village, much to the joy of the townspeople and the relief of the defending militia troops. Sailing toward the eastern side of Islesboro, the British fleet proceeded to Castine (Bagaduce), which was not well defended. Captain Lewis and his small detached company of state militiamen, who were part of Colonel George Ulmer's troops stationed at Castine, fired several shots from their cannons at the approaching British fleet. They quickly abandoned the fort in small boats and made their way to the safety of the mainland and Fort Pine Hill. The British forces quickly captured the undefended fort outpost. After capturing the fort and battery at Castine and setting up a battalion of British troops to secure the Penobscot Bay region, the British Royal Navy and Royal Marine forces continued their push southward toward Philadelphia and Baltimore. Before leaving the Penobscot vicinity, the British fleet delivered a blistering naval attack with broadsides and mortars upon Fort Pine Hill. The British forces caused devastating damage to Fort Pine Hill and the defensive fortifications near the fort. The British fleet destroyed the primary defensive fortification that had served as the American militia headquarters in the Penobscot Bay region and left behind them the burning wreckage of the fort.

Once the threat of further British attack had subsided at Lincolnville and Camden village, Philip Ulmer retired to his home at Ducktrap for needed care of his leg that had been re-injured during the fighting on the Northport/Lincolnville/Camden road. The original injury to Philip's thigh had been received during the Penobscot Expedition in 1779, and the leg had never fully recovered. It caused him continued pain and a permanent limp over the years which led to other health issues.[1541] In spite of his age and physical disabilities, Philip Ulmer continued his involvement with the local veteran militia company, primarily in an advisory and supporting role. Philip continued to serve the town of Lincolnville as a selectman and administrator until the end of the war.

In 1814, Philip Ulmer was appointed by the Massachusetts General Court in Boston as a state deputy customs inspector and pilot stationed at Lincolnville and Camden village. (The village of Camden was formerly known by its Indian name, Megunticook, and was a part of Ducktrap Plantation at one time. Camden village should not be confused with the Camden where Fort Pine Hill was located, near present-day Rockland, Maine.)[1542] Philip Ulmer, serving as a deputy customs inspector, became involved in a dramatic incident with the captured British cargo vessel *Mary* in November 1814. The incident of privateering occurred in late October with several adventurous armed men who left Northport in a dory fishing boat (similar to a whale boat). The young privateers were determined to capture a British cargo transport for profit. The armed men were Major Noah Miller, West Drinkwater, Jonathan Clark and three Duncan brothers: Samuel, John and Kingsbury.[1543] They were intent on patrolling the Belfast Bay and nearby vicinity to prevent supplies from being carried to the British troops at Castine. On November 1, 1814, the young privateers sighted the British sloop *Mary* (some refer to the vessel as a schooner) near Islesboro in the Penobscot Bay. The *Mary* was bound from Halifax to Castine and held a rich cargo of goods valued (at the time) at more than $40,000.[1544] The local privateers, led by militia officer Noah Miller, pursued the sloop and overtook it. They fired a gun and ordered the captain to "heave-to," which the captain would not obey at first. Captain Benjamin Darling, the sailing master, threatened Major Miller and his crewmen. The crewmen rowed along the side of the sloop, boarded and quickly took charge of the vessel. Captain Darling and the supercargo named McWaters, the "King's agent," admitted to Major Miller that the destination of the cargo was indeed Castine.[1545] The British supercargo offered to pay Miller a ransom of ten thousand British pounds, but the leader of the crew, Major Noah Miller, refused the bribe since he had promised to equally share the monetary prize reward with the other men involved with the capture of the sloop *Mary*.[1546] The captain and the supercargo were released on land, and they had to make their way back to Castine on their own.

Major Noah Miller had no authority from the government to take prize vessels from the British, and he had made himself liable for a heavy penalty of being hanged as a pirate if he were caught. Apparently Noah Miller and his crew thought that Miller's commission as a militia major gave him authority to act. Uncertain what to do since he didn't have government authority to capture prize vessels, Noah Miller sailed the sloop to Lincolnville. Miller entered the general store at Ducktrap and asked John Wilson (George Ulmer's son-in-law) what to do about his situation. Wilson advised that Philip Ulmer, the deputy customs inspector, would know what to do in this circumstance. Noah Miller contacted Philip Ulmer, who boarded the sloop and declared the British cargo transport as a prize of the United States.[1547] Major Philip Ulmer, being an experienced and authorized sea coast pilot himself, took the helm of the sloop *Mary* and sailed the vessel to the port at Camden. The U.S. customs inspector for the Penobscot District, Josiah Hook of Castine, was located at Camden with Philip.[1548] Major Noah Miller followed the sloop to Camden by land on foot. Customs Inspector Hook went aboard the sloop and declared the vessel to be a legal prize of the United States. The cargo, mainly satin, silk, lace, shawls, clothes, cloth and other dry goods, was unloaded and taken to Falmouth (Portland) by wagons pulled by teams of oxen.[1549] Customs Inspector Hook made out a revenue commission for Noah Miller and backdated it fifteen days to cover the capture of the sloop *Mary*.[1550] The town officials hired Jonathan Clark, Samuel Duncan and Kingsbury Duncan, and they paid the young men $5.00 each to take the sloop and hide it up the St. Georges River where the British would not be able to find it. The sloop and cargo were sold the following January for the large sum of $69,790.64.[1551] Approximately half of the money was paid to the

United States Treasury, which was the custom. The other half was divided among Customs Inspector Josiah Hook, Noah Miller and his crewmen and Major Philip Ulmer.[1552]

When McWaters, who was King George III's agent, and the British captain reached Castine and reported the loss of the sloop and its valuable cargo, the British commander was enraged and vowed vengeance upon the people responsible for the indignity. The people of Camden were afraid that the capture of the sloop *Mary* would cause great trouble for the town with the British. The British dispatched the frigate *Furieuse* of thirty-eight guns, commanded by Captain Mouncey, to recapture the sloop *Mary*. On November 2, 1814, the *Furieuse*, a French-built frigate that had been captured from Napoleon's French navy, entered the Camden Harbor and anchored outside of the village's rock ledges and out of cannon range. Captain Mouncey demanded the return of the cargo and vessel or the payment of $80,000. Captain Mouncey threatened that "if the demand were not met, Camden and Lincolnville would lie in ashes."[1553] The town authorities held a town meeting and argued about what should be done since the sloop and its cargo had already been sent away from the town. The British captain and the town committee were unable to come to any conclusion, so Robert Chase and Benjamin Cushing, both of Camden, went aboard the frigate *Furieuse* as hostages until the matter could be settled. They were aboard the vessel for several days.

Messengers had been sent to the surrounding coastal towns from Waldoboro to Belfast and Machias on the Penobscot Bay. Since Major Noah Miller came from the militia company at Belfast, another officer was sent with the company to Camden. As the combined militia forces converged on Camden, Captain Mouncey decided to take the two hostages to Castine, where they were placed on parole and held in a guarded house for two weeks. Receiving no satisfaction from the stalemate over the sloop, Captain Mouncey finally released the hostages, and the British captain gave up the idea of retribution upon the townspeople of Camden. The British captain no longer placed the blame for the incident on the residents of Camden and offered a liberal reward for the capture of Major Miller and his crew. In their vengeance and the desire for retribution for the disgrace of the capture of the sloop *Mary*, the British wanted to hang Noah Miller and his crewmen from the ship's mast as pirates.[1554] After many frustrating weeks, the British determined that they would not be able to effectively resolve the stalemate, and they eventually backed away from any further confrontation. British warships eventually had less and less impact on the New England seacoast as the war continued to expand southward along the eastern coastline of America. The strength of the British Royal Navy and Royal Marines were felt by other coastal seaports and river ports in the middle and southern states as Admiral Cochrane's large fleet moved down the eastern coast of the United States.

THE BRITISH ATTACK WASHINGTON AND BALTIMORE

After the surrender of Napoleon Bonaparte and his army in Europe, the British dispatched General Robert Ross from France with 4,500 veteran forces to raid key points on the American seacoast. Admiral Alexander Cochrane, having completed his coastal attacks on the New England states, replaced Admiral Warren at Bermuda, and he became the commander in chief of the North American station. Admiral Cochrane coordinated his Royal Navy fleet with General Ross's British army forces in attacks on vital coastal cities in the middle and southern states of America. The next prong of the planned British military action was to destroy the seat of political and governing power in the capital city of Washington and to destroy Baltimore, the major commercial and industrial port on the Chesapeake Bay. The British Ministry of War also believed that Baltimore Harbor was a protected haven for American privateering activities against British interests in the West Indies, the Mexican Gulf and the southern coast of America. The British government believed that if the political and governing center of the nation was burned and destroyed, and if the major seaport that supplied Washington was also destroyed, the U.S. president and the U.S. Congress would be forced to surrender to the power and authority of the king of England and the British Parliament. The lessons of the Revolutionary War, the first British invasion of colonial America, had not been learned by the governing powers of England. Great Britain's second invasion of America, called the War of 1812, would eventually end the same way as the first. The United States was a democratic republic composed of many sovereign and independent states. It was not governed like Europe, which still had kings and an aristocracy that functioned in a feudalistic and dictatorial way. America had won its freedom from foreign intervention and dominance, and it was determined to retain its freedom, liberty and independence.

To execute the action of the British invasion plan, General Robert Ross and his veteran army forces landed at the mouth of the Patuxent River in Maryland. His objective was to destroy the city of Washington, the governmental seat of diplomatic and political power. In September 1814, the General Ross's well-supplied brigade advanced by land toward the city of Washington without much local resistance. General William Winder, who was in command of the Potomac District, assembled a mixed force of militia, regular troops and several hundred sailors from Commodore Joshua Barney's destroyed flotilla. The American militia troops were easily routed by General Robert Ross's heavily armed British forces. The British troops entered the city of Washington and burned the Capitol building and other public buildings and set fire to the White House. President Madison's wife, Dolley, would not leave the White House until George Washington's famous painting was removed from its frame and taken safely away with other important governing documents such as the Declaration of Independence and the Bill of Rights. It was later admitted by Admiral Cochrane that the burning of the Capitol building and other government buildings and the burning of the White House was in retaliation for the American destruction of the government seat of British political power at York, Canada, in the spring of 1813.

While General Ross's British forces marched on Washington, the local Maryland militia troops around Baltimore had time to hastily strengthen their defenses. General Samuel Smith assembled nine thousand militiamen, including the one thousand men who manned Fort McHenry, which guarded the harbor at Baltimore. The British landed troops at North Point, several miles from the city, where their advancing troops were engaged in a skirmish by the local Maryland militia. During the fierce fighting, General Robert Ross was killed. The British warships of Admiral Cochrane sailed up the Chesapeake Bay and the Patapsco River toward Baltimore Harbor. Fort McHenry was strategically located on Locust Point on two branches of the Patapsco River and defended the entrance to Baltimore Harbor. Admiral Cochrane's warships fired upon Fort McHenry for twenty-five hours, using cannons, bombardments and boat attacks. When the American troops at Fort McHenry did not surrender after the fierce, prolonged attacks, the British admiral decided that a land attack on the fortification would be too costly. Admiral Cochrane finally decided to discontinue the attack on Baltimore Harbor and withdrew his fleet of warships from the Chesapeake Bay to prepare for the next phase of the British invasion plan, an assault on the city of New Orleans. Francis Scott Key, who had been held on board a truce ship in the Chesapeake, had observed the unsuccessful British bombardment of Fort McHenry. He was inspired to write a poem about the event that was entitled "The Defense of Fort McHenry," and it later became known as "The Star-Spangled Banner."

The fourth prong of the British invasion plan was to attack New Orleans and to secure the mouth of the Mississippi River, which was a major center for American commerce, trade and privateering activities throughout the United States, the West Indies and the rest of the commercial markets in the world. Admiral Cochrane assembled a force of approximately ten thousand British troops at Jamaica. In late December 1814, the attack on New Orleans was begun by landing British troops at the western end of Lake Borgne. Unopposed, the invading troops successfully seized control of the area. The initial landing was preparatory to an attempt to seize the city of New Orleans and to secure the lower Mississippi Valley. As the advance forces began to maneuver toward the city, General Andrew Jackson, who was the American commander in chief of the southern states, made a night attack upon the unsuspecting British troops with support from the gunboat *Carolina*. The British troops retreated, enabling General Jackson and his troops to fall back to a location south of New Orleans. Breastworks were hastily built for about a mile along the right flank of the river. A cypress swamp was on the left of the river. A mixed force of militia, regular U.S. forces and reserve troops formed the defensive line. General Sir Edward Pakenham arrived to command the British operation on land. He entrenched his British troops and fought an artillery duel against the American forces. General Jackson's militia forces outgunned the British artillery. After a week, General Pakenham attempted a frontal assault on General Andrew Jackson's breastworks and simultaneously sent a smaller force across the river to attack General David Morgan's defenses. The massed firing from General Jackson's troops, protected by the earthworks which had been reinforced by cotton bales, caused substantial damage to General Pakenham's British Royal Marine troops as they advanced across the open ground in front of the American lines. In less than thirty minutes, the British attack was repulsed, leaving behind 291 killed (including General Pakenham), 1,262 wounded and 48 prisoners, who were taken by General Jackson's American forces. The surviving British troops withdrew to Lake Borgne and left by boat for Mobile, Alabama, where they learned on February 14 that the Treaty of Ghent had been signed, ending the war.

The Treaty of Ghent was finally signed on December 24, 1814, bringing some peace and tranquility to the Lake Champlain region and other parts of the United States. But hostilities continued in the Penobscot Bay area of frontier Maine. The news of the peace treaty didn't reach Camden

(Maine) until February 14, 1815. The territory in Maine, after some delay and reluctance, was returned to the United States on March 23, 1815. The British troops finally left the fort at Castine in April 1815, at which time they took 10,750 British pounds obtained from tariff duties at Castine *after* the Treaty of Ghent was signed. This money was called the "Castine Fund" and was taken to Halifax, Nova Scotia, and used for British purposes. The War of 1812 ended in a stalemate, and the territories captured by the British during the war were returned to the United States.

The news of peace was brought to the village towns of Camden and Lincolnville on February 14, 1815. The stage driver arrived at midnight, blowing the post horn as he rode into town, waking the sleeping and startled residents. The news of peace was met by the firing of guns, the kindling of bonfires and shouts of joy and happiness. The four-pounder cannons in the two forts along the Penobscot Bay began to roar and continued to fire until daybreak. Several militiamen went up to the summit of Mount Battie to take charge of the cannons, two twelve-pounders and one eighteen-pounder, which were fired off to notify the neighboring communities that the war had ended.[1555] The cannons had been placed on the summit of the mountain about seven months before to defend the town and harbor against the invading British fleet commanded by Admiral Cochrane. An account of the historic event stated:

> *As the largest pieces belched forth from its elevated position, in deep, thunder-like tones, the habitations below were shaken to their foundations, while the echo's reverberations were heard resounding over adjacent waters, remote hills, and distant valleys. Thus through the day the firing continued, from all the guns, and the tidings of peace thereby became first announced to the inhabitants of the surrounding towns. The day being spent in demonstrations of joy, the night closed the exhibition by a public dance and a time of festivity.*[1556]

When the news came to the military headquarters in Thomaston, there were shouts of joy everywhere. Guns were fired, and drums beat the news. The one eighteen-pounder cannon that Major Philip Ulmer had installed on the hill near Fort Pine Hill prior to the Penobscot Expedition in 1779 "thundered the happy news from its iron throat which echoes from the lofty crags and [is] heard by the British at Castine, who echoed the joy back again."[1557] The firing of cannons and guns was to celebrate the event and also to signal the townspeople and families to gather together. In Camden, the men from the town and surrounding communities, with the officers and militia soldiers from the barracks, met at the house of Robert Thorndike at Goose River in Waldoboro. When the whole company was gathered, the host called for silence and in simple language related the details of the peace treaty.[1558] The sounds of revelry continued into the night with toasts, songs and food prepared by the women of the towns. Festivities continued through the night, and in the morning, the revelers separated and made their way through the woods to their homes in various communities. After nearly forty years of conflict and two wars for American independence, peace had finally come to America. The hopes and the dreams for a new future of freedom, liberty, national sovereignty and independence from foreign domination and control began to dawn for the American people.

SUMMARY OF THE WAR OF 1812 AND THE END OF BRITISH CONTROL OF THE AMERICAN COLONIES

The Embargo Act of 1807 had no effect on Great Britain or France and was replaced by the Non-Intercourse Act of 1809, which lifted all embargos on American shipping except for those bound for British or French ports. This proved to be unenforceable, and President Jefferson lifted the embargo just three days before leaving office in 1809. The Non-Intercourse Act was replaced in 1810 by Macon's Bill Number 2. This bill lifted all embargos but offered that if either France or Great Britain were to cease their interference with American shipping, the United States would reinstate an embargo on the other nation. Napoleon, seeing an opportunity to cause more problems for Great Britain, declared that France would leave American shipping alone. England continued to exert its naval superiority along the seacoast of America. The United States reinstated the embargo against Great Britain, and the two countries moved closer to declaring war.

The main causes for the war with Great Britain in 1812 were the American desire for expansion into the Northwest Territories following the Louisiana Purchase in December 1803; increased trade restrictions because of the ongoing war in Europe between England and France; British impressments of American merchant sailors and naturalized U.S. citizens into the British Royal Navy; British support of American Indian tribes against the American expansion westward; and the national outrage felt by the American citizens and government officials because of England's continued disregard for their nation's independence and sovereignty that had been won as a result of the American Revolution.

The Napoleonic War occurred at a time that was most advantageous to the United States because the British forces were kept occupied by Napoleon's French forces in Europe, both on land and sea. The situation was particularly serious for the United States because the country was insolvent by the fall of 1814. In New England, opponents of the war with Great Britain were discussing separation from the United States due to the intrusion of the federal government into the affairs of the sovereign states and the implementation of the federal government's authority over the states' militia forces. Stopping short of separation, a number of constitutional amendments to restrict federal power were written and implemented in the Constitution, written in September 1787. The Constitution was ratified in 1788 and replaced the Articles of Confederation. The Bill of Rights was written in 1789 and was ratified on December 15, 1791. These documents clarified the purpose and function of the federal government and the states and the rights and responsibilities of the citizens in the United States.

There were three major theaters of conflict during the War of 1812. At sea, warships and privateers belonging to Great Britain and the United States (and, for a period of time, France) attacked each other's merchant ships. The British Royal Navy's heavy blockade of the Atlantic coast of the United States permitted the powerful British invasion forces to mount large-scale raiding parties on important American coastal seaport towns and villages. This action crippled American navigation and commerce and devastated the fragile American economy. The second theater of action took place on both land and sea, where battles were fought on the frontier borders that ran along the St. Lawrence River and on the Great Lakes in the heart of United States and the North American continent. The third theater of conflict was in the southern colonies and Florida seacoast, in the West Indies and along the Gulf of Mexico coastline. There were major land battles in the southern states in which American forces attacked Britain's Indian allies and defeated the main British invasion at New Orleans. Both British and American army forces invaded each other's territories, but neither army was able to retain control of the captured area, so the invasions were unsuccessful and temporary. The fighting ended on February 18, 1815. Both the British side and American side held parts of the other's territories. The territorial areas were basically restored by the Treaty of Ghent. However, the northern border territories remained in dispute for many years to come.

The significance of the War of 1812 has been overlooked and neglected in our current American history books. The War of 1812 was a complex, four-prong invasion conducted in three theaters of the United States by Great Britain in an effort to bring the young, struggling nation of America to its knees and to restore to Great Britain the subservience of the American colonies. The democratic experiment in America that enabled the thirteen colonies to unite and form a new republic needed to be crushed by the superior might of England's military powers on land and sea. If the British forces had been successful in the second invasion of the United States, American citizens would have been required to take an oath of allegiance to the king of England and to pay heavy taxes to restore the British economy for the two American Revolutions and to pay for Britain's wars in Europe and England's conflicts in other parts of the world. America's extensive unsettled western territories beyond the Mississippi River and its natural resources would have been exploited by the British government, land speculators, investment companies and wealthy capitalists. America's fragile postwar economy and its future as an independent nation and world power would have been destroyed if the British forces had succeeded in their massive invasion of America in 1814–15.

The second invasion of the United States by Great Britain was a last attempt by the British king and British government to reclaim power and control of the American colonies. Although the War of 1812 ended in a stalemate, it confirmed America's sovereignty and decisive separation from England. The United States of America had earned the recognition of the European countries and the countries in the rest of the world. The United States of America had finally proven that it was truly a free, sovereign, respected and independent country.

What the British king and British government didn't understand about America's new republic was that America's governing power rested in the hands of the American people. It was the people of the many sovereign and independent states who elected their representatives to serve in the federal government on their behalf, to write the laws, to provide for the common defense and to tax the population as needed. If the British military forces burned the town or city where the congressional representatives and delegates met, the congressional representatives would move to a safer location where they could meet and continue to conduct the American government's business. Through the capture and burning of the city of Washington and other important cities and major ports along the eastern coastline of America, King George III and the British government believed that the American colonies (states) would be forced into surrendering their governing and economic abilities, and America would again come under the dictatorial control of England. The European concept of governing powers and the rules of war and military engagement were based on the more feudal concepts of dictatorial rulers and monarchies; the palaces of the rulers served as the center of governing power. In America, this was not the case. The new concept was of a democratic republic that was formed by many sovereign and independent states; that had a government that was supported by the American people, who elected their president and legislative representatives; and whose governing officials could be peacefully replaced by the will of the people in state and national elections. This was an idea that was alien to the countries in Europe that were ruled by kings, dictators or warlords. The American experiment with self-government by the common people was expected to fail.

AFTERMATH OF THE WARS WITH ENGLAND

President Madison sent a letter to Congress notifying them that the Treaty of Ghent had been signed on December 24, 1814. The treaty was ratified by the Senate on February 16, 1815, and signed by the president the next day. Peace was proclaimed on February 18, 1815. President Madison congratulated the nation on the conclusion of a war. Madison stated: "[The nation] ages with the success which is the natural result of the wisdom of the legislative councils, of the patriotism of the People, of the public spirit of the militia, and of the valor of the military and naval forces of the country." Almost overnight, the War of 1812 became a glorious success. The fledgling nation had the remarkable good fortune to escape the consequences of a war that had been badly managed from the beginning. The battle at New Orleans, which took place after the actual signing of the Treaty of Ghent, ironically became the most noteworthy incident of the war. The United States Navy received well-deserved popularity and acclaim for many years after the end of the conflict. However, the most significant results of the battle that took place on Lake Champlain did not receive full recognition for another generation or so.

For the American public, the successful results of the War of 1812 were a renewal of self-confidence and faith in the ability of its military to defend the nation's freedom and honor. The conclusion of the war ushered in a period in American history that was referred to as "the era of good feelings" and a time when most Americans felt united behind a common purpose. The enduring legacy of the American Revolution and the War of 1812 was a change in the direction of greater freedom and liberty for the American people. Even in frontier Maine, a new social order and ideology based on individual freedom had developed: freedom from domination and intimidation by the British Empire; freedom of Maine from Massachusetts; the liberty to participate in the political process; freedom from European feudalism and bondage; freedom from the state church; equality under law for the individual; liberty to seek a better future for himself and his posterity; and the opportunity to exploit the country's resources—especially its land. America had become a place where freedom and liberty had a chance to flourish and the individual could become prosperous through hard work and opportunity. The War of 1812 finally convinced the country that it could fend off any foreign threats if they were united in a common cause and that the nation could focus on growth and development with its own national goals.

Following the Louisiana Purchase, President Thomas Jefferson and the Congress designated Lewis and Clark to form an "Expedition of Discovery." The government sent these men and their team of surveyors to map the Northwestern and Oregon Territories and to open the West for exploration and settlement. The federal government made land available to those frontiersmen who dared to settle in the new western territories beyond the Mississippi River. The federal government greatly profited from selling land to wealthy venture capitalists, successful merchants, military veterans who had received land-bounties in payment for their military services and frontier settlers moving westward to stake their claim and develop lands west of the Mississippi River. The new territories offered opportunities to those who had the courage to move westward and invest their energies in developing the land and the natural resources. Land speculation, seemingly limitless opportunities and venture investing (capitalism) became strong incentives for exploration and development of the Western and Northwestern territories.

With the opening up of the frontier regions of Ohio, the Ohio River Valley and the Mississippi River Valley, the westward movement into the new western frontiers of the Indiana Territory and beyond to the Oregon and the Northwest Territories beckoned to the adventurous as well as those who felt exploited in the eastern colonies. There were many Maine settlers, young and old, who moved westward to seek a better climate, a chance to claim more fertile land and an opportunity to make a new life and fortune in a new location. It was the search for prosperity and the hope for a future in a new part of the country where families could flourish and where opportunities abounded. "Manifest Destiny" is the slogan used to describe this new era of exploration and a new spirit of opportunity and discovery.

The stagnation of commerce during the war had brought Massachusetts's economy and trade almost to a halt. With the end of the War of 1812, commerce quickly returned to America, causing an influx of European goods into American markets. The flood of the European goods reduced prices so low that they undercut manufactured and handmade goods, lessening the value of wool and homespun products. Factory- and American-manufactured goods fell in price as well. The war had caused many issues, such as the destruction of homes, businesses and property, as well as many issues concerning societal changes. Weather conditions and droughts, caused by a series of poor growing seasons for agriculture, had a profound effect on the frontier towns in Maine. Trade and commerce were greatly affected, and the fragile economy of towns in frontier Maine was disrupted.

There was a huge eruption of the Tambora volcano in Indonesia on April 11, 1815, that spewed many tons of volcanic ash high into the atmosphere. Ash from the Tambora eruption, along with ash from several other volcanic eruptions in Indonesia and Japan in 1814–15, caused great global changes to climatic conditions and raised many concerns around the world.[1559] In frontier Maine, the growing seasons were very strange in 1815–16. The spring of 1815 was very odd. Some growing seasons were too cold and wet for corn, and other seasons brought drought conditions that were too dry for potatoes and grass to produce much yield. The farmers had to stop their plowing in late May due to a severe snow storm. Volcanic ash continued to spread around the world, causing global famine, epidemics and death everywhere. (Note: In recent reports, it was determined that the Tambora volcano spewed one hundred times more ash into the atmosphere than the eruption of Mount St. Helens on May 18, 1980, in the state of Washington.)

The coldest and most disastrous season on record was 1816. Strangely, there was a dusty fog that blocked the warmth of the sun by day and caused unusual sunsets in the evening. Frost occurred every month of that year. In frontier Maine, the summer of 1816 was very cold, and water buckets standing at the farmers' outer doors froze in place. It was the year without a summer, when birds mysteriously died in flight and fell from the sky. (This same occurrence happened in January 2011, when newspapers reported that thousands of birds mysteriously died in flight and fell from the sky in the southeastern and Gulf states of the United States, likely due to unusual volcanic activity in Iceland and the Philippines the year before.) It was icy cold in June, and multicolored snow fell, covering the landscape. The corn crop was a failure, and very little grain was harvested in July. Haying wasn't begun until the first of August. Disastrous growing seasons, the misfortunes of war and the general business depression that prevailed during this time caused great suffering and deprivation, especially for the people of frontier Maine.[1560] Food supplies were scarce, and starvation and illness were constant concerns. There were famines and epidemics, and typhus killed many thousands of people in Europe. Seeking relief from the extreme climatic conditions, many people from New England, including those from frontier Maine, packed their belongings and moved west toward western Pennsylvania and the Ohio and Indiana Territories.

These were the conditions that Philip Ulmer and his family had to face in the final year of his life. He was distressed over how to continue providing for his wife and children at home and what would happen to them if and when his health should fail. The disastrous growing seasons from 1813 through 1816, the effects of the Tambora volcano eruption and the general business depression that followed the end of the War of 1812 caused great suffering for people who lived in the northeastern region of frontier New England. Many inhabitants of Lincolnville and the surrounding districts in frontier Maine emigrated to western Pennsylvania and Ohio, part of the newly opened western territory in the American heartland of the Ohio and Mississippi River Valleys. Among the war veterans from the frontier were John Wilson of Lincolnville, Reverend Seth Noble of Bangor and other adventurers from Massachusetts and the District of Maine. The expanding western movement of pioneers, adventurers, venture capitalists and land speculators sought to develop the land and seek a better future west of the Mississippi River. Some inhabitants of New England moved to the warmer southern climates in the Carolinas, which offered better business opportunities, longer growing seasons and more productive soil on which to settle and prosper.[1561]

There were a number of Ulmer relatives among the emigration of German settlers from Waldoboro that moved to the Carolinas. Prior to the American Revolution, a number of religious German Lutheran families (called Moravians) from Waldoboro (Broad Bay settlement) decided to emigrate from frontier Maine with their religious leader, Pastor Cilley. They settled on lands to the west of New Bern, North Carolina, where the climate was much warmer than frontier Maine and the prospects for fertile land, security and prosperity were better.[1562] After several years, some of the families in this German Lutheran community near New Bern decided to move farther south to Charleston, South Carolina. These settlers, which also included some Ulmer relatives, moved to the west of Charleston in the marshy river region and started a new German Lutheran community. Many people in the new community died of insect-borne illnesses and other diseases. Several Ulmer families who were involved with the early Ulmer cargo shipping, navigation and trading businesses at the Broad Bay settlement (Waldoboro, Maine) also set up lumber and grain mills on several rivers and developed commercial trading and fur trading businesses with the Indians. The expanding business connections of the Ulmer families from Waldoboro, Thomaston, Rockland and Lincolnville with other Ulmer family members in the more southern states of Pennsylvania and North and South Carolina supported their navigational, cargo shipping and coastal trading businesses on the eastern seacoast of America as well as in Europe and the West Indies.

The extended Ulmer family connections in the southern states had trading connections in the West Indies and traded lumber, firewood, pelts and other needed goods and supplies at the major ports of Savannah, Georgia, and St. Augustine, Florida, as well as ports in the West Indies and New Orleans. As Charleston expanded, the governor of the colony and the governing House of Commons offered land-bounties that included trading incentives and business opportunities on available land and river ports to the west of Charleston. The early settlement of the town of Ulmer, South Carolina (located in the backcountry to the west of Charleston), was settled by some of these hardy German Ulmer pioneers. The Ulmer family in South Carolina built a log trading post and constructed several mills on the river streams in the swampy inland area, where they carried on a successful trading business in lumber, deer hides and other furs, dry goods, naval stores and needed agricultural and manufactured products with the local Indian tribes and settlers.

Ulmer family descendants whose original ancestor, Johannes Jakob Ulmer, first brought the family to America and settled as pioneers in the eastern frontier of the Massachusetts Bay Colony have today successfully spread throughout the United States. Ulmer descendants have been found in parts of Maine, Massachusetts, Connecticut, New York, New Jersey, Pennsylvania, Ohio, Indiana, Illinois, Kansas, Colorado, Arizona, California, the Carolinas, Georgia and northern Florida. All of the Ulmer (von Ulm) descendants in America and in Germany are distantly related to one another. They can trace their original lineage to a single ancestor in Germany who survived the Black Death in Europe. Reginald von Ulm lived at the von Ulm castle in Ulm, which is located in the duchy of Württemberg, Germany. He was the only surviving descendant of the Ulmer family's principal patriarch, Baron Gottfried von Ulm. It is from Gottfried von Ulm's two sons, Waldemar and Friedrick, which the Ulmer families in Germany and in America all descend.

Chapter 19

Last Years of the Ulmer Brothers

RECAP OF PHILIP ULMER'S CAREER

It seems appropriate at this point, as Philip Ulmer's life comes to an end, to reflect on the broad range of Philip's life and military service and to appreciate the scope of his character, his contributions to frontier Maine's diverse society and his service to the nation. Philip Ulmer was an active and devoted citizen of the towns of Waldoboro and Lincolnville, which he faithfully served in many administrative capacities until several weeks before his death. He contributed personally and financially to the communities for the advancement of the roads, business development, schools and the Waldoboro library. In the Federal Direct Tax list of 1798, George Ulmer was the wealthiest taxpayer in Lincolnville. Philip Ulmer was second to his brother in every accounting list.[1563] By the end of the War of 1812, the Federal Direct Tax list of 1815 for Hancock County indicated that Samuel A. Whitney Sr. was the town's wealthiest man with valuable holdings that had once belonged to Philip Ulmer. John Wilson, George Ulmer's son-in-law, was ranked as third-wealthiest in the town. Philip Ulmer was ranked as fifty-third with modest holdings, while George Ulmer no longer possessed any assessable property in Lincolnville and only two small parcels of land in adjoining towns.[1564] Philip and his family lived about a mile inland from the Penobscot shore near his brother on Cobbtown Road, where he lived until his death on October 3, 1816.[1565]

Philip Ulmer served in many official town, county and state leadership positions throughout the years that he lived in Lincolnville. Philip's lifelong devotion and contributions to the Lincolnville (Ducktrap) community have, until recently, been noted only in obscure historical documents, state and federal archives, vague references in ancient journals and letters and in old historical books and town records. It is clear that Philip Ulmer was a principal founder of the town of Lincolnville, which was once a part of the Ducktrap Plantation in frontier Maine. It is also clear from the historical references that he was a trustworthy, highly intelligent and honorable man with a strong sense of duty, love and devotion for his family, friends, community and country.

Philip Ulmer enlisted as a young infantry soldier during the early months of the American Revolution in 1775. He soon advanced in the company ranks to become a versatile military officer, serving in many important leadership roles throughout the eight years of conflict against the British invasion of America during the Revolution. He showed great courage and integrity as a state militia officer in defending the seacoast region of the frontier District of Maine. He took a moral stand on the behalf of the townspeople of Lincolnville against the federal government's Embargo Act of 1809. Major Philip Ulmer jeopardized his position as a U.S. Navy officer in the spring of 1809 because of the stand that he took for Lincolnville's townspeople against unjust decisions of the federal government. He relinquished his government sailing master's warrant in May 1809, just prior to the failed Embargo Act being lifted. This decision must have been personally very difficult for Philip. Since his youth, he had always wanted to serve as a U.S. Navy sailing master in command of his own naval warship. Political conditions and national circumstances beyond his control forced him to give up his lifelong dream as a U.S. Navy commander. Major Philip Ulmer was again called back into the service of his country several weeks after war was declared with England in June 1812. He served the state faithfully until his prior war injury curtailed his ability to actively fight against the invading British forces in 1814. He was assigned to the position of Massachusetts deputy customs inspector and pilot navigator, serving in the Penobscot Bay region.

As a Massachusetts deputy customs inspector, Philip Ulmer became involved in an incident involving the capture of the British sloop *Mary* in November 1814. Few people understood or appreciated the position that Philip Ulmer took in personally defending and protecting Major Noah Miller and his crewmen from British threats of death and from British vengeance aimed at Lincolnville and Camden. Following in his father's footsteps, Major Jacob

Ulmer, eldest son of Philip, served as a colonel of the regiment of militia in the local Hancock and Penobscot region during the War of 1812. Charles Ulmer, Philip's second son, also served as an officer in the local state militia company stationed at Hampden in 1814. Major Philip Ulmer, the son of Philip's uncle John, was an officer in the cavalry. He was actively involved in the War of 1812 with approximately eight to ten other Ulmer relatives.

In the beginning of the War of 1812, British admiral Cochrane and the British Royal fleet attacked the naval shipyard at Hampden, where the warships *Adams* and *Victory* were under repair. Philip Ulmer and other veterans responded to the British attack at Hampden and Bangor by securing the towns to the south that were next in line for attack. Philip Ulmer suffered a re-injury to his previously injured leg during the defensive preparations and hasty retreat on the road from Belfast to Ducktrap. The American militia troops had decided to take a stand at Lincolnville, and barricades were set up on the outskirts of town on the Northport road just to the north of Ducktrap Harbor-cove, where Philip and George lived. Observing the strong defenses at Lincolnville, the British forces changed the thrust of their attack and chose to attack the poorly defended Fort Madison on Castine instead. Major Philip Ulmer's strategic tactics and defensive plans successfully spared the town of Lincolnville and village of Camden from total destruction by British naval and marine forces. The American troops at Castine saw the powerful British naval fleet descending upon them, and after firing several shots, they evacuated the outpost. The British forces quickly took over the peninsula. After securing Castine and leaving enough British troops to secure the region, the British fleet continued their southern advancement, laying waste to the seaports and coastal towns. Before leaving the Penobscot Bay area, the British made a forceful attack on Fort Pine Hill at Camden (near present-day Rockport) and destroyed the Penobscot militia defensive headquarters before moving farther south along the New England seacoast, leaving death and destruction in their wake. A strong force of British troops remained at Castine to secure the Penobscot region with assistance from the British fortress and naval shipyard at Halifax (Nova Scotia).

CIVIC ACCOMPLISHMENTS

Philip Ulmer served as selectman for the town of Waldoboro in 1783–84 before moving to the Ducktrap area after the Revolution. He served as a moderator and the chairman of the selectmen for the town of Lincolnville soon after its incorporation. The petition for incorporation from Ducktrap and New Canaan plantations into the town of Lincolnville in June 1802 was first written with Philip Ulmer's assistance and direction while he served on the town petition committee with his brother, George, and their friend Abner Milliken. He also served in other town administrative positions over the years, such as the town's moderator and surveyor of timber, and he also served on the town committees for roads and schools, just to mention a few. Philip's son Jacob served as the first town clerk while his father was the town selectman. Philip Ulmer often served as the town administrative official who wrote petitions to the Massachusetts Congress with requests for state aid and tax relief or for grievances of the Lincolnville townspeople. He served as a spokesperson and advocate for the townspeople of Lincolnville and local communities, and he addressed the politicians in the Massachusetts legislature in Boston on their behalf.

Philip Ulmer was concerned about the building of schools and roads as well as other infrastructure for the town and surrounding communities. He made sure that his children all had a basic education with reading, writing, arithmetic, science and other disciplines, and he encouraged the development of district schools so that all children in the local community were educated as well. The influence of Philip's grandfather Johannes Jakob Ulmer Sr., who had been a schoolmaster in Germany, could be seen in various aspects of Philip Ulmer's character. Education was so important to him that he contributed money to his hometown of Waldoboro for the purpose of buying books and other reading materials for the establishment of the Waldoboro Library, where Waterman Thomas (Philip and George Ulmer's friend) was chosen to serve as the first librarian. History books mention that Philip Ulmer grew up in Waldoboro, and his military service to Massachusetts was credited to the town during the American Revolution. There have been acknowledgements that Philip Ulmer was an active citizen and contributor to the Waldoboro community. Philip Ulmer's grandfather Captain Johannes Jakob Ulmer Sr. was one of the founding fathers of the Broad Bay settlement in Waldoboro. Philip's uncle John Ulmer was a selectman of the town of Waldoboro, and he was a wealthy businessman in the community. The Waldoboro town records acknowledge that Philip Ulmer served as a town selectman in 1783–84, prior to his relocation to Ducktrap (Lincolnville) with his brother's family.

Philip Ulmer and his brother, George, were early settlers at the Duck Trap Plantation settlement in the fall of 1784, shortly after the end of the Revolutionary War. Philip Ulmer used his experience and leadership as selectman for the town of Waldoboro to help shape the administrative structure and responsibilities of the new Ducktrap settlement, which led to the later incorporation of the Ducktrap and New Canaan plantations into the town of Lincolnville. Philip and two other committee members (his brother, George Ulmer, and Abner Milliken) were designated by the Ducktrap inhabitants to frame the first code of laws and the administrative positions necessary for a town government. Philip Ulmer worked tirelessly as an organizer and leader in the Ducktrap and New Canaan plantation community to help build the town infrastructure for the administrative offices and to define the needs of the town. Philip served on the original committee that wrote a petition to the Massachusetts General Court for incorporation as the town of Lincolnville in 1802.

The town of Lincolnville has only briefly recognized Philip Ulmer's devotion to their community as a public servant and his service as an early founder. Philip Ulmer was an active public servant of Lincolnville (Ducktrap) throughout his adult years and until days before his death in October 1816.[1566] The reversal of Philip's business fortunes in 1797 due to enemy privateering vessels in the West Indies later culminated in 1804 with the sale of his shipbuilding and business complex at Ducktrap and the sale of his home and belongings in 1806. Philip tried to salvage his career by turning to state politics. He was elected to serve Lincolnville and the local county in the House of Representatives in the Massachusetts General Court in 1807. He completed his term of office as an effective state congressional representative for his county constituents and for the townspeople of Lincolnville. Philip wrote a petition to the president of the Massachusetts Congress strongly expressing his constituents' concerns about the possible war with England, the overtaxation in their frontier communities and their economic hardships in the District of Maine prior to the War of 1812. After his public service as a state representative, Philip Ulmer continued to serve the town of Lincolnville as a wartime selectman and justice of the peace. He faithfully attended town meetings as an elder community leader in spite of his increasingly debilitating and painfully infected leg until just days before his death on October 3, 1816.

BUSINESS ACTIVITIES AT LINCOLNVILLE

The townspeople of Lincolnville knew and respected Philip Ulmer's leadership and many contributions to their community. However, the townspeople, even to this day, have expressed an intense dislike of the toll bridge that George Ulmer was directed to build over the Ducktrap stream and maintain with the use of tolls by the Massachusetts General Court in the early 1800s. George Ulmer and his brother, Philip (who was an associate in the toll issue although he received no income from it), were still disliked because of the maintenance taxes for the Ducktrap Bridge in the early years of their town. Philip loved and supported George even though he came under fire for his support of his younger, sometimes confrontational, more politically well-known and flamboyant brother. Philip has seldom been given credit for taking a stand on behalf of the community and local townspeople against some of his brother's controversial and often financially self-serving interests. Philip and George Ulmer worked hard for many years establishing their business complex at Ducktrap Harbor and cove. They provided jobs and services for the area inhabitants during the good business times prior to their slow reversal of fortune around 1797–1807. Inhabitants were involved in all aspects of the shipbuilding, commercial cargo shipping and trading businesses as well as the lime-burning business. The brothers provided jobs for the lumberjacks in clearing the timber land for settlement and for more business development in the Ducktrap watershed and backcountry areas. Philip and George Ulmer regularly extended credit to inhabitants in the Penobscot vicinity who were poor or financially stressed and needed food, provisions and other dry goods for their families. Bartering and the exchange of goods of approximate value made it possible for the local poor to purchase needed provisions and supplies brought back to the Penobscot area aboard the Ulmer cargo vessels and sold in their local stores. At one time, the Ulmer brothers' business enterprises at Ducktrap Harbor, the mill seat and the shipyard cove were the largest employers of inhabitants in the Penobscot Bay region.

Some Indians from the local Penobscot tribe who served with Philip Ulmer during the American Revolution were hired to work at Philip's businesses at "the Trap," where they were paid at the same rate as other local employees. This was a most unusual business practice for this time period. Philip had continued to maintain a good relationship with the local Abenaki-Penobscot Indians at Old Town, and they respected him for his integrity. This fact demonstrates the friendship and strong connection to their respected and loyal Ulmer friends. The Ulmer brothers' treatment of the Indians in the region was unusual since most wealthy trading merchants and most politicians exploited the American Indians at this time. What most people in Lincolnville did not know was that the bond between the Ulmer family of Waldoboro and the local Penobscot Indian tribe had endured as a strong and respectful relationship since the signing of the Dummer's Treaty with Captain John Ulmer Sr. (Philip and George's grandfather) and other Broad Bay witnesses in October 1752.[1567] In later years, one of the relatives of Chief Sabattis, an Abenaki-Penobscot Indian who had served during the American Revolution with Philip and George Ulmer, sought financial support for a military pension from the U.S. government. General George Ulmer was acknowledged in the government petition as lending his support to the authenticity of the military documentation.[1568] As they had always done in previous generations, the local Penobscot Indian tribe continued to use the Ulmer watershed land for hunting and fishing, for gathering clay for their pottery and for collection of the sweetgrass along the shores of the Ducktrap cove for baskets, mats and other uses.

The Ulmer brothers owed their business success at Ducktrap to Henry Knox's monetary support and patronage when they were first starting up their business ventures at Ducktrap Harbor after the Revolutionary War. The Ulmer brothers were given an opportunity to purchase their business complex and watershed acreage from proprietor Henry Knox in 1788 at reduced rates from other land-claim owners in the area. Through Knox's political connections, the brothers received the coveted commissions of justices of the peace.[1569] George Ulmer handled the surveying and lumbering of timber and oversaw the businesses at the sawmill, carding mill, flour mill and lime-burning businesses. The lime was quarried near Coleman Pond and was considered of the best quality. The limestone from the quarry was conveyed to the lime-burning furnace by means of horse-drawn carts. The brothers shared the operation of the general store that sold mercantile goods such as furniture, hardware items, all kinds of dry goods and housewares like candles, cloth and other personal items that were brought back to the Penobscot Bay area in their cargo vessels. Philip Ulmer managed the shipbuilding at "the Trap," the commercial import and export shipping, coastal cargo transports and merchant trading businesses, as well as the ships' chandlery store, which handled sailing and navigational needs of all kinds. The Ulmer brothers' sailing vessels were mostly coasters that traded along the coastline of the United States from Canada as far south as the Gulf of Mexico and the West Indies in the Caribbean. There were several merchant ships that were also built for transatlantic trade with Europe, the Mediterranean and other foreign ports.

Philip and George Ulmer supported and helped each other in their personal, business, political and military lives. Their uncle John, their cousin George Ulmer Jr. and their large families moved from Waldoboro in the mid-1790s to Rockland on the Penobscot Bay, where they built a large shipbuilding, cargo shipping, commercial trading and lime-burning complex near Fort Pine Hill on the shores of Clam Cove and Lermond's Cove that was very successful for many years. Casks made of staves and wooded barrel heads were assembled at the cooper shop by the road near the Ducktrap cove. As many as 1,500 casks at a time were shipped from Ducktrap to Rockland, where their cousin George Ulmer Jr., Uncle John and other family members had their business complex. They had a thriving shipyard, several mills, quarries, cargo shipping, mercantile trading and commercial lime-burning businesses. The Ulmer shipping and commercial trading enterprises eventually became the largest mercantile and lime-producing business complex on the eastern seacoast in the early 1800s, according to historians.

Henry Knox continued to be an intrusive business partner and micromanager in the Ulmer brothers' business complex at Ducktrap Harbor and cove for about twenty years. During this time, Henry Knox continued to receive financial dividends regularly. The Ulmer brothers suffered heavy business losses during the quasi-war with France and Britain that later led to the War of 1812. In 1797 and 1798, Philip Ulmer's cargo shipping business suffered huge financial losses due to the capture of two heavily loaded cargo ships by French privateers on the return voyage to the Penobscot. Over the next few years, the loss of investment interests that Philip held in other Penobscot trading vessels that were captured in the West Indies in the early 1800s became almost too much to bear financially. Since Henry Knox's financial fortunes were closely connected with his patronage in many frontier businesses like the Ulmer business enterprises, he suffered large financial losses as well. Knox's overextended business investments and land speculation caused deep declines in his financial wealth, and he was rapidly going bankrupt. Seeking to pay his mounting debts to creditors, Henry Knox demanded payment on the two business mortgages that he held on the Ulmer brothers' complex at Ducktrap Harbor and cove. The demand for immediate mortgage payment on his shipbuilding and cargo shipping businesses eventually caused Philip to sell his half-ownership in the Ulmer brothers' business complex at "the Trap" to Samuel A. Whitney Sr. around 1804.

In 1806, Philip sold his home as well as other assets which included a large tract of land to Samuel A. Whitney Sr., the greatest part located along the Ducktrap stream. Philip Ulmer had a house and barn built on land that Henry Knox had sold to him in 1798 on the eastern side of the Ducktrap stream next to George's large house.[1570] Jacob Ulmer, Philip's son, later became the second owner of the house near Ducktrap cove, which had been built by his father. Philip moved his family to another plot of land a mile back from the shoreline, where he had another house and barn built near Pitcher Pond. He remained in this house until his death. Samuel A. Whitney Sr. completely replaced Philip Ulmer in every aspect of his business and community life in Lincolnville. Samuel Whitney Sr. became a formidable presence and business competitor in Lincolnville and the Belfast vicinity. Philip continued to serve the Lincolnville community in civic activities and in more political ways as an elected legislator from his town and county to the House of Representatives in the Massachusetts legislature in order to provide for his family's needs. Philip continued to serve the Lincolnville community as a selectman and town moderator, often writing petitions to the Massachusetts General Court supporting the concerns of the county and the Lincolnville townspeople, until days before his death in October 1816.

Masonic and Military Endeavors

Washington never willingly gave independent command to officers who were not Freemasons. Nearly all of the members of his official family, as well as most other officers who shared his inmost confidence, were his brethren in the mystic tie.[1571]
—*Marquis de Lafayette*

Philip Ulmer might have been raised into the Masonic fraternity prior to the American Revolution. There is evidence that he became an active lodge member sometime during the war in the traveling military lodge with General Paterson, Colonel Vose and other army officers with whom he served. He was recorded as a member of the Masonic fraternity with the Massachusetts Grand Lodge after the Revolution, where he served as the Grand Lodge Treasurer, pro tem, representing the Grand Lodge of Massachusetts in the District of Maine.[1572] This would indicate that Philip had already been raised into the Masonic fraternity some years prior to 1794 and was knowledgeable about the Masonic rituals and degrees. The official Masachusetts State records indicate that Philip had already served in a Masonic lodge as a lodge officer and as a Worshipful Past Master in order to officially serve as a Massachusetts Grand Lodge Representative to Maine. Philip Ulmer was a charter member of two Masonic lodges in Maine: Hancock Lodge No. 4 at Castine in 1794 and Amity Lodge No. 6 at Camden in 1801. While under dispensation in 1799–1801, Philip served as the Worshipful Master of the Masonic lodge at Camden village, which met at a local inn. He served as Worshipful Master of the lodge on a number of occasions and in various other officers' stations over the years until his death in 1816. The Masonic lodge where Philip Ulmer was first raised as a Third-Degree Master Mason is still uncertain, but his initiation into the Masonic fraternity might have been at a traveling military lodge, called the American Union Lodge, when he served as a lieutenant in Washington's Continental Army. After this time, Lieutenant Philip Ulmer was often given independent duty and led his own detached company of troops.

General Lafayette developed a personal friendship with Lieutenant Philip Ulmer and Private George Ulmer sometime in early 1778 while stationed at Valley Forge. Lieutenant Ulmer served during the second Canadian Expedition in March 1778 with General Lafayette and with General Johann DeKalb, who spoke German but no English. Lieutenant Philip Ulmer most likely served the foreign generals as an experienced intelligence officer, as an American-German translator and interpreter and as a veteran officer who had served in the Canadian, New York and New Jersey Campaigns of 1776–78. After Philip Ulmer left Valley Forge in early April 1778, having completed his assignment with General Lafayette's cancelled Canadian campaign, his younger brother, George Ulmer, was advanced in rank to sergeant and likely became of service to General Lafayette's division with DeKalb's brigade as a translator and interpreter for his company in the First Massachusetts Regiment. Sergeant George Ulmer remained with the First Massachusetts Regiment after the American troops left Valley Forge, and he was actively engaged in the Battles of Germantown, Brandywine and Monmouth in New Jersey with Lafayette and DeKalb's troops (according to his obituary in January 1826). General Lafayette would have remembered the special service that the Ulmer brothers had rendered to him and to General DeKalb during this phase of the war.

After the Revolutionary War, General Lafayette returned to America for four months, at the invitation of General Washington in 1784, to clear up his military status and secure a settlement for American land grants for his military service. General Lafayette also wanted to thank some of the officers and soldiers in New England for their personal support and service that was given to him during the Revolutionary War. Lafayette made a short four-day visit to Portsmouth, New Hampshire, and the District of Maine accompanied by General Knox.[1573] General Lafayette met with General Henry Knox and General Benjamin Lincoln in Boston in the fall of 1784, and he took a trip to New Hampshire as a part of the "Victory Tour." During this time, Lafayette apparently took a brief sailing trip from Portsmouth along the coast of frontier Maine. The bond of friendship between General Lafayette and the American Patriots was strong enough that during Lafayette's visit to America in 1784, General Lafayette, General Lincoln and General Knox, who served as his host during the visit, paid a social call to the Ulmers at Waldoboro to thank the frontier soldiers for their valiant and heroic service during the Revolutionary War.[1574] Henry Knox, however, had other ulterior motives for hosting Lafayette's tour of Maine's wilderness seacoast. He wanted to show Lafayette and the other dignitaries his vast landholdings and the potential investment opportunities in the frontier Maine region. Knox wanted to show them the entrepreneurial spirit of Revolutionary War veterans like Philip and George Ulmer, who were developing settlements in the wilderness frontier and building new businesses in the Ducktrap watershed on the Penobscot Bay.[1575] The potential for financial investment, business growth and vast wealth was made obvious through the enterprising vision and hard work of frontiersmen like the Ulmer family at Waldoboro and at Ducktrap.

General Lafayette, General Knox and General Lincoln would have heard stories about the Penobscot Expedition in 1779 and the attempt to dislodge the British forces from Fort George on Castine. They would have likely heard about the heroic climb of McCobb's militia captain and his company of soldiers and volunteer U.S. Marines on the dangerous cliffs at Dyce's Head. As many as a third of the marines, militia volunteers, and Penobscot Indians lost their lives within twenty minutes' time in a hail of heavy gunfire. He might have learned about the heroic actions of Philip Ulmer's soldiers and U.S. Marines who had almost caused the surrender of the British forces at Fort George except for the indecision of the commanding officers. General Lafayette had certainly heard about the disastrous retreat of the American fleet up the Penobscot River that resulted in the fiery destruction of the entire American navy fleet commanded by Commodore Saltonstall. Saltonstall's and Lovell's indecision caused half of the American forces on the expedition to either be killed or declared missing. He might have learned that Captain Philip Ulmer had managed to hold his company together and had led General Wadsworth and other disoriented soldiers unfamiliar with the Maine wilderness through the dense forest to the safety of Fort Pine Hill at Camden.

Masonic Connections

The importance of the Masonic philosophy and fraternity was exemplified throughout Philip Ulmer's life. In his Masonic application for membership in the fraternity of Freemasons in frontier Maine, Philip Ulmer simply described himself in the records as "a sailor," and his brother, George Ulmer, described himself as "a surveyor," according to the official records of the Grand Lodge of Maine and at Amity Lodge No. 6 (in present-day Camden). Philip served as a lodge officer in the Hancock Lodge at Castine for some period of time in the 1790s. Philip Ulmer served many times as master, senior warden and treasurer of the lodge. Philip Ulmer was a charter member at the Hancock Lodge No. 4 at Castine in 1794 before it was burned during the British invasion in 1814. (The Hancock Lodge seal was found many years later wedged between two heavy beams of the burned building.) Philip helped to organize the interested men and lodge brothers who wanted to establish a lodge in their local Penobscot area. He helped to prepare the written request for a charter that was sent to the Grand Lodge of Massachusetts. He helped to assemble the necessary items and equipment to establish a successful Masonic lodge at Camden village. When the lodge brothers finally received the official charter from the Massachusetts Grand Lodge, the designated name given to the new lodge was Amity Lodge No. 6. Many of the military officers, state and town leaders and politicians whom Philip and George Ulmer had met and had served with during the American Revolution were also connected to the Ancient Free & Accepted Masons. Men such as General George Washington, Joseph Warren (who served as the first Grand Master of the Grand Lodge of Massachusetts prior to his death at Bunker Hill), General Nathaniel Greene, General Philip Schuyler, Paul Revere (who served as the second Grand Master of the Grand Lodge of Massachusetts), Samuel Adams, John Hancock, Dr. Thomas Warren, Benjamin Franklin, Benedict Arnold, General Lafayette, General John Glover, General von Steuben and many others were all members of the Masonic fraternity. Lodge meetings and initiations of new candidates were held at Morristown, Valley Forge and other encampments by military Masonic traveling lodges and were conducted by some of the officers and Masonic members mentioned above.

Unfortunately, the early Amity Lodge records were burned in a fire, so there is little reliable written evidence remaining about Philip and George Ulmer's years of service to the lodge except in early history accounts written by a few fraternity brothers. The Massachusetts Grand Lodge was able to provide some original Masonic records about Philip and George's lodge affiliations and offices in which they served. Philip Ulmer was one of three Master Masons who wrote the petition for Amity Lodge No. 6 to receive a charter from the Massachusetts Grand Lodge. He served as Worshipful Master of the "Federalist Lodge" (which was the suggested name by the petitioners) from 1799 to 1801 while under dispensation. When the charter was granted two years later, the official name was "Amity Lodge," which was considered a more appropriate name. During the early years of the Masonic lodge, brothers did not have a designated lodge building in which to hold their meetings. They met in a large meeting room at a local inn called "The Megunticook House" (later called "The Elms"), which was located in the village of Megunticook (in present-day Camden village).[1576] Philip's younger brother, George Ulmer, followed Philip's example as worshipful master, and he became the first officially recognized worshipful master of Amity Lodge No. 6, with Philip as his brother's senior warden, in 1801. Prior to Paul Revere's installation as most worshipful grand master of the Grand Lodge of Massachusetts in 1794, Philip Ulmer was recorded by the Massachusetts Grand Lodge in Boston as a charter member at the constitution of Hancock Lodge No. 4 at Castine, where he was seated as Grand Lodge Treasurer pro tem representing the Massachusetts Grand Lodge in the District of Maine on June 9, 1794. Philip and his brother, George Ulmer, were both recorded as charter members at the constitution of Amity Lodge No. 6. Amity Lodge No. 6 has not yet recognized their past worshipful master, Philip Ulmer, or his contributions to the Amity Lodge as an active lodge officer. The earliest Amity Lodge records were burned in a fire and unfortunately no longer exist. What is known about Philip's masonic service to Amity Lodge is that he was a worshipful master, senior warden and treasurer on a number of occasions as well as an officer who served in other lodge seats.

Philip Ulmer's Final Years

Honor does not waver in the wind;
like a rock, Honor must be practiced
in good times and bad, in peace and in war.
—Thomas Jefferson

I hope I shall possess firmness and virtue enough to maintain
what I consider the most enviable of all titles,
the character of an honest man.
—George Washington

On April 25, 1812, the Invalid Act was passed by the U.S. House of Representatives and the U.S. Senate in Washington to provide pension support of persons who were disabled or were invalids due to their military service in the Revolutionary War. The Invalid Act was approved and signed by Henry Clay, Speaker of the U.S. House of Representatives, and by William Crawford, president of the U.S. Senate, pro tem. The president of the United States, James Madison, signed the Invalid Act. The petition requests for government pensions of injured veterans were to be sent to the Department of War. Major Philip Ulmer had a legitimate reason to apply for the U.S. government military assistance program because of his leg injury acquired during the Penobscot Expedition in 1779. For many years, he had suffered with problems from his leg injury, which had never properly healed and had left him with a permanent limp. As Philip aged, it became increasingly difficult for him to perform physical labor and to earn a living. Efforts to provide for the needs of his wife, Christiana, and their young children at Ducktrap (Lincolnville) became an increasingly painful challenge. Philip's injured leg periodically became greatly swollen, and it caused him debilitating suffering in the later years of his life.[1577] In town meetings and during Masonic Ritual at lodge meetings, Ulmer was exempt from standing to read, to recite or to address the assembled gatherings.[1578] Because of his religious beliefs and his personal pride, Major Philip Ulmer refrained from applying for financial assistance when the Invalid Act was first enacted. As time passed, Philip reluctantly had to swallow his personal pride and accept the U.S. government's financial assistance program as an invalid Revolutionary War officer.[1579] Major Philip Ulmer applied for

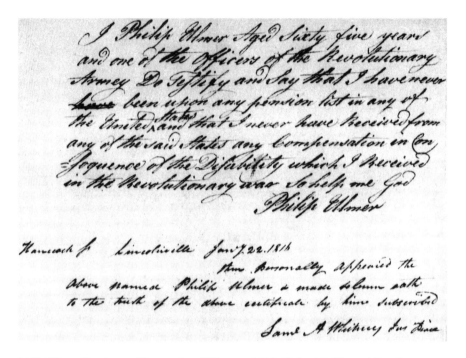

Philip Ulmer, Pension and Bounty Land Warrant, 1816. *National Archives and Records Administration, Washington, D.C.*

federal assistance on October 21, 1814.[1580] After reviewing Philip Ulmer's military petition, the supporting reports from his physical examinations by two government-approved doctors and the supporting documentation concerning the circumstances when Philip received his leg injury during the American Revolution, the U.S. Congress approved his request on January 11, 1815.[1581]

Major Ulmer was granted his military pension by the U.S. Department of War as an invalid officer. The following year, he reapplied for the government pension as an invalid, and it was promptly approved on February 1, 1816.[1582] Sadly, Philip Ulmer died on October 3, 1816, about eleven weeks before his sixty-fifth birthday.[1583] Philip appears to have died of complications from a growing infection in his leg from a war injury. There was no evidence found that either Philip or his widow received a state pension for his military service to the Commonwealth of Massachusetts during the Revolutionary War years or the War of 1812.

Philip Ulmer had suffered for years from his increasingly painful leg, but he seldom complained of his debilitating war injury. The townspeople of

Lincolnville called him "the old man" because of his permanent limp and his use of a cane to walk. Perhaps the term "the old man" was used out of affection, as Martha had referred to her husband, George Washington, or as young soldiers had often referred to their older commanding officers. Few people knew about Philip Ulmer's heroic actions on Lake Champlain in 1776 or at the Penobscot Bay in 1779, where he had received his leg injury during an attack upon the British fort. Fewer still were aware of Philip Ulmer's extensive military service to the fledgling nation or to the state of Massachusetts in defending the frontier coastline. The townspeople for whom he had served as a selectman were unaware of the suffering Philip had endured during the American Revolution or the additional damage to his disabled leg while protecting his family and the Lincolnville community during the War of 1812.

Philip Ulmer's last weeks in Lincolnville were so painful and debilitating that he could no longer stand up on his feet. Philip Ulmer's family and close friends provided him comfort and support during the final weeks and days before his death. Within a short period of time, his painful leg became quite swollen and infected. The infected leg weakened Philip's body, enabling the contamination to spread throughout his body, and soon led to his death. Philip Martin Ulmer died at his house on October 3, 1816, in the backcountry of the Ducktrap watershed near Pitcher Pond.[1584] He died a good death, as the soldiers would relate. Philip had died at his home surrounded by his loving family and not on a bloody battlefield far from home or in some lonely forest to be eaten by wild creatures like many soldiers. The family was comforted by their strong religious faith and readings from favorite family scriptures.

> *Those who wait upon the Lord will renew their strength;*
> *They will mount up with wings like eagles;*
> *They will run and not grow weary;*
> *They will walk and not faint*
> *—Isaiah 40: Verse 31*

> *My soul finds rest in God alone;*
> *My salvation comes from Him*
> *—Psalm 62: Verse 1*

Major Philip Ulmer's family, the military soldiers and officers with whom he served over the years, his Masonic lodge brothers from Amity Lodge No. 6, brother Masons who had once belonged to Hancock Lodge No. 4 and other

Maine lodges and representatives from the Massachusetts Grand Lodge would have attended his funeral service. Dressed in appropriate Masonic attire and in a solemn and dignified manner with muffled drumbeats, as was the custom at this time, the Masonic brothers and the militia officers and soldiers who had served with Major Philip Ulmer during the Revolution and War of 1812 escorted his body from his house and proceeded to the place of Philip's burial on "the Point" at Ducktrap Harbor. Ulmer family members from Waldoboro, Thomaston, Belfast and Lincolnville, as well as town officials, business and political friends and townspeople who knew and respected Philip's public service to the community gathered in the field at Ducktrap cove to attend Philip's funeral service. Being from a devout Lutheran family, Philip received an appropriate burial ceremony as well as the traditional Masonic Ritual funeral service at his gravesite beside the shores of the Penobscot Bay. At the top of Philip Ulmer's white marble headstone was the engraved Masonic square and compass resting upon the open Bible—the "Three Great Lights of Masonry." The open Bible symbolizes God's Holy Word in the writ of Holy Scripture, the square symbolizes truth and honest dealings with others and the compass symbolizes the importance of keeping one's life in bounds with other people. The evergreen sprigs placed upon Philip's chest by his Masonic brothers would symbolize hope of eternal life beyond the grave. Philip wore a white lambskin apron that symbolized purity and innocence before God. All of these Masonic virtues were manifested throughout Philip Ulmer's life. At the end of the Masonic burial ritual, artillery fire was heard echoing from the surrounding hills and adding to the empty feeling shared by the people who attended the burial ceremony. The artillery fire at the end of a military burial ceremony is a tradition that has endured to the present day in honor of our fallen and respected military officers and soldiers.

His body, we consign to Mother Earth;
His memory, we cherish here;
His spirit, we commend to God who gave it.
—Funeral Grand Honors from the Masonic Ritual

Well done, good and faithful servant!
You have been faithful with a few things;
I will put you in charge of many things.
Come and share your master's happiness!
—Matthew 25: Verse 21

Major Philip Ulmer's name, age and death date were inscribed on the white marble headstone below the Masonic symbols, along with his wife Christiana's name, age and, later, her death date. The fine white marble headstone was probably paid for by Philip's brother, George, the Ulmer relatives and possibly by donations from Philip's Masonic brothers. Christiana was left almost penniless, and she had no way of purchasing such a fine stone. Sadly, Major Philip Ulmer received only a short, one-line obituary acknowledgement in the Bangor newspaper with his name, town and the date when he died. Philip Ulmer rests in peace with his wife, with other early frontier settlers of Ducktrap and with a number of other Revolutionary War and War of 1812 military veterans whose graves are beginning to be recognized and honored. Their special resting place beside the Penobscot Bay at Ducktrap Harbor-cove deserves to be recognized and honored with a sign or appropriate plaque to identify these valiant and patriotic men who defended the United States in its darkest hours from enemy invasions from Canada and Europe.

Unfortunately, Philip Ulmer's family was left almost penniless with no means of financial support except from the U.S. government's military pension, which was only a few dollars a month. Philip's wife, Christiana Ulmer, was left as an aging widow with several children between nine and sixteen years of age who were still at home and needed care. As such, Christiana had little choice about her family's dire circumstances, her inability to work and their deteriorating living and health conditions. In desperation, Christiana Ulmer turned to the United States government for a continuance of her husband's small government assistance payment in order to survive and provide for her young children. She sent a private claim petition to the Department of War for a continuance of financial support for Major Ulmer's family and a personal appeal as a destitute widow. Her petition was referred to the U.S. House of Representatives for consideration.[1585] Christiana Ulmer's request was unfortunately rejected on January 29, 1817, about five weeks after her petition was submitted to the U.S. House of Representatives, Pensions and Revolutionary War Claims Committee.[1586] Having lost her husband so recently, the rejection was a terrible blow to the grieving widow and to Major Ulmer's young, dependent children. Major Philip Ulmer had given forty years of personal sacrifice and extensive military service to the state of Massachusetts, to the Lincoln County militia for the seacoast defense of Maine District and to the United States government as a U.S. Continental Army/Navy officer and as a deputy U.S. customs agent—often without receiving any military or government payment for many months or years at a time, if payment was given at all.

Christiana Ulmer's desperate appeal for a renewal of her husband's U.S. military pension was regrettably rejected.

The married children and later descendants of Major Philip Ulmer, Noah Miller and other militiamen who had participated in the November 1814 seizure of the British sloop *Mary* sent a government claim petition to the U.S. Committee of Commerce for the return of monies owed to the Maine Patriots who had captured the prize vessel. The monies from the seized enemy sloop had been delivered to the U.S. Treasury after the signing of the Treaty of Ghent, which ended the War of 1812. After an investigation, the claim petition report concerning the British sloop's capture was presented to the U.S. Senate by Mr. Davis from the Committee on Commerce on February 16, 1838. The claim was found to have strong merits. The Committee on Commerce upheld the claims that the petitioners made on February 16, 1838.[1587] Mr. Woodbridge submitted a report to the U.S. Senate from the Committee on Commerce having re-examined the claim petition referred to them on April 17, 1844, with an accompanying bill: S.156.[1588] It was not until the close of the Franklin Pierce presidency in 1857 that the final resolution about the capture of the British sloop *Mary* in late November 1814 was finally concluded. The federal funds were finally returned to the rightful owners and their heirs. Forty-three years had passed before the return of the government funds to the children and heirs of Major Philip Ulmer and to the families of the other militiamen involved in the November 1814 incident. It is hard to understand why the reimbursement of government funds took so many years since the claim petition was upheld by the U.S. government agencies in February 1838.

Major Philip Ulmer has never been properly recognized for his "continuous military service" to the American cause as a Massachusetts militia officer in the District of Maine from 1775 to 1783.[1589] He has never been properly recognized for his government service as a soldier in the Continental Army with the Massachusetts Line, service in the state militia in Lincoln County or service a naval officer during the most critical periods in the American Revolution. He never sought sympathy or compensation for his permanent leg injury until he was in an invalid state and had no choice but to seek assistance from the government for his prior military services to the country. Few people in the state of Maine know of Major Philip Ulmer's proud history of his military and personal sacrifices to the country and his public service to the state of Massachusetts and to the communities of Waldoboro and Lincolnville (Ducktrap) in Maine. Few know of Philip Ulmer's decision to sacrifice his career opportunity in the U.S. Navy as a sailing master in order to defend his county from unjust government acts and embargoes that threatened the lives and livelihoods of his family, his neighbors and his community. Few people know of his tenure as a Massachusetts congressman in the House of Representatives and the many letters and petitions he wrote on their behalf to the State of Massachusetts and to the federal government seeking relief for their communities and county from heavy taxation. Few people are aware of Philip Ulmer's efforts to salvage and refurbish the cannons and armaments that were sunk in the Penobscot River after the naval defeat in 1779 and use them to defend the coastal towns in frontier Maine from British raiding parties and enemy attacks by sea. Few are aware of his support of frontier Maine's first movements toward statehood prior to the War of 1812 or his service to the community in legal matters as a leader and spokesperson on state, county and local issues that impacted the lives of citizens in frontier Maine. He was man of integrity, and he had a sense of purpose. He was trusted by soldiers who served under his leadership and well respected by fellow officers in all matters assigned to him. Major Philip Ulmer, like so many other unrecognized soldiers, sailors and marines, will never be fully recognized or appreciated for the heroic struggles and sacrifices. Their heroic efforts have enabled future generations to enjoy the blessings of freedom, liberty and the opportunity to pursue their own destiny and prosperity. The vision and desire of our nation's early founders to form a new, united and independent American republic that would secure the civil rights and liberties of American citizens must be carefully guarded and protected.

GEORGE ULMER'S FINAL YEARS

George Ulmer lived for almost ten years after the death of his brother, Philip. There had always been a strong bond between the Ulmer brothers that related on different emotional and spiritual levels, as well as on a family level. Christiana continued to help care for George's invalid wife, Polly, and their adopted child, George Jr., with help from Polly's daughter, Mary Wilson, who had a family of her own by this time. Polly had suffered a debilitating stroke on her right side that had left her paralyzed and a blind invalid some years before 1818.[1590]

John Wilson, the son-in-law of George Ulmer, had bought out George's partnership in the Ulmer businesses at Ducktrap in 1807. John Wilson had become an intense business competitor of Samuel Whitney Sr. at "the Trap" for a number of years. John's partnership ultimately failed in the Ulmer-Wilson businesses at Ducktrap, and he eventually decided to seek his future and his fortune in the western territory of Ohio. The Louisiana Purchase and the Lewis and Clark Expedition had opened up new opportunities in the western frontier for exploration, land speculation, new settlements and new business opportunities for wealthy venture capitalists and adventurous pioneers and settlers. Some of Philip and George Ulmer's family members and cousins migrated westward from Salem, Massachusetts, and from the frontier district of Maine. They sought a new future and new opportunities to prosper in the unsettled and undeveloped western frontier beyond the Mississippi River. John Wilson and other pioneering adventurers like Reverend Seth Noble of Bangor (Maine) sought their fortunes in the new settlements that were springing up in the newly opened western territories—the new American frontier. John Wilson left Lincolnville and his family behind, and he went to the Ohio frontier to seek a new future for himself and his family. After spending several years in Ohio trying to establish a trading and shipping business, John Wilson returned to Lincolnville on horseback, penniless and unsuccessful in his business ventures. Wilson resumed his life with his wife, Mary, and their family in the backcountry of the Ducktrap watershed near Kimball's Brook, later called Kimball's Mill. He resumed a life in farming, land speculation, real estate sales and business trading activities in the Belfast vicinity, where he was very successful.[1591]

By 1815, George Ulmer no longer possessed any assessable property in Lincolnville and only two small parcels, one worth three hundred six dollars and the other sixty-three dollars, in two adjoining towns.[1592] George Ulmer, having lost his fortune and his political offices, retired to the backcountry, where he and Polly lived on his U.S. government pension near their daughter, Mary, and son-in-law, John Wilson.[1593] George Ulmer and John Wilson built a sawmill and gristmill at the Kimball Brook property, where George was able to earn a modest income for several years. In 1820, George remained actively interested and supportive of the Lincolnville community, where he built a town meeting house so that public meetings could be held at one place instead of in private residences or in schoolhouses.[1594] In 1823, George Ulmer's two namesake grandsons provided for their grandfather's needs on the property of Kendall's Mill on Kendall Brook for several years before

George's death. The sales agreement on the property owned by George's grandson at Kimball Brook stated: "It is hereby understood that my Grandfather George Ulmer, and my grandmother Mary [Tanner] Ulmer shall have the use of the Grist mill and Saw mill together with all machinery on the dams, or in the mills, with the use of as much land as they choose to improve during their lives."[1595] George earned a living with income from the store at Kimball's mill. He enjoyed spending time with his Russ and Wilson grandchildren who lived in the nearby Belfast vicinity and helped take care of his invalid wife, Polly.

In March 1820, Maine received its statehood as the twenty-third state under the Missouri Compromise. This allowed Maine to join the Union as a free state, with Missouri receiving statehood a year later as a slave state—preserving the numerical balance between free and slave states in the nation. Inhabitants throughout Maine held parades and had parties to celebrate Maine's statehood. There was a parade in the town of Belfast on Independence Day to celebrate this special event. Apparently, George Ulmer marched in one of the parades, dressed in his Revolutionary War uniform as a Massachusetts state militia major general (a political appointment), complete with his military sword. According to one of the Maine historians interviewed for this book, while the parade moved through the town with bands and people marching, some teenaged boys who were on the sidelines began to laugh, mock and loudly comment about George Ulmer, who was dressed in his old military uniform. General George Ulmer became infuriated with their mockery and disrespectful comments. He apparently attacked the teenagers, threatening them with his sword. General Ulmer and the teenagers had to be physically separated by the other spectators and held for the local Belfast sheriff. General Ulmer and the teenagers spent the night in the local jail, but in separate cells. The Belfast newspaper the *Hancock Gazette & Penobscot Patriot* apparently reported on the Independence Day parade and the unfortunate event between the state militia general and several rowdy teenaged boys. One can only imagine the heated exchange of language between the angry general and the impertinent teenagers. According to the article, General George Ulmer was released the next day, still angry at having been insulted.

General George Ulmer's health soon failed, and he became mostly housebound for the last two years of his life. He and his wife were cared for by family members. On December 23, 1825, George Ulmer died at his residence near Kimball's Mill.[1596] According to Jason Hill of Lincolnville, George Ulmer was buried in the field outside his house (now called the

Kendall House) with an engraved gray slate slab lying upon his grave.[1597] His body was later moved to the small cemetery at Ducktrap cove near his brother and his two children. After George's death, Mary (Polly) Ulmer lived with her daughter, Mary, and son-in-law, John Wilson, on their property in Belfast until her death around 1835 or 1836.[1598] She was buried beside her husband, George. Both George and Mary (Polly) Ulmer's bodies were later moved by his Masonic brothers from Amity Lodge No. 6 to the Mountain View Cemetery at present-day Camden, Maine. General George Ulmer was again buried with appropriate Masonic and military honors. This event occurred on the one-hundred-year anniversary of Amity Lodge's establishment.[1599] The original gray slate headstone marks General George Ulmer's final resting place with an inscription acknowledging his military, civic and political contributions to the state of Massachusetts and Maine, to his county and community and to the Masonic fraternity as the first official worshipful master of Amity Lodge No. 6. There were obituaries written for the local newspapers acknowledging George Ulmer's death and praising him for his many contributions as a successful businessman, magistrate, county sheriff and general in the Massachusetts state militia. Honors were given for his military service in the Revolution and as a senator in the Massachusetts General Court.

CHRISTIANA ULMER'S FINAL YEARS

Christiana Ulmer applied for her husband's military pension compensation on December 25, 1816 (Philip's sixty-fifth birthday), in the hope of receiving some kind of support to help sustain her life and that of her children still living at home in Lincolnville. The petition was reviewed on January 15, 1817, and referred to the Committee of Pensions and Revolutionary Claims. Christiana Ulmer's petition as the widow of invalid war veteran, Major Philip Ulmer, was again reviewed on January 28, 1817, and rejected on January 29, 1817.

Perhaps the town provided some support for the destitute widows, children and other residents in need. This was likely one of the infrastructure arrangements that was made while Philip was an active leader in the town. It is thought that George Ulmer and Philip's married children might have helped with the care of Philip's wife and youngest children still at home. It is probable that Philip's Masonic brothers assisted in the needs of Philip

Ulmer's family after his death. This would have been one of the charges and responsibilities of the Masonic brotherhood. Major Philip Ulmer's white marble footstone and Masonic headstone with the open Bible and the square and compass inscribed upon the top would indicate that he was held in high esteem and respect by his Masonic brothers. The inscription would indicate that Freemasonry was of great importance in Philip's life. His Masonic brothers likely provided the financial means for the impressive white marble stone and Masonic inscription since Christiana could not have afforded such a fine marble headstone and footstone as a marker. Christiana Ulmer died on December 3, 1829, in Lincolnville, Maine. She was buried with her husband and the love of her life, Major Philip Martin Ulmer, at "the Point" (today called Osgood Point) at Ducktrap Harbor-cove in Lincolnville, Maine. Their final resting place is next to their little niece Susanne "Sukey" Ulmer (who drowned at age four in Ducktrap Harbor) and young nephew George "Sudley" Ulmer Jr., both children of General George and Mary (Polly) Ulmer. The Ulmer family members and several other Revolutionary War Patriots who served with Major Philip Ulmer during the American Revolution and the War of 1812 may rest in the oldest burial site in the town of Lincolnville, Maine.

This was a very fitting setting for Philip and Christiana Ulmer's final peaceful resting place, overlooking the Penobscot Bay. In life and in death, Philip and Christiana Ulmer's lives were always connected to the freedom and spirit engendered by the beauty of Maine's wilderness environment and the constant ebb and flow of the sea. Many years have passed since Philip Ulmer and his wife died. Their love for America, their faith in God and their dedication to the townspeople of Waldoboro and Lincolnville have given life and spirit to the kind and generous people who live there. The Ulmer family helped to create the vibrant community and the infrastructure of the seacoast towns that many Mainers are proud to call home.

Conclusion

Major Philip Ulmer gave "continuous service on land and at sea from 1775 until the end of the Revolutionary War." [1600] The life of Philip Martin Ulmer exemplifies the life and times of other military soldiers, sailors and marines during the American Revolution and the War of 1812. Through Major Philip Ulmer's life story, the early history of our democratic American republic and the birth of the United States as a free and sovereign nation can be revealed through the prism of unfolding historical events. The silent voice and exemplary service of this dedicated and honorable American Patriot can finally be heard, recognized and honored. He serves as the quintessential young American citizen whose family came to America as immigrants from Europe and sought a new life in the unsettled wilderness frontier in a new country. They knew the oppressive nature of European monarchs, dictatorial rulers, religious dictates and dogmas and the enslavement of the individual in a feudalistic society. They came to America seeking a better life of freedom, liberty, business opportunities and self-determination. Major Philip Ulmer was among the first generation of American servicemen whose courage and personal sacrifices were far greater than we can even imagine. The profile of Philip Ulmer's life and the times in which he lived is an effort to bring to life one of the silent voices from the distant past who was a native son of eastern Massachusetts in the frontier district of Maine Province. Philip also serves as the quintessential American Patriot of his day—a man who had a deeply abiding religious faith; who was devoted to his family and friends; who loved his new country more than his own life; and who sought to leave behind a legacy of honor, integrity and justice for all people. He was willing to risk his most cherished possessions to ensure that his descendants would be able to live in a country where freedom, liberty and opportunity were protected for everyone.

The Revolutionary War Patriots made great personal sacrifices, they persevered under unimaginable deprivations and illnesses and they managed to survive severe weather conditions with little or no food, clothing, shelter or supplies. Thousands of American Patriots dedicated their lives and fortunes for the American cause, but many thousands never lived to see the results of their sacrifices. The early colonial settlers loved America enough that they were willing to fight and sacrifice their lives and fortunes for the freedom, liberty and opportunities that we take for granted today. The ideology of a democratic republic was a new concept—a great experiment—unknown in European countries, which were ruled by decree in a more feudalistic society.

The American Revolution was brought about by England's exploitation of America's colonial settlers in the thirteen colonies who were struggling to survive on the North American continent. The colonists in America sought to escape from European dictatorial rule and the escalating, imposed taxation of American citizens by an oppressive British government that sought to boost revenue in England's own treasury and lagging economy and to pay

England's war debts from constant warring against its European neighbors, especially France. The French Revolution was brought about by the over-taxation of the French citizens to pay for France's support of the American Revolution and its continuous warring against Great Britain for power, for economic dominance and for military supremacy in Europe and other parts of the world. The sentiments expressed by George Washington are as true today as they were when they were spoken during the American Revolution. In General Washington's address to the troops in 1776, he tried to inspire in the hearts of the soldiers the love of their country and indignation against its European invaders. In his General Orders to the Continental Army, General Washington said:

> *The time is near at hand, which must probably determine whether Americans are to be freemen or slaves; whether they are to have any property they can call their own; whether their houses and farms are to be pillaged and destroyed, and themselves consigned to a state of wretchedness, from which no human efforts will deliver them. The fate of unborn millions will now depend, under God, on the conduct and courage of this army. Our cruel and unrelenting enemy leaves us only the choice of a brave resistance, or the most abject submission. We have therefore to resolve to conquer or to die. Our own, our country's honor, calls upon us for a vigorous and manly exertion; and if we now shameful fail, we shall become infamous to the whole world. Let us then rely on the goodness of our cause, and the aid of the Supreme Being, in whose hands victory is, to animate and encourage us to great and noble actions. The eyes of all our countrymen are now on us, and we shall have their blessings and praise, if happily we are the instruments of saving them from the tyranny mediated against them. Let us therefore animate and encourage each other, and show the whole world that a freeman contending for liberty on his own ground is superior to any slavish mercenary on earth.*

In a later address to his army troops, General Washington urged them to remember that "liberty, property, life, and honour [*sic*] were all at stake; that upon their courage and conduct, rested the hopes of their bleeding and insulted country; that their wives, children, and parents expected safety from them only; and that they had every reason to believe that Heaven would crown with success so just a cause…"

George Washington's own words in his farewell address on September 17, 1796, expressed the struggles and sacrifices suffered by the brave men (and women) who fought for America's freedom and liberty. In President Washington's farewell address, "To the People of the United States," he stated in part:

> *You have, in a common cause, fought and triumphed together; the independence and liberty you possess are the work of joint counsels, and joint efforts, of common dangers, suffering and successes…Here every portion of our country finds the most commanding motives for carefully guarding and preserving the Union of the whole.*[1601]

Just two years after leaving the office of the presidency, George Washington died in his country home at Mount Vernon, Virginia, following a severe respiratory illness. His death on December 14, 1799, at sixty-seven years of age was mourned by American citizens throughout the country. In Europe, accolades and condolences were expressed to the American people and the U.S. Congress by sovereigns and citizens of many European countries. For those who knew George Washington and had served under his leadership, like George and Philip Martin Ulmer, his death was a devastating and personal loss. For months following his death, homage and special memorial services were given in recognition of George Washington in Massachusetts, where the American Revolution had first begun, and throughout the United States. George Washington's memorial service in Massachusetts and frontier Maine was held on February 23, 1800, and was carried out with great ceremony and reverence. America had been set upon a new destiny by men of vision, wisdom and integrity, like George Washington, and there was no turning back. The new republic, the United States of America, was based upon democratic ideals of freedom, justice and liberty, with a national Constitution and Bill of Rights, and was poised to write its own new history on the world stage.

> *With a heart full of love and gratitude I now take leave of you. I most devoutly wish that your later days many be as prosperous and happy as your former ones have been glorious and honorable.*
> —General George Washington, December 4, 1783

Williamstown portrait of George Washington. By Gilbert Stuart. *Courtesy of the Library of Congress.*

AUTHOR'S COMMENTS

On May 5, 2011, a small group of people, members of the Lincolnville Historical Society, made their way to Major Philip Ulmer's gravesite at "The Point" in Lincolnville, Maine, to honor him and to lay an appropriately decorated patriotic wreath upon his grave. He was a brave and honorable Revolutionary War Patriot who deserved to be acknowledged for his many civic, state and military contributions to the American cause. The early May morning was chilly and overcast with thick fog that hung over the Penobscot Bay. The respectful visitors gathered around Philip Ulmer's grave, where the author recalled the merits of Major Philip Ulmer's sacrifices and contributions during the Revolutionary War and the War of 1812, noting his heroic courage and his leadership during the wars. Some of the soldiers who served in Philip Ulmer's militia companies and served under his command throughout the years of enemy conflict are also buried near Major Ulmer at the private cemetery at Ducktrap Harbor-cove. Gratitude was expressed for the perseverance and patriotic service of the officers and soldiers who were willing to give their lives for the establishment of a new nation. The memorial wreath, made by the author, was presented at Major Philip Ulmer's grave with two American flags. The Lord's Prayer was recited, and the author's husband, Richard Hubert, a past master of Hiram Lodge No. 18 in Sandy Hook, Connecticut, and a district deputy for the Grand Lodge of Connecticut, recited the Masonic Funeral Ritual that would have been said 195 years ago at Philip Ulmer's burial. Sprigs of evergreen were laid upon the grave, followed by a minute of contemplative silence in honor of those men who had died. A parting benediction from the King James Bible was given at Philip Ulmer's gravesite, as it had been on the day of his burial:

Well done, thou good and faithful servant;
Thou hast been faithful over a few things;
I will make you ruler over many things;
Enter thou into the joy of Thy Lord.
—Matthew 25: Verse 21

As the ceremony ended, out of the heavy morning mist and thick fog, a young bald eagle suddenly appeared and soared low over the water, close to the tree-covered gravesite on the small peninsula on the shore of the Penobscot Bay. The bald eagle banked sharply, turned and again flew low over the water close to the bushes by the edge of the cemetery at "the Point." As we watched, the young eagle disappeared as quickly as it had come, back into the heavy misty fog over the Penobscot Bay. We were spellbound by the eagle's unexpected appearance and "fly-by." We stood in silence and wonder at what we had seen and experienced. As we left "the Point" and returned quietly along the narrow gravel pathway above the cove toward the cars, we turned back toward the Ducktrap Harbor-cove. We saw the young eagle suddenly reappear out of the mist and gently come to rest upon a treetop above the small cemetery. It was difficult to ignore the significance of the young bald eagle acknowledging our presence during the ceremonial event. It certainly gave the feeling to those present beside Philip's grave that all was well and at peace. It seemed as though Major Philip Ulmer's spirit was somehow present at this very special, sacred place.

EPILOGUE

The author of this book considers it a privilege and an honor to have discovered this remarkable, unknown American Patriot and frontiersman and to have had the opportunity to bring Philip Ulmer's biography to light for the general public to enjoy. He serves as an honorable example of the quintessential man of his generation. He was the son and grandson of European immigrants in the wilderness frontier of easternmost Massachusetts in Maine Province who lived through the French and Indian War, the American Revolution and the War of 1812. At the time of the Civil War (1861–65), there were about two dozen Ulmer men from Maine who fought on the Union side, and there were several in the Carolinas who fought on the side of the Confederacy. One of the young soldiers was fourteen-year-old George Thomas Ulmer, who served as a drummer boy with the Eighth Regiment from Maine beside his older brother, Charley Ulmer. Young George T. Ulmer kept a journal of his adventures during the Civil War entitled *Adventures and Reminiscences of a Volunteer Drummer Boy from Maine*. He wrote of his enlistment in the Eighth Regiment of Maine Volunteers of the Union army and of his wartime experiences with his brother, Charley, in the Southern Theater.[1602] George Thomas Ulmer and his brother, Charley, were two of the four sons of Mary W. (Thomas) and Philip Ulmer, believed to be the youngest son of Christiana and Major Philip M. Ulmer of Lincolnville.[1603] George Thomas Ulmer and his wife, Lizzy May Ulmer, a popular stage actress, eventually moved from the New England seacoast to the Ohio Territory seeking adventure and a new life in the West.

Soldiers who gave military service and received land-bounty claims in lieu of payment from the federal government exercised their land-claim options as western territories became open for settlement. Descendants of Philip and George Ulmer who lived in the vicinity of Lincolnville, Belmont and Belfast moved westward as government land became available in Ohio in the Western Reserve. The descendants of war veterans claimed land using their Patriot ancestor's land-bounty rights from the government. Ulmer cousins who were descendants of Uncle John Ulmer of Waldoboro and Thomaston (Maine) sought their fortunes in the westward movement beyond the Ohio frontier and Indiana Territory. Ulmer relatives have been identified in the states of New York, Pennsylvania, New Jersey, Ohio and in North and South Carolina. Other descendants have been discovered in the states of Georgia and Florida, as well as Illinois, Indiana, Kansas, Colorado, Arizona, California and Washington State.

Although the author is not a direct descendant of Major Philip M. Ulmer from Lincolnville, Maine, there is a connection through the Ulmer family in Ulm and Enzberg in the duchy of Baden-Württemberg, Germany. The author's Ulmer ancestral roots remained in Germany until the 1880s, when the author's great-grandparents, John Jacob (Johann Jakob) and Mary Elizabeth (nicknamed Mae or Maylee) Ulmer, immigrated to America and settled in the Philadelphia vicinity near relatives who had come to America at an earlier time. The author's grandparents were married in Pennsylvania and moved to New Jersey, where they raised two children—a daughter, Frances May Ulmer, and a son, Arthur D. Ulmer. Frances May Ulmer was the author's grandmother. She married an Englishman, George Thomas Miller (the author's grandfather), who was a mechanical and electrical engineer and eventually became a vice-president of the New Jersey Electric Company in the early years of the industry. He became involved in the electrification of the coal mines at Carbondale and at other mining towns in eastern Pennsylvania. George Thomas Miller, who was too old to actively serve in World War II, was involved in the secret development of the atomic bomb in what was known as the Manhattan Project. His skilled knowledge of electrical engineering and mechanical design helped in the development of the trigger and detonating mechanism in the atomic bomb. The devices were later used in the two bombs that were dropped on Japan that swiftly brought an end to World War II.

Frances Mae (Ulmer) and George T. Miller raised three sons—John Robert Miller (the author's father), George Ulmer Miller and Robert Francis Miller—who were involved in World War II in various branches of the American armed services. George Ulmer Miller was injured in a pyrotechnic explosion that blinded him prior to the declaration of war in World War II. Army colonel John R. Miller, a Columbia University graduate, was a mechanical and chemical engineer involved in the research, design and evaluation of the nuclear test trials at the White Sands Proving Grounds in New Mexico. After World War II, he served with Pratt & Whitney Aircraft in Connecticut to develop procedures and designs for jet and turbine engines for aircraft. He later served as an engineer in the design of the propulsion engines and air filtration systems for the Nautilus and Trident class submarines in Groton, Connecticut. These pursuits led to further service with an engineering company that designed the Saturn booster thrusters for NASA. He held six patents in the field of energy production and rocket propulsion systems designed for the Saturn/Apollo space programs in the 1960s. He served on the team of design engineers for the booster and landing thrusters for the space capsule *Eagle*, which resulted in the first successful landing of American astronauts on the moon. He was later involved with the design team for the LEM moon vehicle that facilitated the movement of the U.S. astronauts on the surface of the moon.

Navy chief petty officer Robert F. Miller served in World War II in the Atlantic, Mediterranean and Pacific Theaters, where he served on navy ships that transported troops to their invasion assignments in Europe, Africa, Italy and in the Pacific campaign in the Marshall Islands, Guam, the Marianas Islands and Okinawa. He served with the occupation forces that sailed into Tokyo Harbor, and later Nagasaki Harbor, at the surrender of Japan before returning to the United States. He wrote a journal and documented his experiences during World War II in his book *"The Mighty G": Destroyer DD 423 USS* Gleaves, which was published in 2005 and is presently found in the Library of Congress. George Ulmer Miller served as a congressional lobbyist for a manufacturing company that produced military supplies and provided services to the U.S. government during World War II and the Korean War.

After peace was restored in Europe at the end of World War II, damaged parts of the Baron von Ulm castle were repaired, and the castle was used as a children's home for displaced and orphaned German children. The ancestral castle that once belonged to the von Ulm (Ulmer) family prior to the 1900s still remains on the hilltop overlooking the town of Ulm and the Lutheran Ulm Minster (Ulmer Münster) Cathedral.

In the present generation, one of the Ulmer family descendants, Colonel Lawrence W. Miller (son of John Robert Miller and the author's brother), served as a medical doctor and military advisor for medical needs and services in army hospitals overseas during the Vietnam War in Nuremberg, Germany, and during the Desert Storm and Desert Shield campaigns in Saudi Arabia. Other Ulmer family descendants have carried on the tradition of public and military service, exhibiting a determination to serve the public good through medical research and medical services, education and through work in the field of science and engineering, just as their Ulmer ancestors served many generations before. The Ulmer family history serves as a quintessential example of the many immigrant families who came to America seeking freedom, opportunity and a new way of life in the wilderness frontier of North America. Through hard work, perseverance, educational pursuits and service, they helped create a new nation unlike any other that had existed before.

Whatever the future might hold for America, brave and dedicated soldiers, sailors and marines—like those found in this book—will stand resolute and ready to defend the United States of America. America's servicemen and servicewomen bravely work to uphold the standards and ideals that their forefathers fought, bled and died to achieve for posterity. Their suffering and sacrifices on behalf of our nation have ensured the blessings of freedom, liberty, justice under law and equality that all American citizens enjoy today.

Appendix A

Pension Petition of Philip Ulmer

The following pages show the actual pension petition of Philip Ulmer with his signature.

United States of America

To the Honorable Senate and Honorable House of Representatives in Congress assembled.—The petition of the undersigned respectfully represents, that in the year 1775 he engaged with all the ardor of youth, in the Military service of his Country, first as a Sergeant in a Company of infantry in the 25th Continental Regiment Commanded by Col William Bond, (which Regiment was one of the first that Marched into Canada after General Montgomery's Defeat,) and in the year 1776 he was promoted to an Ensign in said Regiment, and soon after Detached to Command the Schooner Isabella *of eight Guns, in the Rivers St. Laurence ((and)) Sorrell until our Defeat ((---)) Canada, and he then returned to his Station in the Army and early in 1777 Received a first Lieuts. Commission in the first Massachusetts Regiment Commanded by Col Joseph Vose, and in the year 1778 he was Discharged from the Service at his own request on account as was well known at the time by his Superior officers as well as those of his own grade, of his having been Superseded by the appointment of another to fill the vacancy of a Captain to which your petitioner thought he had Senior pretentions—In 1779 your Petitioner had the honor to Command a Detached Company of Melitia [sic] in the unfortunate expedition against the British who had made a Lodgment and fortified on Majorbagaduce on the mouth of the Penobscot, ((and)) in a Sortie made by a Detachment of volunteers on the Day previous to the raising of the Siege (to wit the 14th*

United States of America

To the Honorable Senate and Honorable House of Representatives in Congress assembled — The petition of the undersigned Respectfully represents, that in the year 1775 he engaged with all the ardor of youth, in the Military service of his Country, first as Serjeant in a Company of Infantry in the 25th Continental Regiment Commanded by Col William Bond, which Regiment was one of the first that Marched into Canada after General Montgomerys Defeat, & in the year 1776 he was promoted to an Ensign in said Regiment, and soon after Detached to Command The Schooner Isabella of eight guns, in the Rivers St Lawrence & Sorrell untill our Defeat in Canada, he then returned to his Station in the army and early in 1777 Received a first Lieuts Commission in the first Massachusetts Regiment Commanded by Col Joseph Vose, and in the year 1778 he was Discharged from the Service at his own request on account as was well known at the time by his Superior officers as well as those of his own grade, of his having been Superseded by the appointment of another to fill the vacancy of a Captain to which your petitioner thought he had Senior pretentions — In 1779 your Petitioner had the honor to Command a Detached Company of Melitia in the unfortunate expedition against the British who had made a Lodgment and fortified on Major Bagaduce in the mouth of the Penobscot, & in a Sortie made by a Detachment of vollunteers on the Day previous to the raising of the Seige (To wit the 14th of august) he was wounded in the thigh by a Grape Shot from the Enemys Batterys — the immediate effect was a large Contusion which in two or three weeks mostly Subsided, and indicated no lasting ill Consequences, yet your petitioner has reason to beleive that a pain long and frequently and Severely felt and a Debility Constantly experienced in the limb, owe their origin to the aforesaid wound, This Conclusion is Corroborated by the opinion of Sundry Respectable Gentlemen of the faculty, who have been Consulted upon the Subject — your Petitioner however was not immediately totally Disqualified for the Service, In 1780 he was appointed with the Rank of Major to Command Certain Companies of Detached Melitia, from the Counties of York Cumberland and Lincoln, Stationed at Camden for the Defense of that extreme frontier against the Incursions of the Enemy at Penobscot When the Beams of peace and Independance Dawned upon our Country your petitioner then in the prime and vigor of life, which for a season Maintained an asendancy over the effects of his wound —

Turned his attention to Civil avocations and was thereby enabled to rear and support a Numerous family in a Decent, yet humble grade of life, and while he enjoyed this filicity he felt A Reluctance to making any application to Goverment for assistance — his hopes were Revived when in 1809 he was appointed Sailing Master in the navy of the united States Dismissing other pursuits he was at Considerable trouble and expence to equip and Qualify himself for the Duties of his Station, but by a Circular order from the Navy Department he was Deranged at the expiration of three months from the Date of his appointment — he now finds himself without Resources or employment in the vale of life and Sinking under the Decays of Nature accelerated by his past Services and Sufferings in the Cause of his Country — he is poor or otherwise he would Still be silent without any Certain income or practicable means to Supply the wants of a family which (altho lessoned by the Settlement of some of his Children) is not Small — He appeals to the Justice Generosity and Laws of his Country and prays your Honors that he may receive a pension as Some releif in the eve of life (which Cannot be long) begging leave to Refer your Honors to other Documen (Respecting his Services) which were left on the files of Congress last Session, and pass Such order thereon as Shall be Honorable to the Nation and Equitable to the old Infirm Soldier and as in Duty bound Shall Ever pray

                                                Philip Ulmer

Lincolnville { Dist of M E
October 3rd 1814

Opposite: Philip Ulmer, memorial pension petition, October 1814. *National Archives and Records Administration, Washington, D.C.*

Above: Philip Ulmer, memorial pension petition, page 2. *National Archives and Records Administration, Washington, D.C.*

of august) he was wounded in the thigh by a Grape shot from Enemy Batterys [sic]—
*the immediate effect was a large Contusion which in two or three weeks mostly subsided,
and indicated no lasting ill Consequences, yet your petitioner has reason to believe that
a pain long and frequently and Severely felt and a Debility Constantly experienced in
the limb, owe their origin to the aforesaid wound. The Conclusion is corroborated by the
opinion of Sundry Respectable Gentlemen of the facility, who have been Consulted upon
the Subject—your petitioner however was not immediately and totally Disqualified for
((active)) Service. In 1780 he was appointed with the Rank of Major to Command
Certain Companies of Detached Melitia* [sic], *from the Counties of York, Cumberland
and Lincoln, Stationed at Camden for the Defense of that extreme frontier against the
Incursions of the Enemy at Penobscot—When the Beams of peace and Independence
Dawned upon our Country your petitioner then in the prime and vigor of life, which for
a Season Maintained an ascendancy over the effects of his wound—Turned his attention
to Civil avocations and was thereby enabled to rear and Support a Numerous family in a
Decent, yet humble, grade of life, and while he enjoyed this felicity he felt A Reluctance
to making any application to Government for assistance—his hopes were Revived when
in 1809 he was appointed Sailing Master in the navy of the united States Dismissing
other pursuits he was at Considerable trouble and expence* [sic] *to equip and Qualify
himself for the Duties of his Station, But by a Circular order from the Navy Department
he was Deranged at the expiration of three months from the Date of his appointment—
he now fin((ds)) himself without Resources or employment in the vale* [sic] *of life and
Sinking under the Decays of Nature accelerated by his past Services and Sufferings in
the Cause of his Country—he is poor or otherwise he would Still be silent without any
Certain income or practicable means to Supply the wants of a family which (although
lessoned by the Settlement of some of his Children) is not Small—He appeals to the
Justice Generosity and Laws of his Country and prays your Honors that he may receive
a pension as Some relief in the eve of life (which Cannot be long) Begging leave to Refer
your Honors to other Document((s)) Respecting his Services which were left on the files of
Congress last Session, and pass Such order thereon as Shall be Honorable to the Nation
and Equitable to the Infirm Soldier and as in Duty bound Shall Ever pray.*

*Lincolnville
October 3rd: 1814
Philip Ulmer*
[Good signature in same writing as whole document.]

Appendix B

Pension Petition of Christiana Ulmer

The Petition of Christiana Ulmer, widow of Major Philip Ulmer, for the extension of her husband's Revolutionary War pension to provide for the care of the Ulmer children (still young at home) and for her own care in her elder stage of life. The petition reads:

United States

To the Honor[able] *Senate & House of representatives in Congress assembled,*

The memorial of the undersigned widow of Philip Ulmer lately deceased, respectfully represents that her late husband devoted his early manhood to the service of his country in the revolutionary war, & had the misfortune to be wounded in the thigh by the enemy's shot at the siege of majabigueduce [sic] *on the mouth of the Penobscot river, the painful & debilitating effects of which accompanied him through life & increased with his increasing years…late in life he made application to his country for relief, & your Honors were pleased to place him on the pension List…that within eight months thereafter he died & left your memorial list in circumstances of extreme indigence, houseless, moneyless, friendless, in the vale of years & afflicted with a distress, chronical* [sic] *complaint: wherefore she implores your Honors' commiseration in extending to her the pension settled on her late husband or such part thereof as your honors, in your wisdom & goodness, shall see fit to bestow.*

& as in duty bound will ever pray thee
Lincolnville M.E.
Christiana Ulmer.
Dec. 25, 1816

Christiana Ulmer, memorial pension petition, December 25, 1816. *National Archives and Records Administration, Washington, D.C.*

The petition was referred to the Committee on Pensions and Revolutionary Claims on January 15, 1817. The petition was considered on January 28, 1817, and was reported rejected on January 29, 1817.[1604]

Notes

Overview of Philip Ulmer's Military Life

1. Whitaker and Horlacher, *Broad Bay Pioneers*, 131, 448; Chronology 1770–1779. This includes some of the earliest Revolutionary War muster rolls of the Broad Bay settlement.
2. Ibid., 447–49.
3. Ibid., 131–32; Stahl, *History of Broad Bay and Waldoboro*, 1: 456.
4. Lefkowitz, *Benedict Arnold's Army*, 9–15.
5. General George Ulmer obituary, *Hancock Gazette* and *Penobscot Patriot*, dated January 11, 1826.
6. Ibid.
7. Wright, *The Continental Army*, Colonel Gardner's Regiment; Walton, *The Army and Navy of the United States*, Chronological Record of Battles and Engagements of the Revolution, 1775; Bunker Hill, June 17, 1775. "Paterson's and Gardner's [regiment] with that of General Ward went forward in the afternoon…A part of Gerrish's and a part of Ward's regiment covered the retreat."; Frothingham, *History of the Siege of Boston*, 179.
8. Walton, *The Army and Navy of the United States*, Chronological Record of Battles and Engagements of the Revolution, 1775; Bunker Hill, June 17, 1775; Frothingham, *History of the Siege of Boston*, 179.
9. Frothingham, *History of the Siege of Boston*, 179.
10. Ibid.
11. Commonwealth of Massachusetts, Historical Marker Database: Prospect Hill Markers.

12. Stahl, *History of Old Broad Bay and Waldoboro*, 451, 456.

13. Whitaker and Horlacher, *Broad Bay Pioneers*, 584–85; Stahl, *History of Broad Bay and Waldoboro*, 446–53, 584. Statement on page 452: "The revolutionary service records of the Waldoborough soldiery is a tangled nightmare…In the main, the record of the Waldoborough soldiery in such matters as honorable (service), far above the average." See page 584 for some of Philip's military history with the Continental Army; Massachusetts Continental Line: Ulmer, Philip—"Sergeant in the 25th Regiment of the Continental Army; Continuous service on land and sea from 1775 until the end of the war…"

14. Drake, *History of Middlesex County*, 285; Frothingham, *History of the Siege of Boston*, 180.

15. Commonwealth of Massachusetts, Historical Marker Database: Prospect Hill Markers.

16. Whitaker and Horlacher, *Broad Bay Pioneers*, 453.

17. Ibid.; Nelson, *Benedict Arnold's Navy*, 68, 71.

18. Whitaker and Horlacher, *Broad Bay Pioneers*, 453; Nelson, *Benedict Arnold's Navy*, 94.

19. Stahl, *History of Old Broad Bay and Waldoboro*, 454.

20. Lefkowitz, *Benedict Arnold's Army*, 34–35.

21. Abbot et al., *Papers of Washington Revolutionary War Series*, 2: 432–33.

22. Stahl, *History of Old Broad Bay and Waldoboro*, 452–54.

23. Ibid., 453; Lefkowitz, *Benedict Arnold's Army*, 39.

24. Whitaker and Horlacher, *Broad Bay Pioneers*, 450.

25. Smith, *Arnold's March*, 389; Lefkowitz, *Benedict Arnold's Army*, 148.

26. Stahl, *History of Old Broad Bay and Waldoboro*, 453.

27. Ibid., 452–53; Lefkowitz, *Benedict Arnold's Army*, 41.

28. Stahl, *History of Old Broad Bay and Waldoboro*, 452.

29. Maine Archives, Revolutionary War papers of (Johann) Valentin Minck: "…In 1775 I enlisted to serve on a privateer in army of American Revolutionary War in Mass line and Continental Establishment to serve against the Common Enemy, under Capt Fuller in Bond's Reg't." Sergeant Philip Ulmer also served in Captain Fuller's company with Colonel Bond's regiment; Whitaker and Horlacher, *Broad Bay Pioneers*, 405.

30. Clark, *Naval Documents of the American Revolution*, Volume 2, *Manvide's Journal*, 932; Nelson, *George Washington's Secret Navy*, 190.

31. Department of the Navy, *Dictionary of American Naval Fighting Ships*.

32. Ibid.

33. Commonwealth of Massachusetts, Historical Marker Database: Prospect Hill Markers.

34. Revolutionary War Pension and Bounty-Land Warrant Application Files (Washington, D.C.: NARA); Philip Ulmer, Continental Massachusetts, Pension number: S 19963. Recorded in the Congressional Committee Records in Washington, D.C., Philip Ulmer, October 21, 1814. (See transcript at end of document written by Philip Ulmer.)

35. Ibid.

36. Commission granted by the Continental Congress to Philip Ulmer on April 20, 1776, and signed by John Hancock: *The Bangor Wig and Courier*, September 30, 1887, Volume 54, Number 231; Document in possession of Philip Ulmer's grandson, Captain John Bennett of New York.

37. Whitaker and Horlacher, *Broad Bay Pioneers*, 308; Clark, *Naval Documents of the American Revolution*, 1,078. Revolutionary War Pension and Bounty-Land Warrant Application Files, Philip Ulmer, File number 19963; Force, *American Archives*, 3: 1,693, Return of Provisions, Military Stores, Ordinance and Ordnance Stores on board the schooner *Isabella* and several vessels under the command of Brig. General Prescott, bound for Quebec. November 19–20, 1775.

38. Whitaker and Horlacher, *Broad Bay Pioneers*, 308; Clark, *Naval Documents of the American Revolution*, 1,078. Revolutionary War Pension and Bounty-Land Warrant Application Files, Philip Ulmer, File number 19963.

39. Smith, *The Life and Public Services of Arthur St. Clair*, 1: 25. Taken from the St. Clair Papers; Force, *American Archives*, Fifth Series, 1: 630.

40. Force, *American Archives*, Fifth Series, 1: 630; Ticonderoga, New York: July 28, 1776, Colonel St. Clair, "First Public Reading of the Declaration of Independence," and reported in the *Pennsylvania Evening Post*, August 15, 1776; *New York Journal*, August 15, 1776; *New York Packet*, August 15, 1776; *New York Gazette and the Weekly Mercury*, August 19, 1776.

41. Nelson, *Benedict Arnold's Navy*, 259, 263.

42. Clark, Morgan and Crawford, *Naval Documents of the American Revolution*, 6: 371. Colonel Arnold's letter to General Gates, August 31, 1776; Nelson, *Benedict Arnold's Navy*, 265–66; Sparks, *Correspondence of the American Revolution*; Benedict Arnold letter to Horatio Gates, August 31, 1776.

43. National Archives, Subject file: U.S. Navy, 1775–1910, B.O. Ordnance Equipment, Box 152; Sparks, *Correspondence of the American Revolution*, Volume 1; Benedict Arnold letter to Horatio Gates, August 31, 1776; Maine Archives, Maine 2208; [Act of March 3, 1843] Recorded in Book A, Volume 1, page 4: Petition statement of Miriam Farrow, for widow's

pension of Ezekiel Farrow, Continental (Mass) service ID number: W 23045; Boat service on Lake Champlain 1776; sworn to on July 7, 1838; Probate for the State of Maine, October 13, 1838; service proved by the Honorable Ebenezer Thatcher, Lincoln County Court Judge; Bratten, *The Gondola* Philadelphia, Table 5.1, 57; Nelson, *Benedict Arnold's Navy*, 263; Lundeberg, *The Gunboat* Philadelphia, 30.

44. Revolutionary War Pension files, M804.958; Massachusetts Archives: Continental (Mass.), W# 23045: Ezekiel Farrow: Boat service on Lake Champlain; [Act of March 3, 1843] Recorded in Book A, Volume 1, Page 4; Maine: 2208. Certificate of Pension sent to Ezekiel Farrow's widow, Miriam Farrow, Wiscassett [*sic*], Maine. Recorded in the pension declaration statement: "…in July 1776 he was in service as mate of the *Spitfire* by order of Brigadier General Arnold with Captain Philip Ulmer…" In an oath statement of Ezekiel's brother, John Farrow, who served with his brother in Bond's regiment with Philip Ulmer, he states that his brother "Ezekiel Farrow was taken out of our said company sometime during the summer and put on board a Gun Boat to afsist [*sic*] in manning her and was pointed Lieutenant of her…"

45. Crockett, *Vermont*, 19; "The crewmen from the *New Jersey* were taken aboard the galley *Washington*, and the crew of the *Spitfire* were taken aboard the *Congress*."

46. Sparks, *Correspondence of the American Revolution*, Volume 1; Benedict Arnold letter to General Gates, October 15, 1776.

47. Ibid.

48. Ibid.

49. Wilkinson, *Memoirs of My Own Time*, Volume 1.

50. Crockett, *Vermont*, 23.

51. Wright, *The Continental Army*, 203, 212, 213.

52. Fischer, *Washington's Crossing*.

53. Wright, *The Continental Army*, 203, 204, 212, 213.

54. Revolutionary War Pension and Bounty-Land Warrant, Pension Records: Philip Ulmer, file number 19963.

55. Massachusetts Secretary of the Commonwealth, *Massachusetts Soldiers and Sailors*, 16: 249.

56. Revolutionary War Pension and Bounty-Land Warrant application records, Philip Ulmer, file number 19963; Philip Ulmer's written application statement to Congress about his Revolutionary War service NARA.

57. Hieronimus and Cortner, *Founding Fathers, Secret Societies*, 44–48.

58. Ibid., 45.

59. Wright, *The Continental Army.* Reference: Colonel Vose's Regiment, 1777–1779.

60. Ibid., 203, 212, 213.

61. Massachusetts Secretary of the Commonwealth, *Massachusetts Soldiers and Sailors in the War of the Revolution*, 16: 249. Information also found in the New York State Library, CMA call number: 973.3444 qA2.

62. Ibid.

63. Massachusetts Secretary of the Commonwealth, *Massachusetts Soldiers and Sailors*, 249; Records of Valley Forge; Maine Militia Companies: Colonel Vose regiment; Whitaker and Horlacher, *Broad Bay Pioneers*, 308.

64. Lesser, *The Sinews of Independence*; Valley Forge Muster Roll, Returns of Division and Brigade Commanders in the Continental Army: 4th Division: Maj. Gen. Baron Johann de Kalb; 2nd MA Brigade: Brig. Gen. John Glover; 1st MA. Regiment: Colonel Joseph Vose Regiment. 1st Lieutenant Philip Ulmer is listed in Col. Vose's Regiment at Valley Forge; Sons of the American Revolution, *Maine at Valley Forge*, 42; 4th Division: Maj. Gen. Baron Johann de Kalb; 2nd MA Brigade: Brig. Gen. John Glover; 1st MA. Regiment: Colonel Joseph Vose regiment, Captain Abraham Hunt's company, 1st Lieutenant Philip Ulmer.

65. Goold, *Falmouth Neck in the Revolution*, 49.

66. Stahl, *History of Old Broad Bay and Waldoboro*, 469; Eaton, *History of Thomaston, Rockland, and South Thomaston, Maine*.

67. House of Representatives, *Digested Summary*, Volume 3; Petition Claim of Major Philip Ulmer's widow, Christiana Ulmer; Congress 14, Session 2, Journal Page 205; Referred to Committee on Pension and Revolutionary Claims on January 18, 1817.

68. Revolutionary War Pension and Bounty-Land Warrant application records, Philip Ulmer, file number 19963; Philip Ulmer's application statement to Congress. Also see the testimonies of Ezekiel Dodge, Isaac Bernard, Joseph Coombs and Alexander Kelloch, who were eyewitnesses to "Philip's valor and severe injury to his thigh which left him lame"; Stahl, *History of Old Broad Bay and Waldoboro*; Robinson, *History of Camden and Rockport*; Whitaker and Horlacher, *Broad Bay Pioneers*.

69. Stahl, *History of Old Broad Bay and Waldoboro*; Whitaker and Horlacher, *Broad Bay Pioneers*; Robinson, *History of Camden and Rockport*.

70. Whitaker and Horlacher, *Broad Bay Pioneers*; Stahl, *History of Old Broad Bay and Waldoboro*.

71. Stahl, *History of Old Broad Bay and Waldoboro*.

72. Dunnack, *The Maine Book*, 92.

73. Commonwealth of Massachusetts, *Massachusetts Soldiers and Sailors*, 249.

74. Ibid.; Stahl, *History of Old Broad Bay and Waldoboro*, 584–85.

75. Lincolnville Historical Society, *Lincolnville—Early Days*, 1: 9, 21–23.

76. Callahan, *List of Officers*, U.S. Navy Officers: 1798–1900. "U," Ulmer, Philip: Sailing Master, February 6, 1809. Warrant revoked May 8, 1809; revised edition, Department of the Navy, *Officers of the Continental and U.S. Navy and Marine Corps*.

77. Smith, *Borderland Smuggling*, 2–3.

78. Robinson, *History of Camden and Rockport*, 187.

79. Seymour, *Tom Seymour's Maine*, 10.

80. Robinson, *History of Camden and Rockport*, 158.

81. Williamson, *The History of the State of Maine*, 2: 639.

82. Ibid., 646; Seymour, *Tom Seymour's Maine*, 15.

83. Massachusetts General Court, *Acts and Laws of the Commonwealth of Massachusetts*, Chapter 69 (Boston: Young & Minns, 1796), reprint by Wright & Potter Printing Company, 1896; "Resolve on the Petition of Philip Ulmer and others, allowing them to raise a sunken ship on the Penobscot River"; page 324. The Resolve reads: "On the petition of Phillip [*sic*] Ulmer & others praying for leave to raise the wreck of a Vessell, [*sic*] which was sunk in the Harbour [*sic*] of Cape Jellison at the time of the attack upon Penobscott [*sic*] in the late war. *Resolved:* that Phillip [*sic*] Ulmer, John Pendleton, Hezekiah French, George Ulmer, Adam Rogers be & they hereby are permitted and allowed, at their own expence, [*sic*] to raise the wreck of the Vessell [*sic*] which belonged to the Penobscot Fleet and was sunk in the harbour [*sic*] of Cape Jellison near the mouth of the Penobscot River—and that all the right & title of the Commonwealth in the said Vessell [*sic*] be relinquished to the said Phillip, [*sic*] John, Hezekiah, George & Adam in case they succeed in attempting to raise the same—*Provided* they Effect the purpose aforesaid within one year from passing this Resolve…March 10, 1797."

84. National Archives and Records Administration, Revolutionary War Pension and Bounty-Land Warrant Application Files, (Washington, D.C.) Records of the Department of Veteran Affairs, Record Group 15, Survivor's Pension Application File, NARA. Microfilm publication M804, Roll 2434. Philip Ulmer, Continental Massachusetts, Pension number: S 19963; also Recorded in the *Congressional Committee Records*:

Washington, D.C.; Philip Ulmer, 21 October, 1814. Survivor's Pension Application File, NARA.

85. Lincolnville Town Records; records recently transcribed by staff members of the Lincolnville Schoolhouse Museum and Historical Society.

86. Bangor Gazette, *The Bangor Historical Magazine*, Volume 6 (Bangor, Maine: J.W. Porter, 1891), 156; …Deaths copied from Bangor Gazette Newspaper obituary; Whitaker and Horlacher, *Broad Bay Pioneers*, 308; Lincolnville Historical Society, *Lincolnville—Early Days*. Ulmer family file.

Chapter 1: The Ulmer Family Comes to America

87. Cheney, *Thanksgiving*, 75–76.

88. Timo and Kübrich, *Die Wappen der Deutschen undesländer*. Coat of arms of the Elector Palatinate.

89. Lee, *Genealogical & Personal Memorial of Mercer County*, 1: 358.

90. Stahl, *History of Old Broad Bay and Waldoboro*, 512.

91. Ibid.

92. Lee, *Genealogical & Personal Memorial of Mercer County*, 358.

93. Ibid.

94. Ibid.; Whitaker and Horlacher, *Broad Bay Pioneers*, 305.

95. Whitaker and Horlacher, *Broad Bay Pioneers*, 306–07.

96. Ibid., 305–06.

97. Ibid., 306–07.

98. Ibid., 305–10; Passenger List: 1742 *Lydia*, page 40.

99. Stahl, *History of Old Broad Bay and Waldoboro*, Memoranda and Documents, 747.

100. Whitaker and Horlacher, *Broad Bay Pioneers*, 43, 306.

101. Ibid., 1. German Background.

102. Ibid., 573.

103. Stahl, *History of Old Broad Bay and* Waldoboro, 107.

104. Ibid.; Eaton, *Annals of Warren*; Whitaker and Horlacher, *Broad Bay Pioneers*, 40.

105. Whitaker and Horlacher, *Broad Bay Pioneers*, 39–40.

106. Ibid., 40.

107. Eaton, *Annals of Warren*, 108–09.

108. Leamon, *Revolution Downeast*, 8. Published in cooperation with the Maine Historical Society.

109. Whitaker and Horlacher, *Broad Bay Pioneers*, 126; Broad Bay Land Records, Lot No. 4: Registers of Deeds of Lincoln and York Counties from Massachusetts State Archives: Lot No. 5 belonged to John Ulmer Jr. (once was his father's lot, Johannes Ulmer Sr., at the Medomac Falls also called the Great Falls); John Ulmer Jr. also owned land at the Lower falls of the Medomac Falls, the Great Meadow, Martin's Meadow and Madame Buttaks Meadow; Lot No. 15 belonged to Jacob Ulmer, Philip and George's father; George Ulmer owned property at Moose Meadow Brook and Martin's Meadow; Philip Ulmer owned property at Slaigo Cove.

110. Stahl, *History of Old Broad Bay and Waldoboro*, 291.

111. Whitaker and Horlacher, *Broad Bay Pioneers*, 200.

112. Ibid., 306–07; Stahl, *History of Old Broad Bay and Waldoboro*, 510–11; Eaton, *Annals of Warren*, 62, 115.

113. Whitaker and Horlacher, *Broad Bay Pioneers*, 307; Stahl, *History of Old Broad Bay and Waldoboro*, 510–11.

114. Whitaker and Horlacher, *Broad Bay Pioneers*, 307; Eaton, *Annals of Warren*, 62, 115.

115. Eaton, *Annals of Warren*, 104, 106, 114.

116. Elson, *History of the United States of America*, 168–70.

117. Stahl, *History of Old Broad Bay and Waldoboro*, 291.

118. Eaton, *Annals of Warren*, 120–24; Stahl, *History of Old Broad Bay and Waldoboro*, 291.

119. Whitaker and Horlacher, *Broad Bay Pioneers*, 48; Eaton, *Annals of Warren*, 87, 121–23.

120. Nicolar, *Penobscot Indians* (1895). Quote from a brochure that accompanied the permanent exhibition *As We Tell Our Stories: Living Traditions of* [Indian] *Peoples of Native New England*. Courtesy of the American Indian Archaeological Institute, Washington, Connecticut, and confirmed by the Mashantucket Pequot Museum & Research Center in Ledyard, Connecticut.

121. Chambers, *The Hidden Children*, 107.

122. Sprague, *Sprague's Journal of Maine History*, 6, no. 3. Regarding Soldiers of the American Revolution: *Maine Indians in the Revolution*, 105–12. The article regarding *Sprague's Journal of Maine History: Maine Indians in the Revolution* appeared in the publication *Sentinel* in its issue of June 2, 1897; Foran, *Maine*.

123. Stahl, *History of Broad Bay and Waldoboro*, 399–400. "The migration of Puritans [from the Massachusetts Bay] covered the period from 1765–

1775. It was the most important and influential fact in early Broad Bay history, for it meant the turning point in the future evolution of the isolated and feudal community on the Medomac…These Puritans brought with them and entirely different culture…and interaction was inevitable and fusion unavoidable…The two distinct patterns of life [the Dutch-German and English] influenced and colored one another, but the Puritan being the dominant culture in New England…transformed the feudal practices and views of Broad Bay into a democratic town, specifically English in organization, thought, and action."

124. Grundset, *Forgotten Patriots*, 11–16; Lefkowitz, *Benedict Arnold's Army*, 97, 133, 179, 306; Sprague, *Sprague's Journal of Maine History*, 105–12. Periodicals: Nov. and Dec. 1918, Jan. 1919: Maine Indians in the Revolution, courtesy of Tina Vickery and the Androscoggin Historical Society, 1998.

125. Grundset, *Forgotten Patriots*. See American Indians in the Revolution.

126. Sprague, *Sprague's Journal of Maine History*, 105–12. Periodicals: Nov. and Dec. 1918, Jan. 1919: Maine Indians in the Revolution, courtesy of Tina Vickery and the Androscoggin Historical Society, 1998; Eastport Sentinel, *Maine Indians in the Revolution: Regarding Soldiers of the American Revolution*, article published June 2, 1897. Based on Sprague's Journal of Maine History. U.S. Government War Archives.

127. Lincolnville Historical Society, *Lincolnville—Early Days*, 19; O'Brien, *Ducktrap*, 15–16, 31–39.

128. Stahl, *History of Old Broad Bay and Waldoboro*, 399.

129. Ibid., 398–99.

130. Whitaker and Horlacher, *Broad Bay Pioneers*, 254, 308; General George Ulmer obituary, *Hancock Gazette* and *Penobscot Patriot*, dated January 11, 1826.

131. Whitaker and Horlacher, *Broad Bay Pioneers*, 44, 254.

132. Ibid., 104, 114.

133. Eaton, *Annals of Warren County*, 254; General George Ulmer, (Major) Philip Ulmer's brother, appeared in the *Hancock Gazette* and *Penobscot Patriot*, dated January 11, 1826. It stated: "…his mother [was a native of] some place in Suabia [Swabia], and emigrated to this country before the taking of Louisbourg, at the capture of which his father was present…"

134. Eaton, *Annals of Warren County*, 62–68.

135. Ibid., 96.

136. Stahl, *History of Old Broad Bay and* Waldoboro, 210, 291; Lincoln County Deeds, Book 7, page 90 and Book 22, page 207; Eaton, *Annals of Warren County*, 96–97.

137. Stahl, *History of Old Broad Bay and Waldoboro*, 291.

138. Whitaker and Horlacher, *Broad Bay Pioneers*, 315–16.

139. Ibid., 254, 310; The Massachusetts Vital Records Project-Marriages from 1649 to 1849, *Vital Records of Marblehead Massachusetts to the End of rhe Year 1849*, Volume 2, *Marriages and Deaths*.

140. Eaton, *Annals of Warren County*, 121; Wilson, *Wilson Family History*, 567–68.

141. Stahl, *History of Old Broad Bay and Waldoboro*, 204, 276–77.

142. Ibid.

143. The Massachusetts Vital Records Project-Marriages from 1649 to 1849, *Vital Records of Marblehead Massachusetts to the End of the Year 1849*, Volume 2, *Marriages and Deaths*: Marriages, Orne (Horne), Beckett, Ulmer, etc; The Massachusetts Vital Records Project from 1626 to 1849, *Vital Records of Salem, Massachusetts to the End of the Year 1849*, Volume 4, *Births and Marriages*.

144. Lincoln County Land Deeds, Book 7, page 90, and Book 22, page 207; Stahl, *History of Old Broad Bay and Waldoboro*, 210.

145. Stahl, *History of Old Broad Bay and* Waldoboro, 267.

146. Whitaker and Horlacher, *Broad Bay Pioneers*, 307. "John Ulmer was an Innholder in Broad Bay on 1 Nov 1762, and again on 27 Sept 1763."

147. Ibid., 308.

148. The Massachusetts Vital Records Project-Marriages from 1649 to 1849, *Vital Records of Marblehead Massachusetts to the End of the Year 1849*, Volume 2, *Marriages and Deaths*; The Massachusetts Vital Records Project from 1626 to 1849, *Vital Records of Salem, Massachusetts to the End of the Year 1849*, Volume 4, *Births and Marriages*.

149. Stahl, *History of Old Broad Bay and Waldoboro*, 137.

150. Lincolnville Historical Society, *Lincolnville—Early Days*, 7–8.

151. Stahl, *History of Broad Bay and Waldoboro*, 291, 510–11.

152. Whitaker and Horlacher, *Broad Bay Pioneers*, 307.

153. Ibid., 308.

154. Stahl, *History of Old Broad Bay and Waldoboro*, 291.

155. Ibid., 291, 390–98.

156. Ibid.

157. Ibid., 390–98.

158. Ibid., 291.

159. Lefkowitz, *Benedict Arnold's Army*, 38.

160. Whitaker and Horlacher, *Broad Bay Pioneers*, 453.

161. Stahl, *History of Broad Bay and Waldoboro*, 399, 444–45.

162. Ibid.

163. Bernheim, *History of the German Settlements and the Lutheran Church*, 170–71. *The Javelin*, a Lutheran Church publication, recorded the circumstances of the early German immigration from Maine after the war: "The disappointment and suffering which they (the early German settlers) were made to endure (and) in consequence of the deceptions practiced upon them were trying to the extreme. And with all their troubles, the Indians fell upon them also and destroyed many lives and much substance. Ill-treated, robbed, wronged, and disappointed, many of them, under the guidance of the Moravian clergyman, Rev. Cilley, left the Muscangus (at Broad Bay) and emigrated to the Carolinas in 1773"; pages 228–32 state that during the ministry of Reverend J.G. Friederichs, "a colony of German settlers from Maine settled in North Carolina. They were accompanied by their Pastor Reverend Cilley." J.C. Hope, Esquire, of North Carolina wrote of the early Lutheran settlers there: "In 1763, a Colony of German Lutherans from Maine, accompanied by their Pastor Cilley, joined their brethren in South Carolina, but in time most returned." Reverend Dr. Hazelius stated: "Reverend Mr. Cilley arrived in South Carolina with a colony of German emigrants from Maine in the year 1773. But of his labors and success, no accounts are found." On page 602, it was stated that "About 1773, there were 15 or more families who left Waldoboro and moved to North Carolina." "*Three Old Meeting Houses in Maine*" which appears in the publication Maine Meeting Houses, Walpole: July 24–August 12, 1901, the Waldoboro article also confirms the emigration of 15 or more families from Waldoboro to North Carolina prior to the Revolutionary War.

Chapter 2: The Revolution Begins

164. Fischer, *Paul Revere's Ride*.

165. Stahl, *History of Old Broad Bay and Waldoboro*, 444.

166. Ibid.

167. Ibid.

168. Hutchinson, *The History of the Province of Massachusetts*, 429; Nelson, *With Fire & Sword*, 78.

169. Cahill, *New England's Naughty Navy*, no. 11, 9.

170. Ibid.

171. Ibid.
172. The Massachusetts Vital Records Project from 1626 to 1849, *Vital Records of Salem, Massachusetts to the End of the Year 1849*, Volume 4, *Births and Marriages*.
173. Billias, *General John Glover*, 64.
174. Fogle, *Colonial Marblehead*, 97–98.
175. Ibid., 97.
176. Goold, *Journal of Captain Johnson Moulton's Company*. Poem read before the Maine Historical Society, January 26, 1899.
177. Stahl, *History of Old Broad Bay and Waldoboro*, 204, 447–54. The early militia records of Broad Bay have been described by Jasper Stahl and both Whitaker and Horlacher as "a tangled nightmare." Massachusetts Archives militia rolls indicate that Waldoborough was credited with Philip Ulmer's enlistment and reenlistment in April 1776.
178. American Merchant Marine at War, courtesy of www.USMM.org.
179. Cahill, *New England's Naughty Navy*, Series 11, 9–10.
180. Ibid., 10.
181. Whitaker and Horlacher, *Broad Bay Pioneers*, 451; Porter, *Bangor Historical Magazine*, 2, no. 6, 117; *Hancock Gazette* and *Penobscot Patriot*, January 11, 1826, obituary of General George Ulmer.
182. Secretary of the Commonwealth of Massachusetts, *Massachusetts Soldiers and Sailors in the Revolution*, 16: 248–249.
183. Wilson, *The Ancestors and Descendants of John Wilson*, 232; The *Hancock Gazette*, 1826; George Ulmer obituary: "In his 20th year, while on a fishing voyage, the vessel in which he (George Ulmer) sailed was captured by the frigate, *Lively*, and the vessel and crew carried to Boston, then in possession of the British. He made his escape from the frigate into the town and over the Charles River to the American lines, at the imminent hazard of his life, and then enlisted into the American army and continued until the close of the war—being with Montgomery at Quebec, at Ticonderoga, at the capture of Burgoyne, at the defeat upon Rhode Island, and at the battles of Brandywine and Monmouth."
184. Wilson, *The Ancestors and Descendants of John Wilson*, 233. Some records indicate that Philip's younger cousin, George Ulmer Jr. (son of uncle John Ulmer Jr.) of Waldoboro, was actually the soldier involved in this part of the expedition. However, George Ulmer's U.S. pension material and the "obituary of General George Ulmer" in the *Hancock Gazette* and *Penobscot Patriot*, January 11, 1826, indicate that Philip's

brother, George, participated with Montgomery in the Canadian Expedition.

185. Williamson, "Obituary of General George Ulmer," *Hancock Gazette* and *Penobscot Patriot*, January 11, 1826.

186. Stahl, *History of Broad Bay and Waldoboro*, 275, 456; Whitaker and Horlacher, *Broad Bay Pioneers*, 308.

187. Fischer, *Washington's Crossing*, 75.

188. Martyn, *The Life of Artemas Ward*, 89–121.

189. Dunnack, *The Maine Book*, 3–8.

190. Ibid.

191. Fischer, *Washington's Crossing*, 20–21.

192. Palmer, *George Washington and Benedict Arnold*, 99–100.

193. Ibid.

194. Fischer, *Washington's Crossing*, 147–48.

195. Ibid., 148.

196. Chase, *The Papers of George Washington*, 1: 21–23 (Continental Congress records, dated June 22, 1775, Philadelphia).

197. Palmer, *George Washington and Benedict Arnold*, 99–100.

198. Walton, *The Army and Navy of the United States*. Chronological Record of Battles and Events of the Revolution, 1775, Bunker Hill, June 17, 1775.

199. Wright, *The Continental Army*. See General Washington: Main Army. Massachusetts Regiments of the Continental Army; Colonel Thomas Gardner/Bond's regiment (Fifteenth Massachusetts [MA-09A]; upon the death of Colonel Gardner on July 2, 1775, Colonel William Bond became commander of the regiment; designated Colonel William Bond the Twenty-fifth Continental Regiment [MA-09B] until his death in August 1776. The regiment saw action at the siege of Boston and at Valcour Island when the survivors were assigned to the Third Massachusetts Regiment. The Twenty-fifth Continental Regiment was officially disbanded on January 1, 1777, and merged with Twenty-fourth Continental Regiment to form Heath's/Greaton's Third Massachusetts Regiment 1777–1983) MA-12C.

200. Bonislawski, *The History of Thomas Gardner's Regiment*.

201. Cameron, *American Pioneers of Antigonish*.

202. Swett, Annin and Smith, *History of Bunker Hill*, 30.

203. Nelson, *George Washington's Secret Navy*, 43–44.

204. Palmer, *George Washington and Benedict Arnold*, 98.

205. William Bond Papers, *The Register of William Bond Papers, 1768–1777*, MSS 0080.

206. William Bond Papers, *The Register of William Bond Papers, 1768–1777*; Secretary of the Commonwealth of Massachusetts, "Return" of Officers in Colonel Gardner's Regiment [Fifteenth Massachusetts [MA-09A] on July 6, 1775, Massachusetts Archives; Wright, *The Continental Army*. See General Washington: Main Army. Massachusetts Regiments of the Continental Army; Colonel Thomas Gardner/Bond's regiment (Fifteenth Massachusetts [MA-09A]; upon the death of Colonel Gardner on July 2, 1775, Colonel William Bond became commander of the regiment; This regiment was designated Colonel William Bond's Twenty-fifth Continental Regiment in 1776 [MA-09B]; Bonislawski, *Colonel Thomas Gardner's Regiment*.

207. Wright, *The Continental Army*. Order of Battle—July 22, 1775: Main Army; List of Continental Army Units (1775): Left Wing; Major General Charles Lee's Second Division, in Brigadier General Nathanael Greene's brigade; Gardner's regiment or Fifteenth Massachusetts Regiment.

208. Wright, *The Continental Army*. See General Washington: Main Army.

209. Whitaker and Horlacher, *Broad Bay Pioneers*, 308–09.

210. Nelson, *George Washington's Secret Navy*, 52.

211. William Bond Papers, *The Register of William Bond Papers, 1768–1777*.

212. Hearn, *George Washington's Schooners*.

213. Ibid.

214. Ibid.

215. Stahl, *History of Old Broad Bay and Waldoboro*, 451.

216. Nelson, *George Washington's Secret Navy*, 86–89; Hearn, *George Washington's Schooners*.

217. Cahill, *New England's Naughty Navy*, 60.

218. Nelson, *George Washington's Secret Navy*, 86; Cahill, *New England's Naughty Navy*, 35.

Chapter 3: Expedition to Canada

219. Abbot et al., *Papers of Washington, Revolutionary War Series*, 332–33.

220. Lefkowitz, *Benedict Arnold's Army*, 22.

221. Force, *American Archives*, Fifth Series, 4: 874. Letter from General Washington to Colonel Arnold; Cambridge, January 27, 1776.

222. Abbot et al., *Papers of Washington, Revolutionary War Series*, 368.

223. Wilson, *The Ancestors and Descendants of John Wilson*, 233.

224. Lefkowitz., *Benedict Arnold's Army*, 40–41; Charles Martyn, *The Life of Artemas Ward*, 18.

225. Abbot et al., *Papers of Washington, Revolutionary War Series*, 432.

226. Brown and Peckham, *Revolutionary War Journals of Henry Dearborn*, 37.

227. William Bond Papers, *The Register of William Bond Papers, 1768–1777*, MSS 0080; Box 1, File 14, Mandeville Special Collections Library; 1775, July 17. "A Return of the Number and Name of Men in the late Col. Gardner Regt. [*sic*] that are expert in manging [*sic*] whale boats in the folowing [*sic*] companies."

228. Abbot et al., *Papers of Washington, Revolutionary War Series*, 458.

229. Stahl, *History of Broad Bay and Waldoboro*, 291; Eaton, *Annals of Warren*, 148.

230. Stahl, *History of Broad Bay and Waldoboro*, 449.

231. O'Brien, *Ducktrap*, 37; Taylor, "The Rise and Fall of George Ulmer," 51–66.

232. Stahl, *History of Broad Bay and Waldoboro*, 291.

233. Lefkowitz, *Benedict Arnold's Army*, 37–39.

234. Abbot et al., *Papers of Washington, Revolutionary War Series*, 405.

235. Lefkowitz, *Benedict Arnold's Army*, 56–58.

236. Peter Force, *American Archives*, Fourth Series, 3: 1058. The title of Benedict Arnold's journal is *A Journal of an Intended Tour from Cambridge to Quebeck*, [sic] *via Kennebeck* [sic] *with a Detachment of Two Regiments of Musketeers and Three Companies of Riflers, Consisting of about Eleven Hundred Effective Men, Commanded by Benedict Arnold*.

237. Meigs, *Journal of the Expedition Against Quebec*, 8.

238. Winsor, *Arnold's Expedition Against Quebec*, 5; Lefkowitz, *Benedict Arnold's Army*, 57–59.

239. Richardson, *Standards and Colors of the American Revolution*, 75, 90, 95.

240. Royster, *A Revolutionary People at War*, 24; Martin, *Benedict Arnold, Revolutionary Hero*, 119.

241. Stahl, *History of Old Broad Bay and Waldoboro*, 453–55; Lefkowitz, *Benedict Arnold's Army*, 68, 71, 76; Nelson, *Benedict Arnold's Navy*, 94.

242. Lefkowitz, *Benedict Arnold's Army*, 68, 71, 76; Nelson, *Benedict Arnold's Navy*, 94; Stahl, *History of Old Broad Bay and Waldoboro*, 453–55.

243. Lefkowitz, *Benedict Arnold's Army*, 71, 73–75.

244. Abbot et al., *Papers of Washington*. General Washington's letter to Colonel Arnold, September 14, 1775.

245. Lefkowitz, *Benedict Arnold's Army*, 63.

246. Ibid., 73–74.

247. Ibid., 82.

248. Ibid., 82–83.

249. Ibid., 28.

250. National Society Daughters of the American Revolution, *African American and American Indian Patriots of the Revolutionary War*, 11.

251. Ibid., 13–16; Sprague, *Sprague's Journal of Maine History* 6, no. 3. Regarding Soldiers of the American Revolution; *Maine Indians in the Revolution*, 105–112. The article regarding *Sprague's Journal of Maine History: Maine Indians in the Revolution* appeared in the publication *Sentinel*, in its issue of June 2, 1897, Eastport, Maine; Lefkowitz, *Benedict Arnold's Army*, 98.

252. Ligotti, *Dark Eagle*, chapter 14.

253. Lefkowitz, *Benedict Arnold's Army*, 96.

254. Ibid., 98.

255. Maine Historical Society Collection, Manuscript Document, *Benedict Arnold's Letter Book (1775) and Journal of Lt. John Montresor*, Maine Historical Society; Arnold letter to Washington, Fort Western, September 25, 1775; Procured and presented to the Maine Historical Society by Col. Aaron Burr, 1831; reference Coll. 1765; Lefkowitz, *Benedict Arnold's Army*, 98.

256. Nelson, *Benedict Arnold's Navy*, 94.

257. Stahl, *History of Old Broad Bay and Waldoboro*, 454.

258. Ibid.; reprinted in Roberts, *March to Quebec*.

259. Ibid.

260. Lefkowitz, *Benedict Arnold's Army*, 34–35, 214–15: "More troops eventually joined Montgomery and Arnold. There were 160 Massachusetts troops under the command of Major John Brown, camped at the St. Lawrence River town of Sorel. Ironically, they were the same Massachusetts troops raised and commanded by Arnold early in the war to defend the Lake Champlain region [in May 1775]"; Abbot et al., *Papers of Washington*, 406–09.

261. Lefkowitz, *Benedict Arnold's Army*, 179–80; Force, *American Archives*, Fourth Series, 3: 1,418–19.

262. Ibid., 214–15.

263. Lefkowitz, *Benedict Arnold's Army*, 211.

264. Ibid., 143–49.

265. Abbot et al., *Papers of Washington, Revolutionary War Series*, 2: 425; Frank Squire, ed., "Diary of Ephraim Squire," *Magazine of American History*, no. 2, part 2, (1878), 687–688. The General Orders for the army for

November 25, 1775, included the following: "The Commissioned, Non Commission'd [*sic*] Officers & Soldiers, lately arrived in Camp from Kenebeck [*sic*] river, are to join their respective Corps."

266. Naval Documents of the American Revolution, Volume 2, *Manvide Journal*, 932; Nelson, *George Washington's Secret Navy*, 190–91; Maine Archives, Revolutionary War papers of (Johann) Valentin Minck (cousin of Philip Ulmer and served with the same company and regiment): "…In 1775 I enlisted to serve on a privateer in army of American Revolutionary War in Mass line and Continental Establishment to serve against the Common Enemy, under Capt Fuller in Bond's Reg't…"; Whitaker and Horlacher, *Broad Bay Pioneers*, 405.

267. Bond, *The Register of William Bond Papers*.

268. Stahl, *History of Old Broad Bay and Waldoboro*, 455.

269. Palmer, *George Washington and Benedict Arnold*, 374.

270. Whitaker and Horlacher, *Broad Bay Pioneers*. Muster Rolls.

271. Force, *American Archives*, Fourth Series, 3: 1,710; Abbot et al., *Papers of Washington, Revolutionary War Series*, 2: 494; Lefkowitz, *Benedict Arnold's Army*, 314–15.

272. Abbot et al., *Papers of Washington, Revolutionary War Series*, 2: 452.

273. Irving, *Life of George Washington*, Volume 1, Chapter 8, 191–95.

274. Ibid.

275. Palmer, *George Washington and Benedict Arnold*, 132.

276. Cahill, *New England's Naughty Navy*, no. 11, 23.

277. Nelson, *Washington's Secret Navy*, 133–35.

278. Ibid., 134–35; Cahill, *New England's Naughty Navy*, no. 11, 23.

279. Nelson, *Washington's Secret Navy*, 134.

280. Miller, *Sea of Glory*, 47–49; Cahill, *New England's Naughty Navy*, 23.

281. Nelson, *Washington's Secret Navy*, 143.

282. Ibid.

283. Miller, *Sea of Glory*, 47–49.

284. Nelson, *Washington's Secret Navy*, 143–44.

285. Ibid., 144; Miller, *Sea of Glory*, 47.

286. Miller, *Sea of Glory*, 48; Nelson, *Washington's Secret Navy*, 143–145.

287. Nelson, *Washington's Secret Navy*, 144.

288. Goold, *Falmouth Neck in the Revolution*: Cumberland and Waldo County militia response to the British attack upon Falmouth.

289. Cahill, *New England's Naughty Navy*, no. 11, 23–24.

290. Miller, *Sea of Glory*, 48–49.

291. Ibid.

292. Nelson, *George Washington's Secret Navy*, 145–46.

293. Yerxa, *The Burning of Falmouth*, 149; Nelson, *George Washington's Secret Navy*, 147.

294. Force, *American Archives*, Fourth Series, 3: 1,888–89.

295. Clark, *Naval Documents of the American Revolution*, Volume 2, *American Theatre, September 3, 1775 to October 31, 1775*, 467. Letter from Comte de Vergennes to De Guines; Nelson, *George Washington's Secret Navy*, 146.

296. Chase, *Papers of George Washington, Revolutionary War Series*, 2: 349. Letter from General Washington to John Hancock.

297. Ibid., 333. Letter from George Washington to Richard Henry Lee.

298. George Washington Papers, Letterbook 1, Image 68; Joseph Reed letter to Stephen Moylan (Colonel Glover's aide), Library of Congress.

299. Cahill, *New England's Naughty Navy*, no. 11, 39.

300. Whitaker and Horlacher, *Broad Bay Pioneers*, 131–32. Letter dated February 28, 1776, from Camp Prospect Hill written by Philip Reiser to his father, Martin Razor [*sic*], in Waldoborough, by favor Mr. Acorn: "…send any letters you must Direct them to Prospect Hill in Col. Bond's Regiment and in Capt. Fuller's Company which I belong to. Sergt. [*sic*] Ulmer Remembers his love to you all and his Uncles and aunts family…" Philip Reiser was the cousin of Sergeant Philip Ulmer; Stahl, *History of Old Broad Bay and* Waldoboro, 456.

301. Maine Archives, Revolutionary War papers of (Johann) Valentine Minck. "Abt [*sic*] the Middle of December I enlisted to serve on a privateer in Army of American Revolutionary War in Mass line and Continental Establishment to serve against the Common Enemy, under Capt Fuller in Col. Bond's Reg't…and in Company for Service as Guards in Broad Bay [with] Philip Ulmer's company…"; Whitaker and Horlacher, *Broad Bay Pioneers*, 405.

302. Department of the Navy, *Dictionary of American Naval Fighting Ships*; Paullin, *The Navy of the American Revolution*, 465–66, 518; See Acts and Resolutions of Rhode Island, August 1775; November and December 1776; also May 1778; and Rhode Island Colonial Records, 7, 582; Chadwick, *The First American Army*, 303–04.

303. Naval Documents of the American Revolution, Volume 2, *Manvide Journal*, 932. Dr. John Manvide was a French surgeon with Captain Fuller's company, and he volunteered with other men from the same company to sail on the refitted privateer galleys *Washington* and *Spitfire*. Dr. Manvide served with some of the men from Fuller's company aboard the *Washington* with Captain Martindale, while others sailed

aboard the *Spitfire*. Sergeant Philip Ulmer probably volunteered to serve aboard the *Spitfire*.

304. Maine Archives, Revolutionary War papers of (Johann) Valentin Minck: "In 1775 I enlisted to serve on a privateer in army of American Revolutionary War in Mass line and Continental Establishment to serve against the Common Enemy, under Capt Fuller in Bond's Reg't..." Sergeant Philip Ulmer served in this company and regiment.

305. Nelson, *George Washington's Secret Navy*, 190–91.

306. Maine Archives, Revolutionary War papers of (Johann) Valentin Minck: "In 1775 I enlisted to serve on a privateer in army of American Revolutionary War in Mass line and Continental Establishment to serve against the Common Enemy, under Capt Fuller in Bond's Reg't..." Sergeant Philip Ulmer served with this company.

307. Nelson, *George Washington's Secret Navy*, 153–54.

308. Ibid., 153.

309. Patton, *Patriot Pirates*, 87.

310. Maine Historical Society, "Benedict Arnold's Letter Book (1775)." Arnold letter to Montgomery, November 8, 1775, from "St. Marie, 2½ leagues from Point Levi."

311. Ibid.

312. Wilson, *The Ancestors and Descendants of John Wilson*, 233.

313. New England Historical and Genealogical Society, Manuscript Collections, *Bartlett's Colonial Record of Rhode Island*, 7: 327, 410; Samuel Viall, first mate on the galley *Spitfire* in March 1776; Two schooners furnished by Rhode Island, the galleys *Washington* & *Spitfire* each to carry fifty men, to be refitted at Plymouth as a brig; Sion Martindale as captain of the *Washington*, and Esek Hopkins as captain of the *Spitfire*. Samuel Viall later served as a lieutenant under the command of Commodore Hopkins. He was killed by an explosion of gunpowder on board the brig *Spitfire* on April 2, 1777. Records of Samuel Viall's death can be found in the New England Families Genealogical & Memorial, Series 3, Volume 4, 1690. Samuel Viall's name appears in the Muster rolls in Lincoln County militia and was associated with Philip Ulmer's militia regiment.

314. Department of the Navy, *Dictionary of American Naval Fighting Ships*, Spitfire I; Spitfire II; Paullin, *The Navy of the American Revolution*, 465–66, 518; See Acts and Resolutions of Rhode Island, August 1775; November and December 1776; also May 1778; and Rhode Island Colonial Records, 7, 582.

315. Maine Archives, Revolutionary War papers of (Johann) Valentin Minck: "In 1775 I enlisted to serve on a privateer in army of American Revolutionary War in Mass line and Continental Establishment to serve against the Common Enemy, under Capt Fuller in Bond's Reg't…"

316. Whitaker and Horlacher, *Broad Bay Pioneers*, 404, 405, 420. John Valentin Minck (cousin of Philip Ulmer) states in his Revolutionary War papers: "abt the Middle of Dec 1775 I enlisted to serve on a privateer in army of American Revolutionary War in Mass line and Continental Establishment to serve against the Common Enemy, under Capt Fuller in Col. Bond's Reg't." This was the same company and regiment as Philip Ulmer. He further states that he "served on board State sloop with Capt Curtis."

317. Department of the Navy, *Dictionary of American Fighting Ships*, Ships of the Continental Navy, U.S. Navy row galleys, 1770s ships: USS *Spitfire* (1776).

318. Whitaker and Horlacher, *Broad Bay Pioneers*, 131; Stahl, *History of Old Broad Bay and Waldoboro*, 444; Eaton, *Annals of Warren*, 456.

319. Copied from a letter belonging to Emily Hazelwood of Boston, a descendant of John Martin Reiser.

320. Stahl, *History of Old Broad Bay and Waldoboro*, 275, 456; Whitaker and Horlacher, *Broad Bay Pioneers*, 131.

321. French, *The Siege of Boston*, 254.

322. Ware, *Forgotten Heroes*, 18.

323. Whitaker and Horlacher, *Broad Bay Pioneers*, 131–32. Letter dated February 28, 1776, from Camp Prospect Hill written by Philip Reiser to his father, Martin Razor [*sic*], in Waldoborough.

324. Frothingham, *History of the Siege of Boston*, 295; Drake, *Life and Correspondence of Henry Knox*, 23.

325. Frothingham, *History of the Siege of Boston*, 290–98; Gilman et al., *Theatrum Majorum*, 59.

326. Paige, *History of Cambridge*, 424; French, *The Siege of Boston*, 406; Brooks, *The Boston Campaign*, 224.

327. Paige, *History of Cambridge*, 424–25.

328. Frothingham, *History of the Siege of Boston*, 290–98.

329. Ibid., 297.

330. Ibid., 295.

331. Heath, *Memoirs of Major General William Heath*, 39–43; Paige, *History of Cambridge*, 424.

332. Nelson, *Benedict Arnold's Navy*, 187.

333. Lefkowitz, *Benedict Arnold's Army*, 236.

334. Ibid., 265.

335. Ibid.

336. Whitaker and Horlacher, *Broad Bay Pioneers*, 308; Revolutionary War Pension and Bounty-Land Warrant Application Files, Washington, DC: NARA, Philip Ulmer, Continental Massachusetts, Pension number: S 19963.

337. Revolutionary War Pension and Bounty-Land Warrant Application Files, (Washington, DC: NARA), Philip Ulmer, Continental Massachusetts, Pension number: S 19963. (See transcript at end of document written by Philip Ulmer).

338. Mandeville Special Collections Library, *The Register of William Bond Papers, 1768–1777*, Box 1, Folder 27; General Horatio Gates's orders to General Washington on March 15, 1776, to send relief troops to Canada by way of the Hudson River Valley and Lake George to the Lake Champlain Valley and Richelieu River to the St. Lawrence River, Canada.

339. Nelson, *Benedict Arnold's Navy*, 180.

340. Lanctot, *Canada and the American Revolution*, 126; Nelson, *Benedict Arnold's Navy*, 180.

341. Carroll, *Mission to Canada*, f.n. on 49.

342. Lanctot, *Canada and the American Revolution*, 126; Nelson, *Benedict Arnold's Navy*, 180.

343. Nelson, *Benedict Arnold's Navy*, 180.

344. Ibid., 182.

345. Ibid., 183.

346. Revolutionary War Pension and Bounty-Land Warrant application records, Philip Ulmer, File number 19963; Commission granted by the Continental Congress to Philip Ulmer on April 20, 1776, and signed by John Hancock: *The Bangor Wig and Courier*, September 30, 1887, Volume 54, Number 231; Whitaker and Horlacher, *Broad Bay Pioneers*, 308; National Archives, *Naval Documents of the American Revolution*, 2: 1,078.

347. Commission granted by the Continental Congress to Philip Ulmer on April 20, 1776, and signed by John Hancock: *The Bangor Wig and Courier*, September 30, 1887, Volume 54, Number 231.

348. Whitaker and Horlacher, *Broad Bay Pioneers*, 308.

349. Clark, *Naval Documents of the American Revolution*, 2: 1,078: "Guns and Ordinance Stores Taken on the St. Lawrence River"; Peter Force, *American Archives*, Fourth Series, Volume 3, 1693; "Return of Military Stores on board the several Vessels under command of General Prescott, bound

to Quebec, November 19,1775." Also "Return of Provisions on board several Vessels under command of Brigadier General Prescott, lying opposite La Valtrie, November 19, 1775 signed by Thomas Gamble, Assistant Quartermaster-General." "Return of Ordnance Stores on board different Vessels, November 20, 1775. Signed by Thomas Cooper, Clerk of Artillery Stores." Transcripts by Peter Barranco, May 2008. All returns note the *Isabella* with Captain Bouchat (Bouchet, Bouchette) as Master of the British schooner at the time of capture.

350. Nelson, *Benedict Arnold's Navy*, 180.

351. Coffin, *The Life and Services of Major General John Thomas*, 25.

352. Ibid., 26.

353. Secretary of the Commonwealth of Massachusetts, *Massachusetts Soldiers and Sailors in the War of the Revolution*, 16: 248; Maine Archives, Revolutionary War, U.S. Pension paper of George Ulmer; "Obituary of General George Ulmer," *The Hancock Gazette* and *Penobscot Patriot*, January 11, 1826.

354. Carroll, *Mission to Canada*, 49–50.

355. Nelson, *Benedict Arnold's Navy*, 183–85.

356. Cubbinson, *The American Northern Theater Army in 1776*, 110.

357. Carroll, *Mission to Canada*, 25–33.

358. William Bond Papers, *The Register of William Bond Papers, 1768–1777*.

359. Cubbinson, *The American Northern Theater Army in 1776*, 103–04.

360. Ibid., 104.

361. Coffin, *The Life and Services of Major General John Thomas*, 29–30.

362. Ibid., 29.

363. Palmer, *George Washington and Benedict Arnold*, 163.

364. William Bond Papers, *The Register of William Bond Papers, 1768–1777*.

365. Wallace, *Benedict Arnold*, 20–30.

366. Nelson, *Benedict Arnold's Navy*, 216.

367. Ibid., 216–17.

368. Davies, *Documents of the American Revolution*, 144. Communications from Carleton to Germain.

369. Nelson, *Benedict Arnold's Navy*, 217.

370. Wallace, *Benedict Arnold*, 30.

371. Stanley, *Canada Invaded*, 130–32.

372. Palmer, *George Washington and Benedict Arnold*, 162; Nelson, *Benedict Arnold's Navy*, 217.

373. Nelson, *Benedict Arnold's Navy*, 218.

374. Wallace, *Benedict Arnold*, 30; Stanley, *Canada Invaded*, 130–32.

375. Palmer, *George Washington and Benedict Arnold*, 162.

376. Nelson, *Benedict Arnold's Navy*, 220.

377. Force, *American Archives*, Fourth Series, 6: 1,200. Letter from General Schuyler to General Washington.

378. Nelson, *Benedict Arnold's Navy*, 221.

379. Force, *American Archives*, Fifth Series, 6: 235.

380. Palmer, *George Washington and Benedict Arnold*, 165.

381. Ibid., 165–66.

382. William Bond Papers, *The Register of William Bond Papers, 1768–1777*.

383. Abbott et al., *Papers of Washington, Revolutionary War Series*, 6: 389.

Chapter 4: Defense of Lake Champlain

384. Hazelton, *The Declaration of Independence*.

385. Smith, *The Life and Public Services of Arthur St. Clair*, 25; Force, *American Archives*, Fifth Series, 1: 630.

386. Crockett, *Vermont*, 6; Ketchum, *Saratoga*, 117–18.

387. Force, *American Archives*, Sixth Series, 799. See: Correspondence, Proceedings &c.; General Orders, Head Quarters, July 30, 1776; Commissary supply distribution.

388. Ketchum, *Saratoga*, 118.

389. Nelson, *Benedict Arnold's Navy*, 262. Dr. Stephen McCrea was father or older brother of Jenny McCrea. Jenny McCrea was taken hostage by Mohawk Indians along with a local couple and their six children who lived in the vicinity of Fort Edwards. They would become martyrs of the American Revolution, having been brutally tortured and scalped by the hostile Indians who were under British general Burgoyne's command.

390. Crockett, *Vermont*, 6.

391. Force, *American Archives*, Fifth Series, 630; Smith, *The St. Clair Papers*, 1: 25.

392. Sparks, *The Library of American Biography*, 3: 44; Bratton, *The Gondola Philadelphia & the Battle of Lake Champlain*, 44.

393. National Archives, U.S. Navy 1775–1910, Subject File, B.O. Ordnance Equipment, Box 152. *Gundelow Spitfire Capt. Phillip Ulmer…*; Sparks, *Correspondence of the American Revolution*, Volume 1, Benedict Arnold letter to Horatio Gates; Bratten, *The Gondola* Philadelphia *& the Battle of Lake Champlain*, The American Fleet at Valcour Island, Table 5.1, 57; Nelson,

Benedict Arnold's Navy, 263; Lundeberg, *The Gunboat* Philadelphia *and the Defense of Lake Champlain*, 1776, 30.

394. Nelson, *Benedict Arnold's Navy*, 258.

395. Art Cohn, July 2009 dive and video filming of the *Spitfire* on the bottom of Lake Champlain by the Lake Champlain Maritime Museum dive team. (See the *Spitfire* CD of July 2009 for graphic evidence.)

396. Force, *American Archives*, Fifth Series, 1: 1,268. General Gates letter to John Hancock.

397. Clark, Morgan and Crawford, *Naval Documents of the American Revolution*, 371.

398. Nelson, *Benedict Arnold's Navy*, 266.

399. Clark, Morgan and Crawford, *Naval Documents of the American Revolution*, 371. Letter from General Arnold to General Gates, August 31, 1776; Bratton, *The Gondola* Philadelphia *& the Battle of Lake Champlain*, 48.

400. William Bond, *The Register of William Bond Papers*.

401. Nelson, *Benedict Arnold's Navy*, 266–67.

402. Ibid., 269–70.

403. *Maine Indians in the Revolution*, Eastport, Maine: *Eastport Sentinel*, June 2, 1897; Sprague, *Sprague's Journal of Maine History*, 6: 105–12; Edited later by John G. Deane and Edgar C. Smith in 1918; Courtesy of Tina Vickery and the Androscoggin Historical Society, 1998.

404. Eaton, *Annals of Warren*, 2nd Edition, 1877; October 20, 1752, 87; Whitaker and Horlacher, *Broad Bay Pioneers*, 48.

405. Sparks, *Correspondence of the American* Revolution, Volume 1, Benedict Arnold letter to Horatio Gates, September 7, 1776, from Windmill Point.

406. Clark, Morgan and Crawford, *Naval Documents of the American Revolution*, 6: 734; Letter from Colonel Arnold to General Gates, September 7, 1776; Bratton, *The Gondola* Philadelphia *& the Battle of Lake Champlain*, 49–50; Nelson, *Benedict Arnold's Navy*, 270–71.

407. Nelson, *Benedict Arnold's Navy*, 277.

408. Ibid., 278; Force, *American Archives*, Fifth Series, 2: 532.

409. Nelson, *Benedict Arnold's Navy*, 266.

410. Connecticut Historical Society, *Journal of Bayze Wells*, September 26, 1776 (Collections from the Connecticut Historical Society, 7, 1899), 280–81; Martin, *Benedict Arnold*, 494; Nelson, *Benedict Arnold's Navy*, 266, 282.

411. Clark, *Naval Documents of the American Revolution*, 6: 837.

412. Force, *American Archives*, Fifth Series, 2: 834–35.

413. Millard, *The Battle of Lake Champlain*.

414. Force, *American Archives*, Fifth Series, 2: 1,224; Letter from General Waterbury to the president of Congress, October 24, 1776.

415. Nelson, *Benedict Arnold's Navy*, 294–95.

416. Millard, *The Battle of Lake Champlain*.

417. Nelson, *Benedict Arnold's Navy*, 295.

418. Ibid., 296; Palmer, *George Washington and Benedict Arnold*, 177–78.

419. Hadden, *Hadden's Journal and Orderly Books*.

420. Nelson, *Benedict Arnold's Navy*, 273. The captain of the schooner *Carleton* was James Richard Dacres, who had served as first officer of the British vessel *Blond* on the St. Lawrence River at Quebec, Canada, and had been overseeing the operation of the British warships and bateaux on Lake Champlain. (The son of James Richard Dacres, who also carried the same name as his father, would later appear in American naval history as the captain of the British frigate *Guerriere* (a captured French vessel) that was defeated by the American frigate USS *Constitution* in the War of 1812 off the coast of Maine.)

421. Sparks, *Correspondence of the American Revolution*, Volume 1; Benedict Arnold's letter to Horatio Gates, Schuyler Island, October 12, 1776.

422. Ibid.; Nelson, *Benedict Arnold's Navy*, 300–01.

423. Hadden, *Lieutenant James M. Hadden's Journal and Orderly Books*, 22.

424. Nelson, *Benedict Arnold's Navy*, 300–01.

425. Bratten, *The Gondola* Philadelphia *& the Battle of Lake Champlain*, 64.

426. Sparks, *Correspondence of the American Revolution*, Volume 1; Benedict Arnold's letter to Horatio Gates, Schuyler Island, October 12, 1776.

427. Nelson, *Benedict Arnold's Navy*, 302.

428. Force, *American Archives*, Fifth Series, 2: 1,224; Letter from General Waterbury to the president of Congress, October 24, 1776.

429. Force, *American Archives*, Sixth Series, *Return of the Fleet*, 1,235: Letter from Arnold to Gates, October 1776; Nelson, *Benedict Arnold's Navy*, 302, 307.

430. Nelson, *Benedict Arnold's Navy*, 179.

431. Ibid., 302; Pausch, *Journal of Captain Pausch*.

432. Bratten, *The Gondola* Philadelphia *& the Battle of Lake Champlain*, 64–65.

433. Ibid., 65–66.

434. Stone, *Memoirs, Letters, and Journal of Major General Riedesel*, 71.

435. Roberts, *Rabble in Arms*, 317. The injury was later confirmed by Philip Ulmer's daughter Dolly, who married James Merrill and whose father was one of the main characters in the book by Kenneth Roberts.

436. Sparks, *Correspondence of the American Revolution*, Volume 1; Benedict Arnold's letter to Horatio Gates, Schuyler Island, October 12, 1776.

437. Wigglesworth Papers, *Wigglesworth Family Papers*.

438. Connecticut Historical Society, *"Journal of Bayze Wells,"* September 26, 1776.

439. Force, *American Archives*, Fifth Series, 2: 1,224. Letter from General Waterbury to the president of Congress, October 24, 1776.

440. Stone, *Memoirs, Letters, and Journal of Major General Riedesel*, 71.

441. Hadden, *Hadden's Journal and Orderly Books*.

442. Wigglesworth Papers, *Wigglesworth Family Papers*; Force, *American Archives*, Fourth Series, 6: 1,235; Nelson, *Benedict Arnold's Navy*, 311.

443. Sparks, *Correspondence of the American Revolution*, Volume 1, General Arnold's letter to General Gates: October 12, 1776; Force, *American Archives*, Fourth Series, 6: 1,235.

444. Sparks, *Correspondence of the American Revolution*, Volume 1, Benedict Arnold's letter to Horatio Gates, Schuyler Island, October 12, 1776; Clark, Morgan and Crawford, *Naval Documents of the American Revolution*, 6: 1,235.

445. Wells, "Journal of Bayze Wells," 284.

446. Force, *American Archives*, Fifth Series, 3: 253–54; Benedict Arnold's letter to Philip Schuyler, October 12, 1776.

447. Nelson, *Benedict Arnold's Navy*, 312.

448. Frederick Haldimand Papers, *Correspondence with General Gates, 1758– 1777*, Special Collections, John C. Pace Library, University of West Florida, Pensacola, microfilm; Bratten, *The Gondola* Philadelphia *& the Battle of Lake Champlain*, 69.

449. Bratten, *The Gondola* Philadelphia *& the Battle of Lake Champlain*, 67.

450. Ibid.

451. Wickman, "A Most Unsettled Time of Lake Champlain," 89–98.

452. Wigglesworth Papers, *Wigglesworth Family Papers*; Force, *American Archives*, Fourth Series, 6: 1,235; Nelson, *Benedict Arnold's Navy*, 314.

453. Nelson, *Benedict Arnold's Navy*, 314.

454. Force, *American Archives*, Fifth Series, 2: 1,224, Letter from Waterbury to Gates, October 24, 1776; Bratten, *The Gondola* Philadelphia *& the Battle of Lake Champlain*, 68.

455. Mott et al., *The New York Genealogical and Biological Record*, 245–55. Captain John Thacher was in command of the galley *Washington* at the Battle of Valcour Island in October 1776, where he was wounded, taken prisoner and afterward paroled and subsequently exchanged. John Thacher died on January 16 or 17, 1805, and was buried in the Episcopal burying ground in Stratford, Connecticut, in an unmarked

grave; Force, *American Archives*, Fifth Series, 2: 1,039–40. On file in the New York Public Library; Johnson, *Connecticut Men in the Revolutionary War*, 594, 629, 649; Selleck, *History of Norwalk, Connecticut*, 449–69; Schenck, *History of Fairfield County*.

456. Force, *American Archives*, Fifth Series, 2: 1,224.

457. Clark, *Naval Documents of the American Revolution*, 6: 1,275.

458. Nelson, *Benedict Arnold's Navy*, 316.

459. Thomas W. Baldwin, *The Revolutionary Journal of Col. Jeduthan Baldwin*, 81; Bratten, *The Gondola* Philadelphia *& the Battle of Lake Champlain*, 69.

460. Bratten, *The Gondola* Philadelphia *& the Battle of Lake Champlain*, 69.

461. Nelson, *Benedict Arnold's Navy*, 317.

462. Sparks, *Correspondence of the American Revolution*, Volume 1; Benedict Arnold letter to Horatio Gates, October 12, 1776: "I was obliged myself to point most of the guns on board the Congress, which I believe did good execution."

463. Bratten, *The Gondola* Philadelphia *& the Battle of Lake Champlain*, 69.

464. Bellico, *Sails and Steam in the Mountains*, 158.

465. Clark, *Naval Documents of the American Revolution*, 6: 1,276; Benedict Arnold's report to Major General Philip Schuyler, October 15, 1776.

466. Cohn, "An Incident Not Known to History," 3.

467. Wilkinson, *Memoirs of My Own Times*, 92. Sergeant James Cushing (who later became a brigadier general) served as a marine sergeant on board Arnold's galley *Congress* under his brother, Nathaniel Cushing. James was the younger brother of Nathaniel Cushing from Hingham, Massachusetts, who served as an officer with Colonel Whitcomb's regiment and with Colonel Paterson's regiment on Lake Champlain. These men appear in the muster roll dated November 12, 1776, in camp at Fort Ticonderoga; Secretary of the Commonwealth of Massachusetts, *Massachusetts Soldiers and Sailors in the War of the Revolution*, Volume 4, 296–297.

468. Seelinger, *Buying Time*.

469. Billico, *Chronicles of Lake Champlain*, 222.

470. Wilkinson, *Memoirs of My Own Times*, 91–92.

471. Clark, Morgan and Crawford, *Naval Documents of the American Revolution*, 6: 654. Letter from Arnold to Gates, September 2, 1776; Bratten, *The Gondola* Philadelphia *& the Battle of Lake Champlain*, 69.

472. General Gates, Bulletin of Fort Ticonderoga, October 14, 1776; *Bulletin of the Fort Ticonderoga Museum* 14, no. 1 (Summer 1981): 289–91.

473. Ibid.

474. Ibid.

475. Arnold, *The Life of Benedict Arnold*, 118.

476. Palmer, *History of Lake Champlain*, 131.

477. Trevelyan, *The American Revolution*, 180–81.

478. Stone, *Memoirs, Letters, and Journal of Major General Riedesel*, 79.

479. Mott et al., *The New York Genealogical and Biographical Record*, 44: 251; papers of Rufus Lincoln.

480. Frederick Haldimand Papers, *Correspondence with General Gates, 1758–1777*, Special Collections, John C. Pace Library, University of West Florida, Pensacola, microfilm; Bratten, *The Gondola* Philadelphia *& the Battle of Lake Champlain*, 69.

481. Mott et al., *The New York Genealogical and Biographical Record*, 44: 245–53; State of Connecticut, "Connecticut Men in the Revolutionary War," Third Series, June 1765–May 1820 (Hartford, CT: Connecticut State Library, 1945), 594, Connecticut Archives: Individual Records: "John Thacher, Captain of Navy on Lake Champlain, taken prisoner October, 1776, with General Waterbury." (page 629); Return of American officers and other prisoners on Long Island, August 15, 1778: "Captain Thatcher 'E' (i.e. Exchanged) Conn. Militia, taken October 13th, 1776, on Lake Champlain."; also "Invalid pensioners, residence not stated, John Thacher" (page 649). Also see confirming information in *The New York Genealogical and Biological Record*, 44: 251; Selleck, *History of Norwalk*, 455–56.

482. Selleck, *History of Norwalk*, 455–56.

483. Mott et al., *The New York Genealogical and Biographical Record*, 44: 245–53; State of Connecticut, "Connecticut Men in the Revolutionary War," Third Series, June 1765–May 1820, 629, 649.

484. Nelson, *Benedict Arnold's Navy*, 316.

485. Stone, *Memoirs, Letters, and Journal of Major General Riedesel*, 70–80.

486. Ibid., 79.

487. Sparks, *Correspondence of the American Revolution*, Volume 1; General Horatio Gates letter to General Philip Schuyler, October 31, 1776.

488. Sizer, *The Autobiography of Colonel John Trumbull*, 34; Cubbison, *The Artillery*, 64; Stone, *Memoirs, Letters, and Journal of Major General Riedesel*, 79: "General Riedesel estimated American forces at Fort Ticonderoga as 10,000 men."

489. Stone, *Memoirs, Letters, and Journal of Major General Riedesel*, 79.

490. Sparks, *Correspondence of the American Revolution*, Volume 1; Horatio Gates letter to President John Hancock and Congress, November 5, 1776.

491. Fisher, *Washington's Crossing*, 146.

492. Stone, *Memoirs, Letters, and Journal of Major General Riedesel*, 80.

493. Mahan, *Alfred T. Mahan Collection*.

494. Ibid. "Articles of Captain Mahan on Lake Champlain." Seelinger, *Buying Time*.

Chapter 5: New York and New Jersey

495. Wright, *The Continental Army*, 203, 212, 213. First Massachusetts Regiment, 1777, Colonel Vose's Regiment.

496. Abbot et al., *Papers of George Washington, Revolutionary War Series*, 7: 335. Washington's letter to Lee, December 14, 1776.

497. Fischer, *Washington's Crossing*, 149.

498. Balderston and Syrett, *The Lost War*, 131.

499. Wright, *The Continental Army*. Lineage: Twenty-fifth Continental Regiment; Third Massachusetts Regiment.

500. Fischer, *Washington's Crossing*, 408–10. Appendix P: American Dispositions in New Jersey, January 1, 1777.

501. Wright, *The Continental Army*. Massachusetts regiments of the Continental Army; Fischer, *Washington's Crossing*, 408–10. Appendix P: American Dispositions in New Jersey, January 1, 1777.

502. Massachusetts Secretary of Commonwealth, *Massachusetts Soldiers and Sailors in the War of the Revolution*, 16: 249.

503. Wright, *The Continental Army*, 96; NARA; Lesser, *The Sinews of Independence*, 43–45.

504. Howe, *The Narrative of Lieutenant-General Sir William Howe*.

505. Fischer, *Washington's Crossing*, 113.

506. Irving, *The Life of George Washington*, 424; Fischer, *Washington's Crossing*, 114.

507. Fischer, *Washington's Crossing*, 114.

508. Ibid.; Charles Lee, letter to Adjunct Joseph Reed, November 24, 1776; also found in Reed, *Correspondence*, 1: 305 06.

509. Stryker, *The Battles of Trenton and Princeton*.

510. Gruber, *The Howe Brothers*, 354; Fischer, *Washington's Crossing*, 160–61.

511. Fischer, *Washington's Crossing*, 160–61.

512. Ibid., 126; Tustin, *Diary of the American War*, 18–19. Captain Johann von Ewald's diary.

513. Gruber, *The Howe Brothers*, 135–36.

514. Ibid.; General Howe's letters to Lord Germain, December 20, 1776; Stryker, *The Battles of Trenton and Princeton*, 327–28.

Chapter 6: American Covert Activities in France

515. Isham, *The Deane Papers*, 351; Paul, *Unlikely Allies*, 216–17.
516. Paul, *Unlikely Allies*, 217–18.
517. Ibid., 233.
518. Ibid., 234.
519. Ibid., 218.
520. Ibid., 219.
521. Ibid., 220.
522. Ibid., 246.
523. Fischer, *Washington's Crossing*, 151; George Washington to John Augustine, December 18, 1776; George Washington Papers, 6: 398.
524. Fischer, *Washington's Crossing*, 138.
525. Ibid., 140.
526. Ibid., 141.

Chapter 7: Battles of Trenton, Assunpink and Princeton

527. Fischer, *Washington Crossing*, 150, 195; letter from Major General Grant to General Rall, December 21, 1776.
528. Ibid., 150.
529. Ibid., 202–03.
530. Fischer, *Washington's Crossing*, 202; Reed, *Life and Correspondence of Joseph Reed*; Sparks, *Correspondence of the American Revolution*, GW 7, 426; Joseph Reed to George Washington, December 22, 1776.
531. Sparks, *Correspondence of the American Revolution*, GW 7, 437; General Washington: General Orders, December 25, 1775; Fischer, *Washington Crossing*, 208; Stryker, *Battles of Trenton and Princeton*, 358–59. Officers and noncommissioned officers had white stripes painted on the back of their helmets as a sign for their men to follow their leaders. It was a designation that officers should lead from the front of their troops.
532. Wilkinson, *Memoirs of My Own Times*, 128; Fischer, *Washington's Crossing*, 206.
533. Greenwood, *The Revolutionary Services of John Greenwood*, 80; Fischer, *Washington's Crossing*, 212.
534. Fischer, *Washington's Crossing*, 212–20.
535. Ibid., 219.
536. Wright, *The Continental Army*, Massachusetts regiments of the Continental Army. After the Battle of Valcour Island on Lake Champlain, Philip

Ulmer and the detached Twenty-fifth Continental Regiment (Arnold's brigade), whose commanding officer, Colonel Bond, had died at the end of August at Ticonderoga, were assigned first to Poor's brigade and then to the Third Massachusetts Regiment with Colonel Vose's brigade, an element of the main Continental Army. On December 18, 1776, Vose's brigade was redesigned as McDougall's brigade. On December 22, 1776, McDougall's brigade was part of Sargent's brigade, which operated with Glover's and St. Clair's brigades during the Delaware crossing and the Battle of Trenton. (See Fischer, *Washington's Crossing*, Appendix F, 390–92.) On January 1, 1777, the remnants of the Twenty-fifth Regiment and the Twenty-fourth Continental Regiment and Vose's brigade consolidated and were redesigned as a part of Greaton's Third Massachusetts Regiment.

537. Wright, *The Continental Army*. Massachusetts regiments of the Continental Army; National Archives and Records Administration, *Revolutionary War Pension and Bounty-Land Warrant Application Files*, Philip Ulmer, Continental Massachusetts, Pension number: S 19963. Recorded in the *Congressional Committee Records*: Washington, D.C.; Philip Ulmer, October 21, 1814.

538. Stryker, *The Battles of Trenton and Princeton*, 115, 150.

539. Ibid., 375; Letter from Captain William Hull to Andrew Adams, January 1, 1777.

540. Lancaster, *The American Revolution*, 164; Fischer, *Washington's Crossing*, 230.

541. Ibid., 408–09.

542. Stryker, *The Battles of Trenton and Princeton*.

543. Fischer, *Washington's Crossing*, 247.

544. White, *A Narrative of Events in the Revolutionary War*, 77.

545. Smith, *The Battle of Trenton*, 23; Fischer, *Washington's Crossing*, 251.

546. Dwyer, *The Day Is Ours!*, 259; Fischer, *Washington's Crossing*, 251.

547. Greenwood, *The Revolutionary Services of John Greenwood*.

548. Wilkinson, *Memoirs of My Own Time*.

549. Fischer, *Washington's Crossing*, 183.

550. Ibid.

551. Cresswell, *The Journal of Nicholas Cresswell*, 179–80.

552. Ibid., 182; Sir William Howe's letter to Sir George Germain, December 20, 1776 (Colonial Office records—military records 5/ 92-94, reports from General Howe to his superiors: Public Record Office, Kew, UK); Fischer, *Washington's Crossing*, 182.

553. Smith, *The Battle of Princeton*, 13, 291.

554. Fischer, *Washington's Crossing*, 264.

555. Ibid., 266.

556. Abbot et al., *Papers of Washington*, Colonial Series, 7: 477. General Washington to John Hancock, December 29, 1776.

557. Smith, *The Battles of Trenton & Princeton*, 8–9.

558. Fischer, *Washington's Crossing*, 269.

559. Abbot et al., *Papers of Washington*, Revolutionary War Series, 7: 489–90; General Washington's letter to Robert Morris, December 30, 1776, and Robert Morris's letter to Washington, December 30, 1776.

560. Ibid., 395; Azariah Dunham's letter to Joseph Trumbull, December 21, 1776.

561. Ibid., 489–90. Joseph Trumbull's letter to General Washington, December 13, 1776, and General Washington to Joseph Trumbull, December 16, 1776.

562. Konstam, *Privateers & Pirates*, 16.

563. Ibid., 497; General Washington's letter to Robert Morris, December 31, 1776.

564. Ibid.

565. Fischer, *Washington's Crossing*, 272.

566. Ibid.; Stone, *The Life and Recollections of John Howland*, 71; Olney, *Memoir*, found in *Biography of Revolutionary Heroes*, 193.

567. Abbot et al., *Papers of Washington*, Revolutionary War Series, 7: 500, 504; General Washington's letter to the Executive Committee of Congress, January 1, 1777, and Washington to Hancock, January 1, 1777.

568. Sergeant R——, "The Battle of Princeton" (Wellsborough, PA: Phoenix, 1832). Reprint, *Pennsylvania Magazine of History and Biography* 20 (1896), 515–19; Fischer, *Washington's Crossing*, 272–73.

569. Fischer, *Washington's Crossing*, 272–73.

570. Massachusetts Office of the Secretary of State, *Massachusetts Soldiers and Sailors in the War of the Revolution*, 249.

571. Dwyer, *The Day Is Ours!*, 319; Smith, *The Battle of Princeton*, 15.

572. Fischer, *Washington's Crossing*, 303.

573. Ibid.

574. Smith, *The Battle of Princeton*, 15.

575. Ibid., 17, 33; Dwyer, *The Day Is Ours!*, 327–29; Fischer, *Washington's Crossing*, 310.

576. Fischer, *Washington's Crossing*, 300.

577. Ibid., 299; Smith, *The Battle of Princeton*, 15; Dwyer, *The Day Is Ours!*, 316.

578. Fischer, *Washington's Crossing*, 408; Appendix P: St. Clair's Brigade, Paterson's First Massachusetts Continental Regiment; Chadwick, *The*

First American Army, 193. See Journal of Ebenezer Wild (1776–1781), soldier in Colonel Vose's First Massachusetts regiment; Secretary of the Commonwealth of Massachusetts, *Massachusetts Soldiers and Sailors in the War of the Revolution*, 249. Ulmer, Philip, lieutenant, Col. Vose's regiment; Continental Army pay accounts for service from January 1, 1777, to January 4, 1778; Colonel John Paterson's regiment; list of officers of the Continental Army; commissioned first lieutenant on March 27, 1777.

579. Wilkinson, *Memoirs of My Own Times*, 138; Smith, *The Battle of Princeton*, 16.

580. Smith, *The Battle of Princeton*, 15; Stryker, *The Battles of Trenton and Princeton*, 479; Fischer, *Washington's Crossing*, 301.

581. White, *Narrative of Events*, 77.

582. Dwyer, *The Day Is Ours!*, 323.

583. White, *Narrative of Events*, 77.

584. Dwyer, *The Day Is Ours!*, 323.

585. Fischer, *Washington's Crossing*, 310.

586. Ibid., 304.

587. Fischer, *Washington's Crossing*, 313–14; Smith, *St. Clair Papers*, 30–44; Battles of Trenton and Princeton; Wilkinson, *Memoirs of My Own Times*, 140.

588. Smith, *St. Clair Papers*, 30–44; Battles of Trenton and Princeton; Fischer, *Washington's Crossing*, 314–15.

589. Olney, *Memoir*, 195; Fischer, *Washington's Crossing*, 317.

590. Fischer, *Washington's Crossing*, 318.

591. Ibid., 319.

592. Smith, *Battle of Princeton*, 20.

593. Ibid., 358; Fisher, *Washington's Crossing*, 341–42.

594. Wilkinson, *Memoirs of My Own Time*, 143.

595. Ibid., 147; Rush, *Autobiography*, 128–29.

596. Fischer, *Washington's Crossing*, 334.

597. White, *Narrative of Events*, 78.

598. Bill, *The Campaign of Princeton*, 110–11; Fischer, *Washington's Crossing*, 338.

599. Bill, *The Campaign of Princeton*, 112; Smith, *Battle of Princeton*, 27.

600. Fischer, *Washington's Crossing*, 338–39.

601. Hale, "Letters Written During the American War of Independence," 18.

602. Stryker, *The Battles of Trenton and Princeton*, 458.

603. Freeman, *George Washington*, 357.

604. Wilkinson, *Memoirs*, 148–49.

605. Freeman, *George Washington*, 358.

606. Abbot et al., *Papers of Washington, Revolutionary War Series*, 7: 519–30; George Washington letter to John Hancock, January 5, 1777. (The "military chest" was believed to contain approximately seventy thousand pounds of sterling, according to Washington.); Fischer, *Washington's Crossing*, 340.

607. Fischer, *Washington's Crossing*, 340; Abbot et al., *Papers of Washington, Revolutionary War Series*, 7: 519–30.

608. Ewald, *Diary of the American War*, 50.

609. Ibid., 259–60.

610. Fischer, *Washington's Crossing*, 259–62.

611. Honore-Gabriel Riqueti, Comte de Mirabeau, *Avis aix Hessois et Autre Peoples de l'Allemagne Vendus par Leurs Princes a l'Angleterre* (Cleves, France, 1777), 16; Fischer, *Washington's Crossing*, 261.

612. White, *A Narrative of Events*, 74–79; Fischer, *Washington's Crossing*, 370–79.

613. Fischer, *Washington's Crossing*, 363–70.

Chapter 8: Winter Quarters at Morristown

614. Abbot et al., *Papers of Washington, Revolutionary War Series*, 8: January 28 and February 3, 1777; General Washington's letters to General Sullivan; additional letters to other field officers to assume the initiative and drive events found on pages 66–67, 245, 175, 237; Fischer, *Washington's Crossing*, 353.

615. Ketchum, *The Winter Soldiers*, 212; Fischer, *Washington's Crossing*, 137.

616. Ketchum, *The Winter Soldiers*, 217.

617. Ibid., 216–17.

618. McPherson, "Langdon, Stark, Bennington, and the Triumph of a Private Army, Part 1," *Freedom Daily*, September 2009.

619. Massachusetts Secretary of the Commonwealth, *Massachusetts Soldiers and Sailors in the War of the Revolution*, Volume 16, U, 249. "Ulmer, Philip, Lieutenant, Col. Vose's regt.; appointed Jan. 1, 1777; Continental Army pay accounts from Jan. 1, 1777, to Jan. 4, 1778; also 1st Lieutenant, Capt. Abraham Hunt's co., Col. John Paterson's regt.; list of the Continental Army; Commissioned March 27, 1777; same co. and regt., return on furlough, were in camp on or before Aug. 15, 1777; also 1st Lieutenant, Capt. Hunt's co., Col. Joseph Vose' regt., muster roll for Dec. 1777, sworn to at camp near Valley Forge; reported discharged Feb. 8, 1778 [at his

own request]. He had not been absent subsequently except on furlough, etc., dated Feb. 3, 1779; Captain, in Col. Samuel McCobb's reg't July 8, 1779 to Sept. 24, 1779; 2nd Major, Lieut. Col. Joseph Prime's reg't, under Brig. Gen. Peleg Wadsworth, March 25, 1780; Commissioned March 27, 1780 as 1st Major; Major in Col. Prime's reg't, March 25, to Nov. 25, 1780," MA01: Microcopy 246; Roll 35; Revolutionary War Pension and Bounty-Land Warrant Application Files, Philip Ulmer, Continental Massachusetts, Pension number: S 19963. Recorded in the Congressional Committee Records in Washington, D.C., Philip Ulmer, October 21, 1814. Philip Ulmer, *S 19963*, Series M804, Roll 2434, Frames 137–60.

620. Abbot et al., *Papers of Washington, Revolutionary War Series*, 8: 64. General Washington's letter to John Hancock, January 14, 1777; Fischer, *Washington's Crossing*, 352–53.

621. Ewald, *Diary of the American War*, 132–39.

622. Glaser, *Counterfeiting in America*, 37–39; Craughwell, *Stealing Lincoln's Body*, 33; James Rada, "Revolutionary War Counterfeiting: Attempting to Win War by Weakening Currency," *Colonial America*, September 5, 2008.

623. Davis and Mintz, *The Boisterous Sea of Liberty*. Josiah Bartlett letter to William Whipple, 1777; Gilder Lehrman Document number: GLC 193; University of Houston.

624. Continental Army Books, 18: 243: Philip Ulmer appears with the rank of lieutenant on the "Continental Army Pay Accounts" with Colonel Vose's Regiment for service from January 1, 1777, to January 4, 1778. He reportedly resigned on January 4, 1778, but was not discharged until February 8, 1778; dated February 3, 1779. Other military records indicate a discharge date of February 14, 1778. However, he remained on the muster rolls at Valley Forge until the end of March 1778.

625. Massachusetts Muster and Pay Rolls, 37: 78: Philip Ulmer appears among "A List of Officers of the Continental Army" as 1st Lieutenant in Capt. Abraham Hunt's Company, of John Paterson's Reg't.; dated March 27, 1777. Massachusetts Archives. General Paterson's name also appears as Paterson; Secretary of the Commonwealth of Massachusetts, *Massachusetts Soldiers and Sailors in the War of the Revolution*, 16: 249. Ulmer, Philip.

626. Books—Militia Officers, 28: 75; *A List of Officers of the Massachusetts Militia (Continental Army)*; Philip Ulmer appears as 1st Lieutenant in Capt. Abr'm Hunt's Company, of Col. John Paterson's Reg't.; Commissioned March 27, 1777; Secretary of the Commonwealth of Massachusetts,

Massachusetts Soldiers and Sailors in the War of the Revolution, 16: 249. Ulmer, Philip.

627. Massachusetts Office of the Secretary of State, *Massachusetts Soldiers and Sailors in the Revolutionary War,* 249.

628. Wild, "The Journal of Ebenezer Wild, 78–161.

629. Secretary of the Commonwealth of Massachusetts, *Massachusetts Soldiers and Sailors in the War of the Revolution*, 1: 881. Beckler, Daniel, Waldoborough, enlisted March 18, 1777, by Lieutenant Ulmer at Waldoborough; enlistment three years in Col. Vose's Regiment; Philip Ulmer's brother, George, enlisted January 18, 1777, for three years. Philip's cousin (also named George Ulmer) enlisted in the spring of 1777 with Lieutenant Ulmer, but he often was referred to as George Ulmer Jr. The George Ulmer cousins served together at the same time, while in the same company with Colonel Vose. George Ulmer Jr. was slightly younger in age than his cousin George (Lieutenant Philip Ulmer's brother) so he received the "junior" designation so the two men were not confused.

630. Massachusetts Secretary of the Commonwealth, *Massachusetts Soldiers and Sailors in the War of the Revolution*, 248. George Ulmer "enlisted from 1st Essex County regiment, sworn to at Salem by Joseph Sprague, 1st military officer of Salem, (residence Salem), in Col. John Paterson's Regiment. Reported received State bounty; Private in Capt. Hunt's company, Col. Vose's Regiment; muster roll Dec. 1777, sworn to at camp near Valley Forge. (Appears with Lieutenant Philip Ulmer in Glover's Brigade at Valley Forge) Enlisted Jan. 18, 1777, for three years with Capt. Hunt's company, Col. Joseph Vose's Regiment; also list of men mustered by Nathaniel Barber, Muster Master for Suffolk County, dated Boston, Feb. 2, 1777; Capt. Hunt's company, Col. John Paterson's Regiment. Continental Army pay accounts for service from Jan. 18, 1777 to Dec. 31, 1779. Sergeant, same company, and regiment; pay roll for Nov. 1778, sworn to at Providence (Rhode Island); Order for gratuity, dated Providence, Feb. 13, 1779; Same company and regiment, muster roll for March and April 1779, dated Providence; also Capt. Green's company, Col. Vose's Regiment; Continental Army pay accounts for service from Jan. 1 to Jan. 18, 1780; residence, Waldoborough; credited to town of Salem…"; Whitaker and Horlacher, *Broad Bay Pioneers*, 309. George Ulmer "a private in Col. Joseph Vose Reg't Line of Mass. Continental Establishment [*sic*], Capt. Hunt's Company, enlisted 17 May 1777 served to 7 May 1780, discharged near West Point. Skirmishes at White

Plains and at Flower Town, Rhode Island."; Stahl, *History of Old Broad Bay and Waldoboro,* Volume 1, 584. "Private in 1ˢᵗ Essex County Reg't, Continental Army. Enlisted: January 18, 1777 for 3 years. Discharged: January 18, 1780. Served with Capt. Hunt's Co., Col. Paterson's Regt., Promoted to Sergeant. At Valley Forge and White Plains. Later, became General of Militia." These military records conflict and overlap with each other, and it is very difficult to determine the actual truth about George Ulmer's records. There are so many errors and inaccuracies in the old historical writings.

631. Chadwick, *The First American Army,* 187.

632. Albert Van Dusen, "Connecticut: The First British Raid on Danbury," *New England Quarterly,* April 1777; Reprint, NY: Random House, 1961.

633. Wright, *The Continental Army.* Vose's Regiment.

634. Massachusetts Office of the Secretary of State, *Massachusetts Soldiers and Sailors in the Revolutionary War, 1775–1783,* 16: 249; Sons of the American Revolution, *Maine at Valley Forge,* 42; Those soldiers in Colonel Joseph Vose's Regiment who were recruited as privates under First Lieutenant Philip Ulmer of Waldoborough in the spring of 1777 and served in his company were: Privates John Kelloch, James Kelloch, David Kelloch (three brothers from St. Georges); George Ulmer Jr. and Daniel Beckley from Waldoborough; Charles Wallie from Georgetown; Isaac Bussell and David Bradlee from Penobscot (Bangor); Benjamin Brown from North Yarmouth; and Sergeant John Little from Newcastle.

635. Chambers, *The Hidden Children,* 57.

636. Wright, *The Continental Army.* Massachusetts regiments of the Continental Army; Colonel Joseph Vose's Regiment.

637. Chambers, *The Hidden Children,* 75–76.

638. Wright, *The Continental Army.* Massachusetts regiments of the Continental Army; Colonel Joseph Vose's Regiment.

639. Secretary of the Commonwealth, *Massachusetts Soldiers and Sailors in the War of the Revolution,* 16: 249. Lieutenant Philip Ulmer is present in "same company and regiment in return of men who were in camp on or before August 15, 1777, and who had not been absent subsequently except on furlough." Soldiers' Orders (Continental Line), "A Return"; Volume 10, pages 11, 77. Reported discharged February 8, 1778; dated February 3, 1779; Warrant for gratuity allowed by Council, March 4, 1779. Massachusetts Archives.

640. Wright, "Too Little, Too Late: The Campaign of 1777 in the Hudson Highlands," 30–40.

641. Wright, *The Continental Army*, 203, 212, 213. First Massachusetts Regiment, Colonel Vose's Regiment.

642. M.M. Quaife, "A Boy Soldier Under Washington," 555; Wild, "The Journal of Ebenezer Wild," 78–161; Chadwick, *The First American Army*, 190.

Chapter 9: Battle of Saratoga

643. Fischer, *Washington's Crossing*, 261.

644. Honore-Gabriel Riqueti, Comte de Mirabeau, *Avis aix Hessois*, 16; Fischer, *Washington's Crossing*, 261.

645. Paul, *Unlikely Allies*, 252, 226.

646. Ibid., 226–27.

647. Patton, *Patriot Pirates*, 159; Paul, *Unlikely Allies*, 228.

648. Willcox, *The Papers of Benjamin Franklin*, 548–49; Paul, *Unlikely Allies*, 252.

649. Paul, *Unlikely Allies*, 253.

650. Ibid.

651. Ibid.

652. Ibid., 269.

653. Ibid., 246.

654. Boatner, *Encyclopedia of the American Revolution*. General background information.

655. Gerlach, *Proud Patriot*, 300.

656. Wright, *The Continental Army*. First Massachusetts Line: Vose's Regiment, 1777.

657. Wild, "The Journal of Ebenezer Wild," 78–161; Chadwick, *The First American Army*, 186.

658. Ibid.

659. Ketchum, 145, 337.

660. Saratoga National Park Service, *The Saratoga Campaign of the Revolutionary War.* Original updated publication August 1997 and October 2009. Ulmer, Philip, Massachusetts; Lieutenant, Capt. Abraham Hunt's co., Col. Vose's regt ; Dec. 1777, Jan. 1, 1777, resigned Feb. 1778 at Valley Forge. Ref. MA01 CMA call number: 973.3444 qA2. Also see Vose, Joseph, Colonel, commander of the 1st Mass. Regiment, Glover's Brigade. Ref. SN01, US01.

661. Massachusetts Office of the Secretary of State, *Massachusetts Soldiers and Sailors in the Revolutionary War*, 16: 249. "Ulmer, Philip: 1st Lieutenant,

Capt. Abraham Hunt's co[mpany], Col. John Paterson's reg't.; *also*, 1ˢᵗ Lieutenant,…Col. Joseph Vose's reg't."

662. Wild, "The Journal of Ebenezer Wild," 78–161.

663. Ketchum, *Saratoga*, 337.

664. Ibid., 335–36.

665. Ibid., 336.

666. Abbot et al., *Papers of Washington, Revolutionary War Series*, Volume 1.

667. Ibid., 334.

668. Chadwick, *The First American Army*, 191.

669. Ketchum, *Saratoga*, 339.

670. Chadwick, *The First American Army*, 191.

671. Ketchum, *Saratoga*, 337–38.

672. Burgoyne, *The Remembrancer*, 25; letter from John Burgoyne to George Germain, August 20, 1777.

673. Nelson, *General Horatio Gates*, 114–15.

674. Ketchum, *Saratoga*, 292–95, 340.

675. Ibid., 339.

676. Chadwick, *The First American Army*, 191–93.

677. Ibid., 193–94.

678. Patterson, *Horatio Gates*, 150–53; Chadwick, *The First American Army*, 194.

679. Chadwick, *The First American Army*, 194; Wild, "Journal of Ebenezer Wild," 78–161.

680. Chadwick, *The First American Army*, 194.

681. Fortescue, *History of the British Army*, 204–44. Ward, *The War of the Revolution*, 943–54.

682. Chadwick, *The First American Army*, 194.

683. Ketchum, *Saratoga*.

684. Wild, "Journal of Ebenezer Wild," 78–161; Chadwick, *The First American Army*, 195.

685. Chadwick, *The First American Army*, 195.

686. Wright, *The Continental Army*. Vose's Regiment, Twenty-fifth Massachusetts Regiment—remnants of Colonel Bond's regiment.

687. Essex Institute, letter of John Glover to Azor Orne, September 21, 1777, Historical Collection 5, June 1863 (Peabody Essex Museum, Salem, MA), 101–02.

688. Digby, *The British Invasion from the North*, 274.

689. Chadwick, *The First American Army*, 197.

690. Flexner, *The Traitor and the Spy*, 170–73.

691. Chadwick, *The First American Army*, 198.

692. Ibid., 197–99.

693. Randall, *Benedict Arnold*, 368–69.

694. Wild, "Journal of Ebenezer Wild," 78–161; Chadwick, *The First American Army*, 199–200.

695. Wild, "Journal of Ebenezer Wild," 78–161.

696. Chadwick, *The First American Army*, 200.

697. Wild, "Journal of Ebenezer Wild," 78–161; Chadwick, *The First American Army*, 200.

698. Chadwick, *The First American Army*, 200.

699. Ibid., 199.

700. Ibid., 200.

701. Ibid., 201.

702. Massachusetts Secretary of the Commonwealth, *Massachusetts Soldiers and Sailors in the War of the Revolution*, 16: 249; "Ulmer, Philip; Lieutenant, Col. Vose's regt. [*sic*]; Continental pay accounts for service from Jan. 1, 1777 to Jan. 4, 1778; also 1st Lieutenant, Capt. Abraham Hunt's company, Col. John Paterson's (also written Paterson) regt. [*sic*]; List of officers of the Continental Army."

703. Chadwick, *The First American Army*, 202.

704. Ibid., 203.

705. Wild, "Journal of Ebenezer Wild," 78–161; Chadwick, *The First American Army*, 203.

706. Chadwick, *The First American Army*, 203.

707. Massachusetts Secretary of the Commonwealth, *Massachusetts Soldiers and Sailors in the War of the Revolution*, 16: 249; "Ulmer, Philip; Lieutenant, Col. Vose's reg't: Continental Army pay accounts for service from Jan. 1, 1777 to Jan. 4, 1778."

708. Ebenezer Wild, *Diary of Ebenezer Wild*, 78–161; Chadwick, *The First American Army*, 203.

709. Wild, "Journal of Ebenezer Wild," 78–161.

710. Chadwick, *The First American Army*, 204.

711. Wild, "Journal of Ebenezer Wild," 78–161; Chadwick, *The First American Army*, 204.

712. Ketchum, *Saratoga*, 425.

713. William L. Stone, trans. *Letters and Journals Relating to the War of the American Revolution;* Mrs. Frederika Charlotte Riedesel, (Albany, NY: Joel Munsell, 1867).

714. Ketchum, *Saratoga*, 437; Sewall, *Diary of Henry Sewall*.

715. Stone, *Burgoyne's Campaign*, 120–24, 379; Ketchum, *Saratoga*, 429–30.

716. Ketchum, *Saratoga*, 426–28; Von Riedesel, *Memoirs, Letters, and Journals of Major General Riedesel*, 187–88.

717. Stone, *The Campaigns of Lieut. General John Burgoyne*, 115.

718. Riedesel, *Baroness von Riedesel and the American Revolution*.

719. Stone, *Letters of Brunswick and Hessian Officers*, 128–31.

720. Quaife, *A Boy Soldier under Washington*, 555; Chadwick, *The First American Army*, 204–06.

721. Baxter, *Journal of Lieutenant William Digby*; Furneaux, *The Battle of Saratoga*, 268; Chadwick, *The First American Army*, 205.

722. Ketchum, *Saratoga*, 430.

723. Ibid., 430. See footnote at the bottom of the page: A British officer said, "It was not a little mortifying to us to hear them play that air when their army assembled to be witnesses of our surrender."

724. Riedesel, *Baroness von Riedesel and the American Revolution*; Stone, *Letters and Journals Relating to the War of the American Revolution*.

725. Doblin and Lynn, *The Specht Journal*.

726. Ketchum, *Saratoga*, 431.

727. Ibid.

728. Stone, *Letters of Brunswick and Hessian Officers*, 128–31; General Johann Specht, October 17, 1777; Doblin and Lynn, *The Specht Journal*; Ketchum, *Saratoga*, 432.

729. Doblin and Lynn, *The Specht Journal*.

730. Richard M. Ketchum, *Saratoga*, 432.

731. Ibid.

732. Riedesel, *Baroness von Riedesel and the American Revolution*; Riedesel, *Letters and Journals Relating to the War of the American Revolution*.

733. Ketchum, *Saratoga*, 437; Riedesel, *Letters and Journals Relating to the War of the American Revolution*.

734. Ketchum, *Saratoga*, 437.

735. Ibid., 437–38; Chadwick, *The First American Army*, 206.

736. Stone, *Letters of Brunswick and Hessian Officers*, 128–31; General Johann Specht, October 17, 1777; Doblin and Lynn, *The Specht Journal*; Ketchum, *Saratoga*, 437.

737. Fortescue, *History of the British Army*, Volume 3, Chapter XI, 234–37.

738. Ketchum, *Saratoga*, 438.

739. Brandt, *An American Aristocracy*, 121–22. Nickerson, *The Turning Point of the Revolution*, 405.

740. Ketchum, *Saratoga*, 439.

741. Fortescue, *History of the British Army*, 3: 239–42; Ketchum, *Saratoga*, 435–36.

742. Stahl, *History of Old Broad Bay and Waldoboro*, 462.

743. Wilson, *The Ancestors and Descendants of John Wilson*.

744. Stahl, *History of Old Broad Bay and Waldoboro*, 462; Collections of the Maine Historical Society, Document Series, 15: 266.

745. Stahl, *History of Old Broad Bay and Waldoboro*, 462.

746. Whitaker and Horlacher, *Broad Bay Pioneers*, 489–90.

747. Stahl, *History of Old Broad Bay and Waldoboro*, 462.

748. De Fonblanque, *Narrative and Critical History of America*, 6: 366; De Fonblanque, *Political and Military Episodes*.

749. Ketchum, *Saratoga*, 440–48; Mintz, *The Generals of Saratoga*. General information acquired about the generals and the politics within the military structure during the Revolution.

750. Riedesel, *Letters and Journals Relating to the War of the American Revolution*; Ketchum, *Saratoga*, 369.

751. Ketchum, *Saratoga*, 437; Henry Sewall of York, ME; Diary of Henry Sewall, October 17–18 entry.

752. Chadwick, *The First American Army*, 439.

753. Cutler, *Journal from 1761–1849*, Series 1, Manasseh Cutler Collection, MSS #9, (Ohio University Library: The Mahn Center, Archives and Special Collections.) October 22, 1777; Ketchum, *Saratoga*, 439.

754. Ibid.

755. Fortescue, *History of the British Army*, 3: 243–44.

756. Ketchum, *Saratoga*, 435–37.

757. Willcox, *Portrait of a General*. General information.

758. Ketchum, *Saratoga*, 440–42.

759. Fortescue, *History of the British Army*, 3: 244–45.

760. Benjamin Franklin, *The Papers of Benjamin Franklin*, edited by William B. Wilcox (New Haven, CT: Yale University Press, 1982); October 25, 1777, memorandum by Arthur Lee about his conversation with Franklin; Foreign Affairs Committee, *Communications: Commissioners in France*, (Washington D.C.: Library of Congress); Letters of October 6, 18, and 31, 1777; Ketchum, *Saratoga*, 441.

761. Ketchum, *Saratoga*, 446–47.

762. Chadwick, *The First American Army*, 209.

763. Boatner, *Encyclopedia of the American Revolution*.

Chapter 10: Valley Forge

764. Chadwick, *The First American Army*, 210.

765. Ibid., 206.

766. Ebenezer Wild, *Diary of Ebenezer Wild*, Proceedings of the Massachusetts Historical Society, Volume 6 (Boston: Massachusetts Historical Society, 1890), 78–161.

767. Wild, "Journal of Ebenezer Wild," 78–161; Chadwick, *The First American Army*, 211.

768. Wild, "Journal of Ebenezer Wild," 78–161.

769. Ibid.; Chadwick, *The First American Army*, 211.

770. Wild, "Journal of Ebenezer Wild," 78–161; Chadwick, *The First American Army*, 211.

771. Chadwick, *The First American Army*, 211.

772. Wild, "Journal of Ebenezer Wild," 78–161; Chadwick, *The First American Army*, 212.

773. Ibid.

774. Wild, "Journal of Ebenezer Wild," 78–161; Chadwick, *The First American Army*, 212–13.

775. Chadwick, *The First American Army*, 213.

776. Wild, "Journal of Ebenezer Wild," 78–161; Chadwick, *The First American Army*, 213.

777. Chadwick, *The First American Army*, 217.

778. National Historic Valley Forge, *George Washington's Letter to Governor George Clinton* (Philadelphia: Independence Hall Association, 1996); February 16, 1778.

779. National Historic Valley Forge, *Timeline Leading to Valley Forge*, December 19, 1777; Muster rolls, regiments.

780. Chadwick, *The First American Army*, 236.

781. Ibid., 236–37.

782. Ibid., 210.

783. Ibid., 218–19.

784. Ibid., 218.

785. Massachusetts Muster and Pay Rolls, Volume 48, 332; Muster Roll for Dec. 1777; Philip Ulmer, First Lieutenant; Capt. Abraham Hunt's Company; Col. Joseph Vose's Reg't; sworn to in camp near Valley Forge, January 6, 1778; Massachusetts Archives.

786. Waldo, *Life at Valley Forge (1777–1778)*, excerpted from *American History Told by Contemporaries*, Volume 2, *Building of the Republic*, edited by Albert B. Hart (New York: MacMillan, 1899), 568–72.

787. Ibid.

788. Massachusetts Secretary of the Commonwealth, *Massachusetts Soldiers and Sailors in the War of the Revolution*, Volume 16, U, 249.

789. Valley Forge National Park Service, *Participants at Valley Forge: Muster Roll Data Sheet*: Ulmer, Philip, Lieutenant, Personal ID: MA18825; 2nd MA Brigade, 1MA Regiment, 4th Division, Captain Abraham Hunt's company; General Glover Brigade commander; Muster roll of Jan., Feb., March 1778; Massachusetts Secretary of the Commonwealth; *Massachusetts Soldiers and Sailors in the War of the Revolution*, Volume 16, U, 249. Information also found in the New York State Library, CMA call number: 973.3444 qA2; Massachusetts Muster and Pay Rolls, Volume 48, 332: Muster Roll for Dec. 1777; Philip Ulmer, 1st Lieutenant; Capt. Abraham Hunt's Company; Col. Joseph Vose's Regiment; enlisted January 1, 1777; sworn to in camp near Valley Forge; January 6, 1778. Autograph signature.

790. Revolutionary War Pension and Bounty-Land Warrant Application Files, Philip Ulmer, Continental Massachusetts, Pension number: S 19963. Recorded in the Congressional Committee Records in Washington, D.C., Philip Ulmer, October 21, 1814. (See transcript at end of document written by Philip Ulmer.)

791. Massachusetts Secretary of the Commonwealth, *Massachusetts Soldiers and Sailors in the War of the Revolution*, Volume 16, U, 249; Valley Forge National Park Service, *Participants at Valley Forge: Muster Roll Data Sheet*: Ulmer, Philip, Lieutenant, Personal ID: MA18825; 2nd MA Brigade, 1MA Regiment, 4th Division, Captain Abraham Hunt's company; General Glover Brigade commander; Muster roll of Jan., Feb., March 1778.

792. Stahl, *History of Old Broad Bay and Waldoboro*, 463; Valley Forge National Historical Park, *Maine at Valley Forge: Muster Roll of Maine Soldiers at Valley Forge*, 42. Colonel Vose's Regiment and Captain Abraham Hunt's Company: Lieutenant Philip Ulmer listed with his young recruit privates and sergeant John Little; Massachusetts Secretary of the Commonwealth, *Massachusetts Soldiers and Sailors in the War of the Revolution*, Volume 16, U, 249.

793. Chadwick, *The First American Army*, 223–24.

794. Ibid., 233.

795. Ibid.

796. Boyle, *Writings from the Valley Forge Encampment*, 2: 66–68. Letter from General John Paterson to Thomas Marshall, February 23, 1777.

797. Boyle, *Writings from the Valley Forge Encampment*, 1: 39–40. Letter from Archelaus Lewis to Jesse Partridge, February 1, 1778.

798. Governor and Council Letters, Massachusetts State Archives, Force Mss., Series 7E, (Washington, D.C.: David Library: Library of Congress). Letter of Colonel William Shepard at Valley Forge to the Massachusetts Legislature; Chadwick, *The First American Army*, 236, 799. Benjamin Rush letter to General Horatio Gates, February 4, 1778, Valley Forge Historical Park Collection (Valley Forge, Pennsylvania: Valley Forge Park Authority); Chadwick, *The First American Army*, 225.

800. Chadwick, *The First American Army*, 226–27.

801. Lefkowitz, *George Washington's Indispensable Men*, 232–40.

802. Fitzpatrick, *The Writings of George Washington*, 192–98. George Washington's letter to Henry Laurens, December 23, 1777.

803. Channing, *Students History of the United States*, 210–11.

804. Boyle, *Writings from the Valley Forge Encampment*, 3: 106. Source: Jeremiah Wadsworth Papers: Correspondence, Connecticut Historical Society. Letter from Jeremiah Wadsworth to Ephraim Blane from Camp Valley Forge, April 21, 1778.

805. Chase and Lengel, *The Papers of George Washington*, Revolutionary War Series, Volume 13.

Chapter 11: Political Unrest

806. Paul, *Unlikely Allies*, 190.

807. Ibid.

808. Isham, *The Deane Papers*, 166–70; Paul, *Unlikely Allies*, 190.

809. Paul, *Unlikely Allies*, 240–42.

810. Patton, *Patriot Pirates*, 51–52.

811. Ibid., 76–77. "The supplies delivered aboard Deane's vessels would figure significantly in the Revolution's pivotal battle, the American victory at Saratoga…a battle whose rout of the enemy's attempt to sever New England from the other colonies profoundly shook the prevailing worldview that Britain was invincible."

812. Boatner, *Encyclopedia of the American Revolution*. Thomas Mifflin was removed in October 1777 as quartermaster general; General Greene filled the position of quartermaster general in March 1778; Rossum, *Thomas Mifflin*, 929.

813. Information courtesy of the Independence Hall Association, Valley Forge Historical Society publications, The Conway Cabal: see ushistory.org.

814. Ibid.; Ferling, *The First of Men*, 225.

815. Information courtesy of the Independence Hall Association, Valley Forge Historical Society publications: see ushistory.org.

816. Independence Hall Association, Valley Forge Historical Society publications, The Conway Cabal; Ferling, *The First of Men*.

817. Klos, *Historical Documents of Freedom*; Wilson and Fiske, *Appleton's Cyclopedia American Biography*.

818. Ferling, *The First of Men*, 237–38.

819. Klos, *Historical Documents of Freedom*.

820. Augur, *The Secret War of Independence*, 274.

821. Tower, *The Marquis de La Fayette in the American Revolution*, 241; Smith, *Memoir of the Baron de Kalb*.

822. Case, *Lafayette and the Knight's Templar*, 59–61.

823. Morse, *Freemasonry in the American Revolution*; Hieronimus and Cortner, *Founding Fathers, Secret Societies*, 44–45.

824. Valley Forge Muster Roll: Philip Ulmer; ID Number MA18825; MA State; Lieutenant rank; 1 MA Regiment; 2nd MA Brigade; 4th Division. Service: January, February, March 1778.

825. Lesser, *The Senews of Independence*, Division/Brigade File: 2nd Massachusetts Brigade. Commander: BG John Glover. Part of DeKalb's Fourth Division.

826. Revolutionary War Pension and Bounty-Land Warrant Application Files, Philip Ulmer, Continental Massachusetts, Pension number: S 19963. Recorded in the *Congressional Committee Records*: Washington, D.C.; Philip Ulmer, October 21, 1814.

827. Case, *Lafayette and the Knight's Templar*, 59–61.

828. Ulmer family letter with a brief reference to a visit from Lafayette and written by an Ulmer family descendant. A copy of the letter is in possession of the author and in the Lincolnville Historical Society files.

829. Boyle, *Writings from the Valley Forge Encampment*. Resignation: Lieutenant Philip Ulmer, First Massachusetts Regiment; letters of recommendation from Colonel Vose and Colonel William Shepard, commander; NARA, Record Group 93, M859, Roll 8, Document 2282 and Document 2308; acceptance of Philip Ulmer's resignation, same as above, but Document 2282; Saratoga National Historical Park, *American Participants in the Battles of Saratoga*, Saratoga County: UV, Ulmer, Philip, Lieutenant, Colonel Vose's regiment; from January 1, 1777, resigned January 4, 1778 (or February 8, 1778); also December 1777 at Valley Forge; Ref. MA01. Massachusetts Commonwealth, *Massachusetts Soldiers and Sailors in the War of the Revolution*, Volume

16, 249; Additional information can be found at the New York State Library, CMA call number: 973.3444 qA2.

830. Valley Forge National Historical Park, Valley Forge Muster Roll Data Sheet, Monthly Muster Roll Status; Personal ID: MA18825, Ulmer, Philip; Rank: Lieutenant; Brigade: 2nd MA Brigade; Company: Captain Abraham Hunt's; State: MA; Regiment: 1 MA; Division: 4th Division; Monthly Muster Roll Status: January, February, March 1778; Name on roll without comment...

831. Secretary of the Commonwealth, *Massachusetts Muster and Pay Rolls*, 10: 67. Information copied from microfilm records in the Massachusetts Archives. Massachusetts Archives, *An Account rendered against the United States by the Commonwealth of Massachusetts for amounts for officers and men of Vol. Joseph Vose's Regiment... for wages for the first three years' service in the Continental Army... Account exhibited by Committee on Claims in behalf of Mass. against US, Sept. 21, 1787;* Mass. Archives: Depreciation Rolls, 31: 83.

832. Boyle, *Writings from the Valley Forge Encampment.* Resignation: Lieutenant Philip Ulmer. First Massachusetts Regiment.; letters of recommendation from Col. Vose and Col. William Shepard, Commander; NARA, Record Group 93, M859, Roll 8, Document 2282 and Document 2308; acceptance of Philip Ulmer's resignation, Document 2282.

833. Office of Army Accounts, Paymaster General, *Compiled Service Records of Soldiers Who Served in the American Army During the Revolutionary War, 1775–1785,* Journal American Congress, 4: 237; NARA M881; Continental, Mass.: Ulmer, Philip, number: S. 19963; Book Mark: R & P 436.786; Valley Forge National Park Service, *American Participants at Valley Forge: Muster Roll Data Sheet:* Ulmer, Philip, Lieutenant, Personal ID: MA18825; 2nd MA Brigade, 1MA Regiment, 4th Division, Captain Abraham Hunt's company; Muster roll of Jan., Feb., March 1778; Revolutionary War 1777–1781: Pay Roll of Captain Hunt's Company in Colonel Joseph Vose Regiment, Folder 2; Publication Number: M246; NARA publisher; Shows Lieutenant Philip Ulmer's pay for the months of January, February 1778. Information from Massachusetts Archives indicates "Philip Ulmer appeared on a list of men whose gratuity had *not* been paid for his military service." Records found at the State House in Boston, Massachusetts; Sons of the American Revolution, *Maine at Valley Forge: Proceedings at the Unveiling of the Maine Marker, October 17, 1907 (*Portland, ME: Sons of the American Revolution, 1908), 42; Revolutionary War Pension and Bounty-Land Warrant Application Files, Philip Ulmer, Continental Massachusetts,

Pension number: S 19963. Recorded in the Congressional Committee Records in Washington, D.C., Philip Ulmer, October 21, 1814. (See transcript at end of document written by Philip Ulmer.)

834. Ferling, *The First of Men*, 225.

835. Independence Hall Association, *The Conway Cabal*. Information courtesy of Independence Hall Association: ushistory.org.

836. Patton, *Patriot Pirates*, 194.

837. Wood, *The Radicalism of the American Revolution*, 146.

838. Klos, *Historical Documents of Freedom*.

839. Ferling, *The First of Men*, 238.

840. Independence Hall Association, *General Baron de Kalb*; The official record of DeKalb is found in Weedon's Valley Forge Orderly Book, November 22, 1777. Washington ordered that "the Brigades commanded by Generals Paterson and Learned are to form one division under Major Genl. And Baron DeKalb."

841. Lesser, *The Senews of Independence*, Valley Forge Muster Roll, Division/ Brigade File: DeKalb's Division 4: 2nd Massachusetts Brigade: Commander, BG John Glover: 1st Massachusetts: Colonel Joseph Vose; 4th MA: Colonel William Shephard; 13th MA: Colonel Edward Wigglesworth; 15MA: Colonel Timothy Bigelow.

842. Massachusetts Muster and Pay Rolls, 48: 332: Muster Roll for Dec. 1777: Philip Ulmer, 1st Lieutenant, in Capt. Abraham Hunt's Company, Col. Joseph Vose Regt.: sworn to in camp near Valley Forge, January 6, 1778; located in the Massachusetts Archives; Valley Forge Muster Roll, Lieutenant Philip Ulmer; ID Number MA18825, 2nd Massachusetts Brigade; Colonel Vose's 1st Massachusetts Regiment; Captain Abraham Hunt's Company; 4th Division: January, February, March, 1778; Sons of the American Revolution, *Maine at Valley Forge: Proceedings at the Unveiling of the Maine Marker October 17, 1907: also Rolls of Maine Soldiers at Valley Forge*, 42; Regiment List: Colonel Joseph Vose Regiment: Captain Abraham Hunt's Company: 1st Lieutenant Philip Ulmer, Waldoborough; Secretary of the Commonwealth, *Massachusetts Soldiers and Sailors in the War of the Revolution*, Volume 16, 249; 1st Lieutenant, Capt. Hunt's company, Col. Joseph Vose's regiment; Muster Roll for December 1777, sworn to at Camp near Valley Forge; Lesser, *The Senews of Independence, Monthly Strength Returns of the Continental Army*; See Division/Brigade File; 2nd Massachusetts Brigade; Commander: BG John Glover; 1st MA Regiment: Colonel Joseph Vose,... "Entered Valley Forge in Dec. 1777 and departed in Jun. 1778. Part of DeKalb's Fourth Division. Most men from 2nd Brigade were fishermen

from Marblehead area. They were involved in Washington's [Delaware] river crossings. After their enlistments were up, they became Privateers."

843. Lesser, *The Sinews of Independence*, Valley Forge Muster Roll, returns of division and brigade commanders in the Continental Army.

844. Secretary of the Commonwealth, *Massachusetts Soldiers and Sailors*, 16: 249. Sons of the American Revolution, *Maine at Valley Forge*, 42; Regiment List: Colonel Joseph Vose Regiment: Captain Abraham Hunt's Company: 1st Lieutenant Philip Ulmer.

845. Lesser, *The Sinews of Independence*; See Division/Brigade File; 2nd Massachusetts Brigade; Commander: BG John Glover, part of DeKalb's Division.

846. Ibid. See Division/Brigade File; 2nd Massachusetts Brigade; Commander: BG John Glover; 1st MA Regiment: Colonel Joseph Vose… "Entered Valley Forge in Dec.1777 and departed in Jun. 1778. Part of DeKalb's Fourth Division…"

847. Ferling, *The First of Men*, 238; Valley Forge Historical Society, *Lafayette and the Canadian Invasion*; ushistory.org.

848. Valley Forge Historical Society, *Lafayette and the Canadian Invasion*; ushistory.org.

849. Ibid.

850. Ibid.

851. Boatner, *Encyclopedia of the American Revolution*; Wilkins, *Steuben Screamed*. Courtesy of the National Center of the American Revolution/Valley Forge Historical Society.

852. Wilkins, *Steuben Screamed*; Boatner, *Encyclopedia of the American Revolution*; Bruce Chadwick, *The First American Army*, 240.

853. Chadwick, *The First American Army*, 240.

854. Muster Roll and Pay Abstract for Captain Hunt's Company, Colonel Vose's Regiment at Valley Forge, March 1778.

855. Boatner, *Encyclopedia of the American Revolution*; Wilkins, *Steuben Screamed*. Courtesy of the National Center of the American Revolution/Valley Forge Historical Society.

856. Wilkins, *Steuben Screamed*. Courtesy of the National Center of the American Revolution/Valley Forge Historical Society.

857. Secretary of the Commonwealth, *Massachusetts Muster and Pay Rolls*, 10: 67. Information copied from microfilm records in the Massachusetts Archives. Massachusetts Archives, *An Account rendered*. Massachusetts Archives: Depreciation Rolls, 31: 83.

858. Hieronimus and Cortner, *Founding Fathers*, 44–48.

859. Daughters of the American Revolution, "Application of Amelia Carr Severance, Scituate, Massachusetts" National Number: 254776. Descendant of Philip Martin Ulmer. Application examined and approved by the National Society of the Daughters of the American Revolution on October 9, 1943. Lineage page: Horatio Gates Stevens born December 4, 1820, and died March 31, 1909; child of Paul H. Stevens and Christiana (Ulmer) Stevens, and grandson of Philip Martin Ulmer and Christiana (Young) Ulmer of Waldoboro and Lincolnville, Maine.

860. Boutelle and Burr, "State News: Knox [County]," *Bangor Daily Wig and Courier*, September 30, 1887, Volume LIV, Number 231.

861. Dunnack, *The Maine Book*, 92.

862. Secretary of the Commonwealth, *Massachusetts Soldiers and Sailors*, 249.

863. Williamson, "Obituary of General George Ulmer," *Hancock Gazette and Penobscot Patriot*, January 11, 1826.

864. Library of Congress, *US Statutes at Large*, 6.

865. Cahill, *New England's Naughty Navy*, 44.

866. Boatner, *Encyclopedia of the American Revolution*; Martin, *The Philadelphia Campaign*.

867. Paul, *Unlikely Allies*, 284–85.

868. *Philadelphia Packet*, July 14, 1778, reprinted in Deane Papers, 2: 471–72.

869. Library of Congress, *Washington Papers*, Revolutionary War: Southern Phase, 1778–1781, Manuscript Division (Washington, D.C.); Washington to the Continental Congress, October 22, 1780; Washington to General Nathanael Greene, October 22, 1780.

870. Egret, *La Pré-Révolution Française*, 59; Andress, *1789*, 63.

Chapter 12: Privateering During the Revolution

871. Chadwick, *The First American Army*, 303–05.

872. Ibid., 304.

873. Cahill, *New England's Naughty Navy*, 44.

874. Ibid.

875. Boatner, *Encyclopedia of the American Revolution*; Lampman, "Privateers of the Revolution," *SAR Magazine* 105, no. 4, 20.

876. Lampman, "Privateers of the Revolution," 20.

877. Boatner, *Encyclopedia of the American Revolution*; Lampman, "Privateers of the Revolution," 20.

878. Library of Congress, *Letters of the Delegates to Congress*.

879. Cohn, *Liberty's Children*, 117.

880. Revolutionary War Pension and Bounty-Land Warrant Application Files, Philip Ulmer, Continental Massachusetts, Pension number: S 19963. Recorded in the Congressional Committee Records in Washington, D.C., Philip Ulmer, October 21, 1814.

881. Stahl, *History of Broad Bay and Waldoboro*, 478.

882. Whitaker and Horlacher, *Broad Bay Pioneers*, 420, Revolutionary War statement on Charles Oberlacher; 404, Paul Mink; 405, Valentine Mink. Others mentioned in Captain Philip Ulmer's Company who were involved in building fortifications and sailed for the defense of the frontier were Martin Benner, John Creamer, Conrad Heyer, Paul and John Mink and Charles Hebner.

883. Daughters of the American Revolution, Application for Membership of Amelia Carr Severance, Scituate, Massachusetts, National Number: 254776. Application examined and approved on October 9, 1943, page 3. Amelia Severance is the great-granddaughter of Philip Martin Ulmer.

884. Sons of the American Revolution, Maine Society, *Maine in War: Organization and Officers of the Society, Constitution* (Portland, ME: The Thurston Print, 1897), 92; Commission of Philip Martin Ulmer, 2nd Major; Secretary of the Massachusetts Commonwealth, *Massachusetts Soldiers and Sailors in the War of the Revolution*, 16: 249.

885. Robinson, *History of Amity Lodge*, 55.

886. Whitaker and Horlacher, *Broad Bay Pioneers*, 404–05. See the Revolutionary War statements of Paul and Valentine Mink (Minck).

887. Whitaker and Horlacher, *Broad Bay Pioneers*, 404, 420. See the lineage and pension records of (Johann) Paul Minck and Charles Oberlach who were soldiers in Captain Philip Ulmer's Company. Paul Minck's record states: "private in Capt Ulmer's Co and Col McCobb's Reg't [*sic*], 1 May 1779...and marched by Ulmer to Damariscotta on to Towns end [*sic*], now called Boothbay; transported to Baggaduce [*sic*] where we were landed and took our small arms with us...served on board State sloop, Capt Curtis..." Charles Oberlach's record states: "enlisted May 1779 in Capt Philip Ulmer's Co, and 2 or 3 weeks later marched by Capt Ulmer to Damariscotta, then to Towns End...helped build fort at Cox's Head and erected barracks. The British fired upon the fort & Barracks."

888. Abbott and Elwell, *The History of Maine*, 385.

889. Whitaker and Horlacher, *Broad Bay Pioneers*, 404, 420, 585. See Charles Oberlacher, who served in Major Philip Ulmer's company. He was in

service with Paul and John C. Mink, Conrad Heyer, John Werner (Varner), Martin Brenner, Jacob Bornheimer and John Creamer also served with Philip Ulmer a various times during the Revolutionary War. (Johann) Paul Minck and Charles Oberlach were soldiers in Captain Philip Ulmer's Company. Paul Minck's record states: "private in Capt Ulmer's Co and Col McCobb's Reg't [*sic*]; Charles Oberlach's record states: "enlisted May 1779 in Capt Philip Ulmer's Co, and 2 or 3 weeks later marched by Capt Ulmer to Damariscotta, then to Towns End…helped build fort at Cox's Head and erected barracks. The British fired upon the fort & Barracks." Jacob Bornheimer, (Bornhamer), private in Colonel Samuel McCobb's Reg't: "service a place called Cox's Head, at the mouth of the Kennebec River."

890. Goold, *Falmouth Neck in the Revolution,* 49.

891. Stahl, *History of Broad Bay and Waldoboro,* 465.

892. Ibid.

893. Ibid.

894. Ibid.

895. Whitaker and Horlacher, *Broad Bay Pioneers,* 156–65, Broad Bay Land Records; Stahl, *History of Broad Bay and Waldoboro,* 390.

896. Whitaker and Horlacher, *Broad Bay Pioneers,* 156–65, Broad Bay Land Records.

897. Lincoln County, Deeds, Book 13, 180; Stahl, *History of Broad Bay and Waldoboro,* 396.

898. Whitaker and Horlacher, *Broad Bay Pioneers,* 159, Broad Bay Land Records.

899. Stahl, *History of Broad Bay and Waldoboro,* 464. There is a discrepancy between the two Waldoboro historians, Jasper J. Stahl and Samuel L. Miller, about the Ulmer man who served as selectman in 1778. Samuel L. Miller recorded in his book *History of the Town of Waldoboro, Maine* (1910) that George Ulmer was the Waldoboro town officer in 1778 who served as a selectman. However, George Ulmer (brother of Philip M. Ulmer) was serving at the time with General Washington's Continental Army in New Jersey and Rhode Island until his discharge on January 18, 1780. George Ulmer Jr. (cousin of Philip Ulmer) was also serving with Washington's Continental Army at the same time as his cousin George Ulmer until being discharged in April 1779 and then returned to Waldoboro after a three-year enlistment. Therefore, it is reasonable to determine that John Ulmer (Philip and George Ulmer's uncle) was most likely to have been the selectman of the town of Waldoboro in 1778.

900. Stahl, *History of Broad Bay and Waldoboro*, 464.

901. Ibid., 390.

902. Ibid., 396–97.

903. Whitaker and Horlacher, *Broad Bay Pioneers*, 307.

904. Ibid., 510.

905. Cahill, *New England's Naughty Navy*, 45.

906. Patton, *Patriot Pirates*, 107.

907. Engle and Lott, *American Merchant Marine at War*.

908. Clarke, *Naval Documents of the American Revolution*, Volume 9, 982. George Washington to Brigadier General Heath.

909. Patton, *Patriot Pirates*, 107.

910. Cahill, *New England's Naughty Navy*, 39.

911. Whitaker and Horlacher, *Broad Bay Pioneers*, 131; Stahl, *History of Broad Bay and Waldoboro*, 451. There are discrepancies in the historical accounts concerning the capture of George Ulmer at age twenty while fishing off Marblehead Harbor in 1775. Jasper J. Stahl claims that George Ulmer (son of John Ulmer Jr.) was the young man captured by the British frigate *Lively* in 1775. George Ulmer (son of their uncle John Ulmer Jr.) was born in July 1760 and would have been just fifteen years of age when he lived with his family in Broad Bay. He could not have been present when the attempted impressment took place in 1775 near Marblehead Harbor. However, in the account of Whitaker and Horlacher in *Broad Bay Pioneers*, George Ulmer (brother of Philip Ulmer) was the young man captured at this time when he lived in Salem with his mother and other family members. In the birth records of the two George Ulmers, the only person who was twenty in 1775 when the attempted impressments near Marblehead Harbor took place was George Ulmer, the brother of Philip, who was born in February 1755. Philip's brother, George, would have been twenty years of age at this time.

912. Cahill, *New England's Naughty Navy*, 39.

913. Lesser, *The Sinews of Independence*, Second Massachusetts Brigade, Commander Brigadier General Glover: "Most men from the 2nd MA Brigade were fishermen. They were involved in Washington's River crossing, after their enlistments were up, they became privateers."

914. Cahill, *New England's Naughty Navy*, 39.

Chapter 13: British Attempt to Annex Maine

915. Maine Historical Society, *Collections and Proceedings of the Maine Historical Society*, Second Series, 1: 395; Buker, *The Penobscot Expedition*, 4–5; Bicheno, *Redcoats and Rebels*, 149.

916. Maine Historical Society, *Collections and Proceedings of the Maine Historical Society*, Second Series, 1: 395–96.

917. Ibid.

918. Hoffman and Albert, *Diplomacy and Revolution*.

919. Ward, *War of the Revolution*.

920. Stahl, *History of Broad Bay and Waldoboro*, 466–67.

921. Ibid., 466.

922. Ibid.

923. Buker, *The Penobscot Expedition*, 11; Bicheno, *Redcoats and Rebels*, 149; Stahl, *History of Broad Bay and Waldoboro*, 466.

924. Buker, *The Penobscot Expedition*, 7, 11.

925. Ibid., 14.

926. Stahl, *History of Broad Bay and Waldoboro*, 467.

927. Buker, *The Penobscot Expedition*, 16–36.

928. Patton, *Patriot Pirates*, 131; Cahill, *New England's Naughty Navy*, 48; Paul, *Unlikely Allies*, 14–15. Silas Deane married Elizabeth Saltonstall, the granddaughter of Gurdon Saltonstall, the former royal governor of Connecticut. Her brother was Commodore Dudley Saltonstall.

929. Stahl, *History of Broad Bay and Waldoboro*, 467.

930. Lovell, *The Original Journal of General Solomon Lovell*, 78. See Major Todd's Report; State Archives, 145: 230; Robinson, *The History of Camden and Rockport*, 52.

931. Robinson, *History of Camden and Rockport*, 52.

932. Ibid.

933. Stahl, *History of Broad Bay and Waldoboro*, 584–85; Secretary of the Commonwealth, *Massachusetts Soldiers and Sailors*, 16: 249.

934. Secretary of the Commonwealth, *Massachusetts Soldiers and Sailors*, 16: 249.

935. Ibid., 249. "Ulmer, Philip Martin, Waldoborough, Captain, Col. Samuel McCobb's Regiment." Also found in Massachusetts Archives.

936. Goold, *Bagaduce Expedition*.

937. Secretary of the Commonwealth, *Massachusetts Soldiers and Sailors*, 16: 249.

938. Miller, *History of the Town of Waldoboro*, 87; Stahl, *History of Broad Bay and Waldoboro*, Chapters 4–9: Immigrants… Lists places of origin in Europe, family lineage, and military service.

939. Stahl, *History of Broad Bay and Waldoboro*, 467.

940. Ibid., 454.

941. Ibid., 467. In April 1776, General Thomas was with Ensign Philip Ulmer in Canada, where General Thomas was to assume the command of the Canadian Expedition from Benedict Arnold after the death of General Montgomery during the attack on Quebec in December 1775.

942. Robinson, *The History of Camden and Rockport*, 52.

943. Ibid.; Franks Jr., *A Few Good Men*.

944. Secretary of the Commonwealth, *Proceedings from the Massachusetts Council of War*, Collection of the Revolutionary Period, 1629–1799.

945. Robinson, *The History of Camden and Rockport*, 52.

946. Ibid.

947. Ibid.; Stahl, *History of Broad Bay and Waldoboro*, 468.

948. Buker, *The Penobscot Expedition*, 14.

949. Stahl, *History of Broad Bay and Waldoboro*, 467.

950. Robinson, *The History of Camden and Rockport*, 53; Stahl, *History of Broad Bay and Waldoboro*, 466–68.

951. Ibid.

952. Lovell, *The Original Journal of General Solomon Lovell*, 28–36.

953. Williamson, *History of the State of Maine*, 468–78. William Williamson served as a sergeant in Captain Philip Ulmer's company during the Penobscot Expedition and later became the governor of the state of Maine.

954. Gould, *Storming the Heights*, 46–47.

955. Goold, *Bagaduce Expedition*.

956. Stahl, *History of Broad Bay and Waldoboro*, 468; Robinson, *The History of Camden and Rockport*, 53.

957. Goold, *History of Colonel Jonathan Mitchell's Cumberland County Regiment*, 32.

958. Stahl, *History of Broad Bay and Waldoboro*, 468–69. It included, among others, these men from Waldoborough: Captain Philip M. Ulmer, Jacob Achorn, John Achorn, Michael Achorn, John Benner, Jacon Genthner, Martin Hoch, George Hoffses, John Hunt, Charles Kaler, Paul Mink, Valentine Mink, Christopher Newbert, Henry Oberloch, Peter Orff (Off), Isaac Sargas, Joseph Simmons, John Ulmer Jr. (a cousin from Thomaston), Christopher Walch, John Welt, John Werner and Peter Winchenbach.

All were enlisted for two months. See Massachusetts Secretary of State, *Muster Roll*.

959. Robinson, *History of Amity Lodge No. 6*.

960. Franks Jr., *A Few Good Men*. See Continental Navy.

961. Goold, *History of Colonel Jonathan Mitchell's Cumberland County Regiment*, 32; Wheeler, *History of Castine, Penobscot, & Brooksville*, 50.

962. Stahl, *History of Old Broad Bay and Waldoboro*, 469.

963. Ibid.; Eaton, *History of Thomaston, Rockland, and South Thomaston*, 133.

964. Eaton, *Annals of the Town of Warren*, 1: 176–78; Volume 2, 188.

965. Stahl, *History of Old Broad Bay and Waldoboro*, 471; Robinson, *History of Amity Lodge No. 6*.

966. Eaton, *Annals of the Town of Warren*, 176–78; Whitaker and Horlacher, *Broad Bay Pioneers*, 489. See account of Christopher Newbert, who served in Captain Philip Ulmer's company during the Penobscot Expedition and was severely injured and lost his arm on the assault on Bagaduce, July 28, 1779; Stahl, *History of Broad Bay and Waldoboro*, 469–70.

967. Robinson, *History of Camden and Rockport*, 52–53; Stahl, *History of Broad Bay and Waldoboro*, 469; Eaton, *History of Thomaston, Rockland, and South Thomaston*, 1: 133.

968. Revolutionary War Pension and Bounty-Land Warrant Application Files, M804, Continental Massachusetts, Philip Ulmer, Pension number: S10063; See the Testimonies of Joseph Coombs and Alexander Kelloch.

969. Stahl, *History of Broad Bay and Waldoboro*, 469.

970. Buker, *The Penobscot Expedition*, 42–45.

971. Whitaker and Horlacher, *Broad Bay Pioneers*, 489–90; Stahl, *History of Broad Bay and Waldoboro*, 470.

972. U.S. House of Representatives, *Digested Summary and Alphabetical List of Private Claims Which Have Been Presented to the House of Representatives*, Volume 3, Congress 13, Session 2, Journal page 209; Referred to Committee: Pens. & Rev. Claims; Referred to Committee Whole House; Date: Mar. 28, 1814; U.S. House of Representatives, *Digested Summary and Alphabetical List of Private Claims Which Have Been Presented to the House of Representatives*, Volume 3, Congress 14, Session 1, Journal page 64; Referred to Committee: Pens & Rev. Claims; Senate: Passed; Bill: 171; Congress Date: Apr. 29, 1816; House: Passed; Report: Favorable; Revolutionary War Pension and Bounty-Land Warrant Application Files, Philip Ulmer, Continental Massachusetts; Pension number: S 19963.

973. Revolutionary War Pension and Bounty-Land Warrant Application Files, M804, Continental Massachusetts, Philip Ulmer, Pension number: S10063; See Congressional testimonies of Joseph Coombs and Alexander Kelloch.

974. Ibid.

975. Buker, *The Penobscot Expedition*, 50–52.

976. Ibid.

977. Goold, *Bagaduce Expedition*, Volume 4; Read before the Maine Historical Society, October 27, 1898; General Wadsworth letter to William D. Williamson, January 1, 1828.

978. Ibid.

979. Kevitt, *General Solomon Lovell*, 174–75; Buker, *The Penobscot Expedition*, 52–56.

980. Wheeler, *History of Castine, Penobscot, & Brooksville*, 50.

981. Lovell, *The Original Journal of General Lovell*, 74–81.

982. Ibid., 75. This information can also be located in General Lovell's report in the Massachusetts State Archives, 145: 158.

983. Ibid.

984. Ibid.

985. Ibid.

986. Ibid., 77; General Lovell's Report, Massachusetts State Archives, 145: 158.

987. Stahl, *History of Old Broad Bay and Waldoboro*, 469.

988. Wheeler, *History of Castine, Penobscot, & Brooksville*, 350–52.

989. Castine Historical Society, *1779 Penobscot Expedition*; Lovell, *The Original Journal of General Lovell*, 76.

990. Williamson, *History of the State of Maine*, 468–78; letter from General Wadsworth to William D. Williamson, January 1, 1828.

991. Robinson, *The History of Camden and Rockport*, 52.

992. Lovell, *The Original Journal of General Lovell*, 76.

993. Major Todd's report to the Massachusetts Court of Inquiry, Volume 145, Massachusetts State Archives, 230–37.

994. Williamson, *History of the State of Maine*; letter written by General Wadsworth to William Williamson, January 1, 1828; Published in the *Maine Historical Collections*, Volume 2, Series 2, Folder 153. Contributed by Dr. John S. H. Fogg.

995. Lovell, *The Original Journal of General Lovell*, 76; Major Todd's report to the Massachusetts Committee of Inquiry, 145: 230–37; Massachusetts State Archives.

996. Whitaker and Horlacher, *Broad Bay Pioneers*, 404.

997. Major Todd's report to the Massachusetts Committee of Inquiry, 145: 230–37; Massachusetts State Archives.

998. Records of the Massachusetts Court of Inquiry, *Testimony of Adjutant General Jeremiah Hill, September 29, 1779*; (Washington, DC: NARA Microfilm Publication) Frame 100. The sworn testimony of Jeremiah Hill relates: "…General Wadsworth with a Party went for Cambden [*sic*], I went with a Party for Kennebeck [*sic*], waited there three or four days for General Lovell, hearing that he was Certainly coming that way, he not coming in that term of time, I set out and join'd [*sic*] Gen'l Wadsworth at St Georges, thence to Cambden [*sic*] where I found Captain Ulmer of Col. McCobbs Reg't [*sic*] who had kept his Company from intirely [*sic*] dispersing and was Guarding the Coasts there."

999. Ibid.

1000. Williamson, *History of the State of Maine*, 468–78; letter from General Wadsworth to William D. Williamson, January 1, 1828; Lovell, *The Original Journal of General Lovell*, Chapter 10.

1001. Goold, *Colonel Jonathan Mitchell's Cumberland County Regiment*. Material based on Colonel Jonathan Mitchell's diary.

1002. Lovell, *The Original Journal of General Lovell*, 76; Major Todd's report to the Massachusetts Court of Inquiry, 145: 230–37, Massachusetts State Archives.

1003. Robinson, *The History of Camden and Rockport*, 55.

1004. Ibid.

1005. Records of the Massachusetts Court of Inquiry, *Testimony of Adjutant General Jeremiah Hill*; Testimony states: "…I set out and join'd [*sic*] Genr'l Wadsworth at St. George's, thence to Cambden [*sic*] where I found Captain Ulmer of Col. McCobbs Reg't [*sic*] who had kept his Company from intirely [*sic*] dispersing and who was Guarding the Coasts there."

1006. Secretary of the Massachusetts Commonwealth, *Massachusetts Soldiers and Sailors*, 16: 248–49.

1007. Eaton, *Annals of Warren in Knox County*, 182. Although the commanding officer of the fort at Camden is *credited* to George Ulmer at this time, George was a sergeant in Captain Abraham Hunt's company, with Colonel John Paterson's Regiment until his three-year enlistment in the Continental Army was completed on January 18, 1780. He returned to Waldoboro from Rhode Island, where his regiment had been stationed at the time of the Penobscot Bay expedition, in 1779. Compare George Ulmer's military record with the Continental Army and the Massachusetts state militia records. Stahl, *History of Old Broad Bay and Waldoboro*, 584–85. Captain Philip Ulmer was *actually* the commanding officer for eight months at the fort at Camden when two hundred soldiers were stationed there in 1779–80.

1008. Lovell, *The Original Journal of General Lovell*, 78.

1009. Ibid., 79; Massachusetts Council of Inquiry, 145, 391; Massachusetts Archives; Boston newspaper article, "Chronicle and Advisor," September 23, 1779. General Lovell returns to Boston.

1010. Lovell, *The Original Journal of General Lovell*, 79.

1011. Secretary of the Massachusetts Commonwealth, *Massachusetts Soldiers and Sailors*, 16: 249; Stahl, *History of Old Broad Bay and Waldoboro*, 584.

1012. Goold, *Bagaduce Expedition*.

1013. Goold, "Maine Indians in the Revolution," *Maine Sentinel*, June 2, 1897; *Lewiston Saturday Journal*, "Maine Indians in the Revolution-Proposed Memorial at Oldtown to Patriotic Penobscots: A Record of Their Services," July 8, 1910; Massachusetts Archives, 37: 145; *Bangor News*; Sprague, *Sprague's Journal of Maine* 6, no. 3, 105–12.

1014. Buker, *The Penobscot Expedition*.

1015. Cahill, *New England's Naughty Navy*, Series 11, 54.

1016. Kevitt, *General Solomon Lovell and the Penobscot Expedition*, 174–75.

1017. Nelson, *Washington's Secret Navy*, 326.

1018. Franks Jr. and Ganyard, *A Few Good Men*.

1019. Ibid.; Alpha Bravo Delta Guide to the U.S. Marine Corps: Continental Navy.

1020. Boatner, *Cassell's Biographical Dictionary*, 852.

1021. Wheeler, *History of Castine, Penobscot, and Brooksville*, 42. See footnote about the burial of American soldiers in area above Trask's Rock.

1022. Stahl, *History of Broad Bay and Waldoboro*, 469; Eaton, *History of Thomaston, Rockland, and South Thomaston*, 1: 133.

1023. Williamson, *History of Maine*, 468–78; Stahl, *History of Broad Bay and Waldoboro*, 469.

1024. Wheeler, *History of Castine, Penobscot, & Brooksville*, 332.

1025. Goold, *Penobscot Expedition*; Buker, *The Penobscot Expedition*.

1026. Williamson, *The History of the State of Maine*; "It was afterwards fully ascertained that Gen. McLean was prepared to capitulate, if a surrender had been demanded."; Stahl, *History of Broad Bay and Waldoboro*, 469.

1027. Goold, *Penobscot Expedition*, testimony of Colonel Mitchell and Adjutant-General Hill.

1028. Ibid.

1029. Williamson, *The History of the State of Maine*, 478.

1030. *Maine Historical Magazine*, "Letter of Captain Philip Ulmer," 9: 84.

1031. Baxter, *Documentary History of the State of Maine*, 17: 390, 414–15. Report of General Charles Cushing to the Honorable Jeremiah Powell, president of the Massachusetts Provincial Congress, October 18, 1779. Also see the report of Captain Philip Ulmer to General Cushing, October 28, 1779.

1032. Cornwell, *The Fort*, 456.

1033. Stahl, *History of Old Broad Bay and Waldoboro*, 470.

1034. Castine Historical Society, *1779 Penobscot Expedition*. This statement appears in the display of the event at the Castine Historical Society Museum at Castine, Maine.

1035. U.S. House of Representatives, *Digested Summary and Alphabetical List of Private Claims Which Have Been Presented to the House of Representatives*, Volume 3, Congress 14, Session 1, Journal page 64; Referred to Committee: Pens & Rev. Claims; Senate: Passed; Bill: 171; Congress Date: Apr. 29, 1816; House: Passed; Report: Favorable. See the testimonial of eyewitness Adjutant-General Benjamin Hill; Journals of the House of Representatives of the U.S., *A Century of Law Making for a New Nation: U.S. Congressional Documents & Debates 1774–1875*, Volume 9 (Washington, D.C.: House of Representatives), 881; Library of Congress; Pension petitions for Major Philip Ulmer on 209, 369 and 485.

1036. Williamson, *The History of the State of Maine*, "It was afterwards fully ascertained that Gen. McLean was prepared to capitulate, if a surrender had been demanded."; *Adjutant-General Jeremiah Hill's testimony before the Massachusetts Committee (Court) of Inquiry*: "[Captain] Philip Ulmer performed with great courage and continued to lead his men forwards inspite of his leg injury from grapeshot, brandishing his sword, and encouraging his men forward."; *General Peleg Wadsworth's written report of the exploit upon Dyce's Point*: "They had lost 100 men within 20 minutes time...General Wolfe's heroic ascent to the Plains of Abraham at Quebec."; *Written testimony of Joseph Coombs*: "I observed at the landing of the troops Capt. Ulmer behaved himself as a brave officer, and was much applauded by the Spectators...Captain Ulmer with his officers and upward of fifty men tendered their services in the [enterprisc] in which Captain Ulmer received a severe wound in his thigh [possibly the right] which knocked him down. He was taken from the field by two marines... I was within six feet of him when he fell...before we left this field he resumed the command tho' extremely lame, he showed me the wound, the effect was a large contusion which gave great alarm to the company, as they were warmly attached to him for his bravery."; *Written testimony of Lieutenant Alexander Kelloch*: "Captain Ulmer received a severe wound in his thigh [possibly the right] which knocked him down. He was taken from the field by Lieut. Mathews and one other marine...before we left the field Capt Ulmer returned & assumed the command but was extremely lame & scarcely able to walk, he showed me the wound on his thigh, which was a large contusion. The thigh was very much swollen & turned blackish & discolored. This wound gave great alarm to the company who were very attached to him..."

1037. Maine Historical Society, *Collections and Proceedings*, 391.

1038. Ibid., 414–15. Report of Captain Philip Ulmer to General Cushing, September 28, 1779.

1039. Maine Historical Society, *Collections and Proceedings*, 391.

1040. Ibid., 392.

1041. *Revolutionary War Pension and Bounty-Land Warrant Application*, M804, Roll 2434, (Washington, DC: NARA) Veteran File: Philip Ulmer; National Archives Microfilm Publications: Select Records; Frames 137–158. ID Number: S 19963; Veteran File: Philip Ulmer.

1042. Ibid., National Archives Microfilm Publications: Select Records; Frames 137–58. ID Number: S 19963.

1043. Secretary of the Massachusetts Commonwealth, *Massachusetts Soldiers and Sailors*, 16: 248–49.

1044. Ibid., 249.

1045. Ibid.; Goold, *Falmouth Neck in the Revolution*, 49.

Chapter 14: The War Ends in Maine

1046. *Extracts from the Journals of the Reverend Thomas Smith*, 111–12; Stahl, *History of Old Broad Bay and Waldoboro*, 470.

1047. Stahl, *History of Old Broad Bay and Waldoboro*, 470–71.

1048. Abbott and Elwell, *The History of Maine*, 390.

1049. Stahl, *History of Old Broad Bay and Waldoboro*, 471.

1050. Ibid.

1051. Ibid.; Maine Historical Society, *Collections and Proceedings*, 392.

1052. Stahl, *History of Old Broad Bay and Waldoboro*, 471. Jasper Stahl claims that *George* Ulmer was the Ulmer captain at Fort Pine Hill in Camden in the winter of 1780 when the Penobscot Bay was frozen. This could not have been the case since George Ulmer held the rank of sergeant during this time and was still in military service with the Continental Army at Providence, Rhode Island, during this time. He certainly could *not* have been the officer who walked across the frozen Penobscot Bay in early 1780 as other historians have claimed for the same reason. The Captain Ulmer who had been in charge of Fort Pine Hill was Captain *Philip* Ulmer, who *was* indeed a captain and had been on special assignment to General Wadsworth during this time building forts and defenses in strategic coastal locations. According to state records in *Massachusetts Soldiers and Sailors in the War of the Revolution*, Volume 16, page 249, George Ulmer was still in Colonel Vose's First Massachusetts Continental Regiment, in Captain Green's company, until January 18, 1780. He returned to Waldoboro in late March 1780 (after the ice had thawed) and engaged as an adjutant in Colonel Prime's militia regiment from March 25, 1780, until November 25, 1780, at Camden, where he was with his brother, Major Philip Ulmer. George Ulmer was a second lieutenant in Captain McAllister's company from June 1, 1780, until December 24, 1780. George served in the state militia with his brother, Major Philip Ulmer, off and on during 1781. George Ulmer enlisted as a militia captain on March 13, 1782, and was discharged on November 20, 1782.

1053. Stahl, *History of Old Broad Bay and Waldoboro*, 471; Eaton, *Annals of the Town of Warren*, 181.

1054. Abbott and Elwell, *The History of Maine*, 390; Williamson, *The History of the State of Maine*, 481; Stahl, *History of Old Broad Bay and Waldoboro*, 473.

1055. Secretary of the Commonwealth, *Massachusetts Soldiers and Sailors*, 16: 249; Sons of the American Revolution, Maine Society, *Maine in War*, 92; Commission of Philip Martin Ulmer, 2nd Major.

1056. Secretary of the Massachusetts Commonwealth, *Massachusetts Soldiers and Sailors*, 16: 249; Dunnack, *The Maine Book*, 92; Philip Martin Ulmer's commission to major appears in Whitaker and Horlacher, *Broad Bay Pioneers*, 308; Stahl, *History of Old Broad Bay and Waldoboro*, 584.

1057. Secretary of the Massachusetts Commonwealth, *Massachusetts Soldiers and Sailors*, 16: 249.

1058. Secretary of the Massachusetts Commonwealth, *Massachusetts Militia; Books: Abstracts of Rolls*, 37: 45. "A Pay Abstract: Philip M. Ulmer, Major; (no company or regiment listed) for horse rations while in service at

Camden. Remarks: Under Command of Brig. Gen. Wadsworth, from Mar. 25 to Nov. 25, 1780."

1059. Secretary of the Massachusetts Commonwealth, *Sea Coast Defense Muster Rolls*, 36: 192. Muster and pay roll for: "Philip Martin Ulmer, Major; Col. Primes Regiment, March 25, 1780 to Nov. 25, 1780. Remarks: Service at Camden; also pay abstract for horse rations allowed; 245 days allowance, 1 pass per orders."

1060. Secretary of the Massachusetts Commonwealth, *Massachusetts Soldiers and Sailors*, 16: 249; Stahl, *History of Old Broad Bay and Waldoboro*, 584–85; Whitaker and Horlacher, *Broad Bay Pioneers*, 308–09.

1061. Goold, *Falmouth Neck in the Revolution*, 49.

1062. Stahl, *History of Old Broad Bay and Waldoboro*, 473.

1063. Ibid., 474.

1064. Leamon, *Revolution Downeast*, 128; Maine Historical Society collection.

1065. Ibid.

1066. Ibid.

1067. Maine Historical Society, *Collections and Proceedings*, 393.

1068. *Boston Gazette* article that appeared in print on July 10, 1780. The officer in command of the fort at Camden at the time of this event was Major Philip Ulmer.

1069. Sons of the American Revolution, Maine Society, *Maine in War*, 92; Commission of Philip Martin Ulmer, 2nd Major; Secretary of the Massachusetts Commonwealth, *Massachusetts Soldiers and Sailors*, 16: 249.

1070. Maine Historical Society, *Collections and Proceedings*, 393; Leamon, *Revolution Downeast*, 127–28.

1071. Maine Historical Society, *Collections and Proceedings*, 393; Leamon, *Revolution Downeast*, 128.

1072. Williamson, *History of the State of Maine*, 497. Massachusetts Resolves: 2: 63. "Samuel McCobb succeeded General Cushing. General Wadsworth, being a prisoner, the command of the eastern department was committed to Samuel McCobb of Georgetown, Colonel of the first militia regiment in Lincoln County…promoted to a Brigadier General."

1073. Stahl, *History of Old Broad Bay and Waldoboro*, 476.

1074. Goold, *Falmouth Neck in the Revolution*, 49.

1075. Ibid.

1076. Whitaker and Horlacher, *Broad Bay Pioneers*, 404–05, 420. Philip Ulmer was an officer with this company at this time. See the pension petitions of Paul Mink and Charles Oberlach.

1077. Secretary of the Massachusetts Commonwealth, *Sea Coast Defence* [*sic*] *Muster and Pay Roll*, 36: 192; Revolutionary War Pension Applications of Philip M. Ulmer, (Johann) Paul Minck, Charles Oberlach, Peter Lehr and Charles Hebner of Waldoboro record the building of forts and barracks in strategic locations on the sea coast of Maine and are also found in part in Whitaker and Horlacher's *Broad Bay Pioneers*.

1078. Secretary of the Massachusetts Commonwealth, *Books: Abstracts of Rolls*, 37: 45; A Pay Abstract for Philip M. Ulmer, Major, horse rations while in service at Cambden [*sic*] under Command of Brig. Gen. Wadsworth from March 25 to Nov. 25, 1780; Secretary of the Massachusetts Commonwealth, *Sea Coast Defence* [*sic*] *Muster and Pay Roll*, 36: 192; service at Camden.

1079. Buker, *The Penobscot Expedition*, Chapter 1; Stahl, *History of Old Broad Bay and Waldoboro*, 473.

1080. Buker, *The Penobscot Expedition*, Chapter 1.

1081. Secretary of the Massachusetts Commonwealth, *Massachusetts Soldiers and Sailors*, 16: 248.

1082. Ibid.

1083. Wilson, *The Ancestors and Descendants of John Wilson*, 237–38.

1084. Secretary of the Massachusetts Commonwealth, *Massachusetts Soldiers and Sailors*, 16: 249.

1085. Ibid.; Whitaker and Horlacher, *Broad Bay Pioneers*, 309. A discrepancy appears in the military records at this point. The government information found in *Massachusetts Soldiers and Sailors* states that George Ulmer became a sergeant in Colonel Vose's Regiment in 1778 and served as adjutant at Camden (Maine) in Colonel Prime's regiment for eight months from March 25, 1780, to November 25, 1780, and was then discharged. There is a discrepancy between the above reference and two other historical references about George Ulmer. The information in *Broad Bay Pioneers* states that George Ulmer enlisted as a private in Colonel Vose's Regiment, Massachusetts Continental Line, for three years. He enlisted May 17, 1777, and served to May 7, 1780, with skirmishes at White Plains, New York, and Flourtown, Rhode Island, and was discharged on May 7, 1780, near West Point, New York. The information in Jasper Stahl's *History of Broad Bay and Waldoboro* on page 584 states that George Ulmer enlisted on January 18, 1777, was a private in First Essex County regiment, Continental Army; served with Captain Abraham Hunt's Company, in Colonel Paterson's regiment, promoted to Sergeant and was discharged January 18, 1780. He served at Valley Forge and White Plains.

1086. Secretary of the Massachusetts Commonwealth, *Massachusetts Soldiers and Sailors*, 16: 249.

1087. Ibid.

1088. Leamon, *Revolution Downeast*, 129–30.

1089. Secretary of the Massachusetts Commonwealth, *Massachusetts Soldiers and Sailors*, 16: 249.

1090. Ibid.

1091. Ibid.

1092. Ibid.

1093. Maine Historical Society, *Collections and Proceedings*, 393.

1094. Leamon, *Revolution Downeast*, 135.

1095. Stahl, *History of Old Broad Bay and Waldoboro*, 477.

1096. Leamon, *Revolution Downeast*, 128–29.

1097. Stahl, *History of Old Broad Bay and Waldoboro*, 476–77; Leamon, *Revolution Downeast*, 129; Abbott and Elwell, *The History of Maine*, 391–93.

1098. Leamon, *Revolution Downeast*, 129.

1099. Williamson, *The History of the State of Maine*, 497.

1100. Maine Historical Society, *Collections and Proceedings*, 393; Kidder, *Military Operations in Eastern Maine & Nova Scotia*, 289; Leamon, *Revolution Downeast*, 129.

1101. Maine Historical Society, *Collections and Proceedings*, 393–94; Leamon, *Revolution Downeast*, 129; Kidder, *Military Operations in Eastern Maine & Nova Scotia*, 289.

1102. Leamon, *Revolution Downeast*, 129.

1103. Maine Historical Society, *Collections and Proceedings*, 393; Williamson, *The History of the State of Maine*, 493.

1104. Sons of the American Revolution, *Maine in War*, 134. "General Peleg Wadsworth: served early 1775, Commissioned Captain in Sept. '75, & served in Cotton's and Bailey's reg'ts. Engineer with General Thomas at Dorchester Heights in March 1776; aid to General Ward. In 1778, he was appointed adjutant General of Massachusetts: In 1779 was 2nd in Command of Bagaduce Expedition. He was appointed 1780 as Brig- General and commander the eastern department. In February 1781, he was captured & held in Fort George at Castine. Escaped June 18 & returned home. Prominent man in Portsmouth, ME. First Representative in Congress from District, 1792–1806."; Williamson, *The History of the State of Maine*, 493.

1105. Leamon, *Revolution Downeast*, 129.

1106. Maine Historical Society, *Collections and Proceedings*, 394; Kidder, *Military Operations in Eastern Maine & Nova Scotia*, 289.

1107. Maine Historical Society, *Collections of the Maine Historical Society*, 230; Leamon, *Revolution Downeast*, 130. Reports indicated that the frigate was a Concorde class frigate from Rochefort, France, and carried twenty-four, thirty-two, or thirty-six twelve-pounder guns; approximately 145 feet long, 1,166 tons, and carried a compliment of 255 men.

1108. Maine Historical Society, *Collections of the Maine Historical Society*, 230.

1109. Ibid.; Maine Historical Society, *Collections and Proceedings of the Maine Historical Society*, Second Series, 1: 394.

1110. Maine Historical Society, *Collections and Proceedings of the Maine Historical Society*, 394.

1111. Ibid., 395.

1112. Williamson, *The History of the State of Maine*, 497.

1113. Maine Historical Society, *Collections and Proceedings of the Maine Historical Society*, 395.

1114. Leamon, *Revolution Downeast*, 130.

1115. Kidder, *Military Operations in Eastern Maine & Nova Scotia*, 286.

1116. Ibid.

1117. Ibid. The translation of the letter from the Indian tribes of frontier Maine, represented by the Passamaquody tribal chiefs, to the Massachusetts General Court in Boston can be located on pages 287–88 of this book. The original letter of Colonel John Allen is retained by the Passamaquody Indian tribe.

1118. Leamon, *Revolution Downeast*, 130–31.

1119. Stahl, *History of Old Broad Bay and Waldoboro*, 474.

1120. Leamon, *Revolution Downeast*, 137.

1121. Maine Historical Society, *Documentary History of the State of Maine*, 18: 242; Peleg Wadsworth to the council in Falmouth, April 28, 1780; Maine Historical Society, *Documentary History of the State of Maine*, 18: 366–67; Peleg Wadsworth of the council in Thomaston, August 7, 1780.

1122. Royal Manuscripts Commission, *Report on American Manuscripts*, 209–10; Lieutenant Governor Eyre Massey to Sir William Howe, Halifax, March 15, 1778; Records of the Cumberland County Court of General Sessions of the Peace, October 1782, Maine State Archives.

1123. Leamon, *Revolution Downeast*, 131.

1124. Ibid., 132.

1125. Ibid., 133–34.

1126. Ibid., 138–39.

1127. Abbot, *Papers of Washington, Revolutionary War Series*, Letter of General Washington to John Laurens, president of the Continental Congress, April 9, 1781.

1128. Sumner, *Robert Morris*, 95.

1129. Ibid.

1130. Williamson, *Guns on the Chesapeake*, 215; Bonsal, *When the French Were Here*, 118.

1131. Ketchum, *Victory at Yorktown*, 142.

1132. Davis, *The Campaign That Won America*, 55–57.

1133. Williamson, *Guns on the Chesapeake*, 216.

1134. Ibid., 218.

1135. Ibid., 215; Bonsal, *When the French Were Here*, 118.

1136. Williamson, *Guns on the Chesapeake*, 216.

1137. Selig, "Francois Joseph Paul Comte de Grasse, the Battle off the Virginia Capes, and the American Victory at Yorktown" (article courtesy of AmericanHistory.org).

1138. Williamson, *Guns on the Chesapeake*, 218.

1139. Ketchum, *Victory at Yorktown*, 189.

1140. Williamson, *Guns on the Chesapeake*, 218.

1141. Comte de Rochambeau, Papers, 1780–1784, Accession #7289-c, Albert H. Small Special Collections Library (Charlottesville: University of Virginia, n.d.); Selig, "Francois Joseph Paul Comte de Grasse."

1142. Comte de Rochambeau, Papers, 1780–1784, Accession #7289-c, Albert H. Small Special Collections Library.

1143. Ibid.; Ketchum, *Victory at Yorktown*, 168.

1144. Selig, "Francois Joseph Paul Comte de Grasse."

1145. Tucker, *Norfolk Highlights*, Chapter 14.

1146. Davis, *The Campaign that Won America*, 163–66.

1147. Fitzpatrick, *The Writings of George Washington*. Information found in "The George Washington Papers": Letter from George Washington's Headquarters near York, October 19, 1781, to Congress; Abbott et al., *Papers of Washington, Revolutionary War Series*; October 19, 1781 letter from his headquarters near York: General George Washington to Congress.

1148. Riedesel, *Baroness von Riedesel and the American Revolution*.

1149. Leamon, *Revolution Downeast*, 182.

1150. Maine Historical Society, Documents of the History of Maine, *Representation of the Inhabitants of Falmouth to the General Court, 3 February 1783*, 20: 163–64; Maine State Archives; Leamon, *Revolution Downeast*, 182.

1151. Leamon, *Revolution Downeast*, 182.

1152. *Salem Gazette*, July 11 and July 18, 1782; *Boston Post*, June 15, 1782.

1153. Leamon, *Revolution Downeast*, 182.

1154. Jonathan Sayward Diaries, Volume 23, March 25, 1782; Leamon, *Revolution Downeast*, 182.

1155. Leamon, *Revolution Downeast*, 182; The Resolves of the Massachusetts Senate, March 23, 1784, gives a different date. See Documents of the History of Maine, 20: 334–35. Maine State Archives.

1156. Maine Historical Society, *Documents of the History of Maine*, 20: 321–23; [General] Samuel McCobb to the General Court, May 24, 1784. Maine State Archives; Leamon, *Revolution Downeast*, 183.

1157. Stahl, *History of Old Broad Bay and Waldoboro*, 479.

1158. Ibid., 458.

1159. Miller, *History of the Town of Waldoboro, Maine*.

1160. Leamon, *Revolution Downeast*, 189.

1161. Wright, *The Continental Army*, Lineage Series: First Massachusetts Regiment of the Continental Army.

1162. Massachusetts General Court, *Acts and Laws of the Commonwealth of Massachusetts*, Chapter 69; "Resolve on the Petition of Philip Ulmer and others, allowing them to raise a sunken ship on the Penobscot River"; page 324; The Resolve reads: "On the petition of Phillip [*sic*] Ulmer & others praying for leave to raise the wreck of a Vessell, [*sic*] which was sunk in the Harbour [*sic*] of Cape Jellison at the time of the attack upon Penobscott [*sic*] in the late war.—*Resolved:* that Phillip [*sic*] Ulmer, John Pendleton, Hezekiah French, George Ulmer, Adam Rogers be & they hereby are permitted and allowed, at their own expence, [*sic*] to raise the wreck of the Vessell [*sic*] which belonged to the Penobscot Fleet and was sunk in the harbour [*sic*] of Cape Jellison near the mouth of the Penobscot River—and that all the right & title of the Commonwealth in the said Vessell [*sic*] be relinquished to the said Phillip, [*sic*] John, Hezekiah, George & Adam in case they succeed in attempting to raise the same—*Provided* they Effect the purpose aforesaid within one year from passing this Resolve…March 10, 1797."

1163. Palmer, *George Washington and Benedict Arnold*, 374.

1164. Ibid.

1165. Ibid.

1166. Ibid., 373.

Chapter 15: Changes in Massachusetts after the War

1167. Rose, *Washington's Spies*, 267.

1168. Ibid.

1169. Lomask, "Benedict Arnold: The Aftermath of Treason."

1170. Randall, *Benedict Arnold*, 609–10.

1171. Rose, *Washington's Spies*, 267.

1172. Ibid., 267–68.

1173. Ibid.

1174. Ibid., 269.

1175. Ibid.

1176. Ibid., 269–70.

1177. Taylor, "The Rise and Fall of George Ulmer," 57.

1178. Williams, *French Assault on American Shipping*, 182. Two years later, Samuel A. Whitney Sr. was sailing master and owner of this armed vessel of twelve guns. (See pages 182, 390.)

1179. Ibid., 182.

1180. Rose, *Washington's Spies*, 270.

1181. Ibid., 271.

1182. Ibid.

1183. O'Toole, *Honorable Treachery*, 69–81; Rose, *Washington's Spies*, 271.

1184. Massachusetts Archives, *Committee on Claims in Behalf of Massachusetts against the United States, September 21, 1787*, Depreciation Rolls, 31: 83: "Phillip Ulmer Appears as a Lieutenant on An account rendered against the United States by the Commonwealth of Massachusetts for amounts paid officers and men of Colonel Joseph Vose's Reg't on account of depreciation for the first three years' service in the Continental Army… Account exhibited by Committee on Claims on behalf of Mass. against US, September 21, 1787."

1185. Leamon, *Revolution Downeast*, 192.

1186. Taylor, *Liberty Men and Great Proprietors*, 89.

1187. Stahl, *History of Old Broad Bay and Waldoboro*, 465.

1188. Butler, "The Wadsworths," 4–6.

1189. Leamon, *Revolution Downeast*, 192.

1190. Taylor, *Liberty Men and Great Proprietors*, 39–40.

1191. Leamon, *Revolution Downeast*, 192.

1192. Callahan, *Henry Knox*, 283, 338–50; Leamon, *Revolution Downeast*, 193.

1193. Leamon, *Revolution Downeast*, 191.

1194. Ibid., 193.

1195 Taylor, *Liberty Men and Great Proprietors*, 89-109.

1196. Beverage and Beverage, "Letter Written by an Ulmer Family Descendant." The letter refers to a visit by General Lafayette to the Ulmer family in the fall of 1784 that must have taken place at Waldoboro and/or Ducktrap before Lafayette's return to France. The letter is in possession of the Schoolhouse Museum of the Lincolnville Historical Society, and a copy is with the author of this book. Both Henry Knox and General Lafayette knew Philip Ulmer and his brother, George, during the Revolutionary War. In 1784, the Ulmer brothers were in the process of building a dam and sawmill on the Ducktrap River and a shipyard at Ducktrap harbor-cove. The Ulmer brothers' business ventures at Ducktrap were under construction at this time. The Ulmer brothers' business plan demonstrated the full utilization of nature's resources and water power to produce needed products as well as the construction of sailing vessels to bring the products to market. Philip and George Ulmer had not permanently moved to the Ducktrap cove at this time, but logs were being cut to build homes and other structures at the harbor-cove. General Knox likely wanted to show General Lafayette the Penobscot Bay region and the possibilities for enormous profits that could be made in land speculation and business investments in the developing capitalist society. Lafayette, like other speculators and business investors whom Knox brought to the Ulmer brothers' complex, was probably taken on a tour of the Ulmer brothers' innovative businesses at Ducktrap. Lafayette's second visit to America was in February 1824. Major Philip Ulmer was dead by this time, and George Ulmer was mostly bedridden the last two years of his life, so the meeting could not have taken place then.

Chapter 16: Philip Ulmer after the War

1197. Whitaker and Horlacher, *Broad Bay Pioneers*, 573. Some sources indicate that Christiana was the daughter of Johann Jacob Jung and Anna Marie Lischer (Leissner, sometimes appears Reisser in the old ship lists) from Germany; however, this is probably inaccurate according to Whitaker and Horlacher; Wilson, *Wilson Family History*, Table 30, 573–74; Family of Johann Jacob Ulmer: children: Philip Martin Ulmer.

1198. Whitaker and Horlacher, *Broad Bay Pioneers*, 573–74.

1199. Ibid., 156.

1200. The Massachusetts Vital Records Project, Peabody Essex Museum- Phillip's Library (Salem, MA: The Esscx Institute, 2005–2009). Jacob Ulmer's birth appears in Lincolnville and also Waldoborough.

1201. Eaton, *Annals of the Town of Warren*, 137.

1202. Stahl, *History of Old Broad Bay and Waldoboro*, 396.

1203. Whitaker and Horlacher, *Broad Bay Pioneers*, Chapter 3; Broad Bay Land Records, Lincoln County Courthouse, 159. "Slaigo Cove—Philip Ulmer—1783."

1204. Miller, *History of the Town of Waldoboro*, 266.

1205. Stahl, *History of Old Broad Bay and Waldoboro*, 490.

1206. Collections of the Maine Historical Society, Document Series, 2nd Series, 20, 227; Stahl, *History of Broad Bay and Waldoboro*, 479–80.

1207. Lincolnville Historical Society, *Lincolnville—Early Days*, 1: 18.

1208. O'Brien, *Ducktrap*, 4–15, 117; Lincolnville Historical Society, *Lincolnville—Early Days*, 1: 18.

1209. Taylor, *Liberty Men and Great Proprietors*, 156.

1210. Lincoln County Courthouse (Wiscasset), Lincoln County Deeds, 17, 126; James Getchal to Philip Ulmer, September 23, 1784; Lincoln County Courthouse (Wiscasset), Lincoln County Deeds, 17, 126; James Getchal to George Ulmer, September 23, 1784; Taylor, *Liberty Men and Great Proprietors*, 156.

1211. Taylor, *Liberty Men and Great Proprietors*, 156.

1212. Wilson, *Wilson Family History*, Table 31, 575–76; family of George Ulmer.

1213. Brady, *Martha Washington*, 147.

1214. Taylor, *Liberty Men and Great Proprietors*, 12–13.

1215. Secretary of the Commonwealth of Massachusetts, *Massachusetts Soldiers and Sailors*, 16: 248–49.

1216. Taylor, *Liberty Men and Great Proprietors*, 156.

1217. Lincolnville Historical Society, *Lincolnville —Early Days*, 1: 20.

1218. Ibid., 7, 19–20. The descriptions of the various business enterprises at Ducktrap Harbor were taken, almost without change, from the material found on pages 19–20; O'Brien, *Ducktrap*, 29–39.

1219. Lincolnville Historical Society, *Lincolnville—Early Days*, 1: 19–20.

1220. O'Brien, *Ducktrap*, 9–11.

1221. Smith, *Sprague's Journal of Maine History*, Collections of the Maine Historical Society, Volume 6, Number 3, December 1918–January 1919, 105–112; Goold, "Maine Indian in the Revolution," *The Sentinel*, June 2,

1897: "Pay Roll for a number of Indians for their services at Penobscot on the late expedition tinder command of Lieut. Andrew Gilman, made agreeable to a Resolve of the Gen'l Court of the 17th, Sept. 1779." Massachusetts Archives, Volume 37, 145. Courtesy of Tina Vickery and the Androscoggin Historical Society, 1998; "Maine Indians in the Revolution," *Lewiston Journal: Illustrated Magazine Section*, July 8, 1910, 10.

1222. Stahl, *History of Old Broad Bay and Waldoboro*, 297, 394–96, 510–11; Taylor, *Liberty Men and Great Proprietors*, 156.

1223. Taylor, *Liberty Men and Great Proprietors*, 158–59.

1224. Henry Knox Papers, "Agreement at Ducktrap 1788," Volume 52, Number 5; Taylor, *Liberty Men and Great Proprietors*, 157–59.

1225. Taylor, *Liberty Men and Great Proprietors*, 157.

1226. Ibid., 158.

1227. Ibid., 158–59.

1228. Farrow, *History of Islesborough*, 8: 313.

1229. Henry Knox Papers, "Agreement at Ducktrap, 1788," Volume 52, Number 5; Taylor, *Liberty Men and Great Proprietors*, 158.

1230. Taylor, *Liberty Men and Great Proprietors*, 337; Hancock and Lincoln County Registries of Deeds.

1231. Taylor, *Liberty Men and Great Proprietors*, 157–58.

1232. Ibid., 159.

1233. Henry Knox Papers, 23, "Isaac Winslow, Jr. (quoting William Moliniex) to Henry Knox, January 25, 1789" (Maine Historical Society), 84; Taylor, *Liberty Men and Great Proprietors*, 155.

1234. Henry Knox Papers, 23, "Henry Knox to Isaac Winslow, Jr., March 1, 1789" (Maine Historical Society), 115; Taylor, *Liberty Men and Great Proprietors*, 155.

1235. Taylor, *Liberty Men and Great Proprietors*, 158.

1236. Ibid.

1237. Ibid.

1238. Ibid.

1239. Ibid., 159.

1240. Lincolnville Historical Society, *Lincolnville—Early Days*, 7.

1241. Lincoln County Deeds, Book 13, 180; Stahl, *History of Old Broad Bay and Waldoboro*, 396.

1242. Lincoln County Deeds Book 32, 12; Stahl, *History of Old Broad Bay and Waldoboro*, 396.

1243. Stahl, *History of Old Broad Bay and Waldoboro*, 396; Eaton, *Annals of the Town of Warren*, 132.

1244. Burrage and Stubbs, *Genealogical and Family History*, 2,255.

1245. Henry Knox Papers, 39: 15, Massachusetts Historical Society; letter from Knox to Northport's selectmen (Maine), April 2, 1796; Taylor, *Liberty Men and Great Proprietors*, 161.

1246. Taylor, *Liberty Men and Great Proprietors*, 107.

1247. Ibid.

1248. Ibid.

1249. Resolve 158 (March 17, 1783), *Resolves of the General Court of the Commonwealth of Massachusetts, May 1782–March 1783* (Boston, 1783), E 18026; Taylor, *Liberty Men and Great Proprietors*, 107.

1250. Leamon, *Revolution Downeast*, 207.

1251. Ibid.

1252. Taylor, *Liberty Men and Great Proprietors*, 158.

1253. Lincolnville Historical Society, *Lincolnville—Early Days*, 33.

1254. Taylor, *Liberty Men and Great Proprietors*, 158.

1255. Lincolnville Historical Society, *Lincolnville—Early Days*, 7, 63.

1256. Ibid., 9, 21.

1257. Maine Vital Statistics, Vital Records to the Year 1892, Waldo County; Genealogy Index for Surnames, "U," Maine State Archives. Philip Ulmer, Esq., Justice of the Peace, marriage of Margaret Ulmer (also called "Peggy") and Bezelen Palmer Dalman, February 1, 1812, in Lincolnville; Philip Ulmer, Esq., Justice of the Peace, marriage of Susan (Susanna) Ulmer and Samuel Burkmar, March 20, 1813; Philip Ulmer may have also united his daughter Christiana Ulmer in marriage to Paul H. Stevens in 1808 at Lincolnville, and the marriage of Dolly Ulmer to James W. Merrill in early 1816 at Lincolnville. There many have been other townspeople and family members as well who were married by Justice of the Peace Philip Ulmer, Esq.

1258. Taylor, *Liberty Men and Great Proprietors*, 158; Lincolnville Historical Society, *Lincolnville—Early Days*, 19, 22–23, 31, 63; O'Brien, *Ducktrap*, 31–32.

1259. Taylor, *Liberty Men and Great Proprietors*, 108.

1260. Leamon, *Revolution Downeast*, 209.

1261. Taylor, *Liberty Men and Great Proprietors*, 159; Leamon, *Revolution Downeast*, 193, 207.

1262. Taylor, *Liberty Men and Great Proprietors*, 181–207; Leamon, *Revolution Downeast*, 35, 208.

1263. Taylor, *Liberty Men and Great Proprietors*, 191–93, 198–99.

1264. Ibid., 159.

1265. Hancock County Court of Common Pleas, Record Book 2, case 197, Maine State Archives; Ducktrap Plantation/Lincolnville (front-country), Hancock County; April 28, 1793, Samuel Ely leads a crowd that destroys the milldam belonging to George and Philip Ulmer, leading men who support General Henry Knox's land claim; *Ulmer vs. Ely*, April 1796.

1266. Taylor, *Liberty Men and Great Proprietors*, 159, 265, 337.

1267. O'Brien, *Ducktrap*, 12, 15; Taylor, *Liberty Men and Great Proprietors*, 159.

1268. Taylor, *Liberty Men and Great Proprietors*, 40.

1269. Rose, *Washington's Spies*, 42.

1270. Ibid., 42–43.

1271. Taylor, *Liberty Men and Great Proprietors*, 40–41.

1272. Ibid., 41.

1273. Taylor, *Liberty Men and Great Proprietors*, 40.

1274. Ibid.

1275. Allis, *William Bingham's Maine Lands*, 45; Taylor, *Liberty Men and Great Proprietors*, 41.

1276. Taylor, *Liberty Men and Great Proprietors*, 39–47.

1277. Ibid., 41.

1278. Ibid.

1279. Ibid.

1280. Ibid.

1281. Ibid., 159.

1282. Taylor, "The Rise and Fall of George Ulmer," 56.

1283. La Rochefoucauld-Liancourt, *Travels Through the United States*, 434, 443; Taylor, "The Rise and Fall of George Ulmer," 53.

1284. Ibid.

1285. Eaton, *History of the Town of Warren*, 132; Stahl, *History of Old Broad Bay and Waldoboro*, 573–74.

1286. Huth and Pugh, *Talleyrand in America*, 74, 82; Prince Charles Maurice de Talleyrand-Perigord, "Letter on the Eastern Part of America," Boston, September 24, 1794; Taylor, "The Rise and Fall of George Ulmer," 55–56.

1287. Taylor, "The Rise and Fall of George Ulmer," 54.

1288. Eaton, *History of Thomaston, Rockland, & South Thomaston*, 215.

1289. Taylor, *Liberty Men and Great Proprietors*, 43; Small, *History of Swan's Island*, 45–46.

1290. Taylor, *Liberty Men and Great Proprietors*, 47; Small, *History of Swan's Island*, 45–46.

1291. Small, *History of Swan's Island*, 46.

1292. Taylor, *Liberty Men and Great Proprietors*, 47.

1293. Ibid.

1294. Ibid., 43.

1295. Small, *History of Swan's Island*, 45.

1296. Taylor, *Liberty Men and Great Proprietors*, 43.

1297. Ibid., 43–45, 122; Small, *History of Swan's Island*, 45–46.

1298. Small, *History of Swan's Island*, 46.

1299. Griffiths, *Maine Sources*, 8–9.

1300. Taylor, *Liberty Men and Great Proprietors*, 43.

1301. The General Henry Knox Museum, *Montpelier* (Thomaston, ME: brochure published by The General Henry Knox Museum).

1302. Taylor, *Liberty Men and Great Proprietors*, 43–44.

1303. Ibid.

1304. Small, *History of Swan's Island*, 50.

1305. Ibid.

1306. Taylor, *Liberty Men and Great Proprietors*, 43–44.

1307. Ibid., 159.

1308. Ibid.

1309. Ibid., 191.

1310. Massachusetts Historical Society, Henry Knox Papers, Volume 38, 171: letter from George Ulmer to Henry Knox, March 18, 1796; Taylor, *Liberty Men and Great Proprietors*, 191.

1311. Taylor, *Liberty Men and Great Proprietors*, 159.

1312. Hancock County Court of Common Pleas, Record Book 2, Case 197; Philip and George Ulmer vs. Samuel Ely; Henry Knox Papers, 38; Letter from George Ulmer to Henry Knox, March 18, 1796, page 171; also Henry Knox Papers, 39; letter from George Ulmer to Henry Knox, April 7, 1796, page 23.

1313. O'Brien, *Ducktrap*, 15; Taylor, *Liberty Men and Great Proprietors*, 59.

1314. Taylor, *Liberty Men and Great Proprietors*, 159–60.

1315. Hancock County Court of General Sessions of the Peace files, Box 77, Maine State Archives: George Ulmer's Court, March 1, 1797; Taylor, *Liberty Men and Great Proprietors*, 337.

1316. Taylor, "The Rise and Fall of George Ulmer," 57; Mustapich, "Lincolnville House Named to National Register."

1317. Henry Knox Papers, Volume 55, item number 53, Massachusetts Historical Society; Letter from George Ulmer to Henry Knox: Ducktrap, November 9, 1798; Taylor, "The Rise and Fall of George Ulmer," 57; Mustapich, "Lincolnville House Named to National Register."

1318. Taylor, "The Rise and Fall of George Ulmer," 57; Mustapich, "Lincolnville House Named to National Register."

1319. Taylor, *Liberty Men and Great Proprietors*, 158.

1320. Lincolnville Historical Society, *Lincolnville—Early Days*, Volume 1, 8–10, 18–23.

1321. Ibid., 9.

1322. Taylor, *Liberty Men and Great Proprietors*, 156.

1323. Taylor, "The Rise and Fall of George Ulmer," 52–53; Taylor, *Liberty Men and Great Proprietors*, 156.

1324. Grand Lodge of Masons in Massachusetts, Cynthia Alcorn, Librarian. Membership Records: Major Philip Ulmer; "Major Philip Ulmer is recorded as having been a Charter Member of *Hancock Lodge, No. 4* in Castine, Maine in 1794 and a Charter Member of *Amity Lodge, No. 6* in Camden, Maine in 1801. He is recorded as having served as Grand Treasurer pro tem at the constitution of *Hancock Lodge, No. 4* in Castine, Maine, November 12, 1804."

1325. Alan Taylor, "The Rise and Fall of George Ulmer," 54; Williamson, "Obituary of General George Ulmer," *Hancock Gazette and Penobscot Patriot*, January 11, 1826.

1326. Lincolnville Historical Society, *Lincolnville—Early Days*, 1: 34–35.

1327. Ibid., 34.

1328. Williams, *The French Assault on American Shipping*, 43–371. See the list of reported shipping losses and the lists of cargo and goods aboard the captured vessels taken by the French privateers. Trading ships from the Penobscot appear in the list of captured and lost vessels.

1329. O'Brien, *Ducktrap*, 37.

1330. The Lincolnville Historical Society, *Lincolnville—Early Days*, 34.

1331. Williams, *The French Assault on American Shipping*, 182, 390.

1332. Lincolnville Historical Society, *Lincolnville—Early Days*, 8–9; O'Brien, *Ducktrap*, 37; Taylor, "The Rise and Fall of George Ulmer," 57.

1333. O'Brien, *Ducktrap*, 31; New England Historic and Genealogical Society, *1798 Direct Tax List*; General list of Land, Lots, Buildings, and Wharves; assets of George Ulmer and Philip Ulmer of Ducktrap (Lincolnville).

1334. New England Historical and Genealogical Society, *Massachusetts and Maine 1798 Federal Direct Tax Returns*, "Ducktrap Return," Volume 1.

1335. Maine Historical Society, *Miscellaneous Manuscripts*, 132, 214–22; Hancock County Tax Roll, 1815 Direct Tax.

Chapter 17: The Years After the War

1336. Hudgins, "The Quasi-War," 39–43.

1337. Daughan, *If By Sea*, 280–88.

1338. Rose, *Washington's Spies*, 107–08.

1339. Claypoole, "The Address of General Washington."

1340. Parker, *The Constitution of the Five Nations*; Favor, *The Iroquois Constitution*.

1341. Hieronimus and Cortner, *Founding Fathers and Secret Societies*, 44–45; Morse, *Freemasonry in the American Revolution*, ix.

1342. Cynthia Alcorn, librarian for the Grand Lodge of Masons in Massachusetts, *Historical Records: Maine Lodges under the Grand Lodge of Massachusetts*; letter dated February 4, 2009, was a response to an inquiry about Philip and George Ulmer's Masonic affiliation.

1343. Sachse, *Washington's Masonic Correspondence*, letter to the Grand Lodge of Massachusetts, April 1797; Mackey, *Revised Encyclopedia of Freemasonry*, 1,095. Additional expressions of esteem in the address to the Grand Lodge of Maryland, two months before Washington's death; Hieronimus and Cortner, *Founding Fathers and Secret Societies*, 44.

1344. General Court of the Commonwealth of Massachusetts, *Acts and Laws of the Commonwealth of Massachusetts*, 324. Acts and Resolutions, March 10, 1797.

1345. Daughan, *If By Sea*, 280–388.

1346. Hudgins, "The Quasi-War," 39–43.

1347. Cornwell, *The Fort*, 465.

1348. Knox, *Naval Documents Related to the Quasi-War*, 25.

1349. DeConde, *The Quasi-War*.

1350. Knox, *Naval Documents Related to the Quasi-War*, 6; American State Papers, Volume 2, 28–63; Daughan, *If By Sea*, 280–88.

1351. Taylor, "The Rise and Fall of George Ulmer," 57.

1352. DeConde, *The Quasi-War*.

1353. Taylor, "The Rise and Fall of George Ulmer," 57.

1354. Ibid.

1355. Henry Knox Papers, Volume 41, Item 27: letter from George Ulmer to Knox, Ducktrap, November 14, 1797, Maine Historical Society; Henry Knox Papers, Volume 55, Item 53: letter from George Ulmer to Knox, Ducktrap, December 9, 1797, Maine Historical Society; Henry Knox Papers, Box 4: letter from Henry Knox to Ulmer, Boston, December 7, 1797; Taylor, "The Rise and Fall of George Ulmer," 57.

1356. Taylor, *Liberty Men and Great Proprietors*, 159.

1357. DeConde, *The Quasi-War*.

1358. Hudgins, "The Quasi-War," 42.

1359. DeConde, *The Quasi War*.; Hudgins, "The Quasi-War," 42.

1360. Williams, *The French Assault on American Shipping*, 3–4. See French Spoliation Act issued by Congress.

1361. Hudgins, "The Quasi-War," 42.

1362. Taylor, *Liberty Men and Great Proprietors*, 192.

1363. Ibid., 192–93.

1364. Ibid., 192.

1365. Ibid., 265–67; Hancock County Court of General Sessions of the Peace, Record Book 2, Case 197, Maine State Archives: Ulmer vs. Ely; Samuel Ely leads a crowd that destroys the milldam belonging to George and Philip Ulmer; Henry Knox Papers, 39, page 112, Massachusetts State Archives: Hancock County, Incidents of Extralegal Violence Associated with the Land Controversies; At night, settlers cast loose a boom, setting adrift and scattering spars belonging to George Ulmer, Philip Ulmer, and Henry Knox, July 14, 1796; Henry Knox Papers, 39, page 144, Massachusetts State Archives: Hancock County, Incidents of Extralegal Violence Associated with the Land Controversies; At night, settlers cast loose a boom, setting adrift and scattering spars belonging to George Ulmer, Philip Ulmer, and Henry Knox, September 11, 1796.

1366. Mustapich, "Lincolnville House Named to National Register"; Taylor, "The Rise and Fall of George Ulmer," 57.

1367. Mustapich, "Lincolnville House Named to National Register."

1368. Ibid.

1369. Taylor, *Liberty Men and Great Proprietors*, 198.

1370. Henry Knox Papers, 44, Massachusetts Historical Society, 8: letter from George Ulmer to Henry Knox, dated June 20, 1801; Henry Knox Papers, 44, Massachusetts Historical Society, 13: letter from Robert Houston to Henry Knox, dated June 26, 1801; Taylor, *Liberty Men and Great Proprietors*, 198.

1371. Taylor, *Liberty Men and Great Proprietors*, 194.

1372. Ibid., 198.

1373. Ibid., 194.

1374. Ibid., 164.

1375. Ibid.

1376. Ibid., 217.

1377. Henry Knox Papers, Box 4, Maine Historical Society; letter from George Ulmer to Henry Knox, Ducktrap, November 13, 1801; Taylor,

Liberty Men and Great Proprietors, 217; Taylor, "The Rise and Fall of George Ulmer," 57.

1378. Henry Knox Papers, Box 4, Maine Historical Society; letter from George Ulmer to Henry Knox, Ducktrap, November 13, 1801; Taylor, *Liberty Men and Great Proprietors*, 217; Taylor, "The Rise and Fall of George Ulmer," 57.

1379. Taylor, *Liberty Men and Great Proprietors*, 160.

1380. Ibid., 218.

1381. Ibid., 41.

1382. Lincolnville Historical Society, *Lincolnville—Early Days*, 1: 18.

1383. Ibid., 18–19.

1384. Small, *History of Swan Island*, 47.

1385. Varney, "History of Waldo County, Maine."

1386. Ibid.

1387. Taylor, *"The Rise and Fall of George Ulmer,"* 57.

1388. Williams, *The French Assault on American Shipping*, 390.

1389. Ibid., 182.

1390. Ibid., 182, 390.

1391. Lincolnville Historical Society, *Lincolnville—Early Days*, 1: 8–9.

1392. Taylor, "The Rise and Fall of George Ulmer," 57; Lincolnville Historical Society, *Lincolnville—Early Days*, 1: 8–9.

1393. Williams, *The French Assault on American Shipping*, 182.

1394. Lincolnville Historical Society, *Lincolnville—Early Days*, 34–35; Williams, *The French Assault on American Shipping*, 182.

1395. Wheeler, *History of Castine, Penobscot, and Brooksville*, 391; Lincolnville Historical Society, *Lincolnville—Early Days*, 34–35.

1396. O'Brien, *Ducktrap*, 13.

1397. Lincolnville Historical Society, *Lincolnville—Early Days*, 19.

1398. Ibid., 16; Commonwealth of Massachusetts, *Acts of 1802*, Chapter 16, Petition of Incorporation, June 23, 1802.

1399. General Court of the Commonwealth of Massachusetts, *Acts of 1802*, Chapter 16, Incorporation, June 23, 1802. See Sections 1–3 of the Act of Incorporation; Lincolnville Historical Society, *Lincolnville—Early Days*, 16.

1400. Lincolnville Historical Society, *Lincolnville—Early Days*, 7.

1401. Ibid.

1402. Ibid., 6.

1403. Ibid., 8.

1404. Ibid., 7.

1405. Eaton, *History of Warren in Knox County*, 248.

1406. Lincolnville Historical Society, *Lincolnville—Early Days*, 8.

1407. Ibid., 8–19.

1408. Taylor, *Liberty Men and Great Proprietors*, 158.

1409. Lincolnville Historical Society, *Lincolnville—Early Days*, 19; Taylor, *Liberty Men and Great Proprietors*, 265–67; Hancock County Court of General Sessions of the Peace, Record Book 2, Case 197, Maine State Archives: Ulmer vs. Ely; Samuel Ely leads a crowd that destroys the milldam belonging to George and Philip Ulmer; Henry Knox Papers, 39, page 112, Massachusetts State Archives: Hancock County, Incidents of Extralegal Violence Associated with the Land Controversies; At night, settlers cast loose a boom, setting adrift and scattering spars belonging to George Ulmer, Philip Ulmer, and Henry Knox, July 14, 1796; Henry Knox Papers, 39, page 144, Massachusetts State Archives: Hancock County, Incidents of Extralegal Violence Associated with the Land Controversies; At night, settlers cast loose a boom, setting adrift and scattering spars belonging to George Ulmer, Philip Ulmer, and Henry Knox, September 11, 1796.

1410. "Napoleon Sells Louisiana to the United States," *Texas Landmarks & Legacies*, Volume 2010, Number 120; *Saturday Evening Post*, April 30, 1803.

1411. Ibid.

1412. Taylor, *"The Rise and Fall of George Ulmer,"* 57; Hancock County Supreme Judicial Court, *Abiel Wood vs. George Ulmer; Abiel Wood vs. Samuel A. Whitney; Bank of the United States vs. George Ulmer;* Hancock County Supreme Court Record Book, Volume 1, June 1805, pages 275–81; Henry Knox Papers, Volume XLVI, Items 62 and 91; Letters of George Ulmer to Henry Knox, dated June 30, 1805, Lincolnville, and Ulmer letter to Henry Knox, dated November 10, 1805, Lincolnville.

1413. Taylor, "The Rise and Fall of George Ulmer," 57–60.

1414. Massachusetts General Court Records, *Resolves of the General Court of Massachusetts for the Year 1808* (Boston: Shaw-Shoemaker), number 15545; Resolve 114: February 26, 1808; page 104.

1415. Ibid.

1416. Lincolnville Historical Society, *Lincolnville—Early Days*, 9, 19.

1417. Taylor, "The Rise and Fall of George Ulmer," 85.

1418. Lincolnville Historical Society, *Lincolnville—Early Days*, 9, 19.

1419. Maresh, *Belmont, Maine*; 1830 Census of Belmont, Maine; The Belmont and Morrill Town Register of 1907.

1420. *Acts of the General Court of Massachusetts for the year 1811*, Chapter 99, February 27, 1811 (Boston: Shaw-Shoemaker, Number 23309), 348;

Lincolnville Historical Society, *Lincolnville—Early Days*, 1: 19–23; Taylor, *Liberty Men and Great Proprietors*, 158.

1421. Taylor, "The Rise and Fall of George Ulmer," 54.

1422. Amory, *Life of James Sullivan*, 275.

1423. Taylor, *Liberty Men and Great Proprietors*, 218.

1424. Henry Knox Papers, 46, Massachusetts Historical Society, 129: letter from George Ulmer to Henry Knox, April 12, 1806.

1425. Henry Knox Papers, 46, Massachusetts Historical Society, 129: letter from George Ulmer to Henry Knox, April 12, 1806; Henry Knox Papers, 46, Massachusetts Historical Society, 135: Henry Knox to George Ulmer, May 11, 1806; Taylor, *Liberty Men and Great Proprietors*, 218.

1426. Taylor, *Liberty Men and Great Proprietors*, 218.

1427. Small, *History of Swan Island*, 48.

1428. Ibid.

1429. Ibid., 45.

1430. Paul, *Unlikely Allies*, 324–25.

1431. Taylor, *Liberty Men and Great Proprietors*, 216–18.

1432. Ibid., 210–11.

1433. Ibid., 216–17.

1434. Ibid., 218.

1435. Taylor, "The Rise and Fall of George Ulmer," 87.

1436. Lincolnville Historical Society, *Lincolnville—Early Days*, 9, 21.

1437. Ibid., 8; Howard and Crocker, *A History of New England*, 127.

1438. Lincolnville Historical Society, *Lincolnville—Early Days*, 8.

1439. Taylor, "The Rise and Fall of George Ulmer," 60; Babcock, "The Effects of the Embargo of 1807 on the District of Maine."

1440. Lincolnville Historical Society, *Lincolnville—Early Days*, 10.

1441. Muller, "Smuggling into Canada," 5–21.

1442. Lincolnville Historical Society, *Lincolnville—Early Days*, 10; Records of the Town of Lincolnville, 1809.

1443. Callahan, *List of Officers*. US Navy Officers: 1798–1900 "U"; Ulmer, Philip; Sailing Master, 6 February, 1809.

1444. Ibid.

1445. Babcock, "The Effects of the Embargo of 1807 on the District of Maine"; Smith and Miller, *Borderland Smuggling*, 81–88.

1446. Callahan, *List of Officers*. List of Officers: "U", Philip Ulmer; Rank: Sailing Master; Military Branch: U.S. Navy Officer (1798–1900); Warrant revoked 8 May 1809; Washington Navy Yard, Washington, D.C.: Naval Historical Center.

1447. Hickey, *The War of 1812*; Horsman, *The Causes of the War of 1812*.

1448. Kilby, *Eastport and Passamaquoddy*, 160.

1449. Williamson, *The History of the State of Maine*, 2: 639.

1450. Ibid; Howard and Crocker, *A History of New England*, 2: 127.

Chapter 18: The War of 1812

1451. Feldmeth, "U.S. History Resources."

1452. Williams, *The French Assault on American Shipping*.

1453. Feldmeth, "U.S. History Resources."

1454. Kehne, "The Battle of Plattsburgh, 4.

1455. Pelletier, "The French Connection," 5–7.

1456. Ibid.

1457. Lossing, *Pictorial Field-Book of the War of 1812*. Old song from the War of 1812.

1458. Daughan, *If By Sea*, 420.

1459. Fitz-Enz, *Old Ironsides*; Hickman, *War of 1812*.

1460. Williamson, *History of the State of Maine*, 2: 639.

1461. Porter, "Letter from Major General Henry Sewall of Augusta, 1812." General John Blake's Letters, No. 6, 139; Williamson, *The History of the State of Maine*, 2: 639.

1462. Naval History & Heritage Command, *War of 1812 at Sea, HMS Shannon Captures USS Chesapeake, 1 June 1813* (Washington, D.C.: Department of the Navy, n.d.).

1463. Ibid.

1464. Anderson, *The Scottish Nation*, 102.

1465. Canadian Archives, MSS, Letter of Warren to Croker, January 28, 1814; Mahan, *Sea Power*, 330.

1466. Kehne, "The Battle of Plattsburgh," 4.

1467. Pearson, "Historical Narrative," 34.

1468. Kehne, "The Battle of Plattsburgh," 4.

1469. Ibid.

1470. Ibid.

1471. Lincolnville Historical Society, *Lincolnville—Early Days*, 10.

1472. Ibid.

1473. Smith, "The Trials and Tribulations of Fort Madison."

1474. Ibid.

1475. Ibid.

1476. Williamson, *The History of the State of Maine*, 2: 639.

1477. Robinson, *History of Camden & Rockport*, 187.

1478. Taylor, "The Rise and Fall of George Ulmer," 64; Kilby, *Eastport and Passamaquoddy*, 161–65.

1479. Taylor, "The Rise and Fall of George Ulmer," 62.

1480. Taylor, *Liberty Men and Great Proprietors*, 218; Taylor, "The Rise and Fall of George Ulmer," 58–59; Porter, "General George Ulmer," 118.

1481. Taylor, "The Rise and Fall of George Ulmer," 60–61.

1482. William Eustis letter to George Ulmer, May 6, 1812, Reel 5 of "Letters Sent by the Secretary of War," NARA; William King Papers, George Ulmer letter to William King, July 28 and October 16, 1812, Maine Historical Society; William King to William Eustis, Reel 46; "Letters Received by the Secretary of War," NARA.

1483. Taylor, "The Rise and Fall of George Ulmer," 61.

1484. Wilson, *Wilson Family History*, 248.

1485. Williamson, *The History of the State of Maine*, 639.

1486. William King Papers, George Ulmer letter to William King, October 16, November 9 and November 12, 1812; William King letter to William Eustis, December 6, 1812, Maine Historical Society; Taylor, "The Rise and Fall of George Ulmer," 61.

1487. Williamson, *The History of the State of Maine*, 639.

1488. Ibid.

1489. Ibid.

1490. William King Papers, George Ulmer letter to William King, December 1, December 10 and December 24, 1812, and also January 15 and February 12, 1813; all letters in the William King Papers; Maine Historical Society.

1491. Kilby, *Eastport and Passamaquoddy*, 142–51.

1492. Ibid.

1493. William King Papers, George Ulmer letter to William King on January 15 and February 12, 1813; Maine Historical Society.

1494. Smith, "The Trials and Tribulations of Fort Madison."

1495. William King Papers, George Ulmer letter to William King, December 24 and December 27, 1813 and February 7, 1813; Maine Historical Society.

1496. George Ulmer letter to John Armstrong, April 16, 1813, Reel 58, "Letters Received by the Secretary of War," NARA.

1497. George Ulmer letter to John Armstrong, April 16, 1813, Reel 58, "Letters Received by the Secretary of War," NARA; William King Papers,

George Ulmer letter to William King, January 15, 1813; Maine Historical Society.

1498. William King Papers, George Ulmer letter to William King, December 27, 1812, February 12, 1813 and March 26, 1813; Maine Historical Society.

1499. William King Papers, George Ulmer letter to William King, March 26, 1813; Maine Historical Society.

1500. Kilby, *Eastport and Passamaquoddy*, 161–65.

1501. Ibid.

1502. Taylor, "The Rise and Fall of George Ulmer," 64; Kilby, *Eastport and Passamaquoddy*, 161–65.

1503. Kilby, *Eastport and Passamaquoddy*, 161–65.

1504. Ibid.

1505. Taylor, "The Rise and Fall of George Ulmer," 64.

1506. Kilby, *Eastport and Passamaquoddy*, 161–65.

1507. Letter from Colonel George Ulmer to John Armstrong in 1813, Reel 58 of "Letters Received by the Secretary of War," NARA.

1508. William King Papers, letter from John Armstrong to Colonel George Ulmer, 1813; Maine State Library; letter from Colonel George Ulmer to John Armstrong, 1813; Reel 58, "Letters Received by the Secretary of War," NARA.

1509. Taylor, "The Rise and Fall of George Ulmer," 64.

1510. Taylor, "The Smuggling Career of William King," 19–38.

1511. Brant, *James Madison*, 25; Taylor, "The Rise and Fall of George Ulmer," 64.

1512. Colonel Joseph D. Learned letter to John Armstrong, May 18, 1813; "Letters Received by the Secretary of War," Reel 54; NARA.

1513. Isaac Lane Papers, "Results of the George Ulmer Court of Inquiry, July 3, 1814," Maine Historical Society.

1514. Taylor, "The Rise and Fall of George Ulmer," 64.

1515. William King Papers, letter of William Sterne to William King, July 31, 1813, Maine Historical Society; letter from Thomas H. Cushing to John Armstrong, "Letters received by the Secretary of War," August 16, 1813; NARA.

1516. Smith, *Borderland Smuggling*; Groening, "Maine and the War of 1812."

1517. Isaac Lane Papers, "Results of the George Ulmer Court of Inquiry, July 3, 1814," Maine Historical Society.

1518. Williamson, *The History of the State of Maine*, 639; Lossing, *The Pictorial Field-Book of the War of 1812*, 177.

1519. William King Papers, letter from George Ulmer to William King, August 28, 1813; Maine Historical Society.

1520. William King Papers, letters from George Ulmer to William King, February 24, 1814, and October 27, 1814, Maine Historical Society.

1521. Isaac Lane Papers, letter from Thomas H. Cushing to Isaac Lane, April 15, 1814; Maine Historical Society.

1522. Isaac Lane Papers, "Resolution of the George Ulmer Court of Enquiry, July 3, 1814"; Maine Historical Society. Taylor, "The Rise and Fall of George Ulmer," 65.

1523. "Letters Received by President Madison," Reel 58; letter from George Ulmer to President Madison, March 1, 1814; NARA.

1524. William King Papers, letter from Samuel Dana to William King, November 26, 1814; Maine Historical Society.

1525. Hancock County Supreme Judicial Court Record Book, Volume 4, "George Ulmer vs. Sherman Leland," June 1817, 172–75; Hancock Count Supreme Judicial Court Record Book, Volume 5; "Sherman Leland vs. George Ulmer," June 1821, 31.

1526. Fleming, *The Intimate Lives of the Founding Fathers*, 385.

1527. Lincolnville Historical Society, *Lincolnville—Early Days*, 8.

1528. Ibid., 34.

1529. Williamson, *The History of the State of Maine*, 639.

1530. Ibid.

1531. Lossing, *The Pictorial Field-Book of the War of 1812*, 177–78.

1532. Ibid.

1533. Williamson, *The History of the State of Maine*, 642–49.

1534. Smith, "The Trials and Tribulations of Fort Madison."

1535. Locke, *Sketches of the History of the Town of Camden*, 105.

1536. Robinson, *History of Camden and Rockport*, 158.

1537. Locke, *Sketches of the History of the Town of Camden*, 105.

1538. Ibid.

1539. Sprague and Chapman, *Sprague's Journal of Maine History*, Volume 2, 4; Staff First Brigade, 10th Division, Massachusetts Militia: John Blake, Brigadier-General of Brewer; Charles Blake, Quartermaster of Brewer; Francis Carr, Jr., Aide, of Bangor; Elijah Goodridge, Aide, of Bangor; Charles Ulmer, Aide, at Hampden.

1540. Robinson, *History of Camden and Rockport*, 186–90.

1541. U.S. House of Representatives, *Digested Summary and Alphabetical List*, Volume 3; written testimony of Christiana Ulmer (widow of Major Philip Ulmer); Congress 14; Session 2; Journal page 205. In the written testimony, Christiana wrote that her "late husband devoted his early manhood to the service of his country in the revolutionary war, & had the misfortune to be wounded in the thigh by the enemy's shot at the siege of majabigueduce [*sic*] on the mouth of the Penobscot river, the debilitating effects of which accompanied him through life & increased with his increasing years."

1542. Robinson, *History of Camden and Rockport*, 187.

1543. Ibid., 186.

1544. Ibid.

1545. Ibid., 137.

1546. Ibid., 186–88.

1547. Ibid., 187.

1548. Robinson, *History of Camden and Rockport*, 187; Locke, *Sketches of the History of the Town of Camden*, 137.

1549. Locke, *Sketches of the History of the Town of Camden*, 137.

1550. Ibid.

1551. Robinson, *History of Camden and Rockport*, 187–88.

1552. Ibid. Noah Miller and Customs Inspector Hook received $14,106.34 each; Miller's crewmen received $1,000 each; Major Philip Ulmer, the deputy customs inspector for the Penobscot Region, received $1,000. The men involved in the capture of the sloop *Mary* and its cargo contested the monetary reward payment for the prize vessel. The injustice to Miller's crew and to Major Philip Ulmer in not being paid an equal share of the proceeds from the prize vessel and cargo with Major Noah Miller as promised was finally considered and resolved by the Thirty-fourth U.S. Congress. The survivors of the crewmen or their heirs (like Philip Ulmer's heirs) had refunded to them the money paid to the government in 1815, the amount of $33,213.17. The Thirty-fourth U.S. Congress met in Washington from March 4, 1855, to March 4, 1857, during the last two years of the Franklin Pierce presidency.

1553. Robinson, *History of Camden and Rockport*, 188–89.

1554. Ibid., 192.

1555. Ibid., 196–97.

1556. Locke, *Sketches of the History of the Town of Camden*, 145.

1557. Robinson, *History of Camden and Rockport*, 64–66. Robinson claims on page 55 of his book that "General George Ulmer of Lincolnville took a force to Clam Cove and erected Fort Pine Hill prior to the expedition to Castine and mounted an 18-pounder gun." This could not have happened since Major Philip Ulmer, George's brother, was actually the commander of the company that built Fort Pine Hill and mounted the cannon. George Ulmer was a sergeant stationed with American forces at Rhode Island at the time prior to the expedition on Castine. See *Massachusetts Soldiers and Sailors*, Volume 16, 248–49.

1558. Robinson, *History of Camden and Rockport*, 64–66.

1559. Stothers, "The Great Tambora Eruption," 1:191–98.

1560. Eaton, *Annals of Warren*, 298; Robinson, *History of Camden and Rockport*, 197–98.

1561. Robinson, *History of Camden and Rockport, 198.*

1562. Bernheim, *The History of the German Settlements and the Lutheran Church*, 170–71. *The Javelin*, a Lutheran Church publication, recorded the circumstances of the early German immigration from Maine after the war: "The disappointment and suffering which they (the early German settlers) were made to endure (and) in consequence of the deceptions practiced upon them were trying to the extreme. And with all their troubles, the Indians fell upon them also and destroyed many lives and much substance. Ill-treated, robbed, wronged, and disappointed, many of them, under the guidance of the Moravian clergyman, Rev. Cilley, left the Muscangus (at Broad Bay) and emigrated to the Carolinas in 1773." Pages 228–32 state that during the ministry of Reverend J.G. Friederichs "…a colony of German settlers from Maine settled in North Carolina. They were accompanied by their Pastor Reverend Cilley." J.C. Hope, Esquire, of North Carolina wrote of the early Lutheran settlers there: "In 1763, a Colony of German Lutherans from Maine, accompanied by their Pastor Cilley, joined their brethren in South Carolina, but in time most returned." Reverend Dr. Hazelius stated: "Reverend Mr. Cilley arrived in South Carolina with a colony of German emigrants from Maine in the year 1773. But of his labors and success, no accounts are found." On page 602, it was stated that "about 1773, there were 15 or more families who left Waldoboro and moved to North Carolina." "Three Old Meeting Houses in Maine" which appears in the publication Maine Meeting Houses, Walpole: July 24–August 12, 1901, the Waldoboro article also confirms the emigration of 15 or more families from Waldoboro to North Carolina prior to the Revolutionary War.

Chapter 19: Last Years of the Ulmer Brothers

1563. New England Historical and Genealogical Society, *Massachusetts and Maine 1798 Federal Direct Tax Returns*, Volume 1, "Ducktrap Return."

1564. Maine Historical Society, *Miscellaneous Manuscripts*, 132, 214–22; Hancock County Tax Roll, 1815 Direct Tax.

1565. Lincolnville Historical Society, *Lincolnville—Early Days*, 8.

1566. Ibid., 7–10.

1567. Whitaker and Horlacher, *Broad Bay Pioneers*, 48; Document dated October 20, 1752; Eaton, *Annals of the Town of Warren*, 87.

1568. Sprague, *Sprague's Journal of Maine History*, Volume 6, Number 3 (Washington, D.C.: U.S. Government War Archives, 1918, 1919). Regarding Soldiers of the American Revolution; *Maine Indians in the Revolution*, 105–12. The article regarding *Sprague's Journal of Maine History: Maine Indians in the Revolution* appeared in the publication *Sentinel* in its issue of June 2, 1897, Eastport, Maine.

1569. Taylor, *Liberty Men and Great Proprietors*, 158–60.

1570. Lincolnville Town Records, House Documentation, Lincolnville Historical Society, 69–70.

1571. Morse, *Freemasonry in the American Revolution*, ix; Hieronimus and Cortner, *Founding Fathers*, 44–45.

1572. Massachusetts Grand Lodge of Massachusetts: Official Records. Letter from the secretary of the Massachusetts Grand Lodge confirming Philip Ulmer's Masonic affiliation and service, in possession of the author.

1573. Case, *Lafayette and the Knights Templar*, 59–61.

1574. A Letter written by an Ulmer descendant makes reference to a visit paid by Lafayette to the Ulmer family. This visit must have occurred in 1784 since Philip Ulmer died in 1816 and George was an invalid, confined mostly to his bed during Lafayette's second visit to America in late 1824. The letter is in possession of the Lincolnville Historical Society and Schoolhouse Museum and also with the author. There is also information in the Ulmer family about a Revolutionary War sword from the surrender at Saratoga (October 1777) that has been passed down in the Ulmer family for many generations which was presented by General Washington at Valley Forge in 1778. The sword is presently owned by a relative in the George Ulmer family.

1575. Massachusetts Historical Society, Henry Knox Collection, *Henry Knox Papers I: 1736–1823* (Boston: Massachusetts Historical Society, n.d.).

1576. Stuart Beitler, researcher and transcriber, "'The Elms' Historic Hotel at Camden, ME., Destroyed by Fire," *Massachusetts Lowell Sun*, November 13, 1917. Article reposted October 1, 2008. "…A portion of the hotel was built in 1796 and the first meeting of the Amity Lodge, A.F. and A.M., was held there in 1799, Philip Ulmer, Master. During the War of 1812, it was known as the Megunticook House. It sheltered many distinguished guests."

1577. U.S. House of Representatives, *Digested Summary and Alphabetical List*, Volume 3, Congress 14, Session 2, Journal page 205: Testimony of Christiana Ulmer, widow of Philip Ulmer.

1578. Robinson, *History of Camden and Rockport*. See Chapters 11 and 12.

1579. U.S. House of Representatives, *Journal of the House of Representatives of the U.S.*, Volume 9, *A Century of Law Making for a New Nation: U.S. Congressional Documents & Debates, 1774–1875*; Congressional Record Petitions for Major Philip Ulmer, pages 209, 369, 485; Petitions for General George Ulmer, pages 336, 506, 512. Library of Congress.

1580. U.S. House of Representatives, *Digested Summary and Alphabetical List*; Referred to the Committee of Pensions & Revolutionary War Claims: Accepted; Petition presented to Congress 13, Session 2, Journal page 209.

1581. U.S. House of Representatives, *Digested Summary and Alphabetical List of Private Claims Which Have Been Presented to the House of Representatives;* Referred to the Committee of Pensions & Revolutionary War Claims: Accepted; Petition presented to Congress 14, Session 1, Journal page 64.

1582. Revolutionary War Pension and Bounty-Land Warrant Application Files, Washington, D.C.: NARA, Philip Ulmer, Continental Massachusetts, Pension number: S 19963. Recorded in the Congressional Committee Records in Washington, D.C., Philip Ulmer, October 21, 1814 (See transcript at end of document written by Philip Ulmer); U.S. House of Representatives, *Digested Summary and Alphabetical List of Private Claims Which Have Been Presented to the House of Representatives*, Volume 3, Congress 14, Session 1, Journal page: 64; Referred to Committee: Pensions & Revolutionary War Claims; Senate: Passed; Bill: 171; Congress Date: Apr 29, 1816; House: Passed; Report: Favorable. See the testimonials of eyewitnesses, Adjutant-General Benjamin Hill, Joseph Coombs, and Alexander Kelloch; Journals of the House of Representatives of the U.S., *A Century of Law Making for a New Nation: U.S. Congressional Documents & Debates 1774–1875*, Volume 9 (Washington, D.C.: House of Representatives, n.d.), 881. Library of Congress. See Petitions: Major Philip Ulmer on pages 209, 369, and 485.

1583. Porter, "Deaths Copied from Newspapers."

1584. Lincolnville Historical Society, *Lincolnville—Early Days*, 8.

1585. Greely, *Public Documents of the First Fourteen Congresses*, 820. Petition presented by "Mr. Chappell, on the petition of Christiana Ulmer, widow of Philip Ulmer, asking that his petition be continued to her."

1586. U.S. House of Representatives, *Digested Summary and Alphabetical List*, Volume 3 (Washington, D.C.: Government Printing Office, 1853), Congress 14, Session 2, Journal page 205.

1587. Records of the Senate of the United States, Committee of Commerce, Senate Document Number 204, Congress 25, Session 2.

1588. Records of the Senate of the United States, Committee of Commerce, Senate Document Number 318 and 319, Congress 28, Session 1.

1589. Stahl, *History of Old Broad Bay and Waldoboro*, 584.

1590. Ibid., 310.

1591. Lincolnville Historical Society, *Lincolnville—Early Days*, 9, 19.

1592. Hancock County Tax Roll: 1815 Federal Direct Tax, Miscellaneous Manuscripts, 132, Maine Historical Society, 214–22.

1593. Taylor, *Liberty Men and Great Proprietors*, 235; Howard and Cocker, *A History of New England*, 127; Records of the Office of the Third Auditor of the Treasury, 1818–1872; Ledgers of Payments, 1818–1872 to U.S. Pensioners Under Acts of 1818 Through 1858; National Archives Microfilm Publication T718: 23 rolls; Records of the Accounting Officers of the Department of the Treasury, Record Group 217; National Archives, Washington, D.C.

1594. Lincolnville Historical Society, *Lincolnville—Early Days*, 6, 19.

1595. Wilson, *John Wilson of Tattenhall*, 89.

1596. Howard and Cocker, *A History of New England*, 127; "Obituary of General George Ulmer," The *Hancock Gazette* and *Penobscot Patriot*, January 11, 1826; Porter, *Bangor Historical Magazine* 2, no. 6 (Bangor, ME: 1886), 117.

1597. Quimby, "The Grave of Gen. George Ulmer."

1598. Wilson, *John Wilson of Tattenhall*, 89.

1599. Quimby, "The Grave of Gen. George Ulmer."

1600. Stahl, *History of Old Broad Bay and Waldoboro*, 584.

1601. George Washington Papers: 1741–1799, Series 2, Letterbooks; (Washington, D.C.: Library of Congress); Letterbook 24, George Washington, September 17, 1796, Farewell Address, 224.

1602. Ulmer, *Adventures and Reminiscences*. Entered according to the Act of Congress, 1892.

1603. Maine Vital Statistics, Vital Records to the Year 1892, Waldo County; Genealogy Index for Surnames, "U," Maine State Archives.

Appendix B

1604. U.S. House of Representatives, *Digested Summary and Alphabetical List*, Volume 3 (Washington, D.C.: Government Printing Office, 1853), Presented to Congress 14, Session 2, Journal page 205: Christiana Ulmer, widow of Philip Ulmer.

Bibliography

Abbott, John S.C., and Edward H. Elwell. *The History of Maine*. Augusta, ME: E.E. Knowles & Company and the Brown Thurston Company Printers, 1892.

Abbot, W.W., et al. eds. *Papers of Washington, Colonial Series*. Vols. 1–8. Charlottesville: University Press of Virginia, 1983.

Alcorn, Cynthia. *Historical Records: Maine Lodges under the Grand Lodge of Massachusetts*. Boston: Grand Lodge of Massachusetts A.F. & A.M., 2009.

Allis, Frederick S., ed. *William Bingham's Maine Lands, 1790–1820*. Vol. 1. Boston, MA: The Colonial Society of Massachusetts, 1954.

Amory, Thomas C. *Life of James Sullivan with Selections from His Writings*. Boston, MA: Phillips, Sampson & Company, 1829.

Anderson, William. *The Scottish Nation: The Surnames, Honours and Biographical History of the People of Scotland*. Edinburgh and London: Fullarton Company, 1862.

Andress, David. *1789: The Threshold of the Modern Age*. New York: Farrar, Straus & Giroux, 2008.

Arnold, Isaac N. *The Life of Benedict Arnold: His Patriotism and His Treason*. 4th ed. Chicago: A.C. McClurg & Company, 1905.

Augur, Helen. *The Secret War of Independence*. New York: Duell, Sloan & Pierce, 1955.

Babcock, Blakely B. "The Effects of the Embargo of 1807 on the District of Maine." Master's thesis, Trinity College, 1963.

Baldwin, Thomas W. *The Revolutionary Journal of Col. Jeduthan Baldwin, 1775–1778*. New York: New York Times, 1906. Reprint, New York: Arno Press, 1971.

Baxter, James P. *Documentary History of the State of Maine*. Vol. 17. Portland, ME: LeFavor-Tower Co., 1913.

Baxter, James, ed. *Journal of Lieutenant William Digby of the 53d or Shropshire Regiment of Foot*. Munsell's Historical Series 16. Albany, NY: Joel Munsell's Sons Publisher, 1887.

————. *William Digby, the British Invasion from the North, the Campaigns of Generals Carleton & Burgoyne, with the Journal of Lieut. William Digby*. Albany, NY: Joel Munsell's Sons Publisher, 1887.

Bellico, Russell P. *Chronicle of Lake Champlain—Journeys in War and Peace*. Fleischmanns, NY: Purple Mountain Press, 1999.

————. *Sails and Steam in the Mountains: A Maritime and Military History of Lake George and Lake Champlain*. Fleischmanns, NY: Purple Mountain Press, 1992.

Beverage, Samuel, and Eleanor S. Beverage. Letter written by an Ulmer family descendant. Lincolnville Historical Society, North Haven, Maine.

Bicheno, Hugh. *Redcoats and Rebels: The American Revolutionary War*. London: Harper Collins, 2003.

Bill, Alfred H. *The Campaign of Princeton, 1776–1777*. Princeton, NJ: Princeton University Press, 1948.

Billias, George A. *General John Glover and His Marblehead Mariners*. New York: Holt, Rinehart & Winston, 1960.

Boatner, Mark M. *Cassell's Biographical Dictionary of the American War of Independence, 1763–1783*. London: Cassell & Company, 1966.

————. *Encyclopedia of the American Revolution*. New York: McKay, 1966. Revised 1974.

Bond, William Papers. The Register of William Bond Papers, 1768–1777. MSS 0080. University of California–San Diego, Mandeville Special Collections Library, Geisel Library.

Bonislawski, Michael. *The History of Thomas Gardner's Regiment*. Charlestown, MA: The Charlestown Militia Company, 2010.

Bonsal, Stephen. *When the French Were Here*. Garden City, NY: Doubleday, Doran & Company, 1945.

Boyle, Joseph L. *Valley Forge Encampment of the Continental Army*. Portland, ME: F. Douglas & A. Shirley, 1819.

———. *Writings from the Valley Forge Encampment of the Continental Army, December 19, 1777, to June 19, 1778*. Vol. 2. Bowie, MD: Heritage Books, 2000–04.

Brady, Patricia. *Martha Washington*. New York: Penguin Book Group, 2006.

Brandt, Clare. *An American Aristocracy: The Livingstons*. New York: Doubleday, 1986.

Brant, Irving. *James Madison, Commander-in-Chief*. Indianapolis, IN: Bobbs-Merrill Company, 1961.

Bratten, John R. *The Gondola* Philadelphia *& the Battle of Lake Champlain*. College Station: Texas A&M University Press, 2002.

Brooks, Victor. *The Boston Campaign: April 1775–March 1776*. Conshohocken, PA: Combined Publishing, 1999.

Brown, Lloyd A. and Howard H. Peckham. *Revolutionary War Journals of Henry Dearborn 1775–1783*. Chicago: The Caxton Club, 1939.

Buker, George E. *The Penobscot Expedition: Commodore Saltonstall and the Massachusetts Conspiracy of 1779*. Annapolis, MD: Naval Institute Press, 2002.

Burgoyne, John. *The Remembrancer, 1777*. Vol. 1. Edited by William Stone. Albany, NY: Joel Munsell, 1877.

Burrage, Henry S., and Albert R. Stubbs. *Genealogical and Family History of the State of Maine*. Vol. 4. New York: Lewis Historical Publishing Company, 1909.

Butler, Joyce. "The Wadsworths: A Portland Family." *Maine Historical Society Quarterly* 27 (1988): 2–19.

Cahill, Robert E. *New England's Naughty Navy*. Peabody, MA: Chandler-Smith Publishing House, 1987.

Callahan, Edward W., ed. *List of Officers of the Navy and the Marine Corp from 1775 to 1900*. New York: L.R. Hamersly, 1901.

Callahan, North. *Henry Knox: General Washington's General*. New York: Rinehart & Company, 1958.

Cameron, James M. *American Pioneers of Antigonish*. Antigonish, NS: J.M. Cameron, 1984.

Carroll, Charles, and Allen S. Everest, eds. *Mission to Canada: The Journal of Charles Carroll of Carrollton*. Fort Ticonderoga, NY: Champlain-Upper Hudson Bicentennial Committee, 1976.

Case, James R. "Lafayette and the Knights Templar." Reprint from *Knights Templar Magazine*, Masonic Americana, 1976.

Castine Historical Society. *1779 Penobscot Expedition: An American Naval Disaster*. Castine, ME: Castine Historical Society, n.d.

Chadwick, Bruce. *The First American Army*. Naperville, IL: Sourcebooks, 2007.

Chambers, Robert W. *The Hidden Children*. New York: D. Appleton and Company, 1914. Reprint, Whitefish, MT: Kessinger Publishing, 2004.

Channing, Edward. *Students History of the United States*. New York: MacMillan Co., 1900.

Chase, Philander D., ed. *The Papers of George Washington, Dec. 1777–Feb. 1778*. Revolutionary War Series. Charlottesville: University of Virginia Press, 2003.

———. *Papers of Washington Revolutionary War Series*. Vol. 7. Charlottesville: University Press of Virginia, 1983.

Cheney, Glenn A. *Thanksgiving*. New London, CT: New London Librarium, 2007.

Clark, William, William Morgan and Michael Crawford, eds. *Naval Documents of the American Revolution*. Washington, D.C.: U.S. Government Printing Office, 1964.

Claypoole, David. "The Address of General Washington to the People of the United States." *American Daily Advertiser*, September 19, 1796. Reprinted by James D. Hart and Phillip W. Leininger as "Claypoole's American Daily Advertiser" in *The Oxford Companion to American Literature*. Oxford, UK: Oxford University Press, 1995.

Coffin, Charles. *The Life and Services of Major General John Thomas*. New York: Egbert, Hovey & King, 1844.

Cohn, Arthur B. "An Incident Not Known to History: Squire Ferris and Benedict Arnold at Ferris Bay, October 13, 1776." *Vermont History* 55, no. 2 (1987): 3–88.

———. July 2009 dive and video filming of the *Spitfire* on the bottom of Lake Champlain by the Lake Champlain Maritime Museum dive team. See the *Spitfire* CD of July 2009 for graphic evidence.

Cohn, Scotti. *Liberty's Children: Stories of Eleven Revolutionary War Children*. Guilford, CT: Globe Pequot Press, 2004.

Connecticut Historical Society. "Journal of Bayze Wells of Farmington: May 1775–February 1776." *Collections from the Connecticut Historical Society* 7, (1899).

Continental Army Books. *Continental Army Pay Accounts*. Vol. 18. Washington, D.C: National Archives and Records Service, February 3, 1779.

Cornwell, Bernard. *The Fort: A Novel of the Revolutionary War*. New York: Harper Collins, 2010.

Craughwell, Thomas. *Stealing Lincoln's Body*. Cambridge, MA: Belknap Press, 2007.

Cresswell, Nicholas. *The Journal of Nicholas Cresswell, 1774–1781*. Edited by Samuel Thornely. New York: Dial Press, 1924.

Crockett, Walter. *Vermont: The Green Mountain State*. New York: Century History Company, 1921.

Cubbinson, Douglas R. *The American Northern Theater Army in 1776: The Ruin and Reconstruction of the Continental Force*. Jefferson, NC: McFarland & Company, 2010.

———. *The Artillery Never Gained More Honour: The British Artillery in the 1776 Valcour Island and 1777 Saratoga Campaigns*. Fleischmanns, NY: Purple Mountain Press, 2007.

Cutler, Reverend Manasseh. *Journal from 1761–1849*. Series 1. Manasseh Cutler Collection. Ohio University Library, The Mahn Center, Archives and Special Collections.

Daughan, George C. *If By Sea: The Foraging of the American Navy—From the Revolution to the War of 1812*. New York: Basic Books, 2009.

Davies, K.G., ed. *Documents of the American Revolution, 1770–1783*. Colonial Office Series, Vol. 12. Shannon: Irish University Press, 1972–1981.

Davis, Burke. *The Campaign That Won America: The Story of Yorktown*. New York: Dial Press, 1970.

Davis, David B., and Steven Mintz. *The Boisterous Sea of Liberty*. New York and Oxford: Oxford University Press, 1998.

Declaration of Independence, "First Public Reading of the Declaration of Independence." Ticonderoga, NY, 28 July 1776, Colonel St. Clair. Reported in the *Pennsylvania Evening Post*, August 15, 1776; *New York Journal*, August 15, 1776; *New York Packet*, August 15, 1776; *New York Gazette* and the *Weekly Mercury*, August 19, 1776.

De Fonblanque, Edward B. *Political and Military Episodes in the Latter Half of the Eighteenth Century Derived from the Life and Correspondence of the Right Hon. John Burgoyne, General, Statesman, Dramatist*. London: Macmillan and Co., 1876.

De Fonblanque, Windsor, Justin, ed. *Narrative and Critical History of America*. Vol. 6. Boston and New York: Houghton, Mifflin & Co., 1887.

Doblin, Helga, trans., and Mary C. Lynn, ed. *The Specht Journal: A Military Journal of the Burgoyne Campaign*. Westport, CT: Greenwood Press, 1995.

Drake, Francis S. *Life and Correspondence of Henry Knox: Major-General in the American Revolutionary Army*. Boston: S.B. Drake, 1873.

Drake, Samuel A. *History of Middlesex County, Massachusetts*. Vol. 1. Boston: Estes and Lauriat Publishers, 1880.

Dunnack, Henry E. *The Maine Book*. Augusta: Librarian of Maine State Library, 1920.

Dwyer, William. *The Day Is Ours!* New York: Viking Press, 1982.

Eaton, Cyrus. *Annals of the Town of Warren*. Hallowell, ME: Masters, Smith & Company, 1865.

———. *Annals of the Town of Warren in Knox County: Early History of St. Georges, Broad Bay, and Neighboring Settlements on the Waldo Patent*. Vol. 2. Hallowell, ME: Masters & Livermore, 1877.

———. *History of the Town of Warren: With the Early History of St Georges, Broad Bay, and Neighboring Settlements on the Waldo Patent*. Hallowell, ME: Masters, Smith & Company, 1851.

———. *History of Warren in Knox County*. Hallowell, ME: Masters, Smith & Company, 1851.

Edward, W. *Standards and Colors of the American Revolution*. Philadelphia: University of Richardson Pennsylvania Press, 1982.

Egret, Jean. *La Pré-révolution Française*. Paris: Presses Universitaires de France, 1962.

Elson, Henry W. *History of the United States of America*. New York: MacMillan Company, 1904.

Engle, Eloise, and Arnold S. Lott. *American Merchant Marine at War*. Annapolis, MD: Naval Institute Press, 1975.

Essex Institute. Letter of John Glover to Azor Orne, September 21, 1777. Historical Collection 5, June 1863, Peabody Essex Museum, Salem, MA.

Eustis, William. Letter to George Ulmer, May 6, 1812. Reel 5 of "Letters Sent by the Secretary of War." NARA.

Ewald, Johann. *Diary of the American War: A Hessian Journal*. Edited by Joseph P. Tustin. New Haven, CT: Yale University Press, 1979.

Favor, Lesli J. *The Iroquois Constitution: A Primary Source Investigation of the Law of the Iroquois*. New York: Rosen Publishing Group, 2003.

Feldmeth, Gregory D. "US History Resources." Chart of Key Events & Causes: War of 1812. Courtesy of http://home.earthlink. net/~gfeldmeth/USHistory.html.

Ferling, John E. *The First of Men: A Life of George Washington*. Knoxville: University of Tennessee Press, 1988.

Fischer, David H. *Paul Revere's Ride*. New York: Oxford University Press, 1995.

———. *Washington's Crossing*. New York: Oxford University Press, 2006.

Fitz-Enz, David G. *Old Ironsides: Eagle of the Sea: The Story of the USS Constitution*. Lanham, MD: Taylor Trade Publishing, 2004.

Fitzpatrick, John C., ed. *The Writings of George Washington from the Original Manuscript Sources, 1745–1799*. Washington, D.C.: United States Government Printing Office, 1932.

Fleming, Thomas. *The Intimate Lives of the Founding Fathers*. New York: Harper Collins, 2009.

Flexner, James. *The Traitor and the Spy: Benedict Arnold and John Andre*. New York: Harcourt, Brace & Company, 1957.

Fogle, Lauren. *Colonial Marblehead: From Rogues to Revolutionaries*. Charleston, SC: The History Press, 2008.

Foran, Jill. *Maine: The Pine Tree State*. Mankato, MN: Weigl Publishers, 2002.

Force, Peter, ed. American Archives: Series 4, *From the King's Message to Parliament, of March 7, 1774, to the Declaration of Independence of the United States*. Washington, D.C.: M. St. Clair Clarke and Peter Force, 1843.

———. American Archives: Series 5, *From the Declaration of Independence, in 1776, to the Definitive Treaty of Peace with Great Britain, in 1783*. Washington, D.C.: M. St. Clair Clarke and Peter Force, 1848.

Foreign Affairs Committee. *Communications: Commissioners in France*. Washington, D.C.: Library of Congress.

Fortescue, Sir John. *History of the British Army*. East Sussex, UK: Naval & Military Press, 1899–1930. Reprint of the original in 2004.

Franks, Frederick M. *A Few Good Men: The Revolutionary War*. Edited by Clifton G. Ganyard. Indianapolis, IN: Alpha Books, 2003.

Freeman, Douglas S. *George Washington: A Biography*. Vol. 4. New York: Charles Scribner's Sons, 1948–57.

French, Allen. *The Siege of Boston*. New York: Macmillan Company, 1911.

Frothingham, Richard. *History of the Siege of Boston, and the Battles of Lexington, Concord, and Bunker Hill*. 2nd ed. Boston: Charles Little & James Brown, 1851.

Furneaux, Rupert. *The Battle of Saratoga*. New York: Stein & Day, 1971.

Gates, General Horatio. "Bulletin of Fort Ticonderoga, 14 October 1776." *Bulletin of the Fort Ticonderoga Museum* 14, no. 1 (1981): 22.

George Washington Papers. Joseph Reed letter to Stephen Moylan, Colonel Glover's aide. Library of Congress, Letterbook 1, Image 68.

Gerlach, Don R. *Proud Patriot: Philip Schuyler and the War of Independence, 1775–1778*. Syracuse, NY: Syracuse University Press, 1987.

Gilman, Arthur, et al. *Theatrum Majorum: The Cambridge of 1776*. Cambridge, MA: Lockwood & Brooks, 1876.

Glaser, Lynn. *Counterfeiting in America: The History of an American Way to Wealth*. Philadelphia: Clarkson N. Potter, 1960.

Goold, Nathan. *Bagaduce Expedition, 1779*. Collections of the Maine Historical Society, Vol. 4. Portland, ME: Maine Historical Society, October 27, 1898.

————. *Falmouth Neck in the Revolution*. Portland, ME: Press of the Thurston Print, 1897.

————. "Maine Indian in the Revolution." *Eastport Sentinel*, Vol. 37, June 2, 1897, (*ME*). Massachusetts State Archives. Courtesy of Tina Vickery and the Androscoggin Historical Society, 1998.

Gould, Edward K. *Storming the Heights: Maine's Embattled Farmers at Castine in the Revolution*. Rockland, ME: Courier-Gazette Press, 1932.

Grand Lodge of Connecticut AF & AM. "Benjamin Franklin on Masonic Secrecy." *Connecticut Freemasons Magazine*, November 2009.

Grand Lodge of Masons in Massachusetts, Cynthia Alcorn, Librarian. Membership records copied from the Massachusetts Grand Lodge archives.

Greely, Adolphus W., comp. *Public Documents of the First Fourteen Congresses, 1789–1817*. Washington, D.C.: U.S. Government Printing Office, 1900.

Greenwood, John. *The Revolutionary Services of John Greenwood of Boston and New York*. Edited by Isaac J. Greenwood. New York: De Vinne Press, 1922.

Griffiths, Thomas M. *Maine Sources in* The House of Seven Gables. Waterville, ME: Southworth-Anthoensen Press, 1945. Reprint, Signet Classics, 1961, and W.W. Norton & Co., 2005.

Gruber, Ira D. *The Howe Brothers and the American Revolution*. New York: W.W. Norton & Company, 1972.

Grundset, Eric G., ed. *Forgotten Patriots: African American and American Indian Patriots in the Revolutionary War*. Washington, D.C.: National Society of Daughters of the American Revolution, 2008.

Hadden, James. *Hadden's Journal and Orderly Books: A Journal Kept in Canada and Upon Burgoyne's Campaign in 1776 and 1777*. Edited by Horatio Rogers. Albany, NY: Joel Munsell's Sons, 1884.

Haldimand, Frederick. Correspondence with General Gates, 1758–1777. Special Collections, John C. Pace Library, University of West Florida, Pensacola, microfilm.

Hale, William. "Letters Written During the American War of Independence." Edited by H.C. Wylly. *Regimental Annual, The Sherwood Foresters*. London: Wodehouse, 1913.

Hazelton, John H. *The Declaration of Independence: Its History*. New York: Dodd & Mead, 1906.

Hearn, Chester G. *George Washington's Schooners: The First American Navy*. Annapolis, MD: Naval Institute Press, 1995.

Heath, William. *Memoirs of Major General William Heath*. Edited by William Abbatt. New York: William Abbatt, 1901.

Heaton, Ronald E. *Masonic Membership of the Founding Fathers*. Silver Spring, MD: Masonic Service Association, 1965.

Heline, Corrine. *America's Invisible Guidance*. Los Angeles: New Age Press, 1949.

Heline, Theodore. *America's Destiny: A New Order of Ages*. Oceanside, CA: New Age Press, 1941.

Hickey, Donald R. *The War of 1812: A Forgotten Conflict*. Chicago: University of Illinois Press, 1989.

Hickman, Kennedy. *War of 1812: USS* Constitution *Defeats HMS* Guerriere. Washington, D.C.: Naval Historical Center, 2013.

Hieronimus, Robert and Laura Cortner. *Founding Fathers, Secret Societies*. Rochester, VT: Destiny Books, 2006.

Hoffman, Ronald, and Peter J. Albert, eds. *Diplomacy and Revolution: The Franco-American Alliance of 1778*. Charlottesville: University Press of Virginia, 1981.

Horsman, Reginald. *The Causes of the War of 1812*. Philadelphia: University of Pennsylvania Press, 1962.

Howard, R.H., and Henry E. Cocker, eds. *A History of New England*. Boston: Crocker & Company, 1881.

Howe, William. *The Narrative of Lieutenant-General Sir William Howe in a Committee of the House of Commons on the 29th of April 1779*. London: House of Commons, 1780.

Hudgins, Bill. "The Quasi-War: The Almost War Between America and France in the 1790's." *American Spirit Magazine*, January–February 2010.

Hutchinson, Thomas. *The History of the Province of Massachusetts Bay, from 1749 to 1774*. London: John Murray, 1828.

Huth, Hans, and Wilma Pugh. "Talleyrand in America as a Financial Promoter." 1794–1796, *Annual Report of the American Historical Association for 1941*. Vol. 2. Washington, D.C.: U.S. Government Printing Office, 1942.

Irving, Washington. *Life of George Washington*. New York: G.P. Putnam & Son, 1869. Reprint, Cambridge, MA: Da Capo Press, 1994.

Isham, Charles, ed. and trans. *The Deane Papers, 1737–1789*. Vol. 1. New York: New York Historical Collections, 1886.

Kehne, Caroline. "The Battle of Plattsburgh: A Primer." *Lake Champlain Weekly* 10, no. 6 (2009): 8–14.

Ketchum, Richard M. *Saratoga: Turning Point of America's Revolutionary War*. New York: Henry Holt & Company, 1997.

———. *Victory at Yorktown: The Campaign that Won the Revolution*. New York: Henry Holt and Company, 2004.

Kevitt, Chester B. *General Solomon Lovell and the Penobscot Expedition 1779*. Weymouth, MA: Weymouth Historical Commission and C.B. Kevitt, 1976.

Kidder, Frederic. *Military Operations in Eastern Maine & Nova Scotia: with Notes and a Memoir of Colonel John Allen*. Albany, NY: Joel Munsell, 1967.

Kilby, William. *Eastport and Passamaquoddy*. Eastport, ME: E.E. Shead & Company, 1888.

King, William. Collection: William King Papers, Box 17. Correspondence from George Ulmer to William King, 1812 & 1813. Portland, ME: Maine Historical Society.

Klos, Stanley L. *Historical Documents of Freedom: Marquis de Lafayette*. Originally from Lafayette's Journal, Memoires, Manuscrits et Correspondence du Marquis de Lafayette. 6 vols. Paris, France, 1837–38.

Konstam, Angus. *Privateers & Pirates 1730–1830*. Oxford, UK: Osprey Publishing, 2001.

Lancaster, Bruce. *The American Revolution*. New York: American Heritage Publishing Company, 1971.

Lanctot, Gustave. *Canada and the American Revolution, 1774–1783*. Translated by Margaret M. Cameron. Boston: Harvard University Press, 1967.

Lane, Isaac Papers. Letter from Thomas H. Cushing to Isaac Lane, April 15, 1814. Maine Historical Society.

———. Resolution of the George Ulmer Court of Enquiry, July 3, 1814. Maine Historical Society.

La Rochefoucauld-Liancourt, François Alexandre Frédéric, duc de. *Travels Through the United States of North America*. Vol. 1. London: R. Phillips publisher, 1799.

Leamon, James S. *Revolution Downeast: The War for American Independence*. Portland, ME: Thomson Shore, 1993.

Learned, Colonel Joseph D. Letter to John Armstrong, May 18, 1813. "Letters Received by the Secretary of War." Reel 54, NARA.

Lefkowitz, Arthur. *Benedict Arnold's Army: The 1775 American Invasion of Canada During the Revolutionary War*. New York: Savas Beatie, 2008.

Lesser, Charles H., ed. *The Sinews of Independence*. Chicago: University of Chicago Press, 1976.

Lincoln County Courthouse Wiscasset. Lincoln County Land Deeds, Lincoln County Deeds Book.

Locke, John L. *Sketches of the History of the Town of Camden, Maine*. Hallowell, ME: Masters, Smith & Company, 1859.

Lomask, Milton. "Benedict Arnold: The Aftermath of Treason." *American Heritage Magazine*, October 1967.

Lossing, Benson J. *The Pictorial Field-Book of the War of 1812*. Vol. 1. New York: Harper & Brothers, 1868. Reprint, Whitefish, MT: Kessinger Publishing, 2006.

Lovell, Samuel. *The Original Journal of General Solomon Lovell Kept During the Penobscot Expedition 1779*. Edited by Gilbert Nash. Boston: Wright & Potter Printing Company, 1881.

Lundeberg, Philip K. *The Gunboat* Philadelphia *and the Defense of Lake Champlain, 1776*. Basin Harbor, VT: Lake Champlain Maritime Museum, 1996.

Mackey, Albert G. *Revised Encyclopedia of Freemasonry*. Vol. 2. New York: Macoy Publishing, 1966.

Mahan, Alfred T. *Alfred T. Mahan Collection, 1883–1913*. New York: Charles Scribner's Sons, 1964. Reprint, Princeton, NJ: Department of Rare Books & Special Collections, Princeton University Library, 1985.

Maine Historical Society. *Benedict Arnold's Letter Book 1775*. Portland, ME: Maine Historical Society.

———. *Collections and Proceedings of the Maine Historical Society*. Portland, ME: Maine Historical Society, 1890.

———. *Documentary History of the State of Maine*. Vol. 18. Portland, ME: Maine Historical Society.

———. *Miscellaneous Manuscripts*, 132, Hancock County Tax Roll, 1815 Direct Tax.

Maine State Archives. *Abiel Wood v. George Ulmer, Abiel Wood v. Samuel A. Whitney, Bank of the United States v. George Ulmer*. Hancock County Supreme Judicial Court Record Book, Vol. 1, June 1805.

———. Committee on Claims on behalf of Massachusetts against the United States, September 21, 1787, Depreciation Rolls, Vol. 31. Boston, MA: Wright & Potter Company, 1896.

———. General Lovell's Report, Vol. 145.

———. George Ulmer's Court, March 1, 1797. Hancock County Court of General Sessions of the Peace files, Box 77.

———. *George Ulmer v. Sherman Leland*. Hancock County Supreme Judicial Court Record Book, Vol. 4, June 1817.

———. Governor and Council Letters. Boston, MA: Wright & Potter Company, 1896.

———. Militia Officers, Vol. 28, A List of Officers of the Massachusetts Militia (Continental Army).

———. Petition statement of Miriam Farrow, for widow's pension of Ezekiel Farrow. Maine 2208 (Act of March 3, 1843), recorded in Book A, Vol. 1, July 1838.

———. *Philip and George Ulmer v. Samuel Ely*. Hancock County Court of Common Pleas, Record Book 2, Case 197, April 1796.

———. Records of the Cumberland County Court of General Sessions of the Peace, October 1782.

———. Registers of Deeds of Lincoln and York Counties: Broad Bay Land Records, Lot no. 4. 1760. microfilm.

———. Revolutionary War Papers of Johann Valentin Minck.

———. Revolutionary War, U.S. Pension Paper of George Ulmer.

———. *Sherman Leland v. George Ulmer*. Hancock Count Supreme Judicial Court Record Book, Vol. 5, June 1821.

Martin, David G. *The Philadelphia Campaign, June 1777–July 1778*. Cambridge, MA: Da Capo Press, 1993.

Martin, James K. *Benedict Arnold, Revolutionary Hero: An American Warrior Reconsidered*. New York: New York University Press, 1997.

Martyn, Charles. *The Life of Artemas Ward: The First Commander-in-Chief of the American Revolution*. Port Washington, NY: Kennikat Press, 1921.

Massachusetts, Commonwealth of. *Acts of 1802: Petition of Incorporation*. Chapter 16, June 23, 1802.

———. *Historical Marker Database*. Prospect Hill Markers.

Massachusetts, Secretary of the Commonwealth. *Massachusetts Soldiers and Sailors in the War of the Revolution, 1775–1783*. Vols. 4 and 16. Boston: Wright & Potter Printing Company, 1896.

———. *Proceedings from the Massachusetts Council of War*. Collection of the Revolutionary Period, 1629–1799. Boston: State House, Massachusetts State Archives Collection.

———. *Report to the Legislature of Massachusetts Made by the Commissioners*. Boston: Wright & Potter Printing Co., 1885. Massachusetts Militia; Books: Abstracts of Rolls.

———. *Report to the Legislature of Massachusetts Made by the Commissioners*. Boston: Wright & Potter Printing Co., 1885. Sea Coast Defence [sic] Muster and Pay Roll.

———. "Return of Officers in Colonel Gardner's Regiment on 6 July 1775."(Fifteenth Massachusetts MA-09A). Massachusetts Archives.

Massachusetts Court of Inquiry. Testimony of Adjutant General Jeremiah Hill, September 29, 1779. Washington, D.C.: NARA and Massachusetts State Archives, microfilm.

Massachusetts General Court. *Acts and Laws of the Commonwealth of Massachusetts.* Chapter 69. Boston: Young & Minns, State Printers, 1796. Reprinted by Wright & Potter Company, Boston, MA, 1896.

———. *Acts of the General Court of Massachusetts for the Year 1811.* Chapter 99. Boston: Shaw-Shoemaker, number 23309, February 27, 1811. Boston, MA: Wright & Potter Company, 1896.

———. *Resolves of the General Court of Massachusetts for the Year 1808.* Boston: Shaw-Shoemaker, number 15545, Resolve 114, February 26, 1808. Boston, MA: Wright & Potter Company, 1896.

———. *Resolves of the General Court of the Commonwealth of Massachusetts, May 1782–March 1783.* Boston, number 18026, Resolve 158, March 17, 1783. Boston, MA: Wright & Potter Company, 1896.

Massachusetts Muster and Pay Rolls, vol. 48, Muster Roll for December 1777. Massachusetts State Archives. microfilm.

Massachusetts Vital Records Project from 1626 to 1849. *Vital Records of Salem, Massachusetts to the End of the Year 1849, vol. 4—Births and Marriages.* Salem, MA: The Essex Institute, 2005–09.

Massachusetts Vital Records Project from 1649 to 1849. *Vital Records of Marblehead Massachusetts to the End of the Year 1849, vol. 2—Marriages and Deaths.* Marblehead, MA: Town of Marblehead, MA, 2005–09.

Meigs, Major Return J. *Journal of the Expedition Against Quebec, Under Command of Col. Benedict Arnold.* New York: privately printed, 1864.

Merwin, Henry. *Aaron Burr.* Boston: Small, Maynard & Company, 1899.

Millard, James P. *The Battle of Lake Champlain.* South Hero, VT: The Lake Champlain and Lake George Historical Site, 1997.

Miller, Nathan. *Sea of Glory: The Continental Navy Fights for Independence, 1775–1783.* New York: David McKay, 1974.

Miller, Samuel L. *History of the Town of Waldoboro, Maine.* Wiscasset, ME: Emerson, printer, 1910.

Mintz, Max M. *The Generals of Saratoga: John Burgoyne and Horatio Gates.* New Haven, CT: Yale University Press, 1990.

Morse, Sidney. *Freemasonry in the American Revolution.* Washington, D.C.: Masonic Service Association of the United States, 1924.

Mott, Hopper S. et al., eds. *The New York Genealogical and Biographical Record, Thacher-Thatcher Genealogy.* Vol. 44. New York: New York Genealogical and Biographical Society, 1913.

Muller, H. Nicholas. "Smuggling into Canada: How the Champlain Valley Defied Jefferson's Embargo." *Vermont History*, no. 38 (1970): 5–21.

Mustapich, Susan M. "Lincolnville House Named to National Register." *Camden Herald*, November 9, 2006.

Nash, Gilbert. "The Original Journal of General Solomon Lovell during the Penobscot Expedition." *Chronicle and Advisor*, September 23, 1779.

National Archives and Records Administration. Office of Army Accounts, Paymaster General, *Compiled Service Records of Soldiers Who Served in the American Army During the Revolutionary War, 1775–1785,* Journal American Congress, Col. 4, Washington, D.C.: NARA M881, Continental Massachusetts, Ulmer, Philip, number S. 19963.

———. Record Group 93, M859, Roll 8, Document 2282 and Document 2308.

———. Records of the Accounting Officers of the Department of the Treasury, Record Group 217, Washington, D.C.

———. Records of the Office of the Third Auditor of the Treasury, 1818–1872, Ledgers of Payments, 1818–1872 to U.S. Pensioners Under Acts of 1818 Through 1858, Microfilm Publication T718, 23 rolls.

———. *Revolutionary War Pension and Bounty-Land Warrant Application Files,* Washington, D.C., Records of the Department of Veteran Affairs, Record Group 15, Survivor's Pension Application File, NARA. Microfilm publication M804, Roll 2434.

———. *Revolutionary War Pension and Bounty-Land Warrant Application Files,* Washington, D.C., Philip Ulmer, Continental Massachusetts, Pension number: S 19963. Recorded in the *Congressional Committee Records*, Washington, D.C.; Philip Ulmer, 21 October 1814.

———. *Revolutionary War Pension and Bounty-Land Warrant Application Files*, Washington, D.C.: NARA.

———. Revolutionary War 1777–1781: Pay Roll of Captain Hunt's Company in Colonel Joseph Vose Regiment, Folder 2, Publication Number: M246, NARA.

———. U.S. Navy 1775–1910, Subject File, B.O. Ordnance Equipment, Box #152. *Gundelow Spitfire, Capt. Phillip Ulmer.*

National Society Daughters of the American Revolution. *African American and American Indian Patriots of the Revolutionary War*. Washington, D.C.: National Society DAR, 2008.

Navy, Department of. *Dictionary of American Fighting Ships*. Washington, D.C.: Naval History and Heritage Command: Ships of the Continental Navy, n.d.

———. *Officers of the Continental and U.S. Navy and Marine Corps, 1775–1900*. Washington, D.C.: Naval History and Heritage Command. U.S. Navy Officers: 1798–1900.

———. *War of 1812 at Sea, HMS* Shannon Captures *USS* Chesapeake, *1 June 1813*. Washington, D.C.: Naval History & Heritage Command, n.d.

Nelson, James L. *Benedict Arnold's Navy*. Camden, ME: McGraw Hill, 2006.

———. *George Washington's Secret Navy: How the American Revolution Went to Sea*. New York: McGraw Hill, 2008.

———. *With Fire and Sword: The Battle of Bunker Hill and the Beginning of the American Revolution*. New York: St. Martin's Press, 2011.

Nelson, Paul. *General Horatio Gates: A Biography*. Baton Rouge: Louisiana State University Press, 1976.

New England Historical and Genealogical Society. *Bartlett's Colonial Record of Rhode Island*. Manuscript Collections, Vol. 7.

———. *Massachusetts and Maine 1798 Federal Direct Tax Returns*, "Ducktrap Return." Vol. 1.

———. *1798 Direct Tax List*. General list of land, lots, buildings and wharves, assets of George Ulmer and Philip Ulmer of Ducktrap, Lincolnville.

Nickerson, Hoffman. *The Turning Point of the Revolution: Burgoyne in America.* Boston: Houghton Mifflin, 1928.

Nicolar, Joseph. *Penobscot Indians 1895, As We Tell Our Stories: Living Traditions of [Indian] Peoples of Native New England.* Courtesy of the American Indian Archaeological Institute, Washington, CT.

O'Brien, Diane R. *Ducktrap: Chronicles of a Maine Village.* Lincolnville, ME: Schoolhouse Museum of the Lincolnville Historical Society, 1994.

Olney, Stephen. *Memoir: Biography of Revolutionary Heroes.* Edited by Catherine Williams. Providence, RI: Privately published, 1839.

O'Toole, G.A. *Honorable Treachery: A History of Intelligence, Espionage, and Covert Action from the American Revolution to the CIA.* New York: Atlantic Monthly Press, 1991.

Paige, Lucius R. *History of Cambridge, Massachusetts 1630–1877.* Cambridge, MA: Riverside Press, 1877.

Palmer, Dave R. *George Washington and Benedict Arnold: A Tale of Two Patriots.* Washington, D.C.: Regnery Publishing, 2006.

Palmer, Peter S. *History of Lake Champlain: From Its First Exploration by the French in 1609 to the Close of the Year 1814.* Albany, NY: J. Munsell Publisher, 1866.

Parker, Arthur C. *The Constitution of the Five Nations: The Iroquois Book of the Great Law.* New York: New York State Museum Bulletin no. 184, 1916.

Patterson, Samuel. *Horatio Gates, Defender of American Liberties.* New York: Columbia University Press, 1941.

Patton, Robert H. *Patriot Pirates.* New York: Vintage Books, 2009.

Paul, Joel R. *Unlikely Allies.* New York: Riverhead Books, 2009.

Paullin, Charles. *The Navy of the American Revolution: Its Administration, Its Policy and Its Achievements.* Whitefish, MT: Kessinger Publishing, n.d.

Pearson, Gardner W. *Massachusetts Volunteer Militia in the War of 1812.* Boston: Wright & Potter, 1913.

Pelletier, Robert. "The French Connection: The Battles of Lake Champlain, 1609 and 1812." *Lake Champlain Weekly* 10, no. 6 (2009): 14–16.

Pennsylvania, Historical Society of. "The Battle of Princeton." Journal of Sergeant R--- [*sic*]. *The Pennsylvania Magazine of History and Biography* 20, 1896.

Porter, Joseph W., ed. "Deaths Copied from *Bangor Gazette* Newspaper Obituary." *Bangor Historical Magazine* 6, (1891).

———. "General George Ulmer." *Bangor Historical Magazine* 2, (1887).

Quaife, M.M. "A Boy Soldier under Washington: The Memoir of Dan Granger." *Mississippi Valley Historical Review* 16, March 4, 1930.

Rada, James. "Revolutionary War Counterfeiting: Attempting to Win War by Weakening Currency." *Colonial America*, September 5, 2008.

Randall, Willard S. *Benedict Arnold: Patriot and Traitor*. New York: William Morrow Inc., 1990.

Riedesel, Frederika Charlotte. *Baroness von Riedesel and the American Revolution: Journal and Correspondence of a Tour of Duty, 1776–1783*. Translated by Marvin L. Brown Jr. Chapel Hill: University of North Carolina Press, 1965.

———. *Letters and Journals Relating to the War of the American Revolution, and the Capture of the German Troops at Saratoga*. Translated by William L. Stone. Albany, NY: Joel Munsell, 1867.

Riqueti, Honore-Gabriel, Comte de Mirabeau. *Avis aix Hessois et Autre Peuple de l'Allemagne Vendus par Leurs Princes a l'Angleterre, 1777*. Paris, France: Library Society for Collections of Royal Palace Letters, 1891.

Roberts, Kenneth. *Rabble in Arms*. Greenwich, CT: Fawcett Publications, 1933. Reprint, Garden City, NY: Doubleday & Company, 1947.

Robinson, Reuel. *History of Amity Lodge No. 6*. Camden, ME: Camden Publishing Company, 1897.

———. *History of Camden & Rockport, Maine*. Camden, ME: Camden Publishing Company, 1907.

Rochambeau, Comte de Papers, 1780–1784. Accession #7289-c, Albert H. Small Special Collections Library. Charlottesville: University of Virginia.

Rose, Alexander. *Washington's Spies: The Story of America's First Spy Ring*. New York: Bantam Dell, 2006.

Rossum, Kenneth R. *Thomas Mifflin and the Politics of the American Revolution.* Chapel Hill: University of North Carolina Press, 1952.

Royal Commission on Historical Manuscripts. *Report on American Manuscripts in the Royal Institution of Great Britain: Military Correspondence.* Vol. 1. London: Mackie & Company, 1904.

Royster, Charles. *A Revolutionary People at War.* Chapel Hill: University of North Carolina Press, 1979.

Rush, Benjamin. *Autobiography.* Edited by George Corner. Princeton, NJ: Princeton University Press, 1948.

Sachse, Julius F. *Washington's Masonic Correspondence.* Lancaster, PA: New Era Printing Company, 1915.

Saratoga National Park Service. *American Participants in the Battles of Saratoga.* Saratoga County, NY, 1997.

———. *The Saratoga Campaign of the Revolutionary War, Sept.–October 1777; Participants in the Battle of Saratoga.* New York: Saratoga National Historical Park Service, 1860.

Sayward, Jonathan. *Jonathan Sayward Diaries.* Wooster, MA: American Antiquarian Society, Manuscripts Department, Jonathan Sayward Diaries Collection, 1977.

Schenck, Elizabeth H. *History of Fairfield County.* Vol. 2. New York: Published by author, 1889.

Seelinger, Matthew. *Buying Time: The Battle of Valcour Island.* Washington, D.C.: Army Historical Foundation, 2012.

Selig, Robert A., PhD. "Francois Joseph Paul Comte de Grasse, the Battle off the Virginia Capes, and the American Victory at Yorktown." Article courtesy of AmericanHistory.org.

Selleck, Charles M. *History of* Norwalk. Vol. 1. Norwalk, CT: privately published by the author, 1896.

Seymour, Thomas. *Tom Seymour's Maine: A Maine Anthology.* New York: iUniverse, 2003.

Sizer, Theodore, ed. *The Autobiography of Colonel John Trumbull, Patriot-Artist, 1756–1843.* Privately published, 1841. Reprint, New Haven, CT: Yale University Press, 1953.

Small, Herman W. *History of Swan's Island, Maine.* Ellsworth, ME: Hancock County Publishing Company, 1898.

Smith, John S. *Memoir of the Baron de Kalb.* Maryland Historical Society. Baltimore, MD: John D. Toy, printer, 1858.

Smith, Joshua M. *Borderland Smuggling: Patriots, Loyalists, and Illicit Trade in the Northeast, 1783–1820.* Gainesville: University Press of Florida, 2006.

———. "The Trials and Tribulations of Fort Madison." Paper presented to the Castine Historical Society, February 4, 1998.

Smith, Justin H. *Arnold's March from Cambridge to Quebec.* New York: G.P. Putnam's Sons, 1903.

Smith, Samuel S. *The Battle of Princeton.* Monmouth Beach, NJ: Phillip Freneau publisher, 1967.

———. *The Battle of Trenton.* Monmouth Beach, NJ: Phillip Freneau publisher, 1965.

———. *The Battles of Trenton & Princeton.* Boston: Houghton Mifflin Co., 1898.

Smith, Thomas. *Extracts from the Journals of the Reverend Thomas Smith, 1720–1778.* Portland, ME: Thomas Todd & Company, 1821.

Smith, William H., ed. *The Life and Public Services of Arthur St. Clair.* Vol. 1. Cincinnati, OH: Robert Clarke & Company, 1882.

Sons of the American Revolution. *Maine at Valley Forge.* Portland, ME: The Society of the Sons of the American Revolution, 1908.

———. *Maine in War.* Portland, ME: Thurston Publishing, 1897.

Sparks, Jared. *Correspondence of the American Revolution.* Vol. 1. Boston: Little, Brown & Company, 1853.

Sprague, John F., "Maine Indians in the Revolution." *Lewiston Saturday Journal,* July 8, 1910.

Sprague, John F. and Harry J. Chapman, eds. *Sprague's Journal of Maine History.* Dover, ME: John F. Sprague publisher, 1914.

Squier, Frank, ed. "Diary of Ephraim Squier." *Magazine of American History* no. 2, part 2, (1878).

Stahl, Jasper. *History of Broad Bay and Waldoboro*. Portland, ME: Bond, Wheelwright Company, 1953.

Stanley, George F. G. *Canada Invaded, 1775–1776*. Series Number 8. Toronto: Hakkert Publishing, 1973.

State of Connecticut. *Connecticut Men in the Revolutionary War*. Third Series, June 1765–May 1820. Hartford: Connecticut State Library, 1945.

Stone, Edwin M., ed. *The Life and Recollections of John Howland*. Providence, RI: printed privately, 1857.

Stone, William L. *The Campaigns of Lieut. General John Burgoyne and the Expedition of Lieut. Col. Barry St. Leger*. Albany, NY: Joel Munsell, 1877.

———. *Letters of Brunswick and Hessian Officers During the American Revolution*. Albany, NY: Joel Munsell's Sons, 1891.

———. *Memoirs, Letters, and Journal of Major General Riedesel During His Residence in America*. Vol. 1. Translated by Max von Eelking. Albany, NY: J. Munsell publisher, 1868.

Stone, William T., trans. *Journal of Captain Pausch, of the Hanau Artillery During the Burgoyne Campaign*. Albany, NY: Munsell's Sons Co., 1886.

Stothers, Richard B. "The Great Tambora Eruption in 1815 and Its Aftermath." *Science Magazine* 224, no. 4,654 (1984): 1,191–98.

Stryker, William S. *The Battles of Trenton and Princeton*. Boston: Houghton, Mifflin and Company, 1898. Reprint, Trenton, NJ: Old Barracks Association, 2001.

Sumner, William G. *Robert Morris*. Vol. 2. New York: Dodd, Mead and Company, 1891.

Swett, Samuel, William Annin and George Smith. *History of Bunker Hill, With a Plan*. 2nd ed. Boston: Munroe and Francis, 1826.

Taylor, Alan S. *Liberty Men and Great Proprietors: The Revolutionary Settlement on the Maine Frontier, 1760–1820*. Chapel Hill: University of North Carolina Press, 1990.

———. "The Rise and Fall of George Ulmer: Political Entrepreneurship in the Age of Jefferson and Jackson." *Colby Library Quarterly* 21, no. 2 (1985): 51–56.

———. "The Smuggling Career of William King." *Maine Historical Society Quarterly* 17, no. 1 (1977): 19–38.

Todd, Major. Report to the Massachusetts Court of Inquiry. Vol. 145. Massachusetts State Archives.

Tower, Charlemagne. *The Marquis de La Fayette in the American Revolution: With Some Account of the Attitudes of France Toward the War of Independence.* Philadelphia: J.B. Lippincott Company, 1901.

Trevelyan, George Otto. *The American Revolution.* 2 vols. New York: Longmans Green, 1903.

Tucker, George H. "Norfolk Highlights: 1584 to 1881." *Essays & Artifacts.* Norfolk Historical Society, 1972.

Tustin, Joseph P. *Diary of the American War: A Hessian* Journal. New Haven, CT: Yale University Press, 1979.

Ulmer Papers. Commission granted by the Continental Congress to Philip Ulmer on April 20, 1776, and signed by John Hancock: *The Bangor Wig and Courier*, September 30, 1887, Vol. 54, no. 231. Document in possession of Philip Ulmer's grandson, Captain John Bennett of New York.

———. George Ulmer letter to John Armstrong, April 16, 1813, "Letters Received by the Secretary of War." NARA. Microfilm Reel 58.

———. "Letter of Captain Philip Ulmer." *Maine Historical Magazine* 9. Bangor, ME: Charles H. Glass printers, 1892.

———. "Letters Received by President Madison." Reel 58, Letter from George Ulmer to President Madison, March 1, 1814, NARA.

———. "Letters Received by the Department of War." Letter from Colonel George Ulmer to John Armstrong in 1813, Reel 58 of "Letters Received by the Secretary of War." NARA.

———. Letter that refers to a visit paid by General Lafayette to the Ulmer home. Letter in possession of the Lincolnville Historical Society and Schoolhouse Museum in Lincolnville, ME, and a copy is in the possession of the author.

U.S. Congress. House of Representatives. *Digested Summary and Alphabetical List of Private Claims Which Have Been Presented to the House of Representatives.* Vol. 3. Washington, D.C.: Government Printing Office, 1853.

————. House of Representatives. *Journals of the House of Representatives of the U.S., A Century of Law Making for a New Nation: U.S. Congressional Documents & Debates 1774–1875*. Vol. 9. Washington, D.C.: Library of Congress, 1875.

————. *Instructions to the Commanders of Private Ships or Vessels of War*. Issued by Order of Congress, April 3, 1776. Washington, D.C.: Government Printing Office, 1906.

————. Senate. *Records of the Senate of the United States, Committee of Commerce*. 25th Cong., 2nd sess. Senate Document Number 204, 1875.

————. Senate. *Records of the Senate of the United States, Committee of Commerce*. 28th Cong., 1st sess. Senate Document Number 318 and 319, 1875.

Valley Forge Historical Society. *Lafayette and the Canadian Invasion*. Courtesy of the National Center for the American Revolution, ushistory.org.

Valley Forge Muster Roll. Lieutenant Philip Ulmer, ID Number MA18825, 2nd Massachusetts Brigade, Colonel Vose's First Massachusetts Regiment, Captain Abraham Hunt's Company, 4th Division, January, February, March, 1778.

Valley Forge National Park. *American Participants at Valley Forge: Muster Roll Data Sheet*. Muster Roll of Jan., Feb., March 1778.

————. *The Conway Cabal*. Philadelphia: Valley Forge Historical Society publications, Independence Hall Association, 1997–2010.

————. *General Baron de Kalb*. Philadelphia: Valley Forge Historical Society publications, Independence Hall Association, 1997–2010.

————. *George Washington's Letter to Governor George Clinton*. Philadelphia: Independence Hall Association, 1996.

————. *Lafayette and the Canadian Invasion*. Philadelphia: Valley Forge Historical Society. Courtesy of the National Center for the American Revolution, www.ushistory.org.

————. *Maine at Valley Forge: Muster Roll of Maine Soldiers at Valley Forge*. Portland, ME: Sons of the American Revolution, 1908.

————. Records of Valley Forge, Maine Militia Companies: Colonel Vose Regiment. Philadelphia: Valley Forge Historical Society publications, Independence Hall Association, 1997–2010.

Van Dusen, Albert. "Connecticut: The First British Raid on Danbury." *The New England Quarterly*, April 1777. Reprint, New York: Random House, 1961.

Varney, George J. "History of Thomaston, Maine" and "History of Waldo County, Maine." *A Gazetteer of the State of Maine*. Boston: B.B. Russell, 1886.

Von Riedesel, Friedrich. *Memoirs, Letters, and Journals of Major General Riedesel During His Residence in America*. Vol. 1. Edited by Max von Eelking. Translated by William L. Stone. Albany, NY: J. Munsell, 1868.

Waldo, Dr. Albigence. "Life at Valley Forge 1777–1778." Excerpted from *American History Told by Contemporaries*. Vol. 2, *Building of the Republic*. Edited by Albert B. Hart. New York: MacMillan, 1899.

Wallace, Audrey. *Benedict Arnold, Misunderstood Hero?* Shippensburg, PA: Burd Street Press, 2003.

Walton, William. *The Army and Navy of the United States 1776–1891*. Philadelphia: George Barrie Publisher, 1890.

Ward, Christopher. *The War of the Revolution*. 2 vols. New York: Macmillan Company, 1952.

Ware, Susan. *Forgotten Heroes: Inspiring American Portraits from Our Leading Historians*. Portland, OR: Simon & Schuster, 2000.

Watts, J.J., ed. *Lincolnville—Early Days*. Lincolnville, ME: Lincolnville Historical Society, 1976.

Wells, Bayze. "Journal of Bayze Wells of Farmington: May, 1775–February, 1777: At the Northward and in Canada." *Collections of the Connecticut Historical Society*. Vol. 7. Hartford: Connecticut Historical Society, 1899.

Wheeler, George A. *History of Castine, Penobscot, & Brooksville, Maine*. Bangor, ME: Burr & Robinson, 1875.

Whitaker, W.W., and Gary Horlacher. *Broad Bay Pioneers*. Rockland, ME: Picton Press, 1998.

White, Joseph. *A Narrative of Events in the Revolutionary War, with an Account of the Battles of Trenton, Trenton-Bridge, and Princeton*. Charlestown, MA: J. White, 1833.

Wickman, Donald, ed. "A Most Unsettled Time of Lake Champlain: The October 1776 Journal of Jahiel Stewart." *Vermont History*, no. 64 (Spring 1996): 89–98.

Wigglesworth Papers. *Wigglesworth Family Papers*. Boston: Massachusetts Historical Society, Call Number: Ms. N-114.

Wild, Ebenezer. "The Journal of Ebenezer Wild." *Proceedings of the Massachusetts Historical Society*. Vol. 6. Boston: Massachusetts Historical Society, 1890.

Wilkins, Fred J. *Steuben Screamed but Things Happened and an Army Was Born at Valley Forge*. Valley Forge, PA: Valley Forge Historical Society, 1948.

Wilkinson, James. *Memoirs of My Own Times*. Vol. 1. Philadelphia: Abraham Small, 1816.

Willcox, William B. *Portrait of a General: Sir Henry Clinton in the War of Independence*. New York: Alfred A. Knopf, 1964.

Willcox, William B., ed. *The Papers of Benjamin Franklin*. Vol. 23. New Haven, CT: Yale University Press, 1983.

Williams, Gregory H. *French Assault on American Shipping, 1793–1813: A History and Comprehensive Record of Merchant Marine Losses*. Jefferson, NC: McFarland & Company, 2009.

Williamson, Gene. *Guns on the Chesapeake: The Winning of American Independence*. Westminster, MD: Heritage Books, 1997.

Williamson, Joseph. "Obituary of General George Ulmer." *The Hancock Gazette and Penobscot Patriot*, January 11, 1826.

Williamson, William D. *History of the State of Maine: From Its First Discovery, A.D. 1602, to the Separation, A.D. 1820, Inclusive*. Vol. 2, Chapter 26. Hallowell, ME: Glazier, Masters & Company, 1832.

Wilson, James G., and John Fiske. *Appleton's Cyclopedia American Biography*. New York: D. Appleton & Company, 1887, 1889. Republished by the Gale Research Company, Farmington Hills, MI, 1968.

Wilson, Wendell E., Jr. *The Ancestors and Descendants of John Wilson of Tattenhall, England and Lincolnville, Maine and Allied Families*. Tucson, AZ: Wendell E. Wilson Jr., 2006.

Winsor, Justin, ed. *Arnold's Expedition Against Quebec 1775–1776*. Cambridge, MA: John Wilson and Son, 1886.

Wood, Gordon S. *The Radicalism of the American Revolution*. New York: Vintage Books, 1993.

Wright, Richard K. *The Continental Army, Lineage Series*. Washington, D.C.: Center of Military History, 1983.

Wright, Robert K. *The Continental Army*. Washington, D.C.: Center of Military History, 1989, NARA.

———. "Too Little, Too Late: The Campaign of 1777 in the Hudson Highlands." Master's thesis, College of William and Mary, 1971.

Yerxa, Donald A. *The Burning of Falmouth, 1775: A Case Study in British Imperial Pacification, October 18, 1775*. Portland, ME: Maine Historical Society, 1976.

Index

About the Author

Patricia Hubert is a retired elementary education teacher who lives in Newtown, Connecticut. She is married to Richard Hubert and has two children, Dr. Christopher Hubert and Carolyn (Hubert) Murray, and three grandchildren: Kyle, Julia and Ryan Murray. She is an active member of the Connecticut Daughters of the American Revolution, where she presently serves as the regent of the Mary Wooster Chapter in Danbury, Connecticut. She is a member of the Lake Champlain Maritime Museum, where she is a volunteer and historical researcher of several maritime captains who were involved in battles on Lake Champlain during the American Revolution. Patricia is a member of the Danbury Historical Society and Museum and the Newtown Historical Society in Connecticut. She is a member of the Lincolnville Historical Society and Schoolhouse Museum in Lincolnville, Maine. She has written articles for her local newspapers about Revolutionary War reenactment events as well as several articles for the Lincolnville Historical Society newsletters in Maine. She is an avid reader and researcher about American history, and she enjoys being a colonial reenactor at local historical society events. She is an active member of her church and community in Newtown, and she has been a licensed wildlife rehabilitator for the State of Connecticut for over thirty years. She has given nature programs at local schools and nature centers for many years in the western Fairfield and Litchfield County areas.